Transforming

Transforming

Applying Spirituality, Emergent Creativity, and Reconciliation

Edited by
Vern Neufeld Redekop and
Gloria Neufeld Redekop

LEXINGTON BOOKS/FORTRESS ACADEMIC
Lanham • Boulder • New York • London

Published by Lexington Books/Fortress Academic
An imprint of The Rowman & Littlefield Publishing Group, Inc.
4501 Forbes Boulevard, Suite 200, Lanham, Maryland 20706
www.rowman.com

6 Tinworth Street, London SE11 5AL, United Kingdom

British Library Cataloguing in Publication Information Available

Library of Congress Cataloging-in-Publication Data

Library of Congress Control Number: 2020946386

ISBN 9781498593120 (cloth)
ISBN 9781498593137 (Electronic)

♾™ The paper used in this publication meets the minimum requirements of American National Standard for Information Sciences—Permanence of Paper for Printed Library Materials, ANSI/NISO Z39.48-1992.

Contents

Acknowledgments

The Spirituality, Emergent Creativity, and Reconciliation (SECR) research project, of which this volume is one of the outcomes, was made possible by a three-year grant that was funded initially by Metanexus and then by the John Templeton Foundation. The culmination of the project was an international conference on the theme in May 2012. Additional funding for the conference came from an anonymous donor, to whom we are most grateful.

Participants in a generative dialogue to start the research project included Andrea Bartoli, André Beauregard, Walter Clemens, Zijad Delic, Nadia Delicata, Manal Guirguis-Younger, Iman Ibrahim, Stuart Kauffman, Merle Lefkoff, Richard McGuigan, Steve Moore, Susan Allen Nan, Paul Rigby, Jamie Price, Megan Price, Mac Saulis, Joanne St. Lewis, and Yurim Yi and ourselves. MA students Andrew Coleman and Lara Thacker took note of research questions and who said what, respectively.

Students in several offerings of a graduate course on Spirituality and Conflict Resolution at Saint Paul University contributed to the honing of ideas in this book.

We wish to gratefully acknowledge the support of Saint Paul University for the research project. This included offering a venue for events and supplying a Glasmacher Lectureship for one of the conferences.

As we approached the time to actually publish the two SECR books, we asked the authors for suggestions for titles. It was Catherine Twinn who suggested *Awakening* and *Transforming*; there was an immediate consensus around the appropriateness of her suggestions.

Thanks to Lexington editors Michael Gibson, Mikayla Mislak, Becca Beurer, Chris Fischer, Monika Jagadeesh, and Trevor Crowell who guided us through the details of getting the manuscript in shape for final production.

Bill Buchanan generously provided the photograph for the cover. This is what he said about it in the context of the COVID-19 pandemic:

> These white flowers were not as appealing to the eye as the other more vividly coloured ones and I tended to overlook them altogether when I was out with the camera. I'm fortunate I changed lenses. A closeup look with the macro lens revealed these spectacular, colourful structures within these insignificant little flowers.
>
> Perhaps in these dark times we have to look more closely to see the beauty in the world. It's not gone. It's still there! We just have to look a little harder!

Sometimes the key to transforming lies in looking—and listening—more closely.

Vern Neufeld Redekop
Gloria Neufeld Redekop

Introduction

Transforming—Inside and Out

Vern Neufeld Redekop and
Gloria Neufeld Redekop

"Transforming": the word is jolting, crying out for its cognate cousin, "transformation." But "transforming" is distinguished by its ongoingness; it is both a goal and a process that never ceases. It is like the victim-survivors of atrocities who found that every morning they had to forgive all over again.

The process is not even. There may be key points when a goal is reached, or a new possibility opens up. At any point, a new trajectory may be set that changes everything (Menon 2013). Sometimes a small change—in awareness, framing, or action—can change everything: in "A Tender Agony of Parting," Rumi tells the story of a reed that a craftsman took from the reedbed. After cutting holes in it, the reed was deemed a "human being" that has wailed

a tender agony of parting,
never mentioning the skill
that gave it life as a flute. (2006, 85)

In this case, cutting holes into a reed changes it into a flute; the change is not just physical, it is a change in the ontology—how its existence is framed and what it does, and the skill of the "flute player" that transcends its own physical existence and gives it new meaning. This suggests a transforming shift in consciousness.

When we think of what is confronting humankind in the present era, there is the need for a growth of "psychospiritual" consciousness. Consider the following reflection:

The source of the problems confronting humanity is fundamentally not economic, political or technological, but rather, is to be found within the human

1

psyche. To quote Dr. Stanislov Grof, "In the last analysis, the current global crisis is a psychospiritual crisis; it reflects the level of consciousness evolution of the human species. It is, therefore, hard to imagine that it could be resolved without a radical inner transformation of humanity on a large scale and its rise to a higher level of emotional maturity and spiritual awareness. . . . Radical psychospiritual transformation of humanity is not only possible, but is already underway." This is an important point to consider: There is undeniable evidence that an expansion of consciousness in the human species is not only a remote possibility but is already taking place. Grof concludes, "The question is only whether it can be sufficiently fast and extensive to reverse the current self-destructive trend of modern humanity." In other words, will we wake up in time? (Levy 2020)

Transforming picks up where *Awakening* left off. It involves the ongoing work of bringing new insights into life. It is about not only taking action but also reflecting on the meaning of that action. Action, as seen in chapters by the following authors, ranges from the intrapersonal (Pösel-Steinmair) to the interpersonal (Gagnon), to group (Brodeur) to the large group (Ibrahim, Cleyn, Logie, Hess) to the biosphere (Lefkoff), these authors often showing the interdependence among these dimensions.

It is humbling for us to have had the privilege of weaving into this volume the cream of the authors' research. This involves doctoral dissertations (Chabot, Gagnon, Levesque), master's and post-master's research projects (Cleyn, Logie, Hess), postdoctoral research (Pösel-Steinmair, Moore, and G. Neufeld Redekop), and life's work over decades (Kauffman, Theise, Singh, Brodeur, Hamilton, Ibrahim, Twinn, Lefkoff, and V. Neufeld Redekop). Later we will describe the unique contribution of each to the understanding of the dynamics of transforming, spirituality, emergent creativity, and reconciliation—each addressing a unique combination of these. First, Gloria will "set the stage" with a reflection on the unanticipated impacts of the COVID-19 pandemic and a story of reconciliation that had unanticipated consequences—adjacent possibles. Second, Vern will place the book into the context of the emergence of the Spirituality, Emergent Creativity, and Reconciliation research project. Then we will show how the reflective, research, and experiential threads of the various chapters are woven together to present a whole that is greater than the sum of its parts.

SETTING THE STAGE (GLORIA)

"Transforming"—quite a word to contemplate during this Corona Virus pandemic. A time that is challenging for most of us, and especially for the most vulnerable of our population. What can be transformed during this time of physical distancing? Let us begin with the intrapersonal. Not so easy. There are many who are having mental health challenges. A lot of anxiety and even panic. However, there may be some room for inner transformation to happen. For those of us who are self-isolating, sheltering at home, we have more time to read and contemplate. We may think about what is really most important in life. What am I most grateful for? Thinking about interpersonal transformation, some of us are isolating with either a partner or an entire family; we may be separated from our loved ones. Children are home from school. Sometimes adult children have returned home to isolate with their parents. This presents new challenges. If there is any abuse or violence in the home, this is a very trying time—raising the question of what might transform recrimination and domination to mutual empowerment. Even if there is no history of violence in the home, there is a chance that relationships can be transformed as family members spend more time together. Maybe they do more cooking together. Maybe they watch shows and movies together. Maybe they simply take more time to talk with each other.

There can also be community transformation. Since the COVID-19 outbreak, we Skype daily with a couple whom we have known for many years. Previously, we would have dinner together every month or so. Now we talk every day. One of the spouses is a photographer, and he e-mails one nature photo with a pertinent quote every day. When we talk, we share what we have been doing that day, we talk about the impact of COVID-19, and we have determined to always share something positive. This is community transformation. And there is another personal example. We live in Blackburn Hamlet, a suburb of Ottawa, Ontario. Most of our services are accessible within walking distance—a grocery store, pharmacy, library, banks, doctors, dentists, chiropractor, massage therapists, and even a Dollarama! It seems that most people we encounter on our daily walks are very cognizant of the need for physical distancing during this pandemic. While walking, people are very quick to cross the street as someone approaches. But what is very noticeable is that we wave and smile at each other as we pass. This didn't tend to happen before. And when we pass by homes where people are sitting outside, there is often a little conversation. These are people we have never met before. This is community transformation. And then there are our neighbors, who have volunteered to get groceries for us (and we have taken them up on the offers). Unlike before, whenever we are in our backyard and they are in theirs, there is a lot more conversation than previously. We are alone, yet together!

Another kind of transformation that we see during the COVID-19 pandemic is the beginning of transformation of the biosphere. Positively, various cities that have been shut down have dramatically less pollution and various bodies of water are cleaner than ever. Negatively, there is a rise in the use of plastic; break-ins into stores that are closed down are on the rise as is the incidence of stunt driving on highways. All this is to say that with any emergent new development, like a pandemic, there are significant new possibilities that open up for personal, social, political, and biospheric transformation.

A good example of intrapersonal, interpersonal, and community transformation is evident in the 2019 movie, *The Best of Enemies*, based on the 1996 book, *The Best of Enemies: Race and Redemption in the New South* by Osha Gray Davidson. It is the story of the unlikely friendship between Ann Atwater, a civil rights advocate, and Claiborne Paul (C .P.) Ellis, a Ku Klux Klan leader. The story takes place in Durham, North Carolina, in 1971.

It was a time when integration in the school system had not yet taken place. After a fire in a school where African American children attended, a solution was needed so that these children could continue to go to school. There was no way that Ku Klux Klan members wanted the African American children to attend the same school as their own children. An African American pastor approached a certain Bill Riddick, who was well known for conducting charettes in situations like this. The Miriam-Webster Dictionary defines a charette as "the intense final effort made by architectural students to complete their solutions to a given architectural problem in an allotted time or the period in which such an effort is made" (Miriam-Webster 2019). However, it has also come to mean a meeting of all parties involved in a dispute, with the goal to resolve conflicts and come up with solutions. And that is its meaning in this case.

When Bill Riddick agreed to organize a charette in Durham, he first approached Ann Atwater and C. P. Ellis to be cochairs for the event. After much objection, they agreed. What they had in common was that they were both from the working class and were struggling financially. During the ten days of meeting and eating together, each side had representatives and a vote was taken on the issues confronting them. In the end, the most unbelievable thing happened. In front of the entire assembly, Ellis tore up his Ku Klux membership card. He had become convinced of desegregation. Subsequently, he had many threats to his life in the years that followed. After the charette Ellis and Atwater worked together to form unions and work together to end segregation. When Ellis died in 2005, Atwater gave the eulogy.

In this story, there were a number of transformations that came as surprises. The purpose of the charette was to talk about integration of schools in Durham. However, there were other adjacent possibles that happened as a result of holding the charette.

What we see in this example is, first of all, the intrapersonal transformation of Ellis, who took the great risk of tearing up his Ku Klux Klan membership when his view of segregation became untenable to him. Interpersonal transformation happened between Ellis and Atwater, even to the extent of subsequently working together for thirty years to end segregation, telling their story and inspiring people in other communities. And community transformation resulted from the Ellis/Atwater relationship: previously Ellis did not sell gas to African Americans; now, African Americans in the area lined up to get gas from Ellis's gas station, supporting his business that white people now boycotted. And with the releasing of the movie, there was the possibility that even more people might be affected by what happened in Durham.

THE SPIRITUALITY, EMERGENT CREATIVITY, AND RECONCILIATION (SECR) NARRATIVE (VERN)

In 2008, there were three converging events that led to the possibility of a research project on SECR. First was the need for me to develop a graduate course on Spirituality and Conflict Resolution. Second was my stumbling across the Metanexus exhibit at the American Academy of Religion where they said they could fund the development of my course. Third was the interview on CBC radio with Stuart Kauffman who had just released his book, *Reinventing the Sacred*, in which he developed the concept of "emergent creativity." I subsequently tracked down Kauffman who recommended other complexity thinkers who could join the multidisciplinary team of scholars for the research project—some of whom have chapters in this book (initially Lefkoff and Theise, and later Singh and Peil Kauffman).

The Generative Dialogue (see Redekop 2020) in 2009 was the catalyst for many new insights that were then ploughed into the Spirituality and Conflict Resolution course I taught in the winter of 2010. A second gathering of the research team coincided with one of the classes, which we had in the Courtyard Restaurant—each table of four had two scholars and two grad students—one person from each table moved to another table for each course. We ended with a circle process. The atmosphere was electric, buzzing with new ideas and connections.

The culmination of the research project was an international conference in 2012. It was multifaceted with presentations, Samoan circles, participatory workshops, improv dramas, and creative exchanges. It modeled both compassionate listening (see Gagnon, *Transforming*) and interworldview dialogue (IWVD) (see Brodeur, *Transforming*). The ensuing years involved a series of less formal processes and subprocesses leading to the publication of the two SECR volumes: *Awakening* and *Transforming*. These have led to intra-SECR connections indicated by citations within the volume to chapters in both books.

TRANSFORMING: EMERGING ISSUES AND
ADJACENT POSSIBLES (VERN AND GLORIA)

This book is about transforming processes. Given the interrelated web of insights, it would be profitable for each reader to read the book twice: the first time to grasp what each individual chapter is about; the second time would be to read each chapter in the light of all the others. Indeed, each author has indwelled their particular subject matter to a remarkable degree, and, as noted in chapter 2, indwelling is the key to making a truly creative contribution. In the following paragraphs, we will synthesize the "heart" of each chapter, beginning with a section on Violence, Spirituality, and Reconciliation.

My (Vern) chapter on "Reconciliation as Emergent Creativity" is a synthesis of what I have learned over more than a decade of wrestling with the issue of how complexity theory and emergent creativity can be applied to reconciliation. Reconciliation of deep-rooted conflict has been central to my research since the 1990s. It adds some new dimensions to Stuart Kauffman's concept of criticality—which I have discussed with him—and applies the concept of emergent creativity to the mind as a complex system. I also present hope as a form of active engagement with a challenging issue or question and as a factor that enhances the potential for something creative to emerge.

Katherine Peil Kauffman has indwelled "The Biology of Emotion" for years, drawing on evolutionary biology, neuroscience, theology, philosophy, and other disciplines to present an integrated view of our emotions as the guidance system to our thought, decisions, and volition. This has significant implications for our paradigms of rationality, critical thought, reflexivity, and justice. In this chapter, she shows how an awareness and attentiveness to this emotional guidance system can help us make sense of our own experiences of violation and can lead us to some life-giving approaches to justice-making. It also shows how this well-developed and complex emotional system forms an interface with natural spirituality, showing how important the "heart"—understood as a metaphor for an integrated thought-feeling system—is for how we deal with issues of profound concern to us, including reconciliation.

Petra Pösel-Steinmair, a Girardian theologian, presents the essence of her postdoctoral research project on three women mystics who find constructive ways with dealing with deep suffering and loss associated with World War II. Maria Skobtsova sees every human being, including one's enemy, as an ikon of Christ; in other words, she is able to value the humanity of everyone. This for her was not just a theoretical ideal but the concept is born out of her own experience of confronting those who brought suffering to her and her people. Chiara Lubich uses the concept of *kenosis*—of emptying oneself, a theological notion based on the Apostle Paul's description of Christ "emptying himself"—to provide a basis for unity among people with diverse worldviews (cf. Brodeur). *Kenosis* is not unlike the Buddhist principle of detachment from desire and ego; it is a profound letting go of passions that could be divisive. Dorothy Soelle demonstrates the activist side of mysticism. Out of her experience she presents the important aspect of nonviolently entering into conflict and confronting injustices, such as human rights abuses. All this is in the context of Girard's *Battling to the End* in which he explores the very real possibility of violence going out of control in an escalating spiral of mutually enacted harm to one another. These three mystics shine a light on resources to escape runaway violence.

I (Gloria) went from my doctoral study of Mennonite women's societies, devoted to material help for those in need, to a study of Mennonite women's experience of the Russian Revolution and subsequent civil war and famine. In each case, my research was focused on giving voice to women in contexts where the dominant narrative was male-centric—church and war. In the stories of older women who had been young girls in the early twentieth century, I found instances of resourcefulness, resilience, and care in the face of horrific rape, murder, and plunder. The transforming impact lay in the commitment to do what they did for others who might be suffering and continued to do in their present lives.

The next section on Reconciliation as Spiritual Praxis features scholar-practitioners who have significant experience in engaging people from diverse worlds of culture, religion, and meaning.

Brigitte Gagnon participated in The Compassionate Listening Project (TCLP), using listening to enter into the worlds of Palestinians and Israelis; she then engaged in qualitative and quantitative doctoral research with former participants of TCLP. Her research demonstrated how compassionate listening, with the attendant skills of reflective self-awareness and self-regulation, could have a transforming effect on both the listener and the person listened to. Going from practice to theory development, she developed a model, including a matrix, for a Relational Ecosystem for Peace that shows how attentiveness to the context (safe container), the messenger, and the message can establish conditions conducive to deep connection. The process of connecting with the other in an ever-deeper way is at the heart of this model, offering theoretical and practical clues on how "transforming" and "emerging" from separation (with the other) to communion can happen.

Beginning with his own stirring account of how his own world opened up through dialogue with others, Patrice Brodeur systematically develops the concept of Interworldview Dialogue (IWVD. IWVD incorporates aspects of deep identity that integrates the multiple subidentities that every human beings carries, without reducing or hiding them under any one dominant identity, be it religion or culture, nationality, language, or gender; it shows how understanding complex identity and power dynamics, at the center of all tensions and conflicts, can help bring reconciliation and healing through a realignment of more equitable human dynamics, as a result of an IWVD process. Brodeur theoretically synthesizes the results of over 100 dialogues conducted in several languages over three decades, on all continents. Striking in his account is how challenging it was for him as a young *Québécois* to spend a week living with an Indigenous family in a remote village on the shore of a northeast Pacific coast inlet—it raised questions leading to an indwelling of the world of transcending cultural divides, leading to insights he is publishing for the first time.

As a Canadian Armed Forces (CAF) chaplain serving with the United Nations Protection Forces (UNPROFOR) in Bosnia in the early 1990s, Steve Moore engaged the faith community leaders of the ethnoreligious groups engulfed in the civil war raging at the time. Due to his efforts, and those of chaplains of subsequent tours, the facilitation of dialogue among the local religious leaders was achieved where there had been none for a number of years—seeding reconciliation. The experience left a profound impact on Moore, who eventually pursued doctoral studies to make meaning of this initial impulse of religious leaders turning to chaplains as fellow religious leaders for support in bridging the divide between their faith group communities caused by the war. His groundbreaking research, which included fieldwork with a CAF Muslim padre in Afghanistan (2006), contributed to a global phenomenon of Religious Leader Engagement (RLE). In his chapter, he develops this concept, showing how it can be situated among the variety of stakeholders (whole-of-government) in a conflict situation.

Building on Moore's conceptual development, Karen Hamilton shows how the concept of RLE can be applied to domestic situations that do not involve violent conflict. She is uniquely qualified to do this, drawing on fifteen years of experience as general secretary for the Canadian Council of Churches, a position with diplomatic and strategic challenges nationally and internationally. In this capacity, she indwelled the world of Christian ecumenism. She had and still has a major national and international leadership role in interfaith issues, having recently cochaired the Parliament of the World's Religions.

In terms of a big picture, look at a global pressing challenge for reconciliation; few challenges are as significant as the rift between the Muslim world and "the West." Iman Ibrahim is in a unique position to address this as a Muslim woman who grew up in Egypt and then moved to Canada, where she completed a second bachelor's degree in Carleton University's College of Humanities and a master's degree in international relations and conflict resolution. For years, besides her conflict resolution work, she has played a leadership role in multicultural and dialogue projects including Islamic History Month and in the Canadian Peace Initiative campaign advocating for a Canadian government Department of Peace. Her chapter is a *cri-de-coeur* to bridge the gap between the Muslim world and Euro-based civilizations. She analyzes the Islamic concepts of conflict resolution supporting the transition to democracy and collaborative international relations. A reconciliatory dialogue requires consideration of lessons learned and Muslim societies' needs in order for spiritual leaders to engage more effectively in what Brodeur calls IWVD.

"Heart," as the integrated core of thought, feeling, and spirituality, and as developed by Peil Kauffman, Gagnon, and Brodeur, calls for communication and connection in ways that transcend language. Hence, the need for art and arts literacy in reconciliation processes. This was a focus of Lauren Levesque's doctoral research. In her chapter, she develops the potential for music to make a difference. For this to happen, music literacy is important. The importance of this literacy is discussed with reference to the work of international relations scholar, Roland Bleiker, and the example of the West-Eastern Divan orchestra, which is comprised of Palestinian and Jewish musicians along with youth from across the Middle East and Europe.

The next section on Indigenous Insights and Challenges of Reconciliation addresses a complex array of issues at many different levels. Given the global impact of colonialism with its history of racism, slavery, cultural genocide, paternalism, and domination, there is a profound need for reconciliation that includes structural change, a new form of relationships, healing, transcendence of differences, and a sense of justice.

Joseph Cleyn begins with a chapter on "Transcending Traditional Justice Claims." He shows how colonialism brought a mindset that privileged its own worldview, which included ways of knowing and a set of norms. This meant that the violence of domination included epistemic violence and normative violence—both of these functioning at the level of underlying assumptions, privileging approaches of colonizing Settlers. They empower subtle forms of oppression that continue even after attempts to address concrete forms of cultural oppression, such as residential schools. They call for deep self-critical examination of thought patterns, values, and norms.

Cecil Chabot is in a unique position to examine different worldviews. As a non-Indigenous person raised in an Indigenous context where he was often the only nonaboriginal person in his class, he indwelled the world of the James Bay Cree. Part of that world included stories of Windigo—an individual at the edge of survival that turned cannibalistic. The Windigo concept evolved beyond literal cannibalism to include other forms of personal aggrandizement at the expense of others, taking on mythical and archetypal aspects of character. Chabot's doctoral research was on Windigoes as understood in various Indigenous traditions, using different but related words for the same phenomenon.

Catherine Twinn, a lawyer of Indigenous and European descent, begins with her own experience with addiction, codependency, and enabling within an Indian Act reserve community system, a product of colonization. She sees in the ancient Wihtiko teachings, insights, and warnings that apply as much to today's colonized Indian Reserve communities as to contemporary Western systems. With rare exception, these are addictive systems that, in lockstep with the archetypal leaders such systems beget, cannibalize spirituality, relationships, and life itself. As cannibals, these are undeniably Wihtiko systems. Transcending Wihtiko systems requires the ability to see and understand Wihtiko, which is challenging given the normalization of addiction and codependency within our lives and communities. Wihtiko, as leader and system, consumes many victims—victims who are themselves susceptible to becoming Wihtikos if they lose their soul. We can liberate ourselves from the tyrannical power of Wihtiko leaders and systems enabled by codependent people. Traditional Indigenous teachings point to ways out of Wihtiko domination and destruction, by building one's inner intellectual and psychospiritual power. Developing our intellectual and psychospiritual power can turn every hindrance, impediment, and obstacle into a transformative way forward.

Robert Logie, a Settler with a passion for justice in relation to Indigenous people, takes on the "wicked" challenge of remote Fly-In Indigenous Communities. With a reduced land base making a traditional lifestyle no longer viable, it is a challenge to develop an approach to economic life when the cost of transportation to the urban "south" is so high. Of particular concern to Logie is how the Settler debate is not helpful to Indigenous people. Using an integral theory quadrant-based analysis, he shows how both sides talk past one another and ultimately fail to really engage Indigenous people from remote locations (cf. Cleyn's chapter). With a view to advancing reconciliation and creating space for new opportunities to emerge, Logie calls for an approach that unites integral theory and complexity theory to address feedback loops that are holding these communities back.

Moving from the Canadian context to that of Australia, Sue-Anne Hess examines Aboriginal-Settler relations in the wake of similar colonial injustices. Included are lessons learned about what has happened so far in terms of reconciliation, highlights from Lederach's Moral Imagination as teachings to offer a way forward, and an emphasis on the role of the arts (cf. Levesque's chapter) in advancing reconciliation.

Pervading this volume is a sensitivity to the issue of complexity—this comes to the fore in the next section on Complexity, Community, and Emergent Development. Three complexity specialists from different fields take us into overlapping areas of application.

Liver pathologist and biological scientist, Neil Theise identifies a number of principles of complex adaptive systems, drawn from careful observations from the field of biology. He then shows how these could be applied to human social systems. In this, he is aided by three authors who offer examples from their worlds—Catherine Twinn: Indigenous communities; Gloria Neufeld Redekop: emergence of Mennonite women's societies; and Lissane Yohannes: Eritrean and Ethiopian local communities establishing a border.

Naresh Singh has had a career of reducing poverty by focusing on the assets of poor communities. In the process, he was a pioneer in applying complexity theory to development, noting that in a truly complex environment often the most significant new developments are those that could not have been planned. Hence, the logical frameworks in vogue around the world have severe limitations when it comes to policy and evaluation. He shows how complexity-based approaches can complement log frames to enhance development effectiveness.

Finally, Merle Lefkoff draws on decades of being an environmentalist to reflect on global challenges to the biosphere. As one of the first social scientists to be ushered into the world of complexity science, she is a unique position to draw attention to the adjacent possibles opening up at this time of rapid change to the environment. She does this, not as a lone complexity scientist, but as part of a global scientific community, which she has brought together to generate new insights as to how we as humans can address the cascading challenges facing humanity.

There we have it—an overview of *Transforming: Applying Spirituality, Emergent Creativity, and Reconciliation.* Our own lives have been truly enriched through our engagement with these authors.

REFERENCES

Levy, Paul. 2020. "Quantum Medicine for the Coronavirus." *Tikkun Magazine*, April 16. https://www.tikkun.org/quantum-medicine-for-the-coronavirus?eType=EmailBlastContent&eId=8a4c8f9f-337f-4154-93e8-3a0b906c3ea1.

Menon, Rupa. 2013. "Changing Trajectory: The Role of Karma within a Framework of Reconciliation." In *René Girard and Creative Reconciliation.* Edited by Vern Neufeld Redekop and Thomas Ryba. Lanham, MD: Lexington, 249–268.

Miriam-Webster Dictionary. 2019. *charettete.* https://www.merriam-webster.com/dictionary/charette .

Redekop, Vern Neufeld. 2020. *What is a Generative Dialogue?* Unpublished paper available on request from the author.

Rumi. 2006. *A Year with Rumi: Daily Readings.* Edited by Coleman Barks. New York, NY: HarperCollins.

Part I

VIOLENCE, SPIRITUALITY, AND RECONCILIATION

Chapter 1

Reconciliation as Emergent Creativity

Vern Neufeld Redekop

Reconciliation in the wake of widespread violence demands structural and cultural change.[1] As A. J. Muste pointed out:

> We cannot have peace if we are only concerned with peace. War is not an accident. It is the logical outcome of a certain way of life. If we want to attack war, we have to attack that way of life. (1970)

Changing a "way of life" is a multifaceted challenge involving behaviors, systems, and structures as exterior factors as well as values, culture, orientation, interpretive framework, and emotional memories as interior factors.

Systemic and structural forms of violence, like overt violent actions, deprive victims of a sense of justice, security, and worth (Galtung 1971; Dilts 2012). When victims are not self-flagellating and preoccupied with their own woundedness, they can be obsessed with resentment, revenge, and hatred in relation to those who (unjustly) harmed them (Girard 1976; Minow 1998; Murphy and Hampton 1988). It seems absurd, some would think, to even dare to mention "reconciliation" as an option. Yet it does occur and has grown as a significant concept within the fields of conflict studies and peace studies.[2]

Reconciliation is paradoxical and complex. When it happens, it appears deceptively simple—the dividing walls come down; there is forgiveness; and there is mutual recognition of humanity. However, as anyone who has experienced a deep rift over profound woundedness knows, pressure to forgive or to reconcile at the wrong time can do more harm than good. It results in further victimization, as those who are wounded feel guilty for not reconciling. The very process of reconciliation needs to be open, yet needs direction; it needs to come from the parties involved, yet often they cannot do it alone; sometimes a long period of time is needed for healing, yet it can happen soon after the experience of violence. There is no algorithm or technique that will "make it happen," yet there are processes and teachings that increase its likelihood. These, and many other paradoxes, are indications that reconciliation is a complex phenomenon.

This chapter explores the implications of looking at reconciliation as emergent creativity. In other words, a relational system marked by mimetic structures of violence (Redekop 2002) can be transformed in a manner akin to complex adaptive systems that self-organize when the right elements come together at the right time. This exploration involves the following heuristic operations: first, there will be a definition of emergent creativity, including factors that enhance the potential for something new to emerge; second, recognizing that Girard has shown a form of reconciliation that occurs after scapegoating, I will examine scapegoating as an emergent phenomenon in the history of hominization; this will segue into an examination of blessing-based phenomena leading to an exploration of reconciliation. Finally, I will show that hope, as an aspect of spirituality, can animate the reconciliation process.

EMERGENT CREATIVITY

Stuart Kauffman, one of the leading thinkers of complexity thinking, has contributed significantly to the conceptual development of "emergent creativity," as it occurs in the context of complex adaptive systems (1995). As a cell biologist and a systems biologist, Kauffman noted that evolutionary theory has a lot to say about how some new organisms or species survive but not much to say about how these new specimens emerge in the first place. His theoretical development of emergent creativity speaks to that (Kaufman 2008). He argues that from cells to organisms to large interactive systems there is so much complexity and interactivity among many variables that development cannot be known, predicted, or controlled. They are all complex adaptive systems.

Figure 1.1 shows that within a complex adaptive system are platforms from which new things can emerge. A platform is a context of interaction between elements within a complex adaptive system. It is the specific locus of emergent creativity. When something new does emerge, there are adjacent possibilities that did not exist before. For example, the heart emerges to pump blood but opens up the adjacent possibility of rhythm. The airbag of a fish that is meant to control depth becomes a niche for new organisms. The personal computer opens up the adjacent possibility of the Internet, which is an example of emergent creativity in its own right.

One of Kauffman's most significant observations is that once something new has emerged, it has its own ontology, which cannot be reduced to what

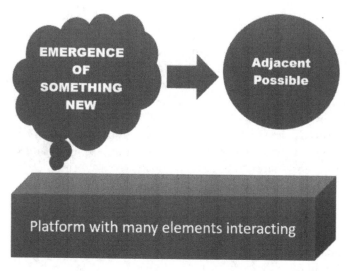

Figure 1.1 **Emergent Creativity.** All figures in this chapter were created by the author.

was before. Quite simply, the emergence of life cannot be reduced to the laws of physics. Kauffman shows how emergent creativity is manifest in the evolution of fields of human activity such as the emergence of economic systems and the common law legal system (2008). Could we then say that the emergence of Spirit cannot be reduced to the organic chemistry of cell biology or even the related fields of neurobiology, physiology, or even systems ecology?

Emergent creativity takes work, which is technically defined as: "the constrained release of energy into a few degrees of freedom" (Kauffman, drawing on Peter Atkins 2008, 90). In this regard, it is the opposite of entropy, which is the random diffusion of energy. There are examples of how even single-celled organisms direct their energy to move in the direction of food sources (Kauffman 2008; Peil Kauffman 2020). Even at that level there seems to be a consciousness at work. Likewise, as Kauffman observes at so many levels, systems engage in the work of directing energy in a relatively focused way.

The world of complexity and complex adaptive system is a nonlinear world in which what emerges is never predictable. There are too many variables to try to account for all of them. The range of possibilities is infinite. In his later work, Kauffman has argued, along with Guissepe Longo and Maël Montévil, that there are no entailing laws that would determine what might emerge (Longo et al. 2012; Kauffman 2020). Put another way, we do not know, and we cannot know, what the future might bring us. The world generally and the smaller worlds of meaning that we indwell are filled with endless possibilities. The future is open.

The fact that we do not know and cannot know what will happen does not mean that we are powerless to do anything about the future. Complexity means neither agnosticism nor despair. Rather, it calls for the kind of humility associated with a sense of awe that there is something that transcends our best efforts and that can impact the future trajectory. The story of Elisha and his servant is a metaphor for this (2 Kings 6:11-19). In the story, they are in a walled city surrounded by a powerful army. The servant is filled with fear. Elisha prays that the servant's eyes might be opened to the creative potential around them. The servant then sees chariots of fire surrounding the city. In the end, they escape danger through a highly creative set of events. In the same way, an awareness of the potential of emergent creativity allows one to "see" that even without knowing what would or could emerge, the potential is there for something to change the situation in a dramatic way.

So, what do we know about complexity that will help us with reconciliation? First, there are conditions under which the probability of something new emerging can be optimized.

Kauffman refers to these conditions as criticality—that is along the line of criticality the probability is high for emergent creativity (2008). Criticality is a function of the number of elements involved and the number of ways of combining these elements. You can have many elements and few ways of combining them and chances are high for emergence (figure 1.2). For instance, in a room filled with several hundred people (many elements), they are asked to form groups based on the main color of the shirt or top they are wearing (few combinations). New groups are likely to emerge in short order. On the other hand, there may be a few elements and many ways of combining them and again chances are high for emergence. A concrete example is a box of Lego blocks—there are relatively few different elements but many combinations of what could be built. If you have few elements and few new ways of combining them, the situation is static—nothing is going to change (the bottom left corner of the graph in figure 1.2). On the other hand, if there are too many elements with many combinations, the result is chaos and the likelihood of anything new emerging is negligible (top right, figure 1.2). While it is impossible to know in advance how many of elements or combinations are optimal, this general understanding can enable one to adjust the situation accordingly.

Beyond the line of criticality, I propose that there is a third axis that impacts the probability that something new will emerge.[3] There are several factors that can enhance the chances for emergent creativity (figure 1.3— note that this is meant to be three-dimensional with the axis of the Number of Elements coming vertically off the page). One of these is desperate need. When there is an emergency, with some extreme needs, new things emerge faster, as is the case in time of war and is currently the case during the

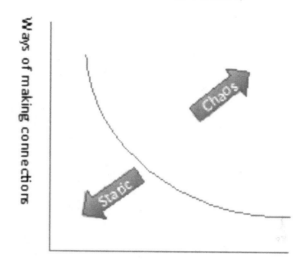

Figure 1.2 Criticality.

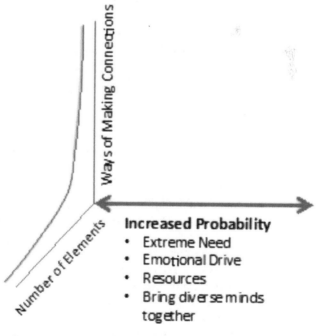

Figure 1.3 Third Axis of Increased Probability.

COVID-19 pandemic. Another is resources; for example, during the 1960s when there was a space race between the United States and the Soviet Union, there was a command economy for space.[4] New items were developed for life in space, and many of them opened adjacent possibilities for life on earth, one trivial example being the powdered orange-flavored drink called "Tang." Another factor that increases the probability for emergent creativity is an emotional drive or intellectual passion to discover something. Related to all of these is the bringing together of diverse experts for the purpose of discovering something new. All of these factors exemplify signs that there is "hope" that something new will emerge; we will return to the theme of hope near the end of the chapter.

René Girard has argued that in archaic societies there was the potential for self-destruction through reciprocal violence and that a scapegoat mechanism emerged that reconciled people, taking them out of the chaotic situation and restoring a social order. I will now examine this phenomenon as a case of emergent creativity.

SCAPEGOAT AND SACRIFICE AS
EMERGENT PHENOMENA

The Girardian hominization narrative (the emergence of humankind) starts with the emergent capacity of humans to imitate the desire of others. "Mimetic desire" is his term (1976, 1987). This capacity builds on mammalian capabilities to imitate behaviors (1987). As Cameron Thomson argues, mimetic desire is an extension of what Tomasello has identified as joint attention—the realization that Self and Other are paying attention to the same thing (2014). This is seen in babies at about nine months when they direct the attention of their parents to some object and show that they are aware that they and an Other are paying attention to the same thing (ibid.). This joint attention can evolve into imagining what the desire of the Other might be and then imitating the desire of the Other—imagining that the Self can have the same thing.

With mimetic desire came a capacity for mimetic rivalry with rivals each wanting what the other had or desired, as well as murder and theft as a way of getting the objects of mimetic desire. These capacities could then extend to all-out reciprocal violence that could destroy archaic communities. What happened, and, according to Girard, happened thousands of times was that a community on the brink of such violence would find a scapegoat and vent all the pent-up violence onto a person they stoned, drowned, or threw off a cliff (1977, 1987, 1989). When this happened, there was a peace that fell upon the community based on a combination of catharsis of violence and everyone having joined in the same activity—a unity in violence. There was also a sense of awe at this wondrous transformation; hence, Girard argues, there was the emergence of a sense of the Sacred (1977) grounded in collective violence.

Through the repetition of this sequence of a build-up of violence through mimetic rivalry ending with a scapegoat catharsis came a realization that this community reconciliation through the death of a victim was desirable and that it should become regular. In the spontaneous emergence of a scapegoat, there was no advance knowledge of who the scapegoat would be, making any community member vulnerable. Furthermore, pushing the violent crisis to the brink of all-out violence made the community as a whole vulnerable.

The adjacent possible opened up by scapegoating was the substitute process of ritual sacrifice (Girard 1977). For most societies, animals were used as sacrifices. This protected humans; it also meant that the meat could be ritually eaten. The sacrifice was a double surrogate. The scapegoat functioned as a surrogate for the enemy of each community member and the sacrificial victim was a surrogate for the scapegoat (ibid.). We can refer to this form of reconciliation as being violence-based reconciliation (Redekop 2014).

The emergence of scapegoating meant the emergence of community reconciliation. Communities developed a shared memory of violent crisis and its denouement through scapegoating. They also developed a social imaginary for reconciliation in the event of violence, resentment, and hatred. That is, a new category opened up for humankind—reconciliation.

One of the characteristics of emergent creativity is that it is nonreducible. That means that its emergence could not have been predicted by what was before nor can it be reduced to the elements existing before its emergence. This would certainly appear to be the case, if Girard has it right. There is nothing built into the situation of a community in crisis that would predict the projection of all violence onto a scapegoat. Once the first scapegoat emerged, there was no turning back—we have been at it ever since.

What about criticality—how does that work within this scenario? We note, first of all, that archaic communities living on the land were relatively small, likely nomadic. It would have been cumbersome for a larger group to travel and the pressure to find food would go up enormously with too large a group. (Note the many problems associated with feeding the Ancient Israelites as they left Egypt and wandered in the wilderness, as described in the Exodus account in the Hebrew Bible.) Everyone would have known all the members of the group. Critical for Girard's sense of emergence was that the proto-scapegoat would have stood out as being different—someone of mixed background, a newcomer to the community, or someone with disabilities.[5] This would have limited the number of potential elements. The combining of someone different with a cathartic violent action is what is new. There are two factors that set up this possibility, however. The first is that intense mimetic rivalry, in Girard's terms, means that the Self lives through the Model-Obstacle, the specific case of Model standing in the way of getting the object of desire. There is already an emotional projection involved whereby the Self identifies with the Model. This sense of identity projection is one of the conditions that makes possible cathartic scapegoating—in effect the scapegoat becomes the rival of everyone. It may be that the scapegoat individual does something unique—kills a large animal, for instance, that makes him the mimetic model for all the men who are hunters. It becomes easier for the one to be rival/enemy of all individuals. The other dynamic is violent contagion. Because of the ripeness of the situation, with all the built-up emotion, as soon as the first stone is being cast, others follow immediately, such that when it is all over, it is impossible to discern who cast the first stone. The fact that the mechanism itself is hidden speaks to this as being an emergent cultural phenomenon of primal communities; they are complex adaptive systems.

We mentioned that crisis or extreme need puts pressure on the system for something new to emerge. In this case, the pressure came from the threat of self-destruction of the community through reciprocal violence. Later, as sacrificial systems were developed, sacrifices were offered at times of grave threat to the community. One example is the human sacrifice of a Greek *pharmakos*—a human sacrifice—when the community was in peril (Girard 1977).

At the level of conscious awareness of a phenomenon, we have in Girard another example of emergent creativity—that of the discovery of phenomena that existed but were hidden from consciousness, in this case, mimetic desire and scapegoating. In other words, the argument is that the human mind is a complex adaptive system and the emergence of new insights happens in line with a general understanding of emergent creativity and that Girard's discoveries are examples of this. With the Girard case, we have a new constellation of elements interacting to produce a new insight: a historian becoming a literary critic and asking new questions; an agnostic reading the Bible with fresh eyes; and expanding engagement with philosophical, classical, biblical, and anthropological texts. We will now take a look at the phenomenon of emergence in the mind, using Girard as a case study.

EXCURSUS—EMERGENCE IN THE MIND

In this section, we will first use concepts of Michael Polanyi and Mihaly Csikszentmihaly to show how the mind could work as a complex adaptive system and then we will turn to the case of Girard. There are aspects of systems-based emergent creativity that resonate with the phenomenon of individual creative action. Michael Polanyi points out that most of our knowledge is tacit—we cannot put it into words (1964). However, out of this tacit dimension emerges language and the capacity to express some of what we know. When we develop a capacity to look at ourselves objectively, we become conscious of the fact that we know something and what it is we know, leading to a more complex level of consciousness (McGuigan and Popp 2015).

Mihaly Csikszentmihaly, in his book on creativity, talks of three phases of significant creative work (1996). The first is to indwell a domain—if you want to write music, you study music, you learn to play, and you become comfortable with music technique, theory, and interpretation—in Polanyi's terms, indwelling contributes to a substantial tacit knowledge base. The second phase is the creative contribution, which emerges out of a decade of indwelling the domain. Mozart wrote his first symphony after ten years of music lessons. Einstein's relativity theory came after years of pondering some paradoxical problems in physics. The third phase is recognition by the field or becoming conscious of the fact that you have done something creative. In other words, the human mind can function as a self-organizing adaptive system—indwelling a world of meaning. This accomplishes two things: first it provides a deep knowledge of the elements involved; second, it explores different ways of combining these elements, eventually eliminating many possible combinations. The indwelling of the field, or the *problematique*, builds up a tacit knowledge base out of which creativity can emerge. The brain works at a tacit level until there is an insight—once there is an insight it cannot be withdrawn, one cannot not know this anymore (Lonergan [1957] 2005). It is the power of knowing something new that propels people forward, motivating them to build on it, perhaps even to die rather than recant.

My spiritual ancestors, the Anabaptists, immersed themselves in the Sermon on the Mount and came up with what for them was an important insight—that normative Christianity demanded a life of discipleship and this implied love for enemies and precluded taking up the sword. Once this became clear for them, they could not undo the insight and thousands died rather than recant. Those in the reform movement of historic Christianity similarly put their lives on the line for a new understanding of Christianity that differed from normative Catholicism—they could not go back. Something new emerged that could not have been predicted and took on a life of its own. Though Csikszentmihaly saw validation by the field as the third phase, he points out that some brilliant people become conscious of the significance of what they have created and do not need external recognition. In any case, this third phase can be framed as bringing to consciousness the fact that something new has emerged. This awareness makes it possible for the emergent reality to extend into the field (see figure 1.4).

The 1950s and early 1960s were years of profound transformation of René Girard. He had come to the United States with a PhD in history from France.

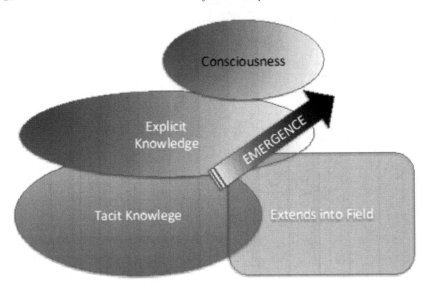

Figure 1.4 Emergence in the Mind.

He ended up teaching French literature. Not being from a literary criticism background, he didn't realize that you don't look for grand patterns and similarities in studying literature. He was interested in what distinguished masterpiece literature from other works of fiction. The big pattern he saw was that masterpiece novelists showed up the mimetic nature of humanity. Their characters were preoccupied in acquiring what their mimetic models had or desired. His examination of five key authors resulted in *Deceit, Desire and the Novel*—the French title is more dramatic, *La Mensonge Romantique et la Verité Romanesque* (The Romantic Lie and the Novelistic Truth). The novelistic truth was that we as human beings do not desire things spontaneously; rather, we desire mimetically. Besides discovering mimetic desire in the 1950s, Girard went through a conversion to Christianity, something he kept veiled in his academic writing for the next decade. In the process, he came to another transformational idea—namely, that the Gospel narratives showed that Jesus as a scapegoat victim was innocent of any wrongdoing that might have led to his death. He saw in the Gospels the unveiling or unmasking of "things hidden since the foundation of the world"[6]—the scapegoat mechanism.

For ten years, Girard indwelled different bodies of literature with these twin insights in mind: mimetic desire and scapegoating. Besides an ongoing odyssey into masterpiece literature (including Shakespeare), he examined the dramas and writings of Ancient Greeks, mastered key works in anthropology, and tackled the philosophy of Heidegger, Derrida, and Lacan and the psychology of Freud. After this decade of intense study in which he was bubbling with new links and connections, he realized "he had bit off more than he could chew" and should publish something. The result was *Violence and the Sacred*, which linked scapegoating with the emergence of sacrifice and the development of cultural taboos. This was followed shortly by *Things Hidden since the Foundation of the World*, a book of interviews arranged according to foundational anthropology, biblical studies, and interdividual psychology. By this time, the key ideas had been published. He kept at it though, using his mimetic hermeneutic to illuminate text upon text, and many books, *To Double Business Bound . . .*, *A Theater of Envy*, *Job: The Victim of His People*, ending with *Battling to the End*, a sustained reflection on the apocalyptic threat that could culminate in the runaway violence envisioned by Clausewitz in his treatise *On War*.

What we see in this narrative, in relation to emergent creativity, is that by approaching two bodies of literature without being conditioned by the field he could make new connections. The study of masterpiece literature led to the emergence of mimetic desire; in his study of the Bible, he examined the text without being conditioned by decades of going to church. The innocent scapegoat victim jumped out at him: first in relation to Jesus; then he saw Job as the victim of his own people; Isaiah's Suffering Servant showed the victim's innocence; and many Psalms gave voice to a scapegoat victim. With these concepts, there were adjacent possibilities—a new take on psychology, hominization, understandings of the economy, a new sense of scientific methodology, and so on. A subsidiary development was a non-sacrificial view of the passion—Jesus did not die to appease God; he died to demonstrate the kind of violent structures that consume us as humans all the time.

RECONCILIATION

We have shown that one form of reconciliation, which occurs through scapegoating, involves a catharsis of violence from a community, resulting in a sense of unity, complete with positive relationships. This change, coming from the violent death or expulsion of a victim, has a sense of immediacy to it and prefigures the development of sacrificial systems that are meant to institutionalize the phenomenon so that there is a periodic reordering of society. One way of framing this is that in a context of mimetic structures of violence, violence-based reconciliation holds the violence at bay: it limits the capacity of violence "to overflow its banks" or to escalate uncontrollably.

Suppose there was a more profound change of relational systems such that the pattern would be more oriented toward creativity, mutual empowerment, and mutual enhancement of the living system. Theoretically, we can talk of

Vern Neufeld Redekop

a transformation of mimetic structures of violence to mimetic structures of blessing (Redekop 2002).

As we can see in figure 1.5, mimetic structures of blessing tend to become increasingly inclusive, and hence, complex. This is in contrast to the closed relational systems in mimetic structures of violence in which it is easy to think of "us" versus "them." Mimetic structures of blessing are generative of more and more options; they are inherently creative. They are marked by a spirit of generosity and are life-oriented, in the sense of celebrating and enhancing the quality of life for all involved. Within a mimetic structure of violence, there are often situations in which people are confronted with minimum choices

Mimetic Structures of

Violence   Blessing

Violence	Blessing
Deep-rooted conflict	*Reconciliation*
Closed	Inclusive
Fewer options	Generative
Acquisitive	Generous
Death oriented	Life oriented
"I had no choice. . .	Choices

Figure 1.5   Reconciliation as Transformation.

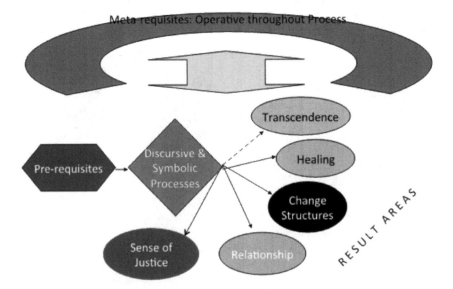

Figure 1.6   Structure of Reconciliation.

with such negative consequences attached that they would think they had no choice but to do something violent. In mimetic structures of blessing, there are choices around how to enhance the lives of one another. Within mimetic structures of blessing, there are clashes of interest, needs, and personalities, but the orientation is such that these conflicts are turned into occasions for creativity. Like mimetic structures of violence, mimetic structures of blessing are constantly in flux, dynamically changing how they manifest themselves.

Reconciliation is both a process and a goal. The goal of reconciliation is to transform a relational system marked by violence and hatred into a situation that allows for healing and flourishing. The process of reconciliation starts with certain prerequisites (see figure 1.6).[7] One of these is a vision and mandate to start a process—to begin the first steps. At the heart of reconciliation are discursive and symbolic processes. These include the open flow of information that marks a true, respectful dialogue and the subsequent opening up of Self and Other to each other. As this happens, there is a realization of hurt and woundedness—sometimes balanced and at other times asymmetrical with a clear victim and a clear perpetrator. In the latter situation, a realization of suffering caused can lead to remorse and apology. This may be answered with forgiveness. The process, expressed so simply, is, in fact, really complex and nuanced. There are emotions that support denial; there are hermeneutical systems that support a justification for violence perpetrated; and there are cultural obstacles to admitting wrongdoing. Popular notions of justice call for retribution. All of these impulses stand in the way of reconciliation.

However, these processes do make a difference to a situation. They are expedited by meta-requisites. These include Gradual Reciprocated Initiatives in Tension-Reduction (GRIT), small trust-building steps, and teachings of blessing—stories, principles, and insights that reinforce reconciliation processes. The results of reconciliation are transcendence (getting "above" the conflict), healing from trauma, a change of political and economic structures, new relationships, and a sense of justice.

In the research project on Spirituality, Emergent Creativity, and Reconciliation (see Redekop 2011), I drew on the following text to develop the Problematique:

> But a stream would rise from the earth and water the whole face of the *adamah* (ground); then *Adonai* God formed *adam* (humankind) from the dust of the adamah, and breathed into his nostrils the breath of life; and the *adam* became a living being. (Genesis 2:6-7)

Mutatis mutandis, we can put it this way: Suppose we have all the elements associated with reconciliation available. It still will not necessarily happen. It is not algorithmic. It is a complex problem with a huge number of variables.

In the Genesis account, the earth-made figure had all the elements of a human being, but it was nothing—nothing until the Spirit was blown into this thing, which became a living being. We can let spirituality stand for that which animates reconciliation, making it come alive (Redekop 2011). Spirituality can be seen as a source for hope, which prompts us to work toward reconciliation and love, which enables us to transcend resentment and negative emotions that stand in the way of forgiveness and renewal of relationships in the wake of hurt and injustice.

Before proceeding with an exploration of the nature of "hope," I would like to reflect on methodology—on how we are proceeding. I am a contextual theologian in the field of deep-rooted conflict and reconciliation. As such, I work in an area where religious-based language can be inflammatory. And, given a history of Christian complicity in hegemonic structures manifest in political power, colonialism, racism, and slavery, not to mention the exclusion of the LGBTQ community, there is a profound academic distrust of Christian-based arguments, particularly those appealing to the Bible as an authority. Within this context, I have been working methodically to find a way to appeal to biblical concepts as having inherent worth based on their hermeneutical and heuristic intellectual fecundity. In other words, I submit that these concepts illumine the human condition such that there is a value added in terms of our capacity to make meaning of our situation and that they work heuristically to help us discover insights of critical importance.

In an earlier publication, I used a hermeneutical circle to look at the words "teaching" and "blessing" to establish the importance of "teachings of blessing" (Redekop 2007b). I first presented *Torah* and *berakhah* in their biblical context. Then I looked at why it might be inappropriate to use these words in a conflict studies environment. Next, I pointed out the opportunities that would present themselves with these concepts. I then reframed the meaning for conflict studies in the light of these considerations. My argument here is that, *mutatis mutandis*, the concept of "hope," as its meaning emerges from the Bible, has intrinsic value and plays a critical role in advancing our understanding of reconciliation as emergent creativity.

HOPE

Hope, within the categories of Paul Ricoeur, becomes an orientation toward the horizon of the future (Ricoeur [1990] 1992). In Charles Taylor's worldview, it can be framed as a particular social imaginary. The word "hope" has been used to translate at least five Hebrew words in the Hebrew Bible. Each of these has its own root metaphors; these tend to be translated by other

English words in other contexts. Assembling these, we have the following concepts feeding into a discursive field for hope:

- *searching*, actively trying to find something new;
- *watching*, looking for something, even scrutinizing the context for signs of something new and positive to emerge;
- *waiting*, being patient with;
- *expectancy*, anticipating something new to emerge without knowing what it might be;
- *trust*, a relational confidence that another will come through for you; and
- *security*, marked by *confidence*.

Given the human capacity for thought and for thought to produce results, as David Bohm maintains (2004), we can think of hope as thoughtful intentionality around an openness for something new to emerge that cannot be defined or described *a priori*.

In other words, hope can be thought of as a confidence in emergent creativity becoming operationalized in a particular context. The time frame can vary from the proximate—something will happen now to the distal—something will emerge over the long term.

Hope can become the basis for another dimension to complement Kauffman's criticality axes of elements and combination. As figure 1.7 suggests, it involves an *imagination* of expectancy that something new could happen. This leads to *actions with anticipation*—research, examination, looking for clues—that could make it happen. Finally, there is the *emergence* of something new—an insight, an "aha" experience, a new configuration. In this regard, hope becomes a concept that has heuristic value in understanding the

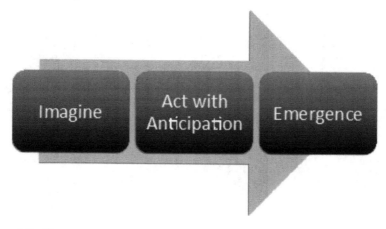

Figure 1.7 Hope.

earlier version of a third axis above—hope keeps people going when there is dire need; hope prompts people to come together to look for solutions to a problem; and hope inspires politicians to set demanding goals for a people.

There is a hitch in that the word "hope" can be used to express an orientation of violence: for example, "I hope he is found guilty and that they lock him up and throw away the key." Another example is George W. Bush's assertion: "Osama bin Laden: Wanted Dead or Alive," expressing a hope that bin Laden would be found and killed or made to suffer. "Hope" is also used to express an intention of blessing: "I hope things go well for you." "I hope you get better soon." "I hope it rains." "I hope that we can find a way to eliminate extreme poverty." Hence, we can imagine the criticality axis of Kauffman being situated in the middle of a bipolar axis with violence in one direction and blessing in the other (figure 1.8). Hope then is an intention oriented toward the future horizon that can have either valence: violence or blessing.

The argument continues that we can do some things to have an impact on the probability of emergent creativity. This is a nonlinear open phenomenon and there is no algorithm that will show what will emerge. However, when you bring a diversity of people together with an intention and with resources, chances increase that something significant will emerge. When it comes to violence, a prime example is a command economy of weapons. What this means is that there is saturation funding to do the research and development to produce weapons that can do particular damage to "bad guys." More neutral, in terms of the violence to blessing continuum, is the saturation funding for the space race in the 1960s and 1970s. When President Kennedy stated that a person would walk on the moon in a decade, that confident hope came

Figure 1.8   Hope as Third Axis.

with saturation funding for space research—any scientist or engineer who had critical skills was hired for the job. Kennedy did not know how it would happen, but he had the confidence in American ingenuity that he could make that statement—which proved to be true, his hope in retrospect was grounded in reality. There were many products and processes that had to be created to make it happen—he had no real conception of exactly how much had to be done.

On the blessing end of the axis, we have challenges as daunting as getting a person to the moon—or even to Mars. These challenges have to do with actualizing reconciliation as the transformation of mimetic structures of violence to mimetic structures of blessing. If, in fact, each instance of reconciliation is nonlinear, nonalgorithmic, open, and with its own dynamics, in other words, if reconciliation is emergent creativity, what can be done to increase the probability that it will occur?[8] One of the factors in this is to have the best stable of concepts that might both help us understand what is needed and have the motivation and imagination to move ahead toward its actualization. To this end I add the concept of love.

LOVE

There are two instances of emergent creativity that are significant in this discourse on love. The first was Rebecca Adams' breakthrough in terms of love defined in terms of mimetic theory. The second was my insight into how the Apostle Paul deconstructed action to highlight the significance of blessing-based love in human affairs.

Back in the 1990s, Rebecca Adams had this gnawing feeling that there was something incomplete in how Girard had developed mimetic theory (2000). In an interview with Adams, he had stated that mimetic desire is neither good nor bad; he had just happened to have concentrated on its violent manifestations. Her own emergent insight into love came through a particular episode of Star Trek (recounted in Redekop 2002, 260–69). Note here that emergent creativity happens when things are combined in a new way. In this case, she combined the experience of the Metamorph in the Star Trek episode with mimetic theory. The Metamorph was a designed humanoid being in the form of a woman. She was programmed to be responsive to the desires of men and was to be a present to the commander of another Starship. Prematurely released, she was creating havoc on Starship Enterprise and Captain Picard insisted she stay in her own cabin. She agreed on condition that he stay with her. Rather than take advantage of her situation, he desired for her the free will that comes with being fully human. She responded to this desire, as she was programmed to do, but in the process was transformed into a being with free will.

Adams then saw that if there is a Wounded Subject with a Model who wishes her well-being, she will then start to value her own self and will take steps to address her problems (figure 1.9). Love, then, is the desire for the well-being of, and relationship with, the desiring Subject on the part of the Model. We are all mimetic models to those around us and as we authentically desire their fullness of being, we can have an impact on their own intentions and actions.

In figure 1.9, we see the Wounded Self prepared to imitate the desire of the Model. The Model desires that the Wounded Self be transformed from woundedness to wholeness. The Wounded Self then has mimetic desire for her own wholeness. This desire for wholeness then can be translated into hope and transformation.

The second emergent insight came when my mother-in-law, Suzie Neufeld, passed away. I was asked to speak on 1 Corinthians 13 at her memorial service. Though I had memorized it as a child, it had been years since I read it. In the meantime, I had done my PhD and digested Ricoeur's *Oneself as Another*, which looks at the structure of action. Hence when I reread it, what jumped out at me was that Paul deconstructs action; in effect, he says that any action can be looked at from the perspective of whether or not it expresses love. The same action as seen objectively, as through a camera lens, could be categorically different based on the interior dimension of the acting Subject. If it would be done without love, it would be empty. With love, it would be full of meaning and enduring impact (for a full development of this concept, see Redekop 2013).

Paul gives a number of action examples. The first is speaking eloquently. This was a highly valued action within Corinth. Gloria and I spent a day in

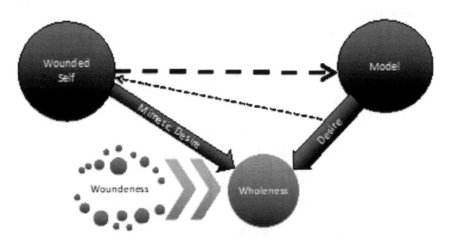

Figure 1.9   Love as Mimetic Desire (Adams).

the ruins of Ancient Corinth a few years ago. We read 1 and 2 Corinthians right there, and these books came alive in a new way. The cobblestone grand entrance to the city leads to a Bema—a raised rock platform on which judgments were made and from which messengers would read important missives. Each of these involved dynamic speech acts. Just outside the city proper was a large amphitheater for dramas, which included great rhetorical moments. Corinth was a place for sophisticated rhetoric. It was exactly this highly valued action that could be vain or meaningful depending on the *agape*—blessing-based love—component.

Other esteemed actions were explaining profound knowledge, changing the world, sharing possessions, and sacrificing one's body. Together they epitomized laudable actions within the historical context. It would be similar to saying, "Though you win the Nobel prize for peace, but have not blessing-based love it is empty; though you win an Olympic Gold Medal, and have not love, it is to no avail."

Love persists in imaging, willing, and desiring the well-being of the other.

PUTTING THIS ALL TOGETHER

It should be clear that how reconciliation happens is not straightforward, especially since to talk of love and forgiveness at the wrong time can only intensify the suffering of victims. There is a complex interplay of dynamics between Self and Other. It is precisely the complexity of how these are implicated that points to each instance of reconciliation as being an instance of emergent creativity. Let us examine a particular case of a reconciliation happening within a reconciliation process to deal with the deep hurt of the Rwandan genocide.

Pierre and Judy Allard lived a shared lifetime of service to marginalized people who were hurt. Pierre had a career as a penitentiary chaplain culminating in being Canada's Director of Chaplaincy and Assistant Commissioner of Corrections. Pierre and Judy invited prisoners into their home and developed community programs of reintegration and restorative justice. Restorative justice was not just a theoretical concept; Pierre had to work through his own anger and hurt over the murder of his brother.

Upon retirement, they set up an NGO called "Just.Equipping." Since Pierre had been the president of the International Prison Chaplains Association (IPCA), he knew chaplains from Rwanda. They invited Pierre and Judy to work with them at the development of Restorative Justice programming to address the release of the *génocidiares* who were involved in the killing of Tutsis during the genocide of 1994. Together a team of chaplains developed a process that involved teachings about taking responsibility for actions, the

Figure 1.10   Reconciliation in Rwanda.

importance of remorse, and the possibility of forgiveness within Rwandan prisons. Following this, hundreds of prisoners wrote letters of remorse, taking responsibility for what they had done, to the family members of victim-survivors. It was clear that they would not receive any special treatment for doing this. Chaplains would then take a letter to a victim, traveling up to five hours into the country. They would describe the letter and give the victim a choice over whether or not to open and read the letter. If a victim would want to meet the one who killed her loved ones, a supportive process was followed to make such a meeting possible.

One such case was that of Alphonse who had killed the mother, brother, and little sister of Teteri. She agreed to meet with Alphonse and responded with forgiveness. He has since been released and returned the village where this happened. Teteri treats him as her son and he works to do what he can for her, helping in her garden (Figure 1.10). Each day that he walks through the village to go to her place, there is a quiet awareness on the part of fellow villagers of the significance of his going to help the one whose family members he killed.

We see in this story emergent creativity at several levels: first there is the emergence of restorative justice and it being a lived reality for the Allards; second, we see the emergence of a well-thought-through process in Rwanda that was implemented by Rwandans; and third, we see the emergence of reconciliation in this particular instance, one of over 300 that have happened so far. We see in this hope for the possibility of reconciliation at every instance—it was hope that prompted the Rwandan chaplains to invite Pierre and Judy to work with them. We also see love as a desire for the well-being of others, motivating people to take action that would result in transformation.

Putting this together:

- We indwell the world of violent conflict with an intention of reconciliation.
- We put together all the elements that might contribute to reconciliation in optimum proportions (criticality).
- We continued to act with a hope that it might come about.
- We breathe into the situation a spirit of love for all the parties, with a desire for their long-term well-being.
- And we wait in hope that reconciliation will emerge.

NOTES

1. Based on the A. J. Muste Lecture delivered by Vern Neufeld Redekop at Hope College on March 26, 2015.

2. Indeed, the concept of reconciliation did not enter the field of social psychology until 1994 (Nadler et al. 2008). Early in the twenty-first century, the concept gained traction academically; note the work of Bloomfield et al. (2004), Bar Tov (2004), Baum and Wells (2004), Abu-Nimer (2001), Long and Brecke (2003), Du Bois and Du Bois (2008), and Daly and Sarkin (2007).

3. I have talked about this with Stuart Kauffman who affirms this line of thinking.

4. A command economy means that there is saturation funding for anything that would advance the goal—in this case putting a person on the moon.

5. It is interesting that one of the few occasions of stoning, which followed the structure of scapegoating, in the Exodus wanderings, involved someone who was half-Egyptian, half-Israelite, who had "cursed God" (Leviticus 24:10–16). There were two signs of difference (cf. Girard 1989)—who he was and what he did.

6. This quotation of Jesus from Matthew 13:35 became the title of Girard's 1987 book.

7. In other publications, I have expanded on the list of prerequisites, discursive and symbolic processes, and meta-requisites. I am only giving a sampling here to provide enough information for the argument I am making.

8. I have advocated for a command economy of peace whereby the best people—scholars and practitioners—would be given saturation funding to develop the concepts, strategies, and practices that would enhance the potential for reconciliation and mimetic structures of blessing.

REFERENCES

Abu-Nimer, M. (ed.). 2001. *Reconciliation, Justice, and Coexistence: Theory and Practice.* Lanham, MD: Lexington Books.

Adams, Rebecca. 2000. "'Loving Mimesis and Girard's' Scapegoat of the Text': A Creative Reassessment of Mimetic Desire." Pp. 277–307 in *Violence Renounced: René Girard, Biblical Studies and Peacemaking*, edited by Willard Swartley. Telford: Pandora.

Bar-Siman-Tov, Yaacov, (ed.). 2004. *From Conflict Resolution to Reconciliation.* Oxford: Oxford University Press.

Baum, Gregory, and Harold Wells, (eds.). 1997. *The Reconciliation of Peoples: Challenge to the Churches.* Maryknoll, NY: Orbis and Geneva: WCC Publications.

Bloomfield, David, Teresa Barnes, and Luc Huyse, (eds.). 2004. *Reconciliation After Violent Conflict: A Handbook.* Stockholm: International IDEA.

Booth, Wayne. 2005. "Introduction: The Rhetoric of War and Reconciliation." Pp. 3–13 in *Roads to Reconciliation*, edited by Amy Benson and Karen M. Poremski. Armonk, NY and London: M.E. Sharpe.

Bohm, David. [1996] 2004. *On Dialogue.* London and New York, NY: Routledge.

Bowker, John, (ed.). 2008. *Conflict and Reconciliation: The Contribution of Religions.* Toronto: The Key Publishing House.

Chanteur, Janine. 1992. *From War to Peace.* Translated by Shirley Ann Weisz. Boulder, CO: Westview Press.

Csikszentmihaly, Mihaly. 1996. *Creativity: Flow and the Psychology of Discovery and Invention.* New York, NY: Harper Collins.

Daly, Erin, and Jeremy Sarkin. 2007. *Reconciliation in Divided Societies: Finding Common Ground.* Philadelphia, PA: University of Pennsylvania Press.

De Waal, Frans. 1989. *Peacemaking among Primates.* Cambridge, MA: Harvard University Press.

———. 2005. "The Law of the Jungle: Conflict Resolution in Primates." Pp. 121–134 in *Roads to Reconciliation: Conflict and Dialogue in the Twenty-First Century*, edited by Amy Benson Brown and Karen M. Poremski. Armonk, NY and London: M.E. Sharpe.

———. 2009. *The Age of Empathy: Nature's Lessons for a Kinder Society.* New York, NY: Three Rivers.

Dilts, Andrew. 2012. "Revisiting Johan Galtung's Concept of Structural … Concept of Structural Violence." *New Political Science*, 34(2), 191–194.

Du Bois, Francois, and Antje du Bois-Pedain. 2008. "Post-Conflict Justice and the Reconciliation Paradigm." Pp. 289–311 in *Justice and Reconciliation in*

Post-Apartheid South Africa, edited by Francois du Bois and Antje du Bois-Pedain. Cambridge: Cambridge University Press.

Fukuyama, Francis. 1992. *The End of History and the Last Man*. New York, NY: Avon.

Galtung, Johan. 1971. "A Structural Theory of Imperialism." *Journal of Peace Research*, 8(2), 81–117.

———. 1992. "The Emerging Conflict Formations." Pp. 23–24 in *Restructuring for World Peace: On the Threshold of the Twenty-First Century*, edited by Katharine Tehranian and Majid Tehranian. Cresskill, NJ: Hampton Press.

———. 2009. *The Fall of the US Empire – And Then What?* Basel: Transcend University Press.

Girard, René. 1976. *Deceit, Desire, and the Novel: Self and Other in Literary Structure*. Translated by Y. Freccero. Baltimore, MD: Johns Hopkins University Press.

———. 1977. *Violence and the Sacred*. Translated by P. Gregory. Baltimore, MD: Johns Hopkins University Press.

———. 1978. *To Double Business Bound: Essays on Literature, Mimesis and Anthropology*. Baltimore, MD: Johns Hopkins University Press.

———. 1987a. *Things Hidden Since the Foundation of the World*. Translated by S. Bann. Stanford, CA: Stanford University Press.

———. 1987b. *Job: The Victim of His People*. Stanford, CA: Stanford University Press.

———. 1989. *The Scapegoat*. Translated by Y. Freccero. Baltimore, MD: Johns Hopkins University Press.

———. [1991] 2000. *A Theatre of Envy*. First published by New York, NY: Oxford University Press. Herefordshire: Gracewing and Surrey: Inigo Enterprises.

———. 2010. *Battling to the End: Conversations with Benoît Chantre*. Translated by M. Baker. East Lansing, MI: Michigan University Press.

Ismael, Jacqueline S. 2007. "Introduction." Pp. 1–18 in *Barriers to Reconciliation: Case Studies on Iraq and the Palestine-Israel Conflict*, edited by Jacqueline S. Ismael and William W. Haddad. Lanham, MD: University Press of America.

Ismael, Jacqueline S., and William W. Haddad, (eds.). 2007. *Barriers to Reconciliation: Case Studies on Iraq and the Palestine-Israel Conflict*. Lanham, MD: University Press of America.

Kauffman, Stuart. 1995. *At Home in the Universe: The Search for Laws of Self-Organization and Complexity*. Oxford: Oxford University Press.

———. 2008. *Reinventing the Sacred: A New View of Science, Reason, and Religion*. New York, NY: Basic Books.

Kim, Sebastian, Pauline Kollontai, and Greg Hoyland. 2008. *Peace and Reconciliation: In Search of a Shared Identity*. Aldershot: Ashgate.

Lonergan, Bernard. [1957]2005. *Insight: A Study of Human Understanding*. [First published by London: Longmans, Green, and Co.] Toronto: University of Toronto Press.

Long, William J., and Peter Brecke. 2003. *War and Reconciliation: Reason and Emotion in Conflict Resolution*. Cambridge, MA: The MIT Press.

Longo, Guiseppe, Maël Montévil, and Stuart Kauffman. 2012. "No Entailing Laws, But Enablement in the Evolution of the Biosphere." *Quantitative Biology*. Accessed May 20, 2015. http://arxiv.org/pdf/1201.2069v1.pdf.

Lopreato, J., and P. Green. 1990. "The Evolutionary Foundations of Revolution." Pp. 107–122 in *Sociobiology and Conflict*, edited by J. Van Der Dennen and V. Falger. New York, NY: Springer.

Lorenz, Konrad. 2002. *On Aggression*. New York, NY: Routledge.

McGuigan, Richard, and Nancy Popp. 2015. *Integral Conflict*. New York, NY: SUNY Press.

Minow, Martha. 1998. *Between Vengeance and Forgiveness: Facing History after Genocide and Mass Violence*. Boston, MA: Beacon Press.

Murphy, Jeffrie, and Jean Hampton. 1988. *Forgiveness and Mercy*. Cambridge: Cambridge University Press.

Muste, A. J. 1967. "Essays by Muste Published." *Anchor*, May 5, 1967. https://hope .edu/offices/muste-lecture-series/resources/Essays%20by%20Muste%20Published %20Anchor%2005-05-1967.pdf.

Nadler, Arie, Thomas E. Malloy, and Jeffrey Fisher. 2008. "Introduction: Intergroup Reconciliation: Dimensions and Themes." Pp. 3–12 in *The Social Psychology of Intergroup Reconciliation*, edited by Arie Nadler, Thomas Malloy, and Jeffrey Fisher. Oxford: Oxford University Press.

Polanyi, M. 1964. *Personal Knowledge: Towards a Post-Critical Philosophy*. New York, NY: Harper and Row.

Redekop, Vern Neufeld. 1995. "The Centrality of Torah as Ethical Projection for the Exodus." *Contagion: Journal of Violence, Mimesis, and Culture*, 2 (Spring), 1995.

———. 2002. *From Violence to Blessing: How an Understanding of Deep-Rooted Conflict Opens Paths to Reconciliation*. Ottawa: Novalis.

———. 2007a. "Reconciling Nuers with Dinkas: A Girardian Approach to Conflict Resolution." *Religion—An International Journal*, 37, 64–84.

———. 2007b. "Teachings of Blessing as Elements of Reconciliation: Intra- and Inter-Religious Hermeneutical Challenges and Opportunities in the Face of Violent Deep-Rooted Conflict." Pp. 129–146 in *The Next Step in Studying Religion: A Graduate's Guide*, edited by Mathieu E. Courville. London: Continuum.

———. 2008. "A Post-Genocidal Justice of Blessing as an Alternative to a Justice of Violence: The Case of Rwanda." Pp. 205–238 in *Peacebuilding in Traumatized Societies*, edited by Barry Hart. Lanham, MD: University Press of America.

———. 2010a. "Healing, Justice, and Reconciliation and Reconciliation." In *The Oxford International Encyclopedia of Peace*. Oxford: Oxford University Press.

———. 2010b. "A Hermeneutics of Blessing as a Meta-Requisite for Reconciliation: John E. Toews' Romans Paradigm as a Case Study." *Journal of Peace and Conflict Studies*, 17(1), 8.

———. 2011. "Spirituality, Emergent Creativity, and Reconciliation." Pp. 585–600 in *Peacemaking: A Comprehensive Theory and Practice Reference*, Vol. II, edited by Sue Allen Nan, Zachariah Cherian Mampilly, and Andrea Bartoli. Westport, CT: Praeger.

———. 2013. "Blessing-Based Love (*agapē*) as a Heuristic Key to Understanding Effective Reconciliation Practices: A Reading of I Corinthians 13 in a Peacebuilding Context." In *Peace on Earth: The Role of Religion in Peace and Conflict Studies*, edited by Tom Matyok. Lanham, MD: Rowman and Littlefield.

————. 2014. "Blessing-Based Reconciliation in the Face of Violence." In *René Girard and Creative Reconciliation*, edited by Vern Neufeld Redekop and Thomas Ryba. Lanham, MD: Lexington.

Ricoeur, Paul. [1990] 1992. *Oneself as Another*. Translated by Kathleen Blamey. Chicago, IL: University of Chicago Press.

————. 2000. *The Just*. Translated by David Pellauer. Chicago, IL: University of Chicago Press.

Thomson, Cameron. 2014. "Mimetic Desire, Aphetic Mimesis, and Reconciliation as the Nexus of 'Letting Go' and 'Turning Around': Conceptual Roots in Tomasello's 'Joint Attention'." Pp. 19–48 in *René Girard and Creative Reconciliation*, edited by Vern Neufeld Redekop and Thomas Ryba. Lanham, MD: Lexington.

Ury, William. 2000. *The Third Side: Why We Fight and How We Can Stop*. New York, NY: Penguin.

Chapter 2

The Biology of Emotion

Implications for Self-Development, Spirituality, and Justice

Katherine Peil Kauffman

EDITOR'S NOTE

In this essay, Katherine Kauffman introduces a new paradigm of how we understand our humanity. Sometimes she refers to this as a "New Story" or "New Science." It involves the role of our emotional selves within the integrated body-mind-spirit consciousness that makes us who we are—individually and collectively. To put this chapter into context, this new paradigm can be contrasted with the paradigm of the human person that emerged after the Enlightenment. This old paradigm featured a clear division between our emotional side and our cognitive side, represented metaphorically by "heart" and "head." In this old paradigm, cognition (logical rationality) was more important than emotion, including passions, expressed in the dictum, "Reason over passion." There are four important corollaries to this paradigmatic framing of humanity. First, there emerged a gender dimension, accentuated by Freud and de Bon. Women were framed as being highly emotional and men as highly rational; hence, men were better suited for professions that involved thinking and good judgment like law, medicine, science, and theology. Second, a la Descartes, humans were first and foremost individual thinkers—I think therefore I am—with individual rights. In this, of course, men as thinkers, voters, and doers were predominant. The sense that we exist within relationships was overlooked. Third, individuals, for their own pursuit of happiness, were self-centered and self-interested—drawing on Darwin, Smith, Locke, and Hume—with interests defined rationally—what is best for ME—and materially. Fourth, there was a racial side to this paradigm that epitomized the white, European male as the highest representation of

41

humanity—that is, having the highest capacity for rationality and intellectual achievement. Though many aspects of this have been repudiated (cf. Cleyn, "Transcending Traditional Justice Claims," Transforming), there is a strong residue of old paradigm thinking that colors values, thoughts, and ideas in many "Western"-based institutions.

In the new paradigm, it becomes apparent that our mind-body is integrated and that emotions drive thought; hence, the objectified apparent rationality of the ideal white male thinker is a thinly disguised veneer over deeply held and passionately defended values that include self-referential chauvinism. The passion for ever greater profits, power, land, and hegemony manifested themselves in colonialism, slavery, and exploitative capitalism in the nineteenth century—all very rational when you plug in the primary value of self-interest. (See Chabot, "Warring with Windigo," and Twinn, "Transforming Wihtiko Systems," Transforming for a concept that develops an entity that feeds off of others and is never satisfied.)—VNR

Human emotions evolved from the early glimmers of pleasure and pain in the first living creatures to the common pallet of human feelings we know so well—feelings like joy, sadness, trust, fear, admiration, envy, love, hate, and so on. But each of these everyday human feelings is actually a package of highly valuable personal information, delivered into consciousness for deeply important biological reasons. Like sounds or colors, feelings are actually informative sensory signals, part of an innate evaluative guidance system long overlooked by science.

According to an emerging new paradigm, the emotional system is the biophysical mechanism that provides the vital functions—animation and guidance—once attributed to spirit or soul. Human feelings embody deep universal values, they color our thoughts, drive our actions, and undergird our learning processes. They serve the ancient function of self-regulation, delivering information to balance, integrate, develop, and actualize all aspects of our identity—body, mind, and spirit (Peil 2012, 2014). As such, our everyday feelings can now be mined for three levels of self-regulatory guidance information: one that informs, preserves, and safeguards optimal physical health; a second that drives mindful individual development and cultural innovation; and a third that guides our socio-spiritual development as one human family, coevolving and cocreating with all other species within one shared and precious biosphere (Kauffman 2020).

I will first show how the emotional side of our existence evolved to help us achieve a capacity to evaluate and make sound decisions. Second, I will show how this emotional dimension is crucial for self-development and what we know about achieving emotional balance and harmony. Third will be an exploration of the implications of this new paradigm for human capacity for relationships—among humans and between humans and other entities. Fourth, I will show that our capacity for making judgments is rooted in our emotional make-up; this then has implications for our understanding of justice and how we respond to violation.

EMOTIONAL EVOLUTION

Single-celled organisms have a capacity to sense toxins in their environment and wiggle away from them; if they need light, they move in that direction. This simple capacity to determine what might harm or help is the beginning of what evolved to be emotions. We can see in this primitive example that this sense provides information that regulates behavior. This "self-regulatory" sensibility then allows organisms' adaptive participation in their own evolution, which not only assists in their survival but also fosters an overall trajectory of variation and complexity. From the simple idea of "what is bad for me" come emotions of fear signaling imminent danger; disgust, protecting us from contaminants and toxins; anger, in response to obstacles to our agency; and sadness informing us of loss, all of which prompt us to form relationships that foster long-term security. The impulse toward "what is good for us" evolves to the emotion of joy with its spin-off emotions of delight, contentment, happiness, and fulfillment.

The Rosetta stone for understanding emotional information is that its binary nature speaks to us of natural values. Feelings arrive in consciousness in pleasurable and painful categories because they encode a deeply *universal evaluative logic*. They say *yes* to this and *no* to that—a *nonnegotiable, life-giving logic* that is central to both our most fundamental evolution and our most complex spiritual impulses. Indeed, as the biophysical guardian of natural values, emotional evaluations undergird all higher-level cognitive and linguistic evaluations, and therefore are shot through all of our most personal judgments, attitudes, and motives. This new paradigm challenges us to reexamine our time-honored sociocultural values within this universal biological context. Even common words such as "good," "bad," "right," and "wrong" must be reevaluated, laundered, and reframed. This will require a seismic shakeup within human consciousness, along with diligent efforts to examine and replace the very foundations of our sociocultural structures, but one that is long overdue.

But this seismic shake-up can be most welcome and rewarding, its benefits vast, indeed global. Accomplishing the task of realigning with our innate value system can deliver all new levels of personal empowerment, well-being, happiness, equitable dignity, social cooperation, and cohesion—states that have long escaped our grasp. Its transcendent lures pleasantly self-reinforcing and iteratively combinatorial, driving an ever-upward positive trajectory—a cocreative spiral—as we rise above the Spiritual Flatland (cf. Wilber 1996) of our own making. For once we reclaim its informational offerings, emotion—the universal wisdom of the heart—can liberate us from our tribal boundaries and human-made prisons of pain to morally and ethically "right" (reactive and proactive) ways of human being and becoming (Kauffman 2020). We can become active participants, aligning with the push of pain and pull of complex pleasure toward ever-better, ever-higher and ever-grander versions of ourselves—*goodness as nature intends.*

Indeed, drawing upon the biological understandings of how positive and negative emotions work together to maintain *critical states of balance.* Then comes the realization that every emotional experience is calling for a systemic balancing, and that each self-corrective rebalancing act forges a new step upon the upward spiral. Over time, we can recover the *optimal ratio* implied within the yes/no logic, something akin to the 80/20 principle (Kauffman, in prep). This means that in a well self-regulated life, humans should experience at least *four times* as many *good feelings* (joy, curiosity, confidence, admiration, wonder, trust, courage, gratitude, compassion, faith, agape love, etc.) as the *basic pains* (sadness, fear, anger, disgust). Only then will we have transcended our current Spiritual Flatland to begin experiencing the 3-D spirituality inherent in our natural design.

Within the new paradigm we begin seeing ourselves as self-aware, sentient co-creators in a living universe, which is the first step away from the shackles of the old materialistic, reductionist worldview as well certain misguided religious assumptions. This new paradigm leads to a new narrative of how we have developed as humans, a narrative undergirded by the insights of this new scientific paradigm of our own evolution.

The New Science: The New Story

To begin, we draw upon polymath economist David Korten to contextualize this new scientific paradigm. Korten suggests that changing the future of humanity for the better requires updating our *sacred story*—the *I AM* story that lies at the center of our human identity. As he puts it: "the practical articulation of the truth in our hearts" (Korten 2015, 18) and "the story in our hearts" (Korten 2015a). Our story embodies the powerful self-fulfilling beliefs that directly impact our thoughts, actions, and our personal and sociocultural trajectories—beliefs that elicit the most powerful feelings.

Korten points out that "[w]e currently organize ourselves as if we are money-seeking robots inhabiting a dead Earth in a dead universe—a potentially fatal error that explains why we are in deep trouble" (Korten 2015a). His project has been "to frame a story that reflects the depth and breadth of human knowledge and points the way to an essential cultural and institutional transformation of our human relationships with one another and Earth" (ibid.).

He offers:

A simple self-evident truth with deep roots in traditional wisdom cultures: That we humans are living beings birthed and nurtured by a living Earth in a living universe. To survive and thrive, we must learn to live as responsible contributing members of the whole of Earth's community of life. The wisdom of traditional peoples, the lessons of religious prophets, and current findings of science together confirm the true story that lives in each human heart and defines our authentic nature. To find our way to a vibrant future, we must acknowledge and share with one another that which we already know. (Korten 2015a)

With this new story all humans can boldly claim: "I am an intelligent, self-directing, participant in a conscious, interconnected, self-organizing cosmos, on a journey of self-discovery, toward ever greater complexity, beauty, awareness and possibility" (Korten 2015, 60).

With elegant simplicity, Korten's new story does indeed synthesize the best science and philosophy presently on offer, shifting our understanding of ourselves to honor our capacities as actively creative agents in a living universe. It emphasizes our accountability and responsibility, a shift away from the idea that we are deterministic machines devoid of legitimate free will, or that our free will defines us as helplessly fallen—"selfish"—children, devoid of any moral compass, and in need of a distant supernatural creator to control or guide us.

However, even within our finest, most complete, big-picture understandings of the human condition, *the functional role of human emotion remains absent* (Peil 2012, 2014; Kauffman 2015). To complete this new story is to understand the biological function of emotion, and its relationship with free will, hardwired behavior, and biological values. Without these crucial yet missing pieces of the human puzzle, we cannot fully understand the nature of violation, of justice or moral value, or even human conscience. We must also ensure that our new story is laundered of any outdated and inaccurate assumptions about what emotion is and what emotion does. For instance, in religions from both East and West, emotion is offered up as the ultimate source of all human suffering, of the "sin" or "evil" in our nature—the powerful, irrational, hedonistic forces of craving and aversion that drive selfish, antisocial, and violent behavior.

This stands in stark contrast with "that which we already know" of the truth and wisdom of the heart; the heart—our emotional system—as the organ of moral conscience, the symbolic center of compassionate care, nonviolence and cooperative grace, and the fount of spiritual revelation—the loving generous, caring, compassionate, and empathic heart that is evidence of moral virtue if not Divine Goodness. Our new story must reconcile these dramatically opposing views of emotion and honor its vital offerings. For all feelings—especially the most complex pains and pleasures—are delivering biologically crucial, nonnegotiable, information. So, I offer these few minor additions (in italics) to complete Korten's new story:

> I am an intelligent, *emotionally sentient, self-regulating* participant in a con-scious, interconnected, self-organizing cosmos, on a *self-actualizing* journey of *Self*-discovery, toward ever greater complexity, beauty, awareness, possibility, and *joy*.

These seemingly minor tweaks change the whole game. For they explicitly define the heart *as* our emotional system, and declare that where there is life, there is *emotional sentience*. As the first "proto" sense to have emerged (well before other sense organs and even brains), emotion serves the primal func-tion of *self-regulation*—an ancient biological blending of sensorimotor control and adaptive immunity, a self-regulatory sense still evident in the chemical circuitry of the simple bacterium (Peil, 2012, 2014). Emotional perceptions (also known as "affective computations") (LeDoux 1989) are different from regular thoughts (cognitive computations) in two ways: They are elicited by stimulus that is "self-relevant" (ibid.)—meaningful to the self, body, mind, even spirit or soul—and they move us to take corrective actions that rebalance us within our "not-self" environment. In terms of the motor components, good and bad feelings trigger approach or avoid behaviors (respectively), yielding "hedonic" behavior (toward that which is beneficial and away from that which is harmful)—a pattern observable across all living creatures (Medicus 1987).

The ingenious *self-regulatory logic* encoded within rudimentary pain and pleasure integrates and unites several biological yin/yang complemen-tarities. These include the foundational evolutionary imperatives of *self-preservation of body* (mediated largely by pain and avoidant behavior) and *self-development* of "mind" (mediated largely by pleasure and approach behavior). These are dual evolutionary *purposes*, if you will, those that offer a subjective reflection of the criteria for natural selection: survival (bodily self-preservation) and "adaptation" (mindful self-development, rather than random mutations), a logic that affords the organism direct participation in the evolutionary process. The more self-development of mind, the less reli-ance on deterministic behaviors and the more adaptively creative use of free will, hence the emergent 80/20 ratio.

Once we understand this self-regulatory logic, we can see how our emotional sense informs us of an ordered sequence of soft-wired "right responses" that should resolve most emotional dissonance without invoking our hardwired fight and flight responses. These right responses are the first-choice self-corrections for every sort of feeling (pleasurable or painful), and they should resolve the lion's share of any form of emotional dissonance. They include *learning* (righting oneself—like a captain would right his sailboat to changing winds), *communication* (righting the social situation by sharing facts, generating resonance, coherence, and social synergy), and *creativity* (righting the environment by working—adding and replenishing need-meeting resources, commodities, and opportunities). For optimal self-regulation, think 80/20 again, with 80 percent right responses, 20 percent fight and flight—the latter advisable only when all previous right responses have been exhausted. So, the phase "self-regulation" packs a meaningful wallop, and once we begin to unpack its logic, we can see how our old, limited—often mistaken—stories have helped perpetuate plenty of self-destructive human folly.

These additions to the story also suggest that the biophysically meaningful self-regulatory information delivered by our emotional sense may emerge from a deep *self-actualizing* impulse within living systems. When we consistently invoke the right responses suggested by our feelings, over time our self-developmental trajectory extends to the self-actualization of all our innate genetic (if not quantum) potentials, what Maslow (1954) noted as one of the highest, most meaningful, of human needs—emotion being how all living systems feel their needs (as Lamarck (1809) once suggested). Indeed, self-actualization seems to be a third self-regulatory imperative, beyond the psychosocial and moral development of mind, extending to a spiritual developmental path—meaning on the broadest and most sweeping scales of time. While we remain largely unaware of it, the emotional system provides an ongoing stream of evaluative sensory information encoded in such complex feeling perceptions as trust, mistrust, courage, worry, gratitude, contempt, admiration, envy, compassion, resentment, love, and hate. Although our outdated stories render us relatively tone-deaf to this divine biological gift, the ever-available flow of emotional messages is actually informing us when, where, and how we can—and that we must—use our creative gifts optimally and wisely. To the degree that our habitual beliefs and sociocultural strategies disengage our emotional awareness, we lose the instinctive endowments of our organism; and to the degree that they *violate* the primary nonnegotiable bio-values encoded in hedonic pleasure and pain, we are unwittingly (but actively) self-destructive in the most literal sense.

SELF-DEVELOPMENT

Yet note also the added capitalization of self in the "journey of Self-discovery" phrase in our new story. In terms of our complex emotional experience, "the self" is a many splendored thing. This capitalization emphasizes the multidimensional and relational aspects of self when mind-as-consciousness is factored in—the entangled, unified, holographic, or hierarchically nested (fractal) collectives or gestalts of consciousness, and ultimately to any Totality of Being—the ultimate Self. This category of "Self" would enfold any notion of "higher self," inner psyche, spirit, or soul, collective soul, and anything like the Jungian collective unconscious, as well as any identity construct through which human beings (or other life forms) maintain an immanent connection to a transcendent creator, God, or All That Is. This expanded notion of Self seems to provide a "not-yet-self" dimensional comparison to the ongoing stream of emotional perception, connoting some deeper perhaps unbounded pool of potentials yet to unfold. So, the self-regulatory logic may ultimately include a foundational complementary relationship between self and Self, wherein the self is at once both an unfolding part and an enfolded whole—a dynamically balanced interaction that may be part of the self-organizing physics themselves.

But even without any of this deeper metaphysical portent, this is another highly relevant, potentially related, and readily observable complementarity that is mediated by binary pleasure and pain, that of a *dialectic mindful self-identity*—in all living systems. Indeed, first-person emotional feelings are integrating and balancing an autonomous individual agent (a "me" identity) and a social entity (a "we" identity)—one very much like and with the same logic as a self/Self binary. In terms of evolution, this is the facet of emotional sentience that gives rise to *group selection*, expanding first-person pleasure and pain to third-party reward and punishment, and expanding the approach and avoid behavioral regimes to include social cooperation and competition. It is this aspect of our emotional self-regulatory logic that the old stories have confounded with the moral notion that "selfishness" is bad and martyred "selflessness" is good—when both are biologically unbalanced—wrong—self-states. We see evidence of this dialectic self-identity and its self-regulatory logic in such physical structures as the sensorimotor chemistry, emotion processing neural structures, and overt behaviors of animals all the way up the evolutionary ladder: from quorum sensing in bacteria, to the dual identity of the slime mold, to the hive mentality of insects (where brains enter the picture), to the territorial and hierarchical behavior of reptiles with "me" taking top priority until the "we" is cooperatively accommodated in the social structure.

Indeed, the reptilian brain is associated with the limbic system and the emergence of the basic emotions. Four out of five of which are painful, the distress signals of sadness, fear, disgust, and anger. This is arguably the source of the 80/20 principle, for with the emergence of basic emotions nature offers us *four times* as much information about *external* environmental conditions that we *must reduce* in order to preserve the body proper—represented within the "selfish" me identity. The avoidant behaviors show up in territoriality, and competitive fight or flight emotional responses, until a long-term cooperative social structure emerges: the dominance hierarchy. With optimal social structures in place, those four basic distress signals will be elicited to further refine them, always *reducing the conditions* that elicit them. In short, the me-self must come first and remain protected within the social structure, for the individual agent always remains the unit of evolution, and emotional information is always relevant to the individual who directly experiences "the feeling of what is happening" (Damasio 1999). All feelings are messages to the self, from the self and about the Self. Nonetheless, with optimal self-regulation the basic pains will be experienced less and less, serving only as corrective signals when universal biologically nonnegotiable needs remain unmet. The upside is that the creature's behavior is then oriented toward more *pleasurable pursuits* such as feeding, mating, and niche building.

Perhaps the most important addition to the new story is the final word: *joy*. Joy is the one positive *basic* emotion—and the grandmother of all complex positive human feelings. For the evaluative logic in pleasure and pain has an evolutionary endgame of ongoing adaptive self-development that is both inspired and rewarded by joy and its complex relatives. Joy is its own intrinsic reward for adaptive learning, ongoing mindful development, and optimal self-regulatory responses. While the basic pains shout "no!" joy sings "yes!" Joy calls our attention to new benefits, affordances, resources, ideas, and social others, and it rewardingly reinforces the best ways to think and act. Joy not only helps us create, protect, and nurture our bodies, it also broadens and builds (Fredrickson 1998), "inspires and rewires" (Haidt 2003) our individual and social minds, moving us to "mend, tend and befriend" (Taylor et al. 2000).

Joy and the Evolutionary End Goal of Self-Development

In terms of evolution, joy and her complex relatives are our rewards for healthy development of the mindful we-self, increasing biological fitness via a broadening empathic expansion to include social others, a trajectory that naturally enlarges the boundaries of one's adaptive ecological niche. It yields cooperation, communication, creative social synergy, and ongoing personal growth—the naturally divine True North goal states of self-regulating life forms within a vitally self-organizing universe. Accordingly, with the emergence of mammals we can readily observe much more joy in animal behavior and even nonverbal expressions of some of the complex positive emotions. Indeed, neuroscientist Jak Panksepp (2005) has mapped the complex and bidirectional emotion processing circuitry of the triune brain, rooting complex emotions much deeper in our evolutionary history than our more anthropocentric old stories suggest. Among mammals, we see playful bonding, loving parental care, empathy (de Waals 2009), morality (fair play is required or social punishment ensues), and altruism (from food sharing to self-sacrificing alarm calls). We also see evidence of an optimal neural and psychosocial developmental trajectory tied to physical health, an epigenetic developmental trajectory influenced physiologically by the care and parental nurturance provided within the foster environment (Jašarević, Rogers, and Bale 2015; Weaver et al. 2004). In primates, the complex bidirectional emotional neural circuitry extends in the prefrontal cortex, the executive control center of the brain, where most complex human feelings are integrated. In monkeys and gorillas, we see evermore complex morality, cooperative social structures, and empathic emotional expressions including grief. In humans, basic joy gives rise to the most desirable hallmarks of human experience: trust, curiosity, confidence, authentic pride, gratitude, admiration, hope, loyalty, wonder, compassion, delight, reverence, faith, authentic happiness, and agape love.

Note also that, like colors or sounds, all feelings bear a unique informational tone (known as the appraisal theme), one uniting the feel good/feel bad polar opposites into meaningful units: Sadness partners with joy to inform us of losses and gains, asking us to reduce the former and increase the latter whenever possible. Fear partners with courage educating us about danger, threat, challenge, and opportunity, moving us to consciously—mindfully—take note of our immediate circumstances and respond accordingly. Anger partners with gratitude, moving us to mediate obstacles and honor resource "affordances" (Gibson 1979), social or otherwise, in our environment. Envy partners with admiration to inform us of our level of self-esteem, personal development, and how we think we stack up against others in the social order; mistrust with trust to keep track of how well we are treated and help decide with whom to bond, cooperate, commune, and rely upon over the long term. With optimal self-regulation over time the flourishing human will indeed experience about an 80/20 ratio of complex pleasures and mostly basic pains.

Unfortunately, humans have largely missed the boat on our emotional sentience and the many levels of evolutionary logic encoded in pleasure and pain, most particularly on how emotion mediates our individual and collective identity structures. We view the self through an outdated Cartesian lens, trying to eclipse emotion with "reason," and fail to see the we/me—I/Thou (Buber 1970) within ourselves; we have gone to town carving up the human family into territorial encampments or rigid dominance castes, and allow our fight and flight responses to run the show. For example, witness the U.S. political arena and the ongoing entrenched conflict between "left-wing liberals" and "right-wing conservatives." While limited and self-defeating to the degree that they oppose one another, they are both half-right.

When stripped to the biological bones, at their best the so-called conservatives are upholding and prioritizing the *body* and the *autonomous* aspects of the self-identity, the individual agency that is biologically required for optimal self-regulation. They are *prioritizing the messages of pain*, honoring the *me-self*, and the self-regulatory imperative of *self-preservation*. They advocate independence, freedom, liberty, spiritual virtue, and personal responsibility for one's actions, as well as conservative use of scarce resources. They emphasize the safety, security, and protection of the individual and the family unit, and demand freedom from excessive or undue regulatory invention.

On the other hand, the so-called liberals uphold the *relational/social* aspects of the human identity, honoring our interdependent nature as well as the collective social mind. Their top priority is the long-term well-being of the group, whether it be a community, a nation, or the entire planet—extending beyond kin to kith. They value cultural diversity, equitable opportunities for growth, optimal health and development, and social justice for all. *They are prioritizing the messages of positive emotion*, the *we-self*, and the self-regulatory imperative of *self-development*.

In a general sense, the Western versus Eastern leadership approaches also prioritize either our *autonomous* or *collectivist* identity constructs, respectively (Markus and Kitayama 1991), while our biology and our now global village demand a balance of both and in the optimal 80/20 ratio.

Indeed, with optimal human development not only are the me-self and the we-self integrated and balanced, but as Singer (1981) suggests, the we-self expands empathically in an ever-wider circle, ultimately to include all members of the human family, even extending to all living systems. This optimal empathic expansion is a meaningfully pragmatic, developmental, unfolding of "self-actualization" and "Self-discovery" in our new story, regardless of any deeper metaphysical implications.

IMPLICATIONS FOR SPIRITUALITY

Accordingly, a central and necessary reinterpretation concerns *spirituality*. Although the word is generally associated with religious ideologies and practices, through this new lens it is defined more narrowly, as a common *variety of human experience*, as William James once described it (James 1985). The claim here is that all of the great religious traditions, as well as secular, humanistic, naturalistic, and Unitarian forms of personal practice, tap into these common "spiritual" impulses and experiences—our *natural spirituality* (Kauffman 2020). Our natural spirituality is the source of the most awe-inspiring experiences of human being, and the context of any enduring existence beyond the earthly life. It moves us to build and maintain a connection with something "greater than the self" in honor of our relational aspects of identity, as well as to create and express the personal capacities that make us a unique individual soul. It is the seat of our moral conscience, our impulses to be and do the best we can, and concerns building some strategy and daily practice to guide and manifest these impulses.

Emotions Offer Spiritual Guidance

In our old religious stories, *the spirit* was considered to be a supernatural force aligned with the soul or with God—all of which were ultimately rejected in light of post-Newtonian mechanistic paradigms. In the old vitalistic paradigm, however, the spirit was defined as the animating, guiding, and vitalizing principle, the *elan vitale* (Bergson 1927), that was held to give life to physical organisms and to play the role of Aristotelian "entelechy" (Von Bertalanffy 1972) in evolution. In our complex systems view, the biophysical mechanism that delivers these animating and vitalizing functions, as well as our direct spiritual experiences, is the *emotional self-regulatory sense.* In other words, our natural spirituality is undergirded by our common biology of emotion, the foundational reservoir of embodied emotional processes that unite and integrate the mind and body, honor and encourage our deepest potentials and capacities, and serve as the motive force that moves, guides, and inspires us to live the fullest, most meaningful and blissfully rewarding life. In short, in our new story, the stream of self-regulatory information offered by the emotional sense is itself the *innate voice of spirit* (Peil 2012).

Our natural spirituality also concerns what seem to be the most serendipitous aspects of life, the portentous coincidences, sacred friendships, and lucky events that befall us—the source of providence and our blessed good fortune. It is also the source of our deepest challenges, our cursed calamities, and the most devastating dark nights of the soul. But in this new view, we are neither at the mercy of divine or evil causal agents behind the scenes nor are random determined victims of physical laws, for we are all *contributing cocreators.* We are willfully and mindfully empowered, active participants in the ongoing creative process, with our daily thoughts and actions calling forth certain experiences from the adjacent possible. With the application of our consciousness and habitual behaviors, we are shaping our own fortunes *as well as those of one another* in the ongoing cocreative adventure. Our emotional sense calls us to not only acknowledge, honor, and embrace our creative power but also mindfully harness it and actualize our immense but latent cocreative potentials as a species.

Our Emotional Unity

Indeed, our natural spirituality tells us that we are *one human family*, biologically, ecologically, and spiritually *undivided*, if not ultimately unified at the deepest levels of self-identity. For despite the myriad faces of humanity, our emotional guidance assures us unequivocally that we are each *equally empowered* as cocreators; that despite the potential pitfalls of the self-regulatory process, we are each worthy of equal human *dignity* and the deepest *respect* as unique individuals. For despite whatever body, race, gender, socioeconomic status, or religious affiliation into which we might be born, we each arrive with distinct creative gifts to deliver, wholly irreplaceable genetic and quantum potentials to develop and express—if not "sacred contracts" to fulfill (Myss 2003). Our naturalistic spirituality tells us that our power comes with both universal human rights and nonnegotiable human responsibilities at both individual and social levels. Understanding and taking accountability for our creative power, both individually and *en mass*, is the central calling of the innate spiritual impulses.

The challenge now, at this hinge of history (Cahill 2010; Kauffman 2016), is to reinvent a shared sense of the sacred (Kauffman 2008) informed by our best science. To acknowledge and honor our natural spirituality as a foundational substrate upon which our cultural and religious diversity can coexist, weave together, and blossom. To, for the first time in human history, transcend the limited identity boundaries that invite entrenched conflict, to equitably honor one another and all living systems, to enhance and share the sacred biosphere that sustains us all. These are the callings of the human spirit that are accompanied by specific guidance that we have long ignored. These are the common callings of the heart, to universally cultivate and practice the genuine respect, compassion, forgiveness, and devotion that we each desire for ourselves. Best of all, they are callings that have long been mired in misconceptions about human nature and our complex identity, callings distorted by our notions of otherness, of sin and evil, thwarted by our external regulatory authorities and institutions that deny our nonnegotiable self-regulatory nature—all born of our lack of understanding of the biological function of emotion.

IMPLICATIONS FOR JUSTICE

In the midst all of this whirling swirling confusion about values, creative empowerment, and the nature of our emotional feelings, we have the twin concepts of *justice* and *violation*—our historical attempts to define right and wrong social states. This new story, however, locates right and wrong states in the biological—emotional and spiritual—flourishing or languishing of the living individual, and recognizes the social distress and eustress as a secondary level of primal self-regulatory pleasure and pain. It suggests that "violation" concerns breaches of our universal rights and responsibilities as human beings.

Emotional Sentience and Ethics

But our new story also weaves religious, moral, ethical, political, and legal notions of human rights and wrongs into the singular context of our common emotional biology. It harkens back to ancient theories of natural law (Delicata 2020), to Plato's unchanging ethical order, to Aristotelian virtue ethics, to the Epicurean pleasure garden, and the Stoic calm—attaining intellectual perfection by transcending false judgment and emotional volatility. It echoes and enhances the "moral sentiments" ethical position advocated by the great Scottish enlightenment philosophers—David Hume, Frances Hutcheson, Adam Smith (Tronto 1993)—uniting also the rationalist, rule, and reason-driven approaches of the Kantian tradition (i.e., the Lockean, justice-as-liberty and the Rawlsian justice-as-fairness approaches (Rawls 1958)) and even the feminist "ethics of care" (Gilligan 1982). As mentioned, the bidirectional emotional processing paths in the brain, as set forth in "dual-process" models of moral cognition (Cannon, Schnall, and White 2011; Greene 2007), suggest that the utilitarian approach, the weighing of specific costs and benefits (Berns et al. 2012), is mediated by the top-down pathway and complex emotions, while the deontological (global rights and wrongs) serves from the bottom-up—via raw pleasure and pain and basic emotion. All of this rich ethical history reflects the many facets of our common emotional biology, "that which we already know" (Korten 2005) through the experience and wisdom of the heart.

Our universal rights and responsibilities as human beings are central to this innate spiritual wisdom, with the ultimate foundational human right being the True-North pursuit of happiness. As John Locke originally put it: "The necessity of pursuing happiness is the foundation of liberty . . . the unalterable pursuit of happiness, which is our greatest good, and which, as such, our desire also follows" (Locke 1690, Book II, para. 52, 243). Likewise, the ultimate foundational human responsibility is offered in a singular moral commandment worthy of the Kantian categorical imperative: "Hurt not others with that which pains thyself," the negative version of the familiar Golden Rule. This fundamental biophysical directive honors the nonnegotiable primacy and universality of pain as compared to the more personally relative, flexible, and developmentally determined nature of the complex pleasures. It avoids the error of assuming or legislating "the good" for others with different sociocultural values, or at different points on the self-developmental spectrum, while also holding up compassion and forgiveness, the common moral strand across every great religion (Armstrong 2004, 2009). Yet this single moral commandment is also implicit within the Western Abrahamic traditions of Judaism, Christianity, and Islam, and explicitly stated in Eastern Hinduism, Buddhism, Jainism, and Confucianism (Rune 1972).

Herein lies the conceptual foundation for justice and violation, both of which concern the emotional dynamics as they play out at interpersonal and group levels of self-regulation. Ultimately, violations are bidirectional breaches of the *social contract* (Hobbs 1651) coming from either internal (breaches of human responsibility) or external (social, institutional, environmental breaches of human rights) sources. Both types of violation are largely motivated (legitimized or justified) by the basic pains (predominantly anger) and the self-preservationary avoidant fight and flight responses to external environmental conditions. But they are also likely undergirded by misguided or limited assumptions, us/them ideologies, and rigid caste structures that also trigger the complex negative emotions (mistrust, shame, contempt, envy, hate, etc.). An external violation is defined as any action (or institution) that unduly interferes with, usurps, or negates one's rightful human dignity and self-regulatory agency. Likewise, it is an internal violation to deny one's *rightful spiritual responsibility* to self-regulate as well as possible. Our optimal sociocultural regulatory strategies will be those that *enable* optimal self-regulation as well as *constrain* and discourage ignorance and irresponsibility with a fourfold emphasis on enablement over constraint, in alignment with the optimal 80/20 ratio of positive/negative emotional experiences of a flourishing individual on the right track (Peil 2012).

Harm Begins with these Two, Deeper, Psychological Violations

While violence is often defined by extreme acts of physical harm, it actually begins with these two forms of *psychological violation*—breaches of human responsibility and breaches of human rights—as they violate the imperatives upheld by our emotional system and lead to the deficiencies of the *wrong-track*. This biological fact is not lost on the World Health Organization, which defines violence as: "The intentional use of physical force or power, threatened or actual, *against oneself*, another person, or against a group or community, that either results in, or has a high likelihood of resulting in, injury, death, *psychological harm, maldevelopment or deprivation*" (Mercy et al. 2003; emphasis mine). The phrase, force "against oneself" is most telling here, as every violation begins as a within-self conflict and its accompanying unanswered distress signals. In fact, this new science offers a clarifying distinction between the terms *power* and *force*, wherein genuine power concerns the optimal physical energy flow through a living system and its application toward healthy self-regulation, ongoing empathic self-development, and creative self-actualization—a combination of well-being and empowerment. Genuine power is associated with cooperative coherence, egalitarian social structures, maximized personal liberty and opportunity, and authentic happiness. Force, in contrast, is the competitive suppression, interruption, or redirection of the energetic flow to attain superior control. Force (whether it be an individual behavior or an institutionalized social strategy) is largely driven by misunderstood distress, defensive behaviors, and competitive conflict, arguably a vestige of primate dominance hierarchies.

But historically, top-down force has been our tactic of choice. For in lieu of using our emotional signals to regulate our own behavior, the ethical strategy of our old understandings has been to *suppressively regulate the behavior of one another* by deliberately inflicting emotional pain. For example, as moral psychologist Paul Rozin has noted, ethical codes are routinely enforced by third-party expressions of the negative emotions (Rozin, Lowery, Imada, and Haidt 1999). Known as the CAD model, they noted how *contempt* enforces codes of *community* (local sociocultural mores); and how *anger* upholds codes of *autonomy* (equal justice, human rights, etc.); and how *disgust* mediates codes of *divinity* (religious mores). Our new story suggests, however, that these third-party expressions likely operate by instilling *first-person* emotions such as shame, embarrassment, guilt, sadness, or fear, and succeed only to the degree that they harness the "flight," submissive, mode of hardwired emotional response (Tangney, Stuewig, and Mashek 2007). This strategy directly violating the prime directive of reducing the basic pains, constructing an entire sphere of human-made suffering that we believe to be normal.

Worse, this strategy can backfire. For it also predicts competitive conflicts between the various ethical codes should they prompt first-person disgust or anger instead, and its naturally aggressive "fight" mode of self-preservationary avoidance (Mullen and Nadler 2008) or elicit such hostile complex emotions as contempt, rage, or hate and "getting even" (the self-regulatory rebalancing) via revenge (DiGiuseppe and Froh 2002). In fact, punitive authoritarian parenting that relies upon shame and humiliation negates the self, invites anger, promotes rage (Scheff, Retzinger, and Suzanne 1991) and self-destructive activity (Milligan and Andrews 2005); and it can lead directly to violent criminal behavior (Athens 1992; Gilligan 1996). In short, while social feedback, punishment, and reward have their time and place, the general social strategy of behavioral constraint upon one another through expressions of negative emotion is violent and biologically self-destructive. It is wrong in every conceivable way.

Multiple Levels of Violation in the Criminal Justice System

Presently, our systems of justice are riddled with assumptions and strategies based on our old stories, most of which are constraint-oriented, with little emphasis on enablement and genuine empowerment. Many of these stories invite escalating exchanges of righteous anger, ongoing conflict, and reciprocal cycles of violation that are both personally and socially self-destructive. We will examine retributive justice, conflation of mental health issues with criminality, legislating morality, and use of deadly weapons. We will then use the example of prohibition of drugs to illustrate how this works.

First is the strategy of *retributive* justice, simple punishment (monetary fines, incarceration, etc.) for misbehavior, which is socially violent and does not work. It simply adds an additional layer of distress to the emotional dissonance that already accompanies both types of violation. It is an ineffective social-level self-preservationary response that further disempowers the already suffering and disenfranchised. Warehouse incarceration can breed subcultures wherein further criminal relationships and strategies can breed, further limiting one's life to a self-destructive wrong track trajectory. Our biology suggests instead that strategies of *restorative* justice (education and rehabilitative and reconciliative approaches) align much better with the pursuit of happiness and the self-developmental imperative, enabling the cooperative impulses and intrinsic motivations.

Second, the confounding of criminal behavior with emotional and behavioral disorder allows issues of public health challenges to masquerade as criminal justice problems. This can lead to proposed solutions that are socially violent, in that they increase universal distress. For example, a high percentage of incarcerated citizens have been diagnosed with mental health disorders. Likewise, children with uncontrollable emotional behavior have been derailed from their educational path, often drugged with questionable psychiatric medicines (Whitaker 2011). As adults, they have been held in solitary confinement, where they are further chemically and developmentally disordered and criminalized, a pattern known as the "school-to-prison pipeline" (Wald and Losen 2003).

Third, the practice of legislating morality in relation to drugs, in denial of free market supply and demand, sets the stage for ongoing conflict, again in violation of the *prime biological directive*. When demand exists (for whatever reason), black markets will predictably emerge, oftentimes in impoverished (perhaps minority) communities lacking in more legitimate economic opportunities. Just as any organism will adaptively exploit changes in its niche, as enforcement approaches evolve, so then do ever more ingenious criminal strategies, if not more desperate and dangerous ways to maintain economic operations. Financial penalties further disempower those already in financial distress, and, to the degree that punitive fines become crucial for income flows for the regulatory authorities, self-organizing dynamics will ensue with both self-preserving and self-developmental impulses that lead to increases in government intervention and spending. In a dynamic systems sense, this is a self-perpetuating positive feedback dynamic that escalates zero-sum competition and chaotic instability to socially destructive levels—the downward spiral opposite to that of our naturally upward trajectory.

Fourth, the use of force and deadly weapons is symbolic of the actual *disempowerment* of both individual agency and social authority, the self-destructive gridlock that is the direct result of dysregulation at both individual and social levels of self-organization. Worse, children, adolescents, and disturbed adults with little hope for a future of genuine flourishing have begun expressing their rage and depression in suicidal massacres, now horrifyingly commonplace occurrences in America, where firearms are supposed to protect our rights as individuals. Although understanding our primal self-regulatory nature offers a strategic way forward, the proliferation of evermore technologically effective and readily available weapons is a symptom of rather profound deviance from our biological optimums, as is our short-term view toward the health of our interdependent biosphere.

Prohibition of Drugs: An Example

For a concrete illustration of these myriad levels of interwoven violation, I now offer the long-standing situation between black youths and police officers, and the illegal drug trade in the United States. While I am not advocating the unhealthy and dangerous use of chemicals in any arena, the ongoing demand for recreational drugs is undeniable. This demand might be due to the simple adult desire to unwind from a busy workweek, the rebellious explorations of youthful curiosity, or even the deeply spiritual investigations of the boundaries of human consciousness. More tellingly, this demand might relate directly to our misunderstood emotional biology. Not only to our misguided social structures but also to increasing biophysical sensitivity to emotional stressors—how experiences of trauma, abuse, neglect, and even socioeconomic inequality get "under the skin" (Hertzman and Boyce 2010). Indeed, we continue to evolve and excessive human-made distress stifles neural development and inviting immune disorder (Dickerson and Kemeny 2004; Meyer-Lindenberg and Tost 2012; Tsankova, Renthal, Kumar, and Nestler 2007) and epigenetic dysregulation (Matttik and Makunin 2010; Worthman 2009; Zhang and Meaney 2010). Together our increasing sensitivity and our ineffective but escalating regulatory constraints perpetuate ongoing suffering and long-term spiritual malaise. With all this suffering, indeed, "epidemic levels of depression" (Seligman 1990), street drugs offer a cheap and easy way to self-medicate, to gain temporary pain relief or grasp a chemically induced moment of joy or ecstasy in an otherwise miserable, meaningless, and hopeless existence. Of course, this is the wrong way to answer emotional distress, but without genuine self-developmental options, it is predictable.

This problem also highlights the economic disparity between those who can afford prescription medicines for mood and pain (or who can import and consume designer drugs in relative privacy of suburban homes) and those who produce, sell, or use bathtub methamphetamine or crack cocaine on the streets. The latter, largely impoverished minority communities, are easier targets for law enforcement who set up institutionalized incentive structures and enforcement strategies with unforeseeable and unintended legal consequences that can further isolate the have-nots and appear racist (Devins, Koppl, Kauffman, and Felin 2015). Worse, the zero-sum competition between the drug dealers and the police, both of which arm themselves with deadly weapons to retain their personal power, creates very real danger and basic fear as well as anticipatory anxiety, worry, and even paranoia, rage, and hate that are factored into perceptual lenses, strategies, and actions on both sides. The headlines of evermore common incidents of fear-driven police assaults against suspected black youths, and the ever-increasing outrage against it should they prove to be innocent, offer examples of the resulting social distress.

This problem of illegal drug markets demonstrates that we have yet to fully learn the lesson of the prohibition of alcohol, a spectacular failure for the same reasons. While drug use can surely be problematic, a good deal of it is essentially the free-market behavior of healthy suppliers and consumers, and (like prostitution, the world's oldest profession) it is not going away anytime soon. To look instead upon the drug problem as a public health issue (as some enlightened governments do), and to provide the structural enablement of legal, equitable access to clean, relatively safe, competitively priced, and taxable designer drugs, would reduce a good deal of the predictable conflict. Coupled with adequate education concerning the emotional system, emphasizing the universal physical manifestations as well as the spiritual portent of uncorrected emotional distress, there would be far less of the unhealthy, escapist, and addictive variety of demand we witness with illegal drug use. Furthermore, with adequate mobility, educational opportunities, apprenticing experiences, and job opportunities that help identify, develop, and actualize individual potentials, the right-track pursuit of happiness can become the dominant motivation, further reducing any unhealthy demand and need for black market employment. Indeed, our common biology suggests that no one truly desires a life motivated predominantly by the simple reduction of pain.

An Enlightened Safety-First Approach

But even with ongoing legal prohibition, such biologically based strategies would emphasize if not prioritize learning and communication—the first-choice right responses—in regulatory approaches. They could openly acknowledge that black markets do provide economic opportunities and fulfill human desires—as well as honestly confront the fact that prohibitive laws predict zero-sum conflict between authorities and dealers, and drive escalating cycles of reciprocal fear and fight and flight reactions on both sides. They could, however, elevate the cooperative goal of *public safety* during the enforcement process above that of prohibition itself via community dialogues. In community policing, for example, public educational forums held in "safe spaces" could invite open dialogue between local black-market agents and police, to forge cooperative agreement upon safety-first interactive strategies in exchange for misdemeanor or reduced charges (Kauffman 2015a; Redekop and Paré 2010; Redekop 2013). Specific safety-first identifying emblems, hand signals, or verbal exchanges during street encounters could validate such agreements, establishing the mutual community trust that can short-circuit the fear-driven cycles of fight and flight defense that ignite us-versus-them violence.

Indeed, such structural enablement would be just the beginning of a social right-track path, where we can begin to harness and influence one another cooperatively and with the complex positive emotions. Moving beyond the negative CAD model of our past (pushing ethical systems on others driven by contempt, anger, disgust) to a strategy inspired by *compassion* for our common human challenges *Awe* for our co-creative gifts along with deep accountability for our autonomous creative agency, and *Devotion* to ourselves as a human family sharing one interdependent biosphere, without the us-versus-them identity boundaries and dominance hierarchies that perpetuate long-term distress. This is the long-term dream, for deconstructing the myriad dysfunctional social structures from our old stories will take time.

Conciliation, Reconciliation, and Justice of Blessing

We can make great strides by honoring, reinforcing, and elevating the aspects of our old story that are on the right track. Those that, as David Korten suggests, have been reflected in "that which we know" (Korten 2015a), the common wisdom of the heart. Indeed, these age-old emotional dynamics have been captured across our philosophical and religious traditions, standing at the center of the most effective approaches to humanitarian justice and reconciliation. I will highlight some of these themes and then show how they have creatively morphed into life-giving approaches to justice.

Successful Themes from Religious Traditions

One example is the practice of *teshuvah* of the Jewish tradition, a strategy of post-violation repentance, to make right a relationship that has gone offtrack (Newman 2010). It works because it honors the trial and error nature of learning, draws upon both human accountability and compassion, reflects a tacit understanding of the two types of violation, and invokes the appropriate right responses. It relies upon honesty, open communication, accountability, correction, and forgiveness. But its deeper success is because its three-step process is an interpersonal reflection of the first-person cycle of emotional self-correction: The victim of any given violation first approaches the perpetrator to point out the violation (communicating the pain to the other, just as the emotion communicates it to the self). The perpetrator (who is often unaware, unless having already experienced some degree of regret, guilt, or shame) then accepts responsibility for the situation (internalizes the message of the pain, openly empathizing and learning rather than protectively denying or justifying the action at issue). This is also where open communication of perceived violations due to limiting beliefs, attitudes, or ideologies can yield learning or cognitive reframing—optimal growth—on both parts (and roles of victim/perpetrator can reverse). The perpetrator then offers a genuine apology and asks the victim how to make it up to them, or to make them whole (just as the individual would rebalance the self-system with a right response). Then, the perpetrator carries out the agreed-upon action, the victim offers genuine forgiveness, and the relationship between them is restored.

The more intrapersonal (first-person) restoration is captured by the Catholic tradition of confession: The perpetrator self-identifies a "sinful" violation through feelings of regret, guilt, or shame—the complex dissonance of a refined moral conscience (themselves the blends and shades of sadness, fear, or self-directed anger or disgust). An honest, accountable acknowledgment of such a misstep to an appropriate religious authority, then invokes the forgiveness and grace of a just and faithful God. The authority then recommends some specific actions or declarations appropriate to the violation, and their heartfelt offering restores the inner spiritual connection between self and Self. Indeed, many criminal justice interventions are due to the lack of accountability implied in the personal confession. Hence, the rituals of confessional atonement are a component of most religions, but in the cases of Buddhism or Islam the confessions require no authoritative intermediary, are kept completive and private, perhaps more in keeping with the personal nature of emotional sensory guidance.

Together, the intra and interpersonal cycles of corrective self-regulation underlie the successful conciliation and reconciliation strategies following even the worst of human on human atrocity, most of which rely on some acknowledgment of our common human bonds, if not our interdependence as living creatures sharing one biosphere. Other positive examples include the concept of *Ahimsa*, the strategy of nonviolence toward all living things, central to the Hindu, Buddhist, and Jain traditions and the African concept of *Ubuntu*, tapping the innate human kindness born of our universal connective bond, following Apartheid or genocidal holocaust.

The Justice of Blessing Model

Placing our traditional religious, social, and political practices in the context of the complexity sciences offers still further evaluative and pragmatic utility. One example is the *justice of blessing* model (Redekop 2002, 2008), which incorporates the concepts of emergent creativity, edge-of-chaos criticality, and the enduring motive power of positive emotion in an enlightened approach to post-violence reconciliation.

The model captures the interpersonal, social-level dynamics, as well as acknowledging many of the individual emotional drivers that perpetuate cycles of violent conflict. It notes the subconscious and low-level default aspects of emotional distress and self-preservationary behaviors, and even how violence-based reconciliation (Girard 1987) can yield emergent self-developmental social unity. It captures how the right track of individual development brings the tacit intuitive (bottom-up) wisdom offered by emotion into conscious awareness and delivers mindful focus and top-down control via the cultivation of the complex positive emotions (Redekop 2014). How establishing community dialogue can begin to break down us/them identity barriers and build genuine public trust. How such feelings as compassion, acceptance, and forgiveness can allow the letting go (Thomson 2014) of entrenched hatred and resentment, can foster empathic unity, and harness the learning and communitive responses to righteous anger—those that undergird successful truth and reconciliation efforts following sweeping historical atrocities (such as Apartheid, genocidal civil war, or even the Holocaust). It honors our innate emotional spirituality as well as borrowing from common religious themes from East and West, wherein a blessing-based life is one of "social and personal justice and attention to right relationships" (Redekop, unpublished correspondence).

It acknowledges that at various points in space and time—despite our best intentions and innate goodness—each of us is both victim and perpetrator of both types of psychological violence. That we are all in the same human boat, and the essence of compassion lies in that universal blanket of forgiveness that we desire for ourselves. It notes the error of "us versus them" thinking and how honoring our common human identity can begin building the mutual trust that feeds back to quiet habitual triggers of fear and anger, even replacing mindsets that breed resentment and revenge. It even implies how taking full accountability can ultimately deliver *gratitude* for the spiritual insights that follow courageous transcendence of our darkest challenges—that from all conflict comes emergent creativity and developmental opportunity should we proceed forward with confidence, courage, agape love, and visionary hope.

When it comes to the aftermath of mass human violence, a justice of blessing can provide an alternative to retributive justice of violence (Redekop 2008). Where perpetrators indwell a deep *teshuvah*—a repentance and willingness to turn things around, they can devote themselves to the well-being of victim-survivors, taking stock periodically how the needs have changed.

CONCLUSION

At this hinge of history, we have collectively forged a broadened philosophical and empirical lens through which to envision and understand our humanity, a view that allows us to tell a newly enlightened story of human identity. We can now make a bold declaration that fully honors our innate capacities as human beings, and a declaration that—if truly embraced—can begin to shift many entrenched but dysfunctional ideas, attitudes, and self-destructive habits:

> I am an intelligent, emotionally sentient, self-regulating participant in a conscious, interconnected, self-organizing cosmos, on a self-actualizing journey of Self-discovery, toward ever greater complexity, beauty, awareness, possibility and joy. (Kauffman adaptation of Korten 2015)

This new story bridges science and religion, honoring the divine revelation written within the Book of Nature as well as that captured within sacred texts of religious traditions from East and West. It allows us to fully acknowledge our God-given creative gifts and their accompanying responsibilities, to understand life as a developmental journey of discovering ever better ways to use our creative apportionment, individually and *en masse*. This new story allows us to transcend more limiting, powerless, or childlike versions of ourselves, and our futile attempts to control one another in lieu of the universal self-regulation of natural design. It rejects the historical dogmas that emerged for that purpose, that we are born sinful, "fallen," deserving of divine punishment for disobedience, or that free will itself was the mistake of a bungling Creator.

But perhaps the biggest addition is that all living creatures also come biologically endowed with a *guidance system*—our emotional sentience— to inform us of the best use of our creative freedom and empowerment, complete with hardwired behavioral safeguards until we awaken to the meaningful information it offers. In terms of religion, it offers a much grander depiction of the "Divine Creator," as the ultimate unified essence of all physical processes, all self-organizing dynamics, and all personal identities, as well as all the enfolded possibilities and self-potentials yet to be—the Self (with a capital S). It offers solid grounding to the perennial *wisdom of the heart*, as the resonance with our innate spirituality, the utilization of our emotional compass, and properly crediting our emotional biology for delivering the fruits of spirit. In terms of science, it fills a conspicuous void in our cannon of self-understanding: how we come to know, promote, and enact *value*—both in our daily lives and in our sociocultural creations. It honors the fact that our feelings encode ancient, innate, and universal evaluations that bubble up from the very physical and dynamical laws of nature, evaluations central to natural selection and evolution, functioning to help us integrate, stabilize, and balance ourselves on an optimally "right" track of being and becoming. It allows us to lay bare how we are going "wrong," reframing the concepts of rights, responsibilities, and violation, reenvisioning what we mean by justice, morality, and virtue, offering all-new approaches to attaining them.

Indeed, add to this brave new vision any personal, social, and global strategies that identify and root out the self-destructive ideologies, attitudes, habits, and institutionalized violations that predict elicitation of the complex negative emotions, yet coming full circle to a healthy curiosity, respect, and genuine gratitude for the information they contain. The transcendence of mindlessly defending overly narrow ego-boundaries, of scapegoating or blaming so-called "evil" others, and of blocking, denying, stifling, or defiling the feelings themselves. For as Pogo put it: "We have met the enemy and he is us" (Kelly 1953), a revelation that must be met with spiritual fortitude and radical accountability. For we have also met the *creator*, and she too is us.

REFERENCES

Armstrong, C. 2004. *The Spiral Staircase: My Climb Out of Darkness*. New York, NY: Anchor Books; Random House, Inc., 293–299.

Armstrong, C. 2009. *A Case for God*. New York, NY: Alfred A Knopf.

Athens, L. 1992. *The Creation of Dangerous Violent Criminals*. Chicago, IL: University of Illinois Press.

Berns, G. S., Bell, E., Capra, C. M., Prietula, M. J., Moore, S., Anderson, B., Ginges, J., & Atran, S. 2012. The price of your soul: Neural evidence for the non-utilitarian representation of sacred values. *Philosophical Transactions of the Royal Society B*, 367, 754–762.

Cahill, T. 2010. *Mysteries of the Middle Ages: And the Beginning of the Modern World*, Vol. 5. Anchor.

Cannon, P. R., Schnall, S., & White, M. 2012. Transgressions and expressions: Affective facial muscle activity predicts moral judgments. *Social Psychology and Personality Science*, 2(3), 325–331.

Damasio, A. 1999. *The Feeling of What is Happening*. Orlando, FL: Harcourt.

Delicata, N. 2020. Reinventing natural law as a school of virtue: Towards a global ethic in the context of emergent creativity." In *Awakening: Exploring Spirituality, Emergent Creativity and Reconciliation*. Edited by V. Neufeld Redekop & G. Neufeld Redekop. Lanham, MD: Lexington.

Devins, C., Koppl, R., Kauffman, S., & Felin, T. 2015. Against design. *Arizona State Law Review*, 47(3) (Fall, December 14). http://arizonastatelawjournal.org/against -design/.

de Waal, Frans. 2009. *The Age of Empathy: Nature's Lessons for a Kinder Society*. New York, NY: Three Rivers Press.

DiGiuseppe, R., & Froh, J. J. 2002. What cognitions predict state anger? *Journal of Rational-Emotive & Cognitive Behavioral Therapy*, 20(2), 133–149.

Dickerson, S. S., & Kemeny, M. E. 2004. Acute stressors and cortisol responses: A theoretical integration and synthesis of laboratory research. *Psychological Bulletin*, 130(3), 355.

Fredrickson, B. L. 1998. What good are positive emotions? *Review of General Psychology*, 2(3), 300–319.

Gibson, J. J. [1979] 2014. *The Ecological Approach to Visual Perception*, Classis edition. Psychology Press.

Gilligan, C. 1982. *In a Different Voice*. Harvard University Press.Gilligan, J. 1996. *Violence: Our Deadly Epidemic and its Causes*. New York, NY: Grosset/Putnam, 10.

Girard, R. 1987. *Things Hidden Since the Foundation of the World*. Translated by S. Bann. Stanford, CA: Stanford University Press.

Greene, J. D. 2007. The secret joke of Kant's soul. In *Moral Psychology, Vol. 3: The Neuroscience of Morality: Emotion, Brain Disorders, and Development*. Edited by W. Sinnott-Armstrong. Cambridge, MA: MIT Press, 35–80.

Greene, J. D., & Paxton, J. M. 2009. Patterns of neural activity associated with honest and dishonest moral decisions. *Proceedings of the National Academy of Sciences*, 106(30), 12506–12511. doi:10.1073/pnas.0900152106.

Haidt, J. 2003. Elevation and the positive psychology of morality. In *Flourishing: Positive Psychology and the Life Well-Lived*. Edited by Corey L. M. Keyes & Jonathan Haidt. Washington, DC, US: American Psychological Association, 275–289.

Hara, M. R., Kovacs, J. J., Whalen, E. J., Rajagopal, S., Strachan, R. T., Grant, W., Towers, A. J., Williams, B., Lam, C. M., Xiao, K., Shenoy, S. K., Gregory, S. G., Ahn, S., Duckett, D. R., & Lefkowitz, R. J. 2011. A stress response pathway regulates DNA damage through β2-adrenoreceptors nd β1-arrestin-1. *Nature*. doi:10.1038/nature10368.

Hertzman, C., & Boyce, T. 2010. How experience gets under the skin to create gradients in developmental health. *Annual Review of Public Health*, 31, 329–347.

Hobbes, T. 1651. *Leviathan*. Edited by C. B. Macpherson. London: Penguin Books, 1985.

Hume, D. 1975. *A Treatise of Human Nature*. London: Oxford University Press, (Selby-Bigge).

James, W. 1985. *The Varieties of Religious Experience*, Vol. 13. Harvard University Press.

Jašarević, E., Rogers, A. B., & Bale, T. L. 2015. A novel role for maternal stress and microbial transmission in early life programming and neurodevelopment. *Neurobiology of Stress*, 1, 81–88.

Kauffman, K. P. 2015. Emotional sentience and the nature of phenomenal experience. *Progress in Biophysics and Molecular Biology*, 119(3), 545–562.

———. 2020. Natural spirituality and the biology of emotion. In *Awakening: Exploring Spirituality, Emergent Creativity and Reconciliation*. Edited by V. N. Redekop & G. Neufeld Redekop. Lanham, MD: Lexington.

———. (In prep).

Kauffman, S. 1996. *Origins of Order*. New York, NY: Oxford University Press.

———. 2008. *Reinventing the Sacred*. New York, NY: Basic Books.

———. 2015. *Personal Communications Concerning Right Response Community Policing Interventions*.

———. 2016. *Humanity in a Creative Universe*. Oxford University Press.

Korten, D. C. 2015. *Change the Story, Change the Future: A Living Economy for a Living Earth*. Berrett-Koehler Publishers.

———. 2015a. Change the Future: A Living Economy for a Living Earth. https://davidkorten.org/changethestory-changethefuture/

Lamarck, J.-B. 1809. *Zoological Philosophy: An Exposition with Regard to the Natural History of Animals*. Translated by H. Elliot. Chicago, IL: University of Chicago Press, 1984 reprint of 1914 edition. First published as Philosophie zoologique, ou exposition des considérations relatives à l'histoire naturelle des animaux, Paris, Dentu.

Locke, J. 1690. *An Essay Concerning Human Understanding*, Book II, para. 52, 243 (Fraser ed., Dover, 1959, 1690).

Markus, H. R., & Kitayama, S. 1991. Culture and the self: Implications for cognition, emotion, and motivation. *Psychological Review*, 98(2), 224.

Mattick, J. S., & Makunin, I. V. 2006. Non-coding RNA. *Human Molecular Genetics*, 15(1), R17–R29.

Maslow, A. 1954. *Motivation and Personality*. New York, NY: Harper Row.

Medicus, G. 1987. Toward an ethnopsychology: A phylogenic tree of behavior. *Ethology and Sociobiology*, 8(3 Suppl.), 131–150.

Mercy, J. A., Butchart, A., Dahlberg, L. L., Zwi, A. B., & Krug, E. G. 2003. Violence and mental health: Perspectives from the World Health Organization's. World report on violence and health. *International Journal of Mental Health*, 32(1), 20–35.

Merryman, J. 2014. *How to Hack Human History*. http://fqxi.org/community/forum/topic/1981.

Meyer-Lindenberg, A., & Tost, H. 2012. Neural mechanisms of social risk for psychiatric disorders. *Nature Neuroscience*, 15(5) (May), 663–668.

Milligan, R.-J., & Andrews, B. 2005. Suicidal and other self-harming behaviour in offender women: The role of shame, anger and childhood abuse. *Legal and Criminological Psychology*, 10(1), 13–25.

Mullen, E., & Nadler, J. 2008. Moral spillovers: The effect of moral violations on deviant behavior. *Journal of Experimental Social Psychology*, 44, 1239–1245.

Myss, C. M. 2003. *Sacred Contracts: Awakening your Divine Potential.* Harmony Books.

Newman, L. E. 2010. *Repentence: The Meaning & Practice of Teshuvah.* Woodstock, VT: Jewish Lights Publishing.

Ostrom, Elinor. 2009. *Nobel Prize Lecture.*

Peil, K. T. 2014. The self-regulatory sense. *Global Advances in Health and Medicine*, 3(2), 80–108. http://www.ncbi.nlm.nih.gov/pmc/articles/PMC401095 7/.

———. 2012. *Emotion: A Self-Regulatory Sense?* EFS International. http://www .academia.edu/7208004/Emotion_The_Self-regulatory_Sense_For_the_Psych_ community_2012_.

Rawls, J. 1958. Justice as fairness. *The Philosophical Review*, 67(2), 164–194.

Redekop, V. N. 2014. Blessing-based reconciliation in the face of violence. In *René Girard and Creative Reconciliation.* Edited by V. Redekop & T. Ryba. Lanham, MD: Lexington.

———. 2013. Mutual respect, complexity and community dialogue: Charting a new path. In *Professional Policing Practice.* Edited by P. A. J. Waddington. Oxford: Oxford University Press.

———. 2008. A post-genocidal justice of blessing as an alternative to a justice of violence: The case of Rwanda. In *Peacebuilding in Traumatized Societies.* Edited by Barry Hart. University Press of America, 205–238.

———. 2002. *From Violence to Blessing: How an Understanding of Deep-Rooted Conflict Opens Paths to Reconciliation.* Ottawa: Novalis.

Redekop, V., & Paré, Shirley. 2010. *Beyond Control: A Mutual Respect Approach to Protest Crowd – Police Relations.* London: Bloomsbury Academic.

Rozin, P., Lowery, L., Imada, S., & Haidt, J. 1999. The CAD triad hypothesis: A mapping between three moral emotions (contempt, anger, disgust) and three moral codes (community, autonomy divinity). *Journal of Personality and Social Psychology*, 76, 574–586.

Rune, D. D. 1972. *The Pictorial History of Philosophy.* New York, NY: Bramhill House.

Scheff, T. J., & Retzinger, S. M. 1991. *Emotions and Violence: Shame and Rage in Destructive Conflicts.* Lexington, MA, USA: Lexington Books/D. C. Heath and Company.

Seligman, Martin E. P. 1990. "Why is there so much depression today? The waxing of the individual and the waning of the commons." In *Contemporary Psychological Approaches to Depression.* Springer US, 1–9.

Selye, H. 1957. *The Stress of Life.* New York, NY: McGraw Hill (Rev. 1978).

Singer, P. 1981. *The Expanding Circle.* Oxford: Clarendon Press.

Spencer, H. 1895. *The Principles of Sociology*, Vol. 6. Appleton, 449.

Tangney, J. P., Wagner, P. E., Hill-Barlow, D., Marschall, D. E., & Gramzow, R. 1996. Relation of shame and guilt to constructive and destructive responses to anger across the lifespan. *Journal of Personality and Social Psychology*, 70(4), 797–809.

Taylor, S. E., Klein, L. C., Lewis, B. P., Gruenewald, T. L.,Gurung, R. A., & Updegraff, J. A. 2000. Biobehavioral responses to stress in females: Tend-and-befriend, not fight-or-flight. *Psychological Review*, 107 (3), 411–429.

Thomson, C. 2014. Mimetic desire, aphetic mimesis, and reconciliation as the nexus of letting go and turning around: Conceptual roots in Tomasello's 'joint attention'. In *René Girard and Creative Reconciliation*. Edited by V. Redekop & T. Ryba. Lanham, MD: Lexington.

Tsankova, N., Renthal, W., Kumar, A., & Nestler, E. J. 2007. Epigenetic regulation in psychiatric disorders. *Nature Reviews, Neuroscience*, 8(May), 355–367.

Tronto, J. 1993. *Moral Boundaries*. New York, NY: Routledge, Chapman & Hall.

Von Bertalanffy, L. 1972. The history and status of general systems theory. *Academy of Management Journal*, 15(4), 407–426.

Wald, J., & Losen, D. J. 2003. Defining and redirecting a school-to-prison pipeline. *New Directions for Youth Development*, 2003(99), 9–15.

Weaver, I. C., Cervoni, N., Champagne, F. A., D'Alessio, A. C., Sharma, S., Seckl, J. R., Dymov, S., Szyf, M., & Meaney, M. J. 2004. Epigenetic programming by maternal behavior. *Nature Neuroscience*, 7(8), 847–854.

Whitaker, Robert. 2011. *Anatomy of an Epidemic: Magic Bullets, Psychiatric Drugs, and the Astonishing Rise of Mental Illness in America*. New York, NY: Broadway.

Wilber, K. 1996. *A Brief History of Everything*. Boston, MA: Shambhala.

Worthman, C. M. 2009. Habits of the heart: Life history and the developmental neuroendocrinology of emotion. *American Journal of Human Biology*, 21, 772–781.

Zhang, T.-H., & Meaney, M. J. 2010. Epigenetics and the environmental regulation of the genome and its function. *Annual Review Psychology*, 61, 439–466.

Chapter 3

Violence, Reconciliation, and the Significance of the Subtle Mystical Dimension in the Light of René Girard's *Battling to the End*

Petra Steinmair-Pösel

Starting from René Girard's analysis of our age as an apocalyptic era, which is in desperate need of deep reconciliation, I will follow the traits of the subtle mystical dimension in *Battling to the End*. Pointing out the fact that, for Girard, cultivating this mystical dimension is the only alternative to human self-destruction, I will consult the works of three contemporary female mystics in order to identify ways in which Christian mystical experience—understood in a broad and thus "democratic" sense—can contribute to deep reconciliation. The Orthodox nun Maria Skobtsova will guide us to an understanding of every human being— even the enemy—as an icon of Christ (bearing within themselves the traits of the divine). Chiara Lubich, founder of the Catholic Focolare Movement, will introduce us to *kenosis*—emptying oneself—as a prerequisite for those who want to advance unity. And Protestant activist and theopoet Dorothee Soelle, by insisting on the prophetic and incompliant dimension of mysticism, will make us aware of the necessity to (nonviolently!) go through conflict instead of simply suppressing it. Thus, these everyday mystics can guide us in opening spaces of emergent creativity (cf. Steinmair-Pösel 2019, 313–413).

GIRARD: BATTLING TO THE END
OR TO CONVERSION

It is in itself an event of "emergent creativity" (cf. Redekop, Reconciliation, *Transforming*) that the French historian René Girard, after immigrating to the United States and teaching there as a professor of French Literature at Johns Hopkins University in the late 1950s, discovered the mimetic nature of human desire as well as the single victim mechanism as the violent *and* violence-restraining foundation of human culture. His basic insights may briefly be summarized in three steps:

1. As human beings we are deeply mimetic. This mimetism isn't restricted to the obvious but superficial level of learning by imitation; rather, the mimetic nature makes human beings desire what they perceive or suspect others to desire, a condition that easily leads to rivalries and conflict (Girard 1980, 1–52). Examined in the context of human history and cultural anthropology, the prevalence of the mimetic character of human beings can be assigned to the verge of hominization: It is a decisive humanizing trait, liberating early humans from the inescapability of instincts and distinguishing them from their animal ancestors.[1]

2. However, the conflictive side of mimetic desire might have caused violence to escalate to the extent of the complete annihilation of entire populations, had there not been an occurrence to halt the contagious violence. Girard discovers traits of such an event in the ancient myths of different cultures and calls this phenomenon the *scapegoat mechanism*. It is a single victim, upon whom mimetically the aggression and violence of the crowd is projected. Consequently, this seemingly evil and monstrous individual is unanimously killed, leaving the surviving group miraculously healed—an effect so positive that the extinguished victim doesn't only appear as demonic culprit but also as divine savior: the archaic Sacred is born—and in the wake of it, myth (sacrificial), rites, and taboos. Hence, archaic religions can be described as a violent way to contain violence, to keep the escalation of antagonistic and undifferentiating mimetic desire at bay: "Humanity results from sacrifice; we are thus the children of religion" (Girard and Chantre 2010, ix). The single victim mechanism as violent means of conflict resolution is therefore not only the root of archaic religions but also the origin of cultures and judicial systems.

3. With the Judeo-Christian tradition something genuinely new enters into that history of violent conflict resolution. Unlike myth, the Bible, for the first time, sides with victims, who are now described as innocent: beginning from Joseph, through the Psalms of lament, to the ultimate victim, Jesus. Revealing their innocence, it disables the scapegoat mechanism, since "a scapegoat remains effective as long as we believe in its guilt. Having a scapegoat means not knowing that we have one. Learning that we have a scapegoat is to lose it forever and to expose ourselves to mimetic conflicts with no possible resolution" (Girard and Chantre 2010,

xiv). In this sense, the Judeo-Christian tradition—in spite of some resemblance of historical Christianity with archaic religions, a phenomenon termed *sacrificial Christianity*[2]—in fact puts an end to sacrificial religion and its violence-taming effects. This bears ambiguous and far-reaching consequences: on the one hand, the biblical knowledge about the innocence of scapegoats, the "intelligence of the victim" (Alison 1998, 79–80), asks for the protection of innocent victims and the avoidance of creating and sacrificing scapegoats; on the other hand, it takes away the fetters that the single victim mechanism put on the escalation of mimetic conflicts. Therefore, Girard characterizes our time as an apocalyptic era, in which "the awareness of the innocence of victims has progressed," yet charity is "facing the worldwide empire of violence" (Girard and Chantre 2010, 216). In the run long, Christianity effectuates that all the social institutions that are rooted in the scapegoat mechanism—like the law (ibid., 108) and our economic system—are doomed. Thereby, as the scapegoat mechanism loses its violence-taming effectivity, in the process of diminishing they demand more and more victims (Palaver 2013, 234–46).

Thus, with Girard we may summarize: "Christianity demystifies religion. Demystification, which is good in the absolute, has proven bad in the relative, for we were not prepared to shoulder its consequences" (Girard and Chantre 2010, x). What exactly are these consequences and what are we lacking to be able to shoulder them?

The consequences are visible in our present situation as Girard describes it in *Battling to the End*: an apocalyptic era marked by deep-rooted conflicts and injustice, open and concealed violence against humans and the environment, an era that could bring the end of "Europe, the Western world and the world as a whole" (ibid., ix). Girard observes an unleashing of violence across the whole world,

> creating what the apocalyptic texts predicted: confusion between disasters caused by nature and those caused by humans, between the natural and the man-made: global warming and rising waters are no longer metaphors today. Violence, which produced the sacred, no longer produces anything but itself . . . Ours is the first society that knows it can completely destroy itself. Yet we lack the belief that could bear up under this knowledge (ibid., x, xiii).

When Girard points to the global threats in the Anthropocene—to the apocalyptically escalating conflicts and struggles for economic and/or military hegemony, which do not only affect human relationships but even include nature and threaten to bring about the end to entire species and biospheres—he doesn't do this as someone who is overly pessimistic or fascinated with doom. Rather, he resembles the Old Testament prophets or Chesterton's cosmic patriot, whose realistic and deeply loyal view, beyond the pessimist's resignation and the optimist's naiveté, is able to raise hope and bring about change (Chesterton 2017, 45–48). Like the Old Testament prophets, he wants to wake up the sleeping consciences of his contemporaries (Girard and Chantre 2010, 217), illuminating for them the profound reasons for the current threats and guiding them into the only direction that might bring about the resolution of deadly conflicts. Instead of battling to the end, he wants us to undergo conversion. But what kind of conversion does he advocate and how can it be done?

The Greek word *metanoia*, which is the New Testament word for conversion, means a turnaround of one's mind. Drawing on the insights of great Romanesque authors like Dostoevsky, Cervantes, Stendhal, and Proust, already in his first book, *Deceit, Desire and the Novel*, Girard describes such an authentic conversion that changes everything: lie makes way for truth, fear for remembrance, restlessness for silence, hatred for love, humiliation for humility, the desire according to the other for the desire according to the self, deviant transcendence for vertical transcendence. Letting go—metaphysical desire, pride, arrogance, the wish to be like God, in a nutshell: letting go of what spiritual masters like Thomas Merton call the *false self*[5] (Merton 2007, 21)—seems to be the gateway to this groundbreaking transformation, a transformation that in many ways reminds us of what the Christian tradition has called the threefold mystical path of purgation, illumination, and union (via *purgativa, illuminativa, unitiva*) (cf. Girard 1996, 45–61, esp. 48).

In *Battling to the End* Girard simply describes the redemptive conversion as starting to be true Christians (Girard and Chantre 2010, x): "To make the Revelation wholly good, and not threatening at all, humans have only to adopt the behavior recommended by Christ: abstain completely from retaliation, and renounce the escalation to extremes" (ibid., xiv).

Since we are facing the current threats only insofar as we adopt the knowledge of the scapegoat but don't let go of our obsessive acquisitive desires, conversion is essential to avoid the deadly escalation of violence. But how, given Girard's assessment of our world as deeply marked by the unleashed rivalrous desire and mimetic conflicts, could it be possible to adopt this alternative behavior—especially as rational insight proves to bear very limited success? Girard presents Christ as an alternative model, whom we should follow.[4] But one might still ask how the model of Christ, which is locally, culturally, and temporally so far away from us, might gain enough attraction, as long as other, ostensibly more attractive models surround us?

To answer this question, let me point to Girard's notion "of an endless chain of 'good imitation,' non-rivalrous imitation" (Girard et al. 2007, 222), which he addresses in *Evolution and Conversion*. It is this kind of imitation Paul invites us to in 1 Corinthians 4:16—"Therefore I urge you to imitate me"—and it is important to note that Paul does not extend this invitation "out of personal pride or self-righteousness but because he himself imitates Jesus, who in turn, imitates the Father" (ibid.). Thus, it is the imitation of a model who will not become a rival as he/she has completely gotten out of the way as an obstacle, requesting nothing for himself/herself (Chantre 2014, 373). Jesus doesn't claim to do anything on his own—quite the opposite: He explicitly says that he only does what he sees the Father doing, and he desires nothing more than to do his heavenly Father's will. Ultimately, Jesus "became independent of mimetic projections," because his "relation to his God had become the innermost core of his own self-experience and of his own person" (Niewiadomski 2005, 495), liberating him from all needs to self-assertion or self-interest.

Thus, there is a chain of peaceful, nonacquisitive imitation, from Jesus through Paul to us—a healing and transforming chain that invites us to let our innermost core be shaped by the experience of gratuitously receiving and giving in return, like Jesus did, passing on love to those around, not claiming anything for himself but opening and making himself permeable for this abundant flow of love. "The 'saints' are the links of this chain" (Girard et al. 2007, 222), and as such—in some ways closer to us than Jesus—they invite us to undergo this conversion and become part of an alternative community, in which peaceful mimesis is cultivated and can be practiced. We cannot do this just by ourselves. As Dorothy Day and Peter Maurin said, we are in need of communities "where it is easier for people to be good" (Day 1997, 280), and of models who won't tear us into the maelstroms of acquisitive mimesis and rivalry but are able to guide us beyond, because—like Jesus—they have gotten out of the way as obstacles.[5] What do these models teach us—with their lives even more so than with their words? How can they help us to overcome the structures of violence and create new structures of reconciliation and blessing (Redekop 2002)?

In the wake of *Battling to the End*, I will now focus on three core concepts, which are part of the necessary *metanoia* in view of the threatening apocalypse: innermost mediation, *kenosis* as a way of effacing oneself before the other, and the nonviolent prophetic resistance as an alternative to violent scapegoating or scapegoating the scapegoaters. I will relate these concepts to the lives and writings of three contemporary Christian mystics who—in their own respective ways—taught and lived out these concepts in an eminent way: Orthodox writer, social worker, and nun Maria Skobtsova; Catholic founder of the Focolare Movement Chiara Lubich; and Protestant theologian, peace advocate, and poet Dorothee Soelle.

MARIA SKOBTSOVA: FINDING THE
RIGHT MODEL TO IMITATE

We have already alluded to the necessity of a chain of positive, nonviolent imitation, though without further explaining how such positive imitation might become possible. In a central passage in *Battling to the End*, Girard is asked about the possibility to escape the conflictual side of mimetism. The question is raised whether *rational models*—who try "to oppose the *mimetic model*, which is always stuck on a single figure who has become a rival or an obstacle" (Girard and Chantre 2010, 131)—might point a way out of the pitfalls of rivalries, but Girard doubts it:

> The rational model cannot thwart mimetism . . . It is absolutely powerless to change the course of events, even though it makes it possible to understand them. The mimetic model constantly forces us back into the hell of desire . . . Given the inevitability of mimetic models, it seems very difficult to describe a model that would remain rational. (Ibid., 131–33)

Though rationality does not seem enough to bring about the necessary change, in the conversation with Benoît Chantre Girard indicates a way that might open up an alternative. And while he seems very pessimistic about the range of people who might take that path—he talks about only geniuses and saints being able to do it—he still describes a possible shift "from heroic temptation to sainthood, from the risk of regression that is inherent to internal mediation, to the discovery of a form of mediation" that Benoît Chantre suggests to call "innermost mediation." Girard agrees to this term and explicates:

> "Innermost mediation" (in the sense of Saint Augustine's *Deos interior intimo meo*), in so far as it supposes an inflection of internal mediation, which can always degenerate into bad reciprocity. "Innermost mediation" would be nothing but the imitation of Christ, which is an essential anthropological discovery. Saint Paul says, "Be imitators of me, as I am of Christ." This is the chain of positive undifferentiation, the chain of identity. Discerning the right model then becomes *the* crucial factor. We imitate Christ less than we identify with the one who, in apocalyptic texts, *will have been* Christ . . . "Truly, I tell you, just as you did it to one of the least of these who are members of my family, you did it to me." (Girard and Chantre 2010, 133)

Therefore, the key to innermost mediation is really to find the right model and to imitate in the right way—a way Girard calls positive undifferentiation or identification. A woman who was profoundly touched by this identification of Christ with "the least of these" and lived out this identification to the end was the Russian Maria Skobtsova.[6] Her eventful life included ups and deep downs, with the loss of her youngest child Anastasia as a radical turning point, bringing about a conversion not unsimilar to that which René Girard describes in *Deceit, Desire, and the Novel*. Like for the poets on whose experiences Girard reflects, for Skobtsova conversion came at the verge of suffering and death— not her own death, but her child's.[7] Reflecting on these experiences she writes:

> The gates have suddenly opened onto eternity, all natural life has trembled and collapsed, yesterday's laws have been abolished, desires have faded, meaning has become meaningless, and another incomprehensible Meaning has grown wings on their backs . . . Everything flies into the black maw of the fresh grave: hopes, plans, calculations, and, above all, meaning, the meaning of a whole life. If this is so, then everything has to be reconsidered, everything rejected, seen in its corruptibility and falseness. (Skobtsova 2003, 127)

For Skobtsova this meant a determined renunciation of what she considered false in her previous existence—and an equally determined commitment to what turned out to be the most profound mystical insight of her life: the deep experience of Jesus Christ's identification with every human being, especially with those suffering and in need, and the wish to be there for them. From now on, as Jim Forest writes, her credo is:

> "Each person is the very icon of God incarnate in the world." With this recognition comes the need "to accept this awesome revelation of God unconditionally, to venerate the image of God' in her brothers and sisters." (Forest 2004)

For her, this meant that you do not have to, and that you must not turn away from this world, to experience God. Rather, in every fellow human being you can really encounter Christ. Skobtsova describes this deep mystical insight, which is the theme of her life, as follows:

> The way to God lies through love of people. At the Last Judgement I shall not be asked whether I was successful in my ascetic exercises, nor how many bows and prostrations I made. Instead I shall be asked, Did I feed the hungry, clothe the naked, visit the sick and the prisoners. That is all I shall be asked. About every poor, hungry and imprisoned person the Savior says "I": "I was hungry, and thirsty, I was sick and in prison." To think that he puts an equal sign between himself and anyone in need . . . I always knew it, but now it has somehow penetrated to my sinews. It fills me with awe. (quoted in Forest 2003, 30)

As a consequence of this profound insight, the inseparability of religious life and social commitment was the *leitmotif* of her life and a recurrent theme in all of her writings. For her, the link between the two was intimate and essential: social action was not "something of the 'second sort,' applied, appended" (Skobtsova 2003, 75) to Christian faith. Rather, concrete, practical love of the other "is the whole key to the mystery of human communion as a religious path" (Skobtsova 2003, 52), the key to true Christianity. In an article entitled *The Mysticism of Human Communion*, she writes: "And it seems to me that this mysticism of human communion is the only authentic basis for any external Christian activity, for social Christianity, . . . for a Christianity turned toward the world" (Skobtsova 2003, 82). In her actual life, after the death of Anastasia, this concretizes as a calling to universal motherhood, which she lives as total commitment for anybody in need.

Herself a Russian émigré in Paris, together with some friends, she founded a house of hospitality for refugees in need. Soon the house became too small, other houses were rented, and the group of those accommodated expanded quickly, including Jews who were provided with false baptismal documents to save them from Nazi persecution. Unlike many of her contemporaries, she understood the persecution of her Jewish brothers and sisters as an attack on Christianity, on the identification of Christ with all human beings. When Maria Skobtsova was finally arrested, a verbal exchange between her and the Gestapo officer Hoffmann, reported by her mother Sophia Pilenko, shows how serious she took her credo of every person being the icon of God incarnate. When the Nazi officer blamed her mother for having badly educated, her Jew-loving daughter, her mother answered that her daughter actually helped everybody: "For a Christian like her there is neither Jew nor Greek, only human beings . . . If you had been in danger, she would have helped you, too" (Pilenko 2011, 107; quotation translated by Petra Steinmair-Pösel). Maria Skobtsova's addition is telling: "Indeed, I would have helped you, too" (Pilenko 2011, 107; quotation translated by Petra Steinmair-Pösel), she said to the officer who was just about to send her on the road to the concentration camp.

Thus, the profound experience that every human being is an icon of God and that Christ has deeply identified with every person and especially the least, in short: the recognition of the divine in every human being makes it absolutely impossible for Skobtsova to demonize another human being, not even her obvious deadly enemy. We might therefore conclude that *innermost mediation*, as described by Girard and exemplified by Skobtsova, immunizes against the conflict-prone ways of mimetic demonization or divinization of the other as model/rival, which always end up with one being the victim of conflictual mimesis. However, Skobtsova clarifies that innermost mediation doesn't mean naive approval of everything other people do—quite the contrary: Recognizing the divine in every human being (without divinizing them) for her also means to recognize the evil forces that obscure this divine core and to struggle for the liberation of the divine core from these distorting evil powers.[8]

CHIARA LUBICH: A MODEL OF EMPTYING ONESELF

In the same paragraph where Girard mentions *innermost mediation* as an alternative to acquisitive, rivalrous mimetic desire, he concretizes what this means, thus addressing a second aspect of the required conversion: "To imitate Christ is to identify with the other, to efface oneself before him [or her]" (Girard and Chantre 2010, 133).

One has to be careful not to misread this passage as advocating a kind of Christian masochism, encouraging one to humiliate oneself. Earlier passages of the Girardian corpus clearly forbid such an interpretation and call for a more differentiated view:

> In the light of our analyses, we are bound to conclude that any procedure involving sacrifice, even and indeed especially when it turns against the self, is at variance with the true spirit of the gospel text . . . self-sacrifice can serve to camouflage the forms of slavery brought into being by mimetic desire. "Masochism" can also find expression in self-sacrifice, even if a person has no knowledge of this, and no wish to reveal it. What might be concealed here is the desire to sacralize *oneself* and make *oneself* godlike—which quite clearly harks back to the illusion traditionally produced by sacrifice. (Girard 1987, 236–237)[9]

So quite opposite to advocating masochistic self-denial as a way out of the pitfalls of rivalrous mimesis, Girard unveils the "pseudo-masochistic structure of mimetic desire" (Girard 1987, 328): "What Freud terms 'primary masochism' is in fact none other than conflictual mimesis—after the point when it sees in the most insuperable rival its model for the most stunning success" (Girard 1987, 332). Thus, there is a way of effacing oneself before the other that turns out to be one of the blind alleys of mimetic rivalry. Here the subject humbles himself/herself before the other not for the sake of the other, but "to become a god mimetically" (Girard 1987, 334), while the other in truth takes the place of the model/rival/obstacle.

Maria Skobtsova in her evaluation of different types of religious life sharp-sightedly points out that such a form of self-sacrifice is in fact more interested in making oneself godlike (in her terms: in the salvation of one's own soul or in ascetic power and perfection) than the welfare of the other. And precisely for this reason it is not in line with an authentic evangelical (in the sense of being in accordance with the Gospel) spirituality, which always seeks the true well-being of the other (Skobtsova 2003, 140–86). The Catholic founder of the Focolare Movement, Chiara Lubich, further introduces us into what we might call the non-masochistic, yet profoundly *kenotic*[10] aspect of following Jesus Christ and its relevance for creating reconciliation, dialogue, and unity.

While *kenosis* becomes very important for her understanding of following Christ, it is not her starting point. Rather, living and promoting unity is the specific vocation Chiara Lubich felt when she founded the Focolare Movement, calling her spirituality the spirituality of communion and saying that "unity is the word that sums up the life of our movement" (Lubich 2007, 16). However, to actually achieve this unity, Chiara sketches a certain way, which necessarily includes the *kenotic* emptying of oneself:

> Before all else, the soul must always fix its gaze on the one Father of many children. Then it must see all as children of the same Father. In mind and in heart we must always go beyond the bounds imposed on us by human life alone and create the habit of constantly opening ourselves to the reality of being one human family in one Father: God. (Lubich 2007, 17–18)

This first step perfectly relates to Skobtsova's aforementioned experience: Seeing all without exception as children of God means seeing their divine core or perceiving them as living icons of God, as Skobtsova describes it using imagery of Eastern Orthodox iconography.

The next necessary step then, according to Lubich, is the emptying of self:

> A virtue that unites the soul to God . . . is humility, the emptying of self . . . The unity of the soul with God, who lives within us, presupposes a total emptying of self, the most heroic humility . . . Humility also leads souls to unity with others: aspire constantly to the "first place" by putting self as much as possible at the service of neighbor. Every soul that wants to achieve unity must claim only one right: to serve everyone, because in everyone the soul serves God . . . The soul that desires to bring about unity must keep itself in such an abyss of humility that it reaches the point of losing, for the benefit and in the service of God in its neighbor, its very self . . . It must live constantly "emptied" because it is totally "in love" with God's will . . . and in love with the will of its neighbor, who[m] it wants to serve for God. (Lubich 2007, 18)

Reflecting on the beginnings of the Focolare Movement, Lubich realizes "that even before we had any ideas about how to achieve unity, we had already been given a model, a figure, life for it. It was the One who truly knew how to 'make himself one' with all people who have lived, who live now and who will live in the future" (Lubich 2007, 19–20). His way to create unity was to love and serve unconditionally and without measure, and he taught that the neighbor to be served is "the person who passes us by in the present moment of our daily life." Lubich concretizes: "We must love that person in such a way that Christ may be born, grow and develop in him or her" (Lubich 2007, 18). However, in a world marked by sin, to love like Jesus will sooner or later include suffering, like it did for Jesus on the cross. While suffering is not something to be sought as such, as it is not a value in itself,[11] under certain circumstances, it is unavoidable if you want to hold on to love. And it is exactly in these moments of suffering that the height of love is revealed like in Jesus forsaken (Lubich 2007, 22–23). Lubich remembers one of her mystical experiences that made her fall in love with Jesus forsaken:

> From the height of the cross he tells me: "I let everything of mine fade away ... everything! I am no longer beautiful, or strong; I have no peace here; justice is dead here; knowledge is gone; truth has vanished. All that is left is my Love, which wanted to pour out *for you* the riches *of God*." (Lubich 2007, 23)

This vision of Jesus in his utmost suffering (seemingly), abandoned by heaven and (certainly by) earth, with "his divine love completely laid open" (Lubich 2007, 22), inspires Lubich and her friends to value their own suffering and more willingly accept and bear it, without in some way or the other passing it on to others. Instead, they read it as an expression of their love to Christ forsaken, as a way to somehow participate in his fate as well as in his redemptive and healing presence: "God was calling us to Unity . . ., and Jesus forsaken was its secret: he was the condition to fulfill Jesus' final testament: 'May they all be one'" (Lubich 2007, 24).

Thus, the spirituality of Chiara Lubich comprises two aspects that can be compared to the two sides of one coin.[12] One side is unity: universal unity among all human beings, but also unity with God. The key to this unity and the other side of the coin is Jesus crucified and forsaken. Lubich recognized him and wanted to embrace him in all the suffering that she encountered in the world: in all the suffering people, in all situations, when she herself was hurt, wronged, or confronted with any other evil. In other words, all the suffering in this world bears the traces of Christ forsaken, and unity can only be understood, lived, and promoted by those who are willing to embrace Jesus forsaken with their whole heart, that is, by those who are ready to follow his *kenotic* path and empty themselves.

In fact, Chiara Lubich put her whole life into this ideal of unity, which should be brought about in and through the Focolare Movement. Her autobiographical book *The Cry* (Lubich 2001) provides an intuition of how much this cost her, how much this was a personal *kenosis* for her—especially the fact of the Focolare Movement not being officially accepted by the ecclesial hierarchy for almost twelve years while being so keen on being united with the church. Moreover, her spiritual journey did not spare her from co-suffering with many of her contemporaries the complete darkness of the absence of God. According to witnesses, she experienced this darkness in the last years of her life and accepted it willingly as the embrace of Christ forsaken. Today her suffering in this respect is understood by the Focolarini as solidarity with a world suffering the absence of God.

And the voluntarily endured suffering turned out to bear rich fruit. In our day, the Focolare Movement is among the largest lay movements within the Catholic Church, working on different levels of dialogue to bring about reconciled unity in diversity: unity within the Catholic Church, unity among different Christian denominations, unity with members of other religions, unity also with nonbelievers and atheists as well as secular culture. Franz Kronreif, a Focolare member who has been committed to the dialogue with nonbelievers and atheists for many years, stresses how much their way of dialogue is a *kenotic dialogue* with roots in the mystical experience of Chiara Lubich and her wish to embrace Jesus forsaken as her only spouse (Kronreif 2012).

Kronreif refers to a difficult mystical yet constitutive and fundamental text to understand the way of dialogue inspired by Lubich. This text also prevents the mistaking of naive and cheap chitchat for dialogue, pointing out the dark, kenotic aspect of voluntary, transformative suffering:

> I have only one Spouse on earth: Jesus forsaken. I have no other God but him. In him there is the whole of paradise with the Trinity and the whole of the earth with humanity. Therefore what is *his* is mine, and nothing else. And *his* is universal suffering, and therefore mine. I will go through the world seeking it in every instant of my life. What hurts me is *mine* . . . Mine all that is not peace, not joy, not beautiful, not lovable, not serene, in a word, what is not paradise. Because I too have *my* paradise, but it is the one in my Spouse's heart. I know no other. So it will be for the years I have left: a thirst for suffering, anguish, despair, separation, exile, forsakenness, torment—for all that is him, and he is sin, hell. In this way, *I will dry up* the waters of tribulation in many hearts nearby and, through communion with my almighty Spouse, in many far away. (Lubich 2007, 95)

In a later text, Chiara Lubich concretizes what this early manuscript means for everyday life, especially for the dialogue inspired by the spirituality of communion. It is a costly dialogue, which demands the complete emptying of oneself to be able to listen without prejudice, to understand before thinking of responses, or counterarguments, to suffer what might be offensive in the discourse without quitting the dialogue. Lubich stresses that in order to love a fellow human being, it is necessary to put aside everything, even the most spiritual things, in the same way as Jesus—out of love for us—even suffered the forsakenness by his heavenly Father. She is convinced: Only a love, which models itself on this love, is able to bring about unity in diversity (Tobler 2002, 267). The fruitfulness of the current Focolare commitment in the field of interreligious dialogue and in dialogue with nonbelievers proves them right (Kronreif 2012).

In September 2015, I was able to participate in a Muslim-Christian dialogue conference near Rome and to witness this distinctive kind of dialogue. Hosted by a group of Focolarini, Christian and Muslim professors dialogued about some of the most sensitive issues in Christian-Islamic relationships, like the history of the perception of the Prophet Muhammed by the Catholic Church or the denial of the Trinity by their Muslim counterparts. Every morning, before entering into discussion, the group, which had been coming together several times over the last few years, renewed a mutual covenant to embark on a *kenotic dialogue*. Thus, all participants explicitly consented to completely empty themselves from their prejudices and ideas, from their will to power and to prevail in the discussions, in order to be able to listen, to understand, to love—without second thoughts. Johannes Vetter, one of the hosts and long-year participants, explained how in the course of their meetings this approach had created a space of mutual trust, a space within which sensitive and painful topics could be addressed, without any side being offended or even leaving the talks in difficult and conflictive situations. And indeed, the progress made by the group is remarkable and keeps inspiring others to work in similar ways toward reconciliation and unity in diversity.

Thus, Lubich with her *kenotic* approach blazed the trail to a way of establishing unity that differs from what we are often used to in our everyday experience: A way that does not rely on exclusion of dissenters, that does not shift the costs of unity to others, but seeks to transform the pain caused by disunity and misunderstanding. She is also very clear about the costs, as she did not conceal the uncomfortable truth that if you want to be an agent of real and deep unity, you must be humble enough to empty yourself, and courageous enough to not flee suffering. Using her metaphor: you have to embrace Jesus forsaken and become a transformer like him.

DOROTHEE SOELLE: A MODEL OF PROPHETIC NONVIOLENT RESISTANCE

While from Maria Skobtsova we have the notion of recognizing the divine in every human being and Chiara Lubich introduced us more deeply into the (non-masochistic) *kenotic* aspect of emptying oneself to bring about reconciled unity in diversity, the Protestant theologian and activist Dorothee Soelle—drawing on the great mystical traditions of not only Christian but also non-Christian origin—introduces yet another, seemingly inconvenient element: mystically inspired, prophetic criticism and nonviolent resistance against all forms of victimization and violence.

In her book *The Silent Cry: Mysticism and Resistance* (Soelle 2001), Soelle elaborates on how the mystical experience of an intimate relationship with God (as mentioned by Girard citing Augustine's *Deos interior intimo meo*) in each religion bears an incompliant and prophetic dimension, which doesn't resign to the powers and systems rooted in scapegoating and violence. What does she mean by that? And why is Soelle's approach important here?

First of all, Dorothee Soelle teaches us something that is central with respect to a question addressed before: Who is approachable by mystical experience? Who can experience the *Deos interior intimo meo* whom Girard mentions with respect to innermost mediation and the overcoming of the pitfalls of mimetic rivalry? While Girard—though not being totally explicit on the matter—seems to only ascribe this kind of grace to geniuses and saints, Dorothee Soelle—drawing on the vast Christian as well as other mystical traditions—intends to democratize mystical experience and show its relevance for all human beings. Her effort is to uncover the mystical sensitivity that is in each of us, to dig it out under the debris of triviality, to disclose its accessibility to everyone, and to encourage people to value their own specific experiences. She is convinced that mystical consciousness must not be reduced to ecstatic and extreme experiences, which are merely open to spiritual elites. Only based on such a democratized understanding of mysticism, the subtle mystical dimension in *Battling to the End* becomes universally relevant.

Second, this democratized understanding of mystical experience is intrinsically related to the praxis of resistance. As Soelle's husband Fulbert Steffensky stresses in their dialogue concluding *The Silent Cry*, insisting that we are all mystics and thus open and receptible to the mystery of the divine, this implies that no human being should be forced to just scrape a living. No one should be condemned to an existence of mere survival. For everybody there should be moments of truth, beauty, and joy, of the enjoyment of life, and God (*fruitio Dei*) (Soelle 2001). In this sense, Soelle's statement that we are all mystics implies a human right to beauty and contemplation.

But if mysticism means "the experience of the oneness and wholeness of life" (Soelle 2001), especially against the background of this experience, the dark and broken side of life, the powers that destroy this oneness and wholeness become all the more visible and unbearable. Thus, mysticism also includes a sensibility to life's brokenness and fragmentation. Perceiving and suffering from this fragmentation is part of mysticism as much as resisting structures and mechanisms that poison and destroy life and love. Therefore, according to Soelle, "the 'and' between mysticism and resistance must be understood . . . radically" (Soelle 2001): you cannot be a mystic without developing some practice of resistance. However, this mystically inspired resistance is exactly the point where Soelle notices a genuine weakness of our political and intellectual culture: "One cannot think what one does not do . . . Our religiously grounded resistance is still so weak, so experientially impoverished, so little practiced that we can hardly think it" (Soelle 2001).

For this reason, we need stories of not only saints but also ordinary people who practice some form of mystically inspired resistance: Stanley Hauerwas and William Willimon have written their book *Where Resident Aliens Live* with this very intention:

> We will tell even more stories, give more instances of fidelity, offer more examples of a church in which ordinary people are called to be saints . . . We offer these examples because we believe that the contemporary church suffers from a lack of political imagination. One reason why the church always focused upon the stories of the saints and the martyrs was to enlarge our imagination. No conversion or growth is possible without imagination. (Hauerwas and Willimon 1996, 20)

For the same reason, the biblical texts—and especially the prophetic tradition—are important for Soelle as well as for other mystics who—by their experience of the divine—were not lead to a spirituality detached from the world but quite the contrary, were driven to engage in the world in their own critical and challenging ways.

Returning to Soelle's understanding of mysticism and focusing on a third important aspect we can derive from her writings, mystical experience for her has to do with the promise and experience of abundance as it is experienced in contemplative praxis, with the experience of a free fall into the vastness of God's love. As Brian Robinette has pointed out, drawing a connecting line to Girard's theory, precisely this contemplative experience of God's unconditional love allows one to "slowly surrender the compulsion to form identity in rivalrous relationship with others, including God" (Robinette 2015). Thus, it changes our relationship to other human beings as well as to God. It frees us—at least to some degree—from our compulsive involvement in the rivalrous mimetic structures that evoke the escalation to extremes mentioned before and it also brings about a profound shift in our notion of God.

In her writings, Dorothee Soelle gives testimony of this fundamental shift. Being a German theologian in the wake of the Holocaust, Soelle herself struggled with and finally dismissed a notion of God who could somehow be mistaken as a rival to human beings—and she did so in an early stage of her theological career (Soelle 2010, 55–63). For her, an all-powerful God, enthroned in heaven, ruling over human history like an absolutist potentate, would have stopped the trains running to Auschwitz and Birkenwald, would have prevented thousands of children from being slaughtered, and atom bombs from being dropped—or this God would be a sadist whom she could never venerate. Therefore, Soelle dismissed the traditional (or at least a naive) notion of omnipotence as a quality of God (Soelle 2006a, 133). Instead, she, existentially as well as theologically, sought and found another notion of God: an empathetic, co-suffering God, very much like Lubich's notion of Jesus forsaken. The God who was on the side of the victims in the concentration camps (Soelle 2006b, 140). The God who needs human beings to cooperate (or become cocreators—cf. Goodhart 2020) in order to make God's love for this world concrete. And making it concrete, for Soelle, also meant making it political.

Cooperating with this God means to resist violence and injustice. It means to struggle for those who are marginalized and victimized—but in a nonviolent way. However, we need to clarify what kind of nonviolence is advocated based on the mystical tradition. Simone Weil, another mystic of the twentieth century, whom Soelle frequently quotes, as well as Mahatma Gandhi and Chiara Lubich have pointed out that it is a form of nonviolence that includes the readiness to suffer. Consequently, nonviolence is not for people lacking courage and readiness to make sacrifices.

In her address to UNESCO on receiving the Prize for Peace Education, Chiara Lubich said: "It is not easy to commit yourself to furthering peace! It demands courage and much suffering" (Lubich 2007, 14). Simone Weil, who had promoted pacifism first, later revised her position criticizing it as naive in the face of Hitler's rise to power and violent conquest of Europe. In this situation and under these preconditions, Weil perceived violent resistance against injustice and violence as necessary, though she always tried to combine this view with her persisting fundamental criticism of violence. Consequently, Weil argued that one has to strive to gradually replace violence in this world with *effective* nonviolence. However, for nonviolence to be ethically justifiable and effective, it must include the readiness to (self-) sacrifice, while Weil criticized the so-called pacifism of those who mix up the detestation of killing and the detestation of dying. This latter form of "pacifism" she perceived among those French "pacifists" who collaborated with the Nazis and she accused them of sacrificing others due to their fear of suffering and death (Cf. Palaver 2010, 470–74). In the same way, Mahatma Gandhi said that in the face of injustice—having to choose between cowardliness and violence— he would advocate violence. By this Gandhi—knowing the momentum of violence—did not mean to promote violence as a means of conflict resolution. He just underlined the fact that nonviolence is not a strategy for those lacking the courage to fight because it might cost their lives (Cf. Palaver 2010, 477).

Besides Weil and Gandhi, Soelle for her understanding of nonviolent resistance also draws on Martin Luther King for whom "an important component of nonviolence ... was the unearned suffering that resulted from the conflicts," which arise as soon as unjust systems and structures are challenged. King "said that there would be rivers of blood," but that they were "determined to make sure that it is not the blood of the enemy" (Soelle 2001). King thus was determined to transform violence by his own suffering. Simone Weil related this way of dealing with violence with her notion of the false gods and the true God, saying that "the false God changes suffering into violence" while "the true God changes violence into suffering" (Weil 2002, 72).

We may therefore conclude that the prophetic struggle against victimization and violence includes brave resistance to the dominant systems and powers, as well as to states, where they victimize and marginalize, but it is fought in the spirit of Gandhi's *ahimsa*, never allowing scapegoating in the name of the victims.[13] It names the injustice, the satanic and sacrificial structures, not to demonize and destroy them but in order to transform them, as Walter Wink points out in *The Powers that Be* (Wink 1999, 13–36).

However, to refrain from being drawn into the logic of escalating violence and the myth of redeeming counterviolence, to remain critical of violence even though in some cases—as the example of Simone Weil has shown—it might not be completely avoidable, one needs to be well grounded in some kind of spiritual practice and experience. Thus, in the last chapter of his book Wink stresses the fundamental importance of a living prayer life to bring about real change (Wink 1999, 180–98). Gandhi also insists that those becoming part of his peace brigade have to have a living faith in nonviolence, which he claimed to be impossible without a living faith in God. He stressed that somebody can only practice nonviolence through the power and grace of God. Without that they would not have the courage to die without anger, fear, or thirst for revenge. For Gandhi, this courage was rooted in the faith that God lives in the hearts of all human beings and that there can be no fear in God's presence (Gandhi 1983, 96).

CONCLUSION

Summing up, Maria Skobtsova, Chiara Lubich, and Dorothee Soelle teach us the mystical dimensions of perceiving the divine core in every human being, of kenotically following Jesus in emptying oneself, and of nonviolently resisting the temptation to scapegoating (in the name of the victims) and violence, which turn out to be essential elements of the conversion that René Girard considers to be indispensable for the vital question of "reconciliation among all members of humanity" (Girard and Chantre 2010, xvii). This conversion will not be brought about by rational insight alone, but requires mystical sources, that allow one to overcome "stumbling blocks," to nonviolently respond to "scandal,"[14] and embrace what seems like "foolishness" in the categories of this world (1 Cor 1:18–23). The invitation to this conversion does not resound like the obtrusive straplines of our times but will remain present in history as a fragile and "silent cry" (Soelle 2001), echoed by those who are willing to listen.

NOTES

1. In his book *I See Satan Fall Like Lightning*, Girard writes: "If our desires were not mimetic, they would be forever fixed on predetermined objects; they would be a particular form of instinct. Human beings could no more change their desire than cows their appetite for grass. Without mimetic desire there would be neither freedom nor humanity. Mimetic desire is intrinsically good. . . . If desire were not mimetic, we would not be open to what is human or what is divine" (Girard 2001, 15–16).

2. Sacrificial Christianity designates a form of interpreting Jesus' life and death in terms of archaic sacrificial religions (Palaver 2013, 246–55, esp. 246–47).

3. According to Merton, this false self—understood as "an illusory person, . . . who wants to exist outside the reach of God's will and God's love" (Merton 2007, 34)—can take the place of God: "It is when we refer all things to this outward and false 'self' that we alienate ourselves from the reality and from God. It is then the false self that is our god, and we love everything for the sake of this self" (Merton 2007, 21).

4. Girard attempts to show that by imitating Jesus we can gain an attitude of *renunciation* that enables us to free ourselves "from the deadly grip of mimetic rivalry" (Palaver 2013, 220).

5. In *Battling to the End*, Girard especially points to the German poet and mystic Hölderlin as such a model, who spent a large part of his life secluded in a tower in Tübingen. I will follow a different path here referring to three women who more actively engaged in the life of this world on the basis of their mystical experience.

6. Born as Elisaveta Pilenko (1891) in Riga (Latvia, then part of the Russian empire), she lived to see both World Wars I and II. While she was nearly killed in the course of the Bolshevik Revolution, she survived, emigrating to France, where the divorced mother of three became an Orthodox nun and finally fell victim to the Nazis, who killed her in the Concentration Camp of Ravensbrück shortly before the end of the war in 1945.

7. U.S.-Franciscan and spiritual director Richard Rohr frequently stresses that great love and great suffering are "the two normal and primary paths of transformation into God, preceding all organized religion" (Rohr 2017), the paths on which we learn to participate in a larger, unconditional love: divine love.

8. Skobtsova speaks about the encounter of "the authentic image of God in man, the very incarnate icon of God in the world, a glimmer of the mystery of the Incarnation and Godmanhood. And man must unconditionally and unreservedly accept this terrible Revelation of God, must bow down before the image of God in his brother. And only when he feels it, sees it, and understands it, will yet another mystery be revealed to him, which demands of him his most strenuous struggle, his

greatest ascetic ascent. He will see how this image of God is obscured, distorted by an evil power. . . . And in the name of the image of God, darkened by the devil, in the name of the love for this image of God that pierces his heart, he will want to begin a struggle with the devil, to become an instrument of God" (Skobtsova 2003, 57).

9. Even though Girard—influenced by Raymund Schwager—gave up his complete rejection of the term *sacrifice* in context of the genuine Christian revelation, his reference to Masochism here makes clear in which sense self-sacrifice is actually opposed to an authentic understanding of the Christian way (Girard 2014, 33–45).

10. The term *kenosis* is derived from the Greek *kenoo*, which means to make something empty. The most relevant Biblical passage in this regard is in Paul's letter to the Philippians. There he writes about the *Logos*: "Who, although He existed in the form of God, did not regard equality with God a thing to be grasped, but emptied Himself, taking the form of a bond-servant, and being made in the likeness of men" (Phil. 2:6–7).

11. This is important to note, as some passages in Lubich's writings—when not balanced with other texts—could be misinterpreted in this way.

12. Lubich writes: "The book of light that God is writing in my soul has two aspects: a luminous page of mysterious love: Unity. A luminous page of mysterious suffering: Jesus forsaken. They are two faces of the same coin" (Lubich 2007, 25).

13. Dorothee Soelle actively participated in and launched nonviolent protests against the rearmament of Germany after World War II, as well as against all kinds of exploitation of humans and nature. For more information on her motivation and commitment, see Soelle's German autobiography *Gegenwind: Erinnerungen* (Soelle 2010).

14. Jeremiah Alberg points to this "scandalous" aspect in his book *Beneath the Veil of the Strange Verses* (Alberg 2013, xv). In his conference paper "On the Beautification of Mimesis," he describes how dealing with scandal in a nonviolent way makes all the difference between revenge and reconciliation. "If 'something has been insulted and defaced' and I, simply as the observer, find that I am 'responsible for restoring it or making reparation for it,' and not for avenging it, then something has changed in our world" (Alberg 2014).

REFERENCES

Alberg, Jeremiah L. 2013. *Beneath the Veil of the Strange Verses. Reading Scandalous Texts.* East Lansing, MI: Michigan State University Press.

———. 2014. "On the Beautification of Mimesis." Unpublished Conference Paper, Presented at the COV&R Conference *'Battling to the End' 1914–2014. The Escalation of Violence and Victimization* in Freising, Germany. *René Girard and Jean-Luc Marion* in Freising/Germany.

Alison, James. 1998. *The Joy of Being Wrong: Original Sin through Easter Eyes.* New York, NY: Crossroad.

Chantre, Benoît. 2014. "Clausewitz und Girard im Zentrum des Zweikampfs." In *Im Angesicht der Apokalypse: Clausewitz zu Ende denken*, 354–380. Berlin: Matthes & Seitz.

Chesterton, Gilbert K. 2017. *Orthodoxy*. Accessed February 1. http://www.ccel.org/ccel/chesterton/orthodoxy.pdf.

Day, Dorothy. 1997. *The Long Loneliness: The Autobiography of the Legendary Catholic Social Activist*. With an introduction by Robert Coles. New York, NY: HarperCollins Publishers.

Forest, Jim. 2003. "Introduction: Mother Maria of Paris." In *Essential Writings*. Translated by Richard Pevear and Larissa Volokhonsky, 13–43. Maryknoll, NY: Orbis Books.

———. 2004. *Mother Maria of Paris: Saint of the Open Door*. Last modified October 18, 2004. Accessed January 31, 2017. https://incommunion.org/2004/10/18/saint-of-the-open-door/.

Gandhi, Mohandas K. 1983. *Ausgewählte Texte*. Goldmann 6577. München: Goldmann.

Girard, René. 1980. *Deceit, Desire, and the Novel: Self and Other in Literary Structure*, 2nd ed. A Johns Hopkins Paperback. Baltimore, MD: Johns Hopkins University Press.

———. 1987. *Things Hidden since the Foundation of the World*. Stanford, CA: Stanford University Press. Research undertaken in collaboration with Jean-Michel Oughourlian and Guy Lefort.

———. 1996. *The Girard Reader*. Edited by James G. Williams. New York, NY: Crossroad.

———. 2001. *I See Satan Fall Like Lightning*. Maryknoll, NY: Orbis Books.

———. 2014. *The One by Whom Scandal Comes*. Studies in Violence, Mimesis, and Culture Series. East Lansing, MI: Michigan State University Press.

Girard, René, Pierpaolo Antonello, and João C. D. C. Rocha. 2007. *Evolution and Conversion: Dialogues on the Origins of Culture*. London: Continuum.

Girard, René, and Benoît Chantre. 2010. *Battling to the End: Conversations with Benoît Chantre*. Studies in Violence, Mimesis, and Culture Series. East Lansing, MI: Michigan State University Press.

Goodhart, Sandor. 2020. "Prophetic Reading and Emergent Creativity in Genesis 1." In *Awakening: Exploring Spirituality, Emergent Creativity, and Reconciliation*. Edited by Vern Neufeld Redekop and Gloria Neufeld Redekop. Lanham, MD: Lexington.

Hauerwas, Stanley, and William H. Willimon. 1996. *Where Resident Aliens Live: Exercises for Christian Practice*. Nashville, TN: Abingdon.

Kronreif, Franz. 2012. *Jenseits des Dialogs: Erfahrungen in der Begegnung der Fokolar-Bewegung mit Atheisten*. Accessed March 17, 2014. http://www.uibk.ac.at/theol/leseraum/texte/964.html#ch3.

Lubich, Chiara. 2001. *The Cry of Jesus Crucified and Forsaken*. Hyde Park, NY: New City Press.

———. 2007. *Essential Writings: Spirituality, Dialogue, Culture*. Edited by Michel Vandeleene, Tom Masters, and Callan Slipper. Hyde Park, NY: New City Press.

Merton, Thomas. 2007. *New Seeds of Contemplation*. With an introduction by Sue Monk Kidd. New Directions Paperbook 1091. New York, NY: New Directions.

Niewiadomski, Józef. 2005. "Extra Media Nulla Salus? Attempt at a Theological Synthesis." In *Passions in Economy, Politics, and the Media: In Discussion with Christian Theology*. Edited by Wolfgang Palaver and Petra Steinmair-Pösel, 489–508. Beiträge zur Mimetischen Theorie 17. Wien: Lɪᴛ-Verlag.

Palaver, Wolfgang. 2010. "Die Frage des Opfers im Spannungsfeld von West und Ost: René Girard, Simone Weil und Mahatma Gandhi über Gewalt und Gewaltfreiheit." *ZKTh*, 132: 462–481.

———. 2013. *René Girard's Mimetic Theory*. Studies in Violence, Mimesis, and Culture Series. East Lansing, MI: Michigan State University Press.

Pilenko, Sophie. 2011. "Elle vous aiderait, vous aussi." In *Le Jour du Saint-Esprit: Sainte Marie de Paris* (Mère Marie Skobtsov, 1891–1945). Edited by Paul Ladouceur, 106–109. Paris: Les Éditions du Cerf.

Redekop, Vern Neufeld. 2002. *From Violence to Blessing: How an Understanding of Deep-Rooted Conflict can Open Paths to Reconciliation*. Ottawa: Novalis.

Robinette, Brian D. 2015. "Contemplative Practice and the Therapy of Mimetic Desire." Paper Presented at the Annual Conference of the COV&R, *The One by Whom Scandal Has Come: Critically Engaging the Girardian Corpus*, St. Louis, July 9–12.

Rohr, Richard. 2017. *Great Love and Great Suffering*. Accessed February 2. http://conta.cc/18eRDFl.

Skobtsova, Maria. 2003. *Essential Writings*. Translated by Richard Pevear and Larissa Volokhonsky. Introduction by Jim Forest. New York, NY: Orbis Books.

Soelle, Dorothee. 2001. *The Silent Cry: Mysticism and Resistance*, Kindle ed. Minneapolis, MN: Fortress Press.

———. 2006a. "Aufrüstung tötet auch ohne Krieg." In *Gesammelte Werke: Band 1: Sprache der Freiheit*. Edited by Ursula Baltz-Otto and Fulbert Steffensky, 12 vols, 117–158. Stuttgart: Kreuz.

———. 2006b. "Leiden." In *Gesammelte Werke: Band 4: Die Wahrheit macht euch frei*. Edited by Ursula Baltz-Otto and Fulbert Steffensky, 12 vols, 9–170. Stuttgart: Kreuz.

———. 2010. *Gesammelte Werke: Band 12: Gegenwind: Erinnerungen*. Edited by Ursula Baltz-Otto and Fulbert Steffensky, 12 vols. Freiburg im Breisgau: Kreuz Verlag.

Steinmair-Pösel, Petra. 2019. *Im Gravitationsfeld von Mystik und Politik. Christliche Sozialethik im Gespräch mit Maria Skobtsova, Dorothee Sölle und Chiara Lubich*. Gesellschaft – Ethik – Religion 16. Paderborn: Ferdinand Schöningh.

Tobler, Stefan. 2002. *Jesu Gottverlassenheit als Heilsereignis in der Spiritualität Chiara Lubichs: Ein Beitrag zur Überwindung der Sprachnot in der Soteriologie*. Theologische Bibliothek Töpelmann 115. Berlin: de Gruyter.

Weil, Simone. 2002. *Gravity and Grace*. With an introduction and postscript by Gustave Thibon. Translated by Emma Crawford and Mario von der Ruhr. London and New York, NY: Routledge.

Wink, Walter. 1999. *The Powers That Be: Theology for a New Millennium*. New York, NY: Doubleday.

Chapter 4

Coming to Terms with Violence and War

The Experience of Mennonite Women and Children in Russia (1917–1925)

Gloria Neufeld Redekop

My interest in the story of the survival of Mennonite women and children during the revolution, war, and famine in Russia grows out of my own grandmother's story of fleeing the revolution in the Ukraine and immigrating to Canada with her family. By interviewing other Russian Mennonite women who experienced the same trauma, I had the opportunity to learn more about my own grandmother's struggle, even though she died over fifty years ago. This documented story gives voice to Russian Mennonite women who lived through this time—as one woman put it, "To give the women the credit, you know." Though Jeanne Vickers does not refer to Mennonite women in particular, her general observations about women in times of war illuminate the experience of the women I interviewed:

> Women suffer greatly in their traditional roles as homemakers, mothers and care givers in times of conflict . . . seeing their young children and aged parents go hungry when food supplies and other necessities are destroyed or sent to the war zones, and when basic necessities like bread become unobtainable . . . Left to sustain the family and endure the loneliness and vulnerability of separation, women suffer great hardships in wartime . . . Their houses may be damaged, or they may flee from home in fear of their lives. (Vickers 1993, 18)

The stories of women and children who struggle to survive in the face of war are beginning to be written (Barstow 2000; Cleaver and Wallace 1990; Gwin 1992; Hunter 1991; Staunton 1991; Vickers 1993). For maternal women, those preoccupied with the care and nurture of children (Ruddik 1995),

91

wartime is not measured by treaties, declarations, and statistics, but by the impact of violence, grief, hunger, loss, fear, pain, and change (Staunton 1991, xi). Their stories are not about winning and losing,[1] but about "the trauma that occurs when the domestic sphere, traditionally a safe place, is disrupted" (Gwin 1992, 3). They struggle to "recreate for themselves and their children safe places . . . albeit temporary ones, in the face of danger and despair" (ibid., 3). As Minrose Gwin puts it, this is a history of "what happens inside the 'house'" (ibid., 18). Women watch while their children, husbands, and friends lose their lives in war. They face torture and psychological distress. They tend the sick and dying. They are raped. When they don't even have enough food for their own families, they have to feed armies of soldiers. They are often left to pick up the pieces of shattered homes and lives.

Social history is written "from the bottom up"—from the experience of ordinary people. Women's social history concentrates on the lives of ordinary women (Neufeld Redekop 1996). This chapter focuses on the experience of women and children in time of violent conflict and famine. What is significant is both their experience and what they remembered about it. Themes discussed in this chapter arose from interviews that were conducted with Mennonite women who experienced the Bolshevik Revolution and subsequent famine in Russia between 1917 and 1925. These themes include children's experiences in war; women's struggles to provide the basic necessities for family survival; the care of orphans and beggars; women's ways of coping with violence and rape; and the role of religious faith. What emerges, upon reflection, is that through the suffering women were agents—they took action to cope, to creatively feed their families when supplies ran out, and to nonviolently protect their families from violence. It becomes clear that their spirituality gave them strength and, conversely, their experiences deepened their own spirituality.

I will first of all provide a brief historical background of the Mennonite experience in Russia (Epp 1962). Then I will describe my interview methodology, after which I will develop the themes identified during the interviews.

HISTORICAL BACKGROUND: WHAT "ORDINARY" MENNONITE WOMEN EXPERIENCED

In the years between 1914 and 1925, people living in Russia, including Mennonites, experienced a world war, a revolution, civil war, and famine. In November of 1914, a decree was issued, prohibiting the use of the German language in public assemblies. This affected the Mennonites adversely because German was their primary spoken language at home and in church. Three years later, Czar Nicholas II was overthrown, and the Bolshevik Revolution began. When the Bolsheviks, under Lenin, seized power in

Russia, Mennonite self-government, as Mennonites had known it, officially ended and settlements were placed under Bolshevik-directed councils. Much violence accompanied this period of change in Mennonite villages.

With the signing of a peace treaty in 1918, Lenin lost control of Russia. Mennonites felt relieved as German troops arrived to occupy the area, since it meant an end to terror. This period of relative peace was short-lived, however, for in the fall of the same year, Nestor Machno, son of a Russian peasant, led an army of peasants against the German invaders. The White Army[2] drove them out and occupied the area until March 1919. For the next two years, South Russia became a battleground of civil war as the White and Red Armies[3] fought for control of the territory, "some villages changing hands as many as twenty times" (Toews 1967, 40). Mennonite-owned mills and factories were confiscated as production and distribution of goods were nationalized. Soldiers, whether of the Red or White Army, were housed and fed in Mennonite homes. With the final defeat of the White Army in November 1920, the Bolsheviks were in control, but by this time, there had been vast devastation. Entire villages had been destroyed. Many women had been raped. Disease was rampant. As if this were not enough, a severe drought was experienced in the Ukraine in the spring of 1921, resulting in the worst winter ever.

What Mennonite women and children suffered during the Bolshevik Revolution and subsequent war and famine in Russia (1917–1925) is a story of fear, loss, violence, hunger, and change. It is a story that is similar to that of women and children in other times and places. What a twelve-year-old girl in Sarajevo wrote in her diary in 1994 could just as well have come from the pen of a Mennonite girl in Russia eighty years before:

> The streets aren't the same, not many people out, they're worried, sad. And there are lots and lots of people and children . . . who are no longer among the living. The war has claimed them . . . [Mommy's] constantly in tears. She tries to hide it from me, but I see everything. I see that things aren't good here. There's no peace. War has suddenly entered our town, our homes, our thoughts, our lives. It's terrible. (Filopovic 1994, 37)

The lengths to which Mennonite women had to go to survive, both physically and psychologically, to keep others alive, is a story that needs to be told.

In the few published diaries and stories written by or about the experience of Russian Mennonite women during this time, there is only scant reference to those "ordinary" activities that women did for basic survival (Epp 1986; Baerg 1985). An exception is Pamela Klassen's *Going by the Moon and the Stars*, the story of two Russian Mennonite women who immigrated to Canada after fleeing from the Soviet Union during World War II (1994). In many cases, these activities were very different from what they were accustomed to doing before the revolution.

While Mennonite women tend to think these activities are too ordinary to mention, they reveal a tremendous amount about the experiences of women during time of war and famine. Only by asking these women, in their eighties and nineties at the time of the interviews, can one arrive at an understanding of the lengths Russian Mennonite women had to go in order to simply survive as a family during this time. There is so much we would like to know. What did women do to protect families and property? Who cared for orphans and beggars? What new roles did women need to take on when husbands had to flee? What was done for women and girls who were raped? Who was responsible for gathering, preparing, and rationing food? What was the role of religion? What has been the effect of these experiences on their present life? What was the role of children? These questions have been ignored, not only by historians, but even Mennonite women themselves have not considered this kind of discussion very important. Invariably, when I contacted women to inquire whether they would be willing to be interviewed, they said, "I don't think I have anything important to say." But it is the attention to what is considered "ordinary" that is so important in recording women's history. Some interviewees did begin to recognize the value of recording the "ordinariness" of their own experience. At the end of one particular interview, suddenly struck by the fact that her own story of survival had been omitted from historical writing, the interviewee remarked, "In my father's books there is nothing about this."

THE INTERVIEWS

I began the discussion of women's role in Russia by talking to women I knew. Through word of mouth, I obtained additional names of women to interview. I also published a call for interviewees in eight Mennonite periodicals: *Mennonite Reporter, Mennonite Brethren Herald, Der Bote, Mennonitische Rundschau, Women's Concerns Report, The Mennonite, Sophia,* and *Window to Mission.* In the end, I interviewed twelve women and one man. Interviews, lasting approximately two hours, were taped and transcribed.

Even though general areas for discussion were determined in advance, I decided not to adopt the traditional method of oral interviewing, which centers "on interviewers' needs to elicit . . . information for various audiences (and) is designed to control the flow of information" (Minister 1991). Instead, I used a framework of oral history that is interactive and open-ended, a framework that gives the person being interviewed the freedom to direct the discussion toward those topics she wishes to pursue. Whatever aspect of their Russian experience these women wanted to talk about, whatever was important to them, became the focus of the interviews. In one case, a woman wanted to talk at length about the traumatic trip through several countries at the time of immigration to Canada. In another instance, a woman went into great detail about the time-consuming process of doing laundry and how difficult this was for her mother when soldiers invaded their home and spent the night.

The women who were interviewed were either small children or teenagers during the revolution and famine. They came from Tiege, Schoenfeld, Blumenhort, Alexanderkrone, Prangenau, Blumstein, Ohrloff, Gnadenheim, Davlekanovo, Eichenfeld, and Ekatarinoslov. They all immigrated to Canada in the early 1920s. At the time of the interviews, some were married, some were widowed, and others were single. Three of the women were from the Mennonite Brethren tradition; the remainder were General Conference Mennonite. A few women still lived in their own homes, some were in seniors' housing, and one lived in a nursing home. One woman, whose story is represented in this paper, had deceased; her story was told to me by her grandson. Most women interviewed were from Ontario; one was from Saskatoon, Saskatchewan. I laughed with them, cried with them, and ate with them—everything from *Zwieback* (dinner rolls) to *Paska* (Easter bread) to *Kotaletten Soppe* (hamburger soup). They sent me on my way with stories, recipes, food for my journey home, and even parsley root for making soup.

I will now recount the highlights of what I heard from these women, including what I learned about children's experiences and responsibilities; women's struggle to provide food and clothing for their families; the care of orphans and beggars; housing of soldiers; women's efforts to minimize violence and cope with rape; and the importance women attributed to faith in God.

THE CHILDREN

First the children. Children were regularly subjected to the effects of violence.

One woman recalled an event she witnessed as an eight-year-old girl during the revolution:

> Katie was a little girl, three years, and she'd run across the yard to the house, and then through the garden. Through the gate came two or three horseback riders and they just about ran over her. I can still see it, a little toddler, they just missed her, the way they were coming at a gallop, they would have trampled her. That was the kind of thing we were confronted with.

Another woman remembered that as a schoolchild she witnessed

> a young lame man being chased by a horseman hacking into his body with a saber until he collapsed and died in front of our house . . . at that same hour, my father was shot and killed while fleeing in our barn. Mother collapsed and was taken to the hospital. We felt like orphans. I wandered from the school to our house. The rebels were gone. Forlorn, I made my way to the barn, saw the pool of blood, fearfully went back into the house, and saw my forty-five-year-old father's body laid out with a bullet hole in his chest.

In one home, when a soldier came to search the house, a girl and her mother were the only ones in the house. She reported that

> he went through the chest of drawers and one of the drawers was mine. I was about fourteen. I was so arrogant. I said, "You have no business going through my drawer, that is mine." He stood up and looked at me and my mother, she was as white as a sheet . . . Then I got scared too when I saw my mother.

One told of the time when bandits entered their house and took her scarf:

> I had got it for Christmas. It was a big kerchief; they used to have it around their shoulders, you know. And one of those bandits had it over his arm. I went and took it from him. I said, "That is my scarf and I got that for Christmas." . . . And he was so angry he shot into the ceiling, but I had my scarf and I brought it to Canada.

Besides the trauma children experienced, watching the violence around them, they also had to take responsibility for the survival of themselves and others, a responsibility that in our society, we say should not belong to children. Before she was fourteen years old, one Mennonite girl cared for her injured father after he had been beaten:

> The Machno (bandits) came and wanted to kill my father, and they took him, and that was in January, a very, very cold day and then they came in the afternoon and took him to kill him. They had let him know they were coming to get him because he was rich. And papa was sitting and reading his Testament and watching and then they came. And then we waited; papa didn't come, papa didn't come. My mother was so restless, she went across the street; there was her sister and I remember I was standing, and I was looking through the window and the house was quite a distance from the street. And then I saw papa coming, barefoot, without pants, just a shirt and a vest. And blood was just streaming down his face and then I grabbed a blanket and ran outside and put it on him

and then I screamed whatever I could. I thought the whole world should hear what they did to my papa. I put a blanket around him . . . and then I helped him to get into bed and then I ran across the street and I screamed what I could and then mama came.

Another woman recalled how her older fourteen-year-old sister gathered all her siblings into a nearby outhouse (an outdoor toilet) when the Bolsheviks came to their house: "We dared not speak for fear of being discovered. After counting heads, she discovered our little three-year-old sister missing. She was out there crying and calling for help. My sister dared to step out and pick her up."

One interviewee said she was an infant at the time. While her sister pushed her in the baby buggy, "soldiers would come and then they'd stand and look at me and they'd talk to me and I would grin, you know. And my sister was so scared they'd take me away. She'd hold onto the buggy, you know."

Christmas is a special time for children. Parents make it so. On one occasion, it was a teenage girl who took the responsibility to make Christmas preparations. This girl's mother had explained to the children that they wouldn't be able to celebrate Christmas because they had nothing left to give.

And then we got up in the morning and there was a little gift. I had a little picture. Everybody had a little picture or a little book. Just Margaret didn't have. Now just imagine, she had had a doll, a VERY beautiful doll, when you press her she would say (in a high voice) "mama, papa." She had given that to a widow (her husband had died and she had one daughter) and this widow had given her little pictures and things like that so that we each had a gift, just Margaret didn't have a gift.

Margaret had taken it upon herself to make sure that her brothers and sisters had Christmas gifts. She had given up her own favorite doll in order to do it.

Children were not shielded from watching others go hungry, and they themselves had to search for food to eat. One woman remembers that as a child she watched a little boy pick up a dead crow and try to eat it: "I saw it from the window, (she starts to cry as she speaks) it was so heartbreaking, he was about a six year old boy; I gave him my portion." Another recalled that, of the many strangers that came to her parents' home to beg for food, one man in particular was quite striking. He used to call the children, "angels of God." She told the story of the days during the famine when her mother was in the hospital just before her death. It was her responsibility to take milk to her mother every morning. It happened that just at that time this "stranger" was also in the hospital; she had to walk past his bed to get to her mother's bed. As she passed by, the "stranger" would say to her, "angel of God, give me something to eat." She felt so badly because she only had enough milk for her mother. Soon after, his bed was empty. He had died.

Children also assisted in burying the dead. In one case, German soldiers had forced Russian men to dig their own graves. As the soldiers shot them, they fell into their own graves. One woman recalled her mother taking her older sister outside with her to bury these Russian men properly, "and they took a shovel, and there were bones and brains, and they hadn't buried them, Germans had shot them in the head and the flesh was lying here and there, and they buried all that."

Children and teenagers also had to take responsibility for financial matters. One woman told at length about her responsibility to carry all the money during her trip out of Russia with her mother and younger brother. As they went from country to country, it was she who changed the money to local currency and was responsible for buying food and other necessities. She told the story of their trip to Germany and the tremendous anxiety she felt as a teenager. At one point, while they were still in Moscow, awaiting exit papers, they ran out of money and wired to a relative in Germany to send money to a German consul in Lithuania. When they arrived at the German consul,

> it was closed and mother knocked, she said, "We have to get in, we have to get in," and he would open the door a little bit only, because it was three o'clock, and my mother, she was only young, she was over forty, and he wanted to close the door and didn't want to let us in because it was closed, and we weren't allowed to stay there. We were supposed to leave and we had no place to stay anyway, so my mother put her foot in the door and didn't let him close it and so we got in and I was so exhausted. There was nobody there; only that man that gave the papers; everybody was gone. I was so exhausted; I was only seventeen (raises her voice), you know, and through all those emotions that we went already. When he said, "what can we do for you?" I sat down on the chair and started to cry; I couldn't say anything. Then mother said we need the papers and we have to leave tomorrow and even [we should have left] today and we have no papers and then I sat and I cried. I couldn't say a word and then he said, "Don't cry. You will go tomorrow." Then he gave us the papers and then we left.

As women reflected on the terror they felt as children, they sometimes wondered how they made it through. They expressed thoughts such as "somehow we got through" and "everybody was in the same situation . . . this was what you had to go through." Children had to comfort each other. When I asked if they had had nightmares as children, one woman answered, "Not me, but my sisters have, maybe a carry-over from our father's murder.

We stepsisters shared a bedroom, and she had such bad nightmares, she was so afraid, I said to her, 'I'm right close to you.' But she got over it, but it was very hard on me too. She was sixteen, I was fifteen."

I heard many stories of the lengths to which the mothers of these children had to go in order to provide enough food for their families. During the years of scarcity and famine, women used their creativity to prepare new kinds of foods to eat, using whatever ingredients they had and inventing dishes they had not eaten before. They described some of the foods their mothers prepared:

When we had milk, we had milk soup, we called it *clungka mousse* (she laughs). Mother had a little bit of flour, and she would mix it with eggs (we had a few chickens), she mixed it with flour and kind of "clunked" it into the hot milk.

We had lots of pumpkins and lots of beets. We made everything from pumpkins—pumpkin mousse, pumpkin this and pumpkin that. We hadn't eaten like that before. She even made jam from beet syrup . . . We always had a cow; in winter there was probably a couple months when we didn't have milk but then we made *prips* (a hot drink from roasted grain).

We had two cows during the famine but we didn't have enough food for the cows. We had milk and that really saved us. We still made butter. We had a little bran but you can't make bran bread, just a flat thing, and we put some butter on it. Both my brothers were swollen from hunger.

We grew a lot of sunflowers, that's how we got our oil. And I remember early in the morning when the sunflowers were beginning to get their seeds, we girls had to get up early and go out in the field and we'd have a tin can and bang, bang, the crows were taking the seeds, we had to get them away. Dad took the sunflower seeds to have the oil pressed out of them; then he could keep the shells that were left. (It's called *makucha*). I can still feel it in my throat. And it was chopped up fine. Then mother would have a little bit of flour and maybe an egg and she would mix that and make it like a bread because there was not enough flour for bread. You made use of absolutely everything. There was a little bit of oil still in it you see. And bake it in a frying pan, it was like a pancake.

They ate whatever was available: "One day Dad made a sling shot and killed sparrows; mom cleaned them. She put them, bones and all, through a food chopper, ground up, like fish . . . and made hamburgers with it." Several women talked about their mothers making thin soups with a special kind of weed that children picked from the fields.

The winter of 1921 was the most difficult. By this time, food was being rationed. Women told how their mothers gave one piece of bread to each family member in the morning to last for the whole day. In one family, the father was the one who did the rationing: "And then my father would take that bread, and each morning, I never forget, and he would get the scale out. Mama stayed away; she couldn't see that. She was in the other room. It hurt her too much when she saw that there wasn't enough food." Most women talked of the time when food arrived from Holland and the United States:

> Then came the wonderful time when packages arrived from USA and Holland. Was that ever wonderful! There came from Holland a mixture for babies and it had all solidified and we ate it like candies but then there came very, very hard sea cakes made of flour and water and salt, shaped like biscuits (Oh I loved it), and sugar and cocoa and a little coffee. Oh, but how we craved for something sweet! American packages . . . —that was when we saw the first margarine, it was all white, we were very, very hungry for some kind of fat, I think that's because we hadn't had enough.

Besides learning new ways to serve food, Mennonite women also found innovative ways to make clothing for their families. Old clothing was taken apart, turned inside out, and remade. Any available material was made into clothing: "Our beautiful curtain between the kitchen and our dining room was made into a dress for me . . . Our chesterfield was supposed to be redone with a beautiful green plush; that was made into a coat for Helga who didn't have anything to wear. Everything you could lay your hands on you converted into something else." Skirts were made from potato sacks and "we embroidered them with the silk from the silkworms. Even our underwear we embroidered." Decorating clothing with embroidery was very important to Mennonite women, even during extreme poverty. It seemed to be one way to preserve their own dignity when so much had been taken away from them.

The revolution left many children, both Mennonite and Russian, without parents. Mennonite villages organized a system of care for these orphans, whereby they would be taken in for a period of time by one family and then move on to another. One woman recalled a particularly heartbreaking experience when her family cared for a Russian orphan named Misha:

> There was a Russian orphanage. There was no more food. And then they put them into our villages. Those poor children, they had to stay one week with one family, the next week with another family. Misha came to us, six years old, and we fell in love with him and he fell in love with us. When we had him one week and then he should go to another home, we said, "Mama, we want to keep him." "Yes, we keep Misha." We didn't have a bed for him, it was a very small house, and then we put chairs together, like six little chairs, that's where Misha slept and then when he went to bed, he always said, "Give me a kiss," and we all had to kiss him. And then was the time he should go to the neighbors, the food was getting very, very scarce, then the neighbor, said, "If we give you a loaf of bread, will you keep him for us?" "YES, we will." And that wasn't enough for a whole week, just a loaf of

bread, so we always had to give him ours, but when we had no more to eat, we said, "No, he has to go to the neighbors, they have food to eat, and we haven't, see," and then he was CRYING—"I want to stay home, I want to stay home." And my brother was big and tall and he had to carry him to the neighbor's screaming and crying, and he kissed us all and we all had to kiss him when he went. It was so heartbreaking. And then when we migrated to Canada, that was the most heartbreaking thing ever. We were at the station, and then when the train blew and we had to get in, and we asked, "Where's Misha?" Here he was sitting under the boxcar, crying. *"Eck vell met nu America comen, eck vell met nu America comen."* (I want to go along to America.) All these seventy years, there's hardly a day where I don't think of Misha and what happened to him. Sometimes when I can't sleep, then I think, "Maybe we should have taken him, maybe we could have hid him. Even now, you know, I think maybe we didn't do right to leave him there."

SHARING FOOD

Besides caring for orphans, there were many beggars walking from village to village during the famine years, begging for food. In one home, the mother drew the blinds while the family was eating, so the beggars wouldn't see them. She knew that if she fed the beggars, her own family would starve. Despite this, she still sometimes gave food to those who came begging. Another woman remembers the day her mother baked bread with the last bit of flour in the house: "I don't know where she (mother) was at that time. I was alone in that room and a girl came (begging) and she was very hungry, and she wanted something to eat, and I looked at her. Quietly I went and reached for that one loaf and cut a piece off and gave it to her. It was the last loaf we had too." In another home, each child received a tablespoon of cooked millet a day. Regularly,

> my sister Margaret . . . she was a saint . . . The windows were very low in our house, and all-day little children would come, we only could see their eyes at the window. They would say, (plaintively), "One mouthful, one mouthful." And that was almost all day you heard that. One child left, the other one came. And then Margaret would take her one spoonful of that millet seed and give it to a child and then she had nothing.

ENCOUNTERS WITH MACHNOVITES
AND OTHER RUSSIAN SOLDIERS

During the ever-changing occupation by Red and White Armies, women were confronted with the problem of housing soldiers, who often brought

filth and disease into Mennonite homes. One woman explained the lengthy
process of doing laundry after soldiers had slept in their beds:

> My grandmother, she had one of those extra beds with high pillows. That was
> just used when company came. And the one soldier with his dirty boots and
> everything, he went right on top of the bed. When they were gone they had
> to delouse everything; they left all kinds of nice lice behind . . . Mother and
> grandmother deloused the bedding and washed it. [They] washed by hand.
> They soaked everything for a whole day. Then they washed it once through.
> Then they let it sit in hot soap water. The next day it was washed again. Then
> it was boiled. Then they rinsed it once and the next day put it through another
> rinse and if there was any starching to do that was done later on . . . a four or
> five day process.

Obviously, the presence of these soldiers posed a threat to the health of
families. One woman remembered her mother warning the children not to
touch the bloody bandages soldiers had left on the straw pile, "because these
men, they had all kinds of things, we don't know what all they had, syphilis
or what."

Averting Violence

Women told of their mothers' role in trying to avert violence and death when
bandits came to their homes. One woman told this story:

> They came at night. We didn't undress; we kept our clothes on day and night.
> And my mother would say, "You stay in bed." See, they raped the women, you
> know. And then she told my dad, "You stay in bed too. If they come, be quiet,
> pretend you are all sleeping." Then when they came to the door with bayonets
> and with their boots, BOOM, BOOM, and my mother went to greet them and
> she had to be very fast. If you wouldn't open the door fast enough, they would
> shoot through the door. I know one lady; she didn't open fast enough, and she
> was just killed through the door. It was her idea and she told papa, "Stay in bed."
> Then she would go and open the door, and she would say, "Oh boys, come in,
> come in, you must be COLD. It is so cold outside, you come in." And most of
> the time they were drunk, and they were swearing and mama said, "Please be
> quiet, the children are sleeping." Well, nobody could be sleeping. But she said,
> "The children are sleeping, and you scare them. Would you be quiet please?
> Then I will make you some tea and I'll give you some sausage." And they just
> loved the Mennonite sausage, raw, just the way it was. And we were lying in
> bed. (It's as plain to me as if it was yesterday.) And they were swearing and
> mother went into the kitchen and made tea for them. We had our heads covered

and we were just listening. And finally, they stopped swearing and then they were eating. And then in between they always said, "Where's the boss? Where's the boss?" They wanted my dad. And my mama said, "He is kind of slow. It takes him so long to get dressed, but he will come. I will call him. But he has to dress first." (He was fully dressed, you know. And she had told papa, "Don't come when they are still angry. You come after they have eaten.") And then papa came out of the bedroom, pulling up his pants, and he said, "Well boys, how are you? Did my wife give you good tea and sausage?" He talked so nice and friendly to them, and then when they had eaten, they couldn't do any harm . . . and then they left.

This mother had carefully orchestrated a plan to save her entire family, and it worked.

The Reality of Rape

In one family, the mother planned ahead how to protect her most vulnerable daughter from rape in the event of being invaded suddenly by bandits. She had instructed the children exactly how to arrange their seating on the couches when bandits would enter the house. The young teenage daughter would sit in the corner with all the others surrounding her so that she would not be noticed as much, and thus, hopefully avoid being raped.

Most of the women knew about the prevalence of rape and several knew women and young girls who had been raped:

A teacher of mine was raped. After that she looked pale and sick. She only married later on when she was in her thirties.

Across the street from us, a woman who was engaged to be married, was raped while milking the cow . . . One woman, six men, one right after the other, and she went insane, she broke down, a nervous breakdown. The anarchists did it.

Martha's (not her real name) dearest friend . . . they took her right in front of the parents and they said, "You come with us." She was only sixteen. And she was raped right there in the home in another room.

I know of one woman, she had given birth to a baby and she was in bed with her baby. And then they came and told her husband, "You show us how you make a baby." And then those anarchists, they raped her afterwards. Terrible.

When women were asked what was done for those who had been raped, most responded that there was really no help for them, except that they might go to the doctor for a physical examination. However, in the town of Eichenfeld, women who had been raped gathered to support each other. Here, many women had been raped while making bread for the 5,000 bandits who entered the village suddenly on October 26, 1919, killing every male fifteen years and older. The next morning, "women gathered in one house in the village and were cared for by a nurse and just supported one another. They stayed together one or two days and then dispersed."

REFLECTIONS ON THE MEANING OF IT ALL

Not only did women tell me their stories, they frequently reflected on what had happened, interjecting comments about how difficult their experiences had been. They talked about the fact that since the whole community was suffering, it made it a little easier. "We were all in the same shoe. And that helped a great deal, that not only we were poor." Some marveled at the inventiveness of their mothers during these hard times: "That's the way we did it. And there were all (raises her voice) kinds of things we had to find out." Two women, reflecting on their reactions to starvation as children, reflected on what war and famine does to people who get habituated to it:

> Those little children, they came to our village begging for bread, and there was nothing, there was nothing to give them and you know they lay there dead with their bellies, when I just think now, we could walk past, we just didn't even look, we just even didn't look, they LAY THERE, the DEAD BODIES LAY THERE. You see, you get so . . . what this time made of people. But those wars that we had, what that made of people . . . The children came to beg for bread and they were so starved—their big bellies . . . I remember as we walked the streets and we saw them laying there, and we didn't even look, we didn't look, I guess we didn't know what to do . . . People get so hard you know, ai-yai-yai-yai-yai, it's no good, it's just no good.

Several women spoke about the lasting effects of their experiences in Russia on their lives today. Several mentioned that being without food as children meant that to this day, they were sure not to waste any food: "The way I save things now, is unbelievable. It's still in me. I can't throw things out. When people go to the restaurant, I could almost cry, the food left on their plates, even in our banquets in the church. Even when we have our family gatherings and the children leave their buns, I cut off the bites and collect them."

Spirituality of Service, Faith, and Gratitude

Two women said that the reason they knit and sew for Mennonite Central Committee (MCC) is because they want to do something for children who are hungry and poorly clothed, like they were. One woman showed me little vests she was making:

> Gloria, I've been knitting vests like this for Rwandan children. I've knit over fifty of them; they want them because the evenings are so cold. When I heard about this I was so happy, because my heart nearly breaks when I see (on television) those little ones lying there with not a stitch on and just a little heap of bones.

Another woman exclaimed, "We have been helped so much, and now we have to help. It is an obligation and a privilege."

Another ongoing effect of these women's experiences is seen in their spirituality. A common theme for these women was their gratefulness to God for bringing them through the hard times. Women talked about the importance of prayer and faith in God:

> Prayer was our only refuge and strength at that time. How often Mama said, "Come let us pray" when papa was away. During that time there were many prayer meetings. Just crying to God, yelling to God, "Help us, help us, do something." . . . There were so many emergencies and then right away there was a prayer meeting called.

One woman recalled how singing hymns helped them cope with the horrors around them. Women were prone to remember those times when God provided for them in special ways:

> We had a big bin, four feet square, that was full of whole wheat flour. We had hardly any potatoes, it had hardly rained, it was crop failure. And this was all the flour we had. We were nine people; grandmother had moved with us too. And then it went down, down, down. We made everything from flour . . . And this bin was empty, except for a little bit of flour in the corner. That's when the miracle happened. My father said, "Children, for how many times (the girls took turns baking bread) will there be flour?" "Papa," we said, "for two more bakings." Then we baked, and papa said, "how much flour is there for baking?" "Oh, for two more," and that went on for quite a long time and papa said, "Children . . ." and it lasted for quite a long time, and that was the miracle.

These experiences contributed to a present-day sense of gratitude for these women. As I left her home, the woman who told the story about the flour bin gave me a big hug and said, "The most important thing is to tell the people what God can do. I just can't stop praising God." Another woman, after recounting, what she called "the biggest miracle" of all, the exit from Russia as the train went through the gate into Latvia, said, "From then on we knew how God's hands were over us and as the train started to go, that was such a feeling, you know. If you went through this, you cannot change, you just take that with you all your life."

LESSONS LEARNED

What we learn from these interviews with women who were children and teenagers during the Bolshevik Revolution and famine is that little girls became "little mothers" as they joined their mothers in roles such as gathering food, feeding people who came begging for food, looking after family finances, preserving family traditions (like Christmas), protecting their families from violence, and burying the dead. We also learn that being forced, for their own survival, to take on adult roles and endure traumatizing experiences had a lifelong impact on their lives. Furthermore, these women, with a faith-based worldview, were able to interpret their experiences in a way that led to a spirit of gratitude.

Through these selected interviews with survivors of war, we have a glimpse into how one group of women and children experienced war and famine at one particular time in history and in one specific location— Mennonite women and children living through the Bolshevik Revolution and subsequent famine in Russia from 1917 to 1925. The stories of these ordinary women and children are a social history that illuminates the experience of those who happened to be living in an area where violent conflict occurred.

Although this analysis is based on a relatively small sample of women, it does demonstrate that a narrative-based social history of women's experience of war produces significant insights for a fuller understanding of historical events. It also shows the human capacity to survive dehumanizing circumstances.

NOTES

1. Robin Morgan, in *The Demon Lover: The Roots of Terrorism* (Toronto: Penguin, 1989), makes the point that women can contribute to violent conflict by making a hero of the violent warrior. In the case of pacifist Mennonite women, generally this would not be an issue; in any case, I am limiting my study to the maternal role of women.

2. The White Army was the traditional army of Russia that supported the Czar and after the death of the Czar, supported the continuity of the traditional system of governance.

3. The Red Army was organized by the Communist Party and was the means to violently overthrow the old order and take control of Russia.

REFERENCES

Baerg, Anna. 1985. *Diary of Anna Baerg: 1916–1924*. Translated and edited by Gerald Peters. Winnipeg: CMBC Publications.

Barstow, Anne Llewellyn, ed. 2000. *War's Dirty Secret: Rape, Prostitution, and Other Crimes Against Women*. Cleveland: The Pilgrim Press.

Cleaver, Tessa, and Marion Wallace. 1990. *Namibia: Women in War*. London: Zed Books.

Epp, Frank H. 1962. *Mennonite Exodus: The Rescue and Resettlement of the Russian Mennonites since the Communist Revolution*. Altona: D.W. Friesen & Sons.

Epp, Peter G. 1986. *Agatchen: A Russian Mennonite Mother's Story*. Translated and edited by Peter Pauls. Winnipeg: Hyperion Press.

Filipovic, Zlata. 1994. *Zlata's Diary: A Child's Life in Sarajevo*. Translated by Christian Pribichevich-Zoric. New York, NY: Penguin Books.

Gwin, Minrose C., ed. 1992. *A Woman's Civil War: A Diary, with Reminiscences of the War, from March 1862*. Madison: The University of Wisconsin Press.

Hunter, Anne E., ed. 1991. *On Peace, War, and Gender: A Challenge to Genetic Explanations*. New York, NY: The Feminist Press.

Klassen, Pamela E. 1994. *Going by the Moon and the Stars*. Waterloo: Wilfrid Laurier University Press.

Minister, Kristina. 1991. "A Feminist Frame for the Oral History Interview." In *Women's Words: The Feminist Practice of Oral History*. Edited by Sherna Berger Gluck and Daphne Patai. New York, NY: Routledge, 27–41.

Morgan, Robin. 1989. *The Demon Lover: The Roots of Terrorism*. Toronto: Penguin.

Neufeld Redekop, Gloria. 1996. *The Work of Their Hands: Mennonite Women's Societies in Canada*. Waterloo: Wilfrid Laurier University Press.

Ruddik, Sarah. 1995. *Maternal Thinking: Towards a Politics of Peace*. Boston, MA: Beacon Press.

Staunton, Irene, ed. 1991. *Mothers of the Revolution: The War Experiences of Thirty Zimbabwean Women*. Bloomington, IN: Indiana University Press.

Toews, John B. 1967. *Lost Fatherland: The Story of the Mennonite Emigration from Soviet Russia, 1921–1927*. Scottdale: Herald Press.

Vickers, Jeanne. 1993. *Women and War*. London: Zed Books.

Part II

RECONCILIATION AS SPIRITUAL PRAXIS

Chapter 5

Relational Ecosystem for Peace (REP)

*From Division to Deep Connection
with Compassionate Listening*

Brigitte Gagnon

Transcending violence includes examining the roots of tension that lie at the core of one's being. This chapter examines ways of engaging conflict at this level by analyzing the various components of the act of compassionate listening (CL). In doing so, it explores the praxis of conflict transformation in zones of violent conflicts, where a certain type of presence is required, demanding a return to a deep interior space where there are powerful emotions and entrenched attitudes concerning the other/the enemy. The challenge involved is developed by John Paul Lederach:

> The act of reaching out emanates from and must return to the deep inner world. Here I refer to the less accessible or empirically observable interior world of the individual where competing voices, anxieties, and debates arise within the potential peacebuilder as she or he encounters perceived and real enemies. A probe into the spiritual and ultimately creative worlds, the inner and outer, invites us to explore the nexus and confluence of tributaries that provide insights into and nurture the quality of presence required to sustain constructive encounter with the enemy-other. (2015, 541)

Conceptualizing the Relational Ecosystem for Peace (REP), which emerged from my doctoral research (Gagnon 2019), generated significant insights on the nexus between practice and spirituality. Through a study of the practice of CL, developed by the Compassionate Listening Project (TCLP), research findings helped envision conditions and factors that facilitate shifts in social connection: from separation to communication and from communication to deep connection or communion.

After presenting some of CL's key features that came to be central in my research, the remainder of the chapter will be on one of the REP's central components: a relational and structural matrix offering a relational platform to help guide shifts to deep connection with others, inspired by the CL practice (see Gagnon and Brodeur 2020, for an overview of the REP).

KEY FEATURES OF THE CL EXPERIENCE

The goal of CL is to transform the energy of conflict or disengagement into an opportunity for further understanding and deep connection (Cohen 2011). This is guided by a curriculum revolving around five core practices: (1) cultivating compassion; (2) developing the fair witness; (3) respecting self and others; (4) listening with the heart, and (5) speaking from the heart (ibid.). Since 1998, TCLP has organized delegations to visit Israel-Palestine, where participants practice CL with guest speakers from diverse perspectives. They hear Israelis and Palestinians share their stories and experiences with the conflict.

Delegates receive a CL introductory training the first day and then put the teachings into practice during one to three listening sessions each day, for about two weeks. Listening sessions take place in guest speakers' homes, community centers, kibbutzim, refugee camps, and other venues. As participants in delegations improve their skills during the listening sessions, it becomes possible for them to affirm their deepest humanity and learn to hold the complexities related to the conflict, with the intention to discover the human being behind stereotypes (Green, in Manousos 2003, 46).

What caught my attention with this practice was the fact that participants reported this experience as life changing and even healing for many (Hwoschinsky 2002). After participating myself in the CL training offered by TCLP, it confirmed my interest in doctoral studies on what underlies these experiences and transformations, as well as the process and type of spirituality at the heart of this approach. I was a participant observer in one of TCLP's delegations and conducted interviews with coparticipants (n = 14); as well I administered an online questionnaire to past CL participants (1998–2015; n = 60). This ground-based research led to the emergence and development of the REP.

One reason for doing a PhD in Religious Studies was to explore the spiritual dimension of human beings. I was curious about what I called the "edge" (the spiritual), aside with other aspects like the physical, mental, emotional, and social in humans when facing a crisis. From my experience as a social worker in health and social services in Canada, as much in clinical functions as planning services and programs, I realized that this aspect—the spiritual—is not discussed. The separation between state and religion in our society, in Canada, is one underlying reason why this reality is overlooked in our case discussions and notes for intervention. Of course, values, convictions, meaning, and sense of life in helping others feed into our motivations, dispositions, and actions; hence, I came to realize that to "elevate consciousness" was central in my work.

This was confirmed to me by many of the youth I helped. Now adults, they came into my life by coincidence even though they are no longer my clients. They reflected on how my intervention had made a big difference in their lives. For example, a young mother whom I helped as a teenager revealed: "My mother talks often about you. We remember how much you helped us. You changed our lives. You believed in us." In this particular case, verbal, emotional, and physical violence was present between mother and daughter and I remember sitting down with them countless hours around the kitchen table trying to establish a safe dialogical space to resolve the crisis at hand. It became a form of laboratory to acquire and practice new dialogical skills, attitudes, and solidify the motivation to consciously replace violence by nonviolence and develop ways to coexist.

Moving forward with steps backward, they got to a point where they could have safe discussions and do problem solving. This, because we became able to put underlying causes of their conflict on the table, which were of psychological and social nature. I knew there was love between them, overshadowed by different traumas, and I saw them shift from attitudes and states of separation with violence involved to communication without violence: the first two of three steps in the REP. The following years it seems they moved from communication to deep love and compassion for one another from what this former client was telling me: the REP's third step that I didn't fully witness, but deep down I knew there were seeds planted in our time together. Most importantly, the home was safe for the child.

Reflecting on this case, along with other similar stories, and the results, which I was made aware of by past clients, I remembered the importance of some factors that I believe made a difference and that are also in the CL practice: trying to see what is most special in each person; feeling equal with clients in our common humanity and not "feeling superior" despite the legal power I had (and had to use when needed for child protection or dangers posed by mental health issues); identifying underlying causes of conflicts, being honest and frank about them and putting a lot of effort into resolving or attenuating them for greater well-being and safety.

So, when I experienced the CL approach in the training TCLP offered, I "knew" (as in ways of knowing) that there was something important to explore further to get to understand what underlies this approach from an experiential and transformational perspective. We lack a vocabulary, methods, and clearer understanding about how spirituality (the "edge") is being deployed in the midst of conflicts. In my research, the notion of the "relational" (aspect of being) replaced the initially named "spiritual" (aspect of being). It resonated in a more integral perspective with other aspects like the mental, emotional, social, and so on. We can be in relation with ourselves, others, the transcendent, and so on. Significant for me is the notion of the "core"—used in CL as referring to the heart of the person.

Pargament and colleagues in the field of psychology and spirituality bring interesting clues on how "sacred core" can be envisioned:

> The term sacred is used inclusively here to refer not only to concepts of God and higher powers but also to other aspects of life that are perceived to be manifestations of the divine or imbued with divine like qualities, such as transcendences, immanence, boundlessness, and ultimacy. (Pargament and Mahoney 2005 in Pargament et al. 2013)

For them, everything that is part of life can be impregnated with the sacred—beliefs, practices, experiences, relations, motivations, nature war, and so on—and the search for the sacred takes place in a continuous journey of discovery and transformation (ibid). They bring the notion of a "sacred core" in human beings with a circle around it with notions like sense, nature, and soul being part of the domain of spirituality (Pargament 2013):

> The "sacred core" refers to ideas of God, higher powers, divinity, and transcendent reality. But the sacred is not restricted to concepts of a Supreme Being or greater reality. Surrounding the sacred core is a ring of other aspects of life that become extraordinary, indeed sacred themselves, through their association with the sacred core. (Pargament 2007, 32)

Pargament adds: "However the sacred core may be defined, it is said to be concerned with earthly as well as heavenly matters" (2007, 37) and linked to the person's experience via thoughts, emotions, behaviors, and motivations (ibid., 39). The challenges linked with spirituality are intrapersonal, interpersonal, and divine (ibid., 112). The data and model (REP) that emerged from my research show pieces of a prism that cover the integral aspect of being in these dimensions.

Using the relational aspect to expose what is taking place in terms of spiritual experiences and transformations in the REP helps to expose what is taking place in the form of an inner template, as a reflection of outer template, of shifts from violence to communication and from there to compassion and deep connection. The vocabulary and model serve as a map of key elements to apply in relationships, especially with so-called enemies, to move to conflict transformation and resolution. This map is complemented by Brodeur's action research.

The interworldview dialogue (IWVD) approach developed by Patrice Brodeur ("Interworldview Dialogue," *Transforming*) complements CL within the REP by adding the interpersonal and intergroup dynamics. Both CL and IWVD approaches include the core elements of transformative learning: experience, critical reflection, dialogue, holistic orientation, appreciation for context, and authentic relationships (Mezirow 2009).

Since my research into TCLP, I have been using key elements of CL and the REP approach in my practice as a trauma and crisis worker and a conflict resolution consultant. The next three features came to be essential in my research and professional practice. Giving conscious attention to them in my practice and exposing them to clients to "elevate consciousness" made all the difference—as if, we finally found a way to name something that we know is central but was not clearly identified.

Quality of Presence

During the TCLP's delegation's listening sessions, it became clear that the quality of presence each person brings to the group is critical, creating new synergy. Gene Hoffman, one of CL's pioneers, explains how a kind of presence is manifest:

> This listening requires a particular mode. The questions are non-adversarial. The listening is nonjudgmental. The listener seeks the truth of the person questioned, and strives to see through any masks of hostility and fear to the sacredness of the individual, and discerns the wounds at the heart of any violence. (Cohen 2011, 10)

John Paul Lederach speaks about the importance of bringing a compassionate presence in peacebuilding, which requires

> that we develop a mind of resilience that courageously faces this tremendous outpouring of ego in the midst of conflict, without replicating its anxious dynamic. And that we nurture the listening heart to live alongside deep trauma without taking over responsibility for healing others. In both instances, compassion suggests a commitment to "alongsidedness" that provides a different quality of presence. This quality of presence requires open vulnerability but not gullible weakness; boundless love with clarity of boundaries and; listening for the fragile voice of truth and choosing to live in truth without arrogance or imposition. (Lederach 2012)

This *alongsidedness* might refer to the type of listening Diana Rehling (2008), an expert in listening in communication, received from visitors while facing an illness at the hospital. She came to call this *compassionate* listening. She compared it with *empathic* listening, where visitors asked her many questions, wanting to understand her condition, which brought her to have preprepared answers, and with *therapeutic* listening, where visitors put an emphasis on fixing the problem, which she said isolated her more, as she felt there was something missing in her to heal. With *compassionate* listening, Rehling explains: "The focus was not on my physical symptoms and specific challenges, but in making sense together. We worked together to create an understanding of the suffering I was experiencing" (2008, 84). This kind of understanding arising from the other was not from psychological compatibility but from shared humanity she says, concluding that it eased her loneliness and allowed her to heal spiritually and begin to grow in her illness (ibid., 86). This resonates with the CL experience during listening sessions and the REP's relational platform to bring a comprehensive way to better understand how this impact unfolds and what is involved in more details.

Authentic Relationships and Resonance to Truth

One delegate pointed to a key aspect of CL—accessibility—in the following reflection:

> In sitting in one of those sessions it struck me that everybody in the room, in that circle, was having a perfect opportunity to express himself or herself exactly as they were and to have their own layers of resistance exposed to themselves if they were conscious and able to learn the steps that we've been looking at here with compassionate listening. Everybody had an opportunity to be exactly as they were and those who were learning the compassionate listening way, were being given a gift by the person who was expressing himself [or herself] in a way that raised the existence in the person that was listening.[1]

CL is accessible and can be achieved by anyone and yet, it is not that easy to do, nor is it "automatic." It needs to be cultivated, as with any contemplative practice with compassion at its center. Yet, it is not always easy to comprehend.

The vocabulary and instructions used in CL training and activities bring a resonance of "truth" in participants. The changes in awareness and practice facilitates a greater sense of connection with the speakers. For example, my research shows there were shifts from judgments made about the guest speakers to finding ways of letting go of these judgments. At times participants had trouble

• feeling and extending compassion when the guest speakers were in a defensive mode;

- staying open and curious toward them despite the difficulties to connect;
- not agreeing with the guest speakers, respecting their own reality;
- controlling personal automatic reactions when triggered by the guest speakers; and
- staying away from too much mental activity so that they could connect deeply with the guest speaker.

They came to the point where they could recognize when their heart was closing and when it was expanding (opening wider), during listening sessions (Gagnon 2019). They reported physiological tensions and unhappiness when having difficulty to connect with the heart, and various states of calmness and inner peace when able to connect. In the midst of these efforts to connect more and more deeply with this awareness of their heart closing and opening, the research showed a form of portal where creativity, spirituality, and emergence of transformative and healing experiences could manifest and be manifested (Gagnon 2019).

The Importance of the Heart

CL is a practice that "integrates cognitive awareness with the wisdom of the heart" (Cohen 2001, 10). Research in neurocardiology shows that an electromagnetic form of communication is a source of information exchanges between people where interaction takes place between the heart of a person and the brain of another, when they are close, or touch each other:

> A head-heart dynamic affects, reflects, and determines our responsiveness outside the field of our conscious awareness. As we become more aware of nature's head-heart dynamic, we begin to cooperate with this mutually interdependent spirit and the collaborative activity between our intelligence and our intellect, our biology and our spirit. The unification and transcendence of our splintered selves may be the next intelligent evolutionary shift. (Koerner 2011, 285)

Combining scientific research about the heart with ancient wisdom gives clues on how the different ways of knowing (physical, mental, emotional, relational, etc.) lead to discernment and wisdom in decision making (see also K. P. Kauffman, "The Biology of Emotion," *Transforming*). Human security depends on it. Discernment manifests in

> the regulating of one's thinking in the acquisition and application of knowledge to make decisions that are right, fair, and just and a relationship with the divine and manifesting itself in one's attitude, motivation, and behavior, expressed in service to others. (Traüffer *et al.* 2010, 178)

From a quiet and centered place, we can "hear the wisdom of our heart and body-mind" selecting options that move toward our well-being as well as that of people around us (ibid., 291).

This is the challenge the CL delegates encountered, leading to the REP's central tool: a relational and structural matrix that can help envision how to get to this level of congruence. In the description of the matrix, I will be attentive to the transformational impact CL can provide in conflicts and the day-to-day interpersonal challenges.

REP: A FUNCTION OF ENVIRONMENT, MESSAGES, AND MESSENGERS

Figure 5.1 shows a relational and structural Matrix as a central feature of the REP. We find three key variables and nine indicators as related to CL.

In this section, we examine the environment, the kinds of messages that are part of CL, and the characteristics of the messenger/listener, as supported by key research findings (Gagnon 2019).[2] All nine structural units in the Matrix are interdependent, so they are like a prism of a Whole in terms of the quality of presence with the heart that is aimed with CL.

The research shows that a synergy created by the interconnectedness between the three variables (format, key messages, and messengers) at the core of CL practice brings a qualitative richness that sets the stage for a potential expansion of consciousness and heart, helping to transcend the polarization at the heart of conflicts (Gagnon 2019). After all, there are a context, key

FORMAT (environment)	KEY MESSAGES (objectives)	MESSENGERS (participants)	MOMENT OF CHOICE (love or not)
Safe container *Well-being*	Look for core essence *Spiritual*	Healing intention *Health*	Degrees of: Hardening of the heart or Expansion of the heart
Non-polarizing *Politics*	Open spirit, open to possibilities *Culture*	Deep connection *Psychology*	
Narratives/Personal stories *Sociology*	Deep Listening *Communication*	Compassionate listening *Ethics*	(vices vs virtues)

(degrees of)
Hardening of the heart or Expansion of the heart (vices vs virtues)

Figure 5.1   Relational and Structural Matrix for the REP. n/a

issues, and people in any situation. So, this can be transposed to any setting as the REP is aiming to create a culture of peace in any environment.

Based on the analysis of the action taking place in the nine structural units of the Matrix, specific types of "responses of the heart" were identified as related to the CL practice, with specific types of intentions and motivations in action.[3] Response of the heart is a characteristic of compassionate love, defined as an "other-centered love," involving an emotional engagement and understanding: "Some kind of heartfelt, affective quality is usually part of this kind of attitude or action, and some sort of emotional engagement. Understanding seems to be needed to love fully in an integrated way" (Fehr et al. 2009).

My research shows that a special combination of listening and compassion in CL's practice fosters a "response of the heart" conducive to transformation and healing to help move from personal and/or group interests at the expense of others to virtues that are other-centered for the Common Good (Gagnon 2019). After all, in any settings, people bring certain "responses of the heart" in what is unfolding and what is presented here can inform them.

Both these elements, structure and process, with the nine units of the Matrix as they are interrelated, inform the type of "agenda of the heart" that can contribute to a culture of peace as defined by the UN as "a set of values, attitudes, modes of behaviors and ways of life that reject violence and prevent conflicts by tackling their root causes to solve problems through dialogue and negotiation among individuals, groups and nations"[4] (Gagnon 2019).

The words that appear in italics in this Matrix (figure 5.1) represent aspects of transformation—well-being, spirituality, and health; branches of society—political, cultural, and psychological; and contributing fields—sociology, communication, and ethics. All contribute to form this relational ecosystem conducive to a culture of peace. Let us now examine the nine structural units of the Matrix based on key research findings (Gagnon 2019) and supported by CL's curriculum to see how this synergy can help integrate this "agenda of the heart." Compassion involves attitude and process (Storolow 2014) and the REP provides clues on both front. Pay attention to elements related to the will (predispositions/intentions with motivations) as well as the capacity (motivations with actions) to move toward greater connection and compassion. Both are interdependent in moments of choice to connect more and more deeply when challenged to do so.

Format or Environment

The format is the environment where activities take place. It includes the following three indicators/concepts: safe container, nonjudgmental and non-adversarial, and personal narratives.

Safe Container

CL research participants recognized the importance of a quality of presence that helps the other feel safe to share his or her thoughts and emotions honestly (Gagnon 2019). The CL approach aims to create a safe space of resilience, connection, and collaboration during listening sessions, through which resolution or transformation can happen—called a "safe container" (Cohen 2011). The response of the heart in this structural unit of the Matrix starts with the intention to create a safe container for honest expression of thoughts and emotions—negative as well as positive. The motivation in action is to project to the others a quality of presence that conveys to them that they are in such an environment. The following two objectives/skills help to actualize this.

First, create a dialogical space of collaboration instead of one of divisive competition. The metaphor of "container" extends our understanding of this space. The etymology of the word "contain" reflects the anticipated outcome: from Latin, contain is *continere* (transitive) "to hold together, enclose," from *com* "with, together" and *tenere* "to hold."[5] A container provides a boundary or enclosure within which what happens within it is delineated from what is outside. This "containment" with CL ensures safety, which allows for the possibility of change that transforms perceptions people have of each other in a conflict and to bring more understanding and respect (Cohen 2011). A key factor in peacebuilding and a culture of peace is an individual orientation toward cooperation that takes into account the other's goals, instead of an orientation toward oneself as in competition (Janssen and Vliert 1996 in Blumberg et al. 2006). All nine structural units can be entry points to guide more connective ways of thinking, being, becoming, and doing within a safe container.

One way to develop a "safe container" emerged in my role as a mediator between two colleagues in a workplace. I explored with them the differences between the paradigms of collaboration versus competition that appeared to be an underlying cause of their conflict. This ignited a synergy of transformation, in combination with other aspects of REP. A safety plan (emotional, physical, and relational) for the de-escalation of the conflict became possible.

Second, the suffering and wounds from the conflict can be held within a safe container—the place and process of encounter. It serves to hold the pain related to personal stories and this can be a healing experience for all: "When participants focus on creating a safe environment, on compassion, empathy and love, the field is determined by those intentions and this provides a safe space for expression of negative as well as positive feelings and experiences" (Cohen 2011, 37). Stolorow calls a "relational home" a space in which the person can "be held, borne, and integrated" as they share emotional pain (2014). Morrison and Severino (2009) see loving environments for humans as relational spaces that are "we-centric." For them, it is not so much a physical space that is important as a space cocreated with the other. It offers vital information equivalent to a "second womb of compassion," the first one being our mother's before we were born (ibid.). These authors associate the word compassion or mercy in Hebrew as *rachamim*, from the same root as the word meaning womb, *rechem*. Delegates sit in silence in front of guest speakers, trying the best they can to listen and connect with the heart, bringing a quality of presence of calm and compassion (Cohen 2011). Compassionate listening is seen as a subset of dialogue characterized by openness, trust, and presence (Hyde and Bineham 2000, in Rheling 2008, 212). It is essential to give space for suffering to be expressed. This can be uncomfortable for many and this is where the other two indicators for the context become essential.

Nonjudgmental and Nonadversarial

CL research participants affirm that a nonjudgmental and nonadversarial environment, open to perspectives from all sides of the conflict, helps listeners soften their own version of "truth" and hear other perspectives (Gagnon 2019). The response of the heart in this structural unit of the Matrix starts with the intention to soften one's version of "truth" in order to hear other perspectives in a nonjudgmental and nonadversarial way. The motivation in action is then to connect with others in accessing one's heart and deepest wisdom in order to intentionally choose to hear and seek to understand different perspectives. The following two objectives/skills help to actualize this.

First, welcome a diversity of perspectives from parties involved in the conflict and the part of truth in each. As a conscious element of the context for this approach, it brings safety in the sense that the idea is not to determine who is right and wrong, what is good or bad, true or false, but to bring perspective. Extensive work on identifying judgments of self and others is part of CL curriculum, as these can block the feeling of compassion. Judgments about others can distract the person from a state of compassion manifest in the language and communication used (Rosenberg 2003). The root of violence is "the thought attributing the cause of the conflict to the 'wrongness' of the other" (ibid., 15). Furthermore, what we believe to be true is not necessarily "the reality" (Ferguson 2010). In the Buddhist philosophy Mdhyamika (*tend del* in Tibetan), the notion of the interdependence of the nature of reality demands that we pay attention to the notion of what constitutes right and wrong, as reality is complex. Things and events are interrelated—with causes and effects and conditions at the heart of reality—so interconnectivity needs to be taken seriously (Dalai Lama 1999).

Second, there is a need to distance oneself from one's own perspective and allow space for other versions of reality. A nonjudgmental and nonadversarial format is one that stays away from polarization; therefore, the development of the "fair witness" is one of CL's core competencies. One must hold both complexity and ambiguity during the listening session, recognizing and containing triggers and judgments made about others that separate us from them (Cohen 2011). LeBaron uses the similar notion of "a state of witness" to bring "a particular quality of listening and talking in conflict resolution," where one "chooses to adopt a spirit of genuine inquiry and curiosity, letting go of judgment in advance" (LeBaron 2002, 71). A conscious choice is involved in listening (Barker and Watson 2000). There is a "filter" of interpretation in the transition from hearing to listening that serves to retain incoming information we find relevant and discard what we find is not (Imhof 2010). In developing a capacity to observe oneself—the ability to know when the heart is open or not during listening—delegates get to recognize what impairs deep listening and address it.

Narrative/Personal Stories

CL research participants recognize that listening and reflecting with an open heart to personal stories/experiences told by the other/others helps listeners gain clarity and understanding (Gagnon 2019). Stories reveal hurt and pain, sometimes from incidents that happened hundreds of years ago, and until some way of addressing them is found, it may be impossible to achieve conflict transformation (LeBaron 2002). The motivation in action is to listen and reflect with the heart on narratives shared by others. The following two objectives/skills help to actualize this.

First, recognize and transcend unhealthy power dynamics created by the drama triangle (aggressor, victim, and savior). As a psychosocial model of human interaction developed in 1968 by Stephen Karpman, the drama triangle shows tendencies in relationships to play out an unconscious scenario in which we spontaneously adopt these roles toward others. Acting out these roles can become a repetitive pattern in particular relational systems. We can learn to shift to healthier roles as presented in *The Empowerment Dynamic* (Emerald and Jaconc 2013): the creator (instead of victim), challenger (instead of perpetrator), and coach (instead of savior). Love and appreciation for others is present in these alternative roles and dynamics, as parties become cocreators interested in the views of others while still expressing what is true for them (ibid.).

Second, identify layers of a story (facts, feelings, values, nonverbal), discerning what is the most important for the other/others. Through the vehicle of story, experiences of relationships, emotions, conflicts, struggles, and responses that are at once personal and universal are revealed (Koerner 2011). The details are unique to the person while the person recognizes himself or herself in the more general patterns of the fabric (ibid.). Stories bring a language and form to communicate the richness of one's own spirituality, that is, the deepness and complexity of the person and its connection with oneself, other persons, the earth, and even the Sacred (ibid., 299). One key exercise in the CL curriculum is to recognize different layers of a story told: facts, feelings, and values. Participants then identify aspects that appear to be very important for the guest speaker. The power of stories is amplified as they learn to know each other from many perspectives, identities, and worldviews.

Key Messages or Philosophy

The key messages (philosophy, instructions, elements at play) related to the conflict at hand can be inspired by the following three indicators for conflict resolution: looking for the core essence, opening one's spirit to new possibilities, and listening deeply.

Looking for the Other's Core Essence

CL research participants affirm that by looking for the other's core essence (what is the most precious and unique in him/her) and encouraging its expression, listeners humanize rather than demonize the guest speaker (Gagnon 2019). The response of the heart starts with the intention to humanize rather than demonize the other/others. The motivation in action is to look and encourage what is the most precious and unique in the other/others. The following two objectives/skills help to actualize this.

First, deliberately connect with our common human identity that unites, focusing on similarities instead of differences. This demands restraint and discipline (His Holiness the Dalai Lama and Cutler 2009). In the research, only a few participants were able to answer a question related to their common human identity with guest speakers, whereas the others had to spend time reflecting on it in order to think of something. Placing the idea of a common identity on top of the list of identities can be a conscious choice. Identifying with guest speakers in their role of parents and grandparents was a promising starting point. We can choose to put our common human identity at the top of the hierarchies of identity factors compared with others, such as religious or political affiliation, which can be exclusive (see Brodeur, "Interworldview Dialogue," *Transforming*, for further elaboration of this aspect).

Second, look for and encourage the expression of the other's core essence. This is enabled by metaphors, which "are useful to bridge worldviews by drawing explicit attention to the presence of fundamental meaning-making differences among parties" (LeBaron 2002, 186). TCLP uses the metaphor of heart to anchor its CL practice:

It starts with the belief that within each individual is the essence of love and compassion but as we move along our journey, we suffer, whether from the pain of judgment, self-doubts, physical or mental abuse, the impacts of injustice, war, poverty, etc. Over the years, we have all developed layers of armor to protect ourselves. And that armor may manifest in one of many behaviors—anger, blame, cynicism, physical attack, withdrawal, etc. Unfortunately, as we arm ourselves against others, we may also close ourselves off to the gifts of our deepest essence, allowing our hearts to shrivel and harden. The work of CL is to re-open and strengthen the pathways back to the heart, particularly when upset or in the heat of conflict. (Cohen 2011, 10–11)

The goal in CL is "to soften the mortar enough to allow the heart to expand and enable new perspective to emerge" from this wall where bricks refer to specific incidents that caused pain, and the mortar is the stories people tell themselves about these events that keep the bricks impermeable and locked in place (ibid.). To help others get to their truth and sharing it, *speaking from the heart* is the core competency that follows *listening from the heart* in a listening session. It is being reflective in asking guests questions or more details on aspects of their story and trying to get at the essence of underlying needs and feelings to give voice to what has truth and meaning for them (ibid., 13).

Opening One's Spirit to Possibilities

CL research participants recognize that in keeping an open spirit during dialogue, one can witness new possibilities—of learning something new or surprising (Gagnon 2019). The response of the heart starts with the intention of keeping an open heart and spirit toward others in light of the situation unfolding during listening sessions. The motivation in action is to become a witness of new possibilities, for oneself and for the other, about the conflict. The following two objectives/skills help to actualize this.

First, create an opening for the softening of positions and the cocreation of wise actions. Conflict resolution can take place in a way least expected. Imagination is recognized as central in conflict resolution (LeBaron 2002, 101): "Surpassing the known, we generate new forms and envision new ways forward. Leaving stereotypes, preconceptions, and assumptions by the old railroad tracks, imagination liberates our minds to conceive new ways of transportation," and can reveal unknown parts of ourselves (ibid., 38–39). Without the regulating influence of the heart's intelligence, our minds easily fall prey to reactive emotions such as insecurity, anger, fear, and blame that divide and bring suffering (Childre et al. 2016, 31). The heart intelligence is seen as "the flow of awareness, understanding and intuition guidance we experience when the mind and emotions are brought into coherent alignment with the heart and with practice, accessing intuition can become integrated into choices and decisions" (ibid.).

Second, go beyond a closeness with the other to letting oneself be surprised. In staying open and continuing to connect with the heart, despite a difficulty to do so, participants reached new and surprising levels of understanding about the guest speaker and the conflict (Gagnon 2019).

Authenticity, inclusion, confirmation, being fully present, a spirit of mutual equality, and a supportive climate are the central characteristics of dialogue (Floyd 1985). In dialogue, each participant leaves himself or herself open and in such vulnerability they risk being changed (Johanessen 2002) with new insights revealed that neither understood prior to the encounter (Rehling 2008). For TCLP, the heart is the best asset for conflict transformation and compassion is its way to use it in a transformational way—a heart can be "wrathful" but with CL it is prosocial and in service of others.

Deep Listening

CL research participants affirm that in calming mental activity (thoughts), in order to be fully present to others with the heart, listeners were better able to get to know the experiences that motivate their perspectives (Gagnon 2019). The response of the heart is the intention of calming the mind in order to be fully present to the other/others. The motivation in action is to sincerely seek to know who they are, what they value, and the experiences that motivate their perspectives. The following two objectives/skills help to actualize this.

First, slow down to the "pace of wisdom" (an expression often used in CL's training) for a qualitatively rich dialogical presence. This slowing down calms one's spirit and centers the self to be fully present to the other. It helps to listen without the "mental chaos" as well as becoming aware of the interpretation at play in listening that comes from the head or mind and from the heart. This is why contemplative practices are used in CL to predispose one to mindfulness and presence (Cohen 2011, 12).[6] This slowed down state manifests as "presence," which in the field of holistic nursing is defined as a multidimensional state of being available in a situation with the wholeness of one's individual being (McKivergin 2005, 234). It has three dimensions: (1) approaching an individual in a way that respects and honors her/his essence; (2) relating in a way that reflects a quality of being with and in collaboration with, rather than doing to, and (3) entering into a shared experience (or field of consciousness) that promotes healing potentials and an experience of well-being (Dossey and Guzzetta 2005).

Second, direct the energy toward the heart during the listening/dialogue and be guided by the process. CL's core competency of listening to the heart demands "shifting the focus from our active minds to the energetic core of our being, and keeping our own stories and interpretations out of the way" (Cohen 2011, 12). Chinese philosopher Chuang-Tzu True explains how empathy requires listening with the whole being:

> The hearing that is only in the ears is one thing. The hearing of the understanding is another. But the hearing of the spirit is not limited to any one faculty, to the ear, or to the mind. Hence it demands the emptiness of all the faculties. And when the faculties are empty, then the whole being listens. There is then a direct grasp of what is right there before you that can never be heard with the ear or understood with the mind. (Rosenberg 2003, 91)

For Gene Knudsen-Hoffman, the type of listening in CL is related to spirituality and discernment:

> I'm not talking about the human ear. I am talking about discerning. To discern means to perceive some things hidden or obscure. We must listen with our "spiritual ear." This is very different from deciding in advance who is right and who is wrong, and then seeking to rectify it. And, it's very hard to listen to people whom I feel are misleading, if not lying. Hard to listen to such different memories of the same event—hard. (Manousos 2003, 313)

Discernment is defined in the scientific literature on leadership as "a multidimensional concept of decision making by logic and reason, by empathy gained through reflection and understanding and by moral ethics determined by one's spirituality" (Traüffer et al. 2010, 177). CL as a practice integrates cognitive awareness with the wisdom of the heart (Cohen 2011); discernment becomes key to achieve this. Remembering that the word intelligence comes from the Latin verb *intelligere*, which means to "pick out" or discern, evidence shows that the more we learn to listen to and follow our heart intelligence, the more balanced and coherent our emotions become (Childre et al. 2016; see Kauffman 2020 for an extensive discussion on matters and importance of the heart in humans and society).

Messengers

The messengers are people involved in the conflict at hand and its transformation and resolution. The following three indicators/concepts are part of this variable: healing intention, connecting deeply, and CL.

Healing Intention

CL research participants recognize that in connecting with the part that is suffering in the other/others, listeners give voice to what has truth and meaning for him/her (Gagnon 2019). The response of the heart starts with the intention to give the other/others a voice for what is true and makes sense for him or her. The motivation in action is to try to connect with the part that is suffering and is meaningful. The following two objectives/skills help to actualize this.

First, allow room for the transformation of wounds and other underlying causes related to the conflict. TCLP sets conditions to support healing out of a belief that people have the capacity to heal themselves. One definition of the healing process in nursing is: "an exchange of energy, truth and communication to help others attune to their own healing capacities in an authentic quality" (McKivergin 2005, 245). Recalling Rehling, an expert on listening, facing an illness, and reporting on the listening received from visitors that she identified as compassionate listening, she felt that they could relate to her experience. This helped her learn what was beyond her medical condition, namely, what it is to be human, to suffer, and to struggle (Rehling 2008). TCLP's perspective is that the listening sessions are as healing and transformative for listeners as for guest speakers (Green 2002, 23).

Second, help the others get to their own truth as close to their heart and healing capacity as possible (Cohen 2011, 13). From a clinical perspective in psychology, when patients are listened to with compassion, they experience their own sacredness and thus enter into a process of healing (Burton 2002). Listening with compassion appears as hearing with the heart, withholding judgment, and maintaining appropriate boundaries (ibid).

Connecting Deeply

CL research participants affirm that in connecting deeply with the guest speakers, listeners get to better know their underlying needs, feelings, and values (Gagnon 2019). The response of the heart starts with the intention to connect deeply with others. The motivation in action is to get to know their underlying needs, feelings, and values, resonating with our common humanity. The following two objectives/skills help to actualize this.

First, create a space of real encounters beyond stereotypes and prejudices. Contact between adversarial individuals and groups can promote compassionate love (Brody et al. 2009). A friendship can be created that has the impact of transforming the perceived relationship as enemies (ibid.). In the *Self-Expansion Model*, Aron and Aron (1986) show how compassion seems to make division boundaries blurred as the other becomes an integrated part of one's own identity. When individuals form a close relationship with another person, they "expand" themselves by including aspects of the other within the self (Aron, Mashek, and Aron 2004, in Brody et al. 2009). A perceived overlap between self and other happens to differing degrees, and the closer individuals become to each other, the more overlap there is between the mental representation of self and other to the point where the two become one (ibid.). The other is treated more like the self and this expansion involves new experiences, perspectives, and identities offered by the other, as well as a change in attitude toward the other that is transformational (ibid.).

Second, connect from heart to heart, spirit to spirit. One CL interview subject reflects about a deep connection she experienced with a guest speaker in a listening session. Being Jewish and this session being in a Palestinian Refugee Camp, she said that she was initially apprehensive about going to that location, but the testimony of one of its inhabitants brought a deep connection[7]:

> I "was" with that person, meaning that I completely understood her at that moment even if I didn't agree. That didn't mean I "was" with her in the sense that we both had the same goals for life. It was that I connected with where she was coming from and I saw no badness, no evil in it, even if I disagreed. It just happened and I could feel it. I could feel an invisible connection, as if there was like a tingling on the back of my neck. I could look at her eyes and I could see our eyes together. It's an indescribable feeling, but I knew I connected. And I also knew that I wouldn't have, if I didn't have the compassionate listening training. I would have intellectualized things and it would not have been as effective. I believe now that if I'm coming from "I'm right and you're wrong and I'm going to tell you the error of your ways" I have no idea if the conversation could get longer. As where I've got that connection, there is this possibility.

Morrison and Severino (2009) bring the notion of resonant attuning that echoes this experience. It is seen as a spiritual experience for both persons involved as they are never alone in the harmonization. According to their theory, the mutual and interactive exchange at the level of emotions and the fact of being an "us" permits to grow in compassion (ibid).

Compassionate Listening

CL research participants recognize that the type of listening involved in CL aims to transform the energy of conflict in giving voice to authenticity and common humanity (Gagnon 2019). The response of the heart starts with the intention of practicing CL. The motivation in action is to present a leadership and presence that aims to transform the energy of conflict in giving voice to authenticity and common humanity. The following two objectives/skills help to actualize this.

First, foster both a will to connect deeply with others and a capacity to bring this about through CL. Attitude and process are related to compassion (Storolow 2014). This is illustrated in figure 5.2, in light of what we have seen in this section.

The will and capacity to connect deeply with others needs to be taken into account for deep connection in light of the research. A person maybe wants

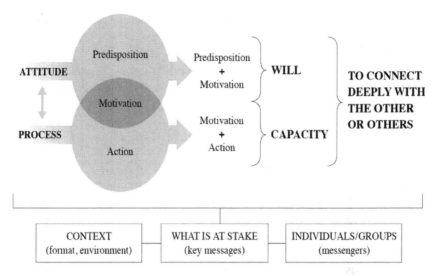

Figure 5.2   Attitude and Process to Connect Deeply According to the REP. n/a

to connect but doesn't have the ability; in another instance, a person has the ability but does not want to. Or one doesn't have either will or capacity. This to say that if the will to do it needs readjustment, look at the elements of intention and motivation that are at stake; where more capacity is needed, motivation and action need fostering, resulting in the practice of effective CL.

Second, shift from shadow zones to light zones (from vices to virtues). A majority of participants in the research experienced one or more than one of the following shifts in their experience with CL (Gagnon 2019):

- From a sense of superiority to a sense of unity or interconnectivity
- From a focus on my own needs or interests to a sense of the nature of the Divine
- From feeling entitled to something (e.g., have one's opinion considered; suffering acknowledged) to setting attention on what is the most important to listen to, with compassion
- From feeling angry to a sense of strength or courage to bear up calmly, to endure
- From blocking the listening to choosing to follow a higher form of truth or knowledge
- From a sense of envy (e.g., at the power of others; something they have) to a deeper understanding
- From wanting to have reasons (e.g., why things happen as they do) to gaining more wisdom

These shifts were inspired and were adapted for the research from the work of Myss (2009, 2010) who presents dualities of vices and virtues as part of human struggles with oneself and others (ibid). Certainly, being part of a group practicing CL is a powerful experience for most listeners (Gagnon 2019), and can ignite mimetic structures of blessings according to Vern Neufeld Redekop:

> When *agapē* includes caring for the agency and full subjectivity of the parties, it could potentially shape the outcome. It is one thing to get people to sign an agreement bringing a formal end to hostilities; it is another thing to reconcile people so that they co-exist peacefully and move beyond that to developing new, mutually supportive relationships. For the latter to happen, it is important to have mimetic models of people who can transcend hurt and difference to allow joy to enter in. (2014, 62)

The author explains that in mimetic structures of blessing, parties in a relational system have an orientation, attitudes, and actions that contribute to the well-being of each other (Redekop 2002). There may be conflict and even rivalries, but given the orientation of blessing, these are turned into creativity, he concludes. I do believe that delegates sitting together during listening sessions, together ignite hope despite the difficulties and pain related to the guest speaker's stories. These guests also convey the joy and hope they carry in their heart, mind, and spirit, despite the conflict surrounding them. Creativity, spirituality, and emergence surround the transformative experiences they live and share in this relational-spiritual space with the clear intention to listen with the heart.

CONCLUSION

This chapter developed a central feature of the REP (see Gagnon and Brodeur 2020 for a description of other features/pillars), represented by a relational and structural Matrix. The REP emerged from ground-based research on the CL approach, complemented by Brodeur's IWVD (see Brodeur, "Interworldview Dialogue," *Transforming*). These dimensions are interrelated and the REP addresses both inner and outer peace factors and conditions to help us move between three stages of social connection: from (1) a feeling or state of separation with others, to (2) a stage of communication, and, from there, to (3) a feeling and state of deep connection and communion (Gagnon 2019).

The Matrix serves as a conceptual tool to bring a compassionate presence conducive to a culture of peace instead of conflict in any environment. Combining structure and processes, it has three variables with three key indicators associated with each, for a total of nine structural units, each with two main objectives and skills. The nine structural units in the Matrix are interrelated and provide clues on how the synergy between all these components creates a form of ecosystem meant to be used as a tool for research and fieldwork.

First, we have indicators related to the format or environment: a safe container created by the type of nonjudgmental and nonadversarial stance required for deep listening to experiences and stories told by parties involved in a conflict. All perspectives being welcome, this gives the chance to see the part of truth in each. Second, key messages at the heart of the dialogical activity include the ability to see what is most unique and precious in the ones sharing these experiences, as well as keeping an open spirit, open to new possibilities for greater understanding and connection and deep listening. Third, the listening brings a healing intention to the activity, opening new avenues for deep connection in the practice of CL that is summed up by all these indicators.

In each of the nine units, we find specific "responses of the heart." The notion of "response of the heart" is inspired by research on compassionate love (Fehr et al. 2009) involving an emotional engagement and understanding: "Some kind of heartfelt, affective quality is usually part of this kind of attitude or action, and some sort of emotional engagement. Understanding seems to be needed to love fully in an integrated way" (Fehr et al. 2009, 8).

We have seen that the will (want to) and the capacity (can) are both important in compassionate listening and for sustainable dialogue. There is no panacea in peacebuilding and someone with violent and/or narcissistic tendencies, for example, may not want to, and/or be able to, communicate. Note the challenges of working with Windagos/Wihtikos (Chabot, "Warring with Windigos"; Twinn, "Warring with Wihtikos in Real Time," *Transforming*). Hence, keeping healthy boundaries is important for CL practitioners, as there is a risk of being taken advantage of without forms of reciprocity in the relationship. At the same time, this is exactly the challenge CL suggests: to love and connect and continue to do so, even with numerous barriers, in order to bring the dialogical encounter to a different level of consciousness, transformation, and healing. The shifts taking place in the research led to an examination of the social connection process from states and feelings of separation to deep connection. It revealed information and insights on a form of portal that opens up in these shifts; this is valuable information for conflict transformation research and fieldwork.

The research on CL showed that it produces significant benefits, including healing and well-being. Healing is defined as the dynamic process of recovery, repair, and renewal, which increases resilience, coherence, and wholeness (Rakel 2017). Participants reported physiological changes in guest speakers showing strong negative emotions and discourse while telling their story and experience of the conflict, becoming more receptive, calm, and communicative as the listening sessions unfolded (Gagnon 2019). They were also able to report healing experiences and changes in themselves in moving from a closing or hardening of the heart to its opening and expansion, along with other facilitating factors, to allow for deeper connection with guest speakers.

Overall, the REP is useful across the field of peacebuilding and conflict transformation, where we need to humanize and shift the connection to a greater level of consciousness to find creative solutions not envisioned before. It emerged and developed within a spiritual research paradigm—one that takes into account and use notions like inner awareness, seen as related to self-knowledge and not limited to the five senses; it is manifest when this awareness goes beyond the self (Lamb 2016). It offers clues on what Lederach sees as "the resilient soul capable of sustaining a healthy self and creative engagement of the other, unveil[ing] the mystery of the pathways that connect the inner world with the ever-present threat of the outer world" (2015, 550). Compassion and a quality of compassionate presence help bridge the inner and outer worlds; the REP, based on a research on the CL approach as developed by TCLP, provides the vocabulary, guidance, and vision to make it happen.

NOTES

1. Interview subject during TCLP's delegation in 2010, part of a research on experiences and transformations TCLP delegates encounter with the practice of CL during the delegations (1998–2015) (n = 75), as well as the examination of the type of processes and spirituality at play in this practice (Gagnon 2019).

2. This Matrix has two main components related to the Basic Social Process Theory (BSPT) (Glaser 2005, 11) on social connection to which the REP emerged: the nine indicators (Basic Social Structural Process) and responses of the heart (Basic Social Psychological Process) as part of each of these nine structural units. Both aspects of the BSPT (Glaser 2005) were validated by participants in our research (n = 80), consisting of TCLP's delegates from 1998 to 2015.

3. The Model for research for compassionate love (Underwood in Fehr *et al*, 2009, 9-18) was used in the research (Gagnon 2019). It has three key components: 1. The Substrate (individual, physical, cultural, environmental, social, emotional and cognitive factors); 2. Motivation and discernment; 3. Actions and attitudes (compassionate love fully expressed) with feedback loops to continue with such expression of compassionate love as a dynamic process. In the REP, these components were seen as a reflection of the Tibetan notion of Kun Long wa, and used to reflect the responses of the heart. The Dalai Lama (1999) explains that the individual's kun long, translated literally, has the participle kun meaning "thoroughly" or "from the depths" and long (wa) denoting the act of causing something to stand up, to arise, or to awaken, is

understood as that which drives or inspires our actions—both those we intend directly and those which are in a sense involuntary—and denotes the individual's overall state of heart and mind. It is considered as central to determine the ethical value to an action.

4. This definition appears under UN Resolutions A/RES/52/13: Culture of Peace and A/RES/53/243, Declaration and Programme of Action on a Culture of Peace: http://www3.unesco.org/iycp/uk/uk_sum_cp.htm.

5. Source: http://www.etymonline.com/index.php?term=contain. March 3, 2017, 17:01.

6. Contemplative practices are used in CL practice as rituals often done at the beginning of the training and listening sessions, for example, lighting a candle with an intention for the group, reading a poem, doing a centration exercise or meditation.

7. Interview subject no. 10, TCLP delegation in Israel-Palestine in May 2010.

REFERENCES

Aron, A., and E. N. Aron. 1986. *Love as the Expansion of Self: Understanding Attraction and Satisfaction.* New York, NY: Hemisphere.

Blumberg, H. H., P. A. Hare, and A. Costin. 2006. *Peace Psychology: A Comprehensive Introduction.* Cambridge: Cambridge University Press.

Briskin, Alan, S. Erickson, J. Ott, and T. Callanan. 2009. *The Power of Collective Wisdom and the Trap of the Collective Folly.* San Francisco, CA: Berrett-Koehler.

Brody, Salena, S. C. Wright, A. Arthur, and T. McLaughlin-Volpe. 2008. "Compassionate Love for Individuals in Other Social Groups." In *The Science of Compassionate Love: Theory, Research and applications.* Edited by Beverley Fehr, Susan Sprecher, and Lynn G. Underwood, 283–305. West Sussex: Wiley-Blackwell.

Burton, L. A. 2002. "The Medical Patient: Compassionate Listening and Spirit-Mind-Body Care of Medical Patients." In *Health Care and Spirituality: Listening, Assessing, Caring.* Edited by R. Gilbert, 163–178. Amityville, NY: Baywood Publishing Co.

Childre, Doc, Howard Martin, Deborah Rozman, and Rollin McCraty. 2016. *Heart Intelligence: Connecting with the Intuitive Guidance of the Heart.* Boulder Creek (Heart Math Institute): Waterfront Press.

Cohen, Andrea S., L. Green, and S. Partnow. 2011. *Practicing the Art of Compassionate Listening.* Bainsbridge Island: The Compassionate Listening Project.

Dossey, Barbara Montgomery, Lynn Keegan, and Cathie E. Guzetta. 2005. *Holistic Nursing: A Handbook for Practice*, 4th edition. Sudbury, MA: Jones and Bartlett Publishers.

Emerald and Zajonc. 2013. "Newsletter: Go Against Yourself || TED* Works – February 8, 2013, based on The Power of TED*." *The Empowerment Dynamic*, by David Emerald. http://powerofted.com/go-against-yourself-2/ (June 2016, 7:15 am).

Fehr, Beverly, Susan Sprecher, and Lynn G. Underwood. 2009. *The Science of Compassionate Love: Theory, Research and applications*. West Sussex: Blackwell Publishing Ltd.

Ferguson, D. S. 2010. *Exploring the Spirituality of the World Religions: The Quest for Personal, Spiritual and Social Transformation*. London: Continuum Books.

Floyd, J. J. 1985. *Listening: A Practical Approach*. Glenview, IL: Scott, Foresman.

Gagnon, Brigitte. 2019. *Écosystème relationnel pour une paix intérieure et extérieure: Modèle issu d'une méthode mixte en recherche sur l'approche de l'écoute compassionnelle selon The Compassionate Listening Project*. Unpublished PhD Dissertation, University of Montreal.

Glaser, Barney G. 2005. "Basic Social Process." *The Grounded Theory Review*, 4, no. 3: 1–15.

Green, Leah. 2002. "Just Listen: Compassionate Listening is Healing – To the Listeners and to Those Who Tell Their Stories." *Yes! A Journal of Positive Futures*, Winter, 20–25.

His Holiness the Dalai Lama, and Howard Cutler. 2009. *The Art of Happiness in a Troubled World*. New York, NY: Doubleday.

Hwoschinski, C. 2001. *Listening with the Heart—a Guide for Compassionate Listening*. Publisher: Example Product Manufacturer. ISBN-10:0971587108.

His Holiness the Dalai Lama. 1999. *Ethics for a New Millennium*. New York, NY: Berkley.

Imhof, M. 2010. "What is Going on in the Mind of a Listener?" In *Listening and Human Communication in the 21st Century*. Edited by A. D. Wolvin, 97–127. West Sussex: Blackwell Publishing Ltd.

Johannesen, R. L. 2002. *Ethics in Human Communication*, 5th edition. Prospect Heights, IL: Waveland Press.

Koerner, JoEllen. 2011. *Healing: The Essence of Nursing Presence*, 2nd edition. New York, NY: Springer.

LeBaron, Michelle. 2002. *Bridging Troubled Waters: Conflict Resolution from the Heart*. San Francisco, CA: Jossey-Bass.

Lederach, J. P. 2015. "Spirituality and Religious Peacebuilding." In *The Oxford Handbook of Religion, Conflict, and Peacebuilding*. Edited by A. Omer, Scott Appleby, and D. Little, 541–569. Oxford: Oxford University Press.

———. 2012. "Compassionate Presence: Faith-Based Peacebuilding in the Face of Violence." Televised Conference of *University of California Television* (UCTV). http://www.uctv.tv/. Posted March 28: https://www.youtube.com/watch?v=0Cp yF9rLs1A.

Manousos, Anthony, Ed. 2003. *Compassionate Listening and other Writings by Gene Knudsen Hoffman: Quaker Peacemaker and Mystic*. Torrance: Friends Bulletin.

McKivergin, M. 2005. "The Nurse as an Instrument of Healing." In *Holistic Nursing: A Handbook for Practice*, 4th edition. Edited by Barbara Montgomery Dossey, Lynn Keegan, and Cathie E. Guzzetta. Sudbury, MA: Jones and Bartlett Publishers.

Mezirow, J., E. W. Taylor, and Associates. 2009. *Transformative Learning in Practice: Insights from Community, Workplace and Higher Education*. San Francisco, CA: Jossey-Bass.

Morrison, Nancy K., and Sally K. Severino. 2009. *Sacred Desire*. West Conshohocken, PA: Templeton Press.

Myss, Carolyn. 2009. *Defy Gravity*. Carlsbad: Hay House.

———. 2010. *Defy Gravity: Healing Beyond the Bounds of Reason*. Audio CD. Abridged, Audiobook, CD.

Pargament, K. I. (Ed. In Chief). 2013. *APA Handbook of Psychology, Religion, and Spirituality, Vol. 1: Context, Theory, and Research*. American Psychological Association.

———. 2007. *Spiritually Integrated Psychotherapy: Understanding and Addressing the Sacred*. New York, NY: The Guilford Press.

———. 1999. "The Psychology of Religion and Spirituality? Yes, and No." *The International Journal for the Psychology of Religion*, 9: 3–16.

Rakel, D. 2017. *Integrative Medicine*, 4th edition. Philadelphia, PA: Elsevier Inc.

Redekop, Vern Neufeld. 2014. "Blessing-Based Love (Agape) As a Heuristic to Understanding Effective Reconciliation Practices: A Reading of I Corinthians 13 in a Peacebuilding Context." In *Peace on Earth: The Role of Religion in Peace and Conflict Studies*. Edited by Thomas Matyok, Maureen Flaherty, Haambes Tuso, Jessica Senehi, and Sean Byrne. Lanham, MD: Lexington.

Rehling, Diana L. 2008. "Compassionate Listening: A Framework for Listening to the Seriously Ill." *International Journal of Listening*, 22: 83–89.

Rosenberg, Marshall. 2003. *Nonviolent Communication: A Language of Life*, 2nd edition. Encinitas: PuddleDancer Press.

Stolorow, Robert D. 2014. "A Non-Pathologizing Approach to Emotional Trauma: Emotional Pain is Not a Pathology." *Psychology Today*. Consulted online, October 20, 2019 at 3:12 pm. https://www.psychologytoday.com/blog/feeling-relating-existing/201412/non-pathologizing-approach-emotional-trauma.

Traüffer, Hazel C. V., Corné Bekker, Mihai Bocârena, and Bruce E. Winston. 2010. "Towards an Understanding of Discernment: A Conceptual Paper." *Leadership & Organization Development Journal*, 176: 176–184.

Chapter 6

Interworldview Dialogue (IWVD)

The Emergence of an Applied Theory for Conflict Transformation and Peacebuilding

Patrice C. Brodeur

Over the years, self-perception changes for any self-conscious human being. How one answers the basic question, "Who am I?" so central to modern identity construction of the self, individually focused more than collectively so, is related to a process of transformation that is inevitably linked to one's own unique set of varied human experiences of reality. The same applies to me, growing up in Montréal, Québec, Canada, and returning to work there after many years of living in various geographical contexts on three different continents.

My formative years were spent in a geographical cocoon composed of three well-knit identities: (1) a Roman Catholic religious and (2) ideologically Québécois majority cultural environment, within a (3) minority French-Canadian national context. At seventeen years old, I left this culturally relatively homogeneous milieu to study near Victoria, British Columbia, a city steeped in an Anglo-Canadian majority. As far as I was concerned, it was like living in a new country, and not only because everything "worked in English here": I soon discovered that "the English," as I had been taught to call all non-French-Canadian others, despite Canada's rich ethnic diversity I was then barely aware of, did not have horns and not all of them were intolerant of Québécois (understood, of course, as the majority identity group within those living in the territory now called Québec).

There was a twist, though, to this more-than-linguistic and cultural immersion: I landed in an international school whose dazzling diversity (more than sixty countries among the 200 student body) propelled me in a paradoxical identity dance that both consolidated and diluted my multiple identities, in ways that have affected me ever since. I have gradually come to this awareness over many years, probably due to other more distant geographical immersions, first in Jerusalem for two years, then in Jordan for one year, followed by fifteen in the United States, and more recently, three in Austria. Surprisingly, in retrospect, the climax of this first, two-year long immersion in a small international community during my late teen years was not in sharing my first-year room with a Palestinian from the Gaza strip, together with an Italian and an Australian, or sharing my second-year room with an Irish, an Indigenous Mayan from Guatemala, and a Malaysian from Borneo island. Nor was it the many challenges faced when trying to make sense of the initial tension between my first-year Palestinian roommate who ended up sharing his second-year room with a newly arrived first-year student from France, who happened to be Jewish. Both became close friends of mine, and their own struggles soon influenced me to study the Middle East, from my first semester at university, several years before the Oslo Accords (1993, 1995). Both my friends were strong in their religious identities and practices, making me discover the results of dialogue before I knew anything about "dialogue." They made me understand the importance of learning through listening and questioning my own ignorance about Judaism and Islam, as well as Middle East politics. Thanks to their patience, they educated me about the crucial importance of learning Arabic and Hebrew, which I did seriously from my very first day at university. I eventually immersed myself in the complex diversity of Jerusalem for two years while studying at the Hebrew University of Jerusalem, and subsequently spent a third year in Amman where I studied at the Sharia College at the University of Jordan. It is because of these two friendships in particular, and my witnessing the often-difficult interactions between them, especially during their first three months, that I embarked on the long path of becoming a religious studies scholar focused primarily on Islam and Judaism, with a later additional specialization in conflict transformation and peacebuilding.

However amazingly transformative these experiences were, precisely because of their multidirectional challenges to my own initially parochial worldview, the greatest of these all came in the way of a "culture shock," during a short, five-day immersion in "my own country of Canada" (at least officially, given my passport, but not necessarily my political ideology, which has fluctuated over time): I was dropped off in a hydroplane to spend a week with a small Indigenous family of four (a mother with her two boys, early teen and preteen, and an older uncle), living in a tiny village of three houses, two of which were empty at the time. This micro-village was on the edge of an impenetrable thick forest, along a small stone beach full of logs. They had drifted into this picturesque cove after a timeless journey floating in the icy Pacific waters of the northern West Coast of the North American continent. The cultural "gap" between my hosts and me could not have been greater—nothing had prepared me for this unexpectedly shocking experience, although in retrospect, profoundly transformative too. Indeed, those days became filled with a search to reach out to my generous hosts, but in ways that were inappropriate, only raising further questions in my head. So many remained unanswered that by the third day, tears took over, not to mention the blisters I had acquired on my hands, not knowing how to cut wood for the fireplace, neither in technique nor in timing (I obviously zealously over-did it). I had never learned how to communicate with others in or through silence, or to be more precise, in a different kind of balance between silence and words, with delayed time in between a question and an answer, if any at all. That single experience of "culture shock," which distressed my identity to the core, remains an endless source of questioning. It represents a moment frozen in time whose memory, by no means idealized, provides me with a constant reminder of just how challenging intercultural dynamics can be, how profoundly nurturing they can be as a source of meaning where deeper waters might help us uncover yet unknown, or yet not-enough-known, parcels of wisdom without which humanity will not survive our current climate, public health, and spiritual crises.

The changing nature of my social and physical environments over these last forty years has not only made me discover slowly how my identity boundaries have been transformed over time; more importantly, they have helped me uncover how identity dynamics function within me and between me and a variety of others I have met in the course of my life journey, as well as among a dazzling variety of others I have either become aware of indirectly through current affairs and media learnings, or through numerous readings about history. These complex identity dynamics characterizing any human being also directly affect, often for the worse because of misguided fears, how human beings have related to a variety of "others" as well as to nature, here and beyond, past and present. This growing awareness of how identity dynamics affect the whole of human history up to the present has also created a renewed sense of flexible and porous identity boundaries in my own self-construction, part of which I can control (personal agency) and part of which are imposed on me (collective agency of many identity kinds that are not of my own choice, but equally real for me about others). In short, this journey has made me discover just how complex identity dynamics are, with various degrees of perceived stillness and shifts in time and over time, affecting how people see themselves in the world, affecting every one of their thoughts and decisions. It has made me realize how I can participate with all human beings, as well as with living and material things, in the universal dance of life, from my own narrow earthly perspective.

What is less well-known, however, is how this dance reflects not only iden-tity dynamics: of equal importance is how identity dynamics are completely

and always intertwined with power dynamics. It took me years before I came
to recognize my own colonial and racist heritage, and how through compassionate listening in particular, I could begin to change my attitude, mind, and
feelings about my own identity in a vastly more complex world than I can
ever imagine. This lifelong observation of these worldwide dynamics has
led to the development of a theoretical framework to make deeper sense of
the intertwined nature of identity and power dynamics that affect all human
beings. This effort has turned into more than a personal intellectual pursuit: it
has become a quest for meaning rooted in perennial values whose embodied
virtues alone can transform humanity into a sustainable and meaningful reality for all. In our time of accelerated climate change with potential threats to
the very viability of humanity on earth, not to mention the public health and
economic crises currently unfolding because of the COVID-19 pandemic
worldwide, it is imperative to discover how each person, and in turn each
collective identity group, can take better responsibility for one's own participation in an intricate human web of interdependent relations that require
sustainable glocal identity and equitable power dynamics.

A key factor in reaching this urgent goal is learning how to communicate
better as human beings, within ourselves, with others, and with all other
forms of life. It has become clearer than ever for me that the current climate
and public health crises are mirrors into a spiritual crisis, at the core of which
lies a lack of deeper internal (both intrapersonal and intraidentity group) as
well as external dialogue with life in its full richness and complexity. Diving
deeper in the meaning of life requires one key daily ingredient: the practice
of dialogue. If I had had this knowledge when I was hosted by this generous
Indigenous family over forty years ago, I know I would have been able to
connect in a much more significant way, less colonial, and more holistically
human. Through various opportunities to practice deeper compassionate listening, including with Indigenous communities of the Turtle continent as well
as various peoples of the Middle East and many other parts of the world, my
own philosophy of dialogue has emerged over the last two decades, a theory
I have chosen to call: "interworldview dialogue" (IWVD).

On a surface literal level, the phrase "interworldview dialogue" is a two-
word expression formed by a simple juxtaposition of the principal noun
"dialogue," preceded by the newly coined word "interworldview," stemming
from the prefix "inter" used before the noun "worldview," itself a compound
word stemming from the concept "view of the world." It is a direct translation from the German *Weltanschauung*, whose origin goes back to Immanuel
Kant (1724–1806) (Naugle 2002). The noun "interworldview" then becomes
an adjective when placed immediately before the noun "dialogue." The Latin
preposition *inter* means "between, among or during." So "interworldview"
literally means *the interaction between* or *among worldviews* or paradigms,

two notions often used synonymously (Creswell and Clark 2011). Here, "paradigm" is understood as used originally by Thomas Kuhn: "a set of generalizations, beliefs, and values of a community of specialists" (Kuhn 1970, in Creswell and Clark 2011, 39). Both Creswell and Clark prefer the word "worldview" to that of "paradigm" (ibid.). "Worldview" can be associated with a specific discipline or community of scholars that suggests the shared beliefs and values of researchers. It can also be associated with an "all-encompassing perspective of the world" (Morgan 2007, in Creswell and Clark 2011, 46). Today, however, the use of the word "worldview" has been popularized to such an extent that it can also be linked to any identity group that thinks of itself as a community.

In this chapter, I present briefly, for the first time, the emergence of this theory of IWVD, with its unique approach integrating both identity and power dynamics. I also elaborate on its core competencies, challenges, and alternative responses for conflict transformation (Lederach 1995) and peacebuilding (Lederach 2005), only scratching the surface of how these two sets of identity and power dynamics intersect and interconnect. (Embryonic elements of this IWVD concept can be found in: WOSM and KAICIID 2018, 32–36.)

IWVD: A NEW APPROACH IN CONFLICT TRANSFORMATION AND PEACEBUILDING

Over the last four decades, using at first a process combining deductive and inductive methods in analyzing my own set of identities as well as consciously adding over the last two decades an action research methodology (Stringer 2014), I developed the "interworldview dialogue" (IWVD) approach to contribute to better interpersonal and intergroup understanding and collaboration, thereby enhancing social transformation toward positive peace (Galtung 2012). This chapter on IWVD represents the cumulative result of leading, a few times with one or two other cotrainers, over 100 workshops in more than seventy countries on five continents. These were conducted mostly in English, sometimes in French, and occasionally also in Spanish, Arabic, or Hebrew (as well as in a few other languages with the help of interpreters). This quantitative and linguistic information helps us understand the various contexts in which IWVD was initially practiced as a hypothesis, then turned into an informal validation process that has included numerous applications in a wide range of cultural and religious contexts. By now, IWVD is no longer only a hypothesis; it has become a theory, with useful transformational applications across the globe and in a multitude of social environments within any one geographical milieu, given the multitude of identities that exist in any human community, however small or large.

As an interdisciplinary scholar rooted initially in theories and methods in the scientific study of religions, with a focus on Abrahamic traditions in particular, as well as in the history of religions and the contemporary geopolitics of religions in international relations, I eventually came to use, in addition to the above action research, a transdisciplinary theory (Jahn, Bergmann, and Keil 2012) and methodology (Nicolescu 2014) to study contemporary intra-, multi-, and interidentity and power dynamics at the heart of any human interaction, wherever it may lie along a spectrum between harmony and conflict.

Over twenty years ago, I first coined the concept "interworldview dialogue" as an alternative to the usage of both "intercultural dialogue" and "interreligious dialogue" (see Marshall 2007 where she interviewed me about IWVD). These two widespread expressions, and their cognates (e.g., interfaith dialogue) (Cheetam, Pratt, and Thomas 2013, 1, fn 1), often show serious limitations in three ways. First, at a conceptual level, the meanings of the root words "religion" and "culture" have emerged from a unique symbiotic relation in the history of modern European ideas, often reflecting an ideological battle between premodern notions of religion as being normative and modern notions of culture(s) as now being normative, within which there may or not exist religion(s), depending on different points of view on how to define "culture." This "battle" has only become more widespread globally in the course of the twentieth century and right up till now. Second, at a practical level, their meanings have been also used in popular discourse in ways that overlap, thus often causing confusion (e.g., is "religion" made up of different cultures or not? Is "culture" potentially made up, at least in part, of elements from different religions or not?). Of course, this confusion stems also from reductive tendencies in defining both terms, often linked to an underlying positivist epistemology. Third, and often unconsciously, these two words have been used in ways that exclude one or more identities, or have greatly reduced the influence of other kinds of identities on the dominant cultural or, if any, religious identity made to be prevalent in one's awareness during the course of specifically "intercultural" or "interreligious" dialogues. For example, in the process of serious dialogical encounters, most people end up feeling uncomfortable with reducing who they are to only, or mostly, one cultural or, if any, one religious identity, given each person's complex identity construction (Leary and Tangney 2012).

The semiotic and etymological tensions between the notion of "culture" and that of "religion" in modern European languages, which arose in the course of the last five centuries with the emergence of modernity first in a European context (Delanty 2015) and then spread worldwide—leading to the concepts of "multiple modernities" (Eisenstadt 2002) or "reflexive modernization" or "liquid modernity" (Lee 2006)—with different degrees of penetration, have resulted in much semantic confusion. At the center of the popular debate as to whether culture includes religion or vice versa, or in other terms, is "culture" superior to "religion" or is "religion" superior to "culture," there is not only an epistemological difference (as mentioned already above) but also a contextual difference as to where geographically one speaks from, and especially since when—the duration of formative time lived in a particular social context and possibly new migratory diasporic location(s). Without relying on any statistics, I have noticed, in my ethnographic observations, that most of those who answer according to the first option live in a predominantly secular society; most of those who answer according to the second option live in a predominantly religious one. This observation needs to be correlated with two scientifically proven facts: first, the more transnational a religion has become over centuries, the more it includes a variety of cultures within its practices; second, the more diverse a society becomes, the more its normative majority culture includes different religions and often, especially with the rise of late and ultramodernity, persons who do not define themselves with any religious identity (i.e., the "non-religious," Lee 2015). The perceptions about these two words and their relation to one another are rooted in a historical tug-of-war between the worlds of politics and religions, which continues to this day, internationally.

To make things more complicated, the emergence of interreligious (or interfaith) dialogue as an organized activity leading to international organizations promoting this particular kind of dialogue (Lehmann 2020) needs to be analyzed as part and parcel of the global colonial project in which a few Western nation-states turned empires, with their particular ideological orientalism, drove much of the search for understanding "others" beyond "the West." Such colonial projects remain in existence to this day, although affecting much smaller geographical areas than in the course of the nineteenth century and first half of the twentieth century. And although our period is often described as postcolonial, some colonial instincts linked to positivistic epistemologies have survived in the form of neoliberal globalization practices and "fundamentalist" discourses, affecting most modern worldviews, whether ideological, secular, or religious (see Cleyn, "Transcending Traditional Justice Claims," *Transforming*), for an analysis of colonial epistemic and normative violence. They all affect, in more or less transparent ways, certain segments of religious communities today, which are often the sources of intrareligious tensions that also limit the prospect for more inclusive interreligious dialogues. Moreover, persons with no religious identity feel excluded from interreligious dialogue circles; and persons with strong religious identities feel often either excluded, or misunderstood, in most intercultural dialogue encounters.

Additional complications come with the recognition of the power dynamics that have often accompanied the introduction/translation of these key concepts into so many non-European languages. These imported words and meanings have also affected the complex processes of their receptions in various host linguistic communities worldwide. Because of the initial tension between the concepts represented by "culture" and "religion" as reflected in the abovementioned symbiotic European history and current diversity of meanings and usages, this challenge of cross-linguistic significations of these two key words has now become much more complex worldwide. A typical example is what happens when we try to identify appropriate synonyms for these two words in a variety of non-European languages in particular (for examples of synonyms for the word "religion," see Alles 2008). In the first phase of a major research project I led between 2013 and 2015 to build a large database of organizations working internationally to promote interreligious dialogue (see the KAICIID Peace Map within the Dialogue Knowledge Hub of the International Dialogue Centre, n.d.), our research team tried to find synonyms for "interreligious dialogue" in ten major languages. The results can be found in a summary of its methodology (Toth-Pickl and Vobecká 2015). At times, such as in the case of Chinese, it was necessary to use several concepts or short expressions pointing as close as possible to how religion is generally understood in Western languages.

In summary, these three kinds of complications affect, in different ways, how "intercultural dialogue" and "interreligious dialogue" are perceived today, simply from the complexity of how their two root words of "culture" and "religion" are perceived. This situation is only rendered more complex when we add the myriad ways the third key word of "dialogue" is understood. In some circles, influenced by the heritage of Greek philosophy, it is possible to find that: "The six basic types of dialogue previously recognized in the argumentation literature are inquiry, negotiation, dialogue, information-seeking dialogue, deliberation, and eristic dialogue" (Walton and Krabbe 1995). As for Rockwell (2003), influenced by the heritage of literary dialogues, he proposes one combined definition for both oral and literary dialogues. Yet, as the word "dialogue" developed in the practice of interreligious dialogue over more than 100 years, there arose many definitions and typologies within that context too (Bohm 1996, 2004).

What has emerged from my personal experiences of both intercultural and interreligious dialogues in different parts of the world is that a variety of persons feel excluded by either of two emphases: (1) when the emphasis is put on the word "culture" (or its adjective "cultural") implicitly understood as a broad concept that includes, as a subset, that of "religion," as a result of the emergence of "a secular age" (Taylor 2007); or (2) when the emphasis is put on the word "religion" (or its adjective "religious") especially in circles promoting "interreligious dialogue," in one form or another.

In the first case, the resulting feeling of exclusion may come from the knowledge and feeling that religion is treated as a subcategory of culture in a way that may be meaningful enough to "cultural Jews, Christians or Muslims," but not sufficiently so for those whose central identity is religious and who, consciously or not, put "culture" as a subsidiary identity in their own self-construction. Those included in this latter group are therefore critical of "intercultural" dialogue or any discourse around "multiculturalism" or "interculturalism" because they feel it is reductive of their own understanding of "religion" as a positive source of transcendent meaning and ethical standards to be believed and practiced in an integrated and paramount religious life.

In the second case, the resulting feeling of exclusion may be either because the word "religion" is understood to mean something that they do not relate to personally (identity and/or belief-practice-wise, being, e.g., "atheist," "agnostic," "humanist," "nonreligious," etc.) or because they prefer using a term that makes sense to them in their own primary linguistic world that does not easily match their understanding of the English word "religion." In both situations, by deduction, the use of the words "religious" or "interreligious" therefore results in feelings of exclusion that go against the value of harmony and peace that underlies most efforts in what is called "interreligious dialogue."

"Interworldview dialogue" is the best solution I found to address seriously the above two sources of "feeling excluded" that exist, though for completely different yet not opposite reasons in two different situations: on the one hand, in so-called "advanced" or "ultra-" or "postmodern" societies where secular ideologies have become dominant over the last century or so, with a parallel rise in nonreligious worldviews, though varying in numeric importance in different secular countries; and, on the other hand, in societies with various combinations of mostly religious but with also different smaller (and at times growing) secular ideologies and nonreligious worldviews, as they are also modernizing and globalizing within nation-state frameworks. I have proposed the alternative concept of "interworldview dialogue" because the simple word "worldview" (Koltko-Rivera 2004) has four advantages over both "religion" and "culture." First, the word "worldview" is more easily translatable in probably most languages. Indeed, this word is devoid of an ideological conflict inherited because of the particular trajectory of how modernity came to develop first in Western Europe, turning "culture" into an alternative all-encompassing word to make sense of group behavior, instead of the older word "religion." Second, a "worldview" can be understood from either a personal or a collective point of view. Third, all human beings have a worldview, whatever the level of self-consciousness each person may have about it, or how well-articulated they can present it. Fourth, worldview is a concept that is highly meaningful precisely because it encompasses all aspects of a person`s life and self-understanding.

For these reasons, and especially the third and fourth ones, the use of "interworldview" does not create any form of exclusion: it includes all human beings with no exception. It therefore transcends the multivalent and at times conflicting concepts of culture and religion to provide a space of meaning that includes all real and/or perceived human perceptions of reality. "Interworldview" thus allows for a more inclusive language in which all human beings can find their place. Already in late 2007, from an earlier phone interview, Katherine Marshall of the Berkley Center at Georgetown University summarized my then concept of "Interworldview Dialogue" as follows: "He describes his vision of 'inter-worldview dialogue' as intended to merge the existing dialogues on culture and religion in an atmosphere of inclusion" (Marshall 2007, preamble online). When using the word "worldview" in the expression "interworldview dialogue," it is thus possible to use a language that helps create a truly inclusive space for dialogue, finally bridging the tension and the many divides between "religion" and "culture." It thus goes a long way to create a "safe space" (cf. "safe container" in Gagnon, "Compassionate Listening," *Transforming*), which is often presented at the first principle or guideline of dialogue (WOSM and KAICIID 2018, 86).

"Interworldview dialogue" can thus be defined as a form of dialogue between any human beings, whether in their own personal capacity or as representatives, formally or not, of one or more identity group or community. In my practice of IWVD in so many different contexts worldwide, reaching over more than a thousand participants, I can attest that, so far, no person has mentioned to me feeling excluded for one reason or another when participating in an IWVD session or training. It would therefore seem that the use of "interworldview dialogue" is a phrase that does not cause "exclusions" the way "religion" and "culture" often do for so many people. Moreover, because IWVD makes explicit the importance of a human being coming to the dialogue space with all of his or her identities and subidentities, both conscious and unconscious, it creates a space that is not only richer in terms of potential themes to dialogue about, but more importantly, it means that a person can be fully him or herself in that space, to the extent that he or she feels safe on the basis of other criteria too.

The concept of "interworldview dialogue" therefore helps overcome the problem that I have encountered so many times, both myself and through listening to other persons sharing how their experience of interreligious dialogue focuses too much on their religious identity, at the expense of other identities. In a nutshell, the concept of IWVD is so inclusive as to encompass many other forms of dialogue, whether intercultural or interreligious (interfaith), or any other for that matter (i.e., intercivilizational, interspiritual, intergroup, interconvictional, etc.). While possibly being the best concept for fully including all human beings, each one in the fullness of their own complexity, it should also be made very clear that IWVD is not intended to become a concept that should replace or supersede the unique specificity of any of the many other forms of dialogue that currently exists.

IWVD is thus simply another form of dialogue, with many advantages as seen above, but also with important limitations. For example, an IWVD may lose the specificity that is provided in particular forms of dialogue focusing on one single kind of identity. For example, it is sometimes necessary for religious people to dialogue with a focus on their religious identities, as it allows specific details of that identity to emerge in ways that recognize both similarities and differences in what pertains to each person's religious identity in comparison with that of other religious persons during such interreligious dialogue. The danger, though, is to avoid essentializing one's own religious identity when practicing interreligious dialogue. The reverse danger is to avoid generalization in sharing one's multiple identities when practicing IWVD. Other examples can be given by replacing the word "religious" in the above first example with that of "culture," or "civilization," or "spirituality," or "group," or "conviction," etc.; the logic of the argument remains valid for all. Each form of dialogue can therefore have a place of usefulness for deepening mutual understanding, at least in those aspects that pertain to the factors associated primarily with that word X turned adjective Y in the expression "inter-Y dialogue."

Another potential limitation in using the phrase "interworldview dialogue" comes from the fact that it is true that any human being is more or less conscious of his or her own worldview and those of others, and more or less able to describe it and them. But this human limitation in self- and other-understanding, which is always present in all human beings, though to different degrees, does not invalidate or prevent anyone from using the concept of "worldview" or that of "interworldview," especially when it comes to linking it with "dialogue" in this new concept of IWVD. If anything, it only creates a new expression that, by virtue of being fully inclusive of all human beings and of all parts of their self-understanding (identities and subidentities), contributes to a more inclusive space that avoids, at least in theory, reductive self- and other-understanding, as can so often be the case in the various practices of both interreligious and intercultural dialogues, among others.

There is general agreement, by both scholars and practitioners of one form or another of dialogue, that dialogue with others is essential to clarify to ourselves what our own identity(ies) is(are), which in turn consolidates what our own worldview is. We know that our thought processes and behaviors depend on our respective worldviews; that they are always the result of both past individual and collective inheritance, with their own sets of unique power dynamics; and that these affect the ongoing process of integrating (or not) our various identities. Persons participating in an IWVD are made aware of the nature and functioning of identity and power dynamics in relation to a combination of personal and collective experiences, both inherited (genes and transmitted memories) and acquired (directly through personal experience and indirectly through reading or hearing stories about others), not to forget the additional layers that come from various levels of structural and systemic influences shaping both identity and power dynamics. All of these levels and kinds of human and spatial dynamics provide vital responses to individual and social needs in ways that avoid reducing reality to political manipulation of an "us versus them" or a simplistic use, for example, of the negatively powerful word "enemy."

The IWVD concept is therefore a kind of meta-paradigm that offers both conceptual depth and flexibility as well as practicality when it comes to serve any human beings engaged in mutual reflection with one or more persons. In short, IWVD is an approach, both theoretical and applied, that seeks to understand, respect, and build upon the multiple identity and power dynamics that are always present during any form of human interaction, including when engaged in dialogue, however defined. IWVD contains the possibility of including any and all the multiple worldviews that exist when any group of persons interact with each other. More specifically, IWVD recognizes the complexity that is inherent in how multiple identities function, always at the intersection of conscious and unconscious power dynamics that shape our interdependent human identity constructions, all of which function within empowering/coercing systems of meaning broader than one person or group of persons can imagine. In this respect, IWVD also includes those aspects of power dynamics so well analyzed in the relatively recent concept of "intersectionality" (Hill Collins and Bilge 2016). Yet, while integrating intersectionality when appropriate (i.e., when those engaged in dialogue feel ready to address it), IWVD also provides a broader framework of identity and power dynamics that seeks to avoid victimization discourses by providing means for taking responsibility to choose how best to move in the Relational Ecosystem for Peace (REP) toward communion with all, rather than disconnection (see Gagnon and Brodeur 2020; Gagnon, "Compassionate Listening," *Transforming*).

INTERCONNECTED DIMENSIONS IN IWVD

The following figure represents various interdependent components linked to the underlying identity and power dynamics necessarily at work in IWVD.

The different dimensions in figure 6.1 are all interconnected to each other. The horizontal axis separates theory (above) from practice (below). The theory part refers to any knowledge one acquires through the mind via reading and listening to ideas about reality, or part thereof, while the practice refers to when information about reality directly comes from a lived experience. Of course, the two are mutually interdependent and complementary.

The vertical axis divides past from future. Within a dialogical space, meaning is derived both from past experiences and the future horizon. The dynamic of the dialogue is situated at the present time. Values, biases, assumptions, and feelings are derived from the past but also inform interpretations of past events; likewise, they shape the imagination of what might happen in the future.

Starting at the convergence of the axes, there is a holarchy, with each holon (Wilber 1996) being both complete and a part of the bigger holon containing it. The movement, from intrapersonal to interpersonal to interorganizational and so on, proceeds outwardly to various circles of increasingly more complex systemic dynamics.

The notion of time (past/future) as well as that of theory versus practice cut across transversally all circles. Perceptions about the past and the future are interrelated, although they are both always perceived in the present. Both dimensions affect constantly how the self and the relationship between self and other are perceived in time, and how they are constantly being constructed in relation to all the other spheres at once. Most interactions happen subconsciously, in a complex set of power dynamics that are rarely perceived directly, and even less so deconstructed within one's own self-understanding.

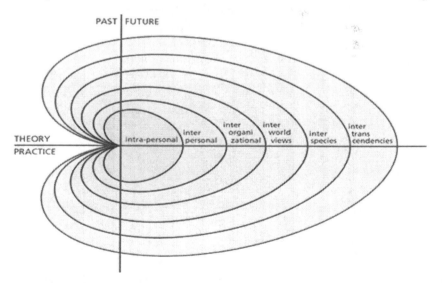

Figure 6.1   Interconnected Dimensions in IWVD.

In addition to this complex set of interrelated dimensions that links inner and outer self with myriad others beyond our body, we can also imagine a camera going down the inner self at the center point of the above schema in order to explore the equally complex world of the inner self, not reflected in this limited schema. Through this introspection, we would probably discover predispositions and motivations in our thinking and feelings to not only deconstruct our own inner and outer identity and power dynamics with the world around us but also begin to take responsibility for how this thinking and our feelings position us along a spectrum from disconnectedness to communion with both self and others (see Gagnon and Brodeur 2020).

Figure 6.1 is one way to reflect the multiple concentric layers of identity dynamics. It also represents one dimension of the third pillar of the REP analyzed in the preceding chapter by Gagnon ("Relational Ecosystem for Peace," *Transforming*). While the REP as a whole makes us understand how the best process for building peace begins from the inside out, moving us from inner to outer peace, this figure 6.1 focuses on showing how the intrapersonal is embedded within several external, or outer, concentric circles that represent different layers of identity dynamics, from the external personal dimensions to the systemic human and even beyond, depending on one's worldview. Yet, on the basis of my own journey and ethnographic observations over many years, the key remains the art of compassionate listening, as studied in depth by Gagnon ("Relational Ecosystem for Peace," *Transforming*). It is essential for deep introspection to unfold more systematically, ultimately allowing the integration of our different levels of knowledge (i.e., cognitive, emotional, social, spiritual, etc.) that makes possible a coherent sense of self.

There is a growing consensus that "selfhood" encompasses an ongoing process of self-evaluation, self-regulation, self-construction, and self-adaptation (Leary and Tangney 2012, 22). The possibilities and potential for the emergence of new perceptions about ourselves, thereby becoming more resilient and potentially better peacemakers within our respective zones of influence, also affect the larger processes of group construction and development. Recent scientific findings converge to make clear that "the self" is not a single system but rather a set of interrelated, functionally interdependent systems interacting in complex ways (Morf and Mischell, in Leary and Tangney 2012, 25). In figure 6.1, each circle represents a layer of identity dynamics, or an identity system of its own. The complexity comes from the ways in which all of these circles/systems function interdependently. The literature on self and group identity is very informative on how worldviews are formed, maintained, transmitted, and sustained over time. One aspect includes how different forms of security (physical, emotional, collective, etc.) have a role in integrative processes of new information related to in-groups and out-groups that affect worldviews (Kritkol-Rivera 2004).

Dispositional and motivational factors leading to wisdom and discernment in dialogue, for participants but especially for facilitators, are explored in the next sections below.

CORE COMPETENCIES IN IWVD

The first competency in IWVD is more theoretical: it requires to understand that, while many definitions of dialogue exist, it is crucial to distinguish first between broad and narrow definitions. When dialogue is defined broadly, it includes many kinds of communication between human beings; "dialogue" becomes an umbrella concept under which these different ways of communicating become subsumed. This is the approach that was taken initially by the Ministry of Education of Quebec, in its program "Ethics and Religious Culture," established in 2008. The real danger of this approach is that it waters down the potentially specific meaning of "dialogue," only creating greater semantic confusion. In contrast, when dialogue is defined narrowly, it can be included as one kind of human communication, alongside many others that fall within a typology of ways human communicate. Dialogue narrowly defined is therefore neither above other communication types (i.e., as if an umbrella word) nor below (i.e., as if a subcategory of meaning attached to one type in particular). A narrow definition of dialogue allows its meaning to be considered on an equal footing with other kinds of human communication within a typology that can include many types, such as: conversation, discussion, deliberation, negotiation, debate, consultation, advocacy, or even conference. Harold Saunders, founder and president of the International Institute for Sustained Dialogue, defines dialogue this way:

> Dialogue is a process of genuine interaction through which human beings listen to each other deeply enough to be changed by what they learn. Each makes a serious effort to take other's concerns into her or his own picture, even when disagreement persists. No participant gives up her or his identity, but each recognizes enough of the other's valid human claims that he or she will act differently toward the other. (2020)

This definition highlights the importance of quality interaction in the dialogue process and differentiates sound dialogue from fake dialogue where contact is unilateral or superficial on the part of one or more of its participants. It also implies that dialogue must be differentiated from debate in which participants focus on securing victory for their own position (see table 6.1 below for a list of elements related to debate, with their counterpart equivalents for dialogue).

Table 6.1 Comparative Table on Notions of Debate versus Dialogue (Yankelovich 1999)

Debate	Dialogue
Tell, sell, persuade	Inquire and to learn
Gain agreement on one meaning	Unfold shared meaning
Evaluate and select the best	Integrate multiple perspectives
Justify/defend assumptions	Uncover and examine assumptions
Assume there is a right answer and I have it	Assume that many people have pieces of the answer and that together, they can craft a solution
Is combative—participants attempt to prove the other side wrong	Is collaborative—participants work together toward a common understanding
Is about winning	Is about exploring common good
Entails listening to find flaws and make counterarguments	Entails listening to understand and find meaning and agreement
Defend my assumptions as truth	Reveal my assumptions for reevaluation
Critique the other side's position	Reexamine all positions
Defend my own views against those of others	Admit that others' thinking can improve my own
Search for weaknesses in others' positions	Search for strength and value in other's positions
Seek a conclusion or vote that ratifies my position	Discover new options

Over the years, the following five broad competencies, acquired through the practice of IWVD (and possibly through other forms of narrowly defined dialogue too), have emerged as foundational to what IWVD can contribute to conflict transformation and peacebuilding:

1. *Knowledge of the theory and practice of IWVD.* This knowledge brings first awareness and then capacity-building to how IWVD promotes better inclusion of diverse kinds of people as well as helps integrate more inclusively the participants' multiple identities in how they approach any topic of dialogue, especially given myriad dialogue contexts.
2. *Identification of one's own multiple identities and how to maximize their use for entering into better connection with others in IWVD, as a means to potential collaboration in ways that can contribute to conflict transformation directly or indirectly through global networking toward peacebuilding.* IWVD participants learn to recognize how their worldview is conditioned by their own set of multiple identities, affecting their thoughts, feelings, and behaviors. They better understand how their own worldview is both the result of and in constant interactions with those of others, within a complex set of power dynamics that affect all the dimensions mentioned in figure 6.1. They get to become more aware

of the impact these have on perceptions about oneself and others, but also on how they can actively change these perceptions too, stepping out of, for example, victimization discourses so central to the drama triangle (Karpman 1968). In becoming conscious of overlapping layers of identities they share with others, in so many different ways, they allow themselves to (re)connect with whom they have been estranged from or with whom they are in varied states of enmity, whether at an individual or group level (i.e., prejudice, discrimination, or even hate speech or crime). They acquire the ability to evaluate better their key assumptions about "truth" and "the other," necessary to practice the next competence.

3. *Awareness and on-the-ground know-how about how to prevent patterns of exclusion that may cause feelings of estrangement, frustration, and anger, which may lead some to radicalization and violence.* With examples and reflection from many on-the-ground examples worldwide, including from their own local contexts, participants become more apt to see the complementarities in the diversity of identities and to open up to the beauty and necessity of differences between human beings. When able to understand better different practices, beliefs, and worldviews, participants can "experience" the other and choose mutual respect of personal choices and practices, even though they may "agree to disagree." A greater degree of inner peace within oneself and in relationship with others results from this process of awareness building, as greater clarity and coherence is reached on selfhood in relations to others.

4. *Compassionate listening to experience deep dialogue, which is necessary for IWVD participants to contribute to conflict transformation and peacebuilding*, including how to learn to put at a distance one's own judgments, thoughts, and feelings about others during the practice of IWVD (see Gagnon, "Relational Ecosystem for Peace," *Transforming*, for a description of compassionate listening).

5. *Taking greater responsibility for one's own personal role in changing negative attitudes and feelings toward more constructive ones, thereby contributing to conflict transformation and peacebuilding.* IWVD participants learn to understand how IWVD relates directly to the REP (Gagnon and Brodeur 2020).

CHALLENGES AND ALTERNATIVE RESPONSES IN IWVD

The research on sociopsychological barriers in conflicts shows that many obstacles can come in the way of practicing IWVD. For example, they may stem from major disagreements about the explicit causes of a conflict:

The long-term preservation of the conflict stems also from the enduring inability to overcome them because of the crystallization and functioning involving cognitive, emotional and motivational processes, combined with pre-existing repertoire of rigid supporting beliefs, world views and emotions that result in selective, biased and distorting information processing. This obstructs and inhibits a penetration of new information that can contribute to the facilitation of the development of the peace process. (Bar-Tal and Halperin 2011, 218)

From an IWVD perspective, groups facing each other in dialogue encounter many challenges. For example, it takes time to understand gradually how our multiple identities are linked to each other not only in complex ways that both tie together and divide all members of both (or more) groups at once during a dialogue. It takes even more time, in general, for participants to get to a point where their knowledge leads them to become aware of how a perception and feeling of sharing a common human identity can emerge from all of these similarities and differences, without denying their importance either. Even longer is the time necessary for participants to figure out how various forms of power dynamics affect, often unconsciously, their own dialogue process in ways that often undermine its lofty aims. This is why the high hopes of initial steps in dialogue only too often crash down later, when one or more challenges emerge in the midst of the dialogue group.

To be more specific, here are seven challenges commonly encountered when IWVD is practiced:

1. The challenge to understand the link between multiple identities and power dynamics within processes that either fuel further one or more cycles of violence or contribute to changing awareness and behaviors that help move toward conflict transformation.
2. The dangers created by various forms of dependencies and codependencies (Twinn, "Warring with Wihtiko in Real Time, *Transforming*) in the power dynamics among the participants and in relation to the organizer(s), within and across their different identity groups; these kinds of challenges need to be counterbalanced with the practice of constructive power dynamics brought about through the acknowledgment of the participants' (including the organizer(s)) interdependency, without which they will not get to create the mutual trust necessary to collaborate in ways that will truly contribute to conflict transformation.
3. The difficulty to make sense of how hierarchies of identities vary comparatively not only across different societies with a large degree of historical, cultural, and religious differences but also across nation-states, even though they may share boundaries and therefore a history of relative proximity.

4. The vital need to recognize what kinds of interests are being privileged by certain identity groups involved in intergroup dynamics, often undermining healthy interdependencies and complementarities across diverse groups.
5. The nonrecognition of the perverse effects created by identity vectors that are perceived exclusively in polarized ways (e.g., majority-minority, visible-invisible, power-powerless, changing-unchanging, etc.) rather than as spectrums along which people and ideas find themselves positioned but with the possibility of shifting positions (i.e., capacity to change).
6. The often-combined low levels of several kinds of literacy (e.g., linguistic, historical, cultural, religious, mediatic, ideological, etc.) about identities beyond one's own multiple identities.
7. The lack of understanding of how identity dynamics both include and exclude at the same time, often ending in opposite results. When they exclude, the results can be seen in increased levels of anger, alienation, humiliation, radicalization, and even violence (psychological and physical). When they include, the results can be seen in increased levels of connectedness, with meaningful creative engagement, compassion, and love.

Fortunately, the practice of IWVD equips participants to face the above challenges through the practice of the following seven alternative responses:

- Emphasize face-to-face encounters for better human transformation, even if these may need to respect social distancing or rely on virtual meetings where that is possible.
- Strengthen common or shared identities rather than different or dividing ones, while not avoiding or dismissing them.
- Change implicit boundaries of reference underlying identity and power dynamics by first making them explicit, so as to then change them by strengthening similarities over differences through joint collaboration for the creation of (re)new(ed) spaces, (re)new(ed) institutions, and (re)new(ed) networks based on more equitable identity and power dynamics.
- Notice tensions as source of dynamic growth before they turn into conflicts, which are to be avoided as much as possible; and if they arise, IWVD still remains one of the best ways to go about finding inclusive, fairer, and transformative solutions.
- Recognize the weight of the past in identity and power dynamics, without making it tip the fragile balance between past-, present-, and future-focused periods within IWVD.
- When developing common collaborative projects, widen the circle of decision makers to include all those affected in a tensed situation or conflict.

- Work also on changing hierarchies of identities so that, in all societies, whether within or across nation-states, at a small local or large global level, a common human identity can emerge at the top of any hierarchy of identities in order to address power dynamics from that common human perspective rather than from divided identities and competing interests.

These responses can be seen in practical terms in how we deal with diversity.

DIVERSITY

Diversity is at the heart of the format we need to develop for a dialogical encounter to be transformative. Diversity is everywhere, but not always consciously so among persons coming to an IWVD. It is the responsibility of the organizer(s) to think ahead and ensure the presence of diverse identities and worldviews among participants, so as to decrease the chances of becoming embroiled in reductive polarities, whether based on identity dynamics or because of power dynamics that might affect how the group ends up polarized by fear of stating one's true, and often nuanced, perspective on any given topic. Such polarization is a reflection of how certain participants, especially the more vocal ones, pass judgments and communicate from a place of adversarial spirit. This can be avoided by good facilitation, which is easier said than done. But one trick is for the facilitator, and the more perceptive participants too, to look constantly for diverse perspectives, including within ourselves sometimes, since we don't always have the same perspective on issues: we evolve, change our mind, alter our thoughts, and even forget things that can change the way we think or feel. So diversity is not just between different persons in a dialogue group that may seem, at least on the surface, to be on a spectrum between very homogenous and very diverse group.

Diversity requires that many choices be made in the format of an IWVD. It needs to enable the greatest number of diverse perspectives to emerge since reality is always perceived and interpreted through different lenses. The case of language is uniquely important in IWVD, because it is the primary means through which communication takes place. If one chooses one particular language, especially in societies with more than one, then of course that may introduce an uneven playing field between those who are fluent and those who are not. If choosing more than one, is translation always necessary? If so, how should it be handled? I recently finished a training of trainers in Cape Verde for the West-African region of the World Scout Organization Movement (WOSM). The twenty-five young adults were divided almost equally between English, French, and Portuguese speakers, most of whom did not know one or both of the other languages. How we managed to set up a relatively equitable trilingual framework to ensure a linguistically safe, that is, equitable space, took some experimentation and quick adjustments, as well as patience and flexibility from all participants. In this particular case, linguistic equity became a core piece in an IWVD approach.

One must also think of diversity from the perspective of other identities too. At a national interreligious dialogue event composed of both senior and youth religious leaders from that Nordic country, the late afternoon sun and relative warmth made it possible to all gather outside for a group picture. We naturally congregated in one open space of the courtyard, where steps allowed us to line up ease so that everyone could be easily seen. Yet, one participant insisted to change the location. At first, I did not know why, until I turned around and looked at what the photograph would see: it immediately became obvious that taking a picture under a large religious sign that made sense to only one religious identity group among this diverse group of persons did not make sense. We cordially all moved about 90 degrees to the right, and the photo was then taken, fully inclusive of all participants.

IWVD is based on the basis that people come from diverse perspectives and have different worldviews. In an IWVD encounter where the IWV notion and approach to reality is emphasized, it offers a conceptual and practical form of metaparadigm able to contain a diversity of worldviews to be shared and respected, although by no means necessary accepted by all.

The challenge of diversity in the world around us remains how to balance the right to say things that can be exclusive of some others, while remaining in a spirit of IWVD where expressing one's truth is as important as respecting that of others, despite at times our possibly profound disagreements. It is the upholding of such tension, with radical respect, that characterizes the best IWVD. The interdependent nature of reality points toward the complex nature of reality as things and events are interrelated by causes, effects, and conditions. One must therefore pay attention to the notion of "true and false" and contextualize any such claims, with the double task of avoiding the extremes in both relativism and objectivist truth claims.

CONCLUSION

This theory of "interworldview dialogue" has emerged over my lifetime to make sense of how to address and impact inclusively and nonviolently the myriad persons and contexts that affect ongoing changes around the globe, for the worst and for the better. It is as much the result of observing intellectually and compassionately outwardly to try to "make sense of the world around me," as it is one of introspection in the mirror of my own deeply needed self-transformation to adapt constructively to this rapidly changing world we all live in as well as to seek greater integrity toward the ideals of positive peace. Indeed, this double process of internal and external self-other examination and analysis is essential to address the challenge often voiced by the Dalai Lama that "problems created by [humanity] can be solved by [humanity]" (Dalai Lama 1999). But for this to happen, more inner and outer dialogue is necessary, from which each one of us learns to take more responsibility for how our respective identities and power dynamics affect our shared planet.

The IWVD competencies, challenges, and alternative responses for conflict transformation and peacebuilding presented in this article offer a new approach to envision more inclusively how to address responsibly and interdependently our numerous common human challenges by recognizing the intricate intersections and interconnections between identity and power dynamics. IWVD requires a more systematic practice of dialogue, at the heart of which lies the transformative power of compassionate listening. One could say that it is a form of deep dialogue requiring what some have called "radical respect," in reaction to so much media attention given to radicalization, especially since 9/11, 2001. Eventually, I hope that the practice of IWVD can influence persons and groups to become more compassionate in their daily lives, and thus contribute toward a holistic culture of peace that includes the latest United Nations efforts toward sustainable development goals.

Ending injustices and violence in our own families, communities, and identity groups starts with the task of ending violence in ourselves (Thich Nhat Hanh 2004). We are all "decision makers," with varying circles of influence, and we are all called to numerous "moments of choices" in our everyday lives, when we decide whether to promote greater connection or greater separation between us and others, as explained so clearly in the REP (see Gagnon, "Relational Ecosystem for Peace," *Transforming*). In small and large ways, through our thoughts, feelings, and behaviors, affecting directly our consumption patterns and social media habits, all human beings participate in making the world the reality it is today.

When presenting the IWVD theory as a means toward more sustainable peacemaking in our respective environments, I am reminded how much I would have benefited from knowing its contents forty years ago when I experienced my first "culture shock" on the coast of the Pacific Ocean. Many wise persons of all religious, spiritual, and ethical worldviews argue that inner peace is a prerequisite for outer world peace to be achieved (Leydon-Rubenstein, cited in Blumberg et al. 2006, 51). Indeed, the reality of our "earthian" world today is only the result, after all, of the aggregate of over seven billion human beings interacting with each other and with the environment. With the IWVD theory, it becomes clearer how these interactions are spurred by their own complex symbiotic internal-external identity and power dynamics. If what we perceive of the contemporary world does not reflect our hopes and aspirations, it is for each one of us to become more responsible as to how we can "make a difference" toward positive peace. There are many valuable ways to go about pursuing this most laudable and timeless aim for any human being of any generation, even more so in our current time of global COVID-19 pandemic. IWVD is more than a theory; by now, it has become one well-tested transformative approach that can improve our understanding of complex human interactions and provide a tangible dialogical and compassionate path toward addressing pragmatically all of our human challenges and crises.

REFERENCES

Abu-Nimer, Mohamed, Khoury, Amal I., and Welty, Emily. 2007. *Unity in Diversity: Interfaith Dialogue in the Middle East*. Washington, DC: United States Institute of Peace Press.

Alles, G. D. 2008. *Religious Studies: A Global View*. London & New York, NY: Routledge.

Aron, A., and Aron, E. N. 1986. *Love as the Expansion of Self: Understanding Attraction and Satisfaction*. New York, NY: Hemisphere.

Aron, A., Aron, E. N., Tudor, M., and Nelson, G. 1991. "Close Relationships as Including Other in the Self." *Journal of Personality and Social Psychology*, vol. 60, pp. 241–253.

Bar-Tal, D., and Halperin, E. 2011. "Socio-Psychological Barriers to Conflict Resolution." In *Intergroup Conflicts and their Resolution: A Social Psychological Perspective*. Edited by D. Bar-Tal. New York, NY: Psychology Press, pp. 217–240.

Blumberg, Herbert H., Hare, Paul A., and Costin, Anna. 2006. *Peace Psychology: A Comprehensive Introduction*. Cambridge: Cambridge University Press.

Bohm, David. 1996/2004. *On Dialogue*. London: Routledge and Routledge Classics.

Brodeur, Patrice. 1997. "Introduction to the Guidelines for an Inter-Faith Celebration." *Journal of Ecumenical Studies*, vol. 34, no. 4, pp. 551–572.

Brody Colin, Salena, Wright, Stephen C., Aron, Arthur, and McLaughlin-Volpe, Tracy. 2008. "Compassionate Love for Individuals in Other Social Groups." In *The Science of Compassionate Love: Theory, Research and Applications*. Edited by Beverley Fehr, Susan Sprecher, and Lynn G. Underwood. West Sussex: Wiley-Blackwell, chapter 10.

Cheetam, David, Pratt, Douglas, and Thomas, David, eds. 2013. *Understanding Interreligious Relations*. Oxford: Oxford University Press.

Creswell, John W., and Plano Clark, Vicki L. 2011. *Designing and Conducting Mixed Methods Research*, 2nd edition. Los Angeles, CA: Sage Publications.

Dalai Lama. 1999. *Ethics for a New Millennium*. New York, NY: Berkley.

Delanty, Gerard. 2015. "Europe and the Emergence of Modernity. The Entanglement of Two Reference Cultures." *International Journal for History, Culture and Modernity*, vol. 3, no. 3, pp. 9–34.

Emerald, Womeldorff, and Zajonc, David. 2013. "Newsletter from the Website of the Author: Go Against Yourself || TED* Works – January 28, 2020, based on The Power of TED*." *The Empowerment Dynamic*, by David Emerald Womeldorff. https://powerofted.com/?s=emerald (Last verified on April 25, 2020).

Fehr, Beverly, Sprecher, Susan, and Underwood, Lynn G. 2009. *The Science of Compassionate Love: Theory, Research and Applications.* West Sussex: Blackwell Publishing Ltd.

Gagnon, Brigitte. 2019. *Écosystème relationnel pour une paix intérieure et extérieure: Modèle issu d'une méthode mixte en recherche sur l'approche de l'écoute compassionnelle selon The Compassionate Listening Project.* PhD Dissertation, University of Montreal, October.

Gagnon, Brigitte, and Brodeur, Patrice. 2020. "The Relational Ecosystem for Peace: An Integrated Heart-Based Approach to Peacebuilding." In *Awakening: Exploring Spirituality, Emergent Creativity and Reconciliation.* Edited by Vern Neufeld Redekop and Gloria Neufeld Redekop. Lanham, MD: Lexington.

Galtung, Johan. 2012. "Peace: Negative and Positive." In *The Encyclopedia of Peace Psychology.* Edited by Daniel J. Christie, vol. 2. Blackwell Publishing, and Wiley Online Library, pp. 758–762.

Glaser, Barney G. 2005. "Basic Social Process." *The Grounded Theory Review*, vol. 4, no. 3, pp. 1–15.

Hill Collins, Patricia, and Bilge, Sirma. 2016. *Intersectionality.* Cambridge, UK and Malden, MA: Polity Press.

Jahn, Thomas, Bergmann, Matthias, and Keil, Florian. 2012. "Transdisciplinarity: Between Mainstreaming and Marginalization." *Ecological Economics*, vol. 79, pp. 1–10.

KAICIID. n.d. *Peace Map within the Dialogue Knowledge Hub of the International Dialogue Centre.* https://www.kaiciid.org/node/6621 (Last verified on April 25, 2020).

Karpman, Stephen. 1968. "Fairy Tales and Script Drama Analysis." *Transactional Analysis Bulletin*, vol. 26, no. 7, pp. 39–43.

Koltko-Rivera, Mark E. 2004. "The Psychology of Worldviews." *Review of General Psychology*, vol. 8, no. 1, pp. 3–58.

Kuhn, Thomas. 1962. *The Structure of Scientific Revolutions.* Chicago, IL: The University of Chicago Press.

Leary, Mark R., and Tangney, June Price. 2012. *Handbook of Self and Identity*, 2nd edition. New York, NY: Guilford Press.

Lederach, John Paul. 1995. *Preparing for Peace: Conflict Transformation across Cultures.* Syracuse, NY: Syracuse University Press.

———. 2005. *The Moral Imagination: The Heart and Soul of Building Peace.* Oxford: Oxford University Press.

Lee, Lois. 2015. *Recognizing the Non-Religious: Re-Imagining the Secular.* Oxford: Oxford University Press.

Lee, Raymond L. M. 2006. "Reinventing Modernity: Reflexive Modernization vs Liquid Modernity vs Multiple Modernities." *European Journal of Social Theory*, vol. 9, no. 3, pp. 355–368.

Leydon-Rubenstein, Lori. 2001. "Peace on Earth Begins with Inner Peace." *Annals of the American Psychotherapy Association*, vol. 4, no. 6, p. 24.

Marshall, Katherine. 27-11-2007. Phone interview entitled: *A Discussion with Patrice Brodeur, Associate Professor and Canada Research Chair on Islam, Pluralism, and Globalization, University of Montreal.* https://berkleycenter.georgetown.ed u/interviews/a-discussion-with-patrice-brodeur-associate-professor-and-canada-re search-chair-on-islam-pluralism-and-globalization-university-of-montreal (Last verified on March 9, 2020).

Merdjanova, Ina, and Brodeur, Patrice. 2009. *Religion as a Conversation Starter: Interreligious Dialogue for Peacebuilding in the Balkans.* London: Continuum International Publishing Group.

Morf, Carolyn C., and Mischel, Walter. 2012. "The Self as a Psycho-Social Dynamic Processing System: Toward a Converging Science of Selfhood." In *Handbook of Self and Identity*, 2nd edition. Edited by M. R. Leary and J. P. Tangney. New York, NY: Guilford Press, pp. 21–49.

Myers, Sondra, and Brodeur, Patrice. 2006. *The Pluralist Paradigm: Democracy and Religion in the 21st Century.* Scranton, PA: University of Scranton Press.

McGonigal, Kelly. 2012. *The Neuroscience of Change: A Compassion-Based Program for Personal Transformation.* Sound True Audio Learning Course.

Naugle, David K. 2002. *Worldview: The History of a Concept.* Grand Rapids, MI: W. B. Eerdmans Publishers.

Nicolescu, Basarab. 2014. "The Methodology of Transdisciplinarity." *World Futures: The Journal of New Paradigm Research*, vol. 70, no. 3–4 on 'Transdisciplinarity', pp. 186–199.

———, ed. 2008. *Transdisciplinarity: Theory and Practice.* New York, NY: Hampton Press.

———. 2002. *A Manifesto of Transdisciplinarity.* New York, NY: SUNY Press.

Rockwell, Geoffrey. 2003. *Defining Dialogue: From Socrates to the Internet.* Amherst, NY: Humanity Books (an imprint of Prometheus Books).

Saunders, Harold. 2020. https://msusd.weebly.com/--what-is-dialogue.html (Last verified on April 29, 2020).

Stringer, Ernest T. 2014. *Action Research*, 4th edition. Thousand Oaks, CA: Sage Publications.

Taylor, Charles. 2007. *A Secular Age.* Cambridge, MA: Belknap Press of Harvard University Press.

Thich Nhat Hanh. 2004. *Peace Begins Here: Palestinians and Israelis Listening to Each Other.* Berkeley, CA: Parralax Press.

Toth-Pickl, Carmen, and Vobecká, Jana. 2015. *Peace Mapping Programme IRD Directory Report: Methodology and Data Collection.* http://peacemap.kaiciid.org/ downloads/IRD-Directory-Report.pdf (Last verified on April 25, 2020).

Wilber, Ken. 1996. *A Brief History of Everything.* Boston, MA: Shambhala.

WOSM and KAICIID. 2018. *Building Bridges: Guide for Dialogue Ambassadors.* Kuala Lumpur, Malaysia: WOSM Publications. https://www.scout.org/sites/de fault/files/library_files/Dialogue%20for%20peace_EN_FINAL_2018_WEB.pdf (Last verified on April 25, 2020).

Yankelovich, Daniel. 1999. "Differences between Debate and Dialogue" adapted from table in *The Magic of Dialogue: Transforming Conflict into Cooperation.* New York, NY: Simon & Schuster.

Chapter 7

The Dénouement of Religious Leader Engagement in the Canadian Armed Forces

S. K. Moore

There is an emerging recognition within the international community that a more comprehensive approach (CA) is needed to effectively intervene in violent conflict situations that continue to confront us globally. As a concept, the CA integrates actors from a number of spheres who could potentially contribute to resolving complex issues. This may include essential allied governments, subject matter experts, functional specialists, nongovernmental organizations, and others as the situation may dictate. As can be appreciated, consultation, coordination, and coherence are critical elements to achieving success (*The Comprehensive Approach* 2010, 4).

Increasingly, religious leaders are being added to the above list of actors. Military leaders, in particular, are coming to more fully appreciate the vital role of religion within civilian populations where mission mandates take them. Western societies tend to be more secular in orientation with religion functioning more in the *private space* versus that of the *public*. These distinctions often do not exist in other parts of the world. In such instances, possessing solely a secular sensibility can present challenges when faced with cultures where religion is pervasive, often resulting in a disconnect of sorts. Religion's resurgence as an aspect of conflict has brought this dichotomy to the fore, resulting in an increasing appreciation for approaches more inclusive of the religious component as it relates to conflict mitigation and peace. Hence, there exists a renewed openness to Religious Leader Engagement (RLE) as an operational capability for chaplains and what its employment may achieve for missions.

This chapter will provide background to RLE development, complete with an overview as to its purpose and function. Brief consideration will be given to the place that extreme versions of religion presently hold as drivers of conflict. Its resurgence is increasingly impacting attitudes within the military, and by extension, the chaplain's operational role as a religious leader, resulting in an expanding *hermeneutic of peace* within the spiritual life and ministry of the military chaplaincy. RLE, as an operational capability, has emerged from this development. Significant attention will be given to the RLE Continuum and its various applications within the categories of *Networking, Partnering*, and *Peacebuilding.*

Of further import to the strategic nature of RLE is its relation to national peacebuilding in a whole-of-government (government departments and agencies collaborating in nation-building efforts) context. Illustrating the *strategic social spaces* of religious peacebuilding at the national level was the experience of UN Special Advisor for Peacebuilding and Development (APD), Ron Kraybill, in Lesotho, where a peaceful transfer of power was made possible.

RELIGION: CONFLICT AND PEACE

We begin by examining religion as a driver of conflict in today's operational environments (OEs). While this concept raises many questions about what is "true religion" and what does it mean for it to "drive" a conflict, we can start with basic observations that religious language is used by people who are violent. Religious leaders play a role in legitimizing violence, and religious bodies are associated in a partisan way with groups in conflict. Against this backdrop we can discern an expanding hermeneutic of peace for chaplains.

Religion as a Driver of Conflict in Today's Operational Environments

While purely religious conflict is rare, there is a rise in hostilities with explicit reference to religion. For those implicated, the clash frequently becomes a struggle between "good" and "evil," rendering violence a sacred duty (Hertog 2010, 10–11). Today's co-optation of religion as a means of deepening existing cultural and political fault lines aids in fueling the justification of militancy and terrorism (Appleby and Cizik 2010, 17). Militant extremism motivated by a religious imperative embraces violence as a divine duty or sacramental act. Holding to markedly different notions of legitimization and justification than their secular counterparts, these organizations indulge without compunction in greater bloodshed and destruction than terrorist groups with solely a political agenda. Noting the role of religious leadership, anthropologist Pauletta Otis notes that "the complexities of conflict may be compounded further when religious leaders who, with their incendiary language, contribute to the congealing of adversarial identity markers, exacerbating the polarization of communities even more" (2004, 20). Appleby puts it this way: "Rather than break down barriers, in short, religion often fortifies them . . . Constructed as inseparable from ethnic and linguistic traits, religion in such settings lends them a transcendent depth and dignity. Extremists thus invoke religion to legitimate discrimination and violence against groups of a different race or language" (2000, 62).

As a vehicle of influence, religion is known for its efficacy, frequently exploited by political leaders prone to supplement their anemic rhetoric with religious ideology as a means to motivate local populations to "extreme patriotism and violent behavior" (Gopin 2009, 37–38). In reference to the Bosnian war, Appleby makes specific mention of how religion, wed to ethnicity, became an identity marker for violence toward the other. He writes that "the demonizers relied on religion to provide 'primordial' and 'age-old' justifications for people intent on hating one another" (2000, 63). The Islamic State, otherwise known as Daesh, perpetrated horrific violence in the name of religion on a scale unknown in living memory. They brought a pathology all of their own.

Realizing operational objectives is paramount. Key to mission success is the recognition that Indigenous populations are the *primary* centers of gravity. An insurgency cannot survive amid the hostile terrain of an unreceptive public (*Land Force* 2008, 5–11).[1] Of import here are actors within Indigenous populations as centers of gravity, a term defined as "strengths that create effects; therefore, they are better defined in terms of people—individuals or groups—that can create effects" (ibid.). "Public opinion," "public will," and "strength of national purpose" are all factors of the abstract and moral perspectives of centers of gravity (English et al. 2005, 318). Shared religious and/or ideological goals serve as centers of gravity, generating a common purpose that can elicit fervency beyond what military leaders and their campaigns can create. As actors within Indigenous populations, religious leaders present as centers of gravity ("Canadian Forces Operations" 2005).

Military chaplains often find themselves in OEs where dynamics such as these have been playing out for an extended period of time. The chaplain interface with religious communities of local populations has always been an integral part of the overall operational experience. Increasingly, engagement of this nature has taken on strategic import. How one responds as an *agent of peace* has been the subject of much debate in recent years, resulting in considerable reflection on the *hermeneutics* of such engagement.

An Expanding Hermeneutic of Peace for Chaplains

Religious traditions constantly face new questions and contextual challenges summoning ardent reflection with respect to sacred texts and belief, leading to new self-understanding and orientation toward the world in which people live. Each religious community remakes itself in light of their present circumstances, something that continues from one generation to the next. In the extreme, the vagaries of war influence such *hermeneutical* processes for faith groups confronted with its banality and the evil it unleashes on all concerned, regardless of loyalties. As such, groups look to their central stories, institutions, traditions, texts, rituals, precepts, and values in a quest to grasp what it means to be a community of faith confronted with situations of extreme violence and how best to live out that faith in light of such realities. R. Scott Appleby notes that "the legal, theological and spiritual resources of a religious tradition . . . are relevant only to the extent that they shape religion as it is lived on the ground, where text and tradition transform, and are transformed by, the concrete realities of daily life" (2003, 239–240). It behooves religious leaders, scholars, and theologians to "seek the good between the inherited wisdom and the specific contemporary situation" (ibid.).

As a multifaith community, military chaplaincy is comprised of a number of religious traditions, each with its own understanding and interpretation of belief based upon the sacred texts and teachings of their particular faith expression. At the core of this interfaith collaboration resides a *hermeneutics of peace* that recognizes peace and justice as sacred priorities to be advanced by peaceable means where possible (Little 2007, 438). Religious leaders in uniform, men and women of faith, often witness horrific acts of violence and its effects in conflict and postconflict environments. These are manifest in the tragic loss of life and livelihood, often accompanied by the staggering movements of refugees in search of safety. Circumstances in time and space such as these challenge one's belief and time-honored traditions, precipitating new self-understandings of chaplaincy.

Demonstrative of this expanding hermeneutics of peace is the impulse among chaplains to draw on the understanding, imagination, and requisite values of their collective faith traditions to aid conflicting groups in rehumanizing the *other*. Hermeneutically, this impulse to engage civilian populations is visible in its many forms among those struggling to rebuild their lives either in the midst of conflict or in its wake. From the humanitarian assistance of earlier times—something that continues today—to building relation with the religious *other(s)* through dialogue—thus spanning the divide of estranged communities (encounter)—to the subsequent collaborative and complementary activities that engender trust and cooperation between estranged groups, chaplains continue to engage the religious *other* as agents of peace. A brief introduction to the OE is in order here as a means of acquainting the reader with the milieu of contemporary operations.

SITUATING RLE

First, the OE has become more complex with an awareness that intervention is in the context of Joint Interagency Multinational including the Public (JIMP). Second, within this OE, there is a continuum of RLE. Third, picking up on one aspect of this continuum we look at the role of networking—building relationships—in conjunction with Religious Area Assessment (RAA). Associated with this, fourth, is the notion that chaplains function as boundary spanners.

The Operational Environment: JIMP

The RLE construct finds its origins in the public space of the JIMP principle, "a [Canadian Armed Forces (CAF)] descriptor that identifies the various categories of players (e.g. organizations, interest groups, institutions) that inhabit the broad environment in which military operations take place" (Gizewski and Rostek 2007, 8).

The environment that JIMP (see Figure 7.1) defines is that of the CA in Operations: "J" represents Joint or the combined nature of operations where the marshaling of different military elements are used in a complementary

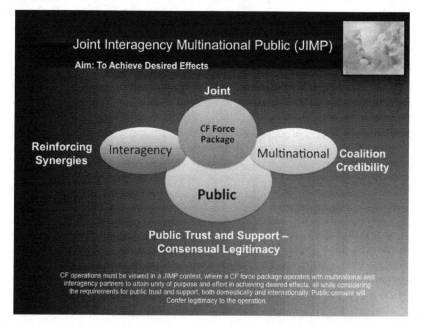

Figure 7.1 Schematic of Joint Interagency Multinational Public Concept (JIMP). (Moore 2013, 109. Used by permission, Canadian Armed Forces Department of Army Doctrine.)

fashion to accomplish the mission; "I" stands for Interagency, which is the whole-of-government domain; "M" or Multinational speaks to international will—numbers of nations coming together under the auspices of the UN, NATO, or other coalitions, bringing to bear all of their combined resources to create stability and effect change where needed; and P, or the Public space, hosts a number of organizations and activities in operations, of which the Indigenous population therein is undoubtedly the most consequential.

Local religious leaders are centers of gravity within Indigenous populations—middle-range actors who, in non-Western societies, where the lines of separation between faith and the public space are markedly less defined, enjoy elevated profiles at community and regional levels. This owes its origins to the seemingly seamless nature existing between religious communities and local culture and, at times, politics. Due to the common ground of the faith perspective, chaplains are able to contribute much as a result of their ability to move with relative ease within religious circles. The following is an overview of the operational role of chaplains.

The Operational Role of Chaplains

The term "Operational Ministry" describes the overall role of chaplains in Operations: in support of the troops and among local Indigenous populations. The primary purpose for a chaplain's presence with a deploying contingent is to administer the sacraments and to provide pastoral support for the troops— the base of the pyramid designated as *Internal Operational Ministry* in figure 7.2. Also benefiting mission mandates is the depicted *External Operational Ministry* that sees the future role of chaplains extended to the strategic realm of (1) advising commanders in terms of the Religious Area Analysis (RAA) of an Area of Operations (AO); and (2) engendering trust and establishing cooperation within communities by engaging local and regional religious leaders—the domain of RLE, spanning in gradations all three categories of *networking, partnering,* and *peacebuilding.*

The RLE Continuum

The emergence of RLE may be viewed through the lens of complexity theory. On the level of human interaction, few milieus present the complexities of today's conflict zones. The numbers of interacting elements are staggering: multinational militaries, the accompanying intergovernmental organizations, and the endless stream of insurgents that come from near and far to oppose them; stressed national, regional, and local governments; and diverse populations presenting a kaleidoscope of political, tribal, cultural, and religious elements. Compounding such complexity further is the ubiquitous presence of international organizations, faith-based and secular nongovernmental

Figure 7.2 Operational Ministry. (Moore 2013,102).

organizations, both domestic and foreign. These and more are known to contemporary OEs.

In recent decades, asymmetric warfare has eclipsed the more conventional forms of earlier times. Military leaders are endeavoring to adapt to not only the unorthodox tactics of insurgents but also to the increasingly interactive OE in which numerous entities function with varying degrees of command and control. Concomitantly, religious extremism of unparalleled fervency has erupted as a dimension of conflict further challenging Western approaches to achieving peace. Enigmatic as well is the upsurge of targeting civilian populations in the West by Islamist extremists from within their own citizenry. As complex adaptive systems theory delineates, all of the above elements are interacting, out of which are emerging some rather unexpected creative methods of grappling with the intense circumstances confronting Western societies. As an operational capability for chaplains, RLE is demonstrative of emergent creativity—an impulse initially visible on an ad hoc basis but opening up the *adjacent possible* of a defined capability in the midst of complexity's interactive elements (see Figure 7.2 for how RLE, an external ministry has emerged out of internal operational ministries).

Today military leaders increasingly acknowledge the strategic merit of building rapport and establishing cooperation with the religious segment of society as critical to the accomplishment of mission mandates.

The RLE Continuum highlights the full spectrum of operational ministry that may engage the services of the chaplain. *Networking, Partnering*, and, in some instances, *Peacebuilding* are depicted here as larger categories under which more specific endeavors are listed. By no means an exhaustive list, however, where employed among local clerics these have proven to be effective means of garnering the much-needed trust of these revered community leaders—a significant development for a more CA to operations.

Networking: RAA

The intent of RAA in operations is to determine the basis for what people do and why they do it with respect to religion. As a capability, deploying chaplains increasingly possess the skills to accumulate and categorize information relating to the religious practices and traditions of Indigenous populations within an AO. This information is gathered from as wide a range of resources as practicably possible in the amount of time allotted prior to deployment. In a very real sense, this analysis remains a living document once *networking* among local religious leaders and their communities becomes a reality, security permitting.

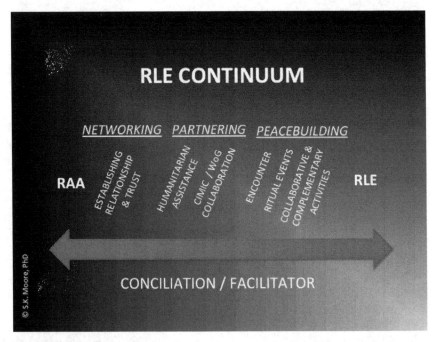

Figure 7.3 RLE Continuum. Diagram by author.

As credentialed clerics, the advanced theological training of chaplains, supplemented by additional skills development, positions them to better interpret the nuances of religious belief that often escape detection—something that could be very costly to a mission. In grasping something of the meaning and reality of the faith perspective, chaplains are more apt to appreciate how the belief system of the grassroots person/community may color their response to given mission initiatives, plans of action, troop movements, and so on. The nature of command often necessitates sending troops into harm's way. As such, the availability of all information pertinent to the decision-making process is vital. Advising commanders of the possible pitfalls or backlashes of given courses of action with respect to religious communities is a crucial aspect of their role (for more information, see Moore 2013, ch. 4).

For this reason, *networking* among religious communities in an AO is an integral aspect of RAA as chaplains engage local faith group leaders, security permitting. It is not uncommon to see *relationship building* with its engendered *trust* develop into the chaplain/religious leader *encounter* becoming a *safe space* for these community leaders to share their concerns and aspirations. RLE activities will naturally flow out of the RAA conducted by chaplains. In this sense, one is built upon the other—both are necessary to the full scope of engagement among local religious communities.

Chaplains as Boundary Spanners

Religious leaders in their own right, military chaplains function quite naturally as *boundary spanners*, moving with relative ease among local leaders and religious communities—security permitting. Credentialed clerics, the training and orientation of the chaplain equips them to better grasp the religious impulses of local communities. If supported, chaplain intervention may mitigate conflict and ameliorate relationships between alienated groups. They share common ground with their local counterparts, deemed trusted individuals—"people of the book" according to the tenets of Islamic teaching.

Of consequence as well is the oft-held perception by religious and community leaders of the global south that Westerners are secularist, and, consequently, a threat to their faith and way of life. Subsequently, the tendency by the religious is to avoid engaging "Westerners," be they military or civilian. This was the experience of Foreign Affairs Canada Political Advisor (PolAd), Gavin Buchan, during his early months in Kandahar, Afghanistan. An experienced diplomat, he acknowledged that the reluctance of the religious leaders of Kandahar Province to engage him in dialogue was due mainly to their concern of his secular views and the adverse influence these views might have. It wasn't until the CAF chaplain, Imam Demiray, arrived that progress was made in opening up a means of communication with the Ulema Council, a body of Islamic scholars (Mullahs) serving as an advisory body to the Governor of Kandahar Province. These exchanges resulted in the Shi'a presence resuming its role on to the predominantly Sunni Ulema Council, effectively bringing them out of isolation. (For a complete account of this documented case study, see Moore 2013, 185–206.)

Chaplains are often able to be a bridge to these influential community leaders, breaking the way for meaningful dialogue with other mission members—military or civilian. It is a great temptation to view RLE as a means of leverage, perceiving a chaplain's relationship with a regional/ local religious leader as a source of crucial information. In such instances, the nuancing of this capability becomes critical. Depending on the OE, communication with religious authorities may be across religious identity boundaries, that is, Christian and Muslim. Imposing undue expectations on what can only be described as fragile relations may jeopardize any engendered trust, transparency, and mutual respect—relations that are often painstakingly established over time. As has been earlier noted, earned trust once lost is extremely difficult to regain. Such is the danger of *instrumental-ism*—reductionism that sees such engagement simply as a device designed to produce an outcome. The benevolence of the actor is at the heart of RLE. This is not to suggest that Command should refrain from communicating to local community or religious leaders through the chaplain. To the con-trary—conveying pertinent information and offering support are always appropriate means of aiding local populations. Chaplains are a natural conduit in this regard.

RLE IN ACTION

"Engagement" is a term implying action. In this section, we deconstruct the range of actions necessary in effective implementation of RLE. Of primary importance is identifying the moderate voice of religion, particularly middle-range actors. Second is partnering as the chaplain engages with civic person-nel in the local population and in the context of Civilian-Military Cooperation (CIMIC). Peacebuilding actions start with encounters that build trust and establish commitments to peaceful coexistence; these actions may lead to ritual events that may range from low-key and relatively private to highly visible public events. There are an array of complementary activities oriented toward internal trust and validation and collaborative activities that build per-sonal trust and contribute to integration. Finally, chaplains weave conciliating and facilitating into the "engagement" dimension of RLE.

Identifying the Moderate Voice of Religion: Middle-Range Actors

Identifying the moderate voices among religious leaders results from *networking* has led to *partnering* and, in some instances, actual *peacebuilding* initiatives. These are faith group leaders—community leaders—often desirous of avoiding conflict; they look for means to reduce tensions and diminish the intransigent positions that can undermine good relations between identity groups. Known as middle-range actors, they enjoy the confidence of the grass roots while moving freely at the higher levels of leadership within their own communities. Their ease of movement affords them relationships that are professional, institutional, and sometimes formal, while other ties are more a matter of friendship and acquaintance. Hence, they have a high degree of social capital within communities (Lederach 1997, 41–42). More notable still, "middle-range actors tend to have pre-existing relationships with counterparts that cut across the lines of conflict within the setting . . . a network or relationships that cut across the identity divisions within the society" (ibid., 42).

Religious leaders are undoubtedly among the more dominant centers of gravity within Indigenous populations—middle-range actors, where, in non-Western societies, the lines of separation between faith and the public space are markedly less defined. They are often revered individuals at community and regional levels. Such esteem owes its origins to the almost seamless nature existing between religious communities and local culture and, at times, politics.

Partnering: The Chaplain and Civic Engagement

As *civic engagement,* the intention of RLE is to see *networking* become *partnering* as relationships are established and friendship deepens with local religious leader and their communities. Local religious leaders are community leaders and, as such, enjoy the confidence of the people. They are uniquely positioned to identify where the greatest needs of the community lie. Through authentic relationships established by chaplains, humanitarian programming may be identified.

Once a given initiative is identified, the role for the chaplain remains one of a *trusted friend* to the religious leaders but segues to becoming *facilitator* as CIMIC teams or whole-of-government members are introduced to the local leadership. Out of necessity, the chaplain remains connected to any such endeavor. Building sufficient levels of trust requires time. The objective of such engagement is not to look for "quick fixes" or "bandage solutions" that will unravel if constant "life support" is not there. The long view must be considered as the most effective approach to achieving lasting results.

Partnering—CIMIC

Operational effectiveness is achieved in a number of ways, CIMIC being one such mechanism. The objective of CIMIC operations and projects is to maintain maximum possible cooperation with civilian authorities, organizations, agencies, and the local population in a commander's AO. In addition, CIMIC programming creates an interface between the local populace and deployed contingents—a two-way information exchange that improves perception while enabling commanders to remain informed. Funds are allocated for various projects that look to enhance the effectiveness of organizations and improve living conditions for local populations (NATO Standard AJP 2013).

I was present on one such occasion at the Kandahar Provincial Reconstruction Team (PRT) in 2006 when a number of new Toyota Crew Cab trucks were presented to the local Kandahar Constabulary of the Afghanistan National Police (ANP). Media, provincial, and city dignitaries and members of the local community were in attendance. Speeches were made, and to the delight of those present, CAF Capt. Imam Suleyman Demiray offered prayers. To express their appreciation, the ANP leadership arranged for a banquet to be held in the PRT compound following the ceremony. Caterers arrived early in the morning to begin the food preparation and cooking of goat meat. By late afternoon, all was prepared and the Canadians and Afghans sat down together to enjoy breaking bread together—the building of relationships and establishing of trust . . . community building.

The significance of RLE at this CIMC event was the effect that Imam Suleyman Demiray had on the Afghans in attendance and the subliminal message that he portrayed. The Imam, as a member of the Canadian contingent, expressed inclusivity and the interconnectedness of all humanity regardless of race, language, or creed. The public appearance of this Muslim cleric in uniform before an Islamic assembly aided in dispelling the long-held belief that Christian and Muslim are foes on the world stage, a snapshot of the pluralism of the Canadian cultural mosaic. This Canadian Forces Muslim chaplain became an opening through which the self-made room for the other within, creating that liminal space where something new came into view out of the mist of misunderstood identities and ideologies. *Mimetically modeled* before this assembled body was the will to embrace, as Demiray's embracing of his Christian brothers and sisters testified to the possibility that in authentic relationship with God and with the other, new experiences . . . new understanding of self and other could be found. Reciprocity of acceptance was exemplified, as Christian and Muslim alike probed the liminal space of a common humanity and common ground upon which to build relationship (for more on this see, Moore and Demiray 2007, 5–8).

Engaging the *other* is all about building relation. Often a prominent local religious leader is a voice of reason within their community and frequently among other faith groups, since they are able to move across ethnoreligious lines easily. Lederach writes, "The centrality of relationship provides the context and potential for breaking violence, for it brings people into the pregnant moments of the moral imagination: the space of recognition that ultimately the quality of our life is dependent on the quality of life of *others*" (Lederach 2005, 35). Chaplains are well positioned to aid CIMIC operations by engaging local religious leaders and their communities.

Peacebuilding: Encounter—the Fragile We of Working Trust and Coexistence

Facilitating, the bringing together of local leadership, most often religious, is the essence of *encounter*. Creating that safe space for dialogue where none has existed provides occasion for altered perspectives to emerge. It is in *encounter* that the rigidity of long-held stereotypes and the constant barrage of propaganda begin to lose their strength. Here one does not simply see the *other* from one's own perspective but such exchanges facilitate viewing oneself through the eyes of the *other*—a double vision of sorts.[2] Where the willingness to engage the *other* begins, a *rehumanizing* of the *other* has a chance to emerge—where the "us" versus "them" softens to the "fragile we."

Peacebuilding: Ritual Events

The building of relation within conflict zones among estranged religious leaders and their faith group communities is exceedingly more than good public relations. Of significance are the occasions where the ritual and symbol of relation are incorporated into schemes within local religious expression and custom. Having established trust, such structures lend themselves to bringing together principals, thus creating opportunities where a renewed vision of the other and *mutuality* begin to come to the fore.

Narratives attuned to one's understanding of life, as well as the meaning of one's relation to the *other*, are often fashioned through ritual and symbol events. These may be *formal* or *informal*. A shared ritual, such as breaking bread together (*informal*), speaks of common culture and heritage; a joint religious celebration (*formal*) underscores identifiable and agreed-upon universals. Such events provide a forum where positive aspects of history may be highlighted; formerly, shared narratives may be revisited. These, in turn, evoke the potential for creating new and positive narratives together: *mutuality*.

As relationships develop and the process of reconciliation deepens, the carefully selected commemoration of sites significant among all groups may further nurture shared narratives: a new community building designated for a multicultural purpose; the dedication of a monument that speaks to a shared history and common future; a memorial park that recalls collective suffering as well as a hopeful tomorrow; and so on. Such ritual and/or ceremonial events among estranged religious communities are highly symbolic and accomplish much in terms of creating meaning as new and shared narratives emerge. Known as *rituals of inversion*, it is the hope that during shared events of this nature strongly held stereotypes of the *other* may be viewed differently. When the religious leaders of opposing ethnoreligious groups come together in public ritual events, at least for the duration of the event, predominant power structures are turned on their head. It may be that those in attendance will leave with the subliminal message of peace and fraternity that will eventually work its way into the conscious.

That being said, care must be taken that shared ritual events are not co-opted for other purposes than what they are intended. These are authentic moments in the life of religious leaders and their communities. Participation in such an event is offered in sincerity, having emerged out of established trust with the chaplain.

Complementary Activities: Toward Internal Trust and Validation

Peacebuilding activities may also take the form of *complementary activities*. Here a chaplain's support may be offered to a local religious leader experiencing a degree of isolation within his or her own faith community due to a desire for more amicable relations across ethnoreligious boundaries—often an unpopular aspiration where intercommunal conflict is a reality. Together, ways may be determined for how more openness toward peaceful themes within the community may be advanced. Over time *internal trust* may develop for religious leaders and their concepts of peace and tolerance for the *other*—validation.

In such instances, the chaplain may aid the local community in facilitating Humanitarian Aid and/or CIMIC projects. Improving life for a local population may also carry with it the benefit of enhancing the credibility of the cleric in question, potentially engendering trust and greater openness to other initiatives.

Religious leaders of moderate voice are invaluable to the furtherance of peace processes in OEs. With respect to *complementary activities*, it may be that during a given operational tour(s), this may be the sum total of what may be accomplished—foundational activity . . . an investment in the present and the future.

Collaborative Activities: Toward Personal Trust and Integration

In circumstances where security and opportunity have been favorable, commanders have authorized chaplains to undertake more intentional *peacebuilding* activities among religious communities. Dialogue and, in some instances, collaborative activities have resulted. Social psychologists currently focusing on the dynamics of intergroup reconciliation note the saliency of *supra-ordinate* goals to such processes. These are jointly agreed-upon objectives that benefit both communities, yet neither group can accomplish them alone, achievable only through *inter*communal cooperation. With thorough needs analysis—an evaluation process facilitated by the chaplain involving the local religious leadership and military/civilian program developers (CA)—a shared project with the right fit may be introduced. As such, nascent integration takes root. Through cooperation of this nature, an identity more inclusive of the *other* begins to develop. It is in such an atmosphere that conflict is transcended, new narratives are written, and the healing of memory begins (Baron 2008, 275–98).

Extended seasons of collaboration create opportunities for building trust. Whereas some contend that trust is a prerequisite for cooperation, field research suggests that it may also be a product of collaborative activity—representing a cross-section of people joining together in common cause (Kramer and Carnevale 2003, 432–50). Establishing trust may also be a way of beginning emotional healing, a level of reconciliation necessitating a higher level of trust: it moves beyond the stage of monitoring if commitments are being honored (coexistence), to "resembl[ing] the trust of friends or family," commonly referred to as *interpersonal* or simply *personal trust* (integration). Through continued interaction, old attitudes are eclipsed by new perceptions of the *other*, an internalization that "over time" leaves its mark on identity. Although old frictions may rear its head—eventualities over which one has no control—the ties forged through such intercommunal collaboration leaves those involved less vulnerable to such situational changes (Kelman 2008, 25)

Conciliation and Facilitation

Conciliation describes a third-party intervening where a dispute has alienated groups, and, by so doing, it results in "correcting misunderstandings, reducing fear and distrust, and generally improving communication between them" (MCDC 2014, 100). Such intervention can lead to dispute settlement or make way for a more intense mediation process. Padres naturally gravitate to building relationships and establishing trust with local religious leaders, thus improving communication and understanding. In the various OEs where this has occurred, "conflict transformation took the form of conciliation" (MCDC 2017, 187). As such, they become a safe space for local religious leaders to share their story, a vital feature of conciliation, improved relations, and an integral component of the reconciliation process. Faith group leaders given to moderate thinking are often found in stressed societies where simmering conflict has yet to break out in overt violence.

Building relationships of trust fosters networks within the OE (ibid., 127). Again, facilitation is a natural role for chaplains, creating "entry points" for other whole-of-government partners—opportunities that would not have otherwise occurred. In some instances, these exchanges have become transformative, as presenting difficulties have been better understood, leading to movement in restoring relations.

The above has been an introduction to RLE, a chaplain operational capability now being integrated into Canadian Army training. It stands as a foray into the complex environment of operations and the religious dimension that await deploying military contingents—a competency that continues to adapt to essential training needs in preparation for application in OEs.

However, how RLE is defined and enacted continues to expand, playing a role in the emerging field of religious peacebuilding. Of encouragement are the increasing numbers of experiences where religious leaders on the national stage have intervened in the midst of political turmoil within their borders, successfully resolving impending crises for their people. Lesotho is one such case where the nation's religious leaders reached out to their government leaders locked in a power struggle on the verge of overt street violence. Of particular note here is the whole-of-government involvement of the UN Special Advisor for Peacebuilding and Development as facilitator. This final section will consider RLE in application, offering the reconciling process enacted in Lesotho as a lens through which to view the efficacy of the Strategic Spaces of Religion.

RLE IN WHOLE-OF-GOVERNMENT APPLICATION: CREATING SPACE IN CIVIL SOCIETY FOR REFRAMING CONFLICT

In 2013, the Economic Community of West African States, the African Union, and the UNDP convened a conference where declarations were signed that committed two of the regional organizations to establishing national infrastructures for peace—the Accra Declaration (U2P 2016, 106).

Of import to this accomplishment were the two years of prior involvement (2010–2012) of Ron Kraybill, then UN Special Advisor for Peacebuilding and Development (APD). The following account draws on his unpublished case study of his time as ADP in Lesotho, depicting the facilitative role he played in the mediation process initiated by the nation's principal faith group leaders (Kraybill 2014; see also Moore 2014a, b).

By way of context, for a number of years President Pakalitha Mosisili of Lesotho and Opposition Leader Tom Thabane were at odds over who should rightfully be governing the country, resulting in a deadlock in Parliament. Unable to resolve their differences, threats of "returning to the streets" to find a lasting solution began to surface, conjuring up fears of the rioting of 1998 with its significant loss of life. Recognizing the imminent danger of the country descending into violence, Kraybill learned of the efforts of the national-level religious leaders: Roman Catholic and Protestant, together representative of 90 percent of the population. The following is a succinct summary of his facilitative and, ultimately, successful efforts in aiding the religious leaders of Lesotho to avert overt violence, arriving at a lasting solution to the crisis. Three additional themes relating to *religion's strategic spaces* will be offered as a means to further amplify how religion's levers may be applied at the various levels of society—a peaceful alternative to violence.

Religion's Strategic Spaces

Some would argue that one of the more salient aspects of religion is the social capital it enjoys within civil society. If such privilege does exist, it is, of course, dependent on certain causal factors within a given culture that create such possibilities. John D. Brewer, Gareth I. Higgins, and Francis Teeny offer clarity to the murky waters of implicating religion in the resolving of conflict, when, normally, the tendency is for many to give such consideration a wide berth (Brewer et al. 2010). They categorize a number of strategic social spaces within civil society that potentially lend themselves to peacemaking and peacebuilding. The intent here is to adapt their research insights to the Lesotho experience. In particular, the following three areas relating to strategic social spaces will be examined for their value to RLE as an emerging construct and capability in operations: social, intellectual, and institutional spaces.

Social Spaces

It is in the "social strategic space" of encounter that religious leaders of moderate voice are able to envision together what others cannot at any particular moment. For many, it would be unthinkable to initiate dialogue with those of an opposing group in search of common ground, much less consider altering prevailing societal conditions that disadvantage another group.

Precipitating the religious leader involvement, explains Kraybill, was the exit of former Botswana president Keitumetse Masire in 2009. After two years of negotiations, it was evident that the *Track I* approach of a high-level clout mediator had failed. As *Track II* mediators, the national religious leaders held credibility and grassroots influence equal to or greater than that of the parties in conflict and the *Track I* mediators.

As noted above, Lesotho's national religious leaders—middle-range actors—enjoyed the confidence of the grass roots while moving freely at the

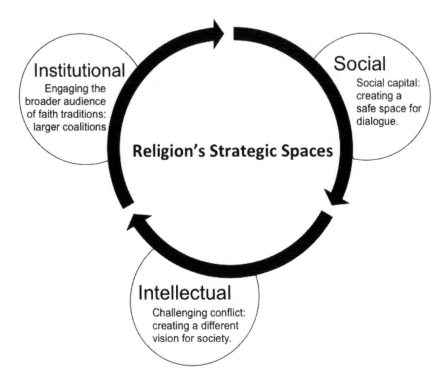

Figure 7.4   Religion's Strategic Spaces. Diagram by author.

higher levels of leadership within their nation. This afforded them relationships that were professional, institutional, some formal, while other ties were
more a matter of friendship and acquaintance, hence a high degree of social
capital within communities. A country 90 percent Christian, preexisting relationships across denominational lines spanned any identity group divisions
within society.

Contributing to their social capital as well, these faith group leaders held
moral authority that simply could not be ignored. Their prominence and
credibility within Lesotho civil society was due largely in part because they
were not politicians and, therefore, not aligned with any one party. Clergy
in Lesotho are widely respected and the Heads of Churches had for some
years prior to this recent impasse played a constructive, nonpartisan role in
resolving an earlier national crisis. Thus, when the nation's principal religious leaders "invited" Mosisili and Thabane to meet and talk, they came.
In fact, they had little choice, for the clergy carried clout of their own—that
of moral authority. To be seen as rejecting a good faith effort for peace by
these highly regarded spiritual leaders would have been detrimental to their
public image.

Intellectual Spaces

Perhaps one of the greatest contributions religion can make to facilitating societal change is its capacity to provide a forum in which to challenge the terms by which a given conflict is understood and to bring forward a different vision for a new society. Religious organizations within civil society constitute as *intellectual spaces* where societal injustice may be opposed.

In Lesotho, the religious leaders employed creative diverse conflict resolution approaches adapted to the context and the requirements of the moment. The initiative, chaired by the Heads of Churches, used tactics rare in traditional diplomacy: a creative blend of relationship and consensus-building, problem analysis, moral and spiritual suasion, input by experts, and appeals to the public that would have been impossible to pull off by mediators based in regional or international political organizations.

These efforts included:

- hours of open dialogue among heads of political parties;
- a series of plenary sessions to define a list of "issues of convergence and divergence";
- prayers at the beginning and end of negotiation sessions that often became robust exhortation for peace;
- two patriotic joint gatherings at Thaba Bosiu, home of the nation's founder, King Moshoeshoe, to honor his renowned commitment to peace;
- hearty meals enjoyed by all in the middle of days of talks; and
- negotiating a code of conduct and signing it before one of the world's leading moral figures.

In traditional diplomacy, it would be rare to use any of the above in mediation; the Heads of Churches built their work around them. Not only are long-held stereotypes of the *other* challenged during such exchanges, leading to a gradual *rehumanizing* of the *other*, encounter of this nature provides the *intellectual space* for the reframing of present hostilities and structurally conceiving how life could improve for their respective peoples—such is positive peace.

Institutional Spaces

It is in the *institutional space* of religious organizations where the intellectual challenges of change are enacted, often extending beyond the local to regional and sometimes international levels in terms of support.

The Lesotho experience reveals that nonstate actors can also be a potent force for peace and stability. Their employment of unconventional approaches to resolving the impasse created opportunities that reached large swaths of the populace— *the institutional space*. These included Sunday morning worship, weekly funerals, local workshops, and community events.

Clergy and development workers of Lesotho were connected to the grass roots in Lesotho in ways few politicians could rival. In the decades since independence, during which politicians repeatedly disappointed, civil society leaders, in contrast, grew in credibility.

This is not to suggest that the religious leader effort did not meet with opposition. Certain politicians opposed to the transfer of power used *provocateurs* at the grass roots in an effort to undermine the peace effort. The Lesotho religious leaders fell back on their authority as Heads of Churches and civil society organizations to advocate restraint and reason among the people. They accomplished this through prepared statements, press conferences, sermons, newspaper ads, and workshops.

They reminded the public repeatedly over the several years of the mediation effort that peaceful agreement was the goal and that dialogue and negotiation was the path required.

Even in the tense final months of campaigning, when a split in the ruling party, the killing of a key opposition leader, and stoning at two rallies put everyone on edge, the vast majority of the key city of Basotho remained calm.

Of significance here is the recognition that religious groups are the most effective when they are part of a general coalition dedicated to future change. With such an integrated approach to whole-of-government initiatives, religious leaders and the groups they represent often emerge as role models and drivers of the process of transformation. The religious leaders of Lesotho saw their efforts enhanced by the contribution of other coalition members, including

- the UN House used for talks,
- the Deepening Democracy Program,
- support to the Independent Electoral Commission,
- staff strategically selected to assist the process, and
- experts in electoral law to aid in guiding upcoming elections.

A key strategy of the Heads of Churches was to assure that the parties went on record with points of agreement or commitments to high standards of conduct. To incentivize the political leaders to abide by their agreement they arranged for the 2009 signing a statement at THABA BOSIU—birthplace of the nation, thus solidifying their resolve to settle their differences through dialogue. Though this pledge looked meaningless for many months as attendance at talks waned, the Heads of Churches leveraged it skillfully at key points to remind political leaders of their responsibility.

Again, *institutional space* became a conduit for conciliatory public events. When things took a turn toward violence in the months just prior to the election, church leaders sponsored Archbishop Tutu's visit with financial and technical support from the UN. In his presence, the parties signed a code of conduct for the election season, pledging to peacefully accept the outcome of election results. Church leaders published pictures and the signed pledge in full-page newspaper ads over the following weeks.

Soon after the election, while memories of an unblemished day were still fresh, church leaders again convened a meeting with politicians. With the threat of a hung Parliament and a prolonged period of uncertainty looming, they reminded the politicians of their pledges. One by one, politicians rose and without qualification gave their endorsements of the election outcomes. This removed a common cause of difficulty following past elections—the tendency of Lesotho's politicians to call into question the legitimacy of entire elections on the basis of technicalities.

With the assistance of an outside expert—Ron Kraybill, UN Special Advisor on Peacebuilding and Development—Lesotho's national religious leaders came together for the common good of their people. Together they were able to mediate a peaceful settlement to a precarious impasse between the incumbent and opposition leader, leading the way to a peaceful election and safe transition of government on June 8, 2012.

CONCLUSION

RLE is a relatively new chaplain operational capability, having emerged quite naturally alongside the primary role of caring for the hundreds of troops with whom they deploy on *expeditionary operations*. Advising Command of the nuances of local religious practice in an AO through well-researched analysis (RAA) has become a welcome resource. Engaging more moderate religious leaders with the view to engendering trust (RLE) and, when possible, promoting dialogue across ethnoreligious boundaries is also being viewed as contributing to greater security.

RLE may also factor into *humanitarian assistance* in the form of *domestic operations* where a natural disaster has occurred necessitating the deployment of military personnel to aid civil authorities unable to cope with the magnitude of a presenting emergency. Interfacing with the leadership of civilian populations is crucial to meeting needs. Religious communities normally have infrastructure at their disposal in the form of large buildings often inclusive of kitchens. As such, numbers of those in need of shelter may find makeshift, yet, readily available accommodation. Chaplains are well positioned to facilitate such arrangements with religious leadership during emergencies.

Salient as well to this discussion has been the significance of the *strategic social spaces* of religion to whole-of-government endeavors: *social, intellectual*, and *institutional*. Collaboration between prominent national/ regional religious leaders and diplomats as a means to mitigate or resolve a crisis may prove to be of strategic merit.

NOTES

1. Again, the authors reinforce the strategic import of local populations to COIN operations (COIN is the abbreviation for Counter-Insurgency Operations): "Generally, within a COIN campaign, strategic centres of gravity are populations and their support of the campaign. The population of the region or nation in question is a centre of gravity over which the insurgents and the COIN elements will fight for support." *Land Force: Counter-Insurgency Operations* 508.6 b. (3), 5–11. See http://info.publicintelligence.net/CanadaCOIN.pdf.

2. For more on Volf's "double vision," see Chapter Three, Part 3, "Reconciliation as Embrace," dissertation of Major S. K. Moore entitled, *Military Chaplains as Agents of Peace: The Theology and Praxis of Reconciliation in Stability Operations* (Ottawa, Canada: Saint Paul University, 2008), 117–43.

REFERENCES

Appleby, R. Scott. 2000. *The Ambivalence of the Sacred: Religion, Violence, and Reconciliation*. Lanham, MD: Rowman & Littlefield.

———. 2003. "Retrieving the Missing Dimension of Statecraft." In *Faith-based Diplomacy: Trumping Realpolitik*. Edited by D. Johnson. Oxford: Oxford University Press. Cited in Hertog 2010.

Appleby, R. Scott, and Richard Cizik. 2010. *Engaging Religious Communities Abroad: A New Imperative for U.S. Foreign Policy*. Chicago, IL: The Chicago Council on Global Affairs.

Baron, R. M. 2008. "Reconciliation, Trust, and Cooperation: Using Bottom-Up and Top-Down Strategies to Achieve Peace in Israeli-Palestinian Conflict." In *The Social Psychology of Intergroup Reconciliation*. Edited by Arie Nadler, Thomas E. Malloy, and Jeffery D. Fisher. New York, NY: Oxford University Press, 275–298.

Brewer, John D., Gareth I. Higgins, and Francis Teeny. 2010. "Religion and Peacemaking: A Conceptualization." *Sociology*, vol. 44, no. 6, 1019–1037.

Gopin, Marc. 2009. *To Make the Earth Whole: The Art of Citizen Diplomacy in an Age of Religious Militancy*. Lanham, MD: Rowan & Littlefield.

Hertog, Katrien. 2010. *The Complex Reality of Religious Peacebuilding: Conceptual Contributions and Critical Analysis*. Lanham, MD: Lexington Books.

Land Force: Counter-Insurgency Operations 508.6 b. (3), 5–11. http://info.publicin telligence.net/CanadaCOIN.pdf.

"Canadian Forces Operations" B-GG-005-004/AF-000 (December 18, 2000), 3–2 cited by King 2005.

Gizewski, Peter (Strategic Analyst), LCD OR Team, and LCol Michael Rostek (DLCD-Land Futures). 2007. "Toward a Comprehensive Approach to CF Operations: The Land Force JIMP Concept." In *Defence R&D Canada: Center for Operational Research and Analysis*. DRCD CORA TM 2007-60, September 2007, 8.

Kelman, Herbert C. 2008. "Reconciliation from a Social-Psychological Perspective." In *The Social Psychology of Intergroup Reconciliation*. Edited by Arie Nadler, Thomas E. Malloy, and Jeffrey D. Fisher. New York, NY: Oxford University Press.

King, C. 2005. "Effects Based Operations: Buzzword or Blueprint." In *The Operational Art, Canadian Perspectives – Context and Concepts*. Edited by A. English, D. Gosselin, H. Coombs, and L. Hickey. Kingston: Canadian Defence Academy Press.

Kraybill, Ron. 2014. *Case Study on the Peace Process Mediated by Lesotho National Religious Leaders*. Unpublished paper by the former United Nations Special Advisor for Peacebuilding and Development for Lesotho.

Kramer, R. M., and P. J. Carnevale. 2003. "Trust and Intergroup Negotiation." In *Intergroup Processes*. Edited by R. Brown, and S. Gaertner. Malden, MA: Blackwell, 432–450.

Land Force: Counter-Insurgency Operations. 2008. *B-GL-323-004/FP-003*. Kingston, ON: Army Publishing Office, 508.6 b (1), 5–11. http://info.publicintelli gence.net/CanadaCOIN.pdf.

Lederach, John Paul. 1997. *Building Peace: Sustainable Reconciliation in Divided Societies*. Washington, DC: United States Institute of Peace.

———. 2005. *The Moral Imagination: The Art and Soul of Building Peace*. New York, NY: Oxford University Press.

Little, David. 2007. *Peacemakers in Action: Profiles of Religion in Conflict Resolution*. New York, NY: Cambridge University Press.

Moore, S. K. 2008. *Military Chaplains as Agents of Peace: The Theology and Praxis of Reconciliation in Stability Operations*. Dissertation. Ottawa, Ontario: Saint Paul University.

———. 2013. *Military Chaplains as Agents of Peace: Religious Leader Engagement in Conflict and Post-conflict Environments*. Lanham, MD: Lexington Books.

———. 2014a. "Military Chaplains as Whole-of-Government Partners." In *Military Chaplains in Afghanistan, Iraq and Beyond: Advisement and Leader Engagement in Highly Religious Environments*. Edited by Eric Paterson. Lanham, MD: Rowman & Littlefield.

———. 2014b. *Presentation given at the Edward M. Kennedy Institute for Conflict Intervention*, Maynooth University, Ireland, November 25, 2014.

Moore, S. K., and S. Demiray. 2007. "The Canadian Forces Chaplain Branch: Modeling Interfaith Cooperation and Pluralism in Afghanistan." *Ecumenism*, vol. 65, March, 5–8.

MCDC—Multinational Capability Development Campaign. 2014. *Understand to Prevent: Practical Guidance on the Military Contribution to the Prevention of Violent Conflict*.

MCDC—Multinational Capability Development Campaign. 2017. *Understand to Prevent.*

NATO Standard AJP – 3.4.9, Allied Joint Doctrine for Civil-Military Cooperation, Edition A. Version 1. Chapter 2—CIMIC in Theatres and Operations, 0202 The Aim and Purpose of CIMIC; 0202.b. Relationships with Civilian Actors: NATO Standardization Agency (NSA) NATO, February 2013.

Ottis, P. 2018. "Religion and War in the Twenty-first Century." In *Religion and Security: The New Nexus in International Relations.* Edited by R. A. Seiple and D. R. Hoover. Lanham, MD: Rowan and Littlefield.

Paterson, Eric, Ed. 2014. *Military Chaplains in Afghanistan, Iraq and Beyond: Advisement and Leader Engagement in Highly Religious Environments.* Lanham, MD: Rowman & Littlefield.

The Comprehensive Approach: Road Map 21 April 2010, Version 4.0, Chief of Force Development, Canadian Forces.

Chapter 8

RLE from the Balcony

The Domestic Application of Religious Leader Engagement

Karen Hamilton

I have subscription tickets to the theater. Each year, as I evaluate the location of my regular seats, I always end up choosing the balcony. From the balcony, one can see down to the whole width and depth of the stage. One can also see up and from side to side, getting a perspective on the space and complexity of the theater and one can see much of the audience and their reaction to the drama before them.

Religious Leaders Engagement (RLE), as articulated by Steve Moore in the context of international peacebuilding, could find a new application in the domestic setting. To begin an exploration of this potential, I will start with a survey of some recent and relevant developments. I will then engage the key aspects of Moore's work through the lens of a unique and original example of domestic application of RLE based on my work and experience, providing a view from the balcony—detailing a wide perspective on the complexity, recent changes, and new opportunities in the religious landscape of the country.

Moore's groundbreaking and unique work focuses on the role of military chaplains and the crucial need for RLE in theaters of conflict and situations of instability, particularly in a global context. His work can be framed as emergent creativity; this always opens up adjacent possibilities: in this case, the categories and parameters of his work can also be applied domestically and would greatly enhance the role of religious leaders and institutions in Canada. This is particularly important domestically at this time because of the large number of Canadians for whom faith is a primary identifier and the awareness that their numbers will grow. What follows is an overview of the religious landscape in Canada to provide a context for the analysis of how RLE has a role domestically.

THE RELIGIOUS LANDSCAPE OF CANADA

There has been a kind of popular wisdom in Western societies for a number of decades that society would and should become more secular. Faith and religion have often been dismissed as unimportant or even destructive. Empirical evidence of the decline in attendance in religious services and the numbers of people claiming adherence to faith traditions has been shown through surveys, books, academic studies, and the popular press. This latter reality is not incorrect but what has proved to be incorrect is the understanding that this would be a permanent trajectory or that it was more of a widespread phenomenon than it actually is.

Acceptance of the Religious Reality

It is certainly true and can be easily demonstrated that attendance at and adherence to many long-standing Christian traditions in Canada has declined dramatically in recent decades. What is also very true, however, is that attendance at and adherence to other Christian traditions and other faith traditions is growing. My experience in this reality, from the vantage point of being in leadership in the Canadian Council of Churches, suggests that it is indisputable, in the Toronto (Ontario, Canada) area alone, to cite just one example; several new, not just churches but cathedrals, have been built in recent years. They have substantial attendance and relationships with both political realities at all levels and local communities.

What was also unforeseen, to cite another example, was the effect of such immigration realities as the recent influx of Syrian refugees. Most of those refugees bring not only an adherence to a particular faith tradition but also an awareness of other traditions and an expectation that faith is not only an identity marker but also an important part of any society. This is not necessarily an uncritical view of religion but a realistic one given global realities. Immigrant and refugee communities in Canada may also maintain strong ties with and an awareness of their countries of origin and the conflicts and religious realities there.

Also of note, based on my observations, is that there is an openness to the general reality of religion in secular publications including *The Economist* and the most recent Christmas Eve editorials in the major Toronto newspapers. Adherence to a faith tradition is both shifting and growing, for reasons such as those stated above. There is also awareness in academic circles that whether or not one is oneself a practitioner of a faith tradition, the fact that many other people are is a phenomenon to be considered in discussions and subject areas of depth. In recent years, I have been invited to speak at two domestic conferences—one academic and one in the area of development and human rights—at which I was the first person of faith to ever be invited to speak. It was recognized that any efforts in human rights and development, particularly at the global level, had to take into consideration the reality of faith as a societal reality and identity marker, in some cases, the most important identity marker.

A concrete expression of the awareness of this new domestic reality is demonstrated by the engagement in the "Our Whole Society" conference, a conference in which academics, journalists, politicians, and religious practitioners debate and discuss the role of religion in Canadian society. The keynote speaker at the third iteration of this conference, John Ralston Saul, who does not speak from a personal faith-based perspective, stated publicly that he accepted the invitation because it came from the faith communities of Canada. Ralston Saul, who some consider Canada's most significant public intellectual, clearly stated his understanding of how important faith is to vast numbers of Canadians. It is also of note that all three iterations of the "Our Whole Society" conference have been at capacity attendance and have included both speakers and participants from the broad spectrum of Canadian society.

Trends in Interreligious Collaboration

It is important to note that the past years and decades have seen a transition in the concrete ways that faith communities and traditions are organized and institutionalized in Canada. In many locations, particularly urban ones where the Christian traditions are those that have been present and prominent in the country for a long time and are now experiencing decline, there has been a similar decline in the membership and activity levels of church councils. Church councils or ministerial associations are those ecumenical, some-what informal gatherings of Christian leaders to build relationships and to engage together on the issues of their locale. Some of such councils have ceased to exist but many have transitioned to become interfaith councils, bringing together representatives of the faith traditions in the area for the same purposes of relationship and joint engagement for the sake of local and regional communities. In addition, there are small but significant dialogue groups that have emerged. Some are dyadic, such as the Muslim-Christian dialogue that has been meeting monthly in Ottawa for nearly thirty years, and some are multifaith. These preexisting relationships and informal structures not only allow for but also encourage and can be a building block for domestic application of RLE.

Another development in recent years is the fact that faith communities have been very active, in a wide variety of ways, in issues of immigration and refugees. Faith communities have always been active and have carried a degree of expertise on these issues but the current global and national context has both heightened involvement and, importantly, visibility in involvement. It has been striking in the last few years, coming from a context in which faith communities often felt ignored by such features of a secular society as the mainstream media, that the vast majority of stories about refugee resettlement/sponsorship in the major media outlets have noted the sponsorship role of a faith community. Mainstream media has noted that sponsorship role very positively.

In line with Moore's articulation of the changes in the nature of violent conflict of the current era, from interstate to intrastate and in dynamic relationship with the rise of social media and communications vehicles globally, there is enhanced awareness domestically of the realities of violent conflict around the world. Through such technological communications vehicles as WhatsApp and Facebook, immigrants, refugees, their sponsors, activists, academics, and the broad public can be aware, on a minute-by-minute basis, with images, of what is transpiring in most regions and localities of violent conflict around the globe.

This leads to broad awareness of what is affecting faith communities, a fact that then can lead to both an awareness of the need for and openness to the broad domestic application of RLE in Canada. In the light of the points stated above—the view from the balcony—I will discuss the domestic applications of RLE through the lens of the 2010 Interfaith Leaders' Summit held in Canada. The paper will conclude with another example of the application of Steve Moore's RLE categories to a domestic context, comments that outline possible contributions of Canadian military chaplains to broad domestic application and some further, future trajectories.

DOMESTIC APPLICATION OF MOORE'S RLE PRINCIPLES CASE STUDY: 2010 INTERFAITH LEADERS' SUMMIT

In 2010, the political G8 and G20 both met in Canada in close chronological proximity. Since 2006, there had been Interfaith Leaders' Summits that had met in such close proximity to the G8. The process leading to these global Interfaith Summits had actually begun the previous year, in 2005, with a Christian, ecumenical summit but since 2006 the faith summits have been interfaith ones. The Interfaith Summit process has continued, though the chronological and geographical proximity is currently focused on G20 political summits because the issues close to the hearts of Interfaith Leaders are now encompassed by the G20. With both the G8 and G20 political summits converging in Canada in 2010, the 2010 Interfaith Leaders' Summit was initiated and implemented through the Canadian Council of Churches. Since I was the organizer and builder of the forty-seven-member interfaith, NGO partnership that hosted the 2010 Interfaith Leaders' Summit, I am in a unique position to make observations about the dynamics of the event.

The Canadian iteration of the Interfaith Leaders' summits brought eighty-five senior faith leaders together from the G8 countries and G20 regions. These leaders met at the University of Winnipeg (Manitoba) for the days prior to the G8/G20 meetings and agreed by consensus on a statement to be presented to the G8/G20. The Canadian iteration of Interfaith Leaders' summits involved a number of unique, creative, and sustainable emergent new possibilities in interfaith summits, receiving a global prize for Best Practices in Interfaith Dialogue. These new possibilities included partnerships with nonfaith-based academic, media, and arts bodies, the involvement of an interfaith youth delegation, a variety of educational processes in numerous venues, and ongoing interfaith coalition building, resulting in the creation of the Canadian Interfaith Conversation, Canada's Interfaith Council.

The discussion below uses the lens of the 2010 Interfaith Leaders' Summit to focus on Moore's RLE categories, indicating their application in the Summit process and the emergent domestic possibilities those categories offer. Note that the application of these principles occurred at the domestic level *within* the countries involved as well as at the international level as representatives interacted *among* one another, spanning national boundaries.

Boundary Spanners

Moore states in his work that military chaplains function naturally as what he terms "boundary spanners" because they are religious leaders in their own right. They are able to move with relative ease among local leaders and religious communities in a wide variety of contexts—global and domestic.

In the domestic application of RLE, the function religious leaders play as boundary spanners is a different one than it would be in regions of overt conflict. Nonetheless, it resonates with Moore's use of the term. In their internal function within faith traditions, the religious leaders contacted about the upcoming Interfaith Leaders' Summit were able to comprehend the meaning, purpose, and implications of the Summit and the relationship of that meaning, purpose, and those implications to the central tenets of their traditions. More logistically, the religious leaders, often those with particular expertise in ecumenism and interfaith dialogue, were able to span the boundaries of their traditions in terms of representation. They were able to determine who within their tradition would be the most effective representative for actual participation in the Summit and to facilitate that participation. The religious leaders initially contacted were boundary spanners in their capacity, knowledge, and vision to ensure effective representation at the Summit table whether that would be the Primate, senior imam, archbishop, president of the temple, moderator, or leaders with expertise in social justice, disarmament, and public policy work. This ensured the maximum impact of the Summit and the respectful reception of its statement by the G8 Summit leaders, along with the ongoing implications of engagement on the basis of its principles.

Crucially, these religious leaders were also often able to span the boundaries external to their own traditions but internal to their region or country. The Summit had requested that all of the G8 countries and G20 regions be represented by delegations representing the faith demographic of their country or region. Because of their reality as domestic boundary spanners within their home context, enormous and often unique strides were taken to fulfil this request. The result was not only the representational presence at the Summit table but also the laying of groundwork in the construction of ongoing relationships in each country and region. Religious leaders knew whom to call whether they had ever previously called them or not.

The story of a phone call I received from a German bishop illustrates this point in an engaging way. The bishop called from Germany to review what was being asked of the interfaith delegation structure hoped for from each G8 country and the G20 regions by the 2010 Interfaith Leaders' Summit. I explained that the anticipated result was that the countries and regions would send delegations that represented, as much as possible, the faith makeup of the country or region. There was a pause as the bishop considered this. He then responded that what this process was asking for was that the various faith traditions in a country or region talk across traditions to each other when they already had difficulty talking within their traditions. The bishop was clear that he both enjoyed the challenge and felt that it was a necessary and visionary step forward in interfaith relations, internationally certainly, but also domestically. Hence, the very process of selecting delegates was a catalyst for the spanning of interfaith divisions within the country.

Networking

The building, implementing, and effectiveness of the 2010 Interfaith Leaders' Summit was only possible because of the coalition of forty-seven partners brought together and formed through both the institutional network of the Canadian Council of Churches and the informal, creative networks that had been established through years of relationship and trust building, shared experiences, visions, and goals. These networks were primarily, but not exclusively, with and through religious traditions. They included the capacity and credibility of religious leaders to have established networks with social justice bodies, parliamentarians, academics, government bureaucrats, and the media.

It is very important to state that the networking that enabled the effectiveness of the Interfaith Leaders' Summit was a combination of institutional and informal networks. In that instance, both were necessary, as was the breath, particularly of the informal networks. Institutional networks gave stability, credibility, accountability, and concrete support to the Summit. They also ensured that the statement issued to the G8 and G20 had institutional traction and an ongoing life within the tradition and its networks. The informal networks brought creativity and dynamism that enabled the Summit to create new structures. In addition, the informal networks ensured that there was a wide range of players gathered around the Summit table—with more government representatives, journalists, human rights advocates, academics, and artists than would otherwise have been the case. In this, they enhanced the critical conditions for emergent creativity.

Middle-Range Actors

Moore's work points to the importance of identifying the moderate voice among religious leaders. The ability to do this results from networking—as one develops trusted partners, it is possible to affirm appropriate partners for specific initiatives—and has led to partnering and, in some instances, actual peacebuilding initiatives.

In situations and regions of overt conflict, these middle-range actors, as he notes, are able to move freely at the higher levels of leadership within their own communities, while at the same time enjoying the confidence of the grass roots of their communities. The vast and, to some degree, still untapped potential of this reality for domestic application was clearly demonstrated by the 2010 Summit. It was the moderate voice among religious leaders that was both reached through previously established networks and which responded to the invitation to participation with enthusiasm and alacrity. In many cases, there were preexisting relationships. What was also very clear, however, was the desire and vision to work together for the benefit of all sectors of Canadian and global society and to build new relationships and networks toward that, if necessary.

The focus of the 2010 Summit statement were the Millennium Development Goals (MDGs), now replaced and amplified by the Sustainable Development Goals (SDGs): climate change and peace, with a particular focus on the abolition of nuclear weapons and the illegal small arms trade. The desire to further these foci for the betterment and amelioration of the life of all peoples on the planet cut across all identity divisions among and between faith traditions and was shared by those that would self-define as moderate in all faith traditions.

Civic Engagement

Moore's emphasis on RLE and civic engagement also has tremendous domestic application, as shown through the lens of the 2010 Interfaith Leaders' Summit, in ways that both increase communication and relationships among various sectors of society and that allow for and encourage the expertise and compassion of faith groups to influence society in positive ways.

A purpose of the Summit process, prior and subsequent to the 2010 Summit, was to produce a statement agreed to by all the faith leaders present. The statement is then presented to the leadership of the G8/G20. In terms of content, the statement focused on commitments shared by the faith communities on such crucial global issues as the SDGs on climate change and peace and security. These were witnessed to and worked toward for the benefit of all the world's peoples and the earth itself. Prior to 2010, such statements would be agreed upon during a faith leaders' summit just prior to the G8/G20 summits and presented to the G8/G20 near the conclusion of those political gatherings.

A crucial turning point in the domestic application of RLE and Civic Engagement occurred in the planning process for the 2010 Summit. The religious leadership in Canada engaged the G8 Sherpa's office to discuss plans for the Interfaith Summit and channels of possible communication and relationship with the political summits. There was a tremendous step forward in both the learning about RLE/Civic Engagement possibilities and the implementation of them in the willingness of the Sherpa's office to engage with religious leaders and the challenge to operate in a more collaborative way with such offices. The Sherpa's office was more than willing to hear from and address the concerns and priorities of the religious leaders and to consider them very seriously, if the religious leaders could accommodate the timeline realities of the Sherpa's office. Concretely, the issues and agendas of the G8/G20 are formulated in the year prior to the political summit and so the previous practice of faith leaders presenting a statement near the conclusion of a political summit could have little effect on that summit. The Sherpa's office was encouraging of the religious leaders submitting a statement nine months prior to the political summit as a way of substantive religious leader engagement with the political process and saw that as beneficial.

This example makes the crucial point that the dialogue of religious leaders with civil society institutions is both important and can be extremely productive. It dismantles any assumption that religious leaders may have about their own timelines and encourages the thinking that religious leadership in

Canada is integral to broad and deep civic engagement and is recognized by the political processes as such.

It is also important to note the importance of religious leaders building and maintaining a network of domestic relationships. The religious leadership of the 2010 Interfaith Leaders' Summit brought an extensive network of not only faith groups but also NGOs, academics, and political contacts into the relationship and Summit process, including media and the global expertise of the G8/G20 Research Group.

Encounter and the Fragile "We" of Working Trust and Confidence

There is often a spiral kind of dynamic to the building of relationship and working trust and confidence. In the case of the 2010 Interfaith Leaders' Summit, it was possible to access a number of base constituencies—the denominations of the Canadian Council of Churches and the global, regional church council relationships built up over the course of a number of years and the long-term interfaith relationships established in Canada. The trust and confidence built in those relationships meant that not only would religious leaders willingly engage in the Summit process, which was something new and unique, but they also willingly engaged in creative consultation in terms of who in their own networks, beyond the networks of the Summit process, should be and could be involved as well.

Relationships already built enabled new relationships to be built. The request from the Summit planning process was for the religious leadership of the G8 countries and G20 regions to attend an interfaith summit in Canada and participate in the creation, both prior to and during the Summit, of a major statement to be received by the G8 and G20. That entailed a kind of external process. The request was also, however, for the religious leader-ship of the G8 countries and G20 regions to consult within their country and region and construct a delegation of faith leaders that represented the faith makeup of the country or region. As noted above, this proved in many cases to be the harder request. A relationship of working trust and confidence was asking religious leaders to create other relationships of working trust and confidence with religious leaders within their own context with whom there had been little engagement and in some cases, mistrust and disagreement.

The request and process worked to a large degree because the initial rela-tionship grounded the others to be built and of course also to speak to one of Moore's crucial points, because in the majority of cases, it was the moderate voice of religion that was being engaged at each level. It required relation-ships, whether familiar or new, in which there was an ability to articulate and hear what was at stake for "the other." The question of who the figures, bodies, and traditions are that represent religion in any context can be very complex and indeed, untidy. There is never a formula of complete certainty; factors and actors change with time and it is ultimately often necessary to step forward in the faith that the representation is right enough. That said, it does have to truly be right enough and it may take extended time of relationship building to ensure that.

Ritual Events

Moore's discussion of ritual events is in close relationship with his discussions of networking and boundary spanners. Religious leaders may indeed be called middle-range actors as those who engage, through ritual events and other means, with the various levels and complexities of any society. Local clergy in most contexts relate both to religious and political hierarchies and the multitude of the people.

In terms of the 2010 Interfaith Leaders' Summit, this meant that the "ritual event" of the Summit was both built by relationships and a spiraling building of relationships and in its actual unfolding built more relationships. Religious leaders who attended that particular "ritual event" were senior leaders of their traditions, with significant experience in engaging with the various hierarchies, not only in faith traditions but in all varieties of national and regional realities. They also had channels to the needs and realities of all peoples in their countries and regions. This enabled a 2010 Interfaith Leaders' Statement to the G8 and G20 that truly spoke to the needs, priorities, and concerns of the lives of the globe's peoples.

This particular ritual event was enabled by and enabled other ritual events. The fact that the first Interfaith Leaders' Summit occurred in 2006, with an ecumenical one occurring the year before, provided the groundwork of trust and to some degree, process, for the subsequent years. The trajectory of successful summits, defining successful as the production of statements and broad, expert, and high-level representation, continued to build. It was also possible, with ritual event following ritual event, to pass on materials and structures that were developed in the ritual event process and then strengthened further ritual events—a kind of spiral process in this example as well as that discussed above.

Complementary Activities

The domestic application of RLE can be seen in the complementary activities of the 2010 Interfaith Leaders' Summit. Although it was religious leaders who were being brought together to engage one another, in new or already formed relationships, one of the main foci of the discussion and subsequent statement, for example, was the MDGs. Because these goals were established by the United Nations, many complementary activities were possible. Adherence to any particular faith tradition was not and is not required in order to participate in the accomplishment of such goals on a national or international level. Relationships were therefore built with parliamentarians, schools, members of NGOs, academics, and research bodies such as the G8 and G20 Research Groups. The MDGs even lent themselves to the development of an interfaith, educational, awareness game for youth that could be used in any kind of educational setting. It was the shared focus that was related to, but not exclusive to, faith bodies that enabled complementary activities.

Collaborative Activities

Moore's discussion of Religious Leader Engagement and *collaborative activities*, as seen through the lens of the 2010 Interfaith Leaders' Summit, is integrally related to the discussion above of *complementary activities*. The goal of fulfilling the MDGs/SDGs cannot be accomplished by faith bodies alone nor by more secular bodies alone. This is particularly the case in the majority of the world's countries and regions where religion plays a more integral role than is perceived to be the case in some Western countries—religion not only plays an integral role in Western countries but also that role will continue to expand (see initial section).

Through the Interfaith Leaders' Summit, collaborative activities were engaged in, and this has established trust that has led to further collaborative activity in areas of concern to both faith bodies and more secular national bodies: palliative care, human trafficking, climate change, and the process and recommendations of the Canadian Truth and Reconciliation Commission (for those in Canada).

Conciliation and Facilitation

The 2010 Interfaith Leaders' Summit played, and such summits continue to play, a role of conciliation and facilitation particularly in terms of the relationships of faith communities with media, educational institutions, and individual politicians. Many past preconceptions were addressed through a shared concern for the MDGs, climate change, and peace possibilities through the control of the illegal small arms trade. Any preconceptions held by media, educational institutions, and local politicians that faith communities had primarily divisive relationships with each other or had as their primary interest conversions or just the good of their own constituents were dispelled. Conciliation was made possible through the visible, active shared concern for the well-being of all peoples of the planet.

ANOTHER EXAMPLE

In the aftermath of the 2010 Interfaith Leaders' Summit, related to it and as an offshoot of it, the "Our Whole Society" conference was created. This is an ongoing, domestic conference that has built on the emergent creativity of the 2010 Summit to open up adjacent possibilities.

As noted above, this conference brings together a wide cross-section of Canadian society to discussion the role of religion in this country. Its creation and ongoing reality as a fully subscribed conference occurring in different national locations every second year is possible because the creators, leaders, and organizers function in and through Steve Moore's categories.

As one of the creators of the "Our Whole Society" conference, I have a particular "view from the balcony" in terms of this important domestic discussion vehicle. The reality of the creators, leaders, and organizers as boundary spanners with both extensive institutional and informal networks enabled and still enables the success of the project. Its premise is to bring together a wide, diverse variety of societal representatives, something that would not be possible without boundary spanners and networkers, religious leaders who embody both of those categories of Moore's defining. Civic engagement is also a key component in this adjacent possibility, forming part of the foundation of the conference. It is not just religious practitioners or faith-based bodies who participate but rather, academics, politicians, media, and social justice actors. They are all Middle-range actors regardless of their particular discipline. The conference itself is, of course, a ritual event according to Moore's definition and complementary and collaborative activities do and can create further adjacent possibilities. Conciliation and facilitation, as Moore defines them, are a particularly strong feature of the OWS conference. The experience of participating in a conference on the role of religion in society has been a new one for numerous participants from sectors of Canadian society not considered particularly religious. Many of those in fields such as media, academia, politics, social justice, and international development were very aware of the importance of the role of religion in the lives of so many in Canada and around the world. Some participants were less accustomed to working and speaking in close collaboration with faith practitioners and in each iteration of the conference, those participants have been impressed by its capacity for deep, broad, informed, and critical discussion on the part of all speakers and attendees. This has led to conciliation amongst diverse Canadian leaders and has facilitated ongoing relationships and an openness to future relationship and collaborative and complementary activities as demonstrated by the global 2018 Parliament of the World's Religions held in Toronto for the first time in the Parliament's over a hundred-year history.

The "Our Whole Society" conference thus demonstrates Moores' categories of RLE in its planning and organization and in its execution. It also demonstrates, as discussed above, the spiral nature in many of these endeavors. The enacting of the roles and categories in emergent creativity builds adjacent possibilities that are not necessarily adjacent by a linear definition of the term. They are adjacent through a broadening, deepening, and solidifying of religious engagement, a kind of spiraling upward of engagement that brings in participants in new ways.

DOMESTIC APPLICATION OF RLE AND MILITARY CHAPLAINCY

This chapter has dealt primarily with the domestic application of RLE and its particular categories as articulated by Steve Moore in terms of a broad RLE primarily through the lens of the 2010 Interfaith Leaders' Summit. It is also crucial to state, however, that Canadian military chaplains will be extremely important to further, broad domestic applications.

The Chaplaincy Branch of the Canadian Forces, through its leadership and its active, well-trained chaplains, would greatly enhance domestic applications in a very wide variety of contexts. Canadian military chaplains bring interfaith awareness, understanding, and concrete applications to any situation. The intentional, structured education and training of military chaplains in interfaith dynamics is unparalleled in the country, especially when set as it is in a context of institutional support and continual enhancement. Military chaplains are accountable to a leadership completely committed to continual education about and practical application of interfaith dynamics.

Military chaplains are engaged domestically and also either engaged globally in theaters of conflict, the effects of which may be imported to Canada, or are very aware through their training and accountability structures, of those realities. Military chaplains could therefore bring an enhanced and needed level of stability to such domestic realities as the newly established interfaith councils and relationships. A commitment by some level of the chaplaincy branch to any domestic application, council, or relationship would bring a level of continuity and knowledge that is possible in some of the larger and more institutionalized faith communities but not possible in others with fewer resources or a more recent history in Canada.

Military chaplains are also a part of a Canadian institutional expression that has a broader geographical expanse than may be possible for some expressions of faith-based traditions in Canada. Military chaplains are boundary spanners who deal with the personal faith of individuals and who deal with institutional structures, from a broad interfaith understanding, and they do

so in a way that encompasses more of the Canadian geographical and demographic reality than most other faith expressions because of the nature of the
Chaplaincy Branch structure within the Canadian Forces.

CONCLUSION

This chapter has articulated past and present examples of RLE in the Canadian
landscape, which, although created independently to Moore's articulation,
both validate its approach and are validated by it. The application of Moore's
work as emergent creativity will also open up crucial adjacent possibilities in
other current and future issues.

Climate change is one of those issues in which domestic RLE could be
enormously beneficial, taking the current, passionate but ad hoc involvement
of religious leaders and institutions to a much greater level. The Holy Texts
of most faith traditions speak clearly about the relationship of humanity to
the natural world. The way that relationship is to be articulated and acted
upon has varied throughout centuries and even decades. In recent decades,
in the context of dire scientific evidence of the destruction and in some
cases irreparable damage to the natural world and the earth's climate made
by human activity, both many secular and religious sectors of Canadian and
international society have become alert to the imperative of changed human
behavior. At this time of writing, the imperative of changed human behavior
is of tremendous pressing concern in both religious and secular contexts. This
issue of global import, global survival even, is of course one of international
scope. It is also one of domestic scope and is a place where Steve Moore's
categories of RLE are not just applicable but may indeed provide some of
necessary forward momentum.

The magnitude of climate change requires boundary spanners. They can
work across and within traditions and religions, engaging with religious leadership and congregants. They can do so in the awareness that the imperative
to ameliorate climate change is very much a "grassroots" movement, which
would be aided by the access to resources and communications vehicles that
faith leadership may have. A similar point may be made about Moore's category of networking. In the institutional and informal networks that religious
leaders both inform and have access to, in the deep listening that is possible in
such networks, may lie the conditions for inspiration and emergent creativity.
Such creativity is desperately needed in the face of the enormity of the issue,
an enormity that can and does lead many to despair.

It is a well-known dynamic of current climate change discussions that there
are those who would not fit Moore's definition of middle-range actors. There
are still those who deny climate change or deny that it is caused in any way

by human behavior. There are also those who, with the best of intentions in the saving of the planet, propose actions that will not happen and the proposal of which can result in a shutting down climate change discussions. Simple examples of this would be those who advocate for the immediate banning of vehicles and airplanes for the goal of dramatic reduction of the damage caused to the environment by fossil fuels. Significant progress in combating climate change will be most likely through the work of middle-range actors who understand the very timely imperative and are able to propose dramatic but doable actions such as a rapid increase in the means of producing sustainable energy sources and a rapid decrease in the consumption of meat.

The category of civic engagement is very clearly crucial in any bringing together of RLE and the issue of climate change. It is to state the obvious to say that the enormity and dire imperative of this issue requires all sectors of society to work together. What is less obvious is a fragmentation among the various actors, nationally and globally, working to ameliorate climate change. It was my privilege to be a part of the consultation process by which the United Nations High Panel created and articulated the SDGs as successors to the MDGs. That process brought together global experts and thinkers representing the regions of the globe. Though there is not a simple understanding of why it is the case, that Panel stated clearly that it is the global climate change actors who are the most fragmented of all the global movements working to improve life for humans and for all aspects of the planet generally. RLE could play an enormous role through networking and boundary spanning, complementary activities, collaborative activities, and facilitation in civil society generally in reducing this fragmentation. There is an imperative to do so. What is also crucial to note, however, is the lesson learned from the engagement of the 2010 Interfaith Leaders' Summit with the Canadian Sherpa's office in the preparation for the G8 and G20 meetings in Canada. Faith groups, especially their religious leaders, must truly work collaboratively in civil engagement, which may mean changing structures and ways of thinking in order to accommodate such things as the need for advance preparation of a draft statement to the G8 and G20. Allowing the space and conditions for emergent creativity may not be easy.

A further avenue of research, action, and transformation could lie in allowing the space and conditions for emergent creativity in the application of Moore's principles of RLE to the calls to action of the Canadian Truth and Reconciliation Commission. It may also not be easy but it is an obvious further avenue for action and transformation and an imperative one.

This chapter has offered a wide perspective on Moore's work in the area of RLE in international peacekeeping, exploring past examples of the application of the categories of his work to the domestic context. It has offered a kind of "view from the balcony" of recent changes and new opportunities in the religious landscape of the country. The chapter has then used the primary example of the 2010 Interfaith Leaders' Summit to demonstrate the comprehensiveness and effectiveness of Moore's categories with the further, related example of the Our Whole Society conference. The fact that the 2010 Interfaith Leaders' Summit was created and executed independently of Moore's work validates that work in its application to a domestic context and Moore's work explicates and validates the effectiveness of the Summit and its foundation for subsequent events such as the Our Whole Society conference. Moore's categories of RLE as emergent creativity provide a crucial template that will enable domestic application. Undertakings such as the Summit and the Our Whole Society conference can be replicated in an intentional way with much potential for adjacent possibilities.

It is also important to note that the application of Steve Moore's work could greatly facilitate the role of religious leaders and institutions in Canada. Neither Moore nor I would advocate for any kind of privileged position for religious leaders and institutions and neither does the Our Whole Society conference. Rather, RLE used domestically in the current Canadian context provides an extremely well-articulated template, with demonstrated successful application of the characteristics of religious leadership, including that of military chaplains, that can enable engagement in a wide variety of societal issues including the imperatives of climate change and the calls to action of the Canadian Truth and Reconciliation Commission. All such engagement can and must be for the good of all Canadian society and beyond.

Chapter 9

Creative Dialogue between Muslim and Western Worlds toward Reconciliation and Addressing Violent Extremism

A Muslim Perspective

Iman Ibrahim

Muslim societies are going through a historical transformation within a complex international context: disenchantment in the modern and postmodern West; the simultaneous rise of secular fundamentalism—"the ideology of nationalism, nurturing the values of unquestioning patriotism and militarism in the modern West" (Falk 2011)—and religion; the despotism of many regimes in Muslim-majority countries; the mistrust in the international institutions' double standards of human rights and security; and the impact of globalization. All have left mixed messages in the minds of Muslims and non-Muslims. These messages influence the development of political Islam, Muslims' reactions to modern and postmodern developments, and the current revolutionary wave that is putting to test capitalist market values, the risky reliance on foreign powers, and the blind revival of the Islamic past. In light of all these dynamics, how have Muslims been seeking reconciliation in the third millennium era? What are the Islamic concepts relevant to conflict resolution and democracy? And how can an understanding of these two factors help Western spiritual leaders dialogue with Muslim counterparts?

In this chapter, I argue that a vision of transformative reconciliation between the Muslim world and the West is possible, in this third millennium era, conditional on both sides establishing democratic societies that practice the prioritization of the values of freedom, justice, ethics, and inclusivity; and that spiritual leaders from both worlds have a role to play in this process. First, I discuss modernity in the West and in the Muslim world and highlight its relevance to the current revolutionary wave in the latter. Then I give examples of Islamic concepts relevant to conflict resolution and democracy. Last, I present points to consider for creative dialogue between Western spiritual leaders and the Muslim world for reconciliation in addition to a collaborative holistic model to address violent extremism.

MODERNITY IN THE WEST AND THE MUSLIM WORLD AND ITS RELEVANCE TO THE CURRENT REVOLUTIONARY WAVE IN THE MUSLIM WORLD

Modernity had its positive aspects in the West, while still leading to a sense of alienation, Orientalism, and, in part, Islamist fundamentalism. Modernity further impacted the Muslim world leading to the emergence of a generation of committed reformers. My purpose is to demonstrate the dialectical relationship between the two worlds over modern times, and the potential to overturn the challenge of extremist tendencies in their current relationship to an optimal "bubbling forth"[1] between their worlds of meaning that serves the higher good of our human societies.

According to Anthony Giddens, "modernity refers to the modes of social life or organization which emerged in Europe from about the 16th century onwards and which subsequently became more or less worldwide in their influence" (Giddens 1990 quoted in Sardar 1995). As the director of the Centre of Postnormal Policy and Futures Studies in Chicago and chair of the Muslim Institute, Ziauddin Sardar explains that modernity involves an obsession with novelty and breaking all taboos, and, in its beginning, it "was associated with direct physical and cultural genocide of the Other" and the "intellectual homicide" of non-Western cultures during colonialism, which gave rise to Orientalism and the denial of the Muslims' civilizational contributions that enabled the Enlightenment and the Renaissance (Sardar 1995).[2] In addition, in modernity, as Kolakowski explains, "the social order . . . is capitalistic in both its economic system and its other institutions . . . taboos must be broken . . . change is global" and "the total commodification of products and wage labour" led to "totalitarianism" with the concentration of the "political, military and ideological power" into fewer hands (Kolakowski 1990 quoted in Sardar 1995). This, Sardar writes, caused "space-time segregation," which produced "fragmented individuals and communities," whose self-sufficiency got replaced "by 'symbolic tokens' like money" and enabled the Western "systemic appropriation of the past to shape the future" by portraying secularism, modernity's core value, as the ideal value; yet, this appropriation did not bring inner peace to the West (Sardar 1995).

Therefore, many Western thinkers voiced the individual's alienation and sought the reconstruction of the social body, leading to redefinitions of key notions such as freedom, order, rights, and ethics in a democracy. Charles Taylor explains his theory as a type of "hierarchical complementarity" in the modern democratic society where individuals seek mutual benefits including the means of living without sacrificing virtue, while securing freedom and individual rights for all, creating a "moral order" that can be embodied in various cultures or "multiple modernities" (Taylor 2004, 19–22, 195). Similarly, Karl Polanyi criticizes market society not for relying on economics but because "its economy was based on self-interest" and insists that freedom relies on "economic collaboration of governments" as well as "domestic freedom" through institutions that balance the freedoms that citizens lose and win to ensure justice and protection of individual rights in practice while separating church and state (Polanyi 2001, 257, 261–62, 264, 267). Interestingly, Hannah Arendt criticizes social sciences that reduce humans to "conditioned and behaving animal[s]" and insists that "neither education nor ingenuity nor talent" can replace the constituents of a permanent "public realm" where humans gather as equals yet distinct in order to produce unpredictable and irreversible "action" that establishes relationships and crosses boundaries (Arendt 1998, 45, 49, 53, 55, 175, 190–91, 220). Charles Taylor, Karl Polanyi, and Hannah Arendt are examples of Western scholars who did not reject modernity but sought to address its negative impact through stressing how democracies need guidelines that are ethical and inclusive of all humans. More recently, the continuing failure of finding fulfillment in the third millennium era and its increasing complexity is reflected in several scholars' call for inclusive networks and adaptive leaderships and systems as seen in the works of Richard McGuigan, Stuart Kauffman, and Merle Lefkoff.

The development of the Muslim world during modernity has been highly influenced by its relationship with the West and the interconnectedness of the temporal and the spiritual in Islam. According to Zaidi, Muslim thinkers attempted to "articulate social-theoretical critiques of the cognitive transformations of modernity from a Muslim perspective—critiques that, in attempting to re-enchant modernity, are implicitly carrying on a dialogue with the Western Social theory" (Zaidi 2006, 72).

Zaidi explains that the first of three rounds of these attempts was focused on synthesis as evident in Iqbal's attempts to demonstrate "the compatibility of Islamic conceptions of God, time and space with the Hegelian and Bergsonian conceptions" (Zaidi 2006, 69–91) and attempts "to synthesize the Sufi concept of *al-insan al-kamil* (the Perfect Man) with the Nietzschean concept of the *Uberman*" (Zaidi 2006, 73–74).

The second round opposed "Western hegemonic cultural penetration" as articulated by neo-revivalists such as Hassan al-Banna Qutb who denounced modernity as the age of *jahilliya* (ignorance) and Maududi who rejected how "the liberal notion of popular sovereignty supersedes the sovereignty of God" (Zaidi 2006, 69–91, 73).

The third round focused on "the recognition of modernity as a *Weltanschauung* and the [need for] reconstruction of knowledge that under-pins Western dominance" as evident in the writings of Nasr and Al-Faruqi (Zaidi 2006, 74). Nasr warns of the threat of secularism and evolutionism, which "suggests that Man [*sic*] can become perfect solely by processes of evolution and progress" and he advocates "a return to the concept of *tawhid* (oneness of God) to reveal the underlying unity and interrelatedness of all that exists" (Zaidi 2006, 74–75).

As Zaidi explains,

Al-Faruqi identifies three shortcomings in Western social science that necessi-tate an Islamic reconstruction: (1) Western social science has not developed the tools to understand the moral and the spiritual realms; (2) by reducing reality to its material level and by arguing for the distantiated, value-neutral observer, Western social science presents a false claim of objectivity; (3) the division of social knowledge into the humanities and social sciences violates the Islamic principle of the unity of truth because questions of ultimate value become the sole domain of the humanities, which pose their inquiry in purely subjective and individualist terms. (Zaidi 2006, 77)

In his project, "*a propos*," Al-Faruqi lays down a twelve-step plan for the Islamization of knowledge and explains that "*tawhid* requires the unification of empirical and normative knowledge, so that human beings may embody God's will on earth," and seeks to redefine the role of Reason as to replace the "pseudo-universalism of Western modernity with the true universalism of an Islamic modernity" (Zaidi 2006, 77–78). As such, ultimate value is not an individual pursuit but is rather manifested in the quality of our human relationships.

THE DEVELOPMENT OF POLITICAL ISLAM

Parallel to these attempts has been the development of political Islam over four sequential movements. As Farhang Rajaee explains, twentieth- and twenty-first-century Islam-centered movements passed through four generations: the apologetic "Politics of Revival 1920s–1960s," the violent nationalist "Politics of Revolution 1963–1991," the totalitarian "Politics of Islamism 1989–1997," and the moderate "Politics of Restoration 1997–2005" (Rajaee 2007, 27, 90, 151, 193, 242–43). The first two generations took place during colonialism, which, along with the despotism of the regimes in postcolonial Muslim-majority countries, led to the emergence of the third generation, the totalitarian Islamists. Colonialism, as Samir Amin explains, was built on Eurocentric "mythical foundations" that denied the original civilizational exchange between East and West and polarized the world into a center—superior Christian Western capitalist states—and periphery—inferior uncivilized Orient that produces natural resources for the West (Amin 1989, Ix–xii, 75–76). Therefore, although Muslims had originally sympathized with the Renaissance's vision of freedom, colonialism's division of the Muslim world by artificial borders and its internal and external injustices invoked varying Muslim responses including (a) some apologetics, (b) the Muslim nationalist movements' rejection of all Western humanistic heritage and Enlightenment, and (c) some extreme interpretations of religious sources that invoke Muslim past traditions and were later manipulated to serve the destructive purposes of terrorism.

To complicate matters, Muslim grievances increased with double standards in implementing international law and human rights as to maintain the *status quo*. Interestingly, Sardar sees Islamist fundamentalism as a "reaction to the crisis of identity created by modernity, to the excess of consumerism, to the powerlessness produced by structural injustices and market democracies"; he sees Islamist fundamentalism as an "opposition to Western market capitalism as a world system" (Sardar 1995).

By contrast, the fourth generation took on a different approach. According to Rajaee, it promoted democracy, accepted reasonable compromises, used intellect, took part in the public arena, and admitted the problems in today's Muslim societies, namely "identity crisis, inequality, intolerance, a battle of values, uncertainty about the future, poverty, addiction," and the tendency to eliminate political opponents (Rajaee 2007, 242). Meanwhile, it has been committed to dialogue, nonviolence, self-examination, as well as a reevaluation of the West and modernity in order to restore Muslims' participation in building civilization (ibid., 243).

Another analysis of Muslim societies by Misbah Islam highlights similar interrelated factors. To begin, poor national policies and incompetent leadership are the causes of a long-time deterioration of Muslim societies. Hence, reformers must address several challenges. First, populations are disempowered due to undemocratic systems. Second, ethical and religious values have deteriorated due to misinterpretation or misapplication of Islam leading to excessive materialism, lack of legal rights and justice (judicial problems), educational deficit, and the role of the elite (Islam 2008). Addressing these challenges is a long, difficult, yet necessary, phase for the development of the Muslim world.

In my view, the emergence and ongoing work of this fourth generation (i.e., the reformers) prepared the way for the mass Muslim revolutions we have been seeing since 2011 despite the highly mixed and unpredictable outcomes. That is because they encouraged many Muslim groups to seek their freedom and socioeconomic and political rights, while creating channels of cooperation and exchange with the world without alienating Muslims from their cultures or spiritual foundation. All this leaves space for nonviolent movements, albeit in a long and unfair battle against extremism, corruption, and abuse by corporate power. This was reflected in nonviolent methodology of the Green Wave Revolution in Iran in 2009, the revolution in Tunisia in 2011, the revolution in Yemen in 2011, and in Egypt in 2011, followed by 2013 anti-government protests by over twenty million Egyptians to overthrow Morsi and the Muslim brotherhood from power. Even the Syrian mass revolt started with nonviolent protests in 2011 before the government's response and other factors turned it into a vicious civil war with several factions fighting against the government and against one another.

Significantly, a wide range of Muslim voices started to play a role in political and constitutional reform. For example, following the ousting of Mubarak's despotic regime in Egypt in 2011, many openly criticized the government for corruption and the gap between rich and poor. Also, under attack were leaders who tried to sabotage the stability of the society using religious divides. For the first time, the people had a voice and they expressed their demands loud and clear: bread, freedom, and justice. They were becoming citizens who could sense their impact and responsibility in shaping the political structure and society through free parliamentary and presidential elections without letting the fear of the unknown cripple their actions. Three significant trends emerged.

First, there was a great diversity among these political actors and parties ranging from the Salafis with their austere form of religious thought; the Muslim brotherhood, with their social and economic network, and their members reflecting varying implementations of Sharia; the Nasirist socialists—figures from the former Mubarak regime promising a new democratic era; and independent candidates with various orientations. Each party's self-presentation and platform became the determinant factor in their level of public support, which marked the spark of a level of accountability and interdependence between authority and the citizens.

Second, none of the parties or candidates expressed reliance on foreign powers, which demonstrated how most players understood that this reform must rely on Egyptian self-determination and their own creativity as leaders, rather than relying on following any foreign policy.

Third, despite the promotion and support of some candidates who presented a singular approach—only socialist, only revivalists of Islamic past, or only opponents of the military—remarkable public support went to candidates who broke these stereotypes by trying to reconcile the opposites, unify the public, and prioritize stability and socioeconomic needs. One example was Mohamed El Baradei who, at the beginning of the revolution, gathered considerable support from groups with diverse affiliations and religions, gender, and age under the National Association for Change, seeking this change within a National Assembly. Nonetheless, due to the continuous need to build effective institutions and fight corruption in order to support good governance, Egypt, similar to many other Muslim societies, continued to experience some of what Roland Paris identifies as "pathologies of liberalization" (2004)[3] in its journey toward a democratic and participatory political system.

Consequently, I can highlight three promising insights from the development of social/political thought for both the West and the Muslim world. First, many on both sides emphasize that reconciliation with modernity necessitates some sort of a democratic/participatory system that prioritizes freedom, order, rights, ethics, and inclusivity, and opens the door to a fair interaction with "others" within the same society (pluralism) and across countries and cultures. This latest movement, which resists the traditional mechanisms of discipline and traditional concepts of progress at the expense of "Others," can lead to mutual promotion of a single international standard of justice and human rights despite the many challenges in this process.

Second, both sides realize that definitions of the notions of freedom and inclusivity are shifting back from abstraction to be strongly linked to concrete socioeconomic benefits connected to human daily practices and needs because it is the practice of these notions that really matters. This recognition promotes ethical scientific advancement. It also extends to the relationship between the Western world and the Muslim world through stressing, at least theoretically, the accountability of governments and of international society—for example, in implementing Responsibility to Protect and Trade Agreements that promote human rights. Due to this shift, calls to reform the UN and create new international reconciliatory/supervisory bodies are increasing, and human rights organizations such as Amnesty International are balancing their emphasis on political rights with an emphasis on socioeconomic rights as explained by Khan (2009). In addition, Western development projects in developing countries increasingly implement performance and results-based evaluations (i.e., measuring impact and multilevel outcomes in people's lives) rather than simply relying on superficial outcome evaluation (i.e., measuring numbers as benchmarks for success).

Third, there is an understanding by many on both sides that this shift to provide more efficient socioeconomic and political benefits is not simply because these benefits have now become ultimate goals in themselves but rather because they are understood as indicators of our rise in consciousness as we mutually acknowledge our basic human values of freedom, ethics, rights, order, and inclusivity in a democratic society with fewer inequalities,

and as we reflect this acknowledgment through certain minimum requirements for the actual implementation of these benefits. This understanding still
leaves room for human creativity in determining the democratic/participatory
structure and form of international collaboration that suit each country and
culture.

In brief, once the growth in our human thought and consciousness clarifies
the "what" and "why" of our quest toward positive peace within the self and
with others (balanced freedom, social justice, public participation, human
unity, and compassion), we can be flexible on the "how" and "when" as
we learn from one another and collaborate in shifting various contexts and
systems.

ISLAMIC CONCEPTS OF CONFLICT RESOLUTION AND DEMOCRACY

There are several Islamic concepts that promote peace with the self and
others, encouraging introspection, nonviolent conflict resolution, and transformation despite the problems we see in the practice of many Muslims
as individuals, groups, and states.[4] Concepts mentioned in the Qur'an and
practiced by the Prophet to peacefully resolve disputes can be used creatively
to support a vision of a just and sustainable peace based on linking together
activities, actors, and institutions at all levels (Philpott and Powers 2010).
Musalaha (reconciliation), *sulh* (mediation), and *tahkeem* (arbitration) imply
acceptance of pluralism and diversity whether within a Muslim state or in
international relations. In mediation, a third party helps bring peace between
conflicting groups without resorting to violence.[5] In arbitration, the quarreling
parties accept a trustworthy and knowledgeable arbiter (or group of arbiters)
to decide.[6]

The Prophet played the role of an interreligious arbitrator between Muslims
and Jews in Medinah and among the Jews themselves using their divine scrip-
tures, as referred to in the Qur'an (5:42–44; Moussalli 1997, 53). In fact, Ibn
Kathir makes "valid arbitration and judgment dependent on justice, equity
and fairness among all" (ibid., 53). Moussalli explains that following the
Prophet's death the

> power of *tahkim* (arbitration) became the prerogative of the *ummah* (the whole
> community of believers regardless of ancestry or geography), the avenue to
> exercising judicial and political rule as well as religious interpretation was in
> theory dependent on *shura* (consultation) as the initiating principle and process
> and on *tahkim* as the principle and process of ratification that might lead to *ijma'*
> (consensus). (Moussali 1997, 58)[7]

The Prophet Muhammad (peace be upon him) set a model for Muslims to prioritize peace in international relations—a notion supported by the Qur'an and Muslim scholars. He used dialogue in international relations as he sent and received ambassadors with full immunity, only fighting the Byzantine Empire and the Persians in self-defense. He sought peace treaties whenever possible, perceiving them as victories (e.g., Treaty of Hudaybia in 628A).[8] Several Qur'anic verses state that Muslims should abide by treaties, never start wars, and if they are compelled to fight to stop conflict between two Muslim groups or fight non-Muslims in self-defense, then they should never transgress the boundaries of stopping the violence (Salmi, Majul, and Tanham 1998, 90)[9] and they should accept peace whenever it is offered. The Qur'anic verses are "Fight in the way of God against those who fight you, but do not begin hostilities" (2:190); "and if your enemy inclines towards peace, do incline towards peace as well" (8:61).

Mahmud Shaltut, who was appointed Shakh al-Azhar in Egypt by presidential decree in 1958, asserted that the Qur'anic verse that can be considered as an Islamic charter concerning the relations between Muslims and non-Muslims is, "Allah does not forbid you respecting those who have not made war against you on account of (your) religion, and have not driven you forth from your homes, that you show them kindness and deal with them justly; surely Allah loves the doers of justice" (Qur'an 60:8; Peters 1977, 37–45). Shaltut explains that Muslims are ordered to fight "those who fight them" due to the "aggression directed against them, expulsion from their dwellings, violations of Allah's sacred institutions and attempts to persecute people for what they believe" and that "the establishment of religious liberty—is the aim upon the attainment of which Muslims should cease fighting" (Peters 1977, 37–45). He refers in his analysis to the verses in which God gave the permission to Muslims to fight non-Muslims based on the latter's unjust actions:

> Permission (to fight) is given to those upon whom war is made because they are oppressed, and most surely Allah is well able to assist them; Those who have been expelled from their homes without a just cause except that they say: Our Lord is Allah. And had there not been Allah's repelling some people by others, certainly there would have been pulled down cloisters and churches and synagogues and mosques in which Allah's name is much remembered. (Qur'an 22:39-41)

Another example of practicing conflict resolution involves Muslim jurists who corrected the deficiency produced by the Ummayad jurists, who divided the world into *dar al-Islam* (land of Islam) and *dar al-harb* (land of war) in order to establish international peace (Sachedina 2001, 32, 34, 43).[10] As such, these subsequent jurists produced other concepts such as *dar al-ahd* (land of treaty) and *dar al-sulh* (land of safety), which the jurist Al-Mawardi considered part of *dar al-Islam* (Salmi, Majul, and Tanham 1998, 74). In recent times, Muslim jurists identified the secular countries where Muslims enjoyed religious freedom as *dar al-hiyad* (land of neutrality) (ibid., 74). Rachid Ghannoushi (Tunis 1980s), interpreted *dar al-Islam* to include "any secular democratic state where religious freedom exists" (Esposito and Voll 2001, 114). Other scholars, such as Al-Ghunaimi, dispensed altogether with all concepts dividing the world and insisted that the Prophet Muhammad entered into treaties for undetermined periods of time, and appreciated jurists who granted equality to Muslims and non-Muslims in the Muslim state (Salmi, Majul and Tanham 1998, 95–96). Al-Ghunaimi further rejected imperialism and exploitation and saw that the normal condition of the world is not to have a pan-Islamic state but rather several political entities coexisting as equals in peace (ibid., 95–96, 102).[11]

This understanding of conflict resolution and managing international relations is one aspect in the analysis of the possible compatibility of Islam and democracy.

Other areas include sovereignty, rights, participation, and equality for women and minorities. There is reference to each area in the Qur'an that can be used to demonstrate conditional compatibility with democratic principles based on interpretation and implementation. Furthermore, there is sufficient literature by scholars, such as Abou El Fadl, Fatima Mernissi, and Sachedina, to demonstrate how Muslim masses were manipulated by their rulers and religious leaders, who became state-paid functionaries, into equating Islam with blind obedience to authority and rigid interpretation of Qur'an and were deprived of originality of thinking and freedom of speech (Mernissi 1992, 38–49 and Abou El Fadl 2004, 23–30). This manipulation took place despite the original progressive seventh-century Muslim jurists' assertion of five fundamental human rights to all regardless of lineage, religion, or color: the right to life (*nafs*), religion (*din*), intellect (*'aql*), property (*mal*), and lineage (*'ird*) (Ceric 2004, 53). In addition, this manipulation led to a reductionist view of original Islamic concepts of consultation (*shura*), consensus (*ijma*), independent reasoning (*ijtihad*), and public good (*istislah*). The gap between Muslims and democracy widened even further due to the impact of colonialism, Muslim nationalist movements' rejection of all Western heritage, postindependence conflicts among Muslim-majority countries, communism, unbalanced Western policies, undereducation or illiteracy among Muslims, and above all the despotic postindependence regimes in Muslim-majority countries.

With the current revolutions and transformation of realities in the Muslim world, starting a genuine yet long process of democratization is possible, even if several groups in the Muslim populace are opposing it. As Irfan

Ahmad argues, "We must shift the debate from the arena of normativity to the domain of practice," because it is a mistake to state that "democracy cannot flourish in Muslim societies unless Muslims become democrats" (Ahmad 2011, 461). Ahmad supports his argument by giving the example of how, at first, Maududi, founder of *Jamaat* in India, asked Muslims not to participate in the elections because they permitted human legislation to replace divine laws, but when opposed by *ulema* (Muslim scholars) and the public, he revised his position and even conducted the debate within *Jamaat* using majority vote (ibid., 464–65).

In short, through reinterpretation of Islamic sources (Qur'an and Hadith), and as I argued elsewhere (Ibrahim 2006), it is possible to conceive of a conditional compatibility between Islam and some form of democracy that allows public participation, ethics, order, individual rights, and inclusivity. In my view, three elements need to be enabled to establish that democracy: (1) a reformed constitution that warrants, at a minimum, accountability, socioeconomic human rights, and repeated honest elections; (2) a radical plan to reform education by making it affordable and accessible, especially to women and minorities, and incorporating relevant fields of humanities, conflict studies, and scientific knowledge being delivered by competent teachers; and (3) free media that does not condone hate. It will be a struggle that takes time, just as the West had a long struggle to establish its democracies (Salem 1997, 12–15).[12] This struggle will further remain highly influenced by the impact of Islamist extremism and by the Western political, economic,[13] cultural, and military domination or involvement in the Muslim world. Despite all uncertainty, Muslims cannot afford to stall this process.

CREATIVE DIALOGUE BETWEEN THE WEST AND THE MUSLIM WORLD

Noting that various concepts through the generations connected the two worlds, we realize that the dialogue between the Muslim world and the West has been taking place for centuries through various forms, whether among intelligentsia (philosophers, scientists) or religious leaders. Western spiritual leaders, even within the Canadian military, can play an active role in dialogue and resolving conflicts in the Muslim world.

Several observations can provide a context for mutual engagement. First, the number and intensity of violent acts related to religion continue to fluctuate, which requires our attention to addressing violent extremism in general rather than a narrow focus on any one or two ideological or religious groups.

On the one hand, violent conflict related to religion rose between 2001 and 2015, especially with the rise of ISIL (Islamic state). The 2010 Human

Security Report shows that there was a 25 percent increase in the number of armed conflicts between 2003 and 2008, especially religion-related ones, and that nine out of thirty-four conflicts between 2004 and 2008 were associated with Islamist political violence (Human Security Report 2009/2010). Also, the 2015 Global Terrorism Index mentions that "deaths from terrorism increased 80% last year to the highest level ever, with 32,685 people killed" and that "Boko Haram and ISIL were jointly responsible for 51% of all claimed global fatalities in 2014" (Global Terrorism Index 2015).[14] We can add to these figures that the Syrian conflict, which involves ISIL, has so far proved to be the worst humanitarian crisis in a generation with over half a million people dead and over 11 million people displaced.

On the other hand, the 2018 Global Terrorism Index shows a fall in deaths resulting from terrorism between 2015 and 2018. It shows a correlation between the impact of terrorism and human rights abuses, social alienation, lack of economic opportunity, and involvement in an external conflict, as well as a rise in far-right and political terrorism (in the United Kingdom, Sweden, France, the United States) mostly by actors with far-right, white nationalists, or anti-Muslim beliefs (Global Terrorism Index 2018). The March 2019 attack in New Zealand on two mosques killing forty-nine Muslims and injuring twenty-nine shows a continuation of an anti-Muslim trend. Adding to the confusion is the lack of clarity concerning what is happening with the ex-ISIL militants following their dismantlement by US-backed forces in 2019, and the question of how best to handle the return of thousands of foreign fighters to Western and Muslim countries.

These observations inform key understandings for the mutual response to the threat of violent extremism. First, the fluctuations of statistics of violent conflict related to religion and lack of clarity necessitate that our response to the threat of violent extremism must be balanced rather than fear-based and must take into consideration the complexity of motivations and processes involving politico-religious radicalization related to individuals and structures in order to disempower terrorist leaders or recruitment groups since these extremists are not united. It is important to keep in mind that Islamist extremism is only one of many types of violent extremism and threats to human security.

Second, religion fuels conflict; yet, it can also be used to manage it and reduce violence. It fuels conflict, as Daniel Philpott explains, "not only by defining the identities and loyalties of communities, but also their very political goals which then becomes *casus belli*" (Peacebuilding Initiative 2009). This understanding can be used to connect with Muslim religious leaders to better understand the layers and web of conflict. Equally important, such understanding can open channels to utilizing these leaders' social functions in peacebuilding through their role in educating and mobilizing their people for creative and constructive engagement within the societies in which they live especially at times of crisis (ibid.). This offers opportunities for Western spiritual leaders to enhance peacebuilding and reconstruction in prevention as well as during conflict and postconflict.

Third, there is a dialectical relationship between the interpretation of religion and aspects of tribal norms in the Muslim world, which stipulates the necessity of integrating and developing the local capacity of target communities in resolving conflicts, albeit in a discretionary manner. In fact, there are recorded examples of NGOs' successful use of tribal norms in conflict mediation in Arab countries where formal justice system is mistrusted, which "shattered the myths and stereotypes about tribal conflict mediation being a backward practice restricted to rural areas" (Safa 2007, 4–5).

At this point, allow me to share some suggestions to Western spiritual leaders to expedite a dialogue that makes sense to both the Muslims and the West, and that creatively addresses violent extremism.

Be Clear about Our Objectives and Equality

Initiators of dialogue need to start with being clear on their objectives. To borrow Viktor E. Frankl's words, they need to determine whether they seek the "will to meaning" and understanding or "the will to power" and "striving for superiority" (Frankl 2006, 99). This will determine whether they see Muslims as the "Other" who needs to be "enlightened" or as equals searching for a meaningful and ethical existence and who must be heard and understood without bias. This will further inform these Western leaders' key messages, methods, and partners and how they use their knowledge of Islamic history and concepts of conflict resolution to find common values and promote freedom, ethics, and inclusivity (also diversity and pluralism). Interestingly, Tariq Ramadan states that the conditions for dialogue "do not lie in the means or ends but in the attitude and frame of mind" and that dialogue should be "approached with humility, concern for coherence and self-criticism, and respect for the other" (2009, 308).

Understand Muslim Culture and Acknowledge the Impact of the Conflict with the West

Western spiritual leaders need to prepare for and conduct the dialogue in context. They need to understand the history and culture of each country targeted for dialogue and acknowledge the realities of the international environment and the dynamics of the current political and economic relationship between Western countries and Muslim-majority countries.

For example, Western spiritual leaders need to acknowledge:

- the impact of Western political and military intervention in Muslim-majority countries as in Iraq, Libya, Afghanistan, and Syria, and the massive suffering of innocent civilians in these countries. As Tariq Ramadan explains, the danger of ignoring political and economic considerations is that "agents of dialogue" will be kept in an "isolated universe" as "the problems are being 'culturalized,' 'religionalized,' or 'Islamized' while they are in actuality primarily social and political in nature" (2009, 306).
- the propaganda against Muslims by much of the Western media, and the right of alternate media to participate in the global communication arena.
- the importance for flexibility concerning the pace and form of democracy that each Muslim-majority country need to take. That is because "being a democracy has never been enough to guarantee the promotion of peace, the respect of human rights, dignity, freedom and autonomy" as evident by the U.S. involvement in many conflicts (ibid., 283).

This will determine these leaders' openness to understand certain actions, explore alternatives that they may suggest to their own coreligionists, governments, or to Muslims leaders.

Use Dialogue as Means for Action

They need to approach the dialogue as means to expose the real causes of conflict and as a platform that leads to action. This is important to give credibility to Western spiritual leaders in the eyes of Muslim leaders and to give ownership of the decision to local groups, which is essential for the implementation. As Ramadan asserts, when discussing dialogue between civilizations, "ideas and values should not only be discussed, but measured through concrete implementation in reality" (ibid., 307).

Here are some ways in which dialogue could mobilize people for transformational action:

1. Make use of the Muslim religious leaders' social functions in peacebuilding through their role in "mobilization" of the masses, "socialization" (education and training) of the elite and poor, "integration" of those shunned by the society, and "substitution for political and partisan-type organizations in particular in times of crisis or closure of the political space" (Peacebuilding Initiative 2009).
2. Involve/invite representatives from all stakeholders in the target country to the dialogue (i.e., be inclusive of various groups) in order to reduce the chance that ignored parties might sabotage the dialogue. Even if some groups refuse to participate formally, reaching out to champions of peace

is an effective strategy to start a discourse in the right direction among members of these groups.

3. Help train Muslim religious leaders in the target country on leadership skills and strategies of nonviolent conflict resolution using their knowledge of Islamic concepts and principles. This will help the exit strategy of the country of these Western spiritual leaders and increase the prospect of success of peace in the target country afterward.

4. Conduct educational/sensitivity training for their own military and government departments related to Muslim culture and explain a basic understanding of relevant Islamic concepts. This would be very important to widen Western decision makers' pool of options to be considered and to avoid an exaggerated perception of an Islamist threat.

5. Help mitigate the impact of hate media. For example, they can help produce a documentary on the reality of sufferings of Muslims in conflicting countries, Muslims' efforts against terrorism as well as the human cost of terrorism on both Muslims and non-Muslims residing in Western countries in order to educate both the locals in the target country and the Western populace.

Train and Use Peace Professionals

Build capacity and transformation within the conflicting communities themselves to help shift the way conflict is seen and managed. Specialized religious-based peace professionals could benefit from applying the approaches of mediation (communicative, facilitative, and directive) to prevent, mitigate, and contain violence especially when the situation reaches a painful stalemate. They can further solicit the assistance from Muslim religious leaders in their own countries who are aware of the language and context of the target country. They can be particularly helpful in the prevention stage (changing attitudes, practices, policies, building peace coalitions). In fact, according to Brian Cox and Daniel Philpott, faith-based mediation/diplomacy has been used as track-two diplomacy and found to be effective in five particular contexts (Cox and Philpott 2011, 20–21): when the conflicting parties define themselves by their religious identities; when charismatic religious leaders motivate reconciliation; when faith-based opposition mobilizes against injustice; when "faith-based diplomats" become "trusted envoys" and use their social networks; and when ideological conflicts are informed by membership to a religion.

Keeping in mind the complexity of the situation, it is also important to be attentive to new emergent and unpredicted developments. These then can open up new adjacent possibles. It is important to give people a mandate to be attentive to these and mobilize timely action.

If a comprehensive and integrative approach is considered, religious peace-building can have a role within the military, civil society, and international coalitions. Steve Moore has written extensively on the need for this approach as well as practical engagement strategies and theology of reconciliation during war in his book *Military Chaplains as Agents of Peace: Religious Leader Engagement in Conflict and Postconflict Environment* (Moore 2013).

Collaborate on a Holistic Approach to Combat Violent Extremism

Violent extremism is one of the most challenging issues both the Muslim and Western worlds face and it is not confined to a particular religious or ideological group. Examples in Canada include the shooting in the 2014 shooting at Parliament Hill by a lone actor supportive of jihadists as well as the shooting at a Quebec mosque in 2017 killing six Muslims. Most recent examples in other countries include the March 2019 shootings in mosques in New Zealand, leaving forty-nine Muslims dead, and the April 2019 bombings of churches and hotels in Sri Lanka, again leaving over 200 killed and hundreds of others injured. All these incidents leave a deep mark of devastation on all our souls. The challenge of violent extremism is not only due to its devastating results but also because addressing it comes with the potential of either a collaboration between polarities (i.e., where our differences bring strength) or a division between duality (i.e., where "us versus them" attitude brings weakness and serves the terrorists' agenda).

All these acts are a reminder of three facts. First, there is no country and no ethnic minority or mainstream society immune to terror; we are all in this together; and we can only face this by uniting together against violent extremism, wherever and however it shows its aggression. Second, acts of terror are merely symptoms and eliminating the symptoms requires recognizing and addressing the root causes, including flawed education and unfair policies. Third, beyond the statements of condemnation and humanitarian support, which we must do, real commitment is overdue to be undertaken by governments, organizations, and communities prior to and once the early signs of violent extremism present themselves.

THE *EPIFANY* MODEL

The approach I propose here is the EPIFANY model, which I created based on many years of research and practical experience in conflict resolution. The violent extremism I refer to here is one that uses any extreme spiritual, political, or social ideals to reject the status quo or undermine expressions of freedom of choice while using violent means to achieve its goals. This EPIFANY model, I am providing below (Figure 9.1), is built on my view that the deep-rooted issue of violent extremism requires a paradigm shift through a creative holistic multidisciplinary approach that aims at transforming individuals, relations, and structures leading to a sustainable progress toward a culture of positive peace. Such model can be seen as an overall umbrella that still allows us to choose the element that we each, an individuals or organizations, can best contribute to without losing sight of the connectedness of the whole. Each letter of the word EPIFANY refers to a certain element and all elements interconnect to enable continuous growth and creativity.

Evolve: Evolve the understanding of the various communities and organizations of positive peace (as analyzed and measured by the Global Peace Index) and their capacities of conflict resolution, embrace pluralism and a shared vision for future generations, explore healthy life purposes and goals (personal and collective), choose healthy partnerships and coalitions.

Prevent: Understand the motivations and processes of drifting into unhealthy ideologies and behaviors that enforce the formation of an extremist identity, understand a higher prospective of accountability, reform corrupt systems domestically or internationally, prevent consciously exacerbating fragile conflict situations.

Intervene: Intervene when harmful actions have already started or violent structures are already entrenched, address unmet needs and deep-rooted causes. People who intervene generally need a mandate. This involves questions about who can provide a mandate, who or which organization is best placed to intervene, and how to take the first step.

Force: Use protective force to stop the violence or harm without crossing over to punitive or revengeful measures that would feed into the narrative of the recruiters of at-risk youth.

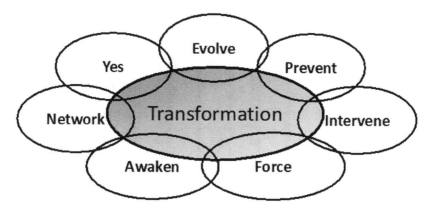

Figure 9.1 EPIFANY. Copyright by Iman Ibrahim.

Awaken: Rehabilitate those who developed an extremist identity and/or drifted into violence by means of: understanding the processes that led to this extremism, evaluating how their past choices failed them in fulfilling their identity needs, and empowering them to explore alternative options that support the transformation of individuals and groups, particularly with those who are especially challenging (see Chabot, "Warring with Windigo," *Transforming*).

Network: Reintegrate those rehabilitated into the community by means of dialogue (Brodeur, "Interworldview Dialogue," *Transforming*), supportive measures (Gagnon, "Heart-Based Communication," *Transforming*), socioeconomic programs, and shared institutional responsibilities. This point requires working on at least four stakeholders: the individuals who need rehabilitation (with attention to age, gender, and role they played in violent conflicts), the governments responsible for these individuals, law enforcement agencies, and host communities. Addressing such network appropriately would produce healthy partnerships capable of evaluating success and lessons learned from the rehabilitation programs and identifying the gaps that require further research.

Yes: Commit the collective (the community, society, and governments involved) to integrating the results of the evaluation of the previously mentioned elements (lessons learned, insights, research needs, and collaborative partnerships) into the Evolve element in order to repeat the EPIFANY cycle with expansion.

Strategies for these elements can be developed in a way that would be amenable to the ever-evolving contexts and identities of the actors involved.

CONCLUSION

Our openness to an empowering, inclusive, needs-based, and action-oriented dialogue between the Muslim World and the West could lead us to an emergent creativity toward reconciliation and addressing violent extremism. Our understanding of our interdependent history, evolving identities and roles, human connections, and universal needs for freedom, justice, and inclusivity is our guiding light to transcend divisions and labels. Integrating interpretations of Islamic concepts that are compatible with democratic values would be a key positive factor in this process. Another key factor is creating peace within and aligning our outer world toward the practical elements that constitute positive peace in our domestic and international relations, which would assist us in overcoming many challenges and going beyond linear thinking and action. The genius of life is manifested as we choose quantum compassion—compassion for ourselves and for all others even for those who harmed us—to break the cycle of violence and transform our structures, and as we choose quantum gratitude—gratitude for everything even painful experiences that helped us grow and connect on a genuine deep level.

NOTES

1. Stuart Kauffmann used this expression of "bubbling forth" in his statement to Muslims at the Spirituality, Emergent Creativity and Reconciliation Conference (*Saint Paul University*, May 24, 2012) to refer to creative yet hidden possibilities.

2. Sardar gives examples of the genocide including the "genocide of the Amerindians, the Australian aborigines," and the "primitive tribes of West and Central Africa."

3. Paris identifies these pathologies as five main problems that societies generally go through: some media that spreads hatred and extremism; opportunistic leaders who dwell on ethnic divisions; the use of elections as a platform for harmful competition that exacerbates societal conflicts; leaders who sabotage democracy to avoid democratic challenges; and speedy marketization that imposes short-term social costs by creating class-based conflicts and political violence (152, 159, 160–68).

4. Qur'anic verse: "and God calls [the human beings] into the abode of peace and guides one who wills onto a straight way" (10:25). The Prophet Muhammad (PBUH) said: "Shall I inform you of merit greater than fasting, charity, and prayer? It is in the conciliation of people" (he said "people" not only Muslims). See also Marc Gopin (2002, 1340).

5. Example: when an Arab tribe intervened between the Muslims in Medinah and Quraysh to avoid war.

6. Example: when the Prophet accepted arbitration with an Arab tribe called Al Anbar.

7. One major example of arbitration following the prophet's death was during the war between Ali (fourth caliph) and Muawiyah (an Ummayad who wanted to usurp the rule using an arbiter who tricked Ali's representative leading to Ali losing the rule and then his assassination by the extremists called *Khawarij*).

8. The Prophet's war with the Byzantine Empire happened after the Roman king killed his messenger and assembled forces to attack the Muslims. The Prophet's war with the Persians started after the Persian King tore Muhammad's letter, sent his governor in Yemen after Muhammad, and ordered the kings of al-Hira to attack the Arab tribes.

9. The authors explain that Ibn Taimiya held that fighting should be confined to the aggressors.

10. AbdulAziz Sachedina explains that this division is a subversion of the Qur'anic spiritual internal division between faith and disbelief (*dar al-iman* and *dar al-kufr*) that was meant to encourage acknowledgment of the lordship of God.

11. The authors explain that Al-Ghunaimi saw evidence in the Qur'an that it is normal to have more than one Islamic state through his interpretation of the verse: 49:9 "If two parties among the Believers fall into a quarrel, make ye peace between

them: but if one of them transgresses beyond bounds against the other, then fight ye (all) against the one that transgresses until it complies with the Command of Allah; but if it complies, then make peace between them with justice, and be fair: for Allah loves those who are fair (and just)." The same understanding of *umma* is shared by another scholar: AbuSulayman.

12. As Paul Salem explains, the Western world needs to remember that it idealized struggle for a long time, as clear in the writings of Hegel and Marx for example, until its countries established national unity, national independence, socioeconomic equality, and democratic governments. This includes eighteenth- and nineteenth-century revolutions and wars in Europe, the United States, and Russia. Revolutions: 1776 in America against Britain (Congress appointed a committee to draft a declaration of independence. Committee members were Thomas Jefferson, Benjamin Franklin, John Adams, Roger Livingston, and Roger Sherman), 1789 in France (against absolute monarchy with feudal privileges for the aristocracy and Catholic clergy, based on Enlightenment principles of nationalism, citizenship, and inalienable rights), 1848 in Europe except for Poland, the Netherlands, Serbia, Russia, and Ottomans (a revolutionary wave, began in Sicily, the French Revolution of 1848, then spread to the rest of Europe), 1917 in Russia, (World Wars I and II).

13. The economic domination has been taking many shapes through direct aid, trade agreement, private investments, and loans through the World Bank and IMF. For example, in John Perkins' book, *Confessions of an Economic Hitman* (2004), he explains how, as an expert in an international consultation firm, his job was to convince less-developed countries to accept multibillion-dollar loans for infrastructure projects and to see to it that most of this money ended up at Halliburton, Bechtel, Brown and Root, and other U.S. engineering and construction companies.

14. This index mentions that "78% of all deaths and 57% of all attacks occurred in just five countries: Afghanistan, Iraq, Nigeria, Pakistan and Syria."

REFERENCES

Abou El Fadl, Khaled. 2004. *Islam and the Challenge of Democracy.* Princeton, NJ and Oxford: Princeton University Press.

Ahmad, Irfan. 2011. "Democracy and Islam." *Philosophy and Social Criticism*, 37(4), 459–470.

Amin, Samir. 1989. *Eurocentrism.* New York, NY: Monthly Review Press.

Arendt, Hannah. 1998. *The Human Condition.* Chicago, IL and London: The University of Chicago Press.

Ceric, Mustafa. 2004. "Judaism, Christianity, Islam: Hope or Fear of Our Times." In *Beyond Violence, Religious Sources for Social Transformation in Judaism, Christianity, and Islam,* Edited by L. James and S. M. Heft, 1st Edition, 43–56. New York, NY, USA: Fordham University Press.

Cox, Brian, and Daniel Philpott. 2011. "Faith-based Diplomacy: An Ancient Idea Newly Emergent." *The Notre Dame Center for Ethics and Culture*, January 14, 2011. https://www.tandfonline.com/doi/abs/10.1080/15435725.2003.9523161.

Esposito, John, and John Voll. 2001. *Makers of Contemporary Islam*. Oxford: Oxford University Press.

Falk, Richard. August 1, 2011. *Warfare and Limits: A Losing Battle*. https://www.alj azeera.com/indepth/opinion/2011/08/20118182137256291.html.

Foreign Affairs and International Trade Canada. 2009. *Departmental Performance Report 2009–2010*. https://www.tbs-sct.gc.ca/dpr-rmr/2009-2010/inst/ext/ext-eng .pdf.

Frankl, Viktor E. 2006. *Man's Search for Meaning*. Boston, MA: Beacon Press.

Giddens, A. 1990. *The Consequences of Modernity*. Cambridge: Polity Press.

Global Peace Index, Institute for Economics & Peace. http://economicsandpeace .org/.

Gopin, Marc. 2002. *Holy War, Holy Peace: How Religion can Bring Peace to the Middle East*. Oxford: Oxford University Press.

Human Security Report 2009/2010. https://www.tandfonline.com/doi/abs/10.1080/0 2255189.2012.664546?journalCode=rcjd20.

Ibrahim, Iman. 2006. *Islam(s) and Democracies, Compatibility and Challenges*. Submitted in a Course on Religion at the College of Humanities at Carleton University.

Islam, Misbah. 2008. *Decline of Muslim States and Societies, The Real Root Causes and What Can be Done Next*. Library of Congress. United States of America: Xlibris Corporation.

Jenkins, Brian Michael. 2016. *Fifteen Years After 9/11: A Preliminary Balance Sheet Testimony of Brian Michael Jenkins Before the Committee on Armed Services United States House of Representatives September 21, 2016*. Rand Corporation. file:///C:/Users/User/Downloads/RAND_CT458.pdf.

Kauffman, Stuart. 2012. "His Statement to Muslims at the Spirituality, Emergent Creativity, and Reconciliation Conference." *Saint Paul University*, May 24, 2012.

Khan, Irene, and David Petrasek. 2009. *The Unheard Truth: Poverty and Human Rights*. New York, NY: W.W. Norton & Co.

Kolakowski, L. 1990. *Modernity on Endless Trial*. Chicago, IL: University of Chicago Press.

Lederach, John Paul. 2003. *Conflict Transformation*. Intercourse, PA: Good Books.

Mernissi, Fatima. 1992. *Islam and Democracy*. Translated by Mary Jo Lakeland. California, NY: Addison-Wesley Publishing Company.

Moore, Steve K. 2013. *Military Chaplains as Agents of Peace: Religious Leader Engagement in Conflict and Postconflict Environment*. Toronto: Lexington Books.

Moussalli, Ahmad. 1997. "An Islamic Model for Political Conflict Resolution: Tahkim (Arbitration)." In *Conflict Resolution in the Arab World*, Edited by Paul Salem, 44–71. Beirut: American University of Beirut.

Paris, Roland. 2004. "The Limits of Wilsonianism: Understanding the Dangers." In *At War's End*. Cambridge: Cambridge University Press.

Peacebuilding Initiative. 2009. *Religion & Peacebuilding: Religion & Peacebuilding Processes*, April, 2009. http://www.peacebuildinginitiative.org/index9aa2.html?p ageId=1827.

Perkins, John. 2004. *Confessions of an Economic Hitman.* San Francisco, CA: Berrett-Koehler Publishers Inc. http://www.amazon.com/Confessions-Economic -Hit-John-Perkins/dp/1576753018.

Peters, Rudolph. 1997. *Jihad in Mediaeval and Modern Islam.* Leiden: E. J. Brill.

Philpott, Daniel, and Gerard F. Powers. 2010. *Strategies of Peace, Transforming Conflict in a Violent World.* New York, NY: Oxford University Press.

Polanyi, Karl. 2001. *The Great Transformation.* Boston, MA: Beacon Press.

Rajaee, Farhang. 2007. *Islamism and Modernism.* Austin, TX: University of Texas Press.

Ramadan, Tariq. 2009. *Radical Reform.* Oxford: Oxford University Press.

Robinson, Bill. 2009. "Canadian Military Spending 2009." *Canadian Centre for Policy Alternatives,* December 2009. http://www.policyalternatives.ca/publications /reports/canadian-military-spending-2009.

Rubin, Jeffrey Z. 1997. "Western Perspectives on Conflict Resolution." In *Conflict Resolution in the Arab World,* Edited By Paul Salem. Beirut: American University of Beirut.

Sachedina, Abdulaziz. 2001. *The Islamic Roots of Democratic Pluralism.* Oxford: Oxford University Press.

Safa, Oussama. 2007. *Conflict Resolution and Reconciliation in the Arab World.* Bergof Research Centre. https://www.berghof-foundation.org/fileadmin/redaktion/ Publications/Handbook/Articles/safa_handbook.pdf.

Salem, Paul. 1997. "A Critique of Western Conflict Resolution from a Non-Western Perspective." In *Conflict Resolution in the Arab World,* Edited by Paul Salem, 11–24. Beirut: American University of Beirut.

Salmi, Ralph H., Cesar Adib Majul, and George K. Tanham. 1998. *Islam and Conflict Resolution.* Lanham, MD: University Press of America.

Sardar, Ziauddin. 1995. *Terminator 2: Modernity, Postmodernism and the Other.* Originally published in June 1992. https://ziauddinsardar.com/articles/terminator -2-modernity-postmodernism-and-other.

Taylor, Charles. 2004. *Modern Social Imaginaries.* Durham, NC and London: Duke University Press.

Willis, Henry. 2017. *The Wrong Terrorism Narrative.* Rand Corporation, Objective Analysis, Effective Solutions, January 2017. http://www.rand.org/blog/2017/01/th e-wrong-terrorism-narrative.html.

Zaidi, Ali Hassan. 2006. "Muslim Reconstruction of Knowledge and the Re-enchantment of Modernity." *Theory, Culture and Society* (SAGE, London), 23(5), 69–91.

2015 Global Terrorism Index, Institute for Economics & Peace. https://reliefweb.int /sites/reliefweb.int/files/resources/2015%20Global%20Terrorism%20Index%20R eport_0_0.pdf.

2018 Global Terrorism Index, Institute for Economics & Peace. http://visionofhuman ity.org/app/uploads/2018/12/Global-Terrorism-Index-2018-1.pdf.

Chapter 10

Arts Literacy and Nonviolent Social Change

Reenvisioning Spirituality through Creative Practice

Lauren Michelle Levesque

The concept of "arts literacy," or the idea of indwelling the arts, has implications for scholarship on spirituality, especially that engaged with nonviolence. More pointedly, scholars have argued that the arts are an under-examined dimension of both nonviolent praxis and processes of reconciliation (Branagan 2013; García 2014). For example, despite acknowledging an increased attention to the arts in peace studies, María Elisa Pinto García argues that much of this research is overly optimistic and anecdotal (2014, 25, 31). She and others suggest that further reflection is needed on the role of the arts in addressing conflict and violence (Bergh and Sloboda 2010, 4).

With this reflection in mind, this chapter explores the potential ways the idea of arts literacy, as related to music and improvisation, can expand thinking on socially engaged and nonviolent spiritualities. In the first section, I discuss my research as an "indwelling" the arts. Second, I examine Edward Said and David Barenboim's thinking on music literacy and why it matters. The third section is an examination of the implications of arts literacy for reenvisioning scholarship on socially engaged and *nonviolent spiritualities*. Fourth, I explore arts literacy in an age of terror, drawing on the work of international relations scholar, Roland Bleiker. Finally, I conclude with suggestions for practice on the intersections between arts literacy and reconciliation. Here, reconciliation is understood as processes that involve transforming "relationships of hostility, mistrust and resentment into relationships of trust and mutual understanding" (Garcia 2014, 28).

INDWELLING THE ARTS

Writing about creative contributions to different areas of knowledge, Vern Neufeld Redekop notes that those making these contributions "have immersed themselves within a domain, usually for about 10 years" (Redekop 2012, 592). Throughout this chapter, I discuss the notion of immersion as it relates to the arts and to scholarship. The idea has relevance, I argue, for reenvisioning scholarship as performance and as creative practice.

Redekop's statement on creative contributions implies a type of "indwelling," or a time when individuals amass extensive knowledge of a particular question and/or issue. This notion of "indwelling" is discussed with reference to "emergent creativity," a concept that comprises thinking on complex adaptive systems as creative environments perpetually moving toward the new (Redekop 2012, 592–94). Redekop states: "Creativity is not reversible; once you've created something, that new thing exits, and you can't go back to a state where it no longer exists" (2012, 592). In this understanding, indwelling a particular question and/or issue takes on certain characteristics, including flexibility and open-endedness.

In my doctoral research, I sought to embody these characteristics with regard to particular questions: What does an adequate approach to protest music performances look like in the discipline of spirituality? What are the implications of such an approach for understanding the role of the arts in nonviolent social and political change? Finally, what implications does this approach bring to understandings of socially engaged and nonviolent spirituality? My answer to these questions required that I do three things. First, I needed to shift my starting points for research from spirituality to music. Second, I employed a responsible interdisciplinarity to discern relevant ideas and frameworks of analysis from literature on contemporary protest music.[1] Third, I immersed myself in these ideas, questions, and frameworks.

Out of this immersion, an approach to contemporary protest music performances emerged, based on the principles of creativity, interdisciplinarity, and music literacy. One of the key insights arising from this work was the need to embrace an expanded and flexible understanding of "creativity" as a theoretical lens and as an integral aspect of research practice. More specifically, indwelling the field of protest music for several years underscored that creativity not only implies the emergence of something new, as Redekop suggests, but also involves openness to other possibilities and the capacity to see other perspectives (Levesque 2012, 100, 111).

Given the commitment to indwelling described above, creativity has become inextricably connected to notions of arts literacy in my work.

More specifically, this understanding was shaped by engaging with Bleiker's research on the role of the arts in international relations theory.[2] Of particular relevance to this discussion are his ideas on the significance of the arts to address the issue of terrorism. Before examining Bleiker's ideas, however, I will explore music literacy as an entré to arts literacy more generally.

WHY MUSIC LITERACY MATTERS

Edward Said was a public intellectual and scholar whose works examined culture, postcolonial theory, and politics (Iskandar and Ruston 2010). Barenboim is a celebrated musician and conductor (Barenboim n.d.). Each has sought to use music as a space where social and political transformation can be imagined and experienced.

Several ideas from Said and Barenboim's conversations are worth exploring as part of the current discussion on arts literacy. Their ideas, in particular those related to the jointly initiated West-Eastern Divan Orchestra, emphasize the value of both music and music literacy for reenvisioning how social and political issues are understood. Addressed below are music as a humanizing space, music literacy as a means of fostering intercultural understanding, and the need for adequate approaches to music as a basis for this literacy.

Music as a Humanizing Space

Ideas about the experience of music formed a bond between Said and Barenboim (Guzelimian 2004, iii). Describing their relationship, Hakem Ruston writes: "The Barenboim-Said friendship was complex and cannot be reduced to the usual dichotomies and labels. Their common affinity for European classical music was the force that brought them together" (2010, 231). Although Said is recognized as a cultural, literary, and post-colonial theorist, he also wrote on music and was an accomplished pianist (Guzelimian 2004, v; Said 1991, 2008). Barenboim is the first and most prominent Israeli musician to have performed in the Palestinian West Bank (Guzelimian 2004, v). Through their individual work and their collaborations, Said and Barenboim strove to understand the impact of music in society and to share this understanding with others until Said's death to cancer in 2003.

As outlined in the book *Parallels and Paradoxes* (2004), their advocacy for music literacy begins with the presupposition that music plays important social and political roles in society. One of these roles is music's capacity to afford individuals and communities a space to resist oppression (Barenboim and Said 2004, 44). In affording this space, music stands in stark contrast to political inhumanity and injustice (Barenboim and Said 2004, 168). According to Said, inhumanity and injustice seek to snub out human creativity and resistance. In contrast, music not only provides but also ignites spaces where people can breathe and feel free (Barenboim and Said 2004, 147).

With this understanding in mind, Said and Barenboim conceptualize musical performance as a preeminent space in which to learn what it means to be human. The conceptualization of music as a humanizing space underpins their lament for the decline of music education in Western societies (Barenboim and Said 2004, 141). This is because, without music education, music literacy declines (Barenboim and Said 2004, 148–150). Barenboim comments:

> But, on the other hand, the study of music is one of the best ways to learn about human nature. This is why I am so sad about music education being practically nonexistent today in schools. Education means preparing children for adult life; teaching them how to behave and what kinds of human beings they want to be. Everything else is information and can be learned in a simple way. To play music well you need to strike a balance between your head, your heart and your stomach. And if one of these three is not there or is there in too strong a dose, you cannot use it. What better way than music to show a child how to be human? (Barenboim and Said 2004, 24)

Here, music literacy represents much more than the technical dexterity with which a musician handles his/her/their instrument. It is also more than information needed to attain commercial success (Barenboim and Said 2004, 146, 168). Music literacy is a source of insight into the complex and multifaceted roles that music plays in society, including spaces of freedom and resistance that are created in its performance. Barenboim explains:

> Another very important point, for me, is that if you study music in the deepest sense of the word—all the relationships, the interdependence of the notes, of the harmonies, of the rhythm, and the connection of all those elements with the speed; if you look at the essentially unrepeatability of music, the fact that it is different every time because it comes in a different moment—you learn many things about the world, about nature, about human beings and human relations. (Barenboim and Said 2004, 122)

Fostering Understanding through Music Literacy

The idea that music can be a humanizing space is illustrated in the jointly initiated West-Eastern Divan Orchestra. Emerging from a 1999 workshop in Weimar, Germany, the orchestra brought together young musicians from different cultural and religious backgrounds (Barenboim 2009, vii; Washington and Beecher 2010, 127–40). Barenboim observes:

> It is not an orchestra; it is much more than that. It is more like a workshop that gives young musicians from different countries of the Middle East a forum to come and study music and then play in concerts. The idea of the West-Eastern Divan comes from Goethe's work of the same title, since he was one of the first Europeans to enjoy and learn from ideas coming from other civilizations. (Quoted in Ruston 2010, 233)

In the intervening years since the initial workshop, the orchestra has made its home in Andalusia, Spain. It is part of a larger foundation, the Barenboim-Said Foundation, whose goals include "the importance of music education for dialogue and reconciliation" (quoted in Ruston 2010, 230).

The orchestra meets annually each summer for several weeks (Cheah 2009, 1–9). The musicians come from various countries: Israel, Palestine, Lebanon, and Spain, among others (Cheah 2009, 1). Elena Cheah, an experienced member of the orchestra, writes:

> I heard in the orchestra's playing a certain unity of purpose in each phrase, an understanding of the cumulative effect of so much unresolved tension, a sensual relationship to the never-ending, continually sustained sound, and an audible comprehension of the harmonic turning points of the piece. (2009, 6)

This sense of musical unity resonates with Said and Barenboim's presuppositions that music is both a humanizing space and plays a role in fostering mutual understanding (Riiser 2010, 19–37). Solveig Riiser comments that the orchestra can be understood as a space for conflict transformation. She underscores, however, that this space is complex and multifaceted, replete with its own internal politics and power dynamics (2010).

Echoing the caution about overoptimistic evaluations of music, questions have been raised about the West-Eastern Divan's contribution to peace and reconciliation in the Middle East. Many have challenged the notion that the orchestra's performances can bring an end to conflict and violence in the region (Washington and Beecher 2010, 138). Those who participate, however, describe small resonances that have impacted their lives, those of their families, and the lives of those who have attended the orchestra's performances. These resonances suffuse the stories that Cheah collected in her study of the orchestra (2009). The members suggest, for example, that by learning about and making music together, their assumptions about other cultures and religions have been challenged, relationships have been built, and new identities forged (For more on the use of music in Israeli-Palestinian peace initiatives, see Brinner 2009). As Said and Barenboim affirm throughout their exchange in *Parallels and Paradoxes*, music literacy is a crucial way of making these resonances possible.

The Need for Adequate Approaches to Music Literacy

The ideas discussed above underscore the significance of having adequate approaches for studying music as a source of insight into social and political issues such as resisting oppression and fostering mutual understanding. Thus, a case could be made that, despite some people's reservations, the West-Eastern Divan Orchestra is itself a source of insight into the individual and communal impacts of conflict and violence in the Middle East (Beckles-Willson 2009). This is because, although a single source pertaining to a particular group of young musicians, the orchestra's performances have been understood as affecting the lives of those participating, their families, and communities. Furthermore, the orchestra was founded on the hope that these impacts would resound in ever-widening circles until peace was a realistic prospect not only in the Middle East but also around the world.

This hope in the possibilities inherent to musical spaces is not exclusive to Said and Barenboim. It is shared by others committed to making music, fostering music literacy, and building the prospects for peace in the region. Kjell Skyllstad comments:

> As a music educator and researcher, involved for many years in international collaboration for peace, I am convinced that music can be a tool for integration, inclusion, group cohesion, collective cooperation, repairing social relationships, and facilitating dialogue between groups in conflict. This has been demonstrated in unique artistic projects bringing together Palestinian and Israelis, as described herein. (2007, 177)

The outcomes of musical projects such as the West-Eastern Divan are difficult to predict. Musical performance is ephemeral, eminently changeable, and unrepeatable.

For individual scholars and musicians such as Said and Barenboim, it is these characteristics that make projects like the West-Eastern Divan so powerful. The emphasis is not only on a particular product or result but also on the possibilities of humanization and mutual understanding that musical spaces can provide. Stated differently, Said and Barenboim seem preoccupied less with measuring the success of their projects, although I am sure that it was and continues to be an important dimension of this work. Rather, they often focus on the interplay of imagination, experience, and literacy that such projects require and encourage. On receiving an award for his efforts with the orchestra, Said stated: "Who knows how far we will go, and whose minds we might change? The beauty of the question is that it cannot be easily answered or easily dismissed" (Said 2009, 277).

IMPLICATIONS OF ARTS LITERACY

The idea of literacy, or indwelling a particular art form, has implications for how scholarship on socially engaged and nonviolent spiritualities is understood and approached. By socially engaged and nonviolent spiritualities, I mean those committed to achieving sociopolitical change through nonviolent praxis. Arts literacy in general and music literacy in particular asks those interested in these spiritualities as an object of study to embrace flexibility and openness in both their understandings and approaches. When appreciated as a source of insight, exploration of a particular art form can help to discern what such flexibility and openness connote.

For example, drawing on her experiences with "embodied improvisation," an improvised practice related to theater, Nisha Sajnani writes that the practice helps art-based researchers to cultivate flexibility, responsiveness, and an embrace of uncertainty (2012, 79–86). It is worth quoting Sajnani's description of this practice in full as it provides a concrete instance of the impacts of these capacities on her research. She observes:

> For example, I invited six colleagues working at a trauma centre to join me in using embodied improvisation to explore their experiences of listening to and working with traumatic narratives. We began with what I refer to as "bodystorming," a process akin to the unfettered play prescribed in DvT [Developmental Transformations] yet with an important difference in that we begin with a theme or a question. The objective of "bodystorming" is to bring to the fore the sounds, movements, images, and scenes salient to our enquiry. The gestures that arose looked like pushing, kicking, roaring, shrinking, sinking and ignoring. These images gave way to short scenes in which individuals oscillated from being cared for and comforted by another to being ridiculed and isolated . . . This experiment invited my colleagues and me to playfully inhabit the tensions we experience on a daily basis, prompting recognition and laughter. In this way, our collective improvisation was also generative in that it disrupted the isolation that often comes with vicarious victimization. (2012, 81–82)

In this example, flexibility and openness are demonstrated through Sajnani's and her colleagues' willingness to be both vulnerable and self-reflexive about their experiences.

A valuable aspect of the improvisation is the emergence of insights that creatively disrupted responses and narratives that had become habitual. Here, to "playfully inhabit" these responses and narratives echoes Premaratna's and Bleiker's notion that theater can provide a model of "experimental spearheading" when hoping to discern other possible ways of addressing an issue and/ or experience (2010, 389–90).

In highlighting this example, I am not suggesting that all scholars interested in socially engaged and nonviolent spiritualities should turn to art-based research. I am suggesting that this and other immersive approaches can expand how these spiritualities are understood and approached. For instance, what would happen if one started his or her research into socially engaged and nonviolent spirituality in improvised music? Or what if the starting point for understanding this spirituality was the notion of improvisioning (Fischlin 2010)? Describing this concept, Daniel Fischlin writes:

> *Improvisioning*—for want of a better word or, perhaps, as the best word to describe this practice beyond words—unifies notions of diverse improvisatory practices with what those practices express, the vision—aesthetic, social, intimate, unspeakable—that only an embodied, live, improvised performance can bring into being. *Improvisioning* then: the irruption of the real of creative vision in the here and now of music in which chance, spontaneity, and unpredictability are active. (2010, 1)

Indwelling an art form with such questions can result in either an affirmation or challenge to one's presuppositions about what social engagement and nonviolent praxis look, feel, and sound like in the context of spirituality. With this in mind, being a practicing artist, musician, or poet is perhaps not as important as the willingness to immerse oneself in or learn with someone who has extensive experience in a particular art form. As Sajnani's research implies, collaboration emerges as an important facet of conducting research into the arts and for acquiring arts literacy.

Taking arts literacy into new territory, we can now examine how it can help address complex conflict-related challenges such as terrorism. In the next section, I explore these possibilities. I suggest that adequate approaches for applying the arts to social and political issues require a willingness on the part of scholars to think expansively, including reaching beyond their own conventional disciplinary understandings. A result of such thinking can be the acquisition of literacy in the arts. Let me now turn to Bleiker's ideas.

THE SIGNIFICANCE OF ARTS LITERACY IN AN AGE OF TERROR

Arts literacy implies, as Bleiker discusses in his volume *Aesthetics and Politics*, that we need to use the "full range of human intelligence" (2009, 1) as we apply the arts as a source of insight to social and political issues such as terrorism. By exploring this turn of phrase in the context of the current chapter, I point to the possibility of its relevance to broadening understandings of and approaches to socially engaged and nonviolent spiritualities. In other words, I suggest that this broadening can help scholars to reimagine how their work impacts on people's engagement with nonviolent sociopolitical change as deeply spiritual endeavors. I turn to Bleiker's ideas below.

Using the Full Register of Human Intelligence

In his engagement with the arts and their role in addressing terrorism, Bleiker refers to the September 11 attacks as generating a "breach in understanding" (2009, 49–50). The idea of a breach implies that, for many, people did not have a category for that kind of thing happening—the terror experienced on that day did not fit into their imaginative frameworks of the world. The experience generated anxiety, fear, and a sense that no one was safe (Mitchell 2011, 12). People's reactions to the attacks, in other words, can be said to have emerged from this break in their understanding.

Bleiker's idea brings to mind a description of terrorism as a tactic that "operates at the level of the imaginary" (Mitchell 2011, 21). An imaginary can be conceptualized as comprising the world of ideas that shape people's justification for and responses to particular events (Strathern and Stewart 2006, 6). Andrew Strathern and Pamela Stewart state: "Our basic argument is that the power of ideas regarding terror does not rest solely on the events of terrorist actions, destructive as they may be. It rests also on the great multiplications of reactions that these acts and the fears that these acts arouse in people's imaginations" (2006, 9). Stated differently, violence can be understood as operating and being registered on several levels, including that of the imagination (Anderson and Menon 2009, 5).

The arts can provide different perspectives from which to not only negotiate the breaches caused by terror but also show how violence is justified as a "legitimate response" (Korp 2008, 254–279). As noted, Bleiker advocates for using the "full register of human intelligence" to address terrorism (2009, 1). The use of this register is needed, in his opinion, because of the failure of militaristic solutions such as in Afghanistan and Iraq to prevent the threat of future terrorist attacks (Bleiker 2003a, 431–32). The perpetuation of violence, in other words, has not led to a more just and peaceful world. This fact underscores the need for different perspectives to understand and explain terrorism (Bleiker 2003c, 387–88).

To broaden perspectives on this issue, Bleiker employs a "problem" or "puzzle-based" approach (2009, 173–79). Here, the underlying assumption is to seek the broadest possible sources of insight into an issue. Rather than relying on conventional sources of insight in international relations, Bleiker turns to the arts. Poetry, for example, is discussed as a window into the experiences of those who have lived with violence and terror in diverse contexts (Bleiker 2009, 128–70). By stretching the boundaries of language, poetry can expand what people believe is possible (Bleiker 2009, 86). Poets, therefore, provide different ways of dreaming up alternative realities.

There are scholarly risks, however, in using a problem or puzzle-based approach. One risk is appearing foolish and/or amateurish because the focus is on breadth rather than depth (Bleiker 2009, 174). A prevailing benefit is enabling a scholar to reach beyond what are considered conventional understandings of the issue in question (Bleiker 2003b, 420). Bleiker observes:

> If a puzzle is the main challenge, then it can be addressed with all the means available, independently of their provenance or label. A source may stem from this or that discipline, it may be academically sanctioned or not, expressed in prose or poetic form, it may be language based or visual or musical or take any other shape or form: it is legitimate as long as it helps illuminate the puzzle in question. (2003b, 420)

It could be said that the focus of this approach is on creative illumination and less on disciplinary boundaries and academic provenance (McGuigan and Popp 2016). With the focus on creative illumination, the approach provides scholars with a space to consider a range of sources of insight, including the arts. Scholars are asked, therefore, to embody openness to possibility and to cultivate a capacity to see other perspectives.

The Arts as a Source of Insight

The arts, as Bleiker suggests, can be an important source of insight for understanding and explaining terrorism. In relation to this issue, they embody what he calls "a reaching for the new, the different, and the neglected" (Bleiker 2009, 11). Here, Bleiker is not suggesting that such frameworks should replace conventional theories and methodologies in international relations (2009, 94–95). Nor is he suggesting that artistic insights are better than those arising from sociopolitical analysis. He is arguing that other frameworks open up spaces in which to rethink an issue, including terrorism. This opening is illustrated with regard to September 11.

The U.S. response to the attacks was to return to "the reassuring familiarity of dualistic thinking patterns that dominated foreign policy during the Cold War" (Bleiker 2009, 51). Bleiker explains that, according to this dualistic thinking, the world is conceived as either "good" or "evil" with the military presented as the only means of protecting the former from the latter. The result of this conceptualization is the generation of new forms of hatred and violence (Bleiker 2009, 51). These consequences warn against falling back on old patterns of thinking, particularly when other perspectives and sources of insight exist such as the arts (Bleiker 2006, 94). He comments:

> Aesthetic sources cannot give us certainty. Embracing them is all about refusing a single-voiced and single-minded approach to politics in favor of embracing multiple voices and the possibility of multiple truths. This is why a novel, a painting, a film or a piece of music can never tell us what to do, whether to go for option A or B. But aesthetic engagements can broaden our ability to understand and assess the challenges at hand . . . They might also reveal that A and B are in fact not the only options—that there is C as well. (Bleiker 2009, 188)

The call for a multivoiced and multiminded approach in relationship to aesthetic sources is an attempt to understand the arts according to their particular dynamics. In other words, the suggestion is made that, when employing the arts as a source of insight, a scholar should consider studying them on their own terms (Bleiker 2005, 191). This means using the frameworks of relevant art-based disciplines in one's research (Bleiker 2005, 193–94).

In doing so, Bleiker sees the role of interdisciplinary scholarship as mirroring that of the poet in effecting social and political change. He writes:

> A poet who wants to function as a chronicler of his or her time must do more than merely reflect the *Zeitgeist* of an epoch. Reflection is not enough. To write poetry that is of poetic and political value, the author must produce more than mirror images of a society. He or she has to distort visions in order to challenge the entrenched forms of representations that have come to circumscribe our understanding of socio-political reality. (Bleiker 2009, 139)

Like the poet, an interdisciplinary scholar does not only reflect the staid understandings and approaches of his or her discipline. He or she challenges these ways of thinking and practice. When the arts are taken up as a centerpiece of such challenges, arts literacy is fundamental.

The Significance of Arts Literacy

In his research, Bleiker situates himself as an international relations scholar interested in the arts (2005, 181). He acknowledges that he is not a trained artist or musicologist and so the "great unread" of arts disciplines is a daunting presence (Bleiker 2009, 183). He negotiates this great unread by being transparent about his biases and presuppositions, including his belief that the arts are foundational to the "quest for knowledge and political thinking space" (Bleiker 2005, 181).

This critical self-reflexivity legitimizes the addition of the arts to his interpretative repertoire. By recognizing his own need for arts literacy, Bleiker respects the integrity of the arts he sets out to analyze. Instead of imposing a sociopolitical analysis, he begins with the presupposition that the arts have something of value to teach the discipline of international relations. In an essay on theater in postconflict Sri Lanka coauthored with Nilanjana Premaratna, he writes:

> Art alone cannot, of course, solve a conflict, but it is part of a larger set of activities that are essential in the process of transforming conflict into peace. Perhaps even more importantly, artistic engagements, as exemplified by the Jana Keraliya theatre group, can serve as a model—a type of experimental spearheading—from which community leaders, politicians, and scholars draw important lessons about larger dynamics at play in peacebuilding processes. (Premaratna and Bleiker 2010, 389–90)

The point I wish to make is that a scholar interested in the arts does not necessarily need to be a practicing artist. Although being an artist, poet, or musician is helpful, what is required is a willingness to engage in "a type of experimental spearheading." The notion of indwelling, however, suggests that this experimentation should include learning from those who are either involved in or who have studied the arts in depth.

In a similar vein, John Witvliet proposes that those interested in the study of music should immerse themselves in musical experiences (2011, 456–57). The idea is that participatory knowledge of music enhances scholarly reflection. This immersion can comprise working with a mentor to learn how to listen, play, or simply better appreciate music's dynamics (Witvliet 2011, 457–58). Witvliet observes: "Part of the value of a master mentor is that we can witness a good model up close—not only a model of good music, but a model of encountering music" (2011, 457). The value of such immersive experience, as Witvliet implies, is a literate understanding of music as a complex, multifaceted human phenomenon.

Bleiker's appreciation for arts literacy is attributed to Alex Danchev (2005, 195), who also turns to the arts as sources of insight into violence and terror. In the introduction to his study *On Art and Terror and War*, he states:

> These essays are dedicated to the proposition that art matters, ethically and politically, affectively and intellectually. Poetry makes something happen after all. Not only does it make us feel—or feel differently—it makes us think, and think again . . . In sum, art articulates a vision of the world that is insightful and consequential; and the vision and the insight can be analyzed. (Danchev 2009, 4)

The arts matter, in Danchev's opinion, because they provide alternative visions of and insights into social and political issues (see also Hyvärinen and Muszynski 2008). Artistic visions and insights are, therefore, worth studying. He also affirms that arts literacy is an important principle with which to undertake the study of these visions and insights.

When applied to scholarship in spirituality, such notions underscore that scholarship is not static or monolithic. There are many ways of understanding and approaching the contemporary spiritual, nonviolent, and engaged life. Furthermore, they emphasize that the ways of understanding and approaching these lives often involve a progression in discernment. By progression, I mean that, from a scholarly perspective, what constitutes the labels "spiritual," "nonviolent," and/or "engaged" is not self-evident. Discerning what these labels mean in particular circumstances may not approximate a straight line. It may resemble an act of improvisioning: a performance characterized by chance, spontaneity, and unpredictability.

In this understanding, scholars can use the idea of creativity and creative practice to reconceptualize themselves as artists with vital roles to play in how to envision and enact socially engaged and nonviolent spiritualities. Acquiring literacy in other sources of insight is simply a different perspective through which to explore these roles. It is a valuable and viable perspective because it has the potential to disrupt presuppositions and, in this disruption, renew understandings of and approaches to spirituality, nonviolence, engagement, and their study in the contemporary world.

Finally, based on what has been discussed throughout this chapter, the concept of arts literacy points to the possibilities of reenvisioning socially engaged and nonviolent spiritualities as performance. Ideas need to be put into action. Often people embody ideas of a more just and peaceful world in their daily lives. Such embodying can take place through the arts, social engagement, spirituality, or a composite of all three. Thus, to conceptualize socially engaged and nonviolent spiritualities as performance attempts not only to draw attention to the everydayness of these activities but also to bridge the spheres of daily life in which they occur.

CONCLUSION

In this chapter, I have engaged with ideas on arts literacy and creative practice. My main argument has been that these ideas have the potential to expand thinking on research into socially engaged and nonviolent spiritualities. As Premaratna and Bleiker note, the arts alone cannot solve conflicts. Similarly, those involved in arts projects acknowledge that these projects alone will likely not bring about reconciliation in regions experiencing deep-rooted conflict such as the Middle East. When taken seriously as having an impact on social, political, and/or spiritual issues, however, the arts can be understood as providing creative illumination into processes of reconciliation.

In particular, arts literacy emphasizes the importance of embodiment and collaboration as part of these processes. For example, Said's and Barenboim's understanding of music literacy suggests that collective embodiment such as in the West-Eastern Divan Orchestra can be especially powerful for creatively addressing social and political issues. This collective immersion in or indwelling music is understood as one avenue through which to engage with questions such as why, how, and where the arts matter in relationship to processes of reconciliation. The idea is that dialoguing about these processes can involve dancing, sounding, and storytelling (e.g., see Nicholls 2010 and Smith 2014). More pointedly, dancing, sounding, and storytelling are important scholarly lenses and methods through which to think through what such dialogues mean in particular contexts.

The scholars and practitioners discussed in this chapter argue that the arts matter. Their ideas and works challenge the undertheorizing of the arts as part of both nonviolent praxis and reconciliation. Concepts such as literacy and creative practice can contribute to this challenge by emphasizing the ways scholarship can both reflect and embody the flexibility and openness that often characterize the arts. Creative illumination, in other words, may require more than reading, discussing, and writing about these human phenomena. It may also require embracing scholarship itself as an embodied performance, one where conventional ways of thinking can be unsettled by the gesture of a hand, the sound of a voice, or the space that emerges after an instrument has fallen silent.

NOTES

1. Philip Sheldrake writes that interdisciplinarity requires more than "a plundering" of the vocabularies and interpretive strategies of other disciplines. A "responsible interdisciplinarity" respects these vocabularies and strategies, recognizing the value of a multipronged approach to a particular issue or topic. For more on this idea, see Sheldrake (2006) and Berling (2006).

2. Since acquiring his PhD in 2000, Bleiker has written and/or edited several books on international conflict and reconciliation—2000; 2005; and Morgan Brigg and Roland Bleiker, eds., *Mediating across Difference: Oceanic and Asian Approaches to Conflict Resolution* (Honolulu, HI: University of Hawai'i Press, 2011).

REFERENCES

Anderson, Patrick, and Jisha Menon. 2009. "Introduction." In *Violence Performed: Local Roots and Global Routes of Conflict*, 1–14. New York, NY: Palgrave Macmillan.

Barenboim, Daniel. n.d. "About." *Daniel Barenboim*. http://www.danielbarenboim.com/index.php?id=86 (accessed February 2, 2012).

———. 2009. "Foreword." In *An Orchestra beyond Borders: Voices of the West-Eastern Divan Orchestra*, edited by Elena Cheah, vii–viii. London, UK: Verso Books.

Barenboim, Daniel, and Edward Said. 2004. *Parallels and Paradoxes: Explorations in Music and Society*. New York, NY: Vintage Books.

Bergh, Arild, and John Sloboda. 2014. "Music and Art in Conflict Transformation: A Review." *Music and Arts in Action* 2, no. 2: 4. http://www.musicandartsinaction.net/index.php/maia/article/view/conflicttransformation/45 (accessed August 10, 2014).

Berling, Judith. 2006. "Christian Spirituality: Intrinsically Interdisciplinary." In *Exploring Christian Spirituality*, edited by Bruce H. Lescher and Elizabeth Liebert, 35–52. Mahwah, NJ: Paulist Press.

Bleiker, Roland. 2009. *Aesthetics and Politics*. New York, NY: Palgrave MacMillan.

———. 2003a. "Aestheticising Terrorism: Alternative Approaches to 11 September." *Australian Journal of Politics and History* 49, no. 3: 430–445.

———. 2006. "Art after 9/11." *Alternatives* 31: 77–99.

———. 2008. "Art against Terror: Nonviolent Alternatives through Emotional Insight." In *Nonviolence: An Alternative for Defeating Global Terror(ism)*, edited by Senthil Ram and Ralph Summy, 169–186. New York, NY: Nova Science Publishers, Inc.

———. 2005. *Divided Korea: Toward a Culture of Reconciliation*. Minneapolis, MN: University of Minnesota Press.

———. 2003b. "Learning from Art: A Reply to Holden's World Literature and World Politics." *Global Society* 17, no. 4: 415–428.

———. 2005. "Of Things We Hear but Cannot See: Musical Explorations of International Relations." In *Resounding International Relations: On Music, Culture, and Politics*, edited by M. I. Franklin, 179–190. New York, NY: Palgrave MacMillan.

———. 2000. *Popular Dissent, Human Agency and Global Politics*. Cambridge, UK: Cambridge University Press.

———. 2003c. "Why, Then, is it so Bright? Towards an Aesthetics of Peace in Time of War." *Review of International Studies* 29: 387–400.

Branagan, Marty. 2013. *Global Warming, Militarism, and Nonviolence: The Art of Active Resistance*. New York, NY: Palgrave MacMillan.

Brinner, Benjamin. 2009. *Playing across a Divide: Israeli-Palestinian Musical Encounters*. Oxford, UK: Oxford University Press.

Cheah, Elena, ed. 2009. "Introduction." In *An Orchestra beyond Borders: Voices of the West-Eastern Divan Orchestra*, 1–9. London, UK: Verso Books.

Danchev, Alex. 2009. *On Art and War and Terror*. Edinburgh, UK: Edinburgh University Press.

Fischlin, Daniel. 2010. "Wild Notes ... Improvisioning." *Critical Studies in Improvisation/Etudes critiques en improvisation* 6, no. 2: 1–10.

García, María Elisa Pinto. 2014. "Music and Reconciliation in Columbia: Opportunities of Songs Composed by Victims." *Music and Arts in Action* 4, no. 2: 24–51. http://www.musicandartsinaction.net/index.php/maia/article/view/musicreconciliationco lombia/97 (accessed August 10, 2014).

Guzelimian, Ara. 2004. "Preface" In *Parallels and Paradoxes: Explorations in Music and Society*, edited by Daniel Barenboim and Edward W. Said, iii–vi. New York, NY: Vintage Books.

Hyvärinen, Matti, and Lisa Muszynski, eds. 2008. *Terror and the Arts: Artistic, Literary, and Political Interpretations of Violence from Dostoyevsky to Abu Ghraib*. New York, NY: Palgrave Macmillan.

Iskandar, Adel, and Hakem Ruston, eds. 2010. *Edward Said: A Legacy of Emancipation and Representation*. Berkeley, CA: University of California Press.

Korp, Maureen. 2008. "Seeing What is Missing: Art, Artists, and September 11." In *Religion, Terror and Violence: Religious Studies Perspectives*, edited by Bryan Rennie and Philip L. Tite, 254–279. New York, NY: Routledge.

Levesque, Lauren Michelle. 2012. *Can a Song Save the World? The Dynamics of Protest Music, Spirituality, and Violence in the Context of the 'War on Terror.'* PhD Dissertation, Saint Paul University.

McGuigan, Richard, and Nancy Popp. 2016. *Integral Conflict: The New Science of Conflict*. Albany, NY: State University of New York Press.

Mitchell, W. J. T. 2011. *Cloning Terror: The War of Images, 9/11 to the Present*. Chicago, IL: University of Chicago Press.

Nicholls, Tracey. 2010. "Speaking Justice, Performing Reconciliation: Twin Challenges for a Postcolonial Ethics." *Critical Studies in Improvisation/Etudes critiques en improvisation* 6, no. 1: 1–15.

Premaratna, Nilanjana, and Roland Bleiker. 2010. "Art and Peacebuilding: How Theatre Transforms Conflict in Sri Lanka." In *Palgrave Advances in Peacebuilding: Critical Developments and Approaches*, edited by Oliver P. Richmond, 376–391. New York, NY: Palgrave Macmillan.

Redekop, Vern Neufeld. 2012. "Spirituality, Emergent Creativity, and Reconciliation." In *Peacemaking: From Practice to Theory*, edited by Susan Allen Nan, Zachariah Cherian Mampilly, and Andrea Bartoli, 586–600. Santa Barbara, CA: Praeger.

Riiser, Solveig. 2010. "National Identity and the West-Eastern Divan Orchestra." *Music & Arts in Action* 2, no. 2: 19–37. http://www.musicandartsinaction.net/inde x.php/maia/article/view/nationalidentity (accessed February 5, 2012).

Ruston, Hakem. 2010. "The Arab/Jewish Counterpoint: An Interview with Daniel Barenboim." In *Edward Said: A Legacy of Emancipation and Representation*, edited by Adel Iskandar and Hakem Ruston, 229–246. Berkeley, CA: University of California Press.

Said, Edward W. 2009. "Appendix: Edward Said's Speech upon his Acceptance of the Principe de Asturias Prize." In *An Orchestra Beyond Borders: Voices of the*

West-Eastern Divan Orchestra, edited by Elena Cheah, 273–277. London, UK: Verso Books.

———. 1991. *Musical Elaborations*. New York, NY: Columbia University Press.

———. 2008. *Music at the Limits*. New York, NY: Columbia University Press.

Sajnani, Nisha. 2012. "Improvisation and Art-Based Research." *Journal of Applied Arts and Health* 3, no. 1: 79–86.

Sheldrake, Philip. 2006. "Spirituality and its Critical Methodology." In *Exploring Christian Spirituality*, edited by Bruce H. Lescher and Elizabeth Liebert, 15–34. Mahwah, NJ: Paulist Press.

Smith, Peter. 2014. "Improvising the Practice of Nonresistance as Creative Mimesis." In *Rene Girard and Creative Reconciliation*, edited by Vern Neufeld Redekop and Thomas Ryba, 149–162. Lanham, MD: Lexington Books.

Strathern, Andrew, and Pamela J. Stewart. 2006. "Introduction." In *Terror & Violence: Imagination and the Unimaginable*, edited by Andrew Strathern, Pamela J. Stewart, and Neil L. Whitehead, 1–39. London, UK: Pluto Press.

Skyllstad, Kjell. 2007. "Salaam Shalom: Singing for Peace Between Palestinians and Israelis." In *Beyond Bullets and Bombs: Grassroots Peacebuilding Between Israelis and Palestinians*, edited by Judy Kuriansky, 177–181. Westport, CT: Praeger.

Washington, David M., and Devin G. Beecher. 2010. "Music as Social Medicine: Two Perspectives on the West-Eastern Divan Orchestra." *New Directions for Youth Development* 125: 127–140.

Willson, Rachel Beckles. 2009. "The Parallax Worlds of the West-Eastern Divan Orchestra." *The Journal of the Royal Musical Association* 134, no. 2: 319–347.

Witvliet, John D. 2011. "Afterword." In *Resonant Witness: Conversations between Music and Theology*, edited by Jeremy S. Begbie and Steven R. Guthrie, 454–463. Grand Rapids, MI: William B. Eerdmans Publishing Co.

Part III

INDIGENOUS INSIGHTS AND CHALLENGES FOR RECONCILIATION

Chapter 11

Transcending Traditional Justice Claims

Challenges of Indigenous-Settler Reconciliation

Joseph Cleyn

The ideal of justice is a fundamental concept for the field of peace and conflict studies. The concept itself is loaded with diverse, yet significant, meanings that can lead to multiple and often conflicting ideas for determining what constitutes a "just society," a "just reconciliation," or a "just peace." These function at the level of epistemological frameworks (how we know or make meaning of something) and normative frameworks (what values we bring to bear on something). Often, a hegemonic, or dominating, framework of justice can control the dialogue over the priorities, objectives, and guiding norms of justice. In such a context, merely conceiving of justice is a contentious endeavor fraught with political implications and consequences. This domination can be surreptitious, or, in some cases, a reality exerted unconsciously. As I wrote this chapter, I tried to reflect on my own normative lens and acknowledge that the vocabulary, methodology, and style of my writing represent my own perspective, ontology, and experience.

Seeking justice in divided societies[1] is a primary objective for conflict scholars and practitioners who aim to transform oppressive relationships (Lederach 1995) by uncovering the roots of violence, whether it is as extreme and blatant as genocide or subtle, yet deep-rooted, as structural violence (Galtung 1969, 1990). Essentially, the goal is to move from violence and oppression of all forms toward a just society, one in which the likelihood of a return to conflict and violence is reduced significantly.

Those engaged with seeking justice in divided societies are faced with an arduous task of weeding through historical injustices and present-day inequalities in order to break down the systems of oppression that stand in

245

the way of a brighter future. An added challenge to this already difficult and complex task is uncovering the systems of oppression present within the epistemological and normative frameworks of justice themselves.

Epistemic violence produces and reproduces inequality by constructing specific frameworks of understanding through hegemonic discourses (Spivak 1985). Put differently, it privileges the language, concepts, rules of rightness, and methods of validation of the dominant group. In this chapter, epistemic violence is used as a conceptual tool to analyze dominant frameworks of justice.

Normative violence as developed by Butler (2009) provides an understanding of the ideological oppression of structural violence. Like epistemic violence, normative violence produces and reproduces inequality; it does so by imposing norms that legitimize oppressive frameworks. More specifically, normative violence is found within norms themselves and therefore it "enables typical violence, while simultaneously erasing the trace of the violence" (Dhawan 2012, 276). In other words, approaching justice in divided societies is particularly difficult because of the potential that the oppressor imposes their own framework of justice. The imposition of epistemological and normative frameworks can reinforce and perpetuate oppression, and therefore constitute a form of violence understood here as epistemic and normative violence.

One example that shows the power of epistemic and normative violence has to do with norms related to property. European societies that engaged in colonial domination were committed to the norm of individual self-interest being expressed within the confines of law. They adopted the Doctrine of Discovery, which basically said that the lands that they were taking over were empty. Hence, the norm of self-interest said that they could claim for themselves whatever land they wanted since there were no legal constraints. There were no rules of validation that would suggest that they first examine the land to see if there were any inhabitants nor did it consider how Indigenous peoples established a sense of connection to particular areas—it was clear to First Nations that there were territories assigned to each nation; there were also conflicts at the fringes of these territories over who had hegemony of the land. The norms of Indigenous peoples were different. Instead of emphasizing individual accumulation and self-interest, what was paramount was sharing. This norm permeated intracommunity relations but it also extended to the newcomers. In fact, without the sharing that occurred, the first Europeans to settle on Turtle Island (North America) would have undoubtedly perished during their first winter.

The concepts of epistemic and normative violence will be used as analytical tools throughout this chapter. They can be considered as ideological forms of structural violence. In other words, they form a part of the invisible deep-rooted systems of power that produce and reproduce inequality (Galtung 1969; Farmer 1996). Evidently, an obfuscating and troublesome challenge for conceiving of the ideal of justice resides within the methodology itself. Both epistemic and normative violence constrain frameworks for conceiving a mutually agreeable and emancipatory ideal of justice. This problem is especially challenging in the context of divided societies and oppressive relationships marred by a colonial past like the Indigenous-Settler relationship in Canada. Here, systems of oppression are embodied in present-day misery, persisting embedded in the process of determining what constitutes justice, truth, and reconciliation.

Colonialism is a particularly pertinent example of the imposition of hegemonic frameworks on other cultures, peoples, or societies. The colonial system of oppression imposed a framework for understanding (epistemic) and valuing (normative) the world based on cosmopolitan ideals of reason, progress, modernization, and enlightenment. Its legacy continues to dominate the methodology and present discourse over ideas of justice, even when the shortcomings of these approaches to justice are becoming evident.[2] Attempting to transition toward justice in a divided society with a history of colonialism or oppression must include understanding that violence may endure within transitional justice mechanisms themselves.

Although this chapter focuses on the colonial system of oppression, the main criticisms, as well as the proposed emancipatory framework, shed light on similar dynamics present in other systems of oppression (i.e., racism, imperialism, or sexism). In shedding light on this problem, several key dilemmas will need to be addressed or, at the very least, kept in mind. In particular, defining legitimate norms in a divided society wherein each group has a different historical, cultural approach, or understanding of justice. This touches on the fundamental tension between universalism and relativism. If justice is to be emancipatory for all, it must be transcultural and transhistorical (i.e., universal), yet each identity group in a divided society has its own interpretation of justice. How, then, can we approach justice without having a certain conception imposed on either side of the divide?

CONCEIVING OF JUSTICE IN DIVIDED SOCIETIES

In the interdisciplinary/transdisciplinary field of conflict studies, the concept of justice is crucial. Often it defines the overall goal of any intervention or peacebuilding program—in the context of postconflict societies—a transition toward a more equitable, peaceful, and just society (Arbour 2007; Galtung 1969; Mani 2005). However, the word "justice" has different meanings within academic fields,[3] and although each of these different understandings of justice is useful in constructing a comprehensive understanding of justice, this chapter focuses on transitional justice.

In most cases, transitional justice refers to postconflict societies like Iraq and Afghanistan, post-genocide Rwanda or Cambodia, or post-Apartheid South Africa. However, it is argued here that transitional justice ought to be the goal for all divided societies in which there are marginalization, oppression, and domination. Although Canadian society is not "postconflict" in the classic sense, the continued marginalization and oppression of Indigenous peoples and the history of colonialism within the Indigenous-Settler relationship reveals the need for a "transition" toward a more just relationship.

In recent years, literature within the field of conflict studies has been calling for a more comprehensive and thicker notion of justice (Mani 2005; McEvoy 2007; Nagy 2013; Oomen 2005), putting into question the legitimacy of the Western conception of peacebuilding as the completion of the liberal project of "enlightenment." Many of the dominant approaches of postconflict justice are rooted in a liberal-democratic approach that prioritizes social cohesion, democratization, industrial and economic reconstruction, and marketization. However, there continues to be much dissatisfaction with the approaches to justice based on liberal-democratic principles.

Ideal frameworks or approaches to transitional justice have been debated within the literature. However, as Betts points out, it is perhaps more important to pose the question: "Who should have the right to conceive of and implement transitional justice" (2005, 737)? Attempting to transition toward social justice in a divided society with a history of oppression must include understanding that violence could in fact be embedded within the principles of transitional justice. It is at this level that this chapter will propose dialogical cosmopolitanism as an epistemic and normative stance for uncovering the seemingly benign systems of oppression in the Canadian context. Furthermore, an analysis of the Canadian Truth and Reconciliation Commission (TRC) will illustrate the challenge at hand for those seeking to transition from oppression, domination, and violence to justice and positive peace. As a transitional justice mechanism, is it able to uncover and eschew the structural violence potentially embedded within its own epistemic and normative framework?

This chapter will proceed in three stages. It begins with a section entitled "The Case of Canada: Truth Reconciliation and . . . Justice?" which outlines the Indian Residential School (IRS) system, the TRC as a transitional justice mechanism, ultimately pointing toward the necessity of identifying and overcoming the dominant epistemic and normative frameworks of justice if reconciliation is to be meaningful. This will be followed by a section entitled "Universal Ideals and Justice," which discusses the difficulty of conceiving of universal ideals of justice in a divided society still caught under the weight of its colonial legacy. The final section, "Reconciliation by Transcending Hegemonic Structures," aims to put forward the epistemological and normative stance of dialogical cosmopolitanism (as opposed to the localized, Eurocentric, idea of cosmopolitanism) as crucial for reconciliation and justice in Canada. Dialogical cosmopolitanism builds on the traditional cosmopolitan ideals of inclusion, global community, and common humanity (cf. Brodeur, "Interworldview Dialogue," *Transforming*) while critically bringing to bear the potential domination inherent in the frameworks for understanding or valuing those very ideals.

THE CASE OF CANADA: TRUTH, RECONCILIATION AND . . . JUSTICE?

This section aims to critically examine the Canadian TRC in order to illustrate the challenges that divided societies face when attempting to address past injustices and transition toward a just and emancipated society. Canada is a crucial example of a liberal democratic society that has been confronted with the fact that its past colonial practices and policies continue to negatively affect the lived experiences of Indigenous peoples. That Canada is a divided society there can be no doubt; it is made clear by the fact that Indigenous people in Canada, when compared with the rest of the Canadian society, suffer higher rates of incarceration,[4] violence and sexual abuse,[5] alcohol and drug abuse,[6] disease,[7] as well as lower rates of education and employment.[8] There is a wealth of literature and research that connects the current marginalization of Indigenous peoples all over the world to the colonial practices of the past (Alfred 2009; Corntassel and Holder 2008; Maddison 2013).

"Not a single Indian . . .": The IRS System

In Canada, the IRS system was a particularly oppressive official policy—one that some authors argue warrants the powerful label of cultural genocide.[9] It began as an official policy of the Canadian government. First institutionalized in the 1880s, its objective was to assimilate aboriginal students into the mainstream working-class culture, and to help Indigenous peoples to adapt better to life in a white-dominated country (MacDonald and Hudson 2012; Woods 2013). Although officially enacted by the Canadian government, the IRS system was administered in cooperation with Christian church organizations, predominantly the Catholic and Anglican churches. The "civilizing mission," legitimized by Enlightenment principles, was the rationale for the Indian Act of 1867, and the IRS system was the means to solve the "Indian problem."

By forcefully taking Indigenous children from their families and communities, and systematically eliminating their culture, language, spirituality, and way of life, the IRS attempted to create fully assimilated individuals that could become part of the hegemonic culture of the colonial state, participating in its economy and abiding by its liberal democratic norms. Furthermore, an "ulterior government motive," Miller writes, "was to minimize and perhaps eventually eliminate the federal government's financial obligations to First Nations" (2003, 368). Essentially, the government's guiding principle was economic; they saw assimilation and forced cultural change as the means to reduce their financial liability.

The words of Duncan Campbell Scott, the head of the Department of Indian Affairs from 1913 to 1932, reveal the motivations of Canada's genocidal policy: "Our objective is to continue until there is not a single Indian in Canada that has not been absorbed into the body politic and there is no Indian question, and no Indian Department, that is the whole object of this Bill" (Scott as cited in Titley 1986, 50). Scott oversaw the expansion of residential schools beginning in the 1920s and culminating in an all-time high of eighty schools in 1931 (Woods 2013). All told, 150,000 students went through the residential system from the 1870s up until 1996, when the last residential school was closed (Nagy and Sehdev 2012, 67).

In addition to losing one's culture, language, way of life, and spirituality, there were other more acute and direct forms of oppression and violence. More specifically, poor living conditions, the negligence of health and well-being, as well as forms of sexual, physical, and emotional abuse were part of the daily life for these Indigenous children. Numerous former students have spoken of the physical and sexual abuse they suffered in the schools, and some children, estimates range from hundreds to thousands, died while in the IRS system (Angel 2013, 200). This form of direct violence has trickled down through the generations. Many of the current challenges faced by Indigenous populations in Canada result from the ongoing intergenerational trauma of the IRS system. The legacy of the abuse and loss of cultural identity continue to afflict current Indigenous communities.

The TRC and Canadian "Transitional Justice"

In 2006, the Indian Residential School System Agreement (IRSSA) was made to address the largest class-action lawsuit in Canadian history against the Government of Canada and particular Canadian church organizations. After failed attempts to address reparations to IRS survivors, and a proliferation of lawsuits against the government, the IRSSA was negotiated as an alternative court-approved agreement that would "expedite the process of providing reparations to survivors while circumventing expensive litigation for each plaintiff" (Henderson and Wakeham 2009). Even though it was designed to "administer the provision of symbolic and material reparations to former students" (Green 2012, 134), the compensation model failed to acknowledge the "intergenerational effects of residential schooling . . . as family members are not eligible to collect payments on behalf of deceased students" (Henderson and Wakeham 2009, 11).

A major component of the IRSSA was the formation of the TRC. It was supported by the TRC Secretariat, a Canadian federal government department. According to the executive summary of the final report of the TRC, its mandate was to "reveal to Canadians the complex truth about the history and the ongoing legacy of the church-run residential schools," as well as "guide and inspire a process of truth and healing, leading toward reconciliation" and to "renew relationships on a basis of inclusion, mutual understanding and respect" (TRC 2015, 23). Essentially, in its five-year mandate, the TRC was commissioned to acknowledge the impact and consequences of the IRS system by providing the opportunity for survivors to tell their stories, and subsequently educate the Canadian public of the legacy of the IRS system. Its ultimate objective was "to transform our country and restore mutual respect between peoples and nations" (TRC 2015, 183). It attempted to do this by gathering survivor statements, preparing a comprehensive historical report, and sharing these with the broader public by facilitating various public events.

In fulfillment of this mandate, it was the hope that the commission would continue the process of healing and reconciliation that began in the 1980s with church apologies, and continued in 1996 with the Royal Commission on Aboriginal Peoples (RCAP), in 2006 with the IRSSA, and in 2008 with the prime minister's apology in Parliament. These moments that mark the path toward the TRC have been criticized for failing to admit the full extent of the colonial legacy of Canada, unfulfilled recommendations, and failure to address the present-day marginalization of Indigenous peoples in Canada (Alfred 2009; Henderson and Wakeham 2009; James 2008). The following are some of the specific criticisms aimed at the TRC, which viewed through the lens of epistemic (meaning-making) and normative (value-making) violence, drive home the point that there is a need for an approach that considers the epistemic and normative power imbalance, decolonizes the relationship, and allows for the reconstitution of the overall framework in general.

Criticisms of the TRC

What entails a legitimate norm in a divided society like Canada, plagued with the colonial policies and practices of the IRS? More generally, in divided societies, where each "group" or "side" has a different historical and cultural approach or understanding of justice, is it possible to conceive of a normative ideal that is emancipatory for both sides? The TRC's mandate to educate the general public with a historical record of the legacy of the IRS system is an important first step toward uncovering enduring systems of oppression and creating new possibilities, new ideals, and new frameworks for knowing and acting. The oppression and marginalization of Indigenous peoples must be heard, made known, and incorporated into the society's consciousness. However, this is only a small part of the process. The following are a number of key criticisms as presented by Stanton (2011), Nagy (2013), Corntassel and Holder (2008), among others, that point to the underlying epistemic and normative violence that continues to constrain the transition to justice and reconciliation.

The fact that the TRC was a state-led mechanism means that its methodology is confined to a liberal-democratic framework rooted in Enlightenment ideals. More specifically, the epistemic and normative framework is preset and does not allow for the diversity and inclusion that is needed to decolonize and mutually transform the Indigenous-Settler relationship. A state-led legal response, the TRC "was not created out of a groundswell of concern about IRS survivors by the public; rather it was agreed to by their government's legal advisers in order to settle costly litigation. Were it not for the enormous financial cost to the government of continuing to defend against the class actions, the TRC would not exist in Canada" (Stanton 2011, 4). As opposed to other TRCs that were part of peace settlements initiated by both sides of the divided society (e.g., South Africa), the dominant Settler society in Canada was not invested in the process. The concern therefore was not to address past or present injustices; it was about managing litigation costs. It is ethically dubious that until the point where the case-action lawsuits became too costly, there was no interest or desire on the part of the state in initiating any transitional justice or reconciliation mechanism.

State-led or top-down transitional justice mechanisms will prioritize the epistemic and normative framework that will continue to legitimize their dominance. In this case, the state manipulated the framework by defining and narrowing the focus to particular injustices instead of the entire colonial system of oppression. Corntassel and Holder (2009) argue that truth commission processes meant to deal with historical human rights abuses of Indigenous peoples have too often trampled on Indigenous concerns with a preemptive focus on regime legitimization and national unity. Canada's TRC can be seen as an attempt to reconcile this dark spot in Canadian history in order to restore Canada's reputation as a world leader in peacekeeping, and protector of human rights globally. In fact, the preface to the executive summary of the TRC final report hints at this state priority by describing the stories of the IRS experience as "difficult to accept as something that could have happened in a country such as Canada, which has long prided itself on being a bastion of democracy, peace, and kindness throughout the world" (TRC 2015, v). Simply put, the narrative surrounding the TRC process is framed by the colonial power that is the Canadian government. This type of framework does not allow for the diversity that is needed for reconstituting the epistemic and normative frameworks necessary for the emergence of an emancipatory transitional justice.

Nagy (2008) pushes for a "thicker" concept of transitional justice that contains the critical reflection needed to decipher the power dynamics hidden in the hegemonic discourse and practice of transitional justice. It is essential to consider this risk of political opportunism and the power dynamics embedded within the epistemic and normative frameworks that shape the discourse for defining justice and dictate the design and priorities of transitional justice mechanisms like the Canadian TRC. McEvoy (2007) contends that it is an openness to other understandings of justice that can promote critical reflection; he argues that there is a need for a broader basis for understanding the meaning of justice in transition, one that is open to forms of knowledge outside of the legal framework.

Lundy and McGovern (2008) argue that transitional justice ought to adopt a participatory approach that allows the "voices of below" (i.e., the dominated, oppressed, and subaltern) to be not only included but also *listened* to. Their approach is critical of dominant interpretations of key transitional justice concepts and calls for a reconstruction of the meaning of justice that includes local knowledge as well as participation. Their argument, that for transitional justice to achieve its ends requires popular participation and local agency, points to the necessity of including diverse and "local" frameworks in forming the epistemic and normative framework of transitional justice.

With these criticisms in mind, it is difficult to view the TRC as a transitional justice mechanism that has the epistemic humility and moral accountability required to accept the conceptions and understandings of the "other." From its normative principle as a litigation management technique, to its narrowed and state-led epistemic focus, the TRC risks legitimizing the colonial legacy and system of oppression. To transform the Indigenous-Settler relationship, there is a need for a transitional justice approach that goes further than recalling the historical injustices of the past, but actually empowers the oppressed voices of today and transcends hegemonic structures. The concept of a "justice of blessing" proposed by Redekop (2008) highlights the importance of transcending hegemonic structures not only for transforming relationships in divided societies but also as a crucial step to reversing continued victimization and cycles of violence. A justice of blessing (as opposed to a justice of violence like retributive or restorative justice) can be used as a heuristic tool to discover new insights and shed light on new meanings of justice in a divided society.

The following section looks at the precarious dynamic inherent in the task of seeking an ideal of justice for both sides of a divided society without enforcing epistemic and normative hegemonic frameworks. It introduces a defense of universalism under the framework of a "new" cosmopolitanism, one that is decolonial, inclusive, encouraging of diversity, and that accepts the pathway to universal ideals as an ongoing process.

UNIVERSAL IDEALS AND JUSTICE

The liberal-democratic ideals that dominate approaches to transitional justice can be traced back to the cosmopolitan principles first enunciated during the European Enlightenment. The enlightenment principle, that all human beings are equal based on their capacity to reason, seems in direct contradiction to the practice of colonialism, imperialism, and any other form of domination. In fact, the project of enlightenment was meant to free people from the chains that constrain and dominate them. It proposed that through reason, humanity is able to dispel all forms of social domination and base society on rational principles, creating a utopian vision of humanity here on earth. However, as Mignolo (2010) and Dhawan (2012) critically argue, these "emancipatory" principles were in fact used to legitimize colonial oppression, and they continue to legitimize epistemological and normative oppression. In the context of this chapter, the task of naming the ideal of transitional justice must also be to uncover the systems of oppression in that process itself. In order to arrive at an ideal of justice that is emancipatory for all sides of a divided society, it is necessary to critically analyze and deconstruct the dominant methodologies and ideologies that support systems of oppression (i.e., colonialism and its roots in the project of enlightenment and modernity that claim universal knowledge). To confront this challenge, it is important to begin with an understanding of the systems of oppression that were founded on the supposedly universal cosmopolitan ideals of the enlightenment.

The Colonial Project and Old Cosmopolitanism

The "old cosmopolitanism"[10] is a product of the Enlightenment, beginning with Immanuel Kant. In fact, the original cosmopolitan framework for determining normative ideals like justice, reconciliation, and peace was developed by Western, European thinkers influenced by the Christian renaissance and enlightenment philosophy. This resulted in the universalization of a localized and particular interpretation of the ideal of justice as well as other normative ideals. The Enlightenment claimed that reason was the ultimate and universal pathway to free humankind from both the material and ideological chains that constrained them. Reason, it was thought, would lead us to the truth, to the universal, and toward the normative ideals that could shape society.

The objective of the Enlightenment and the Kantian cosmopolitan ideal was emancipation and global equality based on natural law; however, in practice, these ideals were used to legitimize colonial domination. Mignolo argues that Kantian cosmopolitanism, based on enlightenment principles, was actually a form of Western expansion and that its method of global expansion was through the colonial "civilizing mission." More specifically, "Kant's cosmopolitanism was cast under the implicit assumptions that, beyond the heart of Europe was the land of those who had to be brought into civilization" (2010, 123). In other words, the Kantian cosmopolitan ideals, even though they were based on emancipation and universal equality through natural law, actually served as justification for European powers to colonize the rest of the world, bringing the "good fortune" of modernity, progress, and science. Wieviorka points out the same "dark side" of the universal enlightenment project. The Kantian cosmopolitan ideals preached progress, emancipation, Christian salvation, and even industrialization; however, in reality they "concealed practices of domination, exploitation or destruction of peoples and individuals" (Wieviorka 2013, 1964).

Normative ideals and epistemological frameworks can become a form of oppression and violence when they are imposed on others under the guise of "universal values" (i.e., cosmopolitan ideals). This was the case for the project of colonialism. The ethnocentric vision of an emancipated global society became an instrument of self-legitimization and concealment for the actual oppression of colonized peoples. According to Wieviorka, the idea of universal ideals "went hand in hand with colonization and legitimated colonial domination. It is a western-centered value and therefore ethnocentric, of which multiple expressions in the present, postcolonial era can still be found" (2013, 1949). A Eurocentric normative and epistemological framework was touted as "universal," and it legitimized the civilizing mission—that it was for the "good" of the colonized to have the "gift" of the Western enlightenment "bestowed" upon them. In other words, "the construction of the 'West' as a normative and epistemological power has left a trail of violent and exploitative systems in the name of modernity, progress, rationality, emancipation, rights, justice and peace" (Dhawan 2012, 268). The same process is subtly played out today.

Take for example neoliberalism: the competition-driven, free market ideological system promoted by the Western powerful nations as enlightened, modern, and therefore just. Farmer (2004) points out that the success of the neoliberal system is in fact indebted to and helps replicate the inequalities of power. In other words, the neoliberal ideology and worldview, which offers a positivist-rationalist explanation of social reality and is upheld by the powerful as the universal perspective, is based on inequality and reinforces and legitimizes oppression. Farmer is interested in looking at the complex relationship between history and current "world systems" and social inequalities. For him, the neoliberal economic system is a continuation of colonial oppression that self-legitimizes using norms found within its own system.

In describing this type of oppression, Farmer (2004) employs the analytical tool of structural violence. However, the concepts of epistemic violence as developed by Spivak (1985) and normative violence as developed by Butler (2009) provide a sharper understanding of the ideological oppression inherent in the colonial system. An example of the ways in which systems of oppression self-legitimize and conceal the trace of structural violence is by controlling the framework for understanding the roots of injustice or conflict. In other words, reframing the causes of the inequalities or injustices away from the underlying structural violence.

Universal Ideals and Cultural Relativism

When the colonizer and the colonized (or the oppressor and the oppressed) come into contact with each other, there are infinite numbers of social, cultural, economic, and political factors that influence their interpretation of meaning. As Goulet points out, "In such circumstances we are likely to unknowingly substitute our own assumptions and categories to those shared, reaffirmed or contested, by local people. Substitution of this sort voids any possibility of understanding others, first and foremost, as they understand themselves" (2007, 208). This is made even more complex since imposed epistemological frameworks and normative ideals actually guide our interpretations. How then is it possible to come to a shared understanding of normative ideals like justice? If our understanding and interpretations are dependent on cultural context, upbringing, language, and other variables, how could we come to understand a transcultural, transhistorical (i.e., universal) notion of justice that is not merely an oppression of one interpretation over the other? Is such a notion even ideal?

Kantian cosmopolitanism began as an emancipatory project but ended up becoming part of the colonial system of oppression. It was oppressive because it forced a Eurocentric epistemic and normative framework on the rest of the world through the civilizing mission of colonialism. Cultural relativists hold this observation, as a key argument against the universality of cosmopolitan ideals. Caney outlines some of the main arguments launched by cultural relativists against cosmopolitanism. Namely, that cosmopolitan ideals, arguments, and frameworks are Western in origin; "they, therefore, do not have validity in non-Western contexts and it would be a form of ethnocentrism and imperialism to seek to act on them" (2000, 528). In other words, cosmopolitan ideals are merely the imposition of a specific system on people who are not part of the cultural context that constructed it. To impose these ideals and the normative framework upon which they are founded is a form of oppression, domination, and subjugation. This form of oppression is understood here as normative and epistemic violence.

A New Approach to Universal Ideals

The relativist critique of "cultural imposition" is a challenge that can be overcome through a decolonizing reconstruction of cosmopolitan ideals. For Wieviorka (2013), this entails a "re-enchantment" of universal values "by showing that their invention is not the monopoly of the Greek, Roman or Christian West and by seeking the sources of an update in other intellectual, moral and political traditions" (1952). In other words, he is pointing out those ideas of universal values like justice, freedom, and democracy that have been conceived in other cultures and at other times. Sen (2003) gives an excellent historical review and analysis of the origins of democracy in India to reveal that ideas that are purported to have originated in Europe and blossomed in the Enlightenment actually have deep histories in other parts of the world. Sen argues that when it comes to understanding democracy, the "intellectual heritages of China, Japan, East and Southeast Asia, the Indian subcontinent, Iran, the Middle East, and Africa have been almost entirely neglected" and that this "has not favoured an adequately inclusive understanding of the nature and the power of democratic ideas" (2003, 31). Essentially, Sen and Wieviorka are advocating for the emergence of a new understanding of universal ideals. Sen argues for it by calling for a more inclusive analysis and knowledge production. Wieviorka calls for a "universalism from below" that challenges the dominant and hegemonic universalism of the West—one that seeks liberation, instead of colonial expansion (2013, 1947). Thus, a universal ideal of transitional justice might be possible in divided societies, as long as it is one that challenges the dominant conceptions and takes into consideration the diverse understandings and cultural approaches to justice.

Arguing along the same lines as Sen and Wieviorka, Mignolo (2011) contends that we must begin by "reducing Kantian legacies to size." More specifically, he means that the Kantian cosmopolitanism that was born out of the enlightenment is merely a "localized" cosmopolitanism. He writes, "Euro-American concepts of cosmopolitanism have the right to exist but have no right to expect to be universal. Cosmopolitan localism means the multiplication of nodes, the active intervention of local cosmopolitan projects from all over the world and the reduction of Western cosmopolitans to its own local history" (Mignolo 2011, 11). In other words, the objective is not to throw away all knowledge rooted in the European enlightenment, but rather, to deuniversalize it. Essentially, the dominance of the Eurocentric version of modernity is a question of the geopolitics of knowledge production.

At least, that is the way that Maldonado-Torres (2004) describes this system of epistemic and normative violence and oppression. He argues that to decolonize the "racist geo-politics of knowledge" requires an inclusive approach—it requires a "radical diversality" for determining universal values. More specifically, he argues for an epistemic framework guided by dialogue with diverse sources of knowledge. The challenge of radical diversality, he writes,

> is to think seriously about Fort-de-France, Quito, La Paz, Baghdad and Algiers, not only Paris, Frankfurt, Rome or New York as possible sites of knowledge. We also need to think about those who are locked in positions of subordination, and try to understand both the mechanisms that create the subordination and those that hide their reality from view to others. There is much in the world to learn from others who have been rendered invisible by modernity. This moment should be more about examining our complicity with old patterns of domination and searching for invisible faces, than about searching for imperial roots; more about radical critique than about orthodox alignments against what are persistently conceived as the barbarians of knowledge. (Maldonado-Torres 2004, 21)

Evidently, it is not purely about including the diverse locations of knowledge, but it is also about raising up and incorporating the historically oppressed voices. In the context of Canada, it is about empowering the voices of Indigenous peoples and having the epistemic humility to include them in an equitable dialogue. This, by any other name, is the project of decolonization.

In describing this movement or school of thought and its relation to universal ideals, Wieviorka (2013) writes, "decolonization is inseparable from the many declarations that in one way or another challenge western arrogance and the idea of universal values" (1949). The idea is to criticize the notion of the "civilizing mission" and reveal the underlying structural, normative, and epistemic violence that were part and parcel of the "gifts" of progress, enlightenment, and modernity.

EPISTEMIC HUMILITY, TRANSCENDENCE, AND RECONCILIATION

Decolonial cosmopolitanism as developed by Mignolo (2010, 2011) and dialogical cosmopolitanism as developed by Mendieta (2009) both offer a platform from which we can emerge out of oppressive systems and create new pathways to mutual understanding. They offer an epistemic and normative standpoint from which hegemonic structures can be reversed, ultimately reducing victimization, empowering the voices of the oppressed, and turning from relations of violence to accountability, humility, and solidarity (i.e., moving from a "justice of violence" to a "justice of blessing"). The former focuses on the need to break down the colonial systems of oppression that universalized a merely *local* epistemic and normative framework. The latter is also decolonial; however, it focuses on the theoretical stance that is needed to move from the "imperial to the dialogical" (i.e., from oppressive to emancipatory). More specifically, it focuses on the epistemic and normative position that one must take in order to include the diverse standpoints of the "other." This type of position allows for the emergence of an emancipatory process "through an engagement with a dialogical imagination that opens up the spaces of mutual transformation" (Mendieta 2009, 254).

Laying Bare Epistemic and Normative Violence

Dialogical cosmopolitanism is a pathway beyond the systems of oppression that dominate through epistemic and normative violence. In fact, Mendieta (2009) describes dialogical cosmopolitanism as a "type of epistemic and moral stance toward the world that is cognizant of both its privileges and thus limits, and which reflects about these from the standpoint of the other, to whom it reaches to learn from and with" (243). In essence, it is a normative ideal and epistemological framework that offers emancipation from dominant conceptions of values like justice, peace, and reconciliation. The idea is that respecting culturally diverse epistemic and normative contexts and including them in a self-reflexive dialogical exchange can decolonize and transform relationships constrained by systems of oppression.

The word "dialogical" has roots in critical theory. Habermas (1987) developed his theory of communicative action as a form of rationality available to every human being "transhistorically." Therefore, each person has the potential to participate in the communicative process (i.e., public discourse or dialogue), which is inherently impartial, and allows the redevelopment of norms that are freed from ideological constraints. Following this Habermasian conception of discourse ethics, Hutchings (2011) argues, the idea of dialogical exchange "remains attractive because it is seen as a way of decentering hegemonic conceptions of knowledge and morality" (64). In other words, it is seen as a pathway to uncovering epistemic and normative violence. Open and impartial dialogue in this sense is the necessary process for "unsettling taken-for-granted truths about the world, specifically the taken-for-granted truths of the powerful" (ibid).

Dialogical cosmopolitanism builds off of this theoretical framework; however, it does so by reflexively acknowledging the historical and cultural roots of that very framework. Essentially, if enlightened, reflexive, and rooted, dialogical cosmopolitanism "is an expectant cosmopolitanism that expands both vertically and horizontally, through local cosmopolitan iterations that defer it making it into a normative ideal that is guided by contextual universalism" (Mendieta 2009, 254). More simply put, dialogue as a mutual process of deliberate self-awareness and willful openness to imagine oneself in the standpoint of the "other" (i.e., perspective or context) can allow for the ongoing process of forming normative ideals.

In this sense then, dialogical cosmopolitanism is not practical everyday discourse. It is a process of imagination, of placing oneself in the other's shoes. Mendieta (2009) describes the dialogical imagination as a process of opening

> a horizon of intelligibility that sets out from recognizing that we imagine others, just as those others imagine us in their own ways. We are always more and less than what we are imagined to be, which is why we must allow others to challenge our "images" and "imagination" of them, and conversely, to allow ourselves to correct our own self-understanding in light of those challenges. Thus, this imagination internalizes the other, alterity, in a non-imperial and non-obliterating way, in order to reconstitute itself. (254)

Dialogical cosmopolitanism in this sense can be analyzed as an "epistemic attitude" that challenges "the monopoly of one worldview" and as a normative principle that commands "the solicitous moral regard for those who are our others" (Mendieta 2009, 208). In other words, there are two parts to dialogical cosmopolitanism: openness to the diverse understandings and a moral accountability to the "other."

Mutual Transformation through Ongoing Dialogue

Perhaps the most important aspect of dialogical cosmopolitanism as a method for decolonizing oppressive conceptions of values like justice, peace, and reconciliation is that it is an ongoing process. The normative and epistemic stance of dialogical cosmopolitanism offers a decolonized framework for uncovering systems of oppression while simultaneously *approaching* universal ideals that cut across culture, time, and space. Essentially, through a willful and deliberate practice of dialogical imagination, diverse and "localized" value systems can be mutually challenged and reformulated. Instead of considering it as a method or process, it is best to consider it as an ongoing epistemological commitment that perpetually approaches an understanding the "other" as well as our own selves. Furthermore, inasmuch as it is an epistemological commitment, it is also a normative one. Specifically, it is a commitment to mutually transform (i.e., decolonize) the relationship by placing oneself in the standpoint of the other.

With the approach of dialogical cosmopolitanism, the Kantian cosmopolitanism vision would be reconstituted in dialogue with other "local" cosmopolitanisms. In other words, instead of universalizing the reasons of white Europeans as the ideal for a cosmopolitan world order, these reasons ought to be discerned, deconstructed, and reconstituted through an "internalization of the other." Mendieta (2009) describes this internalization as allowing others "to challenge our 'images' and 'imagination' of them, and conversely, to allow ourselves to correct our own self-understanding in light of those challenges. Thus, this imagination internalizes the other, alterity, in a non-imperial and non-obliterating way, in order to reconstitute itself" (254).

Dhawam (2012), although not writing from a cosmopolitanism angle, argues for a new ideal of transitional justice by highlighting key aspects contained within the theory of dialogical cosmopolitanism. Specifically, that a decolonization of the idea of transitional justice is necessarily an ongoing process. Dhawam (2012) proposes an approach to justice as a "utopian concept, perpetually deferred, never achieving closure, and, thereby, always open to that which it overlooks or silences. This calls for permanent vigilance from dispensers of (transitional) justice in their efforts to right wrongs" (266). Arguing from a postcolonial-feminist framework, Dhawam contends that determining normative ideals like justice must be a continual process so that any form of "neocolonial" oppression can be identified and weeded out and the "silenced voices of the oppressed" can be empowered. Dialogical cosmopolitanism offers an approach that allows for both of these imperatives to take place. Furthermore, as an epistemic and normative stance, it offers a solution to the problem of affirming an ideal of justice without imposing the dominant conception. In other words, it uncovers the epistemic and normative violence that constrains divided societies from moving forward toward a brighter future of justice, peace, and reconciliation.

In the context of the Indigenous-Settler relationship in Canada therefore, decolonizing and transforming the relationship would require a radical openness to the other's vision of transitional justice. It would take an epistemic humility on the part of the dominant Settler society to arrive at an ideal of transitional justice. If all parts of this divided society repeatedly commit to such an epistemic and normative stance and continually engage with a dialogical imagination, the Indigenous-Settler relationship can be mutually transformed, decolonized, and "unsettled." The ideal of transitional justice will be continually refined and approached and never imposed on either side. From this epistemic and normative stance, there is no fixed single ideal, but rather "a process of arriving at it through an engagement with a dialogical imagination that opens up the spaces of mutual transformation"

(Mendieta 2009, 254). New "spaces" of mutual transformation can allow for an entirely new array of possibilities, ideals, and relationships. Inclusive, diverse conceptions of justice can emerge, transcending the plurality of limited, "localized," and particular historical or cultural frameworks.

A Vision for Reconciliation and the Emergence of New Relationships

On the day the TRC Final Report was released, the chair of the TRC, Justice Murray Sinclair, said, "Today marks the beginning of a new chapter in relations between Indigenous and non-Indigenous Canadians" (Mas 2015). New beginnings can be full of hope and optimism for the future, but transforming relationships takes time. Moving from oppressive relationships to just relationships requires breaking down complex systems of oppression, beginning with the epistemic and normative framework for conceiving of justice, peace, and reconciliation. As a mechanism of transitional justice, the TRC has brought the stories of survivors into public discourse, but will it succeed in going beyond these testimonies by transforming the hegemonic structures and building a path toward positive peace? In other words, can the TRC decolonize the Indigenous-Settler relationship and address the colonial roots of the epistemic, normative, and structural violence that perpetuates the present-day misery of Indigenous peoples?

Regan (2010) argues that for this transformation to take place, there must be an "unsettling of the settler within." More specifically, for mechanisms like the TRC to truly facilitate the transition toward a just society, settler society must accept the colonial history of Canada, but more importantly, confront the epistemic and normative framework that continues to legitimize it. In short, to "unsettle the settler" there must be a critical consciousness within Settler society that uncovers and tears down the different forms of violence of colonialism.

Openness to the testimonies found within the TRC and a moral accountability to those who shared their experiences can dismantle the epistemic and normative violence embedded within the colonial system of oppression. In describing this dismantling of colonial oppression, Angel (2013) argues that in giving their testimony, Indigenous peoples "rupture silences about colonial policies of assimilation and oppression, giving voice to long-denied or stifled experiences" (200). This immense decolonial effort by Indigenous peoples must be met with an equally immense commitment by Settlers to decolonize their own epistemic assumptions and take ownership of Canada's colonial history. To approach the ideal of justice in the Canadian context, Settler society must commit to an epistemic humility, openness to conceptions of justice, and a moral accountability toward Indigenous peoples.

If it is to succeed as an emancipatory process for both sides of Canada's divided society, then the "new relationship" that Justice Sinclair proudly announced must transcend hegemonic structures. This means revealing and dismantling colonialist power in all its forms (Nagy 2013) and transcending hegemonic structures. Transforming the Indigenous-Settler relationship requires a reversal of the imitative cycles of violence and victimization and a move toward cycles of blessing (Redekop 2002). Therefore, it is incumbent upon both sides to focus their orientation, attitude, and actions on blessing the victims of all injustice (Redekop 2002). Such an orientation, coupled with epistemic humility, can promote the continuous cultivation of well-being and the emergence of relationships of solidarity and creativity.

CONCLUSION

It is clear that defining the objectives, processes, and frameworks for achieving, or at least approaching, justice in divided societies is a complex task. In order to build positive peace, past injustices as well as the enduring structural violence must be addressed. Epistemic and normative violence rooted in oppressive colonial practices, both material and ideological, are deeply ingrained in divided societies with a history of colonialism. Canada, examined with its history of colonialism in mind, is a particularly important example of the challenges of transitional justice in divided societies. The ideals and principles of transitional justice can rest on the same "universal" epistemic and normative foundations that legitimized and guided the civilizing mission of colonialism in the first place. The current structural violence that marks the Indigenous-Settler relationship and the transitional justice mechanism of the TRC must be examined under the pretext that "colonial relations still inform how problems are perceived and what solutions are offered" (Dhawan 2012, 264).

The efficiency and effectiveness of different transitional justice mechanisms, practices, and policies ought to be continually refined and improved. However, this chapter is concerned with addressing the systems of oppression that can be embedded in transitional justice frameworks themselves—frameworks that continue to be dominated by hegemonic discourses founded on European enlightenment principles. In other words, this chapter has grappled with the difficulty of uncovering the epistemic and normative violence within liberal democratic society where the majority continues to benefit from the system in place. The overdomination of any particular framework for defining the ideal of justice can do more harm than good in the transition toward a just society.

Breaking down complex systems of oppression surreptitiously legitimized by epistemic and normative violence requires an emergence of new ideals that circumvent localized epistemic and normative principles, and allow new possibilities to creatively emerge. This chapter has suggested dialogical cosmopolitanism as a decolonized epistemic and normative approach for transforming the oppressive Indigenous-Settler relationship into one based on the ideal of justice. Through epistemic humility and openness to other forms of knowledge and a moral accountability to the "other," Settler society can give space to the findings of the TRC and reconstitute their own understanding of justice toward Indigenous peoples. Inclusion of the "other," their perspective, their standpoint, and their experience can reframe the discourse, and allow for new ideas and relationships to emerge.

The *Summary of the TRC Final Report* states, "Reconciliation could not be achieved during the TRC's lifetime, the country could and must take ongoing positive and concrete steps forward . . . it will take many heads, hands, and hearts, working together, at all levels of society to maintain momentum in the years ahead" (TRC 2015, 8). Although, most important for the mutual transformation and reconciliation of the Indigenous-Settler relationship is a spirituality of openness, humility, and moral accountability toward, and solidarity with, the other.

NOTES

1. A divided society can be understood as one where some form of violence or oppression keeps it divided (Guelke 2012). In many cases, divisions within society are marked by ethnicity, religion, class, race, or other group identities (Horowitz 1985). In cases like Canada and the Indigenous-Settler relationship, violence and oppression may remain hidden, deeply embedded within society. This can be considered structural violence, only indirectly observable through the lived experiences of marginalization, poverty, and present-day misery of the oppressed (Galtung 1969; Farmer 1996). In any case, the challenge for all divided societies is to transform oppressive relationships into just relationships.

2. The shortcomings or failures of the liberal-democratic approach to transitional justice will be expanded below. However, for a more in-depth analysis, Paris (1997) gives an encompassing and convincing criticism of "liberal internationalism" in peacebuilding efforts in postconflict countries like Haiti, Bosnia, Afghanistan, and Kosovo. Some other examples of what could be considered failures of the liberal-democratic approach to postconflict peacebuilding and Western models of justice are the cases of Rwanda (Oomen 2005), Cambodia (Call and Cook 2003), or Bosnia (Hoogenboom and Vieille 2010). Although these countries have been able to maintain some level of stability and end extreme violence, in the postconflict context they continue to be marked by fragmentation and a struggle to bridge deepening ethnic divisions.

3. A legal studies perspective might define justice as fair and equitable treatment of all individuals under the law. Legal philosophy, beginning with Plato and Aristotle,

defines justice in terms of "rational principles that uphold equal rights among individuals and promote the fair distribution of scarce resources" (Petersmann 2003). A utilitarian approach to justice, based on John Stuart Mill, is the greatest good for the greatest number of people. In a Marxist fashion, Harvey (1996) defines justice as a powerful mobilizing discourse for political action. Economic or commercial understandings of justice are often based on the principles of Adam Smith or John Locke, specifically, that justice amounts to respecting the property and possessions of others, or rather, to "abstain from taking what others already rightfully and legally possess" (Salter 1994).

4. Indigenous adults are overrepresented in prisons. They accounted for one-quarter (25 percent) of admissions in 2014/2015 while representing around 3 percent of the Canadian adult population (Reitano 2016).

5. The Royal Commission on Aboriginal Peoples found in 1996 that eight in ten Indigenous women experienced violence or abuse and that by sixteen years of age, 51 percent of Indigenous women experienced some form of sexual assault, and 27 percent experienced some form of physical assault; and finally, Indigenous women were eight times more likely, as compared to non-Indigenous women, to be murdered at the hands of their spouse (Kwan 2015). Unfortunately, these trends have not been decreasing. In fact, in 2009, almost half of the women who identify as Aboriginal self-reported experiences of violence or violent victimization (Kwam 2015).

6. Recent data on substance abuse across Aboriginal communities in Canada have not been compiled. The most comprehensive report on substance abuse was completed as part of the Royal Commission on Aboriginal Peoples in 1996. However, Aboriginal communities continue to identify substance use and related harms as some of the biggest challenges currently their people are facing (Firestone et al. 2015).

7. Since contact with European settlers, Indigenous peoples have suffered from higher rates of infectious diseases. However, since the 1980s, chronic diseases like diabetes and cancer are now taking a higher toll on Indigenous populations (Adelson 2005).

8. The unemployment rate of Indigenous peoples compared to the rest of Canadian society is three times higher. On some reserves, there is a 90 percent unemployment rate (McKenzie and Morrissette 2003).

9. The term "cultural genocide" can be understood as the targeted long-term destruction of a group, including their language, traditions, and religions (MacDonald and Hudson 2012). Qualifying past colonial injustices as genocide has political ramifications and there is debate whether or not the IRS system merits the term; however, most authors concede that it was at the very least a cultural genocide (Macdonald and Hudson 2012; Regan 2010; Reyhner and Singh 2010; Woolford and Benvenuto 2015).

10. "Old cosmopolitanism" refers to early modern and Enlightenment philosophical and political ideas, but specifically the Kantian approach—more precisely, ideas like "perpetual peace," the teleological view of nature, and common humanity. Hollinger (2001) writes that the "new cosmopolitanisms" that have appeared over the past few decades, denoted by adjectives like "critical," "national," or "comparative", all have one thing in common; they are trying to make a clear break from the

old cosmopolitanism of Kant and the Enlightenment—one that fails to respond to the plurality, diversity, and complexity of culture, human relations, and society in general (237).

REFERENCES

Adelson, Naomi. 2005. "The embodiment of inequity: Health disparities in Aboriginal Canada." *Canadian Journal of Public Health/Revue Canadienne de Santée Publique, 96,* S45–S61.

Angel, Naomi. 2012. "Before truth: The labors of testimony and the Canadian truth and reconciliation commission." *Culture, Theory and Critique, 53*(2), 199–214.

Arbour, Louise. 2007. "Economic and social justice for societies in transition." *New York University Journal of International Law and Politics, 40,* 1.

Betts, Alexander. 2005. Should approaches to post-conflict justice and reconciliation be determined globally, nationally or locally?. *The European Journal of Development Research, 17*(4), 735–752.

Butler, Judith. 2009. *Frames of war. When is Life Grievable?.* New York, NY: Verso.

Call, Charles, and Susan Cook. 2003. "On democratization and peacebuilding." *Global Governance, 9,* 233.

Caney, Simon. 2000. "Cosmopolitan justice and cultural diversity." *Global Society, 14*(4), 525–551.

Corntassel, Jeff, and Cindy Holder. 2008. "Who's sorry now? Government apologies, truth commissions, and Indigenous self-determination in Australia, Canada, Guatemala, and Peru." *Human Rights Review, 9*(4), 465–489.

Dhawan, Nikita. 2012. "Transitions to justice." In *Gender in Transitional Justice* (pp. 264–283). UK: Palgrave Macmillan.

Farmer, Paul. 1996. "On suffering and structural violence: A view from below." *Daedalus, 3,* 261–283.

———. 2004. "An anthropology of structural violence". *Current Anthropology, 45*(3), 305–325.

Firestone, Michelle, Mark Tyndall, and Benedikt Fischer. 2015. "Substance use and related harms among aboriginal people in Canada: A comprehensive review." *Journal of Health Care for the Poor and Underserved, 26*(4), 1110–1131.

Galtung, Johan. 1969. "Violence, peace, and peace research." *Journal of Peace Research, 6*(3), 167–191.

———. 1990. "Cultural violence." *Journal of Peace Research, 27*(3), 291–305.

Ghali, Boutros Boutros. 1992. "An agenda for peace: Preventive diplomacy." In *Peacemaking and Peacekeeping.* New York, NY: United Nations, 1995 [2nd edition].

Goulet, Jean-Guy. 2007. "Moving beyond culturally bound ethical guidelines." In *Extraordinary Anthropology. Transformations in the Field* (pp. 208–234). Lincoln, NE: University of Nebraska Press.

Green, Robyn. 2012. "Unsettling cures: Exploring the limits of the Indian residential school settlement agreement." *Canadian Journal of Law and Society, 27*(01), 129–148.

Guelke, Adrian. 2012. *Politics in Deeply Divided Societies.* Cambridge: Polity.

Habermas, Jürgen. 1987. *The Theory of Communicative Action Volume Two: Lifeworld and System: A Critique of Functionalist Reason.* Boston, MA: Beacon Press Books.

Harvey, David. 1996. *Justice, Nature and the Geography of Difference.* Oxford: Blackwell.

Henderson, Jennifer, and Pauline Wakeham. 2009. "Colonial reckoning, national reconciliation?: Aboriginal peoples and the culture of redress in Canada." *ESC: English Studies in Canada, 35*(1), 1–26.

Hoogenboom, David, and Stephanie Vieille. 2010. "Rebuilding social fabric in failed states: Examining transitional justice in Bosnia." *Human Rights Review, 11*(2), 183–198.

Hollinger, David. 2001. "Not universalists, not pluralists: The new cosmopolitans find their own way." *Constellations, 8*(2), 236–248.

Hutchings, Kimberly. 2011. "Dialogue between whom? The role of the West/non-West distinction in promoting global dialogue in IR." *Millennium-Journal of International Studies, 39*(3), 639–647.

James, Matt. 2008. "Wrestling with the past: Apologies, quasi-apologies, and non-apologies in Canada." In *The Age of Apology: Facing up to the Past* (pp. 137–153). Philadelphia, PA: University of Pennsylvania Press.

Kwan, Jennifer. 2015. "From taboo to epidemic: Family violence within aboriginal communities." *Global Social Welfare, 2*(1), 1–8.

Lambourne, Wendy. 2009. "Transitional justice and peacebuilding after mass violence." *International Journal of Transitional Justice, 3,* ijn037.

Lederach, Jean Paul. 1995. *Preparing for Peace: Conflict Transformation across Cultures.* Syracuse, NY: Syracuse University Press.

Lekha Sriram, Chandra. 2007. "Justice as peace? Liberal peacebuilding and strategies of transitional justice." *Global Society, 21*(4), 579–591.

Lundy, Patricia, and Mark McGovern. 2008. "Whose justice? Rethinking transitional justice from the bottom up." *Journal of Law and Society, 35*(2), 265–292.

Maddison, Sarah. 2013. "Indigenous identity, 'authenticity' and the structural violence of settler colonialism." *Identities, 20*(3), 288–303.

MacDonald, David B., and Graham Hudson. 2012. "The genocide question and Indian residential schools in Canada." *Canadian Journal of Political Science, 45*(02), 427–449.

Maldonado-Torres, Nelson. 2004. "The topology of being and the geopolitics of knowledge: Modernity, empire, coloniality." *City, 8*(1), 29–56.

Mani, Rama. 2005. "Balancing peace with justice in the aftermath of violent conflict." *Development, 48*(3), 25–34.

Mas, Susana. 2015. "Truth and reconciliation chair says final report marks start of 'new era'." *CBC News,* December 15. Accessed April 25, 2016. http://www.cbc.ca /news/politics/truth-and-reconciliation-final-report-ottawa-event-1.3365921.

McEvoy, Kieran. 2007. "Beyond legalism: Towards a thicker understanding of transitional justice." *Journal of Law and Society*, *34*(4), 411–440.

McKenzie, Brad, and Vern Morrissette. 2003. "Social work practice with Canadians of Aboriginal background: Guidelines for respectful social work." *Envision: The Manitoba Journal of Child Welfare*, *2*(1), 13–39.

Mendieta, Eduardo. 2009. "From imperial to dialogical cosmopolitanism?." *Ethics & Global Politics*, *2*(3), 241–258.

———. 2010. "Interspecies cosmopolitanism." *Philosophy Today*, *54*(Supplement), 208–216.

Miller, Jim. 2003. "Troubled legacy: A history of native residential schools." *Saskatchewan Law Review*, *66*(1), 357–382.

Mignolo, Walter. 2010. "Cosmopolitanism and the de-colonial option." *Studies in Philosophy and Education*, *29*(2), 111–127.

———. 2011. "Cosmopolitan localism: A decolonial shifting of the Kantian's legacies." *Localities*, *1*, 11–45.

Nagy, Rosemary. 2008. "Transitional justice as global project: Critical reflections." *Third World Quarterly*, *29*(2), 275–289.

———. 2013. "The scope and bounds of transitional justice and the Canadian truth and reconciliation commission." *International Journal of Transitional Justice*, *7*, ijs034.

Nagy, Rosemary, and Robinder Kaur Sehdev. 2012. "Introduction: Residential schools and decolonization." *Canadian Journal of Law and Society*, *27*(01), 67–73.

Oomen, Barbara. 2005. "Donor-driven justice and its discontents: The case of Rwanda." *Development and Change*, *36*(5), 887–910.

Paris, Roland. 1997. "Peacebuilding and the limits of liberal internationalism." *International Security*, *22*(2), 54–89.

Petersmann, Ernst Ulrich. 2003. "Theories of justice, human rights, and the constitution of international markets." *Loyola Los Angeles Law Review*, *37*, 407.

Redekop, V. N. 2008. "A post-genocidal justice of blessing as an alternative to a justice of violence: The case of Rwanda." In *Peacebuilding in Traumatized Societies* (pp. 205–238). Lanham, MD: University Press of America.

———. 2002. *From Violence to Blessing: How an Understanding of Deep-Rooted Conflict can Open Paths to Reconciliation*. Ottawa: Novalis.

Regan, Paulette. 2010. *Unsettling the Settler within: Indian Residential Schools, Truth Telling, and Reconciliation in Canada*. Vancouver: UBC Press.

Reitano, Julie. 2016. "Adult correctional statistics in Canada, 2014–2015." *Juristat* (85-002-X). Retrieved April 11, 2016 from Statistics Canada. http://www.statcan.gc.ca/pub/85-002-x/2016001/article/14318-eng.htm.

Reyhner, Jon, and Navin Kumar Singh. 2010. "Cultural genocide in Australia, Canada, New Zealand, and the United States." *Indigenous Policy Journal*, *21*(4), 1–26.

Salter, John. 1994. "Adam Smith on justice and distribution in commercial societies." *Scottish Journal of Political Economy*, *41*(3), 299–313.

Sen, Amartya. 2003. "Democracy and its global roots." *New Republic*, 28–35.

Spivak, Gayatri Chakravorty. 1985. "Three women's texts and a critique of imperialism." *Critical Inquiry*, *12*(1), 243–261.

Stanton, Kim. 2011. "Canada's truth and reconciliation commission: Settling the past?" *International Indigenous Policy Journal*, *2*(3), 2.

Titley, E. Brian. 1986. *A Narrow Vision: Duncan Campbell Scott and the Administration of Indian Affairs in Canada*. Vancouver: UBC Press.

Thomson, Susan, and Rosemary Nagy. 2011. "Law, power and justice: What legalism fails to address in the functioning of Rwanda's Gacaca courts." *International Journal of Transitional Justice*, *5*(1), 11–30.

Truth and Reconciliation Commission of Canada. 2015. *Honouring the Truth, Reconciling for the Future: Summary of the Final Report of the Truth and Reconciliation Commission of Canada*. Retrieved April 11, 2016. http://nctr.ca/assets/reports/Final%20Reports/Executive_Summary_English_Web.pdf.

Wieviorka, Michel. 2013. "The re-enchantment of universal values: Given as the 2013 ERS Lecture at City University London, May 2013." *Ethnic and Racial Studies*, *36*(12), 1943–1956.

Woods, Eric Taylor. 2013. "A cultural approach to a Canadian tragedy: The Indian residential schools as a sacred enterprise." *International Journal of Politics, Culture, and Society*, *26*(2), 173–187.

Woolford, Andrew, and Jeff Benvenuto. 2015. "Canada and colonial genocide." *Journal of Genocide Research*, *17*(4), 373–390.

Chapter 12

Warring with *Windigo/Wihtiko*

Cree and Algonquian Insights into Spirituality, Emergent Creativity, and Reconciliation

Cecil Chabot

The "magnitude of consequence that issued from the collision of European and Indigenous American histories," wrote Steve Stern a quarter century ago, ". . . forces us to consider the problem of meaning: to discover, define, appropriate what 1492 means to human history" (1993, 4). This critical pan-American reconciliation challenge persists, but any attempt to give a single meaning to 500 years of contact to risk closing off sources and examples that are key to finding both meaning and reconciliation.

On the eve of the 500th anniversary of Columbus' arrival, Richard White (1991) argued that the first two centuries of Indigenous and non-Indigenous relations in the Great Lakes region were defined not by European imposition and Indigenous resistance, but by a balance of power that obliged all parties to mutually cocreate, and meet on, a "middle ground." White observed that he was surprised by this conclusion, despite the unambiguous evidence—a surprise echoed by most scholars in his field.

What I found most striking, in contrast, was not his conclusion, but the degree to which so few scholars were able to imagine a situation where Indigenous-European relationships were not defined by an imbalance of power. When White published his book, I was completing high school in a northern Indigenous community, where I had lived all my life: an ancient subarctic Cree summer gathering site where the Hudson's Bay Company had established its second oldest fur-trade post in 1673. With a few temporary exceptions, I was usually the only non-Cree in my class: a fact that some never noticed and a few never let me forget. Yet, with few exceptions, all my Cree classmates had some admixture of Orcadian, Scottish, English, French, or Norwegian ancestry. My hometown of Moose Factory, like much of the James Bay Cree region, has long been defined by what Cree Grand Chief Abel Bosum has called "partnership" (2017). It is an Indigenous-Newcomer "middle ground" that dates back to the seventeenth century but has persisted to the present.

After leaving the north for postsecondary studies that introduced me to the work of White and other scholars, I began to realize how my formative years had given me a perspective that did not fit into an Indigenous versus non-Indigenous binary. This outlook has been shaped by the need to bring the Cree perspectives and traditions in which I had been immersed from birth—and which I took for granted as not only relevant but also indispensable for understanding my world—into dialogue with the French and English perspectives and traditions of my parents, as well as other views and traditions. I needed to do this, because like other youth in my community, I was faced with fundamental human questions and the need to find meaningful and relevant answers to them—and no answer was relevant and meaningful to me if it did not account for the diversity of perspectives and traditions that shaped who I was. This defines the primary objective and approach of my scholarship: to bring Indigenous, Western, Christian, and other traditions into deep dialogue on the fundamental human questions.

This chapter is the fruit of research, conversations, and reflections on the cannibal wihtiko (windigo[1]), as a photographic narrative of fundamental Cree values. I grew up hearing wihtiko stories, some of them shared below. It is not so much the wihtiko, however, but the values it inversely reveals that I propose as a source of critical insights on the theme of "spirituality, emergent creativity and reconciliation."

WINDIGO AS NEGATION OF ALGONQUIAN SPIRITUAL IDEALS AND IDEAS OF EMERGENT CREATIVITY

A long time ago, according to one Cree *ahtalohkan* (mythic narrative), a man became greedy and disrespectful and killed too many fish[2]—a transgression against reciprocity that northern Ontario elder Louis Bird describes as *maahchihew*—"sinning against animals" (2007, 76). This resulted in a great deluge in which male–female pairs of all animal and human persons took refuge on a raft until, working together, they recovered a clump of earth beneath the waters and used it to reconstitute the land. One singular exception stands out in this account of transgression and reconciliation. On the raft was found one category of being that had no mate and remained seated alone in a corner, facing the north. It was known as Windigo.

Windigo is a cannibal monster that epitomizes the perversion of the spiritual values most fundamental for relationship, reciprocity, and reconciliation in Cree and other Algonquian subarctic communities—and perhaps any human community.[3] Windigo destroys all relationships. Although it attained mythic proportions in the traditional spiritual and cultural landscapes of Algonquian peoples, the windigo reflects experience and insights that resonate beyond these landscapes. It emerged and evolved as a unique and creative response to very real crises that any human society could face in similar circumstances. Some of these crises originated from within subarctic Algonquian communities, but others from without—especially at the peak of European colonialism, which both challenged windigo interpretations and prompted new ones that challenged colonialism itself. The emergence, evolution, and interpretations of the windigo—phenomena and concept alike— reveal experiences, ideas, and ideals that are profoundly relevant to questions of spirituality, emergent creativity, and reconciliation.

In the 1970s, northern Saskatchewan Cree elder Marie Merasty recounted a harrowing incident that had occurred a century earlier, in the depths of a particularly difficult subarctic winter. A family of six had found themselves starving. When the father and son failed to return from a critical hunting quest, the mother and her three daughters mustered their remaining strength and left camp in search of their loved ones. After following the trail for some time, they suddenly sighted a frozen body ahead of them.

> "Now we'll be able to eat," exclaimed the old lady. "Here's a young bull moose!" In her hunger, she was hallucinating. The girls seized their mother, their eyes streaming with tears. "Mother, don't say that," one of them urged. "That's my brother!" As if jolted by a startling force, the mother suddenly came back to her senses. (Merasty 1974, 1)

Continuing onward, the four survivors managed to reach and obtain help at an Anglican mission where they eventually recovered from the effects of near-starvation. So ends this *tipachimowin* (historical narrative). For a traditional Cree or Algonquian listener, the reason for the urgent tone in the daughter's plea would have been self-evident, and it is succinctly captured in the title of this narrative—"Almost a Wetiko" (ibid.).

If this woman narrowly escaped going windigo, others were less fortunate. Edward Rae, a northern Manitoba Anishinabe elder, recounted a *tipachimowin* originating with John Thomas (also known as John Doggy), a Norway House fur trader of European and Algonquian ancestry (Fiddler and Stevens 1985, 32). One winter, after a trapper failed to return to his camp as expected, Thomas had become concerned. Recruiting another man for reinforcement, he packed ropes, chains, and tarps and departed in search of the missing trapper. They eventually found him in such a state that they were compelled to subdue and bind him hand and foot before bringing him back to the main camp. With the help of non-Indigenous men, he was then transported across Lake Winnipeg. Rae explains: "When the Windigo woke up, they asked him about his wife and kids. The Windigo replied: 'They are still living. No. I killed them.' Then the Windigo started crying." Upon reaching the rail line, they brought the windigo by train to a psychiatric hospital. There,

> the Windigo woke up for longer periods of time. He asked for his wife and children. Then he said: "I believe I killed my wife and child." Then he started crying. He would stay awake for three hours but he would be crying all the time. The hospital thought he was getting better but he cried all the time.
>
> Soon after, when the Windigo's mind was clear, he was still always crying. He was sure he killed his wife and kids. He had treatment but, eventually, he just died. John Doggy stayed there until the man died, [and] then he went home. (cited in ibid.)

Both these stories—of narrow escape and a more tragic fate—describe people whose responsibility for their windigo-associated behavior appears to have been minimal. Other *tipachimowina* depict more sinister cases. In a 1977 conversation with anthropologist Robert Brightman, northern Manitoba Cree elder Jeremy Caribou gave a very different description of someone who had gone windigo: "That windigo thinks he's the strongest . . . [and] can do what he likes with the other [guy]. Kill him. Even eat him up" (Brightman 1988, 364).[4] In the mid-1950s, northern Ontario and Quebec Cree elders Willie Frenchman and Samuel Iserhoff—the latter an ordained Anglican minister—prefaced another windigo *tipachimowin* with a comment that explains variations between more tragic and more sinister windigo cases: "It has happened before, that when men are hungry they turn cannibals, and this was the case with people who got lost in the bush. Some say that people who are cannibals go mad, others that they go thoroughly wicked."[5]

Cree Spiritual Ideals

The central theme of so many Cree *tipachimowina* and *ahtalohkana*, observes anthropologist Richard Preston, "has to do with the practise of right conduct, and lessons learned from past conduct" (1982, 299). In a subarctic environment fraught with insecurity and the threat of starvation, Cree and other northern Algonquian hunters cultivated high ideals of respectful relationship and reciprocity as well as mental and moral competence in order to preserve human integrity and community when pushed to the edge of its disintegration. Still to this day, comments Preston, the Cree seek to "maintain respect relations, even when they are not reciprocated . . . [in] the hope . . . that respect will eventually be reciprocated" (2010, 287–88). This echoes the comment by one northern Quebec Cree elder in the 1970s: "When we have food, and we are living with others, we give them half our food, and it seems like we find more to replace it" (cited in Feit 1994, 297).

This ethic of respect and reciprocity is not limited to human persons, but extends to other-than-human persons (animal and spirit persons) and the most fundamental mysteries—simultaneously immanent and transcendent—of their contingent existence in an emergent world. Anthropologist Colin Scott explains that for the Cree,

> the world is a place of deep vitality, sometimes restful, sometimes dynamic; pregnant with possibility; a place of emergent, often orderly, sometimes surprising phenomena. Life in this sense, *pimaatsiiwin*, was translated to me as "the continuous birthing of the world." (2006, 61)

Everything that can be named has an animate or inanimate *ačahkw*, which can be translated as form, in the metaphysical sense of this term (Hultkrantz 1953, 488–89) and Algonquian languages define all nouns as animate or inanimate. The "animacy of the lifeworld," observes anthropologist Tim Ingold, "is the dynamic, transformative potential of the entire field of relations within which beings of all kinds, more or less person-like or thing-like, continually and reciprocally bring one another into existence." It is a "condition of being alive to the world" (2006, 3), which is full of emergent creativity, power, mystery, or *manitu*.

Anishinabe scholar Basil Johnston points out that *manitu*, often translated as spirit, "bears other meanings even more fundamental . . . a substance, character, essence, quiddity beyond comprehension and therefore beyond explanation, a *mystery*" (1992, 100–1, emphasis added). By Johnston's description, *Manitu* "imparted life, form, growth, healing, and strength in all things, beings, and places" (ibid.) and is the source of vitality—of *piimaatsiiwin*.

Manitu is the ultimate answer to questions of emergent creativity as well as contingent being, relationship, and knowledge. Yet the historical precontact meaning of *manitu* among Algonquians is unclear (Cooper 1933; Schenck 2011). For many, especially James Bay Cree, *manitu* seems to have commonly connoted a superior benevolent spirit-person of great power, though not necessarily creator. For other Algonquian peoples, the term applies to a plurality of superior other-than-human persons or "powers, which could help and sustain, or harm and destroy" (Schenck 2011, 41). At the same time, as Johnston and Ontario Cree knowledge keeper Greg Spence (personal communication, 2012) confirm, *manitu* sometimes connoted a mysterious force or essence that manifests itself in persons, human, and other-than-human. If

the historical meaning of *manitu* is a mystery, it is not only because historical records and oral traditions are limited. *Mystery* may simply be the most
fundamental meaning of *manitu*. Nevertheless, conceptualizations of *manitu*
are crucial because they shape understandings of the nature of power and contingency as well as human mental and moral competence. A contingent world
in which *manitu* is impersonal mystery-power can easily become a world in
which individuals seek to control that power, whether to help or to harm.
"Adept shamans," writes Landes, "were believed to manipulate the manito
Supernaturals as we do electricity" (1968, 3).

Such a belief may explain why concerns about sorcery appear to have
been more prevalent among some Algonquian people than among others (Preston 1989, 151; Preston 2002, 222; Feit 1994, 303; Rogers 1994,
330–331; Hallowell 1955, 181, 282; Bird 2005, 94–95). Adoption, under
Christian influence, of a belief in *Kitchi-Manitu* was deemed to protect a
person from sorcery (Long 1987, 21), and even the pre-Christian *manitu*,
if conceived as a benevolent and singularly superior spirit-person, was
not subject to manipulation by benevolent or malevolent shamans. Hope
or belief in such a *manitu*, moreover, may have discouraged quests for
manipulative power. It also made hope, in some ways, more important than
power, or to put it differently, it made hope the appropriate manifestation
of power for human persons.

Ehbebukdaet, the eastern James Bay Cree term for hope, Preston points
out, "translates literally into English as untying something, like a knot—plus
the quality of a revealing insight or perception, expressing some new knowledge" (Preston 2002, 208). According to some Cree origin stories or *atalohkana*, the first man and woman arrived from a sky-world—lowered on a rope
woven by Ehep, the great spider. Bird comments that this rope is a metaphor
for mystery (Bird 2007, 16). *Ehbebukdaet* is a mental and spiritual virtue or
strength. It enables a person to endure great hardship not just by accepting
human contingency but also by penetrating deeper into it, by untying knots
in the rope of *manitu*-mystery. Yet it is also directed to *manitu*-person, to
"*pakuseyimakan* ('the one we hope from')" (cited in Long et al. 2006, 481).
Moreover, "if it is successful," writes Preston, it "is transmitted to external
phenomena and influences them . . . a kind of hunting power" (2002, 191). As
such, *ehbebukdaet*—like the Christian "virtue of hope"—is far deeper than
mere optimism.

Manitu may have topped the hierarchy of pre-Christian Cree cosmology,
but animal persons were the primary other-than-human objects of Cree hope
as they were "directly related to the over-riding concern of the Cree—the
food quest" (Long et al. 2006, 472; Preston 2002, 223). Cree *atalohkana*
depict animal persons who experience, think, plan, and communicate like
humans (Bird 2005, 78). Human persons are integrated into the world, not

as lords of the animals, but by "moving into the existing social structure" (Preston 2002, 209; Feit 1994, 295). It is with the help of animal persons that they arrive safely and learn to survive. According to one story, "it was agreed . . . that all animals will have to contribute for the sake of . . . the human [who] can only be alive in the world by using the animals' help—their body, their furs, their feathers and everything" (Bird 2005, 63, 78–80). The purpose of animal persons, at least in part, is to give themselves to the hunter and his family so that they can live. The hunter exercises reciprocity by taking care to show gratitude and respect for animal persons, with specific rituals and gestures (Preston 2002, 200–6; Feit 1994, 297–98).

This Cree view about reciprocity with animals (especially food animals) as persons appears to have emerged as a fundamental expression of hope that their survival in a contingent world was not dependent on mere chance. Their hope translated into a faith that their survival could be ensured by entering into loving relationship with animal persons who would give themselves freely if human persons respected their gift (ibid.). Although, for various reasons, the primary object of Cree hope, faith, and love has since shifted to *Kitchi-Manitu* as creator and owner of the animals, animal persons nevertheless remain important (Chabot 2016, 59).

There were always limits, however, to the reciprocity and parity between human and animal persons. As Preston puts it: "Considerable importance [is] attached to defining and maintaining the distinction between human and other persons. Perhaps their very closeness makes the difference more crucial" (Preston 2002, 210; Bird 2005, 63, 78–80). Anthropologist Regina Flannery found it "'highly significant' that the superior being was described [by Cree in the 1930s] as 'owning everything, every sort of meat and birds, everything on the earth, but not humans'" (cited in Long et al. 2006, 21). "When humans get the terms of their metaphors confused and begin marrying animals or eating other humans," writes Scott, ". . . the results are impossibly comic or tragic" (1996, 75). Scott elaborates: a "fundamental separation and asymmetry between human community and animal community" existed, a separation that translated into a fundamentally different reciprocity among human persons and among animal persons (ibid.). Nevertheless, an ethic of power through respect and reciprocity rather than manipulation or coercion held for relations with food animals as much as for human relations (Flannery and Chambers 1985, 9–10).

Even those who did not adhere to this ideal of respect and reciprocity out of virtue often did so out of social pressure and necessity. Referring to northern Algonquian peoples in the 1930s, legal scholar Julius Lips points out that "if a case should become known where an Indian maliciously disregarded a signal erected in extreme need, he would likewise be disregarded in case of his own need" (1937, 227). Adherence to such ideals on account of social pressure and necessity was fragile. In extreme crisis situations, holding fast to these ideals depended above all on the prior cultivation of personal mental and moral strength.

WINDIGO AS INVERSION OF MORAL IDEALS

Not everyone exhibited such mental and moral strength in the face of hardship, which was understandable, but at times the Cree and Algonquian found themselves struggling to understand and cope with people whose extreme breakdowns of mental and moral competence seemed to push them beyond the edge of humanity—into the category of the monstrous. How could such people be brought back and reconciled with human community, or failing that, prevented from harming it further?

From Cree and Algonquian peoples, there emerged a creative response to this epistemic, moral, and practical dilemma: the concept of the cannibal windigo, a concept that evolved with sufficient ambiguity to allow for a range of causes, manifestations, and degrees of responsibility. It served to prevent or condemn monstrously inhuman actions while preserving or recovering the humanity of those who committed them, or threatened to do so. Even in exceptional circumstances, when execution was deemed necessary for communal safety, the individual deemed possessed by a windigo could be reconciled to the human community. In fact, the windigo was most often killed in order to preserve or release the humanity of a person threatened with possession by it. More rarely, those deemed more fully responsible for monstrous deeds or attitudes were condemned as having lost their humanity—because of their own choices—and transformed into a windigo. When the presence of a windigo threat was much clearer than the responsibility for it, preemptive defensive action could be taken without having to pass final judgment on a person.

Cree and other Algonquian windigo narratives often distinguish between an original supernatural windigo and human windigos, but the origin of the supernatural windigo is itself unclear (Chabot 2016, 68). Some traditions suggest it may have also originated as a human who became severely corrupted by their own will. According to Bird, the first windigos emerged "many years before the European came. People overpopulated the land and over-hunted. They sort of drove themself [*sic*] into starvation. And then some of them became wihtigo—they started to eat each other—many became cannibalistic" (2007, 113; Thompson 1916, 260).

Other James Bay Cree narratives refer to a time "when all the Cannibals lived together." In sharing these stories in the 1930s, Harvey Smallboy, Patrick Stevens, and Frank Rickard made it very clear that this community of cannibals was fragile and short-lived (Flannery et al. 1981). "In olden times,"

according to Smallboy, "two or three families always lived together. . . .
There was a Witiko looking for human victims and he was heading to where
the families were camped." He found one Indian. Knowing he was being followed, the Indian tied brush together in the shape of a man and placed it on
his own trail:

> The Witiko thought the Indian was a moose and when the Witiko came to the
> tied-up brush he thought, "I have caught the Indian at last and he is dead." So
> the Witiko put his carrying strap around the brush and carried it home . . . [to
> his own people, who] said, "He is carrying a bundle of brush." The Witiko said,
> "Brush? This is not brush. This is the moose I was after." They went to work,
> opened up the bundle, and found it was only brush. So the Witiko knew that he
> had not killed the Indian after all. So the Witiko went off again following the
> same Indian's trail. (cited in ibid., 59–60)

The man continued to outwit and avoid the windigo, sometimes with comical results. Finally, the windigo spied the man in the tree and began to shoot
arrows at him, but the man called out: "'Do not fire at your moose. You will
lose his blood.'" The windigo listened and began to climb the tree instead, at
which point, using one final trick, the man succeeded in spearing the windigo
in the back of its neck with the bone spear he had been carrying. "The Witiko
fell down as though he were dead, but then stood up and headed home." The
families at the windigo's camp then tried unsuccessfully to remove the spear.
Finally, the oldest and "wisest" among them told the others to heat the spear
and drive it through rather than pull it out. They did this, and the windigo fell
dead as a result. "All of the people in the tent started to weep for the Witiko."
Then the "wise" person among them instructed the others to have the windigo's wife cook him, so they could all eat him.

> This was done. After they finished eating everyone started to cry and walk off
> from the tent in different directions. All these Witikos kept going. This was the
> last of them. They all turned into Witikos and that is why there are so many
> Witikos all around the world now. (ibid.)

In this account, which is echoed by Rickard's version, the windigo is
identified as such right from the start, but the others in his camp, to whom
he was related by marriage and blood, do not go windigo until the very end.
Until then, they are referred to as human persons, suggesting the first windigo
was also once human. The windigo did not confuse these people with food
animals; moreover, they initially helped him to see that he was only carrying
brush rather than a moose. And the narrator says that the windigo knew then
that "he had not killed the *Indian* after all." Both points suggest he was in the

process of becoming a windigo—he still knew, deep down, that he was hunting a fellow human being, not a moose. Once he was killed and eaten, however, all those in the camp were then obliged to depart in different directions. In killing and eating him, they too had gone windigo, losing their capacity for relationship and their very humanity through such extreme mental and moral incompetence.

Patrick Stevens' story is shorter, omitting the part about the bundle of brush and the first return to camp. It begins by referring to the windigo and all the members of his camp as cannibals: "They say the cannibals have a place where they all live together." If these cannibals started off with a "place where they all live together," they ended up with their relationship completely disintegrated as a result of their cannibalism. The conclusion of Stevens' account is even more explicit on this point than that of Smallboy: "The cannibals said, 'The first two who meet will have a fight and the one who is beaten is the one we will eat next time'" (cited in ibid., 60–61). Stevens' account appears to begin *in media res*, in the middle of things, when the disintegration of their humanity and their community, and their transformation into windigos, is underway but incomplete. They were what Bird calls "half-wihtigo[s]," still capable of living in community—albeit a fragile one—at least until they became full-fledged windigos (2007, 114).

Physical descriptions of windigos sometimes vary greatly, from cunning to dimwitted, gigantic to man-sized. They are thought to be unkempt and terrifying to behold, but some human windigos can also be difficult to detect. If the windigo's physical characteristics are often ambiguous, so too is the nature of "going windigo," which sometimes appears to entail possession and other times transformation. This ambivalence, as suggested already, allows for varying degrees of responsibility. In one story, for example, a mother-turned-windigo refers to her human victims as animals, but knows that this is a lie. She twists reality, deceives and manipulates others, and she is sneaky about her killing and her refusal of normal food. When she is killed, her body takes a long time to burn because her heart had turned to ice—a recurrent theme in windigo stories—which, now melting, repeatedly extinguishes the fire. She had *become* a windigo (Merasty 1974, 3–6). In another story, a man named Pelly is overcome by a windigo and kills others without being sneaky. When his companions kill the windigo, Pelly not only survives but is also cured as a result (Norman 1982, 103–106). He was clearly *possessed* rather than *transformed*.

Possession by a windigo implies the preservation of humanity, perhaps the humanity of a loved one who *could not have committed such a monstrous deed*, and whose execution is not a punishment but liberation from a monster. Even if no monstrous deed had been committed, a hunter could not leave a deranged and potentially violent relative at camp with his wife and children while he hunted. If he stayed at camp to prevent any harm from occurring, everyone might starve. Ultimately, if treatment failed and necessity forced him to take preemptive defensive measures, killing a windigo in possession of his loved one was easier than killing his loved one. In such a case, the "*windigo* effectively separates the person from the problem" (Angell 1997, 179).

However, the windigo can also bind the person to the problem. To say that a person has become the windigo—unless it is transformation through evil acts of sorcery, which clearly frees a person from responsibility—is to condemn a person as having abandoned his or her humanity. "Some of those who became wihtigo were mitews who were capable and powerful," explains Bird, "and they became the worst kind of wihtigos—they were cannibals and mitews at the same time" (2007, 113). They became windigos not because they were too weak to resist a malevolent power or persist under duress, but because they had powerful capacities that they used for malevolent purposes (Teicher 1956, 60). They lost their humanity by their own choice. In many cases, however, the nature of the phenomenon and the degree of responsibility remained ambivalent.

WINDIGO'S SPIRITUAL TRAITS

This ambivalence about responsibility is also present in the nature of the windigo's most defining characteristics, which are not physical but spiritual in nature. Ultimately, the windigo's spiritual traits—its disposition of will, mind, and emotion—are what set it apart and define it. These traits are found consistently across a wide geocultural and historical range of Algonquian narratives: severe loss or abandonment of self-control, or emphasis on manipulative control of others; disconnect with or manipulation of reality or truth; and withdrawal, rejection, or manipulation of relationship (Chabot 2016, 84).

The first of these windigo traits can manifest itself as a severe loss or abandonment of self-control, an incapacity or unwillingness to bring one's actions into conformity with one's understanding. Alternatively, in more sinister cases, the focus of control is displaced from self to others in a quest for manipulative and self-serving power over them (Bird 2007, 112; Johnston 1995, 224). One Cree narrative tells of a manipulative older woman who convinced a younger woman to abandon her new husband and follow her to her winter camp, where she first weakened her and then killed and ate her (Flannery et al. 1981, 72–73). Such cases of manipulative control are far less common than those involving the loss of self-control. An individual who believes himself possessed by the windigo "believes that he has lost permanent control over his own actions" (Teicher 1960, 5). This belief can point to a desperate quest for control in the face of growing powerlessness—a loss or reduction of hope in the face of starvation, death, or an uncertain struggle against "going" windigo. Fatalistic adoption of the windigo identity could follow as an attempt to overcome the reluctance to kill and eat a human person, or escape the anticipated guilt; alternatively, it might be a plea for help in the face of temptations or the fear of giving in to them (Brightman 1988, 337, 354, 363, 372). Loss of self-control could manifest itself as compulsive violence after a period of apparent despondency amidst an interior struggle to overcome either the temptation or the reticence to give in to it. Loss of self-control is reflected in the disheveled and soiled appearance of many windigos (Flannery et al. 1981, 58). Legal scholar John Borrows suggests that the Anishinabe meaning of "windigo" may be "dirty or unkempt" (Personal Communication 2013). According to Johnston, the windigo has an insatiable and uncontrollable appetite for the consumption (literal or figurative) of others if not also self-consumption (1995, 223–24). This could manifest as addictive behavior. In contrast, those who resort to nonviolent starvation cannibalism without "going windigo" are those who maintain their self-control, fully acknowledge their actions, and do not withdraw from society (Flannery et al. 1981, 70).

The windigo's loss of self-control leads to a second fundamental windigo trait: hallucinations and a loss of epistemic capacity or an intentional manipulation of truth to the point that one loses the capacity to see the manipulation of truth for what it is—a lie. This is especially true when a windigo's lack of self-control is manifested primarily as a quest for raw power or manipulative and malicious control over others. In such cases, as Johnston points out, the windigo "exemplifies human nature's tendency to indulge its self-interests, which, once indulged, demand even greater indulgence." Ultimately, this results in an "extreme . . . erosion of principles and values," and the incapacity to direct one's actions toward an understanding of what is good (1995, 224). Having abandoned or rejected the challenge of bringing actions into conformity with an understanding of what is true and good, a windigo imposes a skewed understanding or mode of experience on itself and others. In the extreme, it destroys its capacity to escape its own distortions of what is true or good. Such a windigo is far more dangerous and sinister. Arthur Etherington tells of "an old man . . . [who] would go along with other Indians during the summer. When the winter came *he would think* [suggesting intentional distortion] of the other Indians as becoming animals. He would become a cannibal" (cited in Flannery et al. 1981, 69–70).

The most common manifestations of this windigo trait are less sinister and intentional, usually involving hallucinations induced by desperate conditions. Windigos redefine human beings as edible animals or simply as edible (Flannery et al. 1981, 58; Teicher 1960, 54, 85–87; Bird 2007, 115). This may be a sign of being only "Almost a Witiko." Without helpful intervention, however, the consequences may be disastrous. This trait may also manifest itself as a loss of memory or delirium. Anthropologist A. I. Hallowell recorded the story of a man from northern Manitoba who saw his wife, covered in blood, running toward him from their tent. "He shot her and the children and ate them. For the next month his mind was a blank. Finally, when he recovered sufficiently to tell others what had occurred, he cried" (cited in Teicher 1960, 76). Swift Runner, who was hung by the Canadian state in 1879 after being convicted of killing and eating his wife and children, had gone "on a moose hunt and on his return was close to camp and all he could hear were young moose, nothing but moose. That's when it started on him." Only when he was in court did he regain his senses. "He asked the judge why he was there. The judge told him that he had eaten up his family. . . . He started to cry," and then pleaded for execution, fearing he would reoffend (cited in Honigmann 1953, 309–31). Like Merasty and Rae's stories, cited earlier, these accounts suggest genuine hallucinations, memory loss, and, in varying degrees, a diminished responsibility for monstrous deeds.

The human windigo may lose the capacity, or refuse, to govern his action according to what he once experienced and understood to be true. Either way, the need for unity of the constitutive elements of culture—experience, understanding and action—does not disappear. Therefore, the windigo modifies his perception and conception of reality to fit his behavior. The objective may be to avoid guilt, which suggests a lingering recognition that the forced unity of experience, understanding, and action is a lie. Such a lie can only be maintained by additional lies: by manipulating contradictory perceptions and understandings, by insulating oneself from them, fleeing them, or somehow muting or destroying them. If, as McIntyre suggests (2009, 35), a windigo "cannot be reasoned with," it is not necessarily because of an absence of reason or experiential learning capacity, but rather a completely self-referential and self-serving rationalism and empiricism. This radically individualistic and subjective epistemology results in the destruction of people and relationships, but relationships are also shunned or destroyed simply because they expose or threaten the windigo's circular logic. Because human relationship exposes the distortion of a human person as an edible moose, for example, the windigo retreats or withdraws from relationship, either anticipating or regretting a deviant act (Bird 2007, 113–14; Kohl 1985, 356–57; Johnston 1995, 222; Preston 1978, 61; McIntyre 2009, 38).

This extreme individualism reflects the third windigo trait: withdrawal from relationship, or rejection, manipulation, and destruction of relationship. Johnston says that Windigo "may be derived from *ween dagoh*, which means 'solely for self,' or from *weenin n'd'igooh*, which means 'fat' or excess" (Johnston 1995, 222). Cree elder, scholar, and Anglican minister Edward

Ahenakew refers to the windigo as "He-who-is-alone" (cited in Preston 1978, 61). Anthropologist Morton Teicher writes: "They do not live together as married couples; on the contrary, each windigo is a solitary being. If two of them should happen to meet, then the Indians believe that a violent battle ensues and the one who wins eats the loser" (Teicher 1960, 2, 77, 119). As suggested already, the exceptions to this isolation are temporary and involve what Bird calls "half-windigos" who are not yet fully possessed or transformed (Bird 2007, 113). In one story, a windigo father and two sons attack and kill others, but one son is "accidentally" killed in the process. At first, the father and surviving son lament his death, but they soon stop, and when they eat the dead, the murdered son and brother is the first to be consumed (Flannery et al. 1981, 62). In another version of this story, the surviving windigo son has a snowball fight with the father and sneaks stones into his snowballs (ibid., 65). There is a constant threat of disintegration of their relationship (Teicher 1960, 56). As in the stories cited earlier by Smallboy, Stevens, and Rickard, social disintegration is inevitable. Some exceptionally malicious windigos deceive and manipulate others to such an extent that their evil nature goes unchecked or undetected for a period. They may remain in society, but they are not part of it (Flannery et al. 1981, 62). The windigo described by Cree elder Arthur Etherington is such a one. Most windigos, however, retreat from relationship, if they are not first ostracized. One suspected windigo named Nanusk, for example, would only place his furs on a large stone and refused to interact with others, behavior that immediately aroused suspicion.[6] When he recovered his senses in court, Swift Runner explained that he had killed his last surviving child, not out of hunger, but to remove the last reminder of the gravity of his crime. In his words (translated from the Cree): "The devil suddenly took possession of my soul; and in order to live longer far from people, and *to put out of my way the only witness to my crime*, I seized my gun and killed the last of my children and ate him as I had done the others" (emphasis added, cited in Carlson 2009, 376).

Conversely, reintegration into human relationship and reality was the means by which an almost-windigo could recover mental, moral, and emotional competence—even if it meant a painful coming to terms with the experience and understanding a deviant act done under duress. Bab Wesley tells of one such story:

> There was a man who killed his children and his wife. The man's brother came to him . . . [with] an axe . . . gave him an awful crack but didn't kill him [and] . . . took him back to his own camp. He melted a big bladder full of grease and made the man drink that. It made him vomit bad. At last he started to bring up ice . . . and at last the ice was all yellow . . . And when he started throwing up all that ice he started crying and thinking about what he had done.

His brother did that to him to bring him to his senses. And he was a live
person again. They used to hear him crying because he had killed his wife and
children. (cited in Flannery et al. 1981, 75)

As noted already, humans who go windigo are believed to develop hearts
of ice. They cannot be cured until the ice is removed; alternatively, they
are never fully destroyed until their heart is burnt (ibid., 58, 68, 72). More
than an association with winter and times of famine, the heart of ice represents an interior coldness, an inability to relate to others, and a loss of
capacity for reciprocity. The *wihtiko* is "not a kindhearted one" (Merasty
1974, 7). Emotions and thoughts contrary to the *wihtiko*'s self-centered
epistemology are rejected: "Nothing else matters—not compassion, sorrow, reason, or judgment" (Johnston 1995, 274). The withdrawal from
relationship, however, might not manifest itself as an overt lack of empathy, but as depression resulting from a fatalistic loss of hope. Not surprisingly, therefore, symptoms associated by other cultures with depression
or illness were seen as potentially far more serious from the perspective
of Algonquians.

"Some say that people who are cannibals go mad, others that they go
thoroughly wicked." This explanatory remark, cited earlier, confirms that
the windigo concept accounts for varying degrees of responsibility. Madness
points to a less culpable breakdown in the quest for unity of experience,
understanding, action, and objective reality. It is also seen as treatable,
even if not entirely curable. Wickedness, in contrast, entails culpabil-
ity, perversion, and immorality: a willful and often incurable breakdown
in the quest for unity of experience, understanding, action, and objective
reality. Madness may weaken humanity, but wickedness can pervert or
destroy it.

In Algonquian culture, the concept of mental illness unrelated to malevo-
lence or moral weakness (whether internal or external to the afflicted
person) is a relatively new importation from Western science, which, in
contrast, sometimes reduces evil to mental illness. Australian Criminal psychiatrist, Chris Richardson, comments that she has often faced realities that
her scientific concepts fail to explain or even describe; she can only grapple
with them by having recourse to spiritual concepts such as evil (Richardson
2010, 181–91). The Algonquian used the windigo to understand and cope
with extreme mental and moral incompetence harmful to persons and
society, regardless of the origin of responsibility: "Wetiko was the only
sickness" (Merasty 1974, 1). Insofar as this was the case, manifestations
of windigo traits and the responsibility attached to them were necessarily
ambiguous.

INTERPRETATION, USE, AND ABUSE
OF THE WINDIGO CONCEPT

The windigo concept appears to have originated as an explanation of behavior or symptoms that preceded, accompanied, or followed starvation-related cannibalism. If this was true, the concept was nevertheless adapted to explain similar behaviors or symptoms that may have had different causes. Physical and mental illness, for example, could produce symptoms that were interpreted as windigo possession. This was reinforced when windigo concepts and fears channeled and shaped the specific manifestations of more general mental illnesses. Extremely deviant behavior other than violent cannibalism also came to be explained by the windigo.

Nevertheless, despite the emergence of a wider range of catalysts and explanations for windigo possession or transformation the windigo continued to be perceived as cannibalistic by nature. Furthermore, fear of the cannibalistic windigo prompted Cree and other Algonquians to do anything to avoid even nonviolent cannibalism, which was thought to increase vulnerability to the windigo spirit (Flannery et al. 1981, 59). Non-Algonquians and Europeans often displayed less reticence to engage in nonviolent starvation cannibalism (eating the flesh of the dead in order to survive). On the other hand, as noted already, heightened fear of succumbing to the cannibal windigo spirit could lead some Algonquians to lose hope and fatalistically act out the symptoms and signs of the very thing they most feared. As noted already, this could be an expression of desperate hope for preemptive execution before it was too late to save them from full possession and its destructive consequences. This may explain why some people pleaded with their family members and friends to end their life before the windigo overcame them (Carlson 2009, 373).

Like any other concept relating to good or evil, windigo concepts and fears could also be used or abused to control others. One twentieth-century *tipachimowin* tells how a Cree hunter spread stories of a windigo in order to gain exclusive access to a particular hunting territory (Flannery et al. 1981, 75). In the earliest documentary references to the windigo, dating back to 1636 and 1661, Montagnais individuals used windigo fears to try to prevent neighboring Algonquians from coming into direct contact with the French, which would have eliminated their advantageous middleman position in the fur trade (Thwaites 1896, 9: 113 and 46: 261–63).

The windigo could also be used to scapegoat others, disguise, murder, or justify the killing of the elderly or sick. Even well-intentioned individuals could sometimes be too quick or rigid in their interpretations and responses. Yet, if windigo fears were used to manipulate others or truth or if they prompted rigid interpretations or precipitous executions, it was because these fears were real. Nevertheless, Algonquians were well aware of the potential for abuse or misinterpretation, which is why they often turned to those who had more experience and exhibited prudent discernment. Unfortunately, some scholars have attributed great flexibility of interpretation to the windigo belief itself and almost none to those who held it (Teicher 1960, 2, 220; Hallowell 1951, 7). Although there is some evidence of such rigidity, most cases show far greater evidence of prudent discernment, with execution being resorted to only in extreme cases (Flannery 1981, 59; Brightman 1988, 357–58; Friedland 2009, 120–21).

Weipust's comments in this regard are revealing. Weipust was a Cree elder that Ahenakew respected greatly. Like Ahenakew he was Christian, but had only adopted Christianity as a middle-aged man, and was therefore fully fluent in pre-Christian Cree culture. According to Ahenakew, Weipust had "no doubt that Wetikoos existed in the old days," but only "very rarely." In Weipust's view, "the majority of the reports . . . were untrue—many . . . brought about by some mischievous minded Indian trying to frighten someone else" (cited in Preston 1980, 122–123). As Preston points out, Weipust was "more critical than suggestive, aware of wrongness and wrong-headedness on the part of Indians as well as white men, when they are wondering about such terror-inspiring topics." Windigo narratives could serve many purposes, from keeping children close to camp to explaining the boundary between humanity and inhumanity. Even when it was a question of real people, events, or conditions, the windigo was, "for many Algonkian Indians . . . very uncertain in both appearance and essence." In short, the meaning of the windigo is more flexible, open-ended, and "a matter of attitudes" than acknowledged by those Algonquians and Europeans who tended, instead, "to simplify this variance down to concrete kinds of person (monstrous, symbolic, or other) and condition" (ibid., 124–28).

Whatever changes may have occurred in the interpretation and application of the windigo concept—especially in relation to delirium caused by physical illness—little has changed with regard to the three core traits associated with it. Even more significantly, these core traits point not just to continuities in Cree ideas and ideals but also to commonalities with ideas and ideals that are found in Western culture as well. These points of continuity and commonality have frequently been obscured by the complex evolution of Algonquian and Western struggles to understand and control the windigo (see Chabot 2016), but the ideas and ideals they reveal remain highly relevant to the nexus of mysteries—a free will, moral responsibility, madness, and evil—with which philosophers, theologians, neurobiologists, criminal psychiatrists, anthropologists, and others continue to grapple. As such, these Algonquian ideas and ideals remain also profoundly relevant to understanding deep-rooted conflict and fostering reconciliation.

RECIPROCITY, RELATIONSHIP,
AND RECONCILIATION

The suggestion that profound cultural common ground can be found between Indigenous and Western cultural ideas and ideals is somewhat countercultural in contemporary scholarship, which tends to focus discerning and asserting cultural difference; scholarly literature on the windigo is no exception in this regard (Chabot 2016). Discernment of cultural difference is certainly important for recovering what is uniquely Indigenous in the wake of aggressively assimilationist policies and programs. On the other hand, emphasis on cultural difference sometimes aims at merely inverting—or distancing oneself from—assumptions about Indigenous cultural inferiority that these assimilationist policies were founded on or with which they were justified. For example, Jack Forbes' description of windigo psychosis as a "disease of exploitation, imperialism, and terrorism" largely confined to modern European cultures appears to be a reaction to depictions of the windigo as a culture-bound psychosis of Indigenous peoples (Forbes 2008). It also relies on an analysis of history that juxtaposes the best ideals of Indigenous cultures with the worst failings of Western culture to live up to their own ideals. Forbes is not a solitary example (Chabot 2016).

John Ralston Saul has recently argued for reconceiving Canada as a "people of Aboriginal inspiration . . . a Métis civilization." His argument opens, however, with an emphatic moral judgement of Aboriginal-European cultural differences: "When I dig around in the roots of how we [Canadians] imagine ourselves, how we govern, how we live together in communities—how we treat one another when we are not being stupid—what I find is deeply Aboriginal" (Saul 2008, xvi, 1). This raises the question: if Canadians are Métis, what heritage are they drawing from when they are being stupid? Ultimately, the possibility seems left out that métissage may involve the creative discovery and rearticulation of deeply shared ideals—enriched by diverse experiences of the challenges of living up to them. Saul may have overstated his case for rhetorical purposes, but Bernard Sheehan warned against such rhetoric forty years earlier. "A history of Indian-white relations," he observed in 1969, ". . . can gain nothing, and it might well lose everything, by proposing a mythic natural innocence and proceeding to direct thunderbolts at those who supposedly despoiled it" (267–68, 274).

Implicitly or explicitly, it is sometimes suggested that the problem of abusive power is predominant or inherent in Western culture or in those aspects that have been designated as the scapegoat for Western failings. Yet the Algonquian windigo emerged and evolved as a powerful interpretative concept before Europeans arrived. Moreover, postmodern and decolonial Western cultural currents remain vulnerable—like all human cultures—to the problem of the windigo. The windigo, for example, would certainly approve of the assertion, by Justice Kennedy of the US Supreme Court, of "the right to define one's own concept of existence, of meaning, of the universe, and of the mystery of human life."[7] Postmodern deconstructions of claims to religious, rational, or empirical authority, or assertions of individual moral autonomy, do not free us from the problem of power; rather, they simply change how the problem will manifest itself. To lose sight of this is to lose sight of the valuable Algonquian experiences and insights about spirituality, emergent creativity, and reconciliation that emerge from their struggles with the windigo—whether cannibal or colonialist in appearance.

Cree and Algonquian experiences and insights suggest that relationship, reciprocity, and reconciliation depend upon spiritual ideals and strengths that are rejected or lost by the windigo. The windigo's attitude is that truth, reality, and others can be reduced to objects of self-serving power and desire. The windigo sees its own actions, needs, and choices as the measure of truth or reality, and it seeks to impose conformity with the demands of this radical epistemic and moral autonomy. Those who succumb to this spiritual state are often not malicious; rather, they are frequently weakened by fear of mystery or uncertainty, by isolation, a loss of hope, or lack of an education that fostered self-control or love of truth and goodness.

Reconciliation depends on our quests to bring our understanding into greater unity with a reality in which we are immersed but which also surpasses us. Cree ideas and ideals suggest that we can do this by patiently and prudently unbinding or discerning the rope of mystery and emergent creativity that defines our contingent existence. They also suggest that we cannot do this alone. Rather, we come into being through, in, and for relationships of reciprocity, and it is our relationships that open us to different experiences and understandings that help correct the limitations in our own. The maintenance of relationships of reciprocity, however, requires the cultivation of self-control, which enables us to recognize and live according to the truth we discover rather than define a truth that justifies the way we live. It also depends on our effort to avoid violence except as a last recourse for defense of self and others.

Finally, Cree and Algonquian experiences and insights suggest that reciprocity, relationship, and reconciliation depend on our willingness to maintain sight of the humanity of others, even when confronted with actions—even monstrous ones—that appear to diminish their humanity. On the other hand, a willingness to consider mitigating factors that may reduce responsibility should not blind us to the possibility of evil or the monstrous. For this reason, reciprocity, good relationship, and reconciliation require awareness of our own capacity to go windigo if we do not cultivate the spiritual values and strengths that it negates and rejects.

To be aware of the windigo threat, however, is not to make it a central or defining motivator. Living well together, increasing our freedom by unbinding the rope of mystery, of the true, the good, and the beautiful, cannot be founded on fear or rejection of evil. Windigo was never central to the predominantly Cree world in which I grew up. Nor was this world a static or monocultural world; it was one that had entered into deep dialogue with other cultures and traditions, especially Christianity, a dialogue founded on the virtue of *ehbebukdaet* (hope) in the face of what continues to be a great mystery—*Kitchi Manitu*. In seeking to bring Indigenous, Western, Christian, and other traditions into deeper dialogue on fundamental human questions, I am not doing anything original; rather, I am simply following the example of so many elders and scholars—Cree, non-Indigenous, and others who do not easily fit in such categories—who have been my teachers and mentors.

NOTES

1. There are many variations of this term, including *wihtiko*, *wetiko*, and *wendigo*. *Wihtiko* reflects a Cree pronunciation better, but Windigo, which is of Anishinabe origin, is the sole variant found in the Oxford English Dictionary, and is more widely known and used in the literature. For this reason, I have chosen to use this term. *Kokodjeo*, *atoosh*, and *atchen* are other Cree, Attikamekw, and Montagnais terms. *Chenoo* and *kiwakwe* are other terms of Mi'kmaq and eastern Algonquian origin.

2. LAC (Library and Archives Canada), MG 29, B 15 (Robert Bell Fonds), folder 54, file 12, "Indians. Legends—Charles H. M. Gordon," "The Indian Deluge," 1.

3. Algonquian refers to a broad cultural and linguistic family that includes the Penobscot, Mi'kmaq, Maliseet, Abenaki, Attikamekw, Montagnais, Innu, Naskapi, Cree, Chippewa, Ojibwa, Anishinabe, Algonquin, Blackfoot, and others as well. I use Cree, because there is no other term that easily captures the diverse but related Algonquian peoples this term encompasses, including the Iiyuuch, Mushkegowuk, and so on. I use Anishinabe, because it encompasses peoples who are closely related, both culturally and linguistically, including the Algonquin, Ojibwa, Chippewa, and so on.

4. Robert Brightman, personal communication, August 2016. Brightman gave me the name of the elder, who was not mentioned in his published article. This story was taken from his 1977–1979 fieldnotes for research in Pukatawagan and Granville Lake, Manitoba.

5. Frenchman and Iserhoff, "The Nanusk Stone," DAUL (Division des archives de l'Université Laval), Fonds Jacques Rousseau, P174/D3, folder 51. 1956–1966 was the period that both Iserhoff and Frenchman were in Moose Factory. For more context, see Chabot 2016, 26–27.

6. Frenchman and Iserhoff, "The Nanusk Stone," DAUL, Fonds Jacques Rousseau, P174/D3, folder 51.

7. Planned Parenthood v. Casey, 505 U.S. 833 (1992), https://www.law.cornell.e du/supremecourt/text/505/833 (accessed September 3, 2016).

REFERENCES

Angell, G. Brent. 1997. "Madness in the Family: The Windigo." *Journal of Family Social Work* 2, no. 2: 179–196.

Bird, Louis. 2005. *Telling Our Stories: Omushkego Legends and Histories from Hudson Bay.* Edited by Jennifer S. H. Brown, Paul W. DePasquale, and Mark F. Ruml. Peterborough: Broadview Press.

———. 2007. *The Spirit Lives in the Mind: Omushkego Stories, Lives, and Dreams.* Edited by Susan Elaine Gray. Montreal and Kingston: McGill-Queen's University Press.

Bosum, Abel. 2017. Public lecture on "Indigenous Leadership Governance and Development." McGill University. https://www.youtube.com/watch?v=BdlqsHnx G3I. Accessed October 13, 2020.

Brightman, Robert A. 1988. "Windigo in the Material World." *Ethnohistory* 35 (4), 337–379.

Carlson, Nathan D. 2009. "Reviving Witiko (Windigo): An Ethnohistory of 'Cannibal Monsters' in the Athabasca District of Northern Alberta, 1878–1910." *Ethnohistory* 56 (3), 355–394.

Chabot, Cecil. 2016. *Cannibal Wihtiko: Finding Native-Newcomer Common Ground.* Ph.D. Thesis. University of Ottawa. https://ru or.uottawa .ca/b itstr eam/1 0393/ 33452 /1/Ch abot_ Cecil _2016 _thesis.pdf.

Cooper, John M. 1933. "The Northern Algonquian Supreme Being." *Primitive Man* 6 (3/4), 41–111.

Feit, Harvey. 1994. "Dreaming of Animals: The Waswanipi Cree Shaking Tent Ceremony in Relation to Environment, Hunting and Missionization." Pp. 289–316 in *Circumpolar Religion and Ecology: An Anthropology of the North.* Edited by Takashi Irimoto and Takako Yamada. Tokyo: University of Tokyo Press.

Fiddler, Thomas, and James R. Stevens. 1985. *Killing the Shamen.* Moonbeam, Ontario: Penumbra Press.

Flannery, Regina, Mary Elizabeth Chambers, and Patricia A. Jehle. 1981. "Witiko Accounts from the James Bay Cree." *Arctic Anthropology* 18 (1), 57–77.

———, and M. E. Chambers. 1985. "Each Man has his Own Friends: the Role of Dream Visitors in Traditional East Cree Belief and Practice." *Arctic Anthropology* 22 (1), 1–22.

Forbes, Jack D. 2008. *Columbus and Other Cannibals: The Wetiko Disease of Exploitation, Imperialism, and Terrorism.* New York: Seven Stories Press.

Friedland, Hadley Louise. 2009. *The Wetiko (Windigo) Legal Principles: Responding to Harmful People in Cree, Anishinabek and Saulteaux Societies – Past, Present and Future Uses, with a Focus on Contemporary Violence and Child Victimization Concerns.* MA Thesis, University of Alberta.

Hallowell, A. I. 1951. "Cultural Factors in the Structuralization of Perception." Pp. 164–195 in *Social Psychology at the Crossroads.* Edited by John H. Rohrer and Muzafer Sherif. New York: Harper.

————. 1936. 1951. "Cultural Factors in the Structuralization of Perception." In *Social Psychology at the Crossroads*. Edited by John H. Rohrer and Muzafer Sherif. New York: Harper.

————. 1955. *Culture and Experience*. Philadelphia, PA: University of Pennsylvania Press.

Honigmann, John J. 1953. "European and Other Tales from the Western Woods Cree." *The Journal of American Folklore*, 66 (262), 309–331.

————. 1958. "Attawapiskat—Blend of Traditions." *Anthropologica*, 6, 57–67.

Hultkrantz, Ake. 1953. *Conceptions of the Soul Among North American Indians: A Study in Religious Ethnology*. Stockholm: Ethnographical Museum of Sweden.

Ingold, Tim. 2006. "Rethinking the Animate, Re-Animating Thought." *Ethnos: Journal of Anthropology*, 71 (1), 9–20.

Johnston, Basil. 1992. "One Generation from Extinction." Pp. 99–104 in *An Anthology of Canadian Native Literature in English*. Edited by Daniel David Moses and Terry Goldie. Oxford: Oxford University Press.

————. 1995. *The Manitous: The Spiritual World of the Ojibway*. New York: Harper Collins.

Kohl, Johann Georg. 1985. *Kitchi-gami: Wanderings Round Lake Superior*. Edited by Robert E. Bieder. Translated by Lascelles Wraxall. St. Paul, MN: Minnesota Historical Society.

Landes, Ruth. 1968. *Ojibwa Religion and the Midéwiwin*. Madison, WI, Milwaukee, and London: University of Wisconsin Press.

Lips, Julius E. 1937. "Public Opinion and Mutual Assistance among the Montagnais-Naskapi." *American Anthropologist*, 39 (2), 379–492.

Long, John S. 1987. "Manitu, Power, Books and Wiihtikow: Some Factors in the Adoption of Christianity by Nineteenth-Century Western JamesBay Cree." *Native Studies Review*, 3 (1), 1–30.

————, C. Oberhotlzer, and R. J. Preston. 2006. "Manitu Concepts of the Eastern James Bay Cree." Pp. 451–492 in *Essays in Tribute to Regina Flannery*. Edited by Toby Morantz in Papers of the 39th Algonquian Conference. Edited by Karl S. Hele and Regna Darnell. Winnipeg, MB: University of Manitoba Press.

McIntyre, Erin. 2009. *Evil and Hope in Cree Wittikow Stories*. Masters of Divinity Thesis, University of Saskatoon.

Merasty, Marie. 1974. *The World of the Wetiko: Tales from the Woodland Cree*. Edited by Candace Savage. Translated by Bill Merasty. Saskatoon: Saskatchewan Indian Cultural Centre.

Norman, Howard. 1982. *Where the Chill Came From: Cree Windigo Tales and Journeys*. San Francisco, CA: North Point Press.

Preston, Richard J. 1978. "Ethnographic Reconstruction of Witigo." Pp. 61–67 in *Papers of the Ninth Algonquian Conference*. Edited by William Cowan. Ottawa: Carleton University.

———. 1980. "The Witiko: Algonkian Knowledge and Whiteman Knowledge." Pp. 111–131 in *Manlike Monsters on Trial*. Edited by Michael M. Ames and Marjorie M. Halpin. Vancouver: University of British Columbia.

———. 1982. "Towards a General Statement on the Eastern Cree Structure of Knowledge." Pp. 299–306 in *Papers of the Thirteenth Algonquian Conference*. Edited by William Cowan. Ottawa: Carleton University.

———. 1989. "James Bay Cree Syncretism: Persistence and Replacement." Pp. 147–155 *Papers of the 19th Algonquin Conference*. Edited by William Cowan. Ottawa: Carleton University.

———. 2002. *Cree Narrative: Expressing the Personal Meaning of Events*, 2nd edition. Montreal and Kingston: McGill-Queen's University Press.

———. 2010. "James Bay Cree Respect Relations within the Great Community of Persons: Who Should be Killed and How." Pp. 286–288 in *Nonkilling Societies*. Edited by Joam Evans Pim. Honolulu: Center for Global Nonkilling.

Richardson, Chris. 2010. "Monster or Clown: Bad or Crazy: Who can tell the difference?" Pp. 181–191 *Creating Humanity, Discovering Monstrosity: Myths and Metaphors of Enduring Evil*. Edited by Elizabeth Nelson, Jillian Burcar, and Hannah Priest. Oxford: Inter-Disciplinary Press.

Rogers, Edward S. 1994. "Northern Algonquians and the Hudson's Bay Company, 1821–1890." Pp. 307–343 in *Aboriginal Ontario: Historical Perspectives on the First Nations*. Edited by Edward S. Rogers and Donald B. Smith. Toronto: Dundurn Press.

Saul, John Ralston. 2008. *A Fair Country: Telling Truths About Canada*. Toronto: Penguin.

Schenck, Theresa. 2011. "Gizhe-Manidoo, Missionaries, and the Anishinaabeg." Pp. 39–47 in *Anishinaabewin Niizh: Culture Movements, Critical Moment*. Edited by Alan Corbiere, Deborah McGregor, and Crystal Migwans. M'Chigeeng, Ontario: Ojibwe Cultural Foundation.

Scott, Colin. 1996. "Science for the West, Myth for the Rest? The Case of James Bay Cree Knowledge Construction." Pp. 69–86 in *Naked Science: Anthropological Inquiries into Boundaries, Power and Knowledge*. Edited by Laura Nader. London: Routledge.

———. 2006. "Spirit and Practical Knowledge in the Person of the Bear among Wemindji Cree Hunters." *Ethnos: Journal of Anthropology*, 71 (1), 51–66.

Sheehan, Bernard W. 1969. "Indian-White Relations in Early America: A Review Essay." *William and Mary Quarterly*, 26 (1), 267–286.

Stern, Steve J. 1993. *Peru's Indian Peoples and the Challenge of Spanish Conquest: Huamanga to 1640*. 2nd ed. Madison: University of Wisconsin Press.

Teicher, Morton I. 1956. *Windigo Psychosis: A Study of a Relationship between Belief and Behavior among the Indians of Northeastern Canada*. PhD Thesis, University of Toronto.

————. 1960. "Windigo Psychosis: A Study of a Relationship Between Belief and Behaviour Among the Indians of Northeastern Canada." In *Proceedings of the 1960 Annual Spring Meeting of the American Ethnological Society*. Edited by Verne F. Ray. Seattle, WA: American Ethnological Society, University of Washington.

Thompson, David. 1916. *Thompson's Narrative of his Explorations in Western America, 1784–1812*. Edited by J. B. Tyrell. Toronto: Champlain Society.

Thwaites, Reuben Gold, ed. 1896. *The Jesuit Relations and Allied Documents: Travels and Explorations of the Jesuit Missionaries in New France, 1610–1791, the Original French, Latin, and Italian Texts, with English Translations and Notes*. Cleveland: Burrows.

White, Richard. 1991. *The Middle Ground: Indians, Empires, and Republics in the Great Lakes Region, 1650–1815*. Cambridge: Cambridge University Press.

Chapter 13

Transforming Wihtiko Systems

Catherine Twinn (with thanks to Isaac Twinn)

Upon suffering beyond suffering, the Red Nation shall rise again and it shall be a blessing for a sick world. A world filled with broken promises, selfishness and separation. A world longing for light again. I see a time of Seven Generations when all the colors of [humankind] will gather under the Sacred Tree of Life and the whole world will become one circle again. I salute the light within your eyes where the whole universe dwells. For when you are at that center within you and I am at that place within me, we shall be one.

(Crazy Horse n.d.)

PROLOGUE: CLOSE ENCOUNTERS WITH WIHTIKO SYSTEMS

In 1989 my late husband, Walter Twinn, a Cree-Saulteaux chief, senator, and businessman, began his recovery from an adult life of alcoholism, having spent his childhood in a Canadian Indian Residential School (IRS). With sobriety, he often asked me, "Why is it that everyone I went to residential school with is either dead, drunk or in jail?" The problems Walter was referring to were not entirely new to me: my grandfather was sent to an IRS; my father served in World War II and returned with undiagnosed post-traumatic stress disorder (PTSD) that manifested in addiction, first to alcohol, and then to a religion he applied in a fundamentalist way. However, back in 1989, as an adult child of an alcoholic, I had no answers to Walter's questions.

Beginning in 1989, Walter turned from alcohol, filling his life with ceremonies and a spiritual search for meaning, understanding, and forgiveness. With great pain and remorse, he awoke to the harm his alcoholism caused within a community to which he had given his all. He saw the operationalization of addictions, enabling, and codependency of family, friends, and others within that community system. He saw that addiction consumes; it does not create. In reaching these understandings, Walter overcame human weaknesses—a struggle represented by *Nana'b'oozoo*,[1] a complex character in Anishinaubae teachings: who is not what he appears to be; his real character is hidden; he does not see things as they really are.

In his last years, Walter often remarked, "When I became a [First Nation] chief, I thought our problem was economic and I sought to fix it [and he did], but I now realize our problem is spiritual." The spiritual problem that Walter referred to was the colonial-capitalist inflicted trauma and ideologies valuing materialism and aggressive individualism at the expense of spirituality and creation. Walter nurtured his relationship with self, turning away from a manly reliance on external distractors like alcohol and material success.

He also realized that, as a leader and chief of thirty-one years, his loved ones needed guidance to heal and rebuild community. He engaged a psychologist, Karen Nielsen, to support the community's trauma and grief healing and recovery work. But Walter was just scratching the surface of a very deep and intractable spiritual condition. In his final days, the cumulative stress, heartbreak, and anguish—including the anger of realizing the extent that loved ones lied to him—overtook him. Shaken as he vented about the behaviors of loved ones, he sank into a chair, life's energy draining from him. Two days later, Walter died on October 30, 1997. This was about six months after engaging Dr. Nielsen to work with the community.

Walter's death left the community without a visionary leader, our four young sons fatherless, and a wounded community without a compass for healing. One individual highly coveted Walter's position of chief and his reputation as a respected leader. To at least gain the position of chief, he promised to continue the healing work but resiled immediately after being elected chief in 2003. Lacking a leader's spiritual compass and any mention of healing—interpreted by some as a form of insult—the community healing work stopped in 2003.

While I did not have answers to Walter's questions in 1989, after years of descending through a complex rabbit hole and accessing research into what I have found to be three underlying root issues—colonialism, racism, and unhealed trauma and grief—I now realize that the system that Walter identified as having a spiritual problem is that of a *Wihtiko*[2] system. As I will discuss in this chapter, Wihtiko, as understood in Anishinaabe and Cree cultures, is a spiritually cannibalized human who is defined by three internal traits, qualities, or attitudes:

Severe loss or abandonment of self-control, or the manipulative control of others; disconnect with or manipulation of reality; and abandonment, rejection or manipulation of relationship. The Wihtiko's attitude is that truth, reality, and others can be reduced to objects of self-serving power. (Chabot 2016, 84)

Wihtiko systems mimic and replicate Wihtiko traits, cannibalizing souls and relationships.

At the time of Walter's death, I lacked an adequately developed understanding of Wihtiko systems, and so I personally tried to plead, reason, and negotiate with such a system, expecting humane responses. The late Anishinaabe scholar, Basil Johnston, recounts *Nana'b'oozoo's* heartbreak, realizing colonization's power to alienate us from our spiritual power source and each other:

A storyteller once depicted the alienation of the Anishinaubae people from their cultural heritage and their espousal of Western European civilization as a repudiation of their figurehead, Nana'b'oozoo. In the last story concerning him, Nana'b'oozoo, spurned and scorned, hurt and humiliated by the people who he had loved and served for so many years, gathers all his worldly possessions, stows them into his canoe, and then helps his aged grandmother, N'okomiss, board. He does not want to leave, but he must, for he is no longer welcome in his ancestral home. Still, he tarries and looks longingly in hopes that someone will notice and bid them to stay. But no one gives Nana'b'oozoo and his grandmother a second glance, and they pass beyond the horizon and out of the lives of their kin. (Johnson 1995, 23)

Like *Nana'b'oozoo*, rejected, I withdrew. No one reached out; but I was never far, and when anyone inside the Wihtiko system called out, I was there. With time, I began to see that my heartache was a gift, my pain an impetus, my codependency a sickness. Pushed into recovery and healing, I unmasked, and began to heal my soul.

Wihtiko systems operate both within First Nations as well as globally. These systems are symptomatic of a shared history of racism, colonialism, and unresolved grief and trauma—all of which create the spiritual impoverishment necessary for the onset of Wihtiko systems. Certain minority populations are disproportionately impacted and, consequently, overrepresented across sorrow systems and metrics—child welfare, criminal justice, obesity, diabetes, heart disease, stroke, cancer, mental health, addictions, and now COVID-19, poverty, food scarcity, inequality, and exposure to pollutants. What Lee Macintyre characterizes as today's "Post Truth" era—dangerous, nihilistic, dismissive of science, evidence, facts, and truth (Zakaria 2018)—describes today's Wihtiko system. Unchallenged, Wihtiko systems beget an oppressive and violent force that debilitates, separates, divides, and destroys. Transforming Wihtiko systems requires awakening—seeing and understanding Wihtiko in all its darkness, chaos, and distractions. Awakening is made more difficult, given the normalization of addiction and codependency within our lives and communities requiring inner healing. But soul healing generates an intellectual and psychospiritual power that can transform every hindrance, impediment, fear, shame, and obstacle into a spiritual way forward.

In illustrating the transformation of Wihtiko systems, this chapter begins with Indigenous understandings of the Wihtiko concept. Second, it shows that colonialism is a Wihtiko system, and third, the operationalization of Wihtiko systems and their ensuing consequences. Finally, it illustrates how spirit enables transformation of Wihtiko systems from soul cannibalization to life-giving energy.

INDIGENOUS UNDERSTANDINGS
OF THE WIHTIKO CONCEPT

In early times, the Anishinaabe peoples, which translates to "Good Beings," were taught various basic skills for survival: "life, guardianship, healing and teaching" (Johnston 1995, xvi). The Anishinaabe peoples therefore used their skills to continue with life through the generations (ibid., xvii). However, life was more than survival:

> It has long been assumed that people who were preoccupied with material needs and wants would have little interest in matters of the spirit and the mind. On the contrary, it was this very mode of life, this simple way of meeting simple needs that awakened in man and woman a consciousness that there were realities and presences in life other than the corporeal and the materials. The spirit, the Manitou, the mystery were part of life and could not be separated from it. (Ibid., xviii)

As such, a premium was placed on notions of relationships and reciprocity—any estrangement from these principles could prove to be of grave consequence—leading to the emergence of Wihtiko systems, which caused widespread suffering, misery, and death.

The late Anishinaabe scholar, Basil Johnston, shares Anishinaabe spiritual canons and describes the "ever hungry" and figuratively cannibalistic beings, known as Wihtikos:

> For the unfortunate Weendigo [also known as Wihtiko], the more it ate the bigger it grew; and the bigger it grew, the more it wanted and needed . . . Even the

term Weendigo evokes images of offensive traits. It may be derived from ween dagoh which means "solely for self," or from weenin n'd'igooh, which means "fat" or excess. The Weendigo inspired fear. (Ibid., 222)

As long as its lust and hunger are satisfied, nothing else matters—not compassion, sorrow, reason or judgement. Although the Weendigo is an exaggeration, it exemplifies human nature's tendency to indulge its self-interests, which once indulged, demand even greater indulgence and ultimately result in the extreme—the erosion of principles and values. It is ironic that the Weendigo preys upon and can only overcome ordinary human beings who, like itself, have indulged themselves to excess and hence illustrates the lesson that excess preys and thrives on excess . . . humans must kill the Weendigo to betoken that they must put an end to certain self-serving indulgences or be destroyed. (Ibid., 223–25)

In essence, Johnston conveys that Wihtikos are beings that are excessively for one's self. Moreover, their appetites for self-interest are so grand that it becomes predatory. Such behavior is counter to Anishinaabe principles of thinking about others, the future, and practicing moderation.

Cecil Chabot grew up with the James Bay Cree and interviewed Cree elders who shared stories of Wihtiko, which he describes as "a cannibal monster that epitomizes the perversion of the spiritual values most fundamental for relationship, reciprocity, and reconciliation in Cree and other Algonquian subarctic communities—and perhaps any human community" ("Warring with *Windigo/Wihtiko,*" *Transforming*, 273).[3] He further summarizes its traits as follows:

Ultimately, the wihtiko is defined by three traits related not to physical appearance, but to internal qualities or attitudes: severe loss or abandonment of self-control, or the manipulative control of others; disconnect with or manipulation of reality; and abandonment, rejection or manipulation of relationship. The wihtiko's attitude is that truth, reality, and others can be reduced to objects of self-serving power. (Chabot 2016, 84)

Wihtiko is a demonic, cannibal energy or force that can take human form, whose appetite grows with the eating. It cannot sustain itself without destroying others.

The unchecked development of Wihtiko tendencies in a community creates angry and chaotic family and clan systems, which are often dominated by Wihtiko leaders who blame, gossip, lie, ostracize, exclude, scapegoat, stonewall, deny, manipulate, gaslight, and distort truth, reality, and relationships. Such leaders enforce Wihtiko rules—*don't talk, don't trust, don't feel*—and punish expressions of feelings. One such example is the punishment of female emotional reactions to the misogyny and cruelties served up by such systems. A consequence of the prolonged operationalization of a Wihitko system is the disintegration of community and its households and members. Spurning trust and affection, individuals may medicate by using substances, processes, and hidden forms of addiction.

To prevent the Wihtiko mentality, Indigenous elders emphasized thinking of others and moderation in living. People were to think about the future, not to be greedy for too much and putting the needs of the community and families first. Selfishness, for the Anishinaabek, was the root of social problems, leading to anger, envy, and lust, which create imbalance (Johnston 1995, 223–24). However, the infliction of trauma, including internal disruptions, on Indigenous peoples by the Wihtiko tendencies of imperial Western societies has created a figurative breeding ground for Wihtiko systems within Indigenous communities.

THE WIHTIKO CONCEPT AND COLONIALISM

After exploring how colonialism itself functions as a Wihtiko system, I will show how Christian churches were complicit with Wihtiko systems.

Colonialism as a Wihtiko System

Colonialism has many definitions. I understand it as "power over," and "doing to or for," combined with a practice of subjugation, domination, and exploitation with an economic policy to enrich the dominator at the expense of the dominated. Colonialism is not an historic relic—it still operates—distorting "sovereignty," so it is underpinned by a corrupted and hegemonic political power structure that enriches the few at the expense of many. In the context of the present-day Americas, colonialism has taken the form of "deliberate slaughter and enslavement of ancestors; depopulation by European diseases; removal of ancestors from ancestral lands; discriminatory and sometimes genocidal government policies; loss of lands; theft of property; crooked treaties and unconscionable agreements; and destroyed cultures, languages, sacred sites and religious practices" (Austin 2009, xviii). Raymond Austin goes on to further argue that all this injustice and oppression continue to live on the reservations of Indigenous peoples today; they are just known by different terms (ibid). We now know them as intergenerational trauma, prevalent poverty, poor health, poor educational achievement, alcoholism, drug abuse, and a multitude of social problems (ibid).

Colonialism itself is predicated on the exploitation of lands, resources, and people as an attempt to satisfy the appetites of a few. Like the Wihtiko, colonialism operates out of selfishness and with a lack of compassion. It is also unable to regulate itself to truth and reality, reducing "others" to objects of self-serving power. Consequently, injustices against Indigenous peoples persist in many parts of the world. But the salt on the wound is when Indigenous communities internalize colonialism. Today, Wihtiko Indigenous leaders command the disenrollment, abuse, systemic violence, corruption, and contempt for foundational norms.

Christian Complicity

While racist and capitalist ideologies underpinning colonialism were operationalized throughout Western history, Christendom functioned as a complicit participant. In Canada, one such example is the construction and operation of IRSs whereby Indigenous people later spoke of the abuse they received as children while being students in these schools (see also Truth and Reconciliation Commission 2015). The hand of Christendom in the operation of these types of colonial structures does not only serve as a function of a Wihtiko system but is also contrary to biblical teachings.

Wendell Berry is clear to distinguish the "catastrophic discrepancies" between Christian organizations and behavior from biblical teachings. Berry notes that "modern Christian organizations have kept remarkably quiet about or paid little attention [to several things such as] [w]e humans do not own the world or any part of it" for "the landowner is the guest and steward of God: 'the land is mine, for ye are strangers and sojourners with me'" (1992, 96–97). Berry finds that modern Christianity is culpable for the destruction of the natural world and that Christianity often fails to correct that destruction, despite having aided it. No one can doubt "the complicity of Christian priests, preachers and missionaries in the cultural destruction and the economic exploitation of the primary peoples of the Western hemisphere and other Indigenous cultures throughout the world" (ibid., 94).

But if our understanding stops at this point, it fails to comprehend biblical teachings and cultural traditions that accord with the understandings of Indigenous peoples and universal spiritual values. Yet Western society continues to operate in ways that devastate people and the natural world. The destruction of the Amazon forest and its peoples is the Wihtiko system operating in real time. The Bible gives no license to exterminate or damage or even hold in contempt anything on the earth or in the heavens above it or in the waters beneath it. Berry states that

> destruction of nature is not just bad stewardship, or stupid economics, or a betrayal of family responsibility; it is the *"most horrid blasphemy"* . . . To Dante, *"despising Nature and her goodness was a violence against God"* . . . We

have the right to use the gifts of nature but not to ruin or waste them. We have the right to use what we need, but no more, which is why the Bible forbids usury and great accumulations of property. The usurer, Dante said, *"condemns Nature for he puts his hopes elsewhere"* . . . William Blake . . . said . . . *"everything that lives is holy"* . . . We are holy creatures living among other holy creatures in a world that is holy. Some people know this, and some do not. Nobody of course knows it all the time. (Ibid, 98–99)

Humans, as part of Creation, are spirit and most vulnerable to cannibalization by self-serving excess. Transcending this human tendency is paramount for survival.

THE OPERATIONALIZATION OF
THE WIHTIKO CONCEPT

In contemporary studies of addiction, particularly addictive systems, we can find additional insights concerning how the Wihtiko concept finds concrete expression within organizations and systems. I will show how this applies to the economic system and, most perniciously, within Indigenous governments.

Wihtiko as Addictive Systems and Organizations

The Wihtiko concept today in part functions as addictive systems and organizations, which are hurting systems and organizations that are internally troubled with group behaviors that can be cruel as well as personally and socially destructive. Gabor Maté, who worked with people with addictions in Vancouver's lower east side, sees addictions as going beyond lethal substances to "the frantic self-soothing of overeaters or shopaholics; the obsession of gamblers, sexaholics and compulsive internet users; or the socially acceptable and even admired behaviors of the workaholic" (Maté 2008, 1–2). Similar to the Wihtiko, Maté also utilizes the Buddhist concept of the Hungry Ghost to understand addiction:

> The Inhabitants of the Hungry Ghost Realm are depicted as creatures with scrawny necks, small mouths, emaciated limbs and large, bloated, empty bellies. This is the domain of addiction, where we constantly seek something outside ourselves to curb an insatiable yearning for relief or fulfillment. The aching emptiness is perpetual because the substances, objects or pursuits we hope will soothe it are not what we really need. We don't know what we need, and so long as we stay in the hungry ghost mode, we'll never know. (2008, 1–2)

Like the Hungry Ghost, so too is the Wihtiko plagued by a perpetual hunger for self-satisfaction despite the potential consequences, including the harm to self and others.

Anne Wilson Schaef and Diane Fassel describe individual and family addictions to characterize larger addictive organizations and systems that enable individual addiction. For them, an addiction may be a "process or substance that has taken over our lives and over which we are powerless" (1988, 57). To cover it up we have to lie about it to others and ourselves. As it takes over our lives, it leads to "increasing compulsiveness in our behaviors" (ibid). Like Dr. Maté, Schaef and Fassel argue that addiction extend beyond that of substances to include process addictions—that can include "work, sex, money, gambling, religion, relationships, and certain types of thinking"— which are proven to be similarly potent in putting "a buffer between ourselves and our awareness of feelings" (ibid., 58). Addictive systems replicate the traits of the addict. Schaef and Fassel define "system" as

> an entity that comprises both content (ideas, roles, and definitions) and pro-
> cesses (ways of doing things), and that is complete in itself. A system is made
> up of parts, and the system is larger than the sum of its parts. A system often has
> a life of its own distinct from the lives of individuals within it . . . A corporation
> itself is a being that is greater than the composite of all its workers. This life or
> system has a tradition, a way of doing things, unwritten norms, and expectations
> passed on within the system . . . Systems contain themselves within an entire
> worldview. (Ibid., 60)

An overarching characteristic of an addictive system is that it is closed, presenting "very few options to the individual in terms of roles and behaviors, or even the thinking and perceptions a person can recognize and pursue" (ibid., 61). Norms supporting the addictive behavior are so strong that any who try to escape the toxicity may be punished through social isolation or removal from the community, corporation, or other addictive collective body. Being a closed system, the number, range, and nature of interactions are closed and limited.

An addictive system characteristically uses denial to close itself off from new information that might expose its dysfunctionality or suggest change. It demands that all within the system perfectly adhere to its norms, often centered on a leader who sees any deviance (even questioning) as a threat. There is a preoccupation with control. Ethical and spiritual deterioration are concomitant with toxic stress, dependency, negativism, tunnel vision, and fear (ibid., 62–68). Schaef and Fassel identify six, often hidden, processes that characterize addictive systems: (1) a process that moves us from self-awareness to concentrate on promised expectation; (2) the pseudopodic ego colonizes everything around, instrumentalizing it for its own purposes, bragging about how great the system is, though nothing has been value-added by the system itself; (3) with no real boundaries, there is an external reference to what is outside the self, obliterating the self and denying authentic relationships with others; (4) ideas and experiences that are incongruent with the system are invalidated; (5) anyone who brings unwanted information to the fore is discounted through personality attacks; and (6) complex reality is reduced to black and white choices—two alternatives, two sides, a false dualism—making it easy to categorize friends and enemies and control the situation (ibid., 68–72).

Leaders, or those at the heart of an addictive system, are sustained through codependent relationships. Codependency is itself an addiction—an addiction to relationships. Codependents will do anything to protect the feelings of the addict—lying, excluding, and silencing; unethical proof of loyalty; caring out of a craving for approval; and serving and suffering to the point of giving up any attention to oneself, covering up, fulfilling hatchet roles, and directing rage and anger on threats to this system (ibid., 73–76). An organization may become addictive through having an addict for a leader (ibid., 79–94), replicating addictive processes (ibid., 95–117), having the organization as an "addictive substance" (ibid., 118–36), or the organization itself functioning as an addict (ibid., 137–76).

Addictive systems cannibalize spirituality and relationships—they are modern Wihtiko systems—and therefore take on Wihtiko characteristics, including dishonesty, chaos, confusion, blame, anger, judgmentalism, dualism, denial, entitlement, dependency, rejection, scapegoating, resentment, fear, exclusion, lack of boundaries, negativity, control, rigidity, closed, and the "don't talk, trust or feel" rules. Left unchecked, Wihtiko energies can destroy and consume everything and everyone. We may not only observe the operationalization of the Wihtiko concept in some Indigenous governments, as a consequence of colonial trauma, but in modern capitalist governments as well, the progeny of the originators of privilege, power, excess, and superiority. Wihtikos are alike regardless of where they come from: from Donald Trump to Mohammed Bin Salman, they bring disaster, misery, suffering, and death fueled by an unquenchable greed and excess. As aforementioned, Wihtikos leaders are enabled by organizations and systems populated by people with codependency issues.

As it is estimated that 95 percent of North Americans are codependent—we are poorly prepared to identify and recover from the family, community, and nation-state addictive systems generated by this collective codependency (Whitfield 1991). Hurting, we hope something will save, rescue, fix, or intervene. Numbed, we yield, submit, defer, deny, enable, suffer, and entrust ourselves to the Wihtiko system to quench Wihtiko's appetite. Bruce Alexander in *The Globalization of Addiction: A Study in Poverty of the Spirit* shows that the social circumstances underpinning addiction are built into today's globalizing free-market society whereby people are subject to irresistible pressures toward individualism and competition, which tears rich and poor alike from the close social and spiritual ties that constitute human life (Alexander 2008). Alexander goes on to argue that a large-scale, collective impact social project is required to help people find social integration and meaning in everyday life (ibid).

The Economic Dimensions of Wihtiko Systems

The rapacious appetite of the industrial economy, which functions as a Wihtiko system, has led to the destruction of nature and community. Wendell Berry defines community as a "locally understood interdependence of local people, local culture, local economy and local nature" (Berry 1992, 120). True community safeguards local place, which Berry notes is based on "a culture capable of preserving land and people . . . only within a relatively stable and enduring relationship between a local people and its place" (ibid., 171). The systemic onset and operationalization of the Wihtiko concept destroys any notion of what we might characterize as "true community" as defined by Berry.

The destruction of community and nature begins with making the community's economy subject to an economy that is larger and exploitative (ibid., 126–27). The implications are that:

> If you are dependent on people who do not know you, who control the value of your necessities, you are not free, and you are not safe. The industrial revolution has thus made universal the colonial principle that has proved to be ruinous beyond measure: the assumption that it is permissible to ruin one place or culture for the sake of another. Thus justified or excused, the industrial economy grows in power and thrives on damages to local economies, communities and places. (Ibid., 128)

The present public economy that dispossessed and displaced Indigenous peoples exists to protect the "right" of profit that inevitably gravitates toward the protection of those who profit most, which thereby exists as a political system that safeguards the private exploitation of the public health and wealth (ibid., 138). Such is an exemplary hallmark of a Wihtiko system.

The triumph of technological determinism continues through "surveillance capitalism," which gathers information about us to manipulate and use against us while separating us into two automated groups—the watchers and the watched (Zuboff 2019). Berry notes:

The triumph of the industrial economy is the fall of community. But the fall of community reveals how precious and how necessary community is. For when community falls, so must fall all the things that only community life can engender and protect: the care of the old, the care and education of children, family life, neighborly work, the handing down of memory, the care of the earth, respect for nature and the lives of wild creatures. (Berry 1992, 133)

Indigenous leaders have long commented on the mad cannibalism of colonial nations. For instance, Chief Seattle once remarked that, unlike colonial societies, we do not sell the earth upon which we walk for "we do not inherit the Earth from our Ancestors, we borrow it from our children" (n.d.). Within Chief Seattle's statement is the ideology that, for Indigenous peoples, there is this deeply valued concept of relationships whereby such ought to remain immune to commodification and destruction but preserved with love for all children.

The Systemic Function of the Wihtiko Concept in Indigenous Governments

Despite the sentiment of historic leaders such as Crazy Horse and Chief Seattle, the Wihtiko-like operation of Settler colonialism has proven to be both penetrable and transferrable. Today, Wihtiko-led pandemics in Indigenous communities include epidemics in addictions, disenrollment or exclusion from community, and other structures of violence. Consequently, the tendencies of the Wihtiko concept surface at times in the very communities that were, and are, subject to its focus. Mere mention of these epidemics can invoke furious responses: accusations of stereotyping, attacks on personal integrity, banishment, even judicial attacks. Vicious responses, especially from bully platforms, squelch critical thinking and enable the problem by denying it. There may not often be remedies—especially from colonial Western court structures—for those who question and challenge such operationalization. For instance, although overturned on appeal, an Alberta judge, Justice Denny Thomas, remarked that challenging "the internal decision-making, self-determination, and self-government of an aboriginal community is a serious matter" to support awarding solicitor-client costs against a lawyer who pro bono represented an elderly client excluded from belonging by discriminatory membership norms applied by a First Nation Chief and Council.[4]

One of the outstanding challenges of colonialism's effect on Indigenous communities is how such communities often now mimic the Western modes (and problems) with respect to selecting leadership. The late preeminent Indigenous scholar, Vine Deloria, remarked:

In the old days, leadership depended on the personal prestige of the people whom the community chose as its leaders. Their generosity, service to the community and honesty had to be above question. Today tribal constitutions define who shall represent the tribe in its relationships with the outside world. No quality is needed to assume leadership except the ability to win elections. Consequently, tribal elections have become one of the dirtiest forms of human activity in existence. Corruption runs rampant during tribal elections, and people deliberately vote in scoundrels over honest people for the personal benefits they can receive. Much of the formal resistance to federal programs for increasing tribal independence comes from the Indian people's mistrust of their own leadership, present and future. Many tribes want the tribal lands and assets so restricted that no one can use them to the tribe's detriment—or benefit. (Vine Deloria 2003, 249–50)

Given that many contemporary Indigenous governmental authorities achieve their positions by such trivial measures, it also follows that they may turn to similar means in maintaining their positions. Essentially, the colonized—over time—become colonizers, a cruel mimetic transference.

Disenrollment, or communal exclusion, is one means that contemporary Indigenous governments may use to maintain their position. However, such practice is the antithesis of tribal sovereignty. Gabriel Galanda and Ryan Dreveskracht point out that disenrollment is based upon colonial principles intended to terminate Indigenous values and norms, incentivize the solidification of economic and political clout, and to winnow out those who disapprove of the direction taken by individuals or subgroups aligned with the colonial government (2015, 444). More particularly, disenrollment is either the removal of people from Indigenous community lists or disallowing or ignoring their applications—whether such individuals have a legitimate claim or not. Unless this disenrollment crisis is addressed, Indigenous peoples—who are fractionalizing themselves—could also end up legally terminating themselves.

Galanda and Dreveskracht argue that a result from the colonial process is that the

concepts and assumptions of Indigenous identity reproduce the very social inequalities that have traditionally defined Indigenous oppression. Until these ideologies are disrupted by Indigenous peoples and their governments, the important projects for Indigenous decolonization and self-determination that define Indigenous movements and cultural revitalization efforts today are impossible. (Ibid., 473–74)

The ideologies perpetuating and the "social inequalities" defined by Indigenous oppression, as described by Galanda and Dreveskracht, are products of a Wihtiko system. While Indigenous sovereignty derives from spiritual values, continued cultural integrity, and secure and authentic kinship systems (Ibid, 444), disenrollment, or exclusion from community for selfish gain, deny critical relationships of belonging and identity. These cruelties, symptomatic of a colonized Wihtiko system, will ultimately destroy Indigenous Sovereignty under the lie of preserving it. As Galanda and Dreveskracht point out, tribal sovereignty derives from spiritual values, continued cultural integrity, and secure and authentic kinship systems (ibid., 444). It is less about political power; rather, it "revolves around the manner in which traditions are developed, sustained, and transformed to confront new conditions" (2015, 444). Traditions are a salient aspect of adaptivity within a societal system, essential to produce more adaptive responses to create a healthier, more well-functioning society. Much of the current dysfunction arose historically in response to the systematic suppression of homeostatic social mechanisms of traditional society. Reviving traditions are not just intuitive or nostalgic interventions but also critical to survival when viewed through the principles of the complex systems analysis (Theise, "Harnessing Principles of Complex Systems," *Transforming*, 391–92). Central to adaptivity is community discipline. Tribal sovereignty utilizes

> peace-making, mediation, restitution and compensation to resolve the inevitable disputes that occasionally ar[i]se . . . [and is founded in] spiritual values [and] kinship systems . . . that enabled each Native nation, and the individuals, families, and clans constituting those nations, to generally rest assured in their collective and personal identities and not have to wonder about "who" they are. (Ibid., 444)

Perhaps the greatest challenge facing Wihtiko systems are the enablers that sustain it. Enablers are codependents, crossing all social strata and often occupying power positions. Enablers maintain the addictive system and include insiders and outsiders to that system. Martin Luther King's response to being admonished by eight white clergy over his demand for racial equality captures a universal pain upon realizing that enablers in positions of authority will not help those suffering:

> I must confess that over the past few years I have been gravely disappointed with the white moderate. I have almost reached the regrettable conclusion that the Negro's great stumbling block in his stride toward freedom is not the White Citizen's Councilor or the Ku Klux Klanner, but the white moderate, who is more devoted to "order" than to justice; who prefers a negative peace which is the absence of tension to a positive peace which is the presence of justice; who constantly says: "I agree with you in the goal you seek, but I cannot agree with your methods of direct action"; who paternalistically believes he can set

the timetable for another [person's] freedom: who lives by a mythical concept of time and who constantly advises the Negro to wait for a "more convenient season." Shallow understanding from people of good will is more frustrating than absolute misunderstanding from people of ill will. Lukewarm acceptance is much more bewildering than outright rejection. (King 1963)

Similarly, well-meaning pro-Indigenous members of the "Settler" society can slavishly enable Wihtiko leaders and addictive community systems (cf. Logie, "Transforming 'Wicked' Problems," *Transforming*). Under the guise of supporting self-government and self-determination they can in fact empower and enable addictive systems. Their enabling creates a paradoxical situation: they purport to both respect Indigenous culture and spirituality they have—in their ignorance—conflated with Wihitko leaders and addictive systems. Society must own up to colonialism's legacy that is largely responsible for creating the conditions in which Wihitko leaders thrive. As the German president noted, society must act knowing light from darkness—not from guilt, denial or shame, facing "up to the past . . . what people knew . . . what they had colluded in . . . raising painful questions within families and between generations . . . [and fight] to stop silence and denial from prevailing" (Steinmeier 2020).

TRANSCENDING WIHTIKO HARMS

What do we do about the destructive work of Wihtiko—individual and systemic? First we need to look at the variety of forms of harm and responses to it by those it affects. Second, we need to find teachings that help us transcend the Wihtiko phenomenon.

Categories of Wihtiko By-products

Both Indigenous and non-Indigenous peoples have been the subject of Wihtiko machinations. One plain example is the Jewish Holocaust inflicted by Nazi Germany—Wihtiko systems transcend time and place. Truda Rosenberg, who was one of 300,000 to survive Adolph Hitler's genocidal killing of 2.7 million Jews in Poland, used to say, "I am not a victim; I am not a survivor; I am a victor!" After the war, she had successful careers as a nurse and a clinical psychologist. Her impassioned declaration points to multiple trajectories for those harmed by Wihtikos and the addictive systems that enable them.

However, before more specifically addressing Wihtiko transcendence, I will first outline categories of Wihtikos that function as systemic by-products.

Through my personal observations of many trapped in addictive Indigenous and other communities, I have identified the following: Victim Wihtikos, Tyrannical Wihtikos, Survivors, and Victors. We must keep in mind that Wihtikos can emerge in all manner of cultures and contexts; hence, our final example comes from the entertainment industry.

Victim Wihtikos are deeply wounded emotionally, spiritually, and mentally. As the narcissistic wounded, they have lost a capacity to feel for others as only their pain, their rage, counts. As victims, they manipulate truth, reality, and relationships, lying and distorting to get what they want. They often turn to substances and processes to soothe deep-seated fears and discomforts, compounding harmful behaviors. They consume others to support their addiction. If loved ones confront them on their lies, irresponsible behavior, and addictions, they cannibalize and even discard them. Victim Wihtikos are vulnerable to having their vote "bought off" through a promise of some gain by a Wihtiko politician. These forms of spiritual corruption lead to alienation, isolation, disaffection, disintegration, and even death.

Tyrannical Wihtikos are also on a soul-destroying, narcissistic path, but in their case their drug is power, wealth, privilege, and control. They demand compliance, blind obedience, and loyalty. They engage in capricious self-serving decisions, favoring family and enablers. It can lead to vote-buying, excluding certain people from band membership lists and removing those who fail to supplicate, soothe, and show deference. It can lead to Tyrannical Wihtiko elected leaders enabling drug houses and trafficking on Indian reserves in exchange for support from Victim Wihtikos.

Survivors are those who become aware of their own woundedness and addictions, along with the addictive nature of the systems or communities in which they are living. They reach out for help, acknowledge what they can and cannot control, and continue on a path of sobriety, awareness, and self-empowerment. One example of a survivor that I am personally aware of, by word of mouth, involves a young Indigenous woman. She had reached out to someone and spoke of how she felt worthless and that the only way out was to commit suicide. When she approached her grandmother about the issue, she was told she was acting crazy and was ignored by her grandmother who shut off the heat to the basement where she lived. Distressed, this young woman attempted to hang herself, and when she did, some of her own family in fact encouraged her to do it, as she would be doing them all a favor.

It is evident that this young woman was being cannibalized within a Wihtiko system. However, she made an insightful comment by stating, "You can't heal in the same toxic environment that hurt you." Gabor Maté says "the basic cause of addiction is predominantly experience-dependent during childhood, and not substance-dependent" (2012, 181).

Unfortunately, not only has she been deprived of rich cultural teachings necessary to navigate life's perils, but her developing brain was deprived of a nurturing environment. The role of environmentin brain development is of great importance—particularly because "in the uterus and during childhood [brain development] is the single most important factor in determining whether or not a person will be predisposed to substance dependence and to addictive behaviors of any sort, whether drug-related or not" (ibid., 180). Further, "the expression of genetic potentials is, for the most part, contingent on the environment" (ibid., 181). After birth, human brains grow at the same rate as in the womb—so fast that there are "times in the first year of life when, every second, multiple millions of nerve connections or synapses are established. By age 3, our brain reaches 90% of its adult size, whereas the body is only 18% of its adult size" (ibid., 182). A mother's gaze will instantaneously affect the chemistry of her baby's brain, wiring its circuitry. The environment largely determines which connections survive. Connections and circuits used frequently are strengthened; unused ones are pruned out ("synaptic pruning"). The external experience causes some neurons and synapses and not others to survive and grow (ibid., 183). Hence, as Maté points out, "At any point in this process you have the potential for good or bad stimulation to get in there and set the microstructure of the brain" (ibid., 184). Too much bad stimulation leads to hard core addiction, as will a lack of sufficient good stimulation (ibid., 184). While the human brain continues to develop new circuitry throughout the lifespan, including well into adulthood, the Wihtiko environment of bad stimulation reinforces addiction-driven circuitry. Going to a treatment center would have been an option, but the community system—her environment itself—needed healing; otherwise, the very same Wihtiko machinations that fractured her life—and her brain development and circuitry—would have continued to do so.

Victors are survivors who take additional steps. They redefine their identities; they transcend their trauma cutting off their identity from it. They develop strength to succeed; they hold abusive systems accountable; and they develop an "other-orientation"—reaching out in support of others. Victors can come in many forms. Truda Rosenberg, for reasons described above, is a Victor.

In her own right, Stefani Germanotta (also known as "Lady Gaga") could be characterized as a Victor. Germanotta was bullied as a child in school and raped repeatedly over a period of time as a young woman. In addition, she was ostracized, leaving her with the sense of being outside the community of her peers like a scapegoat victim. The experiences left her with depression, PTSD, and chronic neuropathic pain. One response was to become a cutter: "The only way that I was able to stop cutting and self-harming myself was to realize that what I was doing was trying to show people that I was in pain instead of telling them and asking for help" (Lady Gaga 2019).

There were however a number of things that helped Germanotta turn things around. First, was drastic intervention by a psychiatrist. Second was the support of family and friends (something which the aforementioned survivor lacked). Third was ongoing therapy, and finally were the teachings of blessing she received from her mother who always encouraged her to resort to kindness:

> I've become very mindful of my position in the world and my responsibility to humanity and to those who follow me. And I consider myself to be a kindness punk. I look back at everything I've done, and I look at what I'm doing now, and punks, you know, have a sort of reputation for being rebellious, right? So for me, I really view my career, and even what I'm doing now, as a rebellion against all the things in the world that I see to be unkind. (Ibid.)

Kindness heals the world. Kindness heals people. It is what brings us together and it is what keeps us healthy (ibid.). However, what is also worth noting is Germanotta's mindset: her "responsibility to humanity," and successively, her responsibility to relationships—including to herself. One example of this is when she, together with the World Health Organization (WHO), organized the "One World: Together at Home" concert during the COVID-19 pandemic. It raised money for the WHO and specific charities, while bringing together a wide range of international artists.

Teachings on Transcendence

Had my late husband survived Wihtiko to live a long life, I believe he would have led our community into recovery, to the call of Spirit. As I began my recovery, I understood that concepts such as resentment and bitterness cause great harm to those who carry them, and to engage in compassionate, open, and loving curiosity with myself—to explore the "why" of my behavior—can be life-giving. Nonetheless, truths are tough to arrive at and live. Truth itself may lead to ostracization or even death. Kindness does not necessarily reciprocate kindness—Wihtiko energy often exploits kindness—but we must still practice kindness, love, patience, and acceptance.

Awakening to Wihtiko's machinations that have long controlled us is terrorizing, particularly facing the "mimetic structure of violence": a power far bigger than any individual that overrides individual values and inclinations and stems from a relationship that builds up in such a way that the parties in the relationship say and do things to harm one another (see Redekop 2002, 161–72). A beautiful young woman from an Indian reserve was living a clean life: no sex, drugs, alcohol, or parties. One day, as she walked down the road, a carload of jealous girls came upon her and cut up her face. They took her beauty they did not have. This is the terror of a mimetic structure of violence at work. The girl never recovered from this trauma. No one inside this prism of violence wants to be its target and most avoid stirring this beast. As Redekop argues, a mimetic structures of violence—carried by rage and anger—has within it an intention to harm or get at the other, cowing most people:

> Violence, as *control*, keeps people from achieving their ends, holds them back, and puts obstacles in their way.
>
> Violence, as *force*, inflicts goals, actions, or behaviours on people. It makes people subservient, doing what they do not wish to do . . .
>
> Violence *extracts* from people what they cherish. It may be the theft of possessions or it may mean extracting information through torture, trickery, or treachery.
>
> Violence *diminishes* people. It makes them lose face, humiliates them, and removes all dignity and self-respect.
>
> Violence *hurts* people. It maims them, burns them, makes them bleed, and kills them. With the physical hurt comes the inner hurt of being deceived or betrayed.
>
> Violence can take place at another level—that of *curse*. Curses involve a desire to see the other harmed. It imagines and desires ill for the Other . . .
>
> Violence can also take the form of *withholding help* from someone who is suffering. (Ibid., 163)

Violence can also take the form of administrative violence, "the use of discretionary powers to diminish, harm, or negatively affect people, either individually or as members of a particular group" (Redekop, 2019).

But Redekop holds out the possibility of transforming mimetic structures of violence to mimetic structures of blessing, aided by *teachings of blessing*. It can be done by an inner awakening whereby we develop our consciousness such that we can have compassion for others and ourselves.

However, with inner awakening comes the fact that we must choose to live in Spirit. Elder David Courchene shares with us a story about the laws that help us transcend Wihtiko systems and live in Spirit. More particularly, Elder Courchene calls it the "Seven Sacred Laws" that are foundational. The story begins with a boy who was troubled by how climate change, wars, violence, and hatred indicated a lack of care for the land. He asked his grandfather about what he could do to help the earth. The grandfather was pleased that he had this concern and replied that his question could be answered if the boy went through a specific Anishinaabe ceremony.

It was during this ceremony that the boy learned about the Seven Sacred Laws. In the spirit of the Buffalo, the boy learned of *respect*—one of the secrets to a good life. The Buffalo represented respect because, for Indigenous peoples, the Buffalo gave every part of its physical being to provide food, clothing, shelter, and so forth. Respect is all about giving and sharing by serving humanity and Creation; for the greatest gift one can give is one's own self, which is in part by being a model and example of the Seven Sacred Laws.

Likewise, other animals appeared with a message. The Eagle brought the law of *love*—the essence of the Great Spirit and the spirit of the boy. Mother Earth, Eagle continued, would, out of love, give him all that he needed: "Return that love to her by first loving yourself and who you are . . . I can help heal your spirit. We all need love to heal properly. In love you will defeat all that is evil in your world. Every act of kindness and love will change the universe and change your world" (Courchene 2018; note that subsequent quotes within this story come from the same source).

Next, the boy learned about the laws of *courage* and *honesty*. It was the Bear who brought the Law of Courage. Specifically, the Bear said to the boy: "To walk in courage is to do the right thing—to always take the high moral road . . . [and] become close to Mother Earth who will teach you." Sabe, otherwise known as Saquatch, brought the Law of Honesty, which associated honesty with living a good life: "To be honest is to speak from your heart. Be honest with who you are, and whatever you speak, but make sure your words show kindness for all of Creation." Judgement, said Saba "will not change [people, but] leads to anger, and will only delay teachings that they have to learn."

The law of *wisdom* and *humility* were next in line for the boy to learn. It was the Beaver that brought the Law of Wisdom: "knowing your gifts and using these gifts to serve your fellow human beings. Living your gifts will define your identity and purpose in life." This would "help [one] build a world connected to the Laws we have brought." Knowing oneself helps achieve peace and balance. Just as Beaver would get sick from teeth that kept growing if it did not use them, so not using one's gifts could impact one's health and life. Then the Wolf brought the Law of Humility: "Never put yourself above any of your fellow human beings and never put yourself above Nature because she is our Mother." Humility includes gratitude and treating everyone with kindness.

Finally, grandmother Turtle brought the Law of Truth: "Truth is walking all the laws that have been brought to you by the spirit of the Grandfather Animals that came before me." She reassured the boy that Spirit grandfathers and grandmothers would provide spiritual help, sometimes through dreams or a vision, giving the passion and words to make a difference. She continued:

> I, Turtle, represent Woman, the giver of life—your Mother Earth, and your own mother who gave you life. I bring you the ways of your ancestors, who walked with these Laws. There is so much suffering today because the people have forgotten the Laws and are walking another path that has taken them into darkness.

When the human beings walk with the Seven Sacred Laws, then there will be peace . . . When you are able to do this, you will become free to live what your ancestors lived—*Minopimatiziwin*—a good life.

When he awoke, the boy returned to his grandfather and told the old man about what happened. After listening, the grandfather said:

It is now your choice whether to answer the call of Spirit, my Grandson. You are free to make your choice. The Seven Sacred Laws can make you free. If you live in opposition to these Laws, you will be out of balance. Your troubles as [humankind] began when you lost touch with the Earth, the Original Mother to all life. [Humankind] became cold in the heart and allowed [their] gift of the mind to overwhelm the other gifts. The mind lacked the spiritual foundation to guide its thoughts and actions. It was easy for the dark energies to seize control over the minds of men to destroy life by destroying the Earth. [Humankind] has yet to awaken from this nightmare [they are] in . . . Within the Earth sit the spirits of the Seven Grandfathers who can guide [humankind] to find [their] own spirit again. Only then will [they] wake up. [Humankind] must begin by going back to the land, your mother, who will help awaken anyone who searches for the light, for the truth. You have been given your vision, Grandson. What will be your choice?" (Courchene 2018)

Indeed, it is all of our choices. There is much wisdom to be drawn from these Seven Sacred Laws, but in the context of transcending Wihtiko systems, it is the deep thought into these laws that allows us to better understand our relationships to others, to creation, and to ourselves.

As previously defined, the Wihtiko concept can be understood as a "severe loss or abandonment of self-control, or the manipulative control of others; disconnect with or manipulation of reality; and abandonment, rejection or manipulation of relationship. The Wihtiko's attitude is that truth, reality, and others can be reduced to objects of self-serving power" (Chabot 2016, 84). However, it is with living the Seven Sacred Laws that we can know our place, purpose, and responsibilities within Creation. In understanding and living out these responsibilities, we can influence reform within the community and instill an understanding regarding the importance of relationships. Through this, we can transcend Wihtiko systems.

CONCLUSION

Awakening and transforming is an ongoing struggle. We can remain stuck, silent, isolated, conforming, codependent, seething within a Wihtiko system.

Or we can—lovingly and with curiosity—face our subconscious, deep-rooted conflicts, biases, fears, shame, rage, and defects. Albert Einstein observed, "When I change the way I think, the things I look at change" and moreover that "the consciousness that created the problem will not be the consciousness to solve it" (Einstein n.d.).

In the context of rebuilding Indigenous communities, a Navajo lawyer, professor, and former jurist, Raymond Austin, remarked:

> The revitalization process should motivate many modern Indians to relearn how to think like their ancestors or to "think like an Indian." When modern Indians begin "thinking like Indians" many problems on reservations will disappear . . . Alcoholism, drug abuse, domestic violence, diabetes, obesity and other social and physical ills, and poor educational achievement of Indian children, confront Indian leaders on a daily basis. Instead of looking inward for potential solutions to these problems, Indian leaders tend to look to the non-Indian world for remedies. Problems afflicting Indian peoples on reservations should be seen as prime opportunities for revitalizing, discussing and relearning tribal customs and traditions and applying them as community problem solving tools . . . three foundational [intertwined] doctrines that form the nucleus of this work are described as follows: hozhq (glossed as harmony, balance and peace); k'e (glossed as kinship unity through positive values) and k'ei (Navajo Kinship or clan system). (Austin 2009, xvii–xxii)

There is much depth in the statement to "think like an Indian." Hesitancy is warranted in disregarding this statement because of its Indigenous focus. The reality is that what Professor Austin is referring to is a truth with a universal application. Keep in mind, for instance, that the names for Indigenous nations such as "Anishinaabek" do not translate to "Indigenous" but simply to "Good People."

As we have learned "Indian" or Indigenous thought is really just about evolved human consciousness. Ancient peoples understood that humans must be spiritually formed and continuously guided to prevent becoming a Wihtiko, which unchecked, leads to a collective outbreak of dangerous minds, thoughts, and actions, creating full-blown Wihtiko systems. The call to Spirit is from cradle to grave. Families and communities are the nation's microcosm, determining what the nation will manifest. The ancients understood that survival turned on the effective transmission of these understandings. Story, song, dance, memory, language, art, ceremony, prayer, nature, identity, family, community, belonging, and humor are spirituality's transmitters, holding together life's complex web.

Upon reflecting on the Seven Sacred Laws and my own life's journey, I have learned a number of things that I try to live out. Hold ourselves and others accountable, even when we are afraid. Confront power with truth even if threatened. Enable spirituality; do not cow to cannibalization. Create your support system. Encourage individualism and freedom for every person to be authentic and true to self. Give credit to others and empower them to take action. Communicate openly, honestly, timely, directly. Listen and learn—we are not learning when talking; courage includes listening. Say what needs to be said, when it needs to be said, to whom, and how it needs to be said. Seek improvement, not perfection. Keep going, do not give up, get up. Nurture and live in Spirit. Help build a community that values open, useful interactions. Leave the parched field. Choose the field of flowers. Choose Creation and all that it encompasses.

NOTES

1. According to Johnson (1995, 243), Nana'boozoo was "the youngest son of Ae-pungishimook and Winonah. Some Anishinaubae people regard him as a Manitou; others see him as the all-man, all-woman archetypal human being. Nana'b'oozoo means well, but all too often he is prevented from fulfilling his intentions by the coarser side of his human nature—his passions, drives, whims, and emotions—just as many human beings are often prevented from attaining their purposes and discharging their responsibilities. Like many human beings, Nana'boozoo blunders along and sometimes he is successful. Nana'b'oozoo represents a caricatured understanding of human nature. He is not what he appears to be; his real character is hidden. Nana'b'oozoo himself does not see things as they really are. Despite his misdeeds and violations, perpetrated on his own family and on the world of birds, animals, insects and fish, and his profanation of ceremonies, Nana'b'oozoo . . . reflects the character of many people, timid and unwilling to take risks. Nana'b'oozoo represents that portion of humanity that often gives in to inner weaknesses and exemplifies what ought and what ought not to be done."

2. Wihtiko—defined xxvi, xxvii, xxiii (in accordance with usage by particular groups, the words "Windigo," "Wihtigo," "Weendigo," and "Wihtiko" are used interchangeably, have the same meaning and I will use Wihtiko).

3. Cecil Chabot, Algonquian refers to a broad cultural and linguistic family that includes the Penobscot, Mi'kmaq, Maliseet, Abenaki, Attikamekw, Montagnais, Innu, Naskapi, Cree, Chippewa, Ojibwa, Anishinabe, Algonquin, Blackfoot, and others as well. I use Cree, because there is no other term that easily captures the diverse but related Algonquian peoples this term encompasses, including the Iiyuuch, Mushkegowuk, and so on. I use Anishinabe, because it encompasses peoples that are closely related, both culturally and linguistically, including the Algonquin, Ojibwa, Chippewa, and so on.

4. Justice Denny Thomas, 1985 Sawridge Trust v Alberta (Public Trustee), 2017 ABQB 530, at para 149.

REFERENCES

Alexander, Bruce. 2008. *The Globalization of Addictions: A Study in Poverty of the Spirit*. Oxford: Oxford University Press.

Austin, Raymond. 2009. Navajo Courts and *Navajo Common Law: A Tradition of Tribal Self-Governance*. Regents of the University of Minnesota Indigenous Americas.

Barker, Joanne. 2011. *Native Acts: Law Recognition, and Cultural Authenticity*. Durham, NC: Duke University Press.

Berry, Wendell. 1992. *Sex, Economy, Freedom and Community*. New York, NY: Pantheon Books.

Chabot, Cecil. 2016. *Cannibal Wihtiko: Finding Native-Newcomer Common Ground*. Ph.D. Thesis. University of Ottawa. https://ruor.uottawa.ca/bitstream/10393/33452 /1/Chabot_Cecil_2016_thesis.pdf.

Courchene, Dave nee Nii Gaani Aki Inini (Leading Earth Man). 2018. *A Story of the Seven Sacred Laws*, October 17, 2018. https://www.culturalsurvival.org/news/st ory-seven-sacred-laws-0.

Crazy Horse. https://www.azquotes.com/author/65353-Crazy_Horse.

Deloria, Vine. 2003. *God is Red: A Native View on Religion*, 3rd ed. Golden: Fulcrum Publishing.

Einstein, Albert. n.d. https://www.goodreads.com/quotes/1271307-when-you-chang e-the-way-you-look-at-things-the; https://www.goodreads.com/quotes/320600-we -can-not-solve-our-problems-with-the-same-level.

Evers, Robert Daniel. 2018. "Is Life in a 'Post Truth' World Sustainable?" *A Review of Post Truth by Lee McIntyre*. MIT Press in Pop Matters, March 20. https://www .popmatters.com/post-truth-lee-mcintyre-2549370346.html.

Galanda, Gabe, and Ryan Dreveskracht. 2015. "Curing the Tribal Disenrollment Epidemic: In Search of a Remedy." *Arizona Law Review*, 57(2), 383.

Johnson, Basil. 1995. *The Manitous: The Spiritual World of the Ojibway*. New York, NY: Harper Collins Publisher.

Lady Gaga. 2019. "Interview with Oprah Winfrey, Published November, 2019." *Elle Magazine*. https://www.elle.com/culture/music/a29683686/lady-gaga-haus-labor atories-elle-interview/.

Lancer, Darlene. 2016. *Codependency Stages of Disease and Recovery*. https://www .whatiscodependency.com/codependency-addiction-stages-of-disease-and-recovery/.

Maté, Gabor. 2012 edition. *In the Realm of Hungry Ghosts: Close Encounters with Addiction*. Toronto: Vintage Canada, a division of Random House Canada Limited.

Redekop, V. N. 2002. *From Violence to Blessing: How an Understanding of Deep-Rooted Conflict Can Open Paths to Reconciliation*. Ottawa: Novalis.

———. 2019. "Public-Spirited Leadership and Administrative Blessing." *Presentation at the European Centre for Peace and Development International Conference on "The UN Agenda 2030 to Transform the World,"* Belgrade City Hall, 25 October.

Steinmeier, Frank-Walter. May 8, 2020. *75th Anniversary of the End of WW11*. https:/ /www.bundespraesident.de/SharedDocs/Reden/EN/Frank-Walter-Steinmeier/Rede n/2020/05/200508-75th-anniversary-World-War-II.html.

Schaef, Anne Wilson, and Diane Fassel. 1988. *The Addictive Organization.* San Francisco, CA: Harper and Row.

Seattle, Chief. n.d. https://quoteinvestigator.com/2013/01/22/borrow-earth/.

Sitting Bull. https://www.azquotes.com/quote/704166.

Truth and Reconciliation Commission of Canada. 2015. *Honouring the Truth, Reconciling for the Future: Summary of the Final Report of the Truth and Reconciliation Commission of Canada.* http://www.trc.ca/assets/pdf/Honouring_t he_Truth_Reconciling_for_the_Future_July_23_2015.pdf.

Whitfield, Charles. 1991. *Co-Dependence Healing the Human Condition: The New Paradigm for Helping Professionals and People in Recovery.* Boca Raton, FL: Health Communications Inc.

Zakaria, Fareed. 2018. "Review of Post-Truth by Lee McIntyre." *CNN.* https://mi tpress.mit.edu/books/post-truth.

Zuboff, Shoshana. 2019. "The Age of Surveillance Capital. The Goal is to Automate Us." *Interview in the Guardian*, January 20, 2019.

Chapter 14

Transforming "Wicked" Problems in an Integral Manner

The Case of Fly-In Indigenous Communities

Robert Logie

Watkins and Wilber (2015) define a wicked problem as being multidimensional and involving multiple stakeholders, causes, symptoms, and solutions. Wicked problems are complex—constantly evolving and resist simple solutions. Fly-In Indigenous Communities (FIICs), defined as communities that are only accessible by air for at least part of the year, face wicked challenges related to remoteness such as chronic social problems and lack of economic opportunity. By definition, wicked problems must be addressed holistically. By examining the Canadian media debate on FIICs from 2012 to 2017, I will demonstrate that the absence of an integral approach, including an understanding of complex systems, stymies the emergence of a positive way forward for FIICs in Canada.

This is a matter of concern for this author, who situates himself as a member of Canada's Settler society. The author is a non-Indigenous person of primarily United Kingdom (Scottish and English) ancestry, who now lives on unceded Algonquin territory. The author, his family, and ancestors have enjoyed considerable economic benefits from colonization, but also bear responsibility for the harm it has done to First Nations, Inuit, and Métis in Canada. This chapter seeks to contribute to scholarship on reconciliation between Indigenous and non-Indigenous peoples in Canada by contributing to the debate on FIICs. While a discussion of specific policy options is beyond the scope of this paper, the ultimate goal of this research is to find a way forward that enables Canada's Indigenous peoples (many of them in FIICs) to preserve their language, culture, and connection to the land.

The analysis will show that the media debate was unproductive in that the two sides "talked past each other" and were unable to move to a discussion of concrete, viable policy solutions. This points to the need for an integral approach that creatively takes all perspectives into account in an attempt to find solutions that transcend them all. The lack of traction on the issue of remoteness has implications for efforts to promote reconciliation with and promote well-being and cultural survival of isolated Indigenous peoples. It also points to the need for structural change alongside efforts to pursue reconciliation with Indigenous peoples. This study on Canadian FIICs should also be instructive for those who face wicked problems in other parts of the world.

REMOTENESS AS A WICKED PROBLEM

According to Natural Resources Canada (NRCAN), there are 170 remote Indigenous communities in Canada (CCMEO 2017), of which about 111 are "fly-in" communities that lack year-round road access. However, even though it clearly identifies fly-in communities, NRCAN's Remote Communities Energy Database sees remoteness primarily in terms of access to Canada's energy grid (NRCAN website). In addition, definitions of what constitutes year-round road access or a permanent Indigenous community differ.[1] Finally, due to Canada's vast geography, some Indigenous communities are so far North that they are economically remote even if they have road access. Not only does Canada have many Indigenous groups, it has more FIICs than any other country in the world.

Remote communities face practical challenges such as isolation and high food, fuel, and transportation costs. These are compounded by social and cultural challenges manifest in such things as high rates of youth suicide and erosion of language and culture. Unlike cities and communities in Canada's South, for political, historical, and cultural reasons, many of Canada's FIICs are in locations that are not economically viable. A joint paper of the Harvard Project and the Native Nations Institute for Leadership, Management, and Policy notes that "many First Nations in Canada have been left with miniscule land bases, or are located far from markets and transportation systems" (Cornell 2006, 20). In addition to a lack of arable land or resources that can be profitably exploited, most FIICs lack infrastructure to access global economic opportunities, including high-speed Internet connections. In Nunavut, many resources are located on the interior of Baffin Island, and would require expensive infrastructure to make use of them.

Although Indigenous peoples lived as hunter-gatherers in northern Canada for approximately 15,000 years, the process of colonization and sedentarization has created a profoundly new situation. Remoteness therefore constitutes a wicked challenge: many economic strategies and programs designed for Canada's South will have limited effectiveness in FIICs. Because there is no clear solution at present, the social and economic challenges facing FIICs could even be considered "super-wicked."

To better understand the challenges facing FIICs and the reason that the media debate was unproductive, the first section of this paper will introduce two meta-theories—broad frameworks that give us concepts to sort out and connect a wide array of perspectives. First will be quadrant analysis, which is part of Ken Wilber's *Integral Theory*. Quadrant analysis will provide a way to connect interior phenomena such as culture and identity with external aspects such as concrete economic challenges. Quadrant analysis is supplemented by a multilevel analysis to determine if issues are being discussed on the same level (e.g., high-level drivers versus on-the-ground outcomes such as a high rate of suicide in a community). Second will be *Complexity Theory*, which addresses situations in which there are many interconnected and constantly changing variables. These two meta-theories will be used in the second section to analyze the Canadian media debate on FIICs.

On one side of the debate is the Dominant Discourse camp, which emerged after the Royal Commission on Aboriginal Peoples (RCAP). This camp emphasized Indigenous self-government and identity and the harm done by colonialism. The other side, the Challenger Discourse camp, focused on social and economic problems, putative shortcomings in the governance of FIICs, and the concrete challenges of remoteness. A third section applies *Integral Theory* and *Complexity Theory* to show that the two sides in the public debate "talked past one another" as they spoke to different quadrants and levels of reality. The fourth section addresses the fact that the debate generally left out the voices of Indigenous people in FIICs, suggests ways to reframe the discussion on FIICs, and offers ideas for furthering efforts toward reconciliation that could provide a basis for hope.

A THEORETICAL COMPASS TO ORIENT OURSELVES

This section will provide an overview of two meta-theories—*Integral Theory* and *Complexity Theory*—that we will use to provide a "breadth and depth" analysis of the media debate on FIICs from 2012 to 2017.

Integral Analysis

Quadrant analysis, based on Ken Wilber's *Integral Theory*, divides reality into four quadrants. The Y-axis makes a distinction between singular aspects of reality and plural (group) reality, and the X-axis makes a distinction between the subjective (interior) world—left hand (LH)—and the empirically verifiable exterior world—right hand (RH) (see figure 14.1). For example, theories

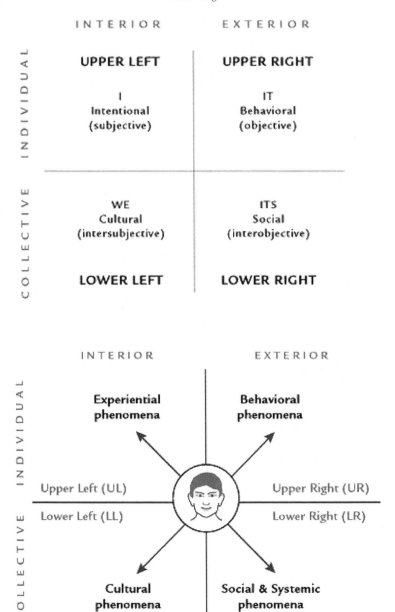

Figure 14.1 The Four Quadrants of Integral Theory. (Esbjorn-Hargens 2009; see also Wilber 2000 and McGuigan and Popp 2016).

and facts related to individual behavior and outcomes are in the upper right quadrant, while economic and political systems would pertain to the lower right (LR) quadrant. Most research disciplines, analytical paradigms, and philosophies focus primarily on one quadrant of reality. However, in the case of hard-to-solve "wicked" social problems, Wilber points out that it is important to look at all quadrants to understand reality in all its complexity.

As can be seen in the second diagram in figure 14.1, in each quadrant there are lines of development from the center toward greater complexity. Wilber, along with McGuigan and Popp, see a key line of development expressed by consciousness—greater development means a greater capacity to deal with complexity. For our purposes, quadrant analysis can be supplemented by multilevel analysis drawn from research on the social determinants of health (SDoH) to provide an integral "breadth and depth" understanding of the debate on FIICs. Reading and Wien (2013) took the various SDoH and other social outcomes and assigned them to three levels (see CSDH 2008; Raphael 2009). The first, the *proximate* level, deals with the most immediate factors such as health behaviors, employment and income, educational attainment, and food security. As such factors are mostly observable behaviors that can be captured by statistics, they fall on the RH of Ken Wilber's schema. However, they would also have a corresponding LH reality related to people's subjective (internal) *experience* of the effects of health challenges such as diabetes and lack of adequate nutrition. *Intermediate* determinants of health consist of healthcare and education systems, community infrastructure, resources and capacities, and environmental policies. Such policies and systems would mostly appear in the LR quadrant (RH side) in Wilber's analysis, again with corresponding experiential LH side realities.

Another *intermediate* determinant of health is cultural continuity, which would fall in the LL quadrant (interior plural). Finally, *distal* determinants are high-level factors that can (but do not always) construct both *intermediate* and *proximate* determinants. These include colonialism and systems of social exclusion, attitudes of deep-seated racism, and the need for a sense of agency and control or self-determination (Reading and Wien 2013, 22). *Distal* determinants generally operate at the group level and would fall under the bottom two quadrants (LL and LR) in Wilber's schema. The fact that they fall under the plural/group quadrants reflects the fact that distal drivers are more complex, involving more people and aspects of reality.

With regards to self-determination and governance for Indigenous peoples, institutional arrangements (e.g., between the federal government and Indigenous groups, including the reserve system) would appear in the LR quadrant, while the feeling of greater empowerment and control that Indigenous people derive from self-government would appear in the LL quadrant of reality. To make it easier for the reader, from this point onward quadrant analysis will primarily focus on the difference between the LH (interior) and RH (exterior) *sides*, rather than specific *quadrants* (e.g., LL vs. LR).

This paper deploys these two theories to provide an "all-quadrant, multi-level" perspective of the challenges faced by FIICs and policy proposals to deal with those challenges.

Complexity Theory and the Potential for Emergence

The paper employs tools from *Complexity Theory* including complex adaptive systems (or CASs for short—for an overview of CASs see Kauffman 1995, 2008; Meadows 1997). A CAS is a complex group of interrelated parts that is adaptive in that the parts spontaneously reorder themselves into a new structure (see Theise, "Harnessing Feedback Loops in Complex Social Systems," *Transforming*, for examples). Redekop (2011) argues that the many actors and variables involved in a deep-rooted conflict can only be understood in terms of a CAS.

According to Naresh Singh ("Development as Emergent Creativity," *Transforming*, 402), CASs contain "many interdependent but autonomous agents interacting with each other and dynamically adapting, co-evolving and self-organizing over time and space." CASs are like a flock of geese whose movements cannot be predicted by simple linear models. Positive and negative feedback loops are an important feature of *Complexity Theory* (Theise, "Harnessing Principles of Complex Systems," *Transforming,* 378). Positive feedback loops exacerbate trends in a system, but their effects can be counteracted by negative feedback loops that bring the system back into balance. A common example of a negative feedback loop is a thermostat that stops a furnace when the temperature of a house becomes too hot (Meadows 1997).

A typical CAS is balanced between stasis and chaos. *Criticality* refers to the number of elements in a system and the number of ways that they can be combined. Figure 14.2 shows that on the line of criticality opportunities for "emergence" (or "emergent creativity"), whereby something new emerges from the system that transforms it, are maximized (see Kauffman 2008; Redekop 2011, 2015). A related insight from *Complexity Theory* is that a necessary condition for emergence is requisite variety or requisite complexity. To be truly adaptive, there should be a sufficient number of nodes or connections in a system, and the complexity of that system should be on a par with the complexity of external systems that it confronts (Allen, Maguire, and McKelvey 2011, 279; see also Widdowson 2008, 2014).

As we have seen, *Integral Theory* provides *"breadth and depth"* analysis, highlighting the quadrants and levels of reality that policies should address. *Complexity Theory* provides additional tools for assessing wicked problems, including the ability to identify feedback loops. The two meta-theories can be employed in a synergistic fashion. Suppose that a policy proposal is put

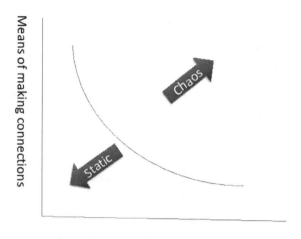

Diversity of Resources

Figure 14.2   Criticality. from Redekop 2015.

forward to address a feedback loop that is exacerbating social problems in many FIICs. *Integral Analysis* can then be applied to determine if the proposed policy operates on the right level and addresses the appropriate quadrants of reality, and therefore has realistic prospects of neutralizing that feedback loop. Due to structural difference between FIICs and cities in southern Canada, economic and social policies may need to focus on different feedback loops that primarily operate on different levels or in different quadrants of reality.

Another policy-relevant insight from CAS is that FIICs have *fewer connections* to the Settler society and the global economy than are available in cities in southern Canada (Theise, "Harnessing Principles of Complex Social Systems," *Transforming*). This puts them at a significant economic disadvantage and makes it more difficult to attain requisite variety so that new solutions to the challenges of remoteness are more likely to emerge.

In the next section, I assess the media debate on FIICs between proponents of the Dominant and Challenger Discourse camps from 2012 to 2017, with particular emphasis on the issue of remoteness.

THE DEBATE ON FIICS

After showing how the Dominant Discourse evolved, I will provide a detailed analysis of the Challenger Discourse. This will be followed by a similar overview and analysis of the Dominant Discourse response to points made by the Challenger group.[2]

Evolution of the Dominant Discourse

Historically, Canada's approach to Indigenous peoples was premised on assimilation. Alan Cairns points out that ironically, assimilation was the strategy of progressive parties such as the New Democratic Party (NDP), its predecessor the Canadian Commonwealth Federation (CCF), and the left wing of the Liberal Party. Progressives felt that separate treatment and federal jurisdiction were not in the interest of Indigenous peoples (Cairns 2000, 56). The debate on Indigenous issues in Canada has shifted dramatically in recent decades, beginning with widespread rejection of the Trudeau Government's 1969 White Paper, which was based on the policy of assimilation of Indigenous peoples (Cairns 2000, 65–66). The Report of the Royal Commission on Aboriginal Peoples (RCAP), released in 1996, was based on parallelism, with Indigenous groups seen as separate from the Settler society and involved in nation-to-nation negotiations with it. The context for RCAP (1991) was the 1990 Oka/Kanehsata:ke crisis during which the Mohawks of Kanehsata:ke resisted the decision of the municipality of Oka, Quebec, to expand a golf course onto their traditional graveyard. Redekop (2002, 2016b) has provided a balanced analysis of the crisis, focusing on (LH side) identity needs. The international embarrassment for Canada from the Oka crisis and the growing gap between Indigenous and non-Indigenous living standards and educational attainment increased pressure on the federal government to change its policies toward Indigenous peoples. While the vast majority of its recommendations were not implemented, the release of the RCAP represented a profound shift. Since then, an increased focus on Indigenous self-government and identity politics favored by the Left have become the Dominant Discourse on Indigenous issues, and assimilationist approaches have been marginalized.

The Left's vision of two nations living side by side is based on the two-row wampum, which is thought to have been presented by Iroquois Mohawks to the Dutch during the negotiation of the 1613 Tawagonshi Treaty (Widdowson 2019, 26–27, 66). According to Alan Cairns (2000), the two-nation theory made more sense in the earlier stages of colonization as there was less of a power and demographic imbalance than at present. Before the mid-1880s the Settler population was small, the fur trade in which Indigenous peoples played a key role was still an important part of the economy, and the colonial powers needed Indigenous peoples "as friends and military allies" (King 2012; Cairns 2000, 142). However, the current power imbalance between the federal government and small FIICs is unlikely to provide a context for a true "nation-to-nation" relationship. While the report of the Truth and Reconciliation Commission (TRC 2015) stresses the importance of the nation-to-nation paradigm, its terms of reference contain only a few weak recommendations to correct this structural imbalance. In practice, the Left's program involves a limited form of self-government for Indigenous communities that does not include all the functions of a modern nation-state. The Yellowhead Institute refers to the transfer of authority in a few areas such as education and family services as "municipalization" (King and Pasternak 2018, 13). Catherine Twinn points out that, under the guise of supporting self-government and self-determination, well-meaning members of the Settler society can end up enabling and empowering addictive and predatory governance systems ("Warring with Wihtiko in Real Time," *Transforming*), with serious repercussions for members of those Indigenous communities.

The Challenger Discourse and the "Move South" Solution

This subsection considers the arguments of representatives of the political Right such as author Tom Flanagan and specifically a series of articles from 2012 to 2017 by two journalists who challenged the Dominant Discourse with regards to FIICs. The first is Jonathan Kay, the former editor-in-chief of *The Walrus* (2014–2017) and of the *National Post* for which he continues to be a prominent columnist and blogger. The second, Scott Gilmore, is a former diplomat who writes and posts blogs for *Maclean's* magazine. In their articles, the journalists make two main arguments: first, that social problems and lack of economic opportunities that FIICs face are difficult to resolve due to their remoteness; second, that governance of FIICs is inadequate and incentives are not aligned with the requirements of the capitalist system. Kay and Gilmore see challenges that Indigenous communities face from remoteness as distinct from the historic effects of colonialism.

Social Problems (RH Side/Proximate Level) Driven by Remoteness

Proponents of the Challenger Discourse point out that every social measure of well-being, including employment and educational attainment, is approximately 50 percent better for Indigenous people in cities than it is in remote communities in Canada's North. Citing Statistics Canada data, Gilmore observes that Indigenous people living in Canadian cities are 40 percent less likely to commit suicide. Indigenous people living in Canadian cities are more likely to have jobs and live longer (Gilmore 2016a, b). According to the 2011 census, only 42 percent of Indigenous youth on reserve aged twenty to twenty-four had graduated from high school, compared with 70 percent living off-reserve (mainly in cities) and 90 percent of Canadians as a whole (figure 14.3). While the 2016 census showed a slight improvement (48 percent, 75 percent, and 92 percent, respectively), the relationship that Gilmore cited remains: high school graduation rates are 50 percent higher for Indigenous people off-reserve (e.g., in cities in the South) than in (often

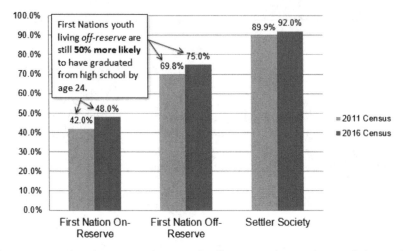

First Nations youth living *off-reserve* are still **50% more likely** to have graduated from high school by age 24.

Figure 14.3 **Education Rates of On- and Off-Reserve First Nations and the Settler Society.** Source: 2011 and 2016 Canadina Censuses.

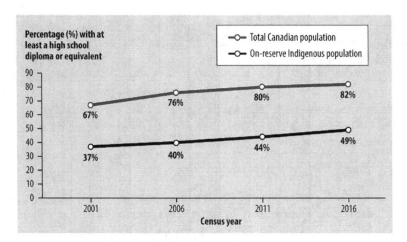

Figure 14.4 **Education Rates of On-Reserve First Nations Versus the Settler Society: 2001–2016.** *Sources*: 2011, 2006, 2011, and 2016 Canadian Censuses and calculations by John Richards (2017) and in Robertson (2018).

remote) reserves (Figure 14.3). Furthermore, the 2001, 2006, 2011 and 2016 national censuses show that the gap in high school graduation rates between on-reserve First Nations and the wider Settler Society has remained consistently high over time (Figure 14.4). For purposes of comparison, according to Inuit Tapiriit Kanatami (ITK 2018), 45 percent of Inuit in Canada reported having a high school diploma in 2016.

A high school diploma is now a requirement for even the most basic employment in Canada. Increased high school graduation rates would improve life chances and social outcomes for Inuit, First Nations, and Métis youth, assuming the availability of employment opportunities upon graduation. According to Richards (2017), at the current rate as measured by Census Canada, it will take thirty-five years to close the education gap between on-reserve Indigenous youth and the Canadian average.

However, the situation may be even worse than this. A pair of audits by Canada's auditor general released in May 2018 found that the education gap between Indigenous and non-Indigenous Canadians has not improved in the last fifteen years. The audit charged that the Department of Indigenous Services Canada did not even measure the education gap on reserves and that the department's method of calculating on-reserve (and off-reserve) high school graduation rates was flawed because it did not account for students who dropped out before Grade 12 (Robertson 2018; Auditor General of Canada 2018). In *Integral Theory*, such data are situated on RH side of reality, and in multilevel analysis it would be located in the *proximate* level of reality. The lack of progress on educational attainment combined with the fact that modern jobs are increasingly knowledge intensive suggests that the education and employment gap between FIICs and the Canadian mainstream may be widening. Failure to pay attention to (RH side) empirical data could lead policymakers to underestimate the challenges or overestimate the economic potential of FIICs, and devise inadequate policy responses.

Substandard Governance and Inappropriate Institutional Arrangements for FIICs

In their articles, Gilmore and especially Kay decried the poor governance of northern Indigenous reserves and the waste of (mostly) federal tax dollars. In a 2013 (b) article, Kay suggested that the housing crisis in Attawapiskat was partly caused by mismanagement of housing funds by that First Nation, and that poor governance went a long way to explaining why 44 percent of housing on Indigenous reserves is inadequate. In the media debate, analysts on the Right often argued that problems facing FIICs originate from poor (RH side/*intermediate* level) institutional arrangements, such as the fact that it is the federal rather than the provincial or municipal level of government that is responsible for FIICs. Kay (2013d) noted that, as they fall under federal jurisdiction, houses built on reserves do not have to conform to provincial building codes. In an impassioned letter to the Ontario College of Physicians, Murry Trussler noted that even though the Kasechewan reserve is on a flood plain, houses on the reserve are often built with plywood (not concrete) basements and immediately become contaminated with mold (Kay 2013c). Trussler recommended that Indigenous peoples be able to access Provincial Public Health services, which would improve health care on remote reserves (but not for communities in Nunavut, which is a federal territory) as health care is normally provided by provinces in Canada (ibid.). Cairns (2000) notes the many governance problems with the "parallel" model implied by the pursuit of Indigenous nationhood that are overlooked by the prevailing orthodoxy.

"Welfarism" and Lack of Alignment with Global Capitalism

Challenger Discourse authors such as Jonathan Kay (2103c) suggest that serious social problems such as family violence, suicide, and substance abuse are exacerbated by welfare dependency that erodes both self-esteem and the work ethic (both internal, LH side concerns). Employment is particularly important for the self-esteem and well-being of young men and for healthy communities more generally (Kay 2016a, b, see also Légaré 2009).

Flanagan (2008) and others describe the advantages of the capitalist system and the importance of integration into the Canadian economy (RH side) so that Indigenous people can fully reap its benefits. Kay suggests that in a capitalist nation such as Canada, "real dignity" for Indigenous communities can only come from knowing that they are not dependent on others "for what they have" (Kay 2013). Kay (2012, 2013b) also states that allowing greater property rights on reserves would, through economic incentives, foster personal responsibility (an interior, LH side value). However, Indigenous communities fear that any move toward private property on reserves is part of an effort by the Settler society to seize their resources and make it impossible for those Indigenous communities to pursue land claims in the future (King 2012). Many on the Left suggest that the Right's concern for Indigenous peoples to benefit from private property should have come much earlier. In the past, the Settler society viewed land given to Indigenous peoples as economically unproductive space. Prime Minister Laurier passed legislation allowing any reserve close to a town with 8,000 people to be moved (generally to a more economically marginal or remote location) if it was deemed to be in the interest of the Canadian public (Coulthard 2014, 174). The TRC (2015) has documented cases where this happened. However, in arguing for increased private property on reserves, Kay (2013a) demonstrates a lack of understanding of the cultural (LH side) and economic/institutional (RH side) reasons that Indigenous groups might want to maintain communal property ownership as well as the historical reasons for preventing the alienation (private selling) of reserve lands.

Frustration over Lack of Progress in FIICs

Among Challenger Discourse authors, there was a palpable frustration at the lack of economic and social progress in FIICs in recent years, despite the implementation of (LH side-oriented) policy proposals rooted in the Dominant Discourse and increased federal government spending. In his article on the problems of Attawapiskat (2016c), Scott Gilmore pointed out that the federal government ministers have been charged with making "real progress" on the challenges facing Indigenous people for three generations. In his articles, Gilmore stressed that it is problematic to assert that increased federal government spending and improved social services will solve the problems of FIICs, for two reasons. First, it does not address the challenges of creating employment in remote areas. Second, it is far more difficult and expensive to provide some services in remote areas. It should be noted that the Left's complaint that FIICs are underfunded is not true in all cases. In an article in the Canadian Medical Association Journal, Young and Chatwood (2011) found that not only were Nunavut's per capita health expenditures 2.5 times greater than the Canadian average, they were the highest in the world (see also Exner-Pirot 2012).

The "Move South" Solution and Its Limitations

In the debate on FIICs, the Right does not propose an economic development strategy except to pursue resource development opportunities where they exist and for residents to move South to find work and gain access to better services (see Kay 2013a, b, c and Gilmore 2016a, b). In a 2016 (a) newspaper article, Jonathan Kay stated bluntly that those living in communities such as Attawapiskat "are doomed to exist in a hellish [*sic*] limbo." Gilmore (2016b) suggested that for people living in communities such as La Loche in Northern Saskatchewan,[3] "the single most effective step they can take to immediately improve their health, education, safety and income is to leave." However, Gilmore (2016c) was careful to clarify that any decision to relocate to cities in the South should be a matter of "choice, not compulsion."

Proponents of the Dominant Discourse often respond that some remote Indigenous communities are doing well economically, implying that the situation of other FIICs could be improved as well. For example, the northern Cree in Quebec have a unique arrangement with the province of Quebec due to the James Bay dam (which flooded much of their traditional hunting grounds) and the Mikisew Cree of Fort Chipeweyan, Alberta, have developed companies that do business in the oil sands. However, such communities generally have two advantages: exceptional economic opportunities (in the North these are generally related to resources or, in the case of the Cree, hydropower) and good leadership that is creatively pursuing those opportunities. The "move south" advice of challengers on the Right such as Kay and Gilmore has to do with FIICs facing very serious social ills that do *not* possess such economic opportunities.

Proponents of the Challenger Discourse are aware of the need of people in FIICs to preserve their culture and connection to the land (a LH side concern), but this is not a primary concern for them. For example, in Maclean's article in 2016 (b), Gilmore muses that Indigenous people who move South should be provided with support so that they can "visit their home reserve."

The Right's "Move South" solution is problematic because it overlooks two factors rooted in the LH (interior) side of reality. First, Indigenous peoples of Canada, largely descended from hunter-gatherers, differ from other groups in modern Canadian society in that they have much stronger spiritual and cultural ties to land. Many believe that Indigenous communities need to survive in their ancestral lands to provide a kind of "cultural home base" in order for any kind of Indigenous diaspora culture in Canadian cities to thrive. Furthermore, Indigenous languages are stronger and still being spoken at home in many FIICs, and tend to be lost within two generations of moving to a city in Canada's South (Kishigami 2002, see also Norris 1998, 2014). For example, Statistics Canada (2019) reports that in 2016, 65.3 percent of the population of Nunuvat considered Inuktitut as their mother tongue, and 73.8 percent reported speaking Inuktitut at home on a regular basis. In the absence of a viable strategy for preserving their culture and connection to the land, many FIICs may see an invitation to "move South" as the latest iteration of Canada's historic policy of forced assimilation of Indigenous peoples.

A second factor that is likely to cause residents of FIICs to resist major policy innovations such as relocation is the effect intergenerational trauma (in Integral Theory, a LH side concern). This includes the shock of colonial contact, past coercive policies including forced relocations, the intergenerational effects of residential schools, and economic shifts such as the collapse of the fur and sealskin trade, all of which have had lasting consequences for Indigenous people in the North. Most residents of FIICs are likely to resist calls from the political Right or any other constituency to relocate to cities in the South with better employment prospects. Individuals and communities would have to consent to any such program. This points to the need for genuine healing of past trauma and reconciliation and an improved dialogue with the Canadian Settler society.

The next section will consider challenges to the Dominant Discourse on FIICs by authors associated with the political Right such as Kay and Gilmore.

The Response of the Dominant Discourse

In this section, I examine the arguments of authors representing the Dominant Discourse (political Left). Rather than addressing Challenger Discourse arguments about remoteness, the Dominant Discourse camp generally focused on the politics of identity and the need to improve services in FIICs.

Accusations of Racism and Colonialism

In the debate on FIICs, the Left doubled down on "the politics of identity" and the focus on LH side issues. Authors on the Left generally saw both Gilmore's "move South" exhortation and the Right's criticism of conditions in FIICs more generally as based on racism, colonialist attitudes, and a policy of assimilation (Vowel 2016a, b; Wilt 2016; Elliot et al. 2017; see Kay 2012; Gilmore 2016b). In this sense the public debate on FIICs was characterized by partisanship and, in the case of the Left, often harsh invective and ad hominem attacks (see Wilt 2016; Vowel 2016a).

Failure to Respond to Arguments about Remoteness

Authors on the Left did not take seriously the Right's arguments with respect to remoteness. They either ignored the issue or they advanced weak or informal arguments that did not really address the connection between remoteness and social and economic problems faced by FIICs. In response to Scott Gilmore's articles in *MacLean's* magazine in early 2016 (a, b), both journalist Vowel (2016a) and lawyers Maggie Wente[4], Michael McClurg, and Bryce Edwards (at the time working at former Ontario Premier Bob Rae's Aboriginal law firm, OKT) employed the same argument: that moving south is not a solution for people in remote Indigenous communities because "urban-dwelling Indigenous people still lag behind" (Wente 2016). However, this does not address the Challenger Discourse argument that Indigenous people living in or near southern cities have better health and educational outcomes than those in FIICs. Statistics on educational attainment from the 2011 and 2016 Canadian censuses support Gilmore's argument (see figure 14.3).

Doubling Down on Identity Politics and Increased Government Spending

In her response to Gilmore's January 2016 article about La Loche, Saskatchewan, Vowel (2016) pointed to a recent decision of the Canadian Human Rights Tribunal (CHRT). The CHRT (2016) had found that child and family services for First Nations children and families living on reserve and those in the Yukon were underfunded relative to the South. Cindy Blackstock points out that the federal government spends less on education per child on reserve than their provincial counterparts (Morin 2017). The call for greater spending on services was taken up by Bob Rae in a February 2016 Globe and Mail op-ed, and in a blog by Wente, McClurg, and Edwards (2016) later that month. In response to Gilmore's June 2017 column on Northern Indigenous communities, four Indigenous authors (Elliot et al. 2017) stressed the need to look at "root causes" of challenges faced by Indigenous communities outlined in the RCAP and TRC reports,[5]

which presumably refer to LH side (interior) and *distal* issues such as racism, gender discrimination, and colonialism. The authors suggested that
after attaining "viable solutions" and improving government services in
areas such as water and policing, it would be possible to address issues such
as unemployment rates (ibid.). However, they present no examples of FIICs
where this approach has worked.

A BREADTH AND DEPTH ANALYSIS: PEOPLE
TALKING PAST ONE ANOTHER

In the debate on FIICs, both the Left and the Right agreed that social outcomes and life chances of Indigenous people living in FIICs are poor and
should be improved. However, while the Right focused on the market
economy and the challenges of remoteness, proponents of the Left assume
that a focus on identity (LH side) issues combined with increased federal
government spending (RH) could resolve those problems. Analyzing both the
Dominant Discourse and that of the Challengers will reveal how each group
was talking past the other.

"Breadth and Depth" Analysis of the Dominant Discourse

The Dominant Discourse based on the politics of recognition has gained
momentum and become the new orthodoxy over the past twenty years even
as chronic social problems affecting FIICs have worsened. Peter Sutton
(2009, 7–8, 41, 69) notes that, largely due to the lack of improvement in
social challenges such as violence and substance abuse in remote Indigenous
communities, the "Liberal Consensus" (similar to the Dominant Discourse)
in Australia began to break down in the mid-2000s. However, during the
public debate in Canada from 2012 to 2017, which did not lead to a serious
discussion on the challenges facing FIICs, Challenger Discourse arguments
did not gain traction. It is reasonable to assume that the Dominant Discourse
will remain in the ascendant for another ten to fifteen years before it faces a
serious challenge.

   In terms of quadrant analysis, due to a focus on LH side issues to the detriment of (RH) political economy concerns, the Left has difficulty "seeing"
the limitations of a model based on limited self-government in a context of
remoteness and continued economic dependency on the federal government.
Despite attaining self-government in 1999, Nunavut has not made progress on a range of social problems, as would be predicted by the Dominant
Discourse model. In fact, outcomes in areas such as education have worsened
(see Légaré 2009; Hicks 2015; Loukacheva 2016).

With regards to multilevel analysis, it has been shown that the Left prefers to focus on *distal* issues such as colonialism and intergenerational trauma.[6] While appearing to give it the high ground in the debate, the Left's lack of focus on the *intermediate* and *proximate* levels has two drawbacks. First, unless (RH side/*proximate* and *intermediate* level) factors such as remoteness, lack of employment opportunities, and welfarism are taken into account, it is difficult to develop a holistic analysis of the significant social and economic challenges faced by remote communities. The distal layer is too far removed to assess lower-level feedback loops (from CAS) that are aggravating wicked social and economic challenges for FIICs.

Second, the policy levers available to the federal government of Canada—which the Left insists should take responsibility for the challenges faced by FIICs—can only address the *intermediate* and *proximate* factors in the near term. Finally, from the standpoint of *Complexity Theory*, it is problematic that proponents of the Dominant Discourse place so much emphasis on high-level (*distal*) intervention points such as "decolonization." Meadows (1997) notes that mindsets and paradigms are the hardest part of a system to change, but problems such as child abuse in FIICs require immediate action.

"Breadth and Depth" Analysis of the Challenger Discourse

Gilmore and Kay both suggested that people in FIICs that do not have an economic base should consider moving South to get access to jobs and better services. In their analysis, they are far more comfortable discussing "external" (RH side) behavioral issues and political and economic factors. Insofar as they address LH side issues (beyond addressing the personal trauma of those in FIICs), they tend to write about the values that underpin the capitalist economic system (Kay 2012—see discussion on private property) or the Settler state (Kay 2013a; Gilmore 2016a). The failure to address LH side factors such as historical trauma and the need for cultural preservation of Indigenous groups combined with the tendency to downplay *distal* factors such as the legacy of colonialism (see Elliot 2017) represents a serious weakness in the analysis of Challenger Discourse authors.

A "breadth and depth" analysis of the media debate on FIICs from 2012 to 2017 has shown that the Left and Right talked past one another and addressed different levels and quadrants of reality (Table 14.1). The media debate failed to generate new, viable, and integrative solutions to the serious economic and social problems faced by FIICs. Predictably, the Left doubled down on the politics of identity and called for (often justified) increases in government spending on services in FIICs. Proponents of the Right called for members of FIICs to "move South" to gain access to jobs and better services but did not otherwise put forward an economic

Table 14.1   The Political Right and Left "Talk Past One Another" When Discussing Fly-In Indigenous Communities

Level/Quadrant	LH Quadrants	RH Quadrants
Distal	Colonialism, entrenched racism, intergenerational trauma	Need to align with market system (global and national), remoteness
Intermediate	Empowerment from self-governance, better outcomes due to revival of language and culture	Workings of political and economic institutions, specific market mechanisms. Indian act and limited self-governance (both)
Proximate	Individual trauma, need for agency	Poor social outcomes (unemployment, family abuse, suicide, education levels)

strategy for those communities. *The bottom line is that, drawing on Integral Theory, an approach that draws on all quadrants and levels of reality is needed.* A debate between two camps, each of which emphasizes only those realities that align with their values and policy preferences, can actually be counterproductive.

IMPLICATIONS FOR RECONCILIATION AND THE NEED FOR HOPE

This section will explore the implications of the broken debate on the challenges of FIICs, including efforts to transform the relationship with Indigenous peoples in Canada.

The debate was conducted by outsiders and rooted in neocolonial assumptions.

In addition to the fact that the two sides of the media debate talked past one another, the debate was dysfunctional in two other ways. First, it was conducted almost entirely by academics and journalists (Indigenous and non-Indigenous) living in the South or nonremote urban centers with access to services and plenty of job opportunities. Boldly asserting that Gilmore "knew nothing" about Indigenous people or the North compared with those who "have spent a great deal of time there," Wilt (associated with the Dominant Discourse) wrote two articles in VICE in which he interviewed, respectively, five Indigenous people (Wilt 2016a) and four experts "who live in and/or have spent a great deal of time" in Canada's North (Wilt 2016b). However, none of the Indigenous people interviewed by Wilt actually lived in FIICs. All interviewees lived in southern cities, with the exception of one who lived in Yellowknife (which is not a remote community or FIIC), and a lawyer from Fort Chipewyan—a community whose members have access to jobs and business opportunities related to Alberta's oil sands to the south.

The media debate raised the interesting question of who should be allowed to speak authoritatively for people in FIICs. Challenger Discourse authors such as Gilmore (2016c) also attempted to seize the high ground on this issue by raising the dire social problems faced by many children in FIICs, including child and family abuse. He asked the elders and adults of Attawapiskat a rhetorical question: "Does their right to live on a remote reserve supersede their children's right to grow up in a healthy and viable community?"

A second problem that the foregoing analysis of the debate on FIICs has brought to light is that arguments advanced by the two sides were infused by paternalistic attitudes and colonial assumptions. Neither the Left nor the Right put forth recommendations outside their ideological "comfort zone." The suggestion from proponents of the Right that people in FIICs should "move South" because there was "no hope" for those communities does not address the desire of Indigenous peoples to preserve their language, culture, and connection to traditional territories. However, the recommendations of authors on the Left were little better. Apart from *pro forma* declarations that treaties should be renegotiated and the *Indian Act* overhauled (Rae 2016; Wilt 2016a, b), there was little indication that authors on the Left were prepared to go beyond the usual prescriptions of a continuation of the politics of identity including limited self-government and demands for higher federal government spending. All of this takes place under a colonial institutional framework that has not produced results for most FIICs. Furthermore, the Left's economic paradigm that is in practice based on welfarism and dependence on resource rents is a recipe for continued dependence on the Settler society and is ultimately paternalistic.[7]

Remoteness is a natural (RH side) barrier that does not fit easily into conflict studies (peace and justice) paradigms designed to tackle structural oppression understood as deeply embedded racist and colonial assumptions (in Integral Theory, found on the LH side) or unjust systems (RH side). Economic sustainability is fundamental to sovereignty and self-esteem. Two paradigms described in this volume may be helpful in overcoming the limitations of Western, Settler-imposed conceptions of justice and in bridging cultural differences between the Settler society and residents of FIICs. First, according to Patrice Brodeur, *interworldview dialogue* ("Interworldview Dialogue," *Transforming*) can integrate both identity and power dynamics of all sides in the discussion. Second, Joseph Cleyn suggests that *dialogical cosmopolitanism* ("Transcending Traditional Justice Claims," *Transforming*) can facilitate openness to diverse sources of knowledge, including from Indigenous groups. In this regard, there is another challenge that needs to be addressed that goes well beyond the usual concerns over representation (who speaks for the community and who speaks for the Settler society? What if the youth disagree with elders on the merits of resource development?). This is the fact that the lack of a clear vision for many FIICs' economic future makes it difficult for them to formulate an "ask" and enter into the dialogic discussion on the shape of a just society and a transformed arrangement with Canada's Settler society. Without clear institutional arrangements that acknowledge their unique rights and situation as Indigenous peoples as well as a solution to the economic challenges of remoteness, people in FIICs are likely to remain trapped in a never-ending transition.

Improving the Dialogue on FIICs

The broken media debate has highlighted the urgency of improving consultation mechanisms and fostering genuine dialogue (Brodeur, "Interworldview Dialogue," *Transforming*) with and about FIICs, including on the challenge of remoteness. There are several steps that could be taken.

First, it might be possible to create a Council of Remote Communities to share analyses and policy approaches to the challenges they face. This could also assist in efforts to lobby the government on issues such as services and infrastructure. Second, there could be more support for Community Dialogues to help people in FIICs come to a better understanding of the challenges they face and come up with their own solutions. As assistant deputy minister in Alberta, Catherine Twinn promoted Community Dialogues to help Indigenous people understand the connections between economic development (a RH side concern) and factors such as reconciliation (among members of the community and with the Settler society), ethics, and spirituality (LH side issues), and ways to end Sorrow Systems that hold back Indigenous community development.

Third, following the insights of *Complexity Theory*, efforts should be made to bring people from the Settler society into contact with people from remote communities and vice versa to increase the number of nodes in the system and increase the chances that something new can emerge (per CAS). One idea would be to create participatory education processes involving settlers and Indigenous peoples coming together and exchanging ideas. Most major Canadian universities offer courses on overseas bilateral development assistance (e.g., to Africa or Latin America). Why not have programs on development in FIICs and Canada's North? University students often try to do at least one year or term at a foreign university. Why not create mechanisms whereby students of teaching, administration, development, and other fields can get credit while working in FIICs? We could build capacity of people in Northern communities and get youth in those communities used to the idea of going to university by flying promising students for summer school in the South to take specialized programs in universities. Meeting other Indigenous people in universities might create a mimetic effect and encourage more youth from FIICs to acquire university degrees, and in the process the expertise and complexity needed to tackle wicked challenges and thrive in the modern global economy. From the fact that many drop out of high school, we can infer that many Indigenous youth don't even consider going to university.

Emergence and "Waiting in Hope"

The previous section has highlighted the importance of a holistic, inclusive dialogue rooted in a postcolonial paradigm that puts people in FIICs at the center of the discussion. However, it remains that many FIICs face a wicked problem in that they do not have a clear and viable path to economic development. In this case, it is important to practice "hopeful waiting" (Redekop 2011) in anticipation of "emergent opportunities" (Redekop 2011; McGuigan and Popp 2016) that would enable FIICs to improve their situation. Redekop has observed that "there are conditions under which the probability of something new emerging can be optimized" (Redekop 2015). Emergent opportunities by definition cannot be foreseen, but two trends bear further analysis. First, the environment in the North is changing rapidly. While the impact of climate change will in many ways be negative, there might be unexpected economic opportunities for FIICs. A second source of emergence could be market and technological shifts. Globalization expert Baldwin (2016) points out that while recent trends have favored those in major cities, it is possible that future technological changes will afford greater opportunities for people in remote communities such as FIICs to capitalize on their unique skills and assets. This highlights the need to resolve issues around education and build human capacity in those communities, both from the standpoint of preserving and recovering Indigenous culture and knowledge while at the same time developing modern economy skills and knowledge in areas such as science, technology, engineering, and math (STEM).

CONCLUSION

This analysis has shown that remoteness is a "wicked" problem that exacerbates the social and economic problems of FIICs. A "breadth and depth" analysis consisting of *Integral Theory* (quadrant and multilevel analysis) combined with insights from *Complexity Theory* has shown that the media debate on FIICs from 2012 to 2017 was unproductive because the Left and the Right addressed different quadrants and levels of reality. Alfred (2016) could have been talking about this debate when he said: "It's hard to have a discussion about the solution when there is no agreement about the nature of the problem."

With regards to multilevel analysis, proponents of the political Right take a "bottom-up" approach. They begin by highlighting serious social and economic problems at the *proximate* level, and move quickly to solutions at the *intermediate* level that align with the global capitalist system embraced by the Settler society. Proponents of the Dominant Discourse, on the other hand, adopt a "top-down" analysis that focuses on *distal*-level drivers such as colonialism and racism. As a result of this emphasis, authors on the Left have difficulty seeing the gravity of social challenges such as family and substance abuse at the *proximate* level or the seriousness of suboptimal institutional arrangements at the *intermediate* level. The CAS analysis combined with *Integral Theory* illuminates the problem: the distal layer of reality alone is not the appropriate frame of reference for designing economic and social policies, though an awareness of that level might help to nuance such projects and increase their ability to effect long-term changes.

With regards to quadrant analysis, the Left focuses almost exclusively on LH side issues, particularly culture and identity, and is ill-equipped to address the natural and observable (RH side) structural challenges related to remoteness. When the Left does focus on RH issues it tends to narrow the debate—with regards to political arrangements, to limited self-government, and with regards to economic challenges, to the necessity of increased federal government spending and treaty renegotiation. The political Right, on the other hand, tends to focus on RH "systemic" issues. However, the neglect of LH side issues such as intergenerational trauma and the need for cultural preservation undermines the Right's "move south" policy prescription. As the two camps in the debate talk past each other, they are unable to find common ground and move to a discussion on concrete policy recommendations.

Another problematic feature of the media debate on FIICs is that it was conducted largely by outsiders and infused with neocolonial assumptions. Both sides of the debate see themselves as the "saviors" of people in FIICs. Furthermore, the lack of a clear path to economic sovereignty and sustainability makes it harder to engage in a dialogic approach to decolonization.

The foregoing analysis highlights the importance of two steps. First, there is an urgent need to promote healthy dialogue on options for FIICs based on inclusive, postcolonial paradigms, and to increase positive linkages between FIICs and the Settler society. Increasing positive connection points between FIICs and the Settler society would help to attain requisite complexity and increase the probability of finding creative solutions to the challenges of remoteness. Measures could include participatory workshops for people in FIICs themselves, increased educational and civil society links, and a more respectful media debate. Second, the fact that the two sides in the Canadian media debate from 2012 to 2017 spoke from narrow perspectives that excluded important factors points to the need for further research: a thorough, integral, multilevel mapping exercise on the challenges facing FIICs, including remoteness. The mapping exercise could incorporate insights from CAS by modeling feedback loops related to remoteness that exacerbate social challenges such as welfare dependency, addiction, and family abuse, and suggesting optimal intervention points in collaboration with people in FIICs. Such an exercise, which might be the next stage in this research project, could assist those who practice "hopeful waiting" (Redekop 2011) to identify "emergent opportunities" for FIICs, which could arise from environmental, technological, or market shifts (among others) in the coming years. There could also be a social shift in both the Settler society and Indigenous groups. In this context, a renewed, inclusive discussion that takes into account all quadrants and levels of reality could lead to new approaches that enable Canada's FIICs to forge a better future.

NOTES

1. Using a looser definition of "permanent community" or "remoteness" (e.g., remote in terms of either power source or road access) yields an estimate of the number of FIICs in Canada that is closer to 200.

2. In this paper, the Dominant Discourse is associated with Canada's political Left and the Challenger Discourse with the Right. Members of the Challenger group such as Jonathan Kay, Scott Gilmore, and Tom Flanagan are generally associated with the Conservative Party of Canada (CPC), while proponents of the Dominant Discourse such as James Wilt and Chelsea Vowel generally position themselves on the Left or far Left.

3. While not an FIIC, La Loche is a five-hour drive from Prince Albert, the nearest major city in Saskatchewan (see Google Maps).

4. Maggie Wente is a member of the Serpent River First Nation, which is located in Ontario on the shore of Lake Huron, close to the TransCanada Highway. She lives in Toronto.

5. Sixteen of the TRC's Calls to Action (CTAs—8, 10, 11, 21, 31, 54, 55, 61, 62, 66–68, 70, 78, and 84) call for increased federal government funding for various services and initiatives (TRC 2015).

6. It is to note that national inquiries related to Indigenous peoples have used progressively stronger language in referring to the problems that Indigenous communities face today (i.e., genocide—see TRC 2015; MMIWG 2019c; Stefanovich 2019).

7. While a full discussion is beyond the scope of this paper, resource rentierism, a term developed by Mahdavy (1970) to describe Middle East petro-states and adapted by Widdowson (2019) for the Canadian context, has limitations that are generally not acknowledged by writers on the Left. First, many FIICs are not located near

viable resources that could sustain them. RCAP (vol. 2, 491) notes that Canadian governments allocated lands without mineral deposits (Nunavut is an exception) to Indigenous groups. Second, it provides fewer incentives to develop skills necessary in a modern economy. As a result, the gap in income and living standards between residents of FIICs and the Settler society will likely remain. Third, this model can actually exacerbate conflict and the gap between "haves" and "have-nots" in Indigenous communities because of the zero-sum nature of decisions on how to distribute resource rents and allocate the relatively few well-paying jobs created by resource extraction (Widdowson 2019, 143, 241). These dynamics are amplified by low educational attainment in FIICs.

REFERENCES

Allen, Peter, Steve Maguire, and Bill McKelvey, eds. 2011. *The SAGE Handbook of Complexity and Management.* Thousand Oaks, CA: Sage Publications.

Auditor General of Canada. 2018. *Spring Report of the Auditor General Report 5—Socio-economic Gaps on First Nations Reserves—Indigenous Services Canada.*

Baldwin, Richard E. 2016. *The Great Convergence.* Cambridge, MA: Belknap Press.

Cairns, Alan C. 2000. *Citizens Plus.* Vancouver: UBC Press.

Canada Centre for Mapping and Earth Observation (CCMEO). 2017. *Natural Resources Canada (NRCAN).*

Canadian Council on Social Determinants of Health. 2013. *Roots of Resilience: Overcoming Inequities in Aboriginal Communities.*

Canadian Human Rights Tribunal (CHTR) Decision. January 26, 2016. "First Nations Child and Family Caring Society of Canada et al. v. Attorney General of Canada (for the Minister of Indian and Northern Affairs Canada)." *CHR Website.*

Commission on the Social Determinants of Health (CSDH). 2008. *Closing the Gap in a Generation: Health Equity through Action on the Social Determinants of Health. Final Report of the Commission on Social Determinants of Health.* Geneva: World Health Organization.

Canada (RCAP), Georges Erasmus, and René Dussault. 1996. *Report of the Royal Commission on Aboriginal Peoples*, vols. 1–5. Ottawa: The Commission.

Cornell, S. 2006. *Indigenous Peoples, Poverty, and Self-Determination in Australia, New Zealand, Canada, and the United States. Native Nations Institute for Leadership, Management, and Policy.* Native Nations Institute for Leadership, Management, and Policy and The Harvard Project on American Indian Economic Development.

Coulthard, G. 2014. *Red Skin, White Masks: Rejecting the Colonial Politics of Recognition.* Minneapolis, MN: University of Minnesota Press.

Elliott, Alicia, Robert Jago, Melanie Lefebvre, and Ryan McMahon. 2017. "The Canada Most People Don't Hear: Four Indigenous Writers Respond to What They Say is a 'Counterproductive' Piece in Maclean's." *Maclean's Website*, June 13, 2017.

Esbjorn-Hargens, S. 2009. "An All-Inclusive Framework for the 21st Century: An Overview of Integral Theory." *Integral Institute*, Resource Paper No. 1, March 2009.

Exner-Pirot, Heather. 2012. "Dead Aid in the Arctic." *Eye on the Arctic.* https://www.rcinet.ca/eye-on-the-arctic/2012/08/16/dead-aid-in-the-arctic/. Accessed April 23, 2020.

Flanagan, T. 2008. *First Nations, Second Thoughts*. Montreal: McGill-Queen's University Press.

Gilmore, Scott. 2016a. "La Loche Shows us It's Time to Help People Escape the North." *Maclean's*, January 27.

———. 2016b. "The Hard Truth about Remote Communities." *Maclean's*, February 9.

———. 2016c. "The Unasked Question about Attawapiskat." *Maclean's*, April 16.

Hicks, J. 2015. *Statistical Data on Death by Suicide by Nunavut Inuit, 1920 to 2014*. Paper prepared for Nunavut Tunngavik Inc., September. http://www.tunngavik.com/blog/2015/09/15/pdf-statistical-data-on-death-by-suicide-by-nunavut-inuit-1920-to-2014.

Inuit Tapiriit Kanatami (ITK). 2018. *Inuit Statistical Profile 2018*. Iqaluit, Nunavut: ITK. https://www.itk.ca/wp-content/uploads/2018/08/Inuit-Statistical-Profile.pdf. Accessed April 23, 2020.

Kauffman, Stuart. 1995. *At Home in the Universe: The Search for Laws of Self-Organization and Complexity*. Oxford: Oxford University Press.

Kay, Jonathan. 2012. "Natives Deserve the Same Property Rights as All Canadians." *National Post*, August 9.

Kay, Jonathan. 2013a. "To Understand How We Got to Attawapiskat, Go Back to the 1905 James Bay Treaty." *National Post*, January 3.

———. 2013b. "Six Lessons from a Brilliant, Scathing Year-Old CBC Report on Attawapiskat's Mismanagement." *National Post*, January 7.

———. 2013c. "What's Wrong with Remote Native Reserves? Let's Ask a Veteran Doctor Who Worked There." *National Post*, January 10.

———. 2013d. "Native Dignity will Come Only from Self-Sufficiency, Not Grand Gestures in Ottawa." *National Post*, January 11.

———. 2013e. "The Looming Crisis Within: Census Shows Rapid Rise in Already Isolated Native Population." *National Post*, May 9.

Kay, Jonathan. 2016a. "Breaking the Cycle." *National Post*, 2016.

———. 2016b. "Moving is the Only Hope for Communities Like Attawapiskat." *National Post*, April 16.

King, Hayden, and Shiri Pasternak. 2018. "A Special Report: Canada's Emerging Indigenous Rights Framework: A Critical Analysis." *Yellowhead Institute*, June 5.

King, Thomas. 2012. *The Inconvenient Indian: A Curious Account of Native People in North America*. Toronto: Anchor Canada.

Kishigami, Nobuhiro, 2002. "Inuit Identities in Montreal, Canada." *Études/Inuit/Studies*, 26(1), 183–191.

Légaré, A. 2009. "Nunavut, the Unfulfilled Dream: The Arduous Path Towards Socio-Economic Autonomy." *The Northern Review*, 30(Spring 2009), 207–240.

Loukacheva, Natalia. 2016. "From Recognition to Reconciliation: Nunavut and Self-Reliance – An Arctic Entity in Transition in From Recognition to Reconciliation." In *Essays on the Constitutional Entrenchment of Aboriginal and Treaty Rights*. Edited by Patrick Macklem and Douglas Sanderson. Toronto: University of Toronto Press.

Mahdavy, Hussein. 1970. "The Patterns and Problems of Economic Development in Rentier States: The Case of Iran." In *Studies in Economic History of the Middle East*. Edited by M. A. Cook. Oxford: Oxford University Press.

McGuigan, R., and N. Popp. 2016. *Integral Conflict: The New Science of Conflict*. Albany, NY: SUNY Press.

Meadows, Donella. 1997. "Leverage Points: Places to Intervene in a System." *The Donella Meadows Project, Academy for Systems Change Website*.

Morin, Brandi. 2017. "First Nations Students Face Continued Funding Shortfalls, Advocate Says." *CBC Website*, August 31.

Natural Resources Canada (NRCAN). 2018. *The Atlas of Canada – Remote Communities Energy Database*. https://atlas.gc.ca/rced-bdece/en/index.html. Accessed April 23, 2020.

National Enquiry into Missing and Murdered Indigenous Women and Girls (MMIWG). 2019a. *Reclaiming Power and Place: The Final Report of the National Inquiry into Missing and Murdered Indigenous Women and Girls*, Vol. 1a.

———. 2019b. *Reclaiming Power and Place: The Final Report of the National Inquiry into Missing and Murdered Indigenous Women and Girls*, Vol. 1b.

———. 2019c. *Supplementary Report: A Legal Analysis of Genocide.*

Norris, Mary Jane. 1998. "Canada's Aboriginal Languages." *Statistics Canada, Canadian Social Trends*, Winter 1998.

———. 2014. "Aboriginal Languages in Canada: Emerging Trends and Perspectives on Second Language Acquisition." *Statistics Canada Website*.

Rae, Bob. 2016. "After La Loche: Mend Hearts, Mend Treaties." *Globe and Mail*, February 3.

Raphael, D. 2009. *Social Determinants of Health: Canadian Perspectives*, 2nd ed. Toronto: Canadian Scholars' Press.

Reading, Charlotte, and Fred Wien. 2013 (2009). *Health Inequalities and Social Determinants of Aboriginal Peoples Health*. Prince George, BC: National Collaborating Centre for Aboriginal People's Health.

Redekop, Vern Neufeld. 1992. *Deep-Rooted Conflict as a Factor in Regional Economic Development*. Unpublished Paper.

———. 2002. *From Violence to Blessing: How an Understanding of Deep-Rooted Conflict Opens Paths to Reconciliation*. Ottawa: Novalis.

———. 2007. "The Relevance of Teachings of Blessing and Justice of Blessing for Reconciliation in Bosnia I Herzegovina." In *Inter-Ethnic Reconciliation, Religious Tolerance and Human Security in the Balkans: Proceedings of the Second ECPD International Conference*. Edited by Takehiro Togo, Jeffrey Levett, and Negoslav P. Ostrjic. Belgrade: European Center for Peace and Development, 287–309.

———. 2011. "Spirituality, Emergent Creativity, Peacemaking and Reconciliation." In *Peacemaking: Practice to Theory*. Edited by Susan Allen Nan, Andrea Bartoli, and Zachariah Mampilly, Chapter 4.3 in Vol. II. Santa Barbara, CA: ABC-CLIO.

———. 2015. *Reconciliation as Emergent Creativity*, A. J. Muste Lecture delivered by Vern Neufeld Redekop at Hope College, March 26.

———. 2016a. *Challenges in Post-Colonial-Authoritarian-Conflict Communities.* Presentation for ECS 5101, Saint Paul University.

———. 2016b. *Reconciliation.* Presentation for ECS 5101, Saint Paul University.

Richards, John. 2017. "Census 2016: Where is the Discussion about Indigenous Education?" *Globe and Mail*, December 13.

Robertson, Dylan. 2018. "Inflated Statistics, Feeble Bureaucrats Blamed for Growing Indigenous Poverty Gap." *Winnipeg Free Press*, May 30.

Statistics Canada. 2011. "Census of Population, 2011." *Statistics Canada Website.*

———. 2016. "Census of Population, 2016." *Statistics Canada Website*, May.

Statistics Canada. 2019. "Evolution of the Language Situation in Nunavut, 2001 to 2016." *Statistics Canada Website*, Released July 9.

Stefanovich, Olivia. 2019. "UN Human Rights Office Calls for Examination of MMIWG Inquiry's Genocide Claim." *CBC Website*, June 16.

Sutton, Peter. 2009. *The Politics of Suffering: Indigenous Australia and the End of the Liberal Consensus.* Melbourne: Melbourne University Publishing.

Taiaiake, A. 2016. *Presentation at University of Ottawa on Indigenous Resurgence*, Ottawa.

Truth and Reconciliation Commission of Canada (TRC). 2015a. *Truth and Reconciliation Commission of Canada: Calls to Action.*

Vowel, Chelsea. 2016a. "Scott Gilmore and the Imaginary Indian." *CanadaLand*, January 29.

———. 2016b. "Vowel: Move South? Here's What Indigenous Peoples Need." *Ottawa Citizen*, April 20.

Watkins, A., and K. Wilber. 2015. *Wicked and Wise, How to Solve the World's Toughest Problems.* Great Britain: Urbane Publications.

Wente, M. 2016. "We Don't Need One More Ride on the Merry-Go-Round. It's Time for Fresh Ideas." *Olthuis, Kleer, Townshend LLP (or: OKTLaw Blog)*, February 10. https://www.oktlaw.com/dont-need-one-ride-merry-go-round-time-fresh-ideas/. Accessed April 23, 2020.

Widdowson, Frances, and Albert Howard. 2008. *Disrobing the Aboriginal Industry: The Deception Behind Indigenous Cultural Preservation.* Montreal and Kingston: Mcgill-Queen's University Press.

Widdowson, Frances. 2016. "The Political Economy of Neotribal Rentierism: A Historical and Material Theory of Aboriginal-Non-Aboriginal Relations in Canada." *Mount Royal University: Paper Presented at the Annual Meeting of the Canadian Political Science Association*, University of Calgary, May 31–June 2, 2016.

———. 2019. *Separate But Unequal: How Parallelist Ideology Conceals Indigenous Dependency.* Ottawa: University of Ottawa Press.

Wilt, J. 2016. "We Asked Indigenous Artists and Thinkers Why Relocating Is Bullshit Here's Why Moving First Nations Isn't the Answer that White Critics Think It Is." *Vice*, April 28.

———. 2106b. "Why Scott Gilmore's Latest Claims about the North Are Bullshit." *Vice*, September 16.

Young, T. Kue, and Susan Chatwood. 2010, February 8. "Health Care in the North: What Canada can Learn from Its Circumpolar Neighbours." *Canadian Medical Association Journal*, 183(2), 209–214.

———. 2017, November 13. "Delivering More Equitable Primary Health Care in Northern Canada." *Canadian Medical Association Journal*, 189(45), 1377–1378.

Chapter 15

Reconciliation in Australia and Lederach's *Moral Imagination*

Sue-Anne Hess

As a non-Indigenous woman of Irish heritage, I grew up with very little aware-ness of the wounded history that surrounded me and my fellow Australians. With a deep appreciation for Lederach's wisdom, I began researching this topic in the light of his theories and was profoundly affected by the injustice and cultural violence to which I had unknowingly contributed. Yet, I was also inspired by the richness of the Indigenous culture, the depth and beauty of their symbols, and the resilience of their communities.

I approached Aboriginal Catholic Ministry in Melbourne with the sole intention to learn. Many times, I sat with the coordinator and did nothing more than listen to her. I was surprised by the warmth of welcome I received, and the generosity with which she would share her stories and culture with me. Despite my comparative ignorance, I was offered a place in the commu-nity and respected for my "white" education.

I was recently invited to edit the final draft of a history book that docu-ments the first thirty years of this group (started in 1986, to be published in 2020). It offered me an intimate glimpse of the courage, friendship, and perseverance of those Indigenous and non-Indigenous Australians who cam-paign daily (despite many setbacks) for real and lasting reconciliation. It is an honor to become a part of their story.

INTRODUCTION

As the world celebrated a new millennium, Australia stepped into the global spotlight by hosting the Olympic Games in Sydney, coinciding with the country's commemoration of its first 100 years as a federated nation. In this historic moment, there was an emphatic focus upon addressing the wrongs of the past, in the hopes that the turn of the century might also mark the moment when all Australians could move forward together in a vision of unity and equality (Tatz 1998). Similar to other colonized nations, the relationship between Indigenous (Aboriginal) and non-Indigenous Australians had previously been characterized by racial inequality, violence, and structural injustice. Consequently, there were fundamental issues to be addressed before Australia could truly claim to be a reconciled and unified nation.

Two decades after that moment, the reconciliation process does not appear to have delivered on the bright future that it had promised and further, the changes that have occurred have been superficial in nature, failing to address the core issues. The status of Indigenous Australians has repeatedly been compared to that of the "Third World" (Halloran 2007, 1), and is regarded internationally as a source of concern. Indeed, in 2011, the then UN High Commissioner for Human Rights, Navi Pillay, stated that national efforts to address disadvantages faced by Indigenous Australians were "being undermined by policies that fail to recognize the right to self-determination for Indigenous people" (UN News 2011).

This chapter will explore some fundamental challenges surrounding the Australian reconciliation process. It will argue that the loss of Indigenous identities and cultural ties is not merely a consequence of the colonial project, but is at the heart of the struggle for agency that continues (Muldoon and Schaap 2012), and, as a result, the description of Australia as a cultural genocide may be applied (Short 2010). Yet, this crisis of identity may also be the key to healing within communities, as well as a powerful resource in the journey toward reconciliation between Indigenous and non-Indigenous Australians.

Further, in reflecting upon Lederach's concept of *The Moral Imagination* (2005), this chapter suggests that a creative approach to reconciliation, including artistic expressions of culture (such as dance, visual arts, and storytelling), might have the potential to serve a twofold healing purpose. First, these creative expressions act as an affirmation of community and identity, which, in light of Nobles' (2008) concept of a "membership theory of apologies," are considered essential to any reconciliation process. A second effect is that these expressions may also act as an opportunity for dialogue, facilitating an "encounter" between different groups, thereby offering a challenge to stereotypes and unhelpful assumptions.

In the following pages, I will provide a brief history of the Settler/Indigenous relationship. This will be followed by some key events of more recent years, including the progression of the "official" reconciliation process. Issues surrounding land rights, apology, and sovereignty will frame the concurrent Northern Territory National Emergency Response (also known as the Intervention). Finally, I will propose a new approach for the healing of identities and the construction of new types of relationships. The political, economic, and legal implications of reconciliation cannot be ignored; yet, this chapter suggests that reconciliation at the relational and cultural levels is an essential foundation upon which to construct social change.

HISTORY OF THE INDIGENOUS/SETTLER RELATIONSHIP: FROM CONTACT, TO COLONIZATION, TO CULTURAL GENOCIDE

Indigenous communities have inhabited the land now known as Australia for more than 40,000 years. Research suggests that hundreds of separate Indigenous nations have existed, with a diverse array of languages, cultural practices, organizational, and meaning systems (Macintyre 1999). Despite the long history, there is still much to be learned from the world's oldest surviving population.

While there is evidence to suggest that first contact happened much earlier, Australia was settled as a British penal colony in the latter part of the eighteenth century (ibid.). The first fleet of convicts and authorities arrived at (what is now known as) Botany Bay in 1788. Surprisingly, the earliest meetings between the local inhabitants and the newcomers have been described as cordial, and characterized by a mutual, yet wary, curiosity. Referencing diary entries and letters scripted by British officers, historian Inga Clendinnen (2003) describes interactions that were fraught with misunderstanding and confusion, and yet not without a sense of openness. As illustrated by the descriptions below, early interactions indicated an eagerness for trade of food, clothing, and tools. Captain Arthur Philip, who described the natives as "friendly and inoffensive," wrote:

> They . . . are fond of any very Soft Musick, and will attend to singing any of the Words which they very readily repeat. But I know very little at present of the people. They never come into the Camp, and I have had few hours to seek them out. There are several roots which they Eat, and I have seen the Bones of the Kangurroo and flying Squirrel at the entrance to their huts, but Fish is their principal support which on these Shores is very scarce and I believe many of them Starving. (Cited in Clendinnen 2003, 26)

Similar other firsthand reports confirmed interactions that were characterized by child-like fascination and amiability. Clendinnen tells of Lieutenant William Bradley, whose first encounter with the local people was as follows:

A remarkably friendly encounter, the British party' being welcomed ashore by unarmed men who pointed out a good landing place and "in the most cheerful manner, shouting and dancing: . . . these people mixed with ours and all hands danced together . . . left their spears in their canoes as a sign of friendship and all proceeded to more dancing and otherwise amusing themselves." (Ibid., 8)

While the texts reflect a marked conviction of superiority by the settlers, it is they who were at the disadvantage, trying to survive in a foreign environment. Clendinnan (ibid.) observes that their efforts at survival may have even appeared comical to the Indigenous people who were well-adapted to the environment. She comments, "What would watching [First] Australians have made of so pathetic a performance from British males, when their own women would take their frail canoes out past the breakers with infants aboard?" (ibid., 91).

Indigenous groups were perceived by the British as savages who had failed to progress in evolutionary terms (Macintyre 1999). Initial attempts to "civilize" them (by means of clothing, modern tools, etiquette behaviors, and language) failed, and as a result, contact between Indigenous and non-Indigenous Australians became hostile in nature. Conflicting interests led to violent attacks and subsequent retaliatory actions (Brennan 1999) as relations between Indigenous and non-Indigenous Australians became increasingly violent and acrimonious (Gunstone 2012). Further, white settlers introduced other dangers, such as smallpox, alcohol, and malnutrition (Short 2010).

Considered the inferior (and therefore weaker) race, Indigenous Australians seemed destined to die out (Maddison 2012). Therefore, the task at hand for Settler communities was to "smooth the pillow of the dying race" (Macintyre 1999, 144). In light of the grave concerns regarding the resilience of the Indigenous cultures, a new approach of "State as Protector" was implemented in the early twentieth century, with the *Aborigines Protection Act*, 1909. Govier describes the action as follows:

The governments of Canada and Australia in the nineteenth and early twentieth centuries believed that a Christian European belief system and way of life were clearly superior for all human beings, they established policies to educate and assimilate Indigenous people according to those values. When they sought to suppress the language, culture and even family relationships of these people, they were doing what they thought was right. (2006, 81)

At the Celebration of Federation (1901), the newly formed Australian nation was determined to establish a unique identity, with an intent focus on building a "White Australia." Immigration from preferred European countries (such as Britain) was encouraged and the assimilation of the local natives into white culture was established by law. In 1951, the Commonwealth Minister for Territories, Paul Hasluck, stated the following: "Assimilation means, in practical terms, that, in the course of time, it is expected that all persons of Aboriginal blood or mixed blood in Australia will live like White Australians do" (Wilson and Dodson 1997, chapter 2).

Well into the twentieth century, a policy was established to support the "cultivation of an Australian sentiment based upon the maintenance of racial purity and the development in Australia of an enlightened and self-reliant community" (Macintyre 1999, 143). In this context, Aboriginal children might be claimed from their parents and communities as Wards of the State, with half-caste and mixed-race children (those who were most likely to successfully transition) as the particular focus (Young 2009). Officially begun around 1909, and continuing through to the 1970s, this practice reflected the belief that these children were better off in state care where assimilation practices might result in a greater chance of employment, education, and other advantages of the superior white culture. To this day, it is unknown how many children were removed either forcibly or by coercion of their parents, with promises of a better future. Some estimate, it may have been as many as 100,000 (Wilson and Dodson 1997).

> The official objective was now "raising of their status" to "the ordinary rights of citizenship," but this in turn was to be achieved by extending the practice of forcible removal of Aboriginal children from their families. By a twisted logic that now horrifies all Australians as it then tormented its victims, the popular association of Aboriginality with dirt, disease and neglect allowed whites to deny the civic rights of the stolen generation and deprive them of their culture. (Macintyre 1999, 187)

Despite the gradual withdrawal of racially based policies through the 1950s and 1960s, it was not until 1997 that an enquiry commissioned by Wilson and Dodson (Human Rights and Equal Opportunity) entitled *Bringing them Home* was published. This document included submissions that described the experiences of hundreds of removed children, sourced from individuals, churches, and government groups. The report referred to a three-year longitudinal study completed during the mid-1980s, comparing outcomes on key lifestyle indicators between children who had been removed from their families and communities and those who hadn't. In a submission to the *Bringing them Home* report, Jane McKendrick provided the following statistics:

Children who have been removed from their families are:

- less likely to have undertaken a post-secondary education,
- much less likely to have stable living conditions and more likely to be geographically mobile,

- three times more likely to say they had no-one to call on in a crisis,
- less likely to be in a stable, confiding relationship with a partner,
- twice as likely to report having been arrested by police and having been convicted of an offence,
- three times as likely to report having been in gaol,
- less likely to have a strong sense of their Aboriginal cultural identity,
- more likely to have discovered their Aboriginality later in life and less likely to know about their Aboriginal cultural traditions,
- twice as likely to report current use of illicit substances, and
- much more likely to report intravenous use of illicit substances. (Wilson and Dodson 1997, submission 310, 22)

The *Bringing them Home* report concluded that the practice of child removal had not only failed in its objectives to improve the lives of Indigenous children, but that considerable pain and hardship had been inflicted. In fact, the resulting loss of culture, identity, shared history, kinship ties, community, and spiritual tradition is now described as genocide:

> Indigenous families and communities have endured gross violations of their human rights. These violations continue to affect Indigenous people's daily lives. They were an act of genocide, aimed at wiping out Indigenous families, communities, and cultures, vital to the precious and inalienable heritage of Australia. (Wilson and Dodson 1997)

This view is reaffirmed by Short (2010), who argues that genocide has occurred and is ongoing. Referring to the works of Lemkin (1944, cited in Short 2010), Short examines the earliest definition of the term "genocide," which is described as an action that can be achieved by one of two methods. The first method, physical genocide, consists of the intentional killing of a population. The second method, cultural genocide, can be achieved by the systematic undermining of a group's way of life, which is "a necessary precondition for the realization of individual needs" (ibid., 47). In this sense, the concept of cultural genocide is not merely symbolic but has tangible, physical effects, as described in the report above. Macintyre also agrees with this view, stating, "All of this was premised on the elimination of Aboriginality, the abandonment of language, customs and ritual, and the severing of kinship ties so that absorption could be complete. It was an impossible condition, and for present day Aborigines it constitutes a policy of genocide" (1999, 145). What is now known as the plight of the "Stolen Generations" has since become the most explicit indicator of a country that is deeply wounded along racial lines.

THE ROAD TO RECONCILIATION

The previous section explored the most prominent policies and actions of the Settler communities against Australian Indigenous groups through the nineteenth and twentieth centuries. Discourse concerning reconciliation, unity, and nationhood took on greater weight as Australia looked toward the twenty-first century. However, the various attempts at recognition and reconciliation have faltered because the underlying structural issues, including the need for self-determination, agency, and cultural integrity, remain unresolved. By extension, there is an essential lack of understanding with regards to the Indigenous relationship with the land. These issues will be discussed in the following section.

Sovereignty and Land Rights

The journey toward reconciliation in Australia may be traced back to the campaign for racial equality in the 1960s. The 1967 referendum was a critical moment in the national psyche, when over 90 percent of the Australian population voted to have discriminatory comments against the Indigenous groups removed from the Constitution (Huggins, in Rothfield et al. 2008). Further, in response to the United Nations Convention on the Elimination of All Forms of Racial Discrimination in 1965, the Australian government created the *Racial Discrimination Act* in 1975. While this document prohibited discrimination on the basis of race, and also helped to reduce state/territory-based policy discrepancies, it was merely a starting point.

A key demand of Australian Indigenous communities has always been the need for a treaty, or formal document of recognition, that recognizes sovereignty and prior land ownership (Auguste 2010). Unlike other countries, such as Canada, New Zealand, and the United States, Australia is the only colonized nation that has never established such an agreement (Davis 2006). In 2017, fifty years after the 1967 referendum, delegates of a four-day First Nations National Constitutional Convention issued a document entitled "Uluru Statement from the Heart." It states the following:

> This sovereignty is a spiritual notion: the ancestral tie between the land, or "mother nature," and the Aboriginal and Torres Strait Islander peoples who were born therefrom, remain attached thereto, and must one day return thither to be united with our ancestors. This link is the basis of the ownership of the soil, or better, of sovereignty. It has never been ceded or extinguished, and co-exists with the sovereignty of the Crown. (Referendum Council 2017)

Nobles states, "To be sure, the absence of treaty-making in Australia has been highly consequential for Aboriginal land and self-government claims of the twentieth and twenty-first centuries" (2008, 44). Samson also writes, "Among many of the world's Indigenous peoples, descents into community-wide trauma and dysfunction have been precipitated by removal from lands" (cited in Short 2010, 53). From an Indigenous perspective we hear:

> We are the people of the land. The land is our mother. For more than 40,000 years we have been caring for this land. We are its natural farmers. Now, after so many years of dispossession, we find once again we are being thrust towards a new dispossession. Our pain and our fear are real. (*Walk with Us* 2011, 47)

This statement, undersigned by seven Indigenous Elders in the Northern Territory, illustrates how the Western conception of land ownership (in the transactional or economic sense) falls far short of the cultural, spiritual, and historical significance understood by Indigenous groups. This is further expressed by Dodson, as below:

> To understand our law, our culture and our relationship to the physical and spiritual world, you must begin with the land. Everything about Aboriginal society is inextricably woven with, and connected to, the land. You take that away and you take away our reason for existence. (Dodson 1997, 41)

Similarly, in 2009, Grieves conducted a comprehensive assessment of Aboriginal social and emotional well-being, which highlighted the "interconnectedness of the elements of the earth and the universe, animate and inanimate, whereby people, the plants and animals, landforms, and celestial bodies are interrelated" (2009, 7).

However, this campaign for recognition of sovereignty is opposed by those who envision an undivided nation, where the way forward lies in solidarity and resistance to any prior land entitlement claim (Maddison 2012). This was most powerfully expressed by Prime Minister John Howard in the year 2000. In an interview with John Laws, he asserted his unwillingness to consider Indigenous claims for a formal document of agreement, stating, "A nation cannot sign a treaty with its own citizens" (Laws 2000, cited in Bennan, Gunn, and Williams 2004, 308). His comment reflected an identification of Indigenous groups as part of the current Australian collective identity, and yet denied their historical relationship with the land.

The 1990s

Through the final decade of the twentieth century, some key events occurred to inspire hope that change was coming. In 1992, the High Court "Mabo" decision was a landmark in the campaign for recognition of the prior land ownership (Brennan 1999). In this case, an Indigenous man, Eddie Mabo, succeeded in his challenge of the legal doctrine of *Terra Nullius*, the colonial notion of "land belonging to no-one" (Nobles 2008, 44). Macintyre observes, "The court did not overturn the sovereignty of the government that had been established in 1788, but recognized the existence in common law of Aboriginal property rights that preceded the European settlement and contin-ued past it" (1999, 476).

In that same year, Prime Minister Paul Keating gave what has since been known as the "Redfern Speech." Regarded by some as one of the greatest Australian speeches, the largely Indigenous audience witnessed the first pub-lic acknowledgment of the wrongs committed through colonization, and the recognition that many of the hardships experienced by Indigenous commu-nities were a consequence of these wrongs. In addition, he acknowledged a deep respect for Aboriginal culture and wisdom (Short 2012, 294). He states:

> The starting point might be to recognise that the problem starts with us non-Aboriginal Australians. It begins, I think with that act of recognition, that it was we who did the dispossessing; we took the traditional lands and smashed the traditional way of life. We brought the diseases. The alcohol. We committed the murders. We took the children from their mothers. We practiced discrimination and exclusion. (Keating, Redfern Speech 1992)

Around the same time, the Council for Aboriginal Reconciliation (CAR) was formed. In 1991, this group had set in place a ten-year plan to propel forward the journey to reconciliation, coinciding with the Centenary of Federation. Made up, in the majority, of prominent members of Indigenous communities, the project aimed to educate the wider community regarding Indigenous culture and issues, address socioeconomic disadvantage, and consider the creation of some form of a reconciliation document (Gunstone 2005). This document, *The Australian Declaration towards Reconciliation*, was presented to the Australian government at an event entitled *Corroborree 2000*. Unfortunately, the document gained little traction, as Corntassel and Holder observe:

> In response to the report, Prime Minister Howard noted that his government would consider its proposals, but essentially dismissed any notion of offering an apology or treaty in keeping with his previously stated positions . . . Clearly in the struggles over the politics of perception, the injustices of history were being memorialized on Australian government terms rather than on Indigenous terms. Consequently, CAR's final report largely disappeared from the public discourse and was no longer considered a viable means for achieving a meaningful dis-course on reconciliation. (2008, 19)

Damien Short, a critic of the reconciliation movement overall, argued that the *Council for Aboriginal Reconciliation Act* (1991) was a further demonstration of the assimilationist policies of the dominant state (2010). He claimed that the moves toward reconciliation were, in fact, a "watering down" of the treaty agenda "that was not the product of consultations with Indigenous peoples" (ibid., 54). Moves toward reconciliation were contrary to the Indigenous claims for the recognition of sovereignty and unique nation-hood. Similarly, Gunstone argues that the popularity of the reconciliation movement rested on the vague ideals of unity and nationalism without seeking to address past wrongs or current injustices (2005). Instead, these popular gestures were a diversion that dismissed Indigenous claims. While there was evidence to suggest that non-Indigenous Australians supported the notion of equal rights and fairness, there was considerably less support for gestures of accountability such as compensation.

Apology

One of the particular recommendations of the *Bringing Them Home* report was the call for a formal apology by the Australian government to the victims, families, and communities of what became known as the Stolen Generation (a term first used by Read (1981)). It was hoped that this gesture would recognize and acknowledge the wrongs of the past and, in so doing, create a new space for Indigenous identities within the broader Australian context (Corntassel and Holder 2008). While some critics might consider the declaration of an apology as mere words (Govier 2006), there was the hope that this symbolic gesture would stimulate concrete actions of political, social, and economic importance.

Prime Minister John Howard continually refused to issue an apology for the government involvement in the Stolen Generation (Short 2010). While numerous voices called for an apology as necessary for moving forward, the prime minister stepped away from this challenge and took the "presentism" position of refusing to apologize for the well-intentioned actions of past generations (Govier 2006). Instead, he proclaimed "genuine regret and sorrow" for the events of the past and declared a commitment to "practical gestures" of reconciliation (Auguste 2010). Nobles provides the following as a possible interpretation for his refusal:

> Conversely, political elites do not offer apologies when they neither support nor seek to advance Indigenous or minority group claims. They do not recognize group rights, nor do they believe that the facts of historical injustice require them to do so. Nor do they define reconciliation in expansive ways, choosing instead to view reconciliation in narrowly and in largely affective

ways, without referring to fundamental political, legal or economic alterna-
tions. (2008, 33)

Many within the Indigenous community were disappointed and disillu-
sioned by the prime minister's refusal to take accountability. For example,
Govier, citing Human Rights Watch, explains, "It is impossible to expect 'reconciliation' if part of the population refuses to accept that anything was ever
wrong, and the other part has never received any acknowledgement of what it
has undergone, or of the ultimate responsibility for that suffering" (2006, 45).

It wasn't until 2008 that the formal apology was issued by the then prime
minister, Kevin Rudd. At the time, it was viewed as a potentially significant
moment for the future of the Australian nation (Auguste 2010). Hopes were
raised that the words of apology might then be followed by policies and
provisions to make it effective (Short 2012). Indeed, there was the hope that
patterns of past injustice might be broken. However, by the time the apology
occurred, it was overshadowed by other developments, which are discussed
below.

The Intervention

In 2010, the concluding comments from the United Nations Committee on
the Elimination of Racial Discrimination (CERD 2010) meeting with representatives from Australia expressed ongoing concerns regarding the status
of Indigenous peoples. In particular, it highlighted limited legislative protection regarding racial discrimination (13), higher incarceration rates (20), and
inadequate resources invested in Indigenous legal and interpretive services in
the criminal justice system (19). Significantly, despite a declared emphasis on
the importance of Indigenous cultures and rights, they also observed a lack
of investment of resources into their promotion (21). Altman and Hinkson
had previously also noted that "at the heart of the government's coercive
approach lies a clear intent to bring to an end the recognition of, and support
for, Aboriginal people living in remote communities pursuing culturally distinctive ways of life" (2007, 5).

Perhaps the best illustration of this issue can be found in the Northern
Territory Intervention. In 2007, the *Ampe Akelyernemane Meke Mekarle*
"Little Children are Sacred (LCAS)" report was released. This was ten years
after the *BTH* (1997) report had identified a range of serious and unresolved
issues for Indigenous Australians, and was released at a time when issues of
treaty, land ownership, political empowerment, and self-determination were
hotly debated topics (Short 2012). The *LCAS* report not only outlined the
incidents of child sexual abuse in remote Northern Territory communities but
also identified other concerning issues, as follows:

A breakdown of Aboriginal culture has been noted by many commentators. A number of underlying causes are said to explain the present state of both town and remote communities. Excessive consumption of alcohol is variously described as the cause or result of poverty, unemployment, lack of education, boredom, and overcrowded and inadequate housing. The use of other drugs and petrol sniffing can be added to these. Together, they lead to excessive violence. In the worst case scenario it leads to sexual abuse of children. (Wild and Anderson 2007, 12)

Hinkson argues that the rationalization of "protecting children" justified "draconian" measures, which included the suspension of the *Racial Discrimination Act* and other violations of rights while simultaneously reconfirming the Aboriginal stereotype of drunk, lazy, violent savages, who need to be protected from their own destructive patterns (2008). The seriousness of the claims and the descriptions of unacceptable living conditions were used to justify the hasty and drastic measures that followed. These included alcohol restrictions, welfare payment restrictions, banning of X-rated pornography, enforced school attendance, and compulsory health checks for children. Further, there were acquisitions of property by government, increase in policing and monitoring, removal of the permit system of common areas for communities, introduction of market-based rents and "normal" tenancy arrangements, and the appointment of managers to all government businesses within these communities (ibid., 2).

Initially, the decision to take immediate and definitive action regarding these concerns was welcomed as a means to address the existing social challenges (Anderson 2011). However, this quickly turned into disappointment and fear as these measures were implemented with little or no consultation with Indigenous communities, their leaders, or representatives (Hinkson 2008). Instead, the Intervention was played out as a moral rescue of the helpless and vulnerable who, in keeping with stereotype, seemed oriented toward self-destruction. Punitive actions, such as those mentioned above, were implemented by police and military in an indiscriminate manner, resulting in the treatment of these communities as "a problem to be solved" (Maddison 2009, 1). Hinkson quotes Sue Gordon, who was the head of the Northern Territory's Emergency Task Force. Gordon commented, "I appreciate people's concerns as to a lack of consultation. But . . . very clearly this was an emergency. If you have an emergency, like a tsunami or a cyclone, you do not have time to consult people in the initial phase" (2008, 7).

While the proponents of the Intervention claimed to have the welfare of Indigenous children as a driving force, Maddison (2009) reports that the authors of the *LCAS* report were "devastated" by the effects of their document, especially because very few, if any, of the ninety-seven recommendations of their report were implemented:

> The Intervention strategy made no reference to the "Little Children are Sacred" report on which it purported to rely. It has followed none of the recommendations. "Little Children are Sacred" specifically noted in its first recommendation that consultation with and the involvement of Aboriginal people in developing responses to child sexual abuse is critical. (Behrendt et al. 2008, 15)

Most importantly, as described below, the NTER not only failed to acknowledge the issues of structural racism that had contributed to these findings, but it also did nothing to strengthen or empower Indigenous culture from within:

> Why are welfare payments being tied to school attendance when there are not enough teachers and classrooms in the Northern Territory to cater for all Indigenous students? Why were mandatory physical examinations of children proposed when this not only breaches the rights to privacy and overrides the need for parental consent, but there are not enough doctors on the ground to perform such examinations or provide effective follow-up? Where are the health and counselling services needed to deal with such problems? Why aren't community medical services—which have been crying out for more resources for decades—being funded? (Ibid., 16)

Instead of creating solutions within the Indigenous communities based on careful consultation, the Intervention appeared to have land rights issues at its core, as described below:

> Minister Brough had presented a proposal to the Central Land Council offering to address basic housing repairs in exchange for the lease back of their land for ninety-nine years. The Council rejected his offer, saying that the people concerned did not want to sacrifice their control over land, especially for basic infrastructure, which should not be bartered for by government. (Behrendt, Watson, McCausland, and Vivian 2008, 17)

In *Walk with Us* (2011), the Aboriginal Elders' response to the Intervention, Rev Dr. Djiniyini Gondarra OAM (Galiwin'ku) shared similar concerns that a policy that appeared to be driven by humanitarian intent was driven by another motivation:

> The truth is that these Governments have used the Little Children are Sacred report as a Trojan horse to get what they really wanted. We believe the Northern

Territory Government and Federal Government are using the Intervention as an excuse to take our land. Aboriginal communities are communities where there are a lot of rich minerals and other resources that Government would use. (Ibid., 27)

A further complaint against the Intervention is that it failed to achieve its intended outcomes. In 2015, a research study was conducted to evaluate the success of the Intervention policies. This study demonstrated that only four of the thirteen "closing the gap" targets have seen improvement in the eight years since its implementation. Of the other nine measures, there has been either no improvement or decline in the quality of life scores (Gray 2016).

Similar to the Canadian example of justice issues, described by Cleyn in the current volume, the Intervention provides a clear illustration of a colonial "solution" firmly rooted in existing structures of power imbalance and oppression. Former prime minister of Australia, Malcolm Fraser, described the Intervention as "paternalistic and demeaning to Aboriginal people" (*Walk with Us* 2011, 5).

Huggins suggested that reconciliation in Australia is about three important elements, which may be paraphrased as follows: (1) recognizing the right of the Aboriginal and Torres Strait Islander peoples, as the First Australians, to express their cultures and participate on an equal footing in all aspects of Australian life; (2) achieving respectful and productive relationships between Indigenous and non-Indigenous peoples in all spheres; and (3) being able as a society, through the way institutions and communities operate, to acknowledge, value, and allow for difference (cited in Rothfield et al. 2008, xiv). In light of these criteria, it is clear that the journey toward reconciliation for Indigenous and non-Indigenous Australians had progressed very little, if at all, and only by superficial measures.

A CHANGE OF APPROACH

So far, this chapter has provided a summary of the relationship between Indigenous and non-Indigenous Australians and sketched out a brief history. As discussed, the inequalities and injustices have continued over the years, as the underlying imbalance remains unchanged. Tatz describes this it as follows:

There is a gulf between Aborigines and non-Aborigines. No other people, in Maureen Watson's words, have been so "wedded, enslaved, whitewashed and saved." Very few minorities have suffered anything like the duration and extent of the gun and the whip, the neck chains and the rape, the exile to remoteness, the break-up of families, the forcible removal of children, the indefinite periods of legal wardship and minority status, the levels of want, poverty, deprivation, and exclusion as of now. For the vast majority of Aborigines and Islanders, the past is not a foreign country. What present governments say they (may) have endured, the Indigenous Australians still endure: wholesale imprisonments, constant removal of children to institutions of various kinds, gross ill-health, appalling environmental conditions, unemployability, increasing illiteracy, family breakdown, increased internal violence, and almost unbelievable levels of youth suicide. (1998, 3)

For this reason, gestures of reconciliation that operate within existing hegemonies are limited in their effectiveness. A new approach needs to be considered—one that is grounded in an appreciation of the political, relational, and spiritual dimensions of the issue. Redekop (2002) offers a five-point framework for conceptualizing the needs and motivations of communities who have experienced deep-rooted violence (colonization is included in this category). According to Redekop, these *Human Identity Needs* of meaning, connectedness, security, recognition, and action provide a useful framework for illustrating the ways in which groups are affected by these experiences of injustice. The colonization experience has deeply wounded Indigenous Australians according to each of these needs—destroying their meaning system, damaging relationships among people and the land, threatening security, diminishing agency, and definitely not providing recognition of dignity and rights. This may, in part, explain why "closing the gap" strategies employed by the government have not achieved their objectives as hoped. As stated below:

For many years, the predominant government policy was informed by the view that practical measures of overcoming disadvantage can operate in isolation from the spiritual aspects of reconciliation. In reality, it is impossible to separate attempts to better employment, housing, education, health or income status of Indigenous Australians from the attainment of greater respect for and recognition of difference in culture, historical perspective and priorities. How you feel about yourself—the sense you have of who you are—is intrinsic to how you behave. If you believe you're beaten, then you're beaten. If you believe you're an outsider, then you're an outsider. For all intents and purposes, if you believe that the rest of Australia has no respect for you or your culture, then it does not. (Huggins, xiv, cited in Rothfield et al. 2008)

In light of Redekop's *Identity Needs* model, the remainder of this chapter will be dedicated to reflecting on a framework that has been developed by John Paul Lederach, a prominent voice in the field of peacebuilding and community healing. Lederach describes reconciliation in the following way:

Reconciliation, we have seen, is focused on building relationships between antagonists. The relational dimension involves the emotional and psychological aspects of the conflict and the need to recognize past grievances and explore future interdependence. Reconciliation as a locus creates a space for the encounters by the parties, a place where the diverse, but connected energies and concerns driving the conflict can meet, including the paradoxes of truth, mercy, justice and peace. (1997, 34)

Lederach's understanding of reconciliation moves away from top-down model of change. Instead, it is to be understood as a process, or a journey, rather than as a final point (2005). Too often, he comments, governments and groups envision a reconciliation journey as having a finite time frame restricted to a term of government office, or even shorter, which he considers unrealistic when considering the delicate nature of human relationships. This is absolutely the case in Australia, where the direction of the reconciliation agenda has changed multiple times over recent decades, according to the mindset of the government in power (Maddison 2009).

Most significantly, he offers an opportunity to reframe the case through the lens of *The Moral Imagination.* This, he explains, is "the capacity to imagine something rooted in the challenges of the real world, yet capable of giving birth to that which does not yet exist" (Lederach 2005, ix), and it demonstrates Lederach's core belief that it is the human capacity to be creative that can yield the most surprising and hopeful results. *The Moral Imagination* incorporates four key elements as fundamental to the peacebuilding process. They may be summarized as follows: (1) conceptualizing a web of relationships, (2) sustaining paradoxical curiosity, (3) maintaining a belief in and the pursuit of the creative act, and (4) an acceptance of inherent risk (ibid., 5). Each of these four elements work as powerful guideposts in providing opportunities for healing and reconciliation. Even though these could helpfully be adopted by all sides in a conflict, it should be noted that the burden of responsibility falls on the Settler group to embody these principles.

Conceptualizing a Web of Relationships

The first of the four requires that parties perceive themselves and one other as participants in a "web of relationships." He states that "peacebuilding requires a vision of relationship. Stated bluntly, if there is no capacity to imagine the canvas of mutual relationships and situate oneself as part of that historic and ever-evolving web, peacebuilding collapses" (ibid., 35). In support of this view, Govier makes the following point:

> It is exactly because people must live together and work together that reconciliation matters. If past divides persist to structure present and future relationships,

there will be little security in the new structures. In all this, relationships are fundamental: it matters how people see each other and how they feel about each other . . . Even when large groups of people are involved, feelings and attitudes matter. (2006, 17)

By conceptualizing interdependence, parties are drawn into encounter and dialogue to achieve constructive outcomes. Too often in conflict situations, parties withdraw from engagement and sever connections. This disconnection results in ignorance, stereotyping, and oversimplifying the motive of the "enemy" group.

Lack of understanding, particularly by Settlers toward Indigenous communities, remains an inhibiting factor in the Australian case. W. E. H. Stanner (an influential voice in the anthropological study of Aboriginal culture) affirms this view by observing "that the grossly unequal relationship . . . found their root in the British failure to comprehend, much less to tolerate, legitimate difference." This incomprehension has continued to this day, because "a different tradition leaves us tongueless and earless towards this other [Aboriginal] world of meaning and significance" (cited in Clendinnen 2005, 58). This claim is affirmed by Indigenous writers who identify understanding between groups as critical to the reconciliation process. By extension, it is a lack of understanding that serves as an underlying factor in experiences of Indigenous disadvantage at a social, economic, and political level. For example, Patrick Dodson states, "Australia is a nation that is paralysed by [its] failure to imagine any relationship with first peoples other than assimilation" (Dodson, cited in Collingwood Whittick 2009, 127).

By contrast, Lederach's concept of a *web of relationships* may be a starting point upon which to build a foundation of trust between groups. As Govier states: "What is crucial for reconciliation is that relationships of animosity and fear be replaced by better relationships, characterized by acceptance and respect, and at least some degree of trust" (Govier 2006, 18). This sentiment is articulated repeatedly by Indigenous leaders and other prominent voices, as illustrated below:

I would envisage dialogue to take place . . . with the people of Australia, accepting each other as human beings first and foremost, being proud of the diversity of cultures that is now evolving in Australia . . . most of all being proud that we have one of the longest continuing cultures in history. (*Walk with Us* 2011, 41)

Similarly, the 2017 *Uluru Statement from the Heart* pronounces that

Makarrata is the culmination of our agenda: the coming together after a struggle. It captures our aspirations for a fair and truthful relationship with the people of

Australia and a better future for our children based on justice and self-determination. (Referendum Council 2017)

In July 2006, Mick Dodson, a prominent Indigenous academic and spokesperson, standing alongside Prime Minister Howard, presented a clear commitment to moving forward together in partnership, stating: "I am here today to tell the Prime Minister that I am ready to walk alongside him in taking the next steps towards reconciliation. I believe that you, Prime Minister, are here for the same reason." He concludes, "The time is right to take the next step. Together" (Maddison 2009, xxxiii).

As the Australian nation journeys toward reconciliation, it is hoped that previous "paternalistic" approaches may be replaced by a relationship of equals that is "just and mature" (National Congress of Australia's First Peoples 2016). Lederach's concept of a *web of relationships* allows for equal consultation to be at the forefront of any future directions. Northern Territory Anti-Discrimination Commissioner, Mr. Cubillo states:

> There needs to be a change of view. Aboriginal people want to be involved. I hear a lot about making changes, but no-one has actually listened to how the Aboriginal people want to do that . . . the best people to give you advice on it are the people living there themselves. (Harris 2012, 26–27)

Sustain Paradoxical Curiosity

Consistent with the conceptualization of a *web of relationships* is the importance of cultivating of "paradoxical curiosity" by all parties toward one another. Lederach explains this second element in the following way:

> When the two terms are combined, we have *paradoxical curiosity* which approaches social realities with an abiding respect for complexity, a refusal to fall prey to the pressures of forced dualistic categories of truth, and an inquisitiveness about what may hold together seemingly contradictory and even violently opposed social energies together. (2005, 36)

As previously discussed, processes of reconciliation may be hindered by parties who hold rigid, narrow, and outdated conceptions of one another. Therefore, the challenge is to step away from dualistic "right/wrong" or "us/them" classifications and to allow for complexity and ambiguity. Paradoxical curiosity requires that parties relax these preconceived ideas, and become open to learning the histories, narratives, and meanings of the other without judgment or critique.

In Australia, there has been an ongoing denial of Indigenous story and narrative as a part of the nation's history. Australia's collective identity has been built around sanitized ideas of mateship, a "fair go," and courageous support of military allies (Macintyre 1999). However, the "Great Australian Silence" that was famously heralded by W. E. H. Stanner in the 1960s (cited by Short 2012) has continued, driven by a firm resistance against telling of stories and acknowledging how these experiences of the past may be contributing factors to the disadvantage of today.

For many Australians, the 1997 *Bringing Them Home* report was significant in revealing the extent of the damage caused by child removal policies. The authors of the report dedicated it to the courage and generosity of hundreds of Indigenous contributors who were willing to share memories, stories, and experiences, many of which were distressing and painful to tell. Since then, other stories of injustice, violence, and murder have come to light, and are expected to continue for years to come. As recently as November 2019, a map indicating locations and details of Indigenous massacres was published by a University of Newcastle research team (Ryan et al. 2019). This resource continues to be amended and modified as new data come to light. According to Maddison, this type of work (building a shared understanding of the stories of the past) is critical to moving toward reconciliation. She states, "It is only when a nation has found the ability to acknowledge past wrongs and break the bonds of solidarity with the perpetrators of historic injustice that the past can become history" (Maddison 2012, 12).

Finally, *paradoxical curiosity* makes room for difference without a need to absorb dualities. This concept was endorsed by a number of community members during the Northern Territory consultations in 2011, during a discussion around the structure of education. "You have to recognise both . . . Learn both Indigenous and the Western. Put it together. If you want to learn our culture, come, fit in, sit with us, learn our culture" (Harris 2011, 41; note Cecil Chabot's chapter on Windigo is a good example of this, *Transforming*). Another community member states: "You are looking at this education is [*sic*] Western side, but why not accepting our education model, our culture, our stories, our knowledge, our future for our future children to pass our knowledge as one? Why has that not been recognised?" (ibid., 42). Paradoxical curiosity allows for multiple, concurrent truths without the need for one to dominate another. In this sense, groups have the freedom to coexist and cooperate without acceding identity or uniqueness.

Belief and Pursuit of the Creative Act

The first two elements of Lederach's *Moral Imagination* describe the need to conceptualize all parties in a *web of relationships* where history, culture, and engagement are characterized by a sense of *paradoxical curiosity*. From this point of view, Lederach highlights the particular role of the artist as a speaker of truth and identifies *belief in and the pursuit of the creative act* as the third key element for facilitating engagement and reconciliation. Creative arts (dance, poetry, painting, and storytelling) might then be understood as a means of communication between Indigenous and non-Indigenous communities. Through this type of expression, the artist not only represents the reality of the world around him/her but also invites its witness to be open to the possibility of something more. He says, "Creativity and imagination, the artist giving birth to something new, proposes to us avenues of inquiry and ideas about how we know the world, how we are in the world and most important, what in the world is possible" (2005, 39). It is the deep immersion in the present as well as the hopeful sense of a transcendent "other" that makes the artist both essential to their community and simultaneously positioned as an outlier (ibid.).

While mainstream approaches may advocate for creative practices as a periphery to other project-based, "practical" strategies of reconciliation, Lederach places an emphasis on simple expressions of human experience and identity at the core of peacebuilding. Once more, his approach is well-aligned to Redekop's theory of *Human Identity Needs* (2002). As Lederach states, "Culture links individual and collective identities, providing symbols (some of the deeply invested with affect or emotion) that connect individuals to others 'like them' while at the same time separating those individuals from 'unlike others'" (2002, 79). Symbols are sources of *meaning* and *recognition* that open up new possibilities for *empowerment* (action) and *connection*.

Aboriginal Catholic Ministry, in the city of Melbourne, has demonstrated the effectiveness of this type of initiative. In the front garden of their suburban office, there is an outdoor art exhibition that was created by an Indigenous artist. Each of the eight stations tells stories (both painful and uplifting) of the past, and shares hopes for the future. They are a talking piece of history and an opportunity for education. Elsewhere throughout the property wall murals, artworks, and other symbols are featured to immerse visitors in the richness of Indigenous culture. The office, sponsored by the Catholic Archdiocese of Melbourne and managed by an Indigenous coordinator, has the following vision statement:

> To be perceived as an Aboriginal Community recognised for its commitment to Aboriginal and Torres Strait Islander Peoples having their rightful place in the Church and the wider community.
>
> Inspired by the Gospel, we are committed to the dignity of each person, to open hospitality, to truth-telling about dispossession, to be a place of connection.
>
> We work for reconciliation in partnership with those who believe that there can be an alternative to the present order. (ACM 2020, 15)

It is the artwork, in all of its expressions, that facilitates this conversation, and draws people into a deeper understanding of the struggle, resilience, and hope of Indigenous Catholics in Victoria.

The Willingness to Risk

The final element identified by Lederach is the willingness to risk. He states, "To risk is to step into the unknown without any guarantee of success or even safety. Risk by its very nature is mysterious" (2005, 39).

During the 1990s, there were some pioneering reconciliation initiatives, particularly at the popular level (Halloran 2007). Community-based education resources and "study circles" that were introduced by the CAR in the 1990s were popular and well received (Gunstone 2005). A further advancement was the quarterly publication of *Walking Together* (1991–2001), which covered key issues in the reconciliation journey. It emphasized positive steps taken and reached a distribution of approximately 75,000 copies. Another significant highlight was the national *Sorry Day* celebration, where hundreds of thousands of people walked across the Sydney Harbour Bridge in a public declaration of unity in May of the year 2000.

A particular example can be seen in the Australia Day celebrations in the New South Wales township of Lismore. Patrick McAllister describes the event in detail below:

> A distinctively different Australia Day performance was created through an innovative reworking of old elements (for example, adding the reconciliation award to the established set of awards), through changing the content of certain aspects (for example, directing the nature of speeches), through accentuating certain elements at the expense of others (for example, reconciliation at the expense of blind patriotism), through redefining meaning (for example, the meaning of loyalty to the nation through the group RockOnciliation singing the national anthem) and through the introduction of elements taken from different contexts that served to refashion relationships symbolically (for example, the "welcome to country"). (2009, 177–78)

Overall, the event was regarded as a success. Beyond winning the NSW Statewide award for "Most Creative Australia Day," this community celebration achieved an outcome infinitely more impressive:

> In a report written by a member of the organizing Committee (LCC 1998, 7–9), the ceremony was described as "an uplifting and powerful experience . . . It felt like we were in a cocoon, a time capsule, cut off from the rest of the world . . . we were sharing something very special together." There was a

"whole-heartedness, honesty and depth of feeling in the speeches [that] took everyone present to a deeper space in their hearts, to a place where we experienced our humanity, and appreciated the joy, pain and opportunity that we, as Australians, have in common." It was an event "creative in the deepest sense of the word: it connected us to our sense of community, built cultural bridges, and it felt good to be there." (Ibid., 168–69)

This example of Lismore's Australia Day Celebrations illustrates how local acts of creativity, communication, and inclusion are capable of transforming attitudes and building powerful connections. It illustrates Lederach's assertion that "time and again, social change that sticks and makes a difference has behind it the artists' intuition" (2005, 73).

CONCLUSION

Contrasted against a 40,000-year history, the journey toward reconciliation for Australia's Indigenous and non-Indigenous communities is only a few decades old. As with similar countries, the damage caused by the colonization project is only recently finding its place in public discourse. In Australia, stories of subjugation, disease, dispossession, and massacre are being shared, in many instances, for the first time. While a formal apology has been issued for the forced child removal policies of the twentieth century, other strategies geared toward a "unified" nation appear to disregard the unresolved injustices of the past. Recognition of equal status and rights, prior land ownership, and self-determination continue to be the objectives at the heart of Indigenous activism.

Many of the challenges faced by Indigenous communities today are a result of the White Australia assimilation policies. The damage that has been caused to Indigenous cultures—the forced removal of Aboriginal children from their families and communities, the absence of legislative frameworks of the protection of rights and representation, the lack of recognition of a diverse array of traditions and values, and the absence of any meaningful consultation—indicate that cultural genocide, initiated more than 200 years ago, is still at work.

Yet at a deeper level, this crisis is about the struggle for identity, culture, and voice. Removal from ancestral lands and communities has a strong, spiritual dimension for Indigenous groups, and the consequential disconnect from language and story, as well as familial and traditional ways, is an assault against their fundamental Human Identity Needs.

Lederach's *Moral Imagination* provides an opportunity to consider ways forward in light of these needs and a framework for facilitating healing and reconciliation between Australia's diverse communities. Recognizing a *web of relationships*, and acknowledging ways in which a lack of understanding of one another has created damaging distance and isolation, might be an important step forward. Understanding the need to learn about one another, hearing stories, and allowing for multiple truths and realities may also be a way to exercise *paradoxical curiosity*. In creative cultural expression, there is hope that communities may be reaffirmed in shared identities and values as well as providing a medium of communication that allows for an understanding of difference. Finally, *The Moral Imagination* calls for a *willingness to risk*. That is, to be open to the emergence of new directions, symbols, meanings, and connections.

This chapter argues for a reconceptualization of the relationships between communities in Australia. It suggests that within Lederach's framework, where artistic expression of culture, historical narratives, and values are given central importance, there exists the opportunity to express, acknowledge, and heal the wounds of the past. In reaffirming the essence of diverse, but not unequal identities, we can be empowered to create positive social and structural justice.

REFERENCES

Aboriginal Catholic Ministry. Forthcoming 2020. *The Seed Has Grown: Our Story.* Thornbury: Aboriginal Catholic Ministry.

Aborigines Protection Act, 1909 (No. 25). Accessed online July 15, 2014. https://www.legislation.nsw.gov.au/acts/1909-25.pdf.

Altman, Jon, and Melinda Hinkson. 2007. *Coercive Reconciliation: Stabilise, Normalise, Exit Aboriginal Australia.* North Carlton, Australia: Arena Publications Association.

Anderson, Pat. 2011. "Pat Anderson: Intervention Neither Well-intentioned nor Well-evidenced." *Crikey Pat Anderson Intervention Neither Well-Intentioned nor Well-Evidenced Comments.* Accessed July 21, 2015. https://www.crikey.com.au/2011/05/05/pat-anderson-intervention-neither-well-intentioned-nor-well-evidenced/.

Auguste, Isabelle. 2010. "Rethinking the Nation: Apology, Treaty and Reconciliation in Australia." *National Identities*, 12(4). Taylor & Francis Group, Routledge. Accessed November 19, 2014. http://www.tandfonline.com/doi/abs/10.1080/14608944.2010.520984#.VGorgvnF9tU.

Behrendt, Larissa, Nicole Watson, Ruth McCausland, and Alison Vivian. 2008. *Submission to the Review of the Northern Territory National Emergency Response.* University of Technology Sydney Jumbunna Indigenous House of Learning. Accessed online October 28, 2019. https://www.uts.edu.au/sites/default/files/NTNER_Submission_1.pdf.

Brennan, Gerard. 1999. "Reconciliation." *University of New South Wales Law Journal*, 22(2), 595. Accessed online August 1, 2015. http://classic.austlii.edu.au/au/journals/UNSWLawJl/1999/10.html.

Clendinnen, Inga. 2003. *Dancing with Strangers*. Melbourne: Text Pub.

Collingwood-Whittick, Sheila. 2012. "Australia's NT Intervention and Indigenous Rights on Language, Education and Culture: An Ethnocidal Solution to Aboriginal 'Dysfunction'?" In *Indigenous Rights in the Age of the UN Declaration*, edited by E. Pulitano and M. Trask. Cambridge: Cambridge University Press. Accessed online October 25, 2019. https://www.academia.edu/39609842/Australia_s_NT_intervention_and_Indigenous_rights_on_languala_education_and_culture?email_work_card=view-paper.

Corntassel, Jeff, and Cindy Holder. 2008. "Who's Sorry Now? Government Apologies, Truth Commissions, and Indigenous Self-Determination in Australia, Canada, Guatemala, and Peru." *Human Rights Review*, 9(4), 456–489.

Council for Aboriginal Reconciliation Act 1991 (No 127). Accessed online January 10, 2020. https://www.legislation.gov.au/Details/C2004C03090.

Davis, Megan. 2006. "Treaty, Yeah? The Utility of a Treaty in Advancing Reconciliation in Australia." *Alternative Law Journal*, 31(3), 127–136.

Dodson, M. 1997. "Land Rights and Social Justice." In *Our Land is Our Life: Land Rights – Past, Present and Future*, edited by Galarrwuy Yunupingu (pp. 39–51). Australia: University of Queensland Press.

Govier, Trudy. 2006. *Taking Wrongs Seriously: Acknowledgement, Reconciliation, and the Politics of Sustainable Peace*. Amherst, NY: Humanity.

Gunstone, Andrew. 2005. "The Formal Australian Reconciliation Process, 1991–2000." *Proceedings of National Reconciliation Planning Workshop, May 30–31, 2005*, Old Parliament House, Canberra. Accessed online July 24, 2015. https://pdfs.semanticscholar.org/7600/034853d481c56dd655d118c09ce205506637.pdf.

Gunstone, Andrew R. 2012. "Reconciliation and the 'Great Australian Silence'." In *The Refereed Proceedings of the 2012 Australian Political Studies Association Conference*, edited by R. Eccleston, N. Sageman, and F. Gray (pp. 1–17). Melbourne, Vic, Australia: Australian Political Studies Association. Accessed online July 10, 2015. https://www.auspsa.org.au/sites/default/files/reconciliation_and_the_great_australian_silence_andrew_gunstone.pdf.

Gray, Steven. 2016. "Scoring the Intervention: Fail Grades on Closing the Gap, Human Rights." *Indigenous Law Bulletin*, 8(23), 10–14. Accessed online November 1, 2019. http://classic.austlii.edu.au/au/journals/IndigLawB/2016/9.pdf.

Grieves, Vicki. 2009. *Aboriginal Spirituality: Aboriginal Philosophy, the Basis of Aboriginal Social and Emotional Wellbeing*. Aboriginial Health Discussion Paper Series, Publication Number 9. Casuarina, NT: Cooperative Research Centre for Aboriginal Health. Accessed online November 12, 2019. http://www.crcah.org.au/publications/downloads/DP9-Aboriginal-Spirituality.pdf.

Halloran, Michael J. 2007. "Indigenous Reconciliation in Australia: Do Values, Identity and Collective Guilt Matter?" *Journal of Community & Applied Social Psychology*, 17(1), 1–18.

Harris, Michelle, ed. 2011. *NT Consultations Report 2011: By Quotations.* Notting Hill, Vic: Vega Press.

Harris, Michelle, ed. 2012. *A Decision to Discriminate: Disempowerment Aboriginal in the Northern Territory.* East Melbourne: Concerned Australians.

Hinkson, Melinda, and Jeremy Beckett. 2008. *An Appreciation of Difference WEH Stanner and Aboriginal Australia.* Canberra, ACT: Aboriginal Studies Press.

Huggins, Jackie. 2008. "Preface: The Human Face of Indigenous Australia." In *Pathways to Reconciliation: Between Theory and Practice*, edited by Philipa Rothfield, Cleo Fleming, and Paul A. Komesaroff (pp. xiii–xvii). Aldershot, England: Ashgate.

Keating, Paul. 1992. "Year for the World's Indigenous People." *Speech in Redfern Park by Prime Minister Paul Keating*, December 10, 1992. Accessed online April 30, 2015. https://www.creativespirits.info/aboriginalculture/politics/paul-keatings -redfern-speech#toc2.

Laws, J. 2000. "Interview with John Howard, Prime Minister of Australia (Sydney, May 29, 2000), in Bennan, S. Gunn, B. and Williams, G. 2004, 'Sovereignty' and its Relevance to Treaty-Making Between Indigenous Peoples and Australian Governments." *Sydney Law Review*, 26(3), 308.

Lederach, John Paul. 1997. *Building Peace: Sustainable Reconciliation in Divided Societies.* Washington, DC: United States Institute of Peace.

Lederach, John Paul. 2005. *The Moral Imagination: The Art and Soul of Building Peace.* Oxford: Oxford UP.

Macintyre, Stuart. 1999. *A Concise History of Australia.* Cambridge, UK: Cambridge UP.

Maddison, Sarah. 2009. *Black Politics: Inside the Complexity of Aboriginal Political Culture.* Crows Nest, NSW: Allen & Unwin.

McAllister, Patrick. 2009. "National Celebration or Local Act of Reconciliation? Public Ritual Performance and Inter-Ethnic Relations in an Australian City." *CANF Anthropological Forum*, 19(2), 163–183.

Muldoon, Paul, and Andrew Schaap. 2012. "Aboriginal Sovereignty and the Politics of Reconciliation: The Constituent Power of the Aboriginal Embassy in Australia." *Environment and Planning D: Society and Space*, 30(3), 534–550.

National Congress of Australia's First Peoples. 2016. *Aboriginal and Torres Strait Islander Peak Organisations Unite: The Redfern Statement*, 9 June. Accessed online December 8, 2019. http://nationalcongress.com.au/wp-content/uploads/ 2016/10/The-Redfern-Statement-9-June-2016.pdf.

Nobles, Melissa. 2008. *The Politics of Official Apologies.* New York, NY: Cambridge UP.

Read, Peter. 1981. *The Stolen Generations: The Removal of Aboriginal Children in New South Wales 1883 to 1969.* New South Wales, Surry Hills: New South Wales Department of Aboriginal Affairs.

Redekop, Vern Neufeld. 2002. *From Violence to Blessing: How an Understanding of Deep-Rooted Conflict Can Open Paths to Reconciliation.* Ottawa, ONT: Novalis.

Referendum Council. 2017. *Uluru Statement from the Heart.* Accessed online November 1, 2019. https://ulurustatement.org/the-statement.

Short, Damian. 2012. "When Sorry Isn't Good Enough: Official Remembrance and Reconciliation in Australia." In *When Sorry Isn't Good Enough: Official Remembrance and Reconciliation in Australia.* SAGE. Accessed online November 17, 2014. http://mss.sagepub.com/content/5/3/293.

Short, Damien. 2010. "Australia: A Continuing Genocide?" *Journal of Genocide Research,* 12(1–2), 45–68. Accessed online April 30, 2015. https://www.research gate.net/publication/47412860_Australia_a_continuing_genocide/link/02e7e528 3447f28248000000/download.

Tatz, Colin. 1998. "The Reconciliation 'Bargain'." *Melbourne Journal of Politics,* 25(1), 120–130.

Ryan, Lyndall, William Pascoe, Jennifer Debenham, Stephanie Gilbert, Jonathan Richards, Robyn Smith, Chris Owen, Robert J. Anders, Mark Brown, Daniel Price, Jack Newley, and Kaine Usher. 2019. *Colonial Frontier Massacres, Australia (Date Range: 1780 to 1930).* Australia: University of Newcastle. Accessed online January 8, 2020. https://c21ch.newcastle.edu.au/colonialmassacres/map.php.

UN Committee on the Elimination of Racial Discrimination (CERD). 2010. *Report of the Committee on the Elimination of Racial Discrimination: Seventy-Sixth Session (15 February–12 March 2010), Seventy-Seventh Session (August 2–27, 2010),* A/65/18. Accessed online, July 10, 2015. https://www.refworld.org/docid/4ef1 977f2.html.

UN News. May 25, 2011. "Australia: UN Urges Rethink of Policies on Indigenous Peoples and Asylum-Seekers." Accessed online February 2, 2016. https://news.un .org/en/story/2011/05/376282-australia-un-urges-rethink-policies-indigenous-peop les-and-asylum-seekers.

Wild, Rex, and Pat Anderson. 2007. "Ampe Akelyernemane Meke Mekarle Little Children Are Sacred." *Report of the Northern Territory Board of Inquiry into the Protection of Aboriginal Children from Sexual Abuse.* Northern Territory Government, April 30, 2007. Accessed online October 10, 2014. http://www.inqu irysaac.nt.gov.au/pdf/bipacsa_final_report.pdf.

Wilson, Sir Ronald, and Pat Dodson (Commissioners). 1997. *Bringing Them Home Report of the National Inquiry into the Separation of Aboriginal and Torres Strait Islander Children from Their Families.* Sydney: Human Rights and Equal Opportunity Commission. Accessed online May 30, 2015. https://www.humanrig hts.gov.au/our-work/bringing-them-home-report-1997.

Young, Robin. 2009. "The Stolen Generation." *Psychotherapy in Australia,* 16(1), 59.

Walk with Us: Aboriginal Elders Call Out to Australian People to Walk with them in their Quest for Justice. 2011. East Melbourne: Concerned Australians.

Part IV

COMPLEXITY, COMMUNITY, AND EMERGENT DEVELOPMENT

Chapter 16

Harnessing Principles of Complex Systems for Understanding and Modulating Social Structures

Neil D. Theise with Catherine Twinn,
Gloria Neufeld Redekop, and Lissane Yoannes

Complex systems, with many constantly changing and interacting parts, adapt to new situations in surprising ways, without any single participating member being in control. The regulating characteristics of complex systems, which encourage the creativity of adaptive self-organization, will be reviewed with reference to a variety of examples, cells in the creation of living tissues, organs, and organisms; ants as they organize into colonies; and, in particular, humans self-organizing into social structures. From the mathematical point of view of complex systems theory, there are no significant differences between these various examples, because it is a special feature of such systems that the principles, processes, and outcomes are scalable, applying across all scales of size. Indeed, not only at cellular and the social levels are these principles found, but throughout existence from the smallest scales of the quantum realm (Theise and Kafatos 2013a, b, 2016), to the biochemical and cellular realms (Theise 2005; Theise and Harris 2006; Theise 2006), to the realm of flocking birds, schools of fish, and ant colonies (Theise and Kafatos 2013a, b, 2016), to humans and their societies and cultures, and still further upward to ecosystems (Johnson 2001; Kauffman 1993, 2019; Lewin 1999), the planetary self-organization enshrined in James Lovelock's Gaia hypothesis (Theise & Kafatos 2013b, 2016) and the supra-galactic scales of the universe (Theise and Kafatos 2016).

Systems of individuals will self-organize into larger-scale adaptive structures when they fulfill four criteria (Johnson 2001; Lewin 1999; Theise 2006): (1) sufficient numbers to generate a diversity of creative interactions; (2) predominance of negative, homeostatic feedback loops over positive feedback

Table 16.1 Definitions

	A Definition	Synonyms
Systems	Groups of interacting individuals.	
Complex systems	Groups of interacting individuals that, fulfilling certain criteria, give rise to *emergent self-organization* that is *adaptive*.	Complex systems Complex adaptive systems Dynamical systems Complex dynamical systems
Complexity theory	Theoretical understandings and mathematical descriptions of the behavioral/functional criteria that lead to the features of complex systems.	Complex systems theory
Emergent self-organization	Large-scale structures that arise—in a bottom-up, unplanned fashion—from the local interactions between individuals comprising a complex system at the smaller levels of scale.	Emergent properties Emergence
Adaptive	The ability to alter the forms of self-organization so that the system as a whole can survive changes in the environment.	
Homeostasis	The tendency toward a relatively stable equilibrium between interdependent elements.	
Negative feedback loop	Best defined by example: A heater turns on when the temperature of a room drops to a certain low point. When the temperature rises to a certain high point, the heater turns off. Thus, negative feedback loops tend to keep a system in *homeostasis*. When negative feedback loops that govern interindividual interactions predominate over positive feedback loops, adaptive self-organization is possible.	Homeostatic feedback loop
Positive feedback loop	Best defined by example: When a room warms up a heater turns on. The hotter it gets, the more the heater is turned up. Thus, homeostasis is not achieved and any system governed by positive feedback loops will eventually consume all available energy for its sustenance.	

Table 16.1 (*Continued*)

	A Definition	Synonyms
	In systems, a predominance of positive feedback loops governing interactions does not preclude emergent self-organization. However, these structures will be energy expending and self-limited rather than adaptive. Examples: normal cells become cancerous, healthy economies have hyperactive bubbles that end in collapse, war fevers overtake communities and war follows.	
Quenched disorder	The limited, low-level randomness present in all complex systems. Too much randomness: the system can't self-organize in sustainable ways. Too little randomness: the system's structures can't change in response to environmental changes leading to large-scale (perhaps systemwide) collapse. *Quenched disorder* results in production of *adjacent possible* (see below) by creating unplanned changes in modes of self-organization.	Criticality
Adjacent possibles	Unplanned modes of self-organization enabled by quenched disorder in the system. Most adjacent possibles may never occur or may be nonadaptive and thus not give rise to emergence. However, all successful adaptations that allow a complex system to thrive begin as an adjacent possible.	Adjacent possibilities Emergent creativity

loops; (3) important interactions are local, not global—no member of the system is truly monitoring the status of the whole or planning its organizational interactions; and (4) limited randomness or *quenched disorder*. A corollary to these is the inevitability of partial or complete mass extinction events that occur when systems fail to adapt to evolving conditions with sufficient speed (e.g., the coronavirus pandemic is an unfortunate current/recent event). Definitions of the key terms for this chapter are summarized in Table 16.1

CRITERIA FOR COMPLEX ADAPTIVE EMERGENCE

In the realm of human affairs in which there might be a capacity to reflect upon and consciously influence conditions, consideration of the criteria that promote emergent creativity in a system can play a helpful role in enhancing the potential for novel, beneficial, adaptive creativity to emerge. What follows is an elaboration on these four criteria. Note: This is not to say that we can then exercise "global sensing/top-down planning" to control emergence! But, of course, the systemic interventions we might consider have their effects on the local conditions.

Numbers Matter

One needs sufficient numbers of interacting individuals to create emergent self-organization. "Numbers matter" (Johnson 2001). Three ants do not make a colony, though twenty-five ants are sufficient. Out of such diversity, there is self-organization of tunnel digging, food line formation, and designation of space for a "cemetery" where bodies of dead ants are placed and dumps are established for depositing refuse. This can be readily seen in the self-contained ant farms sold for children (or curious adults). The twenty-five ants contained in the small-scale environment produce all the above structures, but as ants gradually die off, these become less and less well organized until finally, with only a small number of ants, such self-organization disappears altogether.

Not only will any system need a minimum number of individuals to accomplish adaptive self-organization, but the greater the numbers of individuals in the system, the more complex and elaborate will be their emergent structures. Thus, an ant colony comprising twenty-five ants is not as complex as one with a hundred, or a thousand, or ten thousand, or a super colony made up of small or large subcolonies. In human terms: a village is not a city is not a megalopolis.

One reason for this increasing complexity is that with increasing numbers, exponentially greater diversity of interactions can take place, resulting in greater production of adjacent possibles. Diversity is key. Thus, one can generate greater complexity by increasing diversity, by enlarging the group, or by creating new modes of interaction that increase the interactivity between them.

Homeostasis Maintained by Feedback Loops

It is not only the number and range of interactions that govern the ability and likelihood of emergent self-organization but also the nature of those interactions. Interactions can often form *feedback loops*, which may be classed as *negative* or *positive* (Johnson 2001; Lewin 1999). These are easily defined with reference to temperature control in a room.

A negative feedback loop is how temperature control is normally maintained. When a room is sufficiently cold, a heater turns on. When the temperature rises to the appropriate temperature, the heater turns off. Thus, the room is always kept within set boundaries. In this example, the boundaries are set by the person who occupies the room. In the complex systems of nature, the setting of boundaries itself is an emergent property called *homeostasis*, the comfortable state of equilibrium. Living systems keep aspects such as nutritional status, body temperature, and sleep/arousal systems within healthy boundaries that allow the system (the ant, the person, the ecosystem) to survive. In fact, all biological systems, inclusive of human social systems, are not rigidly stable, but oscillating between boundaries under the influence of such negative, homeostatic feedback loops.

Positive feedback loops can also exist within complex adaptive systems. An example would be a room in which the heater turns on when it gets warmer to make the room even hotter. If present, positive feedback loops are usually constrained by the interfering predominance of negative feedback loops. However, if they are insufficiently opposed by negative feedback then, while self-organization may still occur, it will be energy expending and self-limited, rather than adaptive. Examples to consider would include weather patterns such as hurricanes or tornadoes and normal tissues that undergo genetic events eliminating homeostasis and resulting in cancers. Socially, we might consider sustainable economic growth versus "bubbles" and sustained peace versus war fever.

Note that the use of the words "positive" and "negative" does not indicate moral or qualitative judgments such as "good" or "bad"; rather, "positive" is like the accelerator of a car and "negative" is like the brake and steering wheel—all are needed to get where you want to go. Prevention of calamitous economic policies or descent into the chaos of war may therefore be approached from the perspective of encouraging robust feedback loops that are homeostatic—leading to a sustainable state of affairs—between members or functional aspects of society as well as early recognition of expanding positive feedback loops that may be modulated by social and educational policies.

No Global Sensing or Top-Down Control

No individual within the system is monitoring the global state of the system as a way of driving self-organization and adaptation; all members of the system are simply reacting to local stimuli (Johnson 2001; Lewin 1999). So, no ant is assessing whether the colony has enough food or needs a bigger tunnel system (the "queen" serves only a reproductive function; she is not, in fact, a governing monarch). Instead, each ant is simply responding to local cues, such as pheromones produced by other ants or touch (e.g., direct contact with terrain, other ants, potential food). Likewise, no cell in our bodies is noting whether we're tired, hungry, thirsty, and so on. Each cell simply responds to interactions with other cells, or with a connective tissue matrix in their environment, or nutrient status coming via the blood, or signaling molecules dispersed from cells near (e.g., neurotransmitters between nerves) or far (e.g., hormones like insulin or estrogen that are produced by one organ that influence cells dispersed throughout the body).

That global sensing and top-down control are not necessary for explaining emergent self-organization, even when it appears as though there must be such features in operation is proved by the ability of computer modeling of these local interactions of these same systems. If one programs "virtual ants" to sense and respond to their environments and to each other the way their real-life counterparts do, larger-scale structures, such as food lines, tunnel digging, and establishment of a cemetery, arise, even though the programmer did not program these structures. Bottom up, not top down.

That an illusion of global sensing and the appearance of top-down design can be mistakenly identified in these features lies, at least, in two facts. The first is that some self-organized systems themselves actually do supervene over others. So, in the example of circadian rhythm above, it would appear that the internal "clocks" in the brain and perhaps elsewhere are creating a top-down control; these clocks are themselves only clusters of cells relating to local cues such as molecular mechanisms that happen to be cyclical and sensation of light by the eyes, skin, and pineal gland. But no clock in the body is "thinking" of a twenty-four-hour cycle. The twenty-four-hour cycle at the global level is an emergent property arising from local cues.

In human society, things, not surprisingly, are a little more complex. Individuals (such as kings, presidents, prime ministers, CEOs, pundits) may think that they are globally sensing, but they are never able to truly monitor every aspect of the system. This is, in part, why political and social life is so unpredictable and uncontrollable. The illusory appearance of global monitoring and control may persist for limited times (think communist economic systems), but inevitably aspects that escape monitoring and control will lead to unexpected outcomes, including collapse of the system.

And attempts at top-down control and planning are simply not as likely to give rise to adaptive changes: a now historical example from American political life is the electoral primary campaigns of Hillary Clinton and Barack Obama prior to the 2008 American presidential election (Poon 2010). The utility of the example is in the clarity of the contrasting strategies in the campaigns. The Clinton campaign attempted a traditional top-down organization, but often could not respond quickly to sudden real-world events that impacted on the campaign. The Obama campaign, essentially designed as a bottom-up process from the grass roots of volunteers in local communities, could much more rapidly, creatively, and adaptively respond to every political, social, and economic turn during the campaign in ways that were, moreover, specific to each state and local system in which it was embedded. The Clinton campaign, ultimately, could simply not keep up.

There is a role for leadership, however. Some individuals who may have a somewhat higher-level view than others and, by virtue of the different view, have different modes of interaction can change the nature of the emergent self-organization (Lichtenstein and Plowman 2009). Nonetheless, even so, this leadership plays out through local interactions. By "local" in this context, we don't just mean physically adjacent (face-to-face interactions) but interactively adjacent (e.g., messages sent by other means such as phone or Web-based systems).

Limited Randomness

This is perhaps the most surprising (at first glance) element of complex adaptive systems. There has to be a low level of randomness in the system (Johnson 2001; Lewin 1999). If there is no randomness in the system, then there will be no possibility for exploring new states of being when the environment changes; the system will behave like a machine. Without randomness, the system will always self-organize, machine-like, in precisely the same way and, thus, when the environment changes there will be no adaptation. The result: systemic collapse.

On the other hand, if there is too much randomness, then the "noise" in the system will undermine the stability of any possibly emerging structures and self-organization will be insufficient or impossible. Therefore, there must be a low level of randomness, also referred to as *quenched disorder.* This duality—not too much, not too little—is another way of framing Stuart Kauffman's concept of criticality (Kauffman 1993, 2019).

Back to the ant colony for another example. Food lines, from a distance, look like straight lines with all the ants going to the food source and back to the colony in the shortest, most efficient possible distance. This food line arises from how ants deposit pheromones in response to food and to other ants' pheromone signaling. However, if one kneels down to look more closely, one will always find that some ants are not following the line. These ants are not different per se to the other ants, but for one reason or another (often random itself) they have not encountered the signals that have brought the other ants into the emergent structure.

Computer modeling confirms that it is precisely these divergent ants that are responsible for finding the quickest route around an obstacle (like your foot) if the food line is interrupted or discovering a new food source to begin establishing another food line. An excellent example of the importance of such computer modeling is that done at Bell Labs in the early 1970s. The goal: model ant colonies (Johnson 2001). The result: programming virtual divergent ants into the phone circuits, thereby so rapidly finding a new link to connect two people that not only would the phone connection not be lost but doing so with such rapidity that the interruption was too short to be noticed by the people conversing.

One could argue that in human societies, artists, philosophers, and scientists might be considered such "divergent ants," finding new possibilities for self-organization. In fact, every person, like every ant, may perform that function, every moment containing the possibility of an unexpected, unpredictable new choice that leads somewhere new. Such events are often cusp phenomena—sudden rapid states of change that overtake an entire system. The Arab spring of 2011 would be an example, having started with one person burning himself as a protest in Tunisia (Noueihed 2011). Rather than an organized, top-down, planned event, there was a spontaneous reorganization of social structures from the changing, often random interactions of ordinary individuals, most of whom were not practicing activists in the first place.

This quenched disorder is the fundamental source of the Kauffman's "adjacent possibles." Randomness happens. New structures nascently arise. Some are gone in the flash of a moment, some persist for brief periods, others for longer. None of them are planned or intended for a purpose ("no global sensing": there is no One to intend a purpose let alone have the absolute capacity to achieve it). So, just as there is quenched disorder at the level of the individuals of the system, there is also quenched disorder at the level of emergence. But then the environment changes, perhaps sufficiently so that an old form of self-organization no longer is adaptive; those structures collapse. But one of the many "adjacent possibles" turns out, by chance, to be suited to persist and thrive as an adaptive response. Thus, does quenched disorder allow for the possibility of the group as a whole to adapt and survive? At critical times in the life of a complex system, there is a failure to adapt in a timely manner; the result: mass extinction.

A COROLLARY: MASS EXTINCTIONS

One last important theme needs to be addressed, separate from the above because it is not a description of the nature of interactions between individuals, but, rather, an outcome of how complex systems behave as a whole. This theme is that of mass extinction events, either of major populations within the system or of the system as a whole. These are inevitable and inherent in the mathematics that describe all complex systems (Lewin 1999). As such, the details are beyond the scope of this chapter, though they have been well described for nonmathematicians elsewhere (Kauffman 1993). Suffice it to say that inherent in the behavior of complex adaptive systems, sooner or later, despite the ability to adapt, there is a failure to adapt and a part of the system or the whole system will essentially disintegrate.

For biological beings like us, this means that eternal life and a fountain of youth are impossibilities. To be adaptive, that is, to be alive, means, *necessarily*, to die. On the social level, this means that despite the best intentions and the best application of the most sophisticated tools for influencing societal outcomes, the system will eventually be overcome by changes in the environment to which it cannot respond or to changes in interactions within the system so that adaptation does not occur.

At the human level, such changes in the environment might be natural disasters, plagues, or military invasions by another nation. Global climate change is an obvious looming possibility that makes the idea of civilization-scale and species-wide extinction events a vivid potential. This chapter is being written during the global COVID-19 pandemic, a time when extinctions of all manner of human systems are readily evident. Interestingly, what is a mass extinction event on the one level (an end of car traffic and airplane travel) is adaptive at another (unprecedented decline in continental air pollution). This highlights the relative nature of "good" versus "bad" when considering complex systems.

Accepting this inevitability (though unpredictability) of collapse as an inherent aspect of the world, of course, can lead to nihilistic pessimism (perhaps a form of psychosocial collapse, itself). On the other hand, it is also the fount from which new possibilities emerge. Since every system eventually collapses, the worst of human social organizations likewise will come to an end. And while healthy, adaptive systems will also come to an end, the ones that follow, regenerating from the individuals who are still alive, will lead to new, creative ways for humans to self-organize socially. A complexity analysis of human systems is, in a way, beyond pessimism or optimism. Our classification of it in one direction or the other is not about the value of the systems, but what we each bring to our viewing and study of the system.

HEURISTIC EXAMPLES: THEORY TO PRACTICE

In this section, we will look at several instances of how emergent creativity occurs in different contexts by examining some heuristic examples that help us discover how awareness of them can lead to strategic actions that will enhance community well-being.

Historically Administered Indian Affairs Reservation Communities (Contributed by Catherine Twinn)

"Reservations" set apart and administered by Indian Affairs in Canada and the United States experienced, among other things, severe disruptions to their cultures, languages, laws, social organization, economies, and systems of governance. Navajo jurist, Raymond Austin described some of today's outcomes:

> Alcoholism, drug abuse, domestic violence, diabetes, obesity and other social and physical ills, and poor educational achievement of Indian children, confront Indian leaders on a daily basis. . . . Indian leaders tend to look to the non-Indian world for remedies. (Austin 2009, xxii)

This failure to create self-sustaining economic and social structures that are healthy, sustainable, and self-actualizing is shackled by conditions that include widespread clinical depression, substance abuse, and high rates of inter- and intrafamily violence, which impede adaptive self-organization. These are not simply physical, social, or economic challenges. They are complex challenges ultimately requiring spiritual solutions.

A traditional non-Indigenous approach to solving these problems is to take each one and apply standard, contemporary "therapies." Substance abuse can, for example, be treated with pharmacologic interventions and attempts by law enforcement to eliminate the creation or distribution of substances of abuse. Clinical depression can be treated pharmacologically and/or with "talk therapies" (either one on one or in group). Interpersonal violence can be dealt with as a problem requiring psychosocial therapies or as a criminal problem left to the police, courts, and jail systems. While these symptomatic efforts have some role to play, they respond to symptoms, not root causes, and can sometimes make matters worse. Even when well-funded, staffed, and expertly executed, they are not focused on healing root causes that alone can lift and restore these communities to a high-functioning state. Such Western approaches clearly do not lead to enduring, robust changes; they are costly, time-consuming, and, most importantly, culturally and spiritually inappropriate, deriving from cultural traditions outside those First Nations. Raymond Austin describes it this way:

> Problems afflicting Indian peoples on reservations should be seen as prime opportunities for revitalizing, discussing and relearning tribal customs and traditions and applying them as community problem solving tools. (Austin 2009, xxii)

Complexity theory—which some thinkers see as aligned with Natures' Laws as understood by Indigenous peoples—suggests an alternate conceptual approach that may yield new kinds of interventions. One thing all of these problems have in common is that they tend to limit the number and variety of interactions between people. Depressed people are isolative with low levels of social functioning. Addicted individuals increasingly limit their interactions to those involved in maintaining the addiction or the cognitive/psychological effects of the addiction make it harder to interact with others. Interpersonal violence creates emotional states that also diminish interactivity: fear, anxiety anger, guilt, and shame felt by victims and perpetrators alike, and their families and communities. These features represent a loss of interactive diversity and a diminished capacity for creative emergence through that loss. As complexity criterion #1 indicates: numbers matter, the number of interacting individuals, but also the number of ways in which those individuals can interact.

So, while specific, contemporary interventions have a role, another, complementary, concurrent, and culturally appropriate approach includes other ways that increase the likelihood of meaningful and diverse interactions—approaches that are not specifically goal or outcome directed, but generate new, diverse interactive possibilities. Some of these may be a matter of reviving or strengthening traditional cultural forms such as small or large talking circles, community conversations, societies, ceremonies, fasts, feasts, clan systems, celebrations, harvesting, gathering, growing food, hunting, and caring acts of kindness and generosity. It may be a focus on the robust renewal of tribal structures, bodies, and systems of governance. It will include restoring the teachings of Natures' laws to develop well-formed and self-regulating human beings. And it may take the form of creatively generated new societal groups or forms. Traditionally, Bands were open, organic, fluid, forming, and reforming, dividing and amalgamating. Unlike today's tightly closed and controlled relational system, employing discriminatory rules derived from federal assimilation and termination principles intended to terminate Indigenous values and principles. Either way, Indigenous approaches and wisdom work in conjunction with Western problem-oriented, contemporary approaches; each being a spoke in a strong wheel.

The reader may note some other features of this case study that merit further discussion. For example, an essential feature is that the possible solutions are not "top down," but "bottom up." Also, such interventions are not goal-directed. In the absence of expected outcomes, how does one measure success (see Singh, "Development as Emergent Creativity," *Transforming*)? This complexity analysis, however, suggests that not only global outcomes can be measured (changing rates of violence, substance abuse, depression, and suicide) but also local ones such as measuring numbers and diversity of types of interactions among members of a community.

The Emergence of Mennonite Women's Societies in Canada (Contributed by Gloria Neufeld Redekop)

When Russian Mennonites first immigrated to Canada in the 1870s, forming their own religious communities was very important to them, both for
men and women. However, the institutional church was male-dominated
and women were not allowed to preach or take part in church business
meetings. This was based on a literal reading of the biblical text I Timothy
2:8:15: "Let a woman learn in silence with all submissiveness. I permit
no woman to teach or to have authority over men; she is to keep silent"
(Revised Standard Version, verses 10-11; see Neufeld Redekop 2012, chapter 6 for an in-depth exegesis of the Timothy text, pointing out how it has
been mistranslated).

But because women wanted to be more involved in the church, they
formed their own societies, connected with the churches in which they were
members.

In my book *The Work of Their Hands: Mennonite Women's Societies
in Canada*, I sent surveys to 304 Canadian Mennonite women's societies
in the two largest Mennonite denominations in Canada—the Mennonite
Brethren and General Conference Mennonite (now called Mennonites in
Canada) (Neufeld Redekop 1996). The survey was completed by 230 groups.
Evidence that these women were pleased to have their history recorded was
that not only did they complete the survey, but many groups also submitted
their constitutions, annual reports, financial reports, and minutes of meetings.

Their empowerment as Mennonite women was evident in that these societies were generally organized on their own, without any directive from
central church agencies—a true bottom-up emergence. Even though across
Canada these groups were similar in their work and activities, each society
decided what their own activities would be and what their groups would be
called. While many were called "Sewing Circle" or "Mission Society," other
names included Willing Helpers, Friendship Circle, Helping Hands, Ladies
Fellowship, Prayer Band, and Open Door Fellowship. It is interesting to note
that there were strong similarities in organizational structures and prioritization of group activities for social "good" across the groups—the emergent
properties tended to be similar, reflecting perhaps the uniformity of structures
and behaviors of the male-dominant, traditional (and traditionalist) communities dispersed across the continent.

While the institutional church was involved in supporting the work of
"missions," these women's groups made their own decisions as to which
"mission" to support. And it meant that their gifts as women were being used
to further good causes. One example is of one group in Saskatchewan that
during World War I, at the request of the Red Cross, knit and sewed items for

men overseas. The same happened during World War II when, as one group put it, "many boxes of yarn were brought to the church to be divided among the sisters and worked into hats, scarves, mitts, gloves and socks in varying sizes" (Leamington Mennonite Brethren Church Women's Societies Minutes n.d., 38). This kind of involvement was one of the ways Mennonite women were able to feel empowered to do something that was particular to their skill set of working with their hands to help those in need. Another use of their handwork was to organize auctions where they would sell the items they had knit or sewed. And then the proceeds went to projects they chose to support.

Besides the handwork these women did in order to meet certain needs, they had regular meetings. These meetings had several components. As one group reported, "The meetings always had a strong spiritual emphasis with different sisters taking part in scripture reading, devotionals, prayers, and singing our favourite hymns" (ibid., 38). The specific worship pattern they adopted was similar to that of the worship in the institutional church: Bible reading, prayer, singing, and a devotional that they sometimes called a sermonette. They also ate together, which is something often done in the church itself. Mennonites love to eat together. The major difference between what happened in the church and what happened in women's society meetings was that one was male led and the other, female led. Without being explicit about it, these women were able to essentially be their own "church," organizing a parallel church, a context where they could decide how to meet their own spiritual needs, study the Bible for themselves, decide which songs to sing, and determine which needy causes they would like to support. They were self-empowered through their societies.

I end with a personal note. When I was asked to present my research to an assembly of Mennonites, I had a little trepidation because I knew there would be Mennonite women present who were members of these kinds of societies. What would they say? Would they deny my proposal that Mennonite women were in fact acting as a parallel church? To my surprise, a woman approached me after my presentation and said, "What you said, that is exactly what we were doing."

The Emergence of a New Border between Ethiopia and Eritrea (Contributed by Lissane Yohannes)

With Eritrea's breaking away from Ethiopia in 1993, the stage was set for an all-out conflict between the two countries starting in May 1998. The conflict involved long-standing rivalries that manifested in contesting the border. Eventually the war claimed the lives of 100,000 people and left over a million displaced.

There was an internationally negotiated Algiers Peace Agreement in June of 2000. Despite the conclusions of the Algiers Agreement, the border remained undemarcated. Ethiopia offered a six-point proposal for a complete normalization and Eritrea rejected the offer and insisting on the unconditional implementation of the agreement. This resulted in a "no war—no peace" situation with skirmishes from time to time. It affected the people on both sides of the border socially and economically for the past twenty years.

It is interesting to note that despite the two states insisting on their positions, the people on both sides of the borders had some form of interaction among themselves despite a heavy presence of security forces:

1. It was quite natural for people who were so closely related to be determined to sustain relationships, including weddings, while separated by borders and existing conflict.
2. The weddings took place during the night, which allowed the people to cross the border and celebrate their respective weddings. One might call these cross-border weddings!
3. The people on both sides of the borders supported and respected their interests. Whenever cattle crossed the borders while grazing, the people on the other side of the border would make sure these animals were returned to their owners. If and when the Eritrean army slaughtered some of the cattle crossing from Tigrai, the Eritrean peasants would compensate the loss.

These examples illustrate that the people on both sides of the borders were merely interested in a peaceful coexistence. Their assertion of their own interests in the face of a top-down structure, designed to undermine them, is an example of the actual absence of top-down control in the face up of bottom-up interventions. Also, the interventions can be seen as examples of homeostatic negative feedback loops, using naturally arising and historic practices to restore balance between neighbors across the official "border."

At one point, local groups of Eritreans and Ethiopians said to one another, "We know which families traditionally owned which land and we could determine between us where the boundary should be." Based on that realization, small groups from the two sides met all along the contested border. When all the decisions of the local groups were consolidated, there was a recommendation to settle the border dispute once and for all, at least from one side of the border, for where the entire border should be that had been agreed upon by all the people living along the border.

Consequently, the border opened for a time, albeit without demarcation, and the people were able to cross from both sides. While the border, unfortunately, is again closed, diplomatic relations continue, and airlines fly between the two countries. Of course, there remains a lot to be done to normalize relations between the two countries. Nonetheless, these local solutions, generated locally, led to an end of the rigid impasse with its perpetuation of the "no war—no peace" situation. Hence, the people on both sides of the border are central and their initiative must be respected.

SUMMARY POINTS

Human societies are examples of complex adaptive systems and are therefore dependent upon and conditioned by the same properties as are all such systems: the number of members and the diversity of interactions, the predominance of homeostatic negative feedback loops governing interactions, the creativity of bottom-up self-organization arising from interactions at the local level, and the presence of some degree of randomness in the system to stoke creative, adjacent possibles.

They are both embedded in other complex systems, such as the natural world, the larger civilization, and the global economy, and give rise to subsystems of their own like neighborhoods and associations. As such, they are both examples of emergent self-organization of the larger system even as they modify themselves in continual recreative self-organizing of their own emergent structures. Changes to the environment in which human societies are embedded have the capacity for bountiful adaptations in response to changing environments, though occasional collapses of parts or the whole system are an inevitable corollary to the systems inherent creativity.

We have offered three heuristic examples of how a complexity perspective can highlight salient aspects of what is both adaptive and maladaptive within a societal system. One example (Indigenous societies) shows a system trapped in profound dysfunction; in this instance, the complexity analysis points to possible interventions that may produce more adaptive responses that lead to a healthier, more well-functioning society. It is of particular note that so much of the dysfunction arose historically in response to the systematic suppression of homeostatic social mechanisms of traditional society. Possible modifications of current practice to revivify those traditions become not only intuitive or nostalgic interventions but those that reflect the principles of the complex systems analysis. This analysis may therefore help to guide choices in societal shifts, but also suggests ways to measure possible outcomes at the level of the individuals *as the intervention is made* not just awaiting more global shifts in community behaviors.

In the second case, Mennonite women's societies are an example of how bottom-up solutions to social problems sometimes just arise. No plan. No intention. Just a local response to a local need. And perhaps because of the uniformity of the male-dominated societies in which these women found themselves and their own uniformity as women in this particular culture; however dispersed they were across a continent, similarities of emergent structures were seen throughout. And yet, at the same time, the specificities of each location and church and social circumstance led to creative diversity, as well, reflecting the dynamism arising within the diversity of a complex systems.

Finally, there is the transitional state of the Eritrean-Ethiopian "no war—no peace" situation. At one point a bottom-up self-organized process to self-organize a boundary that reflected historical needs and obligations resulted in a top-down decision to respect the new boundary. Before this, there had been a de facto decision to let local people engage in cross-border activities like weddings, simply setting up the circumstances and conditions for a creative solution: all the relevant neighbors on either side produced the diversity of memories and meanings. The means of interaction to promote creativity along with the homeostatic nature of interactions *as they had persisted locally* despite the conflict and a reliance on bottom-up approach yielded a significant solution. A change was sought; conditions were fostered that allowed a solution to arise.

Thus, we see that not only do societies function as complex systems, but they also display all the possible outcomes of such systems: including dysfunction that leads to collapse, creative adaptation that gives rise to a sustainable and healthy future, and, most importantly, the possibility of rationally applying the principles of complex systems theory to make changes. It is not to *design* a solution but to *foster* the conditions that are more likely to manifest in adaptive, emergent societal changes of benefit.

REFERENCES

Austin, R. D. 2009. *Navajo Courts and Navajo Common Law.* Minneapolis, MN: University of Minnesota Press.

Johnson, S. 2001. *Emergence: The Connected Lives of Ants, Brains, Cities, and Softward.* New York, NY: Scribner.

Kauffman, S. 1993. *Origins of Order: Self-Organization and Selection in Evolution.* Oxford: Oxford University Press, Technical Monograph.

———. 2008. *Reinventing the Sacred.* New York, NY: Basic Books.

———. 2020. "The Re-enchantment of Humanity: The Implications of no Entailing Laws." In *Awakening: Exploring Spirituality, Emergent Creativity, and Reconciliation.* Edited by Vern Neufeld Redekop and Gloria Neufeld Redekop. Lanham, MD: Lexington.

Leamington Mennonite Brethren Church Women's Society Minutes. n.d. unpublished.

Lewin, R. 1999. *Complexity: Life at the Edge of Chaos.* Chicago, IL: University of Chicago Press.

Lichtenstein, B. B., and D. A. Plowman. 2009. "The Leadership of Emergence: A Complex Systems Leadership Theory of Emergence at Successive Organizational Levels." *The Leadership Quarterly,* 20: 617–630.

Neufeld Redekop, Gloria. 2012. *Bad Girls and Boys Go to Hell (or not): Engaging Fundamentalist Evangelicalism*. Eugene, OR: Wipf & Stock.

———. 1996. *The Work of Their Hands: Mennonite Women's Societies in Canada*. Waterloo: Wilfrid Laurier University Press.

Noueihed, L. 2011. "Peddler's Martyrdom Launched Tunisia's Revolution." *Reuters*, January 20. https://www.reuters.com/article/us-tunisia-protests-bouazizi/peddlers-martyrdom-launched-tunisias-revolution-idUSTRE70J1DJ20110120.

Poon, O. A. 2010. "Did Obama have an 'Asian Problem'?" In *Race 2008: Critical Reflections on an Historic Campaign*. Edited by Myra Mendible. Boca Raton, FL: Brown Walker Press.

Theise, N. D. 2005. "Now You See It, Now You Don't." *Nature*, 435: 1165.

———. 2006. "Implications of 'Post-Modern Biology' for Pathology: the Cell Doctrine." *Laboratory Investigation*, 86: 335–344.

———. 2009. "Beyond Cell Doctrine: Complexity Theory Informs Alternate Models of the Body for Cross-Cultural Dialogue." *Annals of the New York Academy of Sciences*, 1172: 263–269.

Theise, N. D., and M. D'Inverno. 2004. "Understanding Cell Lineages as Complex Adaptive Systems." *Blood Cells, Molecules, and Diseases*, 32: 17–20.

Theise, N. D., and M. Kafatos. 2013a. "Sentience Everywhere: Complexity Theory, Panpsychism, and the Role of Sentience in the Self-Organizing Universe." *Journal of Consciousness Exploration & Research*, 4(4): 378–390.

———. 2013b. "Complementarity in Biological Systems: a Complexity View." *Complexity*, 18: 11–20.

———. 2016. "Fundamental Awareness: An Framework for Integrating Science, Philosophy and Metaphysics." *Communicative & Integrative Biology*, 9: e1155010.

Theise, N. D., and R. Harris. 2006. "Postmodern Biology: (Adult) (Stem) Cells are Plastic, Stochastic, Complex, and Uncertain." *Handbook of Experimental Pharmacology*, 174: 389–408.

Chapter 17

Development as Emergent Creativity

Naresh Singh

A huge gap continues to exist between what is known and possible and what is actually being done to reduce crisis, foster resilience, and support international development cooperation. There continues to be a mismatch between a complex systems reality on the ground and the use by the international community of linear deterministic tools designed for engineering projects during the Cold War era. This chapter seeks to make available principles, tools, and practical applications of complexity theory and complex adaptive systems (CASs) to humanitarian and development workers around the world. These tools are not new; they have been in use in different fields for at least twenty-five years. However, despite noteworthy attempts to get the international humanitarian and development community to use them and so bring their practice closer to the problems they seek to solve, uptake has been slow.

In some ways, ready embrace has not occurred because of the language used, with words such as "complexity" (which by the way does not mean complicated), "adaptive," and "systems," which all seem sensible, but at the same time theoretical and impractical. The real difficulty, however, for us is to accept that we are not in full control, that the outcomes we seek cannot be determined with certainty, that we will fail sometimes, and, perhaps more often than not, and especially, if we use tools not suited to the problem. It will be argued that if we use a logical framework slavishly, we will be blind to the emergence of new options, and even if we see emergence, we will not have room to incorporate novelty since we have already fully determined the way our project must be implemented. It must be clear from the outset that uncertainty, emergence, and adaptability do not in any way mean reduced accountability, but what we seek to count and how we do our monitoring and evaluation (M&E) will change.

I first encountered complexity theory in the mid-1990s while at the International Institute for Sustainable Development in Winnipeg, Canada. Since sustainable development sought a balance among the economic, social, and ecological systems, an economic theory alone could only be partial. Could economic, social, and ecological theories somehow work together to provide a functional theoretical framework that would allow policy and program development and evaluation with indicators to measure progress? In that search, complexity adaptive systems theory shone a clear light on much that had to be understood differently and done differently. I have since being using these insights in my work on developmental evaluation (DE), in working in conflict zones and in teaching, policy, and program design and evaluation in complex situations.

The next section provides an overview of the historical evolution of development cooperation from World War II to now and what lessons have been learned in aid effectiveness for development cooperation in stable countries. Following this, we will describe the challenges facing development cooperation in Fragile and Conflict Affected Situations (FCAS) and the lessons learned to date in these situations. This section will be followed by a section that shows how complexity theory is providing a framework that can yield highly relevant and practical policy and program ideas for governments, as well as multilateral and NGO actors, engaged in development cooperation whether in stable countries or in FCAS. Subsequently, the intersections between development, conflict, and complexity are discussed before looking at the limitations of current development cooperation through a complexity lens. Finally, we discuss practical applications of insights from complex adaptive systems for development and conflict management in areas of program design, M&E, and policymaking.

INTERNATIONAL DEVELOPMENT COOPERATION: HISTORICAL EVOLUTION AND LESSONS LEARNED

Just after the end of World War II, the ideas of development and underdevelopment were significantly influenced by the dominant world position of the United States. In order to consolidate that hegemony and make it permanent, they conceived a political campaign under the guise of a global development agenda. In the words of President Truman at his inauguration in 1949:

> We must embark on a bold new program for making the benefits of scientific advances and industrial progress available for the improvement and growth of underdeveloped areas . . . The old imperialism—exploitation for foreign

profit—has no place in our plans. What we envisage is a program of development based on the concepts of democratic fair dealing. (In Sachs 2012, 3)

Reflecting on this statement, Gustavo Esteva commented:

On that day (January 20, 1949), 2 billion people became underdeveloped. In a real sense, from that time on, they ceased being what they were in all their diversity, and were transmogrified into an inverted mirror of others' reality: a mirror that belittles them and sends them off to the end of the queue, a mirror that defines their identity, which is really that of a heterogeneous and diverse majority, simply in terms of a homogenizing and narrow minority. (In Sachs 2012, 4)

Esteva further notes that, since then, development has connoted an escape from an undignified condition called underdevelopment and concludes that for someone to conceive the possibility of escaping from a particular condition it is necessary first to feel that one has fallen into that condition. The real tragedy of the pursuit of development since then has been the acceptance of that view by the leading economists of the developing countries and so development as the search for the way of life of the West began!

It is enlightening then to take a quick look at the journey that followed, so we are well positioned to avoid repeating what we have done before and now expect different results. In the first decade of international development after World War II, development was conceived of purely as economic growth in average GNP per capita. Issues of distribution, inclusion and equity, and jobs creation were not considered. Unsurprisingly then, social problems remained and, in many cases, increased, so the next decade focused on social development. But that only led to the realization that development required both economic growth and social development—one was not possible without the other. And so socioeconomic development as a more integrated approach was adopted. When this approach did not seem to work as well as was hoped for, a shift from a focus on the development of things to a development of people occurred and the human development paradigm was born. A decade later, it was observed that the human development approach was not delivering as well as it was imagined it would, and so the development community decided that it would focus only on the basic needs of human development. That too did not do well, as was hoped for, and a shift on the "how" of development took place. That ushered in participatory and endogenous approaches to counter the top-down and outside-driven approaches. While this evolution was proceeding, another evolutionary branch had started as result of environmental pollution problems and this finally led to the sustainable development paradigm that seeks to achieve development objectives without damaging the natural environment.

Fast forward to the present era. During the second decade of the twenty-first century we have observed the twentieth anniversaries of the United Nations world summits held in the 1990s on various dimensions of development including education (Jomtein, 1990), human rights (Vienna, 1991), sustainable development (Rio, 1992), women (Beijing, 1993), population (Cairo, 1994), social development (Copenhagen, 1995), human settlements (cities) (Istanbul, 1996), food (Rome, 1999), and the Millennium Summit with its millennium development goals (MDGs) (New York, 2000). Half way through the decade, in 2015 the targets of the millennium declaration were to be achieved. Results were mixed with four of the twenty-one targets possibly achieved (UN 2015). The important global goal of reducing extreme poverty by half compared to 1990 levels was achieved several years before 2015.

The lessons learned in development cooperation over the prior decades have been articulated in the seminal document: *Shaping the 21st Century* (OECD 1996) in which many of the goals that became the MDGs were first articulated. The lessons learned were articulated in the form of commitments by the OECD:

> First, by a willingness to make mutual commitments with our development part-
> ners, supported by adequate resources; second, by improving the co-ordination
> of assistance in support of locally-owned development strategies; and third, by
> a determined effort to achieve coherence between aid policies and other policies
> which impact on developing countries. (Ibid., 2)

Over the last decade, the OECD has further elaborated Aid Effectiveness Principles working in partnership with civil society and developing country governments and convening four high-level fora in Rome (2003), Paris (2005), Accra (2008), and Busan (2011). These principles if put into practice would constitute what most in international development circles would consider state-of-the-art development cooperation. The Paris Declaration was based on five key principles: country ownership, alignment, harmonization, managing for development results, and mutual accountability. The Accra Agenda for Action reaffirmed these principles and translated them into specific commitments to accelerate action. Busan brought together a diverse set of actors into partnership that recognized

> a more complex architecture for development co-operation, characterised by
> a greater number of state and non-state actors, as well as co-operation among
> countries at different stages in their development, many of them middle-income
> countries. South-South and triangular co-operation, new forms of public-private
> partnership, and other modalities and vehicles for development have become
> more prominent, complementing North-South forms of co-operation . . . As we

partner to increase and reinforce development results, we will take action to facilitate, leverage and strengthen the impact of diverse sources of finance to support sustainable and inclusive development, including taxation and domestic resource mobilisation, private investment, aid for trade, philanthropy, non-concessional public funding and climate change finance. At the same time, new financial instruments, investment options, technology and knowledge sharing, and public-private partnerships are called for. (OECD 2011, [paragraph 14])

In 2015, the International Community adopted the sustainable development goals (SDGs) also called the post-2015 or 2030 agenda. The seventeen SDGs replace the MDGs but have a much more comprehensive agenda going beyond the basic social needs' focus of the MDGs to include issues of growth, governance, conflict and peace, and related sustainable development issues. While the MDGs addressed the needs of the developing world, the SDGs constitute a truly global agenda that incorporates the lessons learned as described above. Financing for the SDGs was discussed at the Financing for Development conference in Addis Ababa (also in 2015) and a range of innovative financial mechanisms identified including social impact investment mechanisms such as blended finance and development impact investment bonds. Official aid over the last few years (2016–2018) has flattened out at about USD150B while the financial gap to pay for the implementation of the post-2015 agenda is of the order of USD2.5 trillion. This financial gap will be very difficult, if not impossible, to bridge, so other fundamental transformations become necessary.

FCAS IN TODAY'S WORLD

About 1.5 billion people live in fragile states, most of which have seen conflict since 1989, and none of which is likely to achieve any of the SDGs, although about 30 percent of ODA (Official Development Assistance) is spent in these countries. Transitioning out of fragility is long, arduous political work that requires country leadership and ownership. Processes of political dialogue have often failed due to lack of trust, inclusiveness, and leadership. International partners often bypass national interests and actors, providing aid in overly technocratic ways that underestimate the importance of harmonizing with the national and local context, supporting short-term results at the expense of medium- to long-term sustainable results brought about by building capacity and systems (International Dialogue on Peacebuilding 2011).

Roughly 400 million extremely poor people live in fragile states, a number that has remained essentially unchanged since 1990. Although this is only about one-third of the total global population living in extreme poverty, the trend is for this to increase to one-half; hence, the challenges of extreme poverty will increasingly be found in fragile states. Ending extreme poverty, then, will not be possible without understanding and tackling the sources of fragility (USAID 2014).

While not all fragile states end up in conflict, most do. Conflict becomes more likely when segments of society question governments' fairness and inclusivity; and the consequences of conflict include destroyed assets and options for livelihoods and diversion of public investments from development to security (ibid.). Drivers of fragility and conflict range from lack of resources, like land and water, or abundance of a single resource, like oil, or poverty. Religious or ideological differences, along with issues of ethnicity, race, class or language, divide communities in toxic and deadly ways, particularly in a context of weak state institutions and powerful social groups seeking political and economic power. Perhaps the most defining feature of conflict in today's world apart from being intrastate is that more than 75 percent of those killed are noncombatants (The World at War n.d.).

The context for development cooperation as described earlier, even in stable situations is fundamentally a CAS with interacting economic, social, and ecological subsystems—and myriad actors and networks. It would readily be appreciated then that FCAS are even more complex, turbulent, and adaptive. The Paris Declaration and Accra Agenda for Action encourage partners to work toward aligning their programs with the policies and priorities of recipient states. Aligning with Indigenous processes of reform can be challenging, especially where political leadership and consensus are still being built. Alignment is difficult where strategic priorities are not clearly identified or where priorities are not focused on longer-term peace and development. So, in Accra, members of the g7+ dialogue process led by nineteen fragile states, building on the Paris Principles and on the DAC 2007 Principles for Aid Effectiveness in Fragile States, agreed to the New Deal for effective engagement in fragile states as defined by their five peacebuilding and state-building goals (PSGs) as follows[1]:

- "Legitimate Politics—Foster inclusive political settlements and conflict resolution;
- Security—Establish and strengthen people's security;
- Justice—Address injustices and increase people's access to justice;
- Economic Foundations—Generate employment and improve livelihoods, and
- Revenues & Services—Manage revenue and build capacity for accountable and fair service delivery."

   The PSGs are intended to guide the identification of peacebuilding and state building priorities at the country level. They are to inform global and country-level funding decisions to help ensure that all fragile countries, and their key peacebuilding and state building priorities, are supported. (International Dialogue on Peace Building and State Building, OECD 2015, 131)

Recognizing the inherent complexity of the undertaking, the dialogue partners also outlined the principles of how they would proceed to develop *focus* and *trust* by conducting periodic country-led assessments on the causes and features of fragility, along with sources of resilience, as a basis for one vision, one plan. A compact would then be agreed among stakeholders as the key mechanism to implement the one vision, one plan, supported by transparent, timely, predictable aid flows. While a compact may take different forms in different contexts and at different points in transition out of fragility, it will ensure harmonization and donor coordination, reduce duplication, fragmentation, and program proliferation. A compact can also guide the choice of aid modalities and can provide a basis to determine the allocation of donor resources aligned to the country-led national priorities, in line with good aid effectiveness principles.

Clearly, much progress has been made in development cooperation over the years in both stable and FCAS countries. However the financial instruments—whether as projects, sector-wide approaches, structural adjustment programs, or budgetary support— have used tools largely based on the logical framework, or some logic model that is predetermined, as the theory of change, assumes high levels of predictability of outcomes and a casual linear chain of inputs leading to outputs, outcomes, and desired impact. The success of this approach in complicated engineering projects was so widespread that it was automatically assumed it would work in CASs that characterize socio-economic development contexts of all kinds. As will be shown below, this assumption is often erroneous. The challenge then is to recognize the value as well as the limitations of this approach and to find ways of overcoming the limitations while building on its strengths. The CAS approach will not provide a panacea to existing limitations, and certainly will have limitations of its own, but its insights and tools need more attention than they currently receive.

COMPLEX ADAPTIVE SYSTEMS

My journey into exploring the value of complexity theory for understanding developmental challenges originated during my tenure at the International Institute for Development Studies while I was searching for a theory for sustainable development that would go beyond the standard economic varieties that were clearly inadequate, if not harmful. The theory would have to explain or at least provide insights into understanding what happens at the intersection of economic, social, and ecological systems that would allow us to develop policies and programs that support the functioning of these systems in harmonious balance. This would not be a fixed state of harmony but a constantly evolving, adaptive, and interactive process. This search led me to the study of complexity theory and CASs. This section will review the characteristics of such systems and show how they might be applied. A CAS is comprised of many interdependent but autonomous agents interacting with each other and dynamically adapting, coevolving and self-organizing over time and space. Some examples of what CASs are and are not will help to make the concept concrete (These are from OECD 2009).

The human brain is a complex system. The firing of certain neurons affects the firing of other neurons and the result in the whole-brain system can then influence the individual neurons. This dynamic ultimately produces some profoundly hard-to-predict phenomena of mind such as ideas, metaphors, and dreams (c.f. Redekop, "Reconciliation," *Transforming*).

Two Nobel Prizes in Economics have been awarded for complex systems research. Thomas Schelling found that residential segregation tends to emerge in a system of independent citizens if they hold only a few simple, unobjectionable preferences for being near others like themselves (i.e., no hatred or racism is necessarily required). His Nobel Prize in 2005 was more directly for enhancing our understanding of conflict and cooperation using game theory (Schelling 1960). Paul Krugman has been able to explain the existence of clusters of economic activity and regional growth disparities by examining economies as CASs. This work has already influenced city planners and economic geographers, among others. He has also shown how models of self-organization can be applied to many economic phenomena—how the principles of "order from instability," which explain the growth of hurricanes and embryos, can also explain the formation of cities and business cycles; how the principles of "order from random growth" can explain the strangely simple rules that describe the sizes of earthquakes, meteorites, and metropolitan areas (Krugman 1996).

Many others have described the economy in terms of CASs including Arthur (1996), Kauffman (2008), Omerod (2001), and Simpson (2002).

Terrorist groups and guerilla fighters follow CASs principles with distributed cells of self-organizing activity more than deterministic hierarchical models of the formal military with their chains of command. No wonder then the mismatch between fighting tactics of the two when engaged in battle.

Many other examples exist from ant colonies to cities and markets but the above examples should suffice to clarify the concept (cf. Theise, "Harnessing," *Transforming*). These CASs show a set of generalizable characteristics that follow:

Nonlinearity: Changes in one property of the system is not proportional to changes elsewhere in the same or a coupled system. So, a small change could result in huge impact, like the flapping of a butterfly wings in one part of the world, which could cause a hurricane somewhere else. Or a large effort might have little or no effect like heavy bombing of a distributed terrorist network might affect one or two cells.

Adaptability: Complex systems are formed by independent constituents that interact, changing their behaviors in reaction to those of others, thus adapting to a changing environment. The interactions need not be direct or physical; they can involve sharing of information, or even be indirect; for example, as one agent changes an environment, another responds to the new environmental condition.

Emergence: Novel patterns that arise at a system level that are not predicted by the fundamental properties of the system's constituents or the system itself are called emergent properties. What emerges is beyond, outside of, and oblivious to any notion of shared intentionality. Each agent or element of pursues its own path but as paths intersect and the elements interact, patterns or interaction emerge and the whole of the interactions becomes greater than the separate parts.

Adjacent Possibles: Each emergent element—material change, product, process, idea, or organization—opens up new possibilities, called "adjacent possibles." For example, widespread distribution of personal computers opened up the adjacent possible of the Internet. The actualization of any particular adjacent possible is not entailed by the new conditions even though it is made possible by them. The actualization may itself be an instance of emergent creativity.

Self-organization: A system that is formed and operates through many mutually adapting constituents is called self-organizing because no entity designs it or directly controls it. Self-organizing systems will adapt autonomously to changing conditions, including changes imposed by policymakers. For example, a market operates through all the independent decisions of buyers and sellers. Prices evolve through interactions. While markets can be influenced, they cannot be directly controlled. They will make their own—sometimes surprising and undesirable—responses to direct interventions.

INTERSECTIONS: DEVELOPMENT, CONFLICT, AND COMPLEXITY

Bearing in mind the characteristics described above, almost all development and conflict situations would seem to more closely exhibit the features of

CASs than of linear deterministic (even if complicated) systems. To further illustrate, any developing country, fragile or not, is likely to have pockets of conflict, areas of relative stability, areas prone to natural disasters, well-to-do areas, and areas with chronic poverty. In fragile countries, conflict is likely to be more widespread and protracted with government exercise of a legitimate monopoly over violence highly constrained. The country will have urban and rural settings with people making their livelihoods in a range of socioecological settings such as coastal, arid and semiarid, forest, savannah, and mountain zones. The country is likely be organized in a nested *holarchy*[2] of households in villages/municipalities in communities, in districts in provinces/states/governorate. Each unit of organization will have some degree of autonomy and yet be interdependent with others. Autonomy of lower-level units is likely to be greater in decentralized democracies and a spectrum of lower to higher levels of autonomy is likely to be found across the range of developing countries. Capacities to provide public goods and services will be increasingly limited with increasing levels of poverty and conflict.

Political governance in association with government capacity to provide public goods and services including security will define the relative freedoms people will have to participate in politics, markets, and the economy including in the private sector—especially in regard to setting up new businesses and obtaining affordable credit. Human capabilities will in part be defined not only by health and education opportunities but also by the other freedoms, all interacting with each other. In some countries, various ethnic, ideological, religious, or tribal groups will exploit weak governance structures and use force and violence to obtain resources such as land, water, political power, and money. Corruption will be present in varying degrees and likely to increase with higher levels of poverty and conflict. Most of these societies are likely to be closed-access societies in which those with political power keep a tight-knit group seeking economic rents from those with economic power, who in return seek political patronage.

The question that now arises is to what extent the above situations are described by fixed rules in a linear deterministic manner, and to what extent by nonlinearity, adaptability, self-organization, emergence, dynamic coevolution, and uncertainty? The answer to this question will help determine the kinds of models and tools that are likely to be most useful. One must of course bear in mind their ease of application will be determined by cost, ability to communicate what is being done, and, of course, acceptance in a world dominated by a deterministic mindset in which control and certainty are highly prized both by international agencies and by local officials and politicians. Little surprise then that international development cooperation is still dominated by linear logical frameworks, whether in stable countries or countries in conflict, and still hope to be faithful to the Paris and Busan principles of aid effectiveness, development cooperation, and the New Deal for working in FCAS. In cases of sudden crises requiring humanitarian relief, there can be exceptions for emergency relief operations, which are often based on a flash appeal to meet immediate needs, while consolidated appeals are used for more predictable needs in protracted or postconflict situations.

LIMITATIONS OF CURRENT APPROACHES TO INTERNATIONAL COOPERATION

There are two different contexts to be considered when it comes to international cooperation—those in which countries are relatively stable and those in which there is fragility, often accompanied by violent conflict.

Stable Countries

The most common development cooperation instrument continues to be the project. Projects are typically designed using linear logic models as their theories of change for design, implementation, monitoring, and evaluation. In this framework, inputs such as money, knowledge, and people's time are assumed to lead to desirable outputs, which in turn are to lead to outcomes, some in the short term, others in the longer term, and these interact with other factors to produce impacts. So, there is usually some branching toward the impact stage in what is otherwise an essentially linear logical causative chain. Projects designed and implemented as such are usually evaluated (formative evaluations) at midterm to monitor progress and to see whether they are on track. Some changes might be required for course correction but this is usually difficult to do, especially if there are budgetary implications. The validity of the preplanned goals is not usually questioned even if the circumstances have changed.

Now consider that a single agency might be funding several partners to carry out many different projects in the country sometimes even in the same sector! In addition, there are usually many different agencies funding different partners at the same time. And somehow each of these projects with their individual internal logic models are supposed to subscribe to the Paris Principles on harmonization, alignment, country ownership, mutual accountability, and so on. So maybe we can think of integrated log frame per donor agency and then a super integrated log frame at the national level that brought together all the development cooperation initiatives in the country in one coherent log frame! Even if this were possible it would still be an attempt at using an essentially linear model to work in a nonlinear environment with many autonomous agents. For these reasons, other approaches have been used with varying degrees of success. These include sector-wide approaches in which a sector as whole is supported by different partnerships, structural adjustment programs, especially by the World Bank in which loans are made to governments in return for macroeconomic policy adjustments, or budget support in which various forms of accountability are agreed upon but which allows a great deal of flexibility. Complex systems research offers insights and tools that could be helpful in policy making, program design, and M&E.

Fragile and Conflict-Affected Situations

FCAS countries might be in one or more of three common situations: fragile without conflict; be in actual conflict, recent or protracted; or in postconflict, where a peace agreement has been reached. The challenge in postconflict situations is peacebuilding and peacekeeping, prevention of relapse into widespread conflict, reconstruction, and long-term development including resilience building. In fragile countries without conflict, the challenge is state-building and building resilience in economic, social, ecological, and political systems while addressing causes of vulnerability. The priority in countries with active conflict is saving lives, reducing suffering, restoring dignity, reduction of harmful and violent forms of conflict, peacemaking, and reconciliation, followed by postconflict actions. In many countries, various combinations of actions are required depending on context and neat categories as proposed here are not evident.

In many cases, humanitarian relief is highest priority. Effective ways of humanitarian relief in which its primary goals of saving lives and livelihoods, reducing suffering, and restoring dignity are met without making conflict worse or foreclosing options for longer-term sustainable development continue to be contentious as the following quotes show:

> Although aid agencies often seek to be neutral or non-partisan toward the winners and losers of a war, the impact of their aid is not neutral. . . . When given in conflict settings, aid can reinforce, exacerbate, and prolong the conflict; it can also help to reduce the tensions and strengthen people's capacities to disengage from fighting and find peaceful options for solving problems. Often, an aid program does some of both. But in all cases aid given during conflict cannot remain separate from that conflict. (Branczik 2004)

And

> A commonly cited example of aid perpetuating a conflict is that of Sudan, where civil war has lasted for well over a decade, and over two billion dollars have been spent on humanitarian aid. Both rebel leaders and aid workers openly

acknowledge that humanitarian aid, in addition to saving many lives, is a large factor in making it possible for the belligerent groups to continue fighting. (Ibid.)

The central premise of the New Deal is country-led and country-determined actions even though a multistakeholder compact is a key feature. But how is this to be implemented in situations where governments have little or no control over violence or capacity for service delivery. In some cases, there might not even be a government that has legitimacy and enough support to be credible.

In all of these situations, CASs offer insights into general approaches to problem solving, policymaking, program/project design, and M&E.

APPLICATIONS OF INSIGHTS FROM CAS TO DEVELOPMENT COOPERATION

In this section, I will begin by highlighting key insights that are drawn from the world of complexity thinking. I will then show how these can be applied to different aspect of the development process from design, to implementation, to evaluation.

Emergence, Adjacent Possible, and Innovation

Even a casual observation of natural ecosystems and nature in general presents compelling evidence of ceaseless creativity as Kauffman describes it (2008). Billions of cells and a multiplicity of organisms and energy pathways are creating new cells, organisms, and niches—none identical to what was there before. In Darwinian evolution, it is noted that an organ like the heart could have causal features that were not the function of the organ and had no selective significance in its normal environment. But in a different environment, those causal features might have selective significance. This preadaptation is abundant in biological evolution and when one occurs a novel functionality comes into existence. According to Kauffman, the profound implication of this is that any feature or interconnected set of features in the right selective environment can turn out to be a preadaptation and will give rise to a new functionality in the universe. Since we have no way of predetermining this, the evolution of the biosphere is unpredictable in its invasion of the adjacent possible. Hence, we cannot follow a deterministic approach to evolution of the biosphere; this has ramifications of how we do science generally. It can be argued that this unpredictability holds true as well for how the economy or human culture in general evolves.

Johnson drawing from Kauffman's notion of the adjacent possible describes it
as a kind of shadow future hovering on the edges of the present state of things,
a map of all ways in which the present can reinvent itself. . . . What the adjacent
possible tells us is that at any moment, the world is capable of extraordinary
change, but only certain changes can happen. The strange beautiful truth about
the adjacent possible is that its boundaries grow as you explore those boundaries. Each new combination ushers in new combinations into the adjacent possible (2010, 30).

The global economy with its more than 10 billion goods and services with
complements (like a nail and a hammer) or substitutes (like a screw and a
screwdriver) would have contained only a few hundred goods and services
50,000 years ago. This expansion or evolution can be traced to invention of
new uses for existing products (with the appropriate Darwinian preadaptation) and the satisfaction of existing needs in new ways leading to a constant
invasion of the adjacent possible and unpredictable economic evolution.
Exponential explosion in the evolution of goods and services occurs since the
adjacent possible goods and services that are complements or substitutes are
more than one per good. As Kauffman describes it:

When the car was invented it created the conditions for oil industry, the gas
industry, paved roads, traffic lights, traffic police, motels, car washes, and
suburbia in what is called a Schumpeterian gale of creative destruction. The
destruction side of the story is then extinction of the horse buggy, saddlery,
smithy, and pony express. The creative parts of the Schumpeterian gale are all
complements of the car. Together they make a kind of autocatalytic, mutually
sustaining economic-technological ecosystem of complements that comman-
deer economic and capital resources into that autocatalytic web and can create
vast wealth. (2008, 160–61)

All of this suggests that a kind of bottom-up innovation is the natural way
the world works. Recently, Joi Ito, head of MIT media lab, suggested that
in today's world the approach to innovation should be building quickly and
improving constantly without waiting for permission or proof that you have
the right idea (2014). This kind of bottom-up innovation, he says, is seen
in the most fascinating futuristic projects emerging today, and it starts with
being open and alert to what is going on around you right now. This has now
become possible because of the Internet—allowing low-cost collaboration,
developing a prototype, and deploying right away so that market testing can
begin immediately. He concludes that the cost of innovation is now so low
that it need not be reserved for big companies and universities. It is more
about figuring out how to use the resources available, how to learn quickly,

and use the changing opportunities landscape by being fully present in the now.

So, can these alternative ways of thinking about creativity and innovation help in supporting development and reducing conflict in developing countries?

For stable developing countries, the implications are that we need to start with their assets, their innovative capacities, and their preadaptations to build their capacities to recognize and exploit the adjacent possible, which is constantly emerging. Most importantly, this will require a fundamental shift in mindset and new way of thinking about development cooperation. The tools in current use in development cooperation are not well suited to this new worldview, but we must not throw the proverbial baby out with the bath water. The current tools are overrestrictive and focused more on accountability and compliance to a predetermined set of goals criteria. Endogenous creativity and innovation are thus stifled. We must therefore seek more flexibility, recognize the characteristics of the complex systems we are dealing with, and plan accordingly. But such planning must not fall prey to the traditional development planning we have so far witnessed in which so-called development experts set predetermined goals such as making poverty history and then set out to use aid and linear logic models to do achieve the goal. Rather, we would need to take more of a searching approach by asking questions such as, what aid does well to help these countries meet their aspirations? Or better still, how does aid help the poor get out of poverty in terms they define? Such an approach has been well described by Easterly in what he called "searchers vs planners" (2005).

For FCAS countries, an examination of the way conflict is being addressed and the ways in which humanitarian relief and development assistance are being delivered, through the lens of CAS, should be enlightening. We are likely to see, for example, that intrastate conflicts are driven by many simultaneous forces such as resource scarcity, ideology, ethnicity, terrorism, and so on—unless addressed in a comprehensive multistakeholder bottom-up manner are unlikely to successful. This is probably already known but some of the emerging tools to be described later are not in common use. Humanitarian aid and development assistance as illustrated earlier can easily have perverse impacts because of the complexity of the situation in which they provided. There is a continuing divide between humanitarian and development agencies in their struggle to obtain larger pieces of the aid pie. The result is recurrent humanitarian crises because relief is not designed to lead to early recovery and longer-term sustainable development. The solution seems to lie in the idea of resilience building in which the capacity of communities affected by conflict are strengthened to help them cope, recover, and transform during conflict, so they are able to develop sustainable livelihoods. Tools derived from CAS are very well suited to building resilience, but the again the mindset and thinking of relevant international agency and local leaders will have to change to see resilience for what it is worth. Unfortunately, the idea is already being co-opted for resource mobilization of individual agencies. A fundamental leadership shift is required as well as described in the following passage:

> We need to respond to the current waves of disruptive change from a deep place that connects us to the emerging future rather than by reacting against patterns of the past, which usually means perpetuating them . . . The ability to shift from reacting against the past to leaning into and presencing an emerging future is probably the single most important leadership capacity today. It is a capacity that is critical in situations of disruptive change, not only for institutions and systems but also for teams and individuals. (Scharmer and Karfer 2013, Loc 72, Kindle Version)

While mindset and leadership changes are perhaps the most important insights, we can derive by looking through the CAS lens, there are some more practical changes that are also emerging. Some of these are described below.

Program Design

In order to capture the insights described above in practical program/project design, one approach will be to facilitate the following steps:

- A multidimensional assessment of the assets/activities and coping/adaptive strategies of would-be beneficiaries of development cooperation. Assets include human, social, physical, natural, economic, and political capital.
- Establishment of the vision of a life worth living or a more sustainable livelihood.
- Define what the communities can/will do on their own to get to their vision.
- Then finally define what help they need from outsiders such as development agencies.

The simple sequence of steps outlined above can, in the hands of a skilled facilitator, help build on the dominant log frame to incorporate several dimensions of CAS. For example, the starting point is not *needs* but assets. This helps set the stage for building on local strengths and endowments and encourage innovation. Human capital assessment, for example, moves us away from the common assumption that the only form of human capital that the poor have is labor, and opens up a wider conversation that includes their creativity. Similarly, each of the forms of capital assessment opens up a wide range of avenues through which alternative pathways to the local vision can be pursued. The indicators to be used in the program design emerge from the communities themselves during the visioning exercise in which they define a better life. Yet the need to a have a framework with action plans and goals, which the funders would ask for, is not lost.

Monitoring and Evaluation

The main reasons for M&E of development cooperation programs have changed over time from assessments of inputs to assessments of results. The focus on results and results-based management is now so widespread that it is difficult to conceive of donors measuring their performance in terms of the extent to which they reached their spending targets. And while that remains an important dimension of accountability for promises made, the focus of M&E must clearly be on the purpose for which cooperation was intended. In the linear logic model, M&E commonly assess outputs and outcomes at immediate and intermediate levels. Ultimate outcomes are often used to describe impacts. And some programs even assess the process used to arrive at the various results. In current terminology, outputs are not always considered results, which in these cases refer to development outcomes only.

The design of any M&E exercise must at the outset consider questions such as: What is nature and purpose of the project, program, or policy to be evaluated? Was it designed for social innovation or merely to deliver services and goods such as sanitation, wells, or vaccines? Were the results intended to be additive $(1 + 1 = 2)$, synergistic $(1 + 1 > 2)$, or transformative (in which fundamental social economic or political changes take place)? Was the context simple, complicated, or complex? Are we interested only in progress toward intended results or in unintended effects as well?

And of course, we need to consider as well the more routine questions such as: How will the report be used and who are the likely users? Is this about accountability or learning or both? What data sets will be required, and are these available? Are relevant baselines available for comparison? What are the budget, time, and political constraints?

Answers to these questions help to determine what type of evaluation will be needed. Traditionally, development projects would undergo a formative evaluation at midterm and an end-of-project summative evaluation. More recently, DE, inspired by complexity theory, has been introduced to enhance innovation and to deal with programs that reflect the characteristics of CAS (Patton 2010; Gamble 2008; Dozois et al. 2010).

DE provides the opportunity to learn and gain insights into the emergence of any novelty that might arise as a new, innovative, and complex undertaking is being implemented, especially if the goal is more to learn than to judge. In this regard, it is different from formative or summative evaluations, which essentially seek to assess whether a program is delivering what it said it would. DE applies to situations in which both the path and the destination are evolving. It differs from making improvements along the way (formative evaluation) to a clearly defined goal and is intended to support innovation in a context of uncertainty. It is intended to make visible the intuitive and the tacit. DE is therefore a part of the program design process and the assessment occurs in real time as the program is being implemented. The evaluator becomes part of the project team, fully participating in decisions and facilitating discussions about what and how to evaluate, and encouraging good reflective practice. The evaluator helps team members conceptualize, design, and test new approaches in a long-term process of continuous development, adaptation, and experimentation, keenly sensitive to unintended results and changes in the environment. Insights are used for changes in the ongoing program implementation, taking innovations to scale, facilitating rapid assessments in crisis situations, as well as for the design of similar future offerings.

Donors would of course consider such a situation impossible to deal with, at least in their traditional way of doing business using artificial rational abstracts and linear logic models to deal with complex dynamic adaptive realities on the ground. The challenge is to bridge this chasm in a way that is acceptable to all stakeholders involved.

Small strategic shifts might be most productive. We could consider using more SPICED indicators (Roche 2003):

Subjective: using insights from informants (beneficiaries/stakeholders).
Participatory: indicators should be developed with stakeholders.
Interpreted: easily interpreted to different stakeholders.
Cross-checked: comparing indicators and using different stakeholders, methods to ensure validity.
Empowering: the process should allow stakeholders to promote their own agency.
Diverse: indicators should be different, from a range of groups and across genders.

These can be contrasted with traditional SMART indicators (OECD 2014): *Specific, Measurable, Attainable, Realistic*, and *Timely*. Also move from evaluation for single-loop learning (formative/summative) to evaluation for double-loop learning. In single-loop learning, changes are made to improve immediate outcomes as the difference between actual and desired outcome is evaluated. Double-loop learning involves questioning the assumptions, policies, practices, values, and system dynamics that led to the problem in the first place and making changes to the underlying system either to prevent the problem or embed the solution in a changed system. Finally, we might consider proposing evaluations, which follow the adaptive cycle on innovation rather than a single linear chain. A schema (Figure 17.1) of the adaptive cycle originally developed by Holling (2001) for ecosystem adaptation and modified by Gamble (2008) is shown below with proposed types of evaluations for different stages of the social innovation cycle.

The design and evaluation stages start together with DE in the upper left-hand quadrant through formative evaluation and single-loop learning in the bottom left hand to summative evaluation at maturity in the top followed by deep reflection of what worked and what did not and then second-loop learning and redesign in DE as the cycle repeats itself.

The real-world constraints to evaluations, budget, time data, and politics must be constantly borne in mind and these can be addressed in similar ways as for standard evaluations (Bamberger 2006).

Making Policy in the Face of Complexity

The increasing connectedness of the global economy, the pace of change, and the scale of impact of our actions mean that policy makers must make decisions in a world of increasing uncertainty and change not unlike a CAS. However, almost by definition public policy must include statements of future desirable social goals and so must have a degree (preferably a high degree) of predictability. On the other hand, uncertainty in CAS is high and

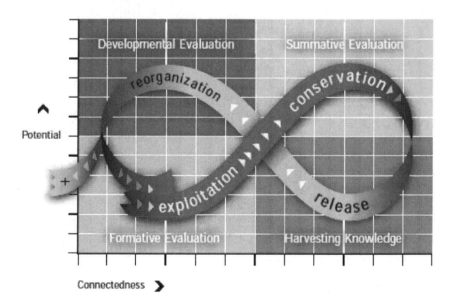

Figure 17.1. Stages of the social innovation cycle. n/a n/a

predictability low. So, a contradiction arises, requiring careful management. It will be unwise to suddenly abandon well-accepted traditional tools of policy analysis such as cost-benefit analysis. As in the case of evaluation, it will be better to gradually bridge the gap between policymaking assumptions of a deterministic clockwork universe to an evolutionary adaptive and uncertain world. A few practical strategies of making such a transition are described in this section.

The first is to start with existing policy analysis tools and make change incrementally. One such approach is described by Roe (1994). The value, limitations, and assumptions of the common policy assessment tool, cost-benefit analysis, are reviewed. The limitations of using this tool in complex development or conflict situations are identified and ways of addressing them are developed. Some additional tools such as narrative policy analysis, Girardian economics, critical theory, or local justice systems approaches are discussed. Narrative policy analysis involves an assessment of stakeholders' stories of the public policy issue from which a meta-policy narrative is derived for further analysis. The following are used as additional tools to develop a richer picture of the policy context and develop alternative policy options for decision makers (Roe 1998): Girardian theories of herd behavior in economics; critical theory in which stakeholders are encouraged and trained to question economic, social, and political structures as an input to policy making; and local justice systems in which local people discuss justice and fairness and set up local standards. More recently, application of Girardian mimesis has been applied to reconciliation efforts for reducing violent conflict and might offer important insights, in combination with other tools mentioned here, to making policy in complex conflict situations (Redekop and Ryba 2014).

Second is the approach to creating adaptive policies. Rihani (2002) has observed that basically development is what nations do as CASs, and what they do can be described as uncertain evolution that has no beginning or end, nor shortcuts, and few signposts on the way. He concludes that rigid plans and policies are inappropriate and that the only feasible approach is for nations to exercise flexibility and pragmatism in order to survive, learn, and adapt over and over again. Adaptive policies are able to navigate toward successful outcomes in settings that cannot be anticipated in advance. This can be done by working in concert with certain characteristics of CASs including: enabling the self-organization and social networking capacity of communities; decentralizing governance to the lowest and most effective jurisdictional level; promoting variation in policy responses; and formal policy review and continuous learning (Swanson and Bhadwal 2009).

Third is the approach of macro-micro policy linkages assessment. In many developing countries, especially those characterized by widespread poverty, or protracted conflict, or both, the poor, excluded, and marginalized often do not have a voice in the policy or national political process. Their livelihood realities are not taken into account in national policy. The result is that policies and laws are at best indifferent to local realities and more often than not are disruptive to local livelihoods efforts. Even when policies or laws are intended to be supportive, because of the complex nonlinear policy transmission mechanism from national to local levels, perverse impacts can be expected. An approach to addressing this is an assessment of local impacts of relevant national policy and then providing feedback to policy makers.

Generally, there are three interacting levels: national, district or regional, and local. Macroeconomic, sectorial, and fiscal policies are set at the national level. The district or regional level requires the institutional arrangements and organizational capacity to implement policies as well serve as the platform for a two-way conversation between national and local levels facilitating bottom-up and top-down policy communications. The local level is where policies have the most visible impacts on the livelihoods of people. These levels are mutually interdependent and the successful promotion of local livelihoods will need supportive policy actions at all three levels.

In FCAS countries, accelerating the transition from humanitarian relief to stabilization, recovery, and sustainable livelihoods is both mandatory and urgent. Helping to build resilience of communities to crisis will contribute to arresting and reversing the downward vicious cycle in which conflict destroys livelihoods and destroyed livelihoods fuel conflict. Policies that can accelerate the transition and reverse the downward cycle are therefore urgently required. A recent multidimensional assessment of livelihoods in Yemen, a country in protracted conflict, revealed that even the better communication of existing policies that support and protect livelihoods at the local level would a good first step. While policy reform takes time, existing supportive policies could be made much more effective by better articulation and communication, so the local people would know what they were and could demand enforcement. Reference was made to simple issues such as the levels of compensation being offered to internally displaced persons, returnees, and host communities. Information on what was to be expected and what not would prevent exploitation of the poor by those with connections to the authorities. General information on credit and related interest rates or on tax policies on small enterprises could avoid exploitation of petty traders and owners of small businesses by corrupt tax collectors.

The OECD report on complexity science and public policy provides brief descriptions on some of the most important complexity tools being used in public policy domains at this time such as agent-based or multiagent models, network analyses, data mining, scenario modeling, sensitivity analyses, and dynamical systems modeling (2009).

CONCLUSION

As we promise to try and provide development assistance, whether in stable, crisis, or postcrisis situations, to support holistic and transformative actions we need to reflect on what we have learned and what is now required. This chapter provides a summary of the lessons learned in development cooperation over the last seventy years and looks at what will now be required through the lens of the CASs on the ground, with which we need to work. It provides concrete strategies to support the shifts that will be required in program design, M&E processes, and policymaking. While development cooperation started at a time when the best tools were linear logic models, and we were forced to fit a complex reality into simplistic models to meet our needs for accountability and measuring progress, we now have tools that can help us deal more directly with that complexity. All that remains is for us to show a bit of courage, work with best of what we already have, but recognize the limitations of what we have been doing so far and try some new thinking.

NOTES

1. International Dialogue on Peace Building and State Building, *A New Deal for Engagement in Fragile States*, 2011, www.pbsbdialogue.org.
2. The word "holarchy" has been used by complexity theorists in place of hierarchy to denote autonomy and interdependence within the structure, not following one-way top-down instructions as in a hierarchy.

REFERENCES

Arthur, W. B. 1996. *Increasing Returns and the New World of Business*. Harvard Business Review, July–August.

Bamberger, M. et al. 2006. *Real World Evaluation: Working under Budget, Time, Data and Political Constraints*. Sage.

Branczik, A. 2004. *Humanitarian Aid and Development Assistance*. www.beyondi ntractability.org.

Esteva, G., and W. Sachs. 2012. *The Development Dictionary*. Zed. Books. Ebook. Loc.420.

Dozois, E. et al. 2010. DE 201. *A Practitioner's Guide to Developmental Evaluation Cycle*. J. W. McConnel Family Foundation.

Easterly, W. 2005. *The White Man's Burden*. The Penguin Press.

Gamble, J. 2008. *A Developmental Evaluation Primer*. J. W. McConnell Family Foundation.

Holling, C. S. 2001. Understanding the Complexity of Economic, Ecological, and Social Systems. *Ecosystems*, 4(5): 390–405.

International Dialogue on Peace Building and State Building. 2011. *A New Deal for Engagement in Fragile States*. www.pbsbdialogue.org.

Ito, J. 2014. Want to Innovate? Become a "now-ist." *Ted Talks*, July 2014.

Johnson, S. 2010. *Where Good Ideas Come From*. Riverhead Books. Penguin.

Kauffman, S. 2008. *Reinventing the Sacred*. Basic Books.

Krugman, P. 1996. *The Self Organising Economy*. Wiley- Blackwell.

OECD. 2015. *International Dialogue on Peace Building and State Building*.

OECD. 2014. *Measuring and Managing Results in Development Cooperation*.

OECD. 2011. *Busan Partnership*.

OECD. 2009. *Applications of Complexity Science for Public Policy*.

OECD. 1996. *Shaping the 21st Century*. Contribution of Development Cooperation.

Patton, M. 2010. *Developmental Evaluation. Applying Complexity Concepts to Enhance Innovation and Use*. Guilford Press.

Omerod, P. 2001. *Butterfly Economics*. Basic Books.

Redekop, V. N., and T. Ryba. 2014. *René Girard and Creative Reconciliation*. Lexington Books.

Sachs, W. ed. 2012. *The Development Dictionary*. Zed Books. E-book. Loc.308.

Rihani, S. 2002. *Complex Systems Theory and Development Practice. Understanding Non-Linear Realities*. Zed Books.

Roe, E. 1998. *Taking Complexity Seriously: Policy Analysis, Triangulation and Sustainable Development*. Kluwer.

———. 1994. *Narrative Policy Analysis: Theory and Practice*. Durham, CT: Duke University Press.

Scharmer, O., and K. Kaufer. 2013. *Leading from the Emerging Future. From Ego-system to Ecosystem Economies*. Kindle E book. Berrett-Koehler Publishers Inc.

Schelling, T. 1960. *The Strategy of Conflict*. Harvard University Press.

———. 1978. *Micro-Motives and Macro-Behaviour Reflect Agent Based Computational Modeling in Complex Systems*. W.W. Norton & Co.

Simpson, D. 2002. *Rethinking Economic Behaviour*. Palgrave MacMillan.

Swanson, D., and S. Bhadwal. 2009. *Creating Adaptive Policies. A Guide for Policy Making in an Uncertain World*. IDRC/Sage.

The World at War. www.globalsecurity.org.

United Nations. 2015. *Millennium Development Goals Report*.

USAID. 2014. *Ending Poverty in Fragile Contexts*. Discussion Paper. www.usaid.gov/sites.

Chapter 18

Sacred Diplomacy as "The Adjacent Possible Praxis"

Transforming Peacebuilding to Meet the Challenges of a Warming Planet

Merle Lefkoff

This chapter relates a personal journey culminating in the following insight, which will be explained in the course of the narrative:

> In order to build a peaceful noetic polity in an imagined Ecozoic future, what we need is a newly designed Sacred Diplomacy that facilitates face-to-face dialogue in numinous, spirit-welcoming spaces. Let us visit the imaginary space where negotiated futures become actualized, based on the adjacent possibles ready to help people and planet flourish within the boundaries of the living systems providing balance for our beloved home in the universe.

My primary concern is the relationship between integrative peacebuilding, the uncertain future we face in a time of postnormal planetary disturbance, and the possibility of a new facilitated dialogue praxis we can apply to the unprecedented peacebuilding challenges emerging from global warming and species extinction. The question guiding my discoveries is the following:

Can we now harness the power of our emergent creativity to help keep the peace in the likely chaos and possible violence accompanying the unknowable future on an altered planet?

After briefly sharing a deeply formative experience of being in Nature, I introduce complex adaptive systems science as the basis for a new praxis for addressing some of the most significant complex challenges represented by global warming, where two of the primary planetary threats are the melting Arctic and massive deforestation in the Amazon. I then consider our responsibility to acknowledge several primary societal effects of climate change,

419

instructing us to do whatever we can to become cocreators with Nature during a time of turbulent social and ecological transition. This will lead to an elaboration of how complexity science can shape our peacebuilding practices as we address complex problems in a new way. Following a discussion about our responsibility for what happens next, I will introduce Sacred Diplomacy as a praxis that might help avoid the violence that often accompanies rapid change, offering a message of hope.

Before I fast forward to thoughts about a new approach to the present vulnerability of people and planet, some definitions are in order. The "Anthropocene" is the term that captures the main point about the new epoch following the Holocene: that human alteration of the living systems that govern our planet has progressed to a point where the survival of our species is at risk, along with the ongoing and rapid extinction of millions of nonhuman species (Anthropocene Working Group 2019; Zalasiewicz and Waters n.d.).

I am aware that the name Anthropocene describes the most distinctive aspect of the new epoch, not its whole character. And I am careful not to use the term as though all of the diverse human groups on the planet are equally responsible for our present dilemma. They are not. Indigenous peoples and those living in poor countries have contributed much less to the problem, and even worse, they are the populations most likely to be affected.

I adopt a definition of "diplomacy" that concentrates on "Track Two" (back-channel) interventions by third-party neutrals skilled in nonviolent "gentle action" (Peat 2008) to affect the behavior and decisions of people holding adversarial positions, who might otherwise resort to violence (Jones 2015). Track Two diplomacy emerged in the twentieth century out of a recognition that there were limits to official Track One diplomacy that could be accommodated by dealing with people who were a step removed from elected leaders and official spokespersons for a country but still in a position to have significant influence. Eventually, the term "Multitrack Diplomacy" was introduced to include meaningful contact with people, at all levels, from both sides of a conflict.

For our purposes here, the term "Sacred" refers to peacebuilding processes that facilitate dialogue in a numinous space of hope (producing a spiritual feeling of awe and wonder), one in which emergent creativity uncovers possible conditions for sustainable peace in an adjacent future. Sacred includes regarding something with "great respect and reverence" (Oxford 2020) and of great value. As such, "Sacred Diplomacy" refers to valuing the people, the process, the biosphere, and the ultimate goal of finding a way of contributing to the well-being of all (cf. Brodeur, "Interworldview Dialogue," *Transforming*). As Redekop suggests, our present challenges might "well usher in a new era of blessing-based human civilization and consciousness" (Redekop 2020, 180).

In addition to "diplomacy," I will be referring to "dialogue" as well. Physicist David Bohm has always been my guide as a facilitator of community-based conflict resolution. His belief that entering into dialogue creates the potential for solving problems by communicating freely in a creative moment is still the basis for a hopeful transition from enmity to trust (Bohm 1996). His understanding is that in dialogue people can "think together."

The *Ecozoic Era*, a term coined by ecotheologian Thomas Berry, refers to the future possibility of a different way for humans to live on the planet, based on the notion of planet Earth, and not us humans as the center of the universe. Berry suggests a framework for the transition, outlining an eight-point approach for change (Eaton 2014).

This emerging paradigm of Sacred Diplomacy suggests that through radical new transdisciplinary group process, which includes both scientists and nonscientists indwelling the language of complexity, metaphor, and storytelling, in addition to the more traditional "case study" approach to solving problems, we humans might be brought back to the many forgotten laws of Nature—the natural laws of mutual reciprocal interdependence and responsibility that govern both robust ecosystems and social systems. We can no longer afford to see ourselves as separate from Nature. The coming of the Anthropocene is forcing a reckoning requiring us to return to our abandoned home. We *are* Nature, and we, her human progeny, are presently in the grips of an unthinkable future that includes violent conflict, one we should seriously be thinking about right now.

MY JOURNEY BEGINS

My journey begins with a walk, years ago, through the fabled "Marshes of Glynn" on the Georgia Coast. I was accompanying my teacher, biologist Eugene Odum, known as the visionary father of modern ecology, who wrote the first textbook, *The Fundamentals of Ecology* (1953). He insisted that we learn how the marshes actually worked as a critical living system that we humans partnered with for mutual survival, in addition to celebrating their beauty.

Back in cityscape Atlanta where I lived, I had been told that filling in "swamps" to erect buildings was a sign of economic progress. Odum reminded us that the root of the word "ecology" is the Greek word *oikos* meaning "house," and I realized that much economic development was destroying the "house" that we lived in.

As we walked, Odum remembered a poem about the marshes that envisioned "the souls of [people]" dwelling together with the creatures underneath the waters covering the marshland, in a spiritual, sacred union with

Nature. I have never forgotten that walk. It has helped guide my life choices. Each careful step in the wetlands changed my life. Forever.

Years later, after much difficult and sometimes harrowing work as an international mediator assisting negotiations in conflict zones around the world, I was living and working in the Rocky Mountains in Santa Fe, New Mexico. There I discovered another exciting and emerging science, known at the beginning as "complex systems theory." The theoretical work found a home at what became the Santa Fe Institute (SFI). Established in 1984 by Los Alamos scientist George Cowan with David Pines and others, the founders were holistic thinkers, worried about increasing specialization in the sciences. Their remedy was to establish a new independent research institute that would combine disciplines traditionally kept isolated from one another in academia and government agencies. Included in their efforts were pioneers from the past such as cyberneticist Gregory Bateson and others, who recognized the necessity of studying human-in-nature from a systems perspective (Bateson 1972).

The SFI pioneers called their new discipline the science of "complex adaptive systems." What started as an interdisciplinary approach became a transdisciplinary approach, combining older scientific disciplines to form a completely new science often open to extended peer communities comprising a diversity of nonacademic practitioners trying to solve global problems.

After a few years of heartbreaking work in the Balkans during the war in the 1990s, I was searching for something new that might transform traditional diplomacy. At the same time back home, I was working intimately with Indigenous colleagues cofacilitating dialogues to resolve conflicts within Native communities in New Mexico. They introduced me to a recent synthesis between Indigenous and Western science, both based on Nature's systems that can teach us how to adapt to rapidly changing initial conditions on the ground that are unpredictable in their future impact. This scientific framework weaves the Native cosmology of the First Peoples, principles from complexity science, and successful conflict transformation methodologies from both Native and Western practice. Tewa scholar Gregory Cajete, from Santa Clara Pueblo, writes, "Today, with the creative theory of chaos and quantum physics, a new scientific cultural metaphor has begun to take hold. The insights of this new science parallel the vision of the world long held in Indigenous spiritual traditions" (Cajete 2000, 16).

THINKING ABOUT THE UNTHINKABLE

In the last few years, worldwide attention is helping to mobilize a growing network of civil society groups, scientists, and young activists, alarmed over the implications of climate catastrophe and species extinction, perhaps the most important among the many challenges we face. The major indicators of human and planetary well-being signal endlessly recurring positive feedback loops driving our human and natural systems toward social, economic, political, and planetary collapse (Theise, "Harnessing Principles of Complex Systems," *Transforming*).

There are a number of continuously changing and complex physical and information systems that interact with one another to produce our present dilemma. At a primary level, I will first discuss the *physical* changes to the planet as the result of human contributions to global warming, taking up the examples of Arctic melting and deforestation, particularly in the Amazon. Second, I will look at the challenge of getting good information on what is happening.

Global Warming

As Wallace-Wells observes, "Never in the earth's entire recorded history has there been warming at anything like this speed—by one estimate, around ten times faster than at any point in the last sixty-six million years" (2019, 65). No place is warming faster than the Arctic. A complex, nonlinear cooling system for the planet, the ice-rich Arctic permafrost is melting faster than anticipated, outstripping the climate models, sending out greenhouse gases that speed up climate change (Shea, 48–55). The Antarctic ice sheet melt has tripled, from 49 billion tons per year in 1997 to 2,019 billion in 2017 (Wallace-Wells 2019, 64).

The largest, densest, and second longest-living forests in the world are the temperate rainforests in southern South America. The *Fitzroya cupressoides* trees ("Alerce" in Spanish) live for 1,600 years. Old Growth are, per unit area, the most long-lived stores of carbon in the terrestrial biosphere. Their aboveground biomass has been accumulating for millennia, and their protection is critical to mitigating global warming and the rapid extinction of masses of critical insect populations.

Recent research on the importance of preserving our tropical rainforests has found that CO_2 emissions from land are even more important than emissions from fossil fuels. Landcover change since the beginning of the Industrial Revolution is estimated to be the source of 40 percent of present-day total anthropogenic warming and species extinction. When researchers examine the combination of both forest loss and agricultural emissions, the impact is even greater. What is clear is that tropical deforestation has global warming and species extinction impacts at a planetary scale.

In 1990, at the request of the Organization of American States (OAS) and the International Rainforest Alliance, I was asked to join a large research team to address protection of the remaining Alerce forest in southern Chile (Christian 1990). A new threat to the forest had emerged from the furniture manufacturing industry, since the wood is highly prized for its beauty and because it is amazingly waterproof. We spent several weeks getting to know the forests, taking advantage of the welcoming warmth and native wisdom of the Indigenous Mapuche tribes who somehow managed to live in the forest despite all obstacles. We spent days riding their tough little ponies from village to village as we assessed what could be saved.

During my time in Southern Chile, I formed an intense, emotional relationship with the Alerce rainforest as I had earlier with the wetlands of the Georgia coast, strengthening my resolve to help preserve forest ecosystems. The negotiations with the businessmen and officials at the "table" were delicate because of the enormous profits from the Alerce wood for the manufacturers and the Chilean government. I remember my grief when I made only limited progress with the forces of capitalism and consumption. I began to challenge traditional conflict resolution and negotiations methodologies as insufficient for reaching agreement in the more complex global issues emerging at the end of the twentieth century.

The Information Challenge

Getting accurate *information* about rapid ecological changes and their impacts is especially challenging. Just as academic researchers in the social sciences are slowly waking up to the new norm of planetary disruption, climate scientists are often forced to report their latest findings with great caution. For example, the U.S. State Department's Bureau of Population, Refugees and Migration (PRM) has warned document authors that their analysis must be reviewed by donors who can remove funding if they don't agree with the analyses presented (Stoakes 2019).

At best, with the exception of alarms coming from the United Nations, national security analysts, and environmental activists massing in protest, along with a growing number of young academics, we now have primarily speculative reports on the possible impacts of global warming on the potential for near and future conflict. Nevertheless, at the recent UN Climate Action Summit, mobilized by UN secretary-general Antonio Guterres because of inaction at the UN COP ("Conference of Parties") meetings, he used the dire warnings of the latest IPCC report to push for specific action plans on several fronts: (1) stop construction of coal facilities; (2) stop fossil fuel subsidies and commit to net-zero carbon emissions by 2050; and (3) tax polluters while cutting taxes for people (Guterres 2019).

Alongside the primary physical challenges are many *social and political* changes as a result of global warming, from mass migration to housing issues, food security, availability of water, and so on, linking back to information as a political tool. The social and political dimensions are connected to the global economy as well as to changes in the biosphere, including the role of income disparities between rich and poor at both the individual and collective levels. They all demand creative and comprehensive action.

AN INTEGRATIVE PEACEBUILDING APPROACH

When I was invited in 2010 to join the Integrative Peacebuilding (IPB) group at Saint Paul University in Ottawa, the different paths of my ongoing journey began to converge. The IPB initiative was turning new ideas from complexity science toward the search for peace. The group of scholars and practitioners looked at ways people could get out of their silos to address complex problems with many stakeholder groups. It evolved to integrate complexity theory, integral theory, and mimetic theory along with an ethical vision giving priority to enhancing the capacities and well-being of the most vulnerable people (Redekop 2019). I started to see that IPB offered insights, theories, and a methodology that could address the complex challenges related to global warming. For me, an integrative approach starts close to home, bringing insights from the First Peoples of where I live into conversation with my global concerns.

I have the privilege of living and working in a diverse cultural community informed by traditional stories of Indigenous forms of knowledge. The original part of my adobe house in the small farming community of La Cienega south of Santa Fe is 250 years old. But it is built on land that had been originally occupied by my present neighbors in *Cochiti Pueblo* to the South— descendants of remarkable Native farmers popularly known as the *Anasazi*, a Navajo word meaning "the ancient ones." La Cienega historians William H. Schneider and Carl Perkins, who have deep knowledge of our local past, have alerted me to the fact that as long ago as the tenth and eleventh centuries CE, the Anasazi might well have developed the first agricultural settlements where I live in the American Southwest (personal conversation).

Archaeologist David E. Stuart writes that what archaeologists call the *Chacoan Culture* created "the grandest regional social and political system in prehistoric North America" (Stuart 2014, 7). However, after 700 years of development, the Chacoan society lasted only 200 years "collapsing spectacularly in a mere forty." Stuart asks the questions: "Why did such a great society collapse? If another catastrophe befell us in our own time, who would survive and become a new future—the present?" (ibid.). Stuart surmised a lesson for our own time as he wrote about conditions that worsened with the arrival of extended drought "that ripped apart the very fabric of the Chaco phenomenon" (ibid., 120).

Our present extended drought conditions are amplified by the unintended consequences of our relentless drive toward the next technological break-through, no matter how destructive. This juggernaut of emergent creativity has brought us close to or even past the tipping points that provide the bound-ary conditions for the web of life. In the following section, I explain how I sought to combine my interest in complexity science, Indigenous knowledge, and my later research in integrative peacebuilding, with my concern about ecological and social impacts and the possibility of profound social unrest. I wondered, *how might an integrative peacebuilding approach to the disrup-tions accompanying the Anthropocene transform my traditional praxis in conflict resolution and Track Two back-channel negotiations?*

Transforming to a New Praxis

During the mid-1990s, I was working on the ground as a mediator in the Balkans in the midst of a genocidal war. My experience was that traditional diplomacy was not creative enough to adapt to the rapid changes in the world following the collapse of the Soviet Union. Back in Santa Fe, I started having regular lunches with Cowan and Pines, the founders of the Santa Fe Institute, asking them to help me understand how complexity science, based on a com-bination of natural sciences like physics, biology, and mathematics, might open a door for a social science practitioner like myself to discover novel roadmaps for global coexistence.

They suggested that I seek a research grant, and when I came to them, donor funding in hand, they opened the door to a little-known think tank at Los Alamos National Laboratory called the Center for Non-linear Studies (CNLS) where, along with the Santa Fe Institute, complexity science was being advanced and applied. I spent four years at the Center after 9/11 as guest scientist and affiliate studying complexity science for peacebuilding with colleagues who were mostly physicists, mathematicians, and computer scientists simulating the emerging threat of international terrorism.

At the same time, I was also invited to become a member of several national security teams, including one at the U.S. Marines Warfighting Laboratory, modeling the unprecedented and complex threat of nonstate actors and groups (Lawlor 2005). This experience gave me an international mediator devoted to peacebuilding, unique access, and insight into how complexity science was being applied to war and peace.

What I learned, watching computer simulations of dynamic "agents" inter-acting on the screen, was that the seemingly random behavior of the agents, programmed with very simple rules (the "initial conditions"), emerged into a complex order that was not predetermined by the programmers. The outcomes were "nonlinear," the initial conditions changing dramatically because of the dynamic and unpredictable self-organizing interactions among the agents, without a "leader" in charge. I was fascinated by this new idea of "emergence"—that by changing just a few simple rules, the relationships among the agents emerged into very different and more complex arrangements that were almost always a surprise. In order for troops to survive, especially in urban combat, rapid adaptation, without instructions from the top, was essential at a "local" level, which challenged the command/control culture of combat.

I started thinking about peacebuilding as an intervention in the initial conditions on the ground, stopping the positive feedback loops that continuously escalated the violence, allowing peace to become an emergent property of intervention at the grassroots level of civil society, dynamical and self-organizing—perhaps even "leaderless" in the traditional sense—from the bottom up, not the top down.

The Northern Ireland peace process is a good example. Betty Williams happened to witness the horrific killing of three children when an automobile spun out of control as the result of ongoing violence on the streets of Belfast. In response, she gathered 200 women to march for an end to the violence. The initial march quickly became a mass movement of 50,000 protestors. When the dead children's aunt, Mairead Corrigan Maguire, joined the movement eventually called "Peace People," the two women became powerful and courageous leaders in demanding that an official peace process begin. Monica McWilliams and May Blood, also Protestant and Catholic women leaders working together, formed the Northern Ireland Women's Coalition, a new political party that enabled them to have a seat at the table during the peace negotiations that led to the Belfast Agreement/Good Friday Agreement.

The Belfast women worked relentlessly across partisan lines in their communities, often in back-channel meetings and cross-sector dialogues as they pushed for a more holistic agenda for the negotiations to include mixed housing, societal integration of prisoners back into society, and public education. In a final act, they were instrumental in organizing the campaign that helped assure agreement for the negotiated peace in the public referendum in 1998. Later, Monica McWilliams wrote that when the international chair of the peace negotiations thought about the outcome, he stated that "the emergence of women as a political force was a significant factor in achieving the Agreement" (McWilliams 2015, 13).

COCREATING THE UNKNOWABLE FUTURE

I was privileged to meet award-winning complexity scientist Stuart Kauffman, an early theorist at the Santa Fe Institute, whose work I came to admire. He and I originally met at the Lindisfarne Fellowship meetings (Thompson n.d.).

The Lindisfarne Association was founded by cultural historian and social philosopher William Irwin Thompson who wrote extensively on his idea of the evolution from "every little nation-state" as the primary means of governance and group identity, to what he terms a "noetic polity," where human mindfulness enables the emergence of a new planetary civilization resulting from the collapse of the old systems and cultures.

I came to believe with Kauffman that it is the emergent creativity of human ingenuity, combined with the dualistic separation of Society/Nature—particularly in what some call "The Capitalocene"—that has given our species the power to alter our home in the universe beyond its ability to support the health of ours and other species. Jason W. Moore, coordinator of the World-Ecology Research Network, argues that the biosphere's tipping points have emerged from the overpollution that comes when capitalism runs out of spaces to dump the waste (Moore 2015).

Recent scholars writing about "The Great Acceleration" of human power to transform the planet point to the industrial upswing in a postwar recovery beginning about 1945 (McNeill and Engelke). Moore, however, makes clear that dating capitalism's rise to global dominance at the beginning of the Industrial Revolution in the 1850s and leaping forward to the post-World War II period is a mistake. Humans began their "environment-making revolution" at least 400 years earlier in continuing loops of emergent creativity (Moore 2015).

I choose to join others in dating planetary transformation as the result of human wealth accumulation much earlier, about 10,000 to 12,000 years ago when we settled down to till the soil and grow and store food. "The Shape of History with Stuart Kauffman" traces the human journey of "growing differentiation and the complexities of the values of goods . . . to the power elites of today" (Kauffman 2019). And now we find that it is politically impossible for today's power elites, whose wealth is more concentrated than at any moment in human history, to find the will to abandon their privilege so that the Earth can restore itself to balance.

Many international diplomats and especially youth are worn out from toxic politics, overriding militarism, and positional bargaining for land, money, energy, and power that define present international relations. In the absence of action by government and institutional leaders around the world, collective direct action is spreading as populations abandon hope for justice and conflict resolution under the failed leadership of global economic and political elites.

Radically inclusive and newly self-empowered global citizen activists, when released into the new world of post-COVID-19, will hopefully once more climb the barricades and demand political and economic change.

"Occupy Wall Street" changed the global conversation about the inequality of unfettered market economies before the movement dispersed around the world (Levitin 2015). Indigenous First Nations women leaders successfully organized "#IdleNoMore" to demand justice for the taking of their lands by Canadian colonists (Coates 2015). The Standing Rock Sioux tribe on the Missouri River gathered thousands of protesters from hundreds of Indigenous nations, every U.S. state, and many foreign countries, to join them in stopping the building of the Dakota Access Pipeline (#NoDAPL) across their lands. The protests continue on behalf of Indigenous land rights worldwide. Sweden's autistic savant, young Greta Thunberg, is leading a worldwide revolution of young people who are protesting the probable loss of their future to biosystems collapse as a result of the failure of global leadership (Thunberg 2019).

Massive resistance often works when all other change strategies fail. A wonderful example of an earlier campaign that was successful in stopping contamination of the biosphere resulted in an agreement to stop the consumption and production of products responsible for the depletion of ozone. The success was detailed in a 2019 UN report that looked at the positive results that came about after mobilization of mass joint action by scientists, government officials, and civil society groups. The agreement to end destructive practices included ongoing monitoring, which helped provide a path to implementation, aided by research from the private sector that developed substitutes for former products adding to ozone depletion. A win/win all the way around (UN News 2017).

Today, in their latest handbook for activists, *This Is Not a Drill*, one of the new political movements, "Extinction Rebellion," begun in the United Kingdom and rapidly engaged in self-organizing global action, asks the question, "So what is your place in these times of unravelling, dissolving, transformation?" (Extinction Rebellion 2019). They conclude, "This is an international rebellion, aligned with all peoples living with struggles to protect life on Earth. This is sacred" (ibid., 186).

CLIMATE CHANGE AND CONFLICT

In a speech in Rome on World Food Day, October 16, 2018, David Beasley, head of the World Food Programme, sent out a global warning:

> A potent combination of hunger, climate change and [human]-made conflicts are creating a "perfect storm." . . . After a decade of decline, the number of chronically malnourished people in the world has started to grow again—by 38 million, largely due to the proliferation of violent conflicts and climate-related shocks . . . Global hunger—after showing decreasing trends for decades—is on the rise again since 2016, due to factors that include the combining effects of climate change and conflicts. (Agence France-Presse 2018).

Reporting on a recent study for the university's Stanford News, Devon Ryan wrote:

> The study estimates climate has influenced between 3% and 20% of armed conflict risk over the last century and that the influence will likely increase dramatically. In a scenario with 4 degrees Celsius of warming (approximately the path we're on if societies do not substantially reduce emissions of heat-trapping gases), the influence of climate on conflicts would increase more than five times, leaping to a 26% chance of a substantial increase in conflict risk, according to the study. Even in a scenario of 2 degrees Celsius of warming beyond preindustrial levels—the stated goal of the Paris Climate Agreement—the influence of climate on conflicts would more than double, rising to a 13% chance. (Ryan June 12, 2019)

Academic research on direct connections between climate change and conflict has led to an ongoing debate about whether the world is getting more or less peaceful. Agreement is likewise still elusive on appropriate definitions, indicators, measurement, and evaluation (see Singh, "Development as Emergent Creativity," *Transforming* for an approach to evaluation in complex situations). However, there is new evidence regarding a link between climate change, conflict, and migration. Researchers from the International Institute for Applied Systems Analysis in Austria, the University of East Anglia, and others "found that in specific circumstances, the climate conditions do lead to increased migration, but indirectly, through causing conflict" (Abel et al. 2019a, b).

In his foreword to the 2018 climate risk report to the Australian Senate, Admiral Chris Barrie, member of the Global Military Advisory Council on Climate Change, shared the implications for Australia's national security. "I told the inquiry," he wrote, "that after nuclear war, human-induced global warming is the greatest threat to human life on the planet" (Barrie 2018). The policy recommendations at the conclusion of the report laid out the worst-case near-term scenario, in order to frame the "existential threat" as a present global emergency that insists on military preparedness. "I could paint a scenario where unregulated migration—as we've seen in Europe in recent years—unregulated migration might easily overwhelm any of the efforts we could put out to stop it from happening," Barrie said. "You can see the numbers. They are really quite frightening" (ibid.). The admiral also questioned whether Australia had enough troops and equipment to deal with "concurrent" threats, using the example of simultaneous floods in Queensland, bushfires in Victoria, and a humanitarian crisis in the Pacific (Elton-Pym 2018).

Conflict's effect on worsening food insecurity as a result of global warming is just beginning to be studied. Of the seventy-seven studies included in a recent risk modeling analysis, only seven looked at the effect of conflict, including ten years of famines in Nigeria and Somalia, where political conflict and violence is rampant from groups like Boko Haram (MERIAM 2018).

The headline in National Geographic's September 2019 issue was "The New Cold War." Competing countries are racing to gain a foothold in the melting Arctic, their correspondents reported, "setting the stage for conflict at the top of the world" (Shea 2019). Graphic photos of U.S. and Canadian soldiers conducting training exercises "derived from the Winter War, fought between Finland and the Soviet Union in World War I," and parachuting into Alaska to prepare for coordinated operations in extreme cold-weather environments, are accompanied by equally chilling maps of the military bases and airfields ringing the eight nations that comprise the Arctic countries. In the world above sixty-six degrees latitude, the new frontier now "open for business" offers the riches of new shipping lanes and vast mineral deposits (ibid.).

OUR RESPONSIBILITY FOR WHAT HAPPENS NEXT

Every year since 1951, Nobel Laureate scientists get together in Landau, Germany. Young scientists can apply to join them. In the long-standing history of the Lindau Nobel Laureate Meetings, there have been only two sociopolitical requests: the Mainau Declaration of 1955 appealing for a ban on the use of nuclear weapons and the Mainau Declaration on Climate Change at the sixty-fifth meeting in 2015 that issued an urgent warning about the consequences of global warming. The Declaration was timed to coincide with the upcoming UN Climate Change Conference in Paris later that year. "Failure to act," the thirty-six signatories warned, "will subject future generations of humanity to unconscionable and unacceptable risk" (Mainau 2015).

By most measures, the melting Arctic being perhaps the most important, planetary disruption continues to mount at a rapid pace. A growing but hesitantly stated scientific consensus confronts the possibility that we can neither stop nor slow the onset of looming climate catastrophe and associated challenges such as the terrifying global extinction of species, extreme weather events, runaway capitalism, population growth, loss of topsoil to grow food, and decimation of the world's forests.

In *Awakening*, Kauffman put forward the notion that we, as humans, are cocreators of the unfolding reality (Kauffman 2020). While we cannot prestate the conditions of the future potential collapse, Kauffman reminds us that as part of Nature we also help cocreate the emerging future. While this happens in a context in which we do not know and cannot know what will happen, because we are deeply responsible for what *has* happened we are equally responsible to prepare for what might happen in the future. (Indigenous teachings add that we should consider the consequences of our decisions and actions for at least seven generations to come.)

Among these challenges, in a world already experiencing endless war, is the specter of unprecedented human displacement, migration, and violent conflict. In *The Birth of the Anthropocene*, Jeremy Davies writes that the start of the Anthropocene "provides a framework for understanding the modern ecological catastrophe, rather than a prescription. It is a way of seeing, not a manifesto" (Davies 2016, 193). Thus, we in the peacebuilding community have a special responsibility to begin immediately to find a way to facilitate the cocreation of stories about *future* environmental, sociopolitical, economic, and governance landscapes that are *peaceful* and flourishing because of a changed collective consciousness about planetary limits.

My concern continues to grow about global warming and the rapid extinction of species, along with a rise in "climate migrants" as possible precursors to conflict and violence accompanying the competition for resources that might ensure survival. At the same time, it is clear that both the past pleas of the scientific community and civil society advocacy have failed so far to stem the tide of rapidly advancing chaos. Perhaps this is because agents of change in the academy and among civil society nongovernmental organizations do not share the same conversation and decision-making platforms. Indeed, even inside those sectors, expertise is now so overspecialized and issue advocacy so siloed, it's no wonder meaningful action has been absent.

Bob Lamb, CEO of the Foundation for Inclusion, has been warning about the inability of our present problem-solving systems to successfully address large-scale social problems. Our present frameworks, he writes, show "not that some problems are harder to solve than others, rather that complex problems are *fundamentally unsolvable* using linear methods" (Lamb 2018, 4).

SACRED DIPLOMACY AS AN
ADJACENT POSSIBLE PRAXIS

I was a consultant in Washington, DC, in the 1980s for a variety of government agencies, including the U.S. Environmental Protection Agency and the U.S. Department of Energy. At that time, the data about global warming and carbon emissions brought about by fossil fuels extraction was well known and accepted as a global threat that needed a bipartisan response, which was framed as early as 1979 at the World Climate Conference in Switzerland. Scientists agreed that there was still time to win the race against catastrophic global warming if we could get an international treaty to limit carbon emissions. But as Lamb noted, old thinking kept us from crossing the finish line. Many tried, and this tragic failure is a largely forgotten story of opportunity lost to an unspoken agreement among leaders in the rich countries to take only those actions that did not compromise the economic privileges and conveniences bought by unfettered economic growth. What would have happened to our chances for a peaceful future survival back then, I wondered, if traditional rules of engagement had shifted in order to get a meaningful treaty passed that limited the emissions beginning to cause worsening climate effects?

As the effects of climate disruption began to enter mainstream discourse, I extended my search for new dialogue processes that might break through paralysis and anxiety about global warming, returning once more to Kauffman and his new work on what he terms "the adjacent possible" (TAP). Kauffman was taking a deep dive into the "Shape of History" and the evolution of a global economic system based on ownership and profit, influenced by an emergent and restless human creativity that searched earlier inventions and breakthroughs in order to combine them to make more and more efficient and complex technologies, keeping the new combinations that worked (Kauffman 2019).

Most exciting to me was Kauffman's understanding that each introduction of a new technology was accompanied by an opening to additional adjacent possibles waiting in the wings for the next explosion of emergent human creativity. TAP tells a compelling and clarifying story of the emergent creativity that has propelled human progress over many millennia. With the advent of agriculture (10,000–12,000 years ago), humans learned to grow and store food, creating "increased GDP and per capita GDP" along with increasing inequality, partly because we pass our stored wealth on to our descendants. We continue to evolve as we combine previous adjacent possibles into new products that are more complex and more valuable than those invented earlier. Simpler designs become more sophisticated combinatorial technology, with increasingly problematic unintended consequences for life on Earth.

If we think of this story as a graph, it appears in the form of a hockey stick, lying on its side with the blade pointing up. GDP and its accompanying adjacent possible technologies shoot upward more rapidly on the blade after the start of the Industrial Revolution (about 1850), toward a probable outcome—a higher reach of human evolution that hurtles off the edge of chaos into a dark unknown of worsening inequality, more dramatic weather events, migration, conflict, species extinction, and human misery. This rapid change is represented by the blade of the hockey stick on the graph, showing where we are now.

It is with this long-standing indwelling of the world of complexity and its present extension into the adjacent possible that I became convinced that this way of thinking about the uncertain future provides the missing problem-solving tool that Lamb was searching for in order to deal with the potentially catastrophic events associated with global warming, species extinction, and adjacent planetary risks. The Center for Emergent Diplomacy in Santa Fe, New Mexico, where I serve as executive director (emergentdiplomacy.org), has recently adopted the TAP theory as a metaphor to guide experimenting with a new methodology for diplomatic negotiations and community-based dialogues. The intent is to discover and develop unprecedented foresight scenarios about an unknown and mysterious future, existing only in the adjacent possible.

Neither personal experience of extreme weather nor decades of reports pointing toward ever-increasing climate emergency have changed the political will to take the actions necessary to mitigate the worst biosphere losses. As indicated above, my colleagues and I believe that we are past the tipping point to remain in our present thinking, helpless to stop or slow down the relentless positive feedback loops driving global systems toward the brink of collapse. We are all familiar with the daily barrage from journalists reporting on worsening climate impacts for 3.2 billion poor people and an ever more potentially dystopian future for the rest of us if we don't find a way to birth new ideas for a future of living differently.

Borrowing the best of many ideas from our colleagues, we decided to combine principles from Western complex science, Native spirit-welcoming practice, and integrative peacebuilding—using the metaphor of the adjacent possible—into a praxis that can help keep the peace during a turbulent transition in planetary history. The methodology of the "Playbook" and workshops for facilitators uses a systems-thinking approach with a focus on quickly building capacity for community dialogues and self-organizing collective resilience as we enter the unknown future. We continue to explore how to enter the adjacent possible by applying a praxis that can help prepare for and avoid the violence accompanying rapid change.

Believing that it is too late to continue framing and reframing old questions as we try to adapt and transition and survive constant change, we begin our workshops by asking the following:

- How will we live on an altered planet?
- What would a global economy look like on a future Earth, and is one even possible?
- Can we imagine an emergent web of diverse economies that self-organize into robust and appropriate local sharing communities and structures of governance?
- And even though we often know what to do, why don't we do it? How can an Indigenous past—before the advent of destructive technology—help us discover a robust future?

These are a few of the questions that can help lead us into the adjacent possible space.

Our brains find it difficult to think about an unknown future without using the past and present as a guide. We humans think—erroneously and tragically—that we can predict the future by using information from past and current cycles and trends. In our Sacred Diplomacy praxis, we use past history to remind us of what went wrong, avoiding the past and present as a guide to the future we desire. These are unprecedented times in human history, requiring a complete reset of our past operating systems. Possible terms of a new civilization and consciousness go beyond the cause and effect thinking of the past and present. It is difficult to start from a blank slate, but not impossible. We invite change agents into dialogue who are eager to imagine a future that has yet to emerge. As Einstein once famously said, "Imagination is more important than knowledge." That quote has never been more appropriate than now.

The Sacred Diplomacy workshops and training materials for building a new learning community of futurists, both dreamers and activists, have some of the following key elements:

- A safe, spirit-welcoming space
- Room for experiential exercises and play
- No prepared agenda
- Privilege listening over responding
- Diversity and inclusion
- No stated goals, objectives, or outcomes
- Spontaneous circles for emergent ideas
- *Gedanken* ("thought") experiments
- Journaling
- Short stories about a thriving future
- Biomimicry (when in doubt, ask nature for advice)
- Ideas to action: scenarios to carry forward
- When possible, conduct dialogue processes outdoors

What is needed first for peacebuilding is a methodology that is rigorous enough to establish truth claims and bring clarity to discourse but not so confining that the "spirit" necessary to deep dialogue is forgotten.

The new Sacred Diplomacy process we are continually refining is diverse and inclusive, and also involves inviting a group of who are rich in "cognitive diversity" to join the parties at the table, providing what complexity scientist Scott Page calls "the diversity bonus" (Page 2007). The bonus refers to better outcomes as the result of the inclusive and cognitive diversity at work in the negotiations. "This brings different representations, categories, heuristics, models and frameworks into the deliberations" (ibid.). Page thought about what kind of group was needed "to create what Stuart Kauffman called different adjacent possibles. A smart person can be stuck on a problem and another person might present a new adjacent possibility and get that person unstuck. New adjacent possibilities create the diversity bonus" (ibid.).

We have gathering evidence that the creativity and productivity of negotiations soar when the process includes meetings that start by enlisting an inclusive group with diverse cognition. They are enhanced by not starting meetings with preset agendas specifying linear outcomes (see Stanley and Lehman 2015) that are designed to allow the self-organization of small groups often in circular settings to encourage spiritual reflection and listening as the basic norms of dialogue. Needed are special tools to navigate both positive and negative feedback loops as discussion deepens; strategic planning is replaced with storytelling and scenario building. The process gives priority to a holistic analysis of problems after they are sliced and diced into siloes for preliminary analysis. Native peoples have taught us that human beings can find answers to the most intransigent dilemmas by meeting face-to-face; sharing stories in addition to data; and above all privileging *listening, instead of responding.*

Our need for hope forces us to offer solutions that try to preserve our present lives on a largely flourishing planet of the past. But these attempts do not open the doors to the adjacent possible that might offer us an escape from the present collapsing systems in which we are all implicated and perhaps fatally stuck. The TAP methodology presents such a possibility, an unprecedented opportunity in which to navigate a return to the laws of nature that are always available to us when we pay respectful attention to its limits, the "re-enchantment" with Nature that Kauffman calls for (Kauffman 2020).

I can imagine innovative solutions emerging from thriving, diverse local community networks, entering into reflective problem-solving dialogues that break down the dominant and destructive hierarchies of the past and present, taking into action the best future scenarios for a just and robust transformation from the Anthropocene to the Ecozoic. Those who gather at the Center for Emergent Diplomacy invite collaboration as we continue to refine and implement a radical new model for synchronous spiritual transdisciplinary negotiations and dialogue at a time of troubled transition. I continue to be inspired by visionary thinkers and teachers and the stirrings of a shift in global consciousness.

Because the future is immediate, even though unknowable, one of the main challenges as practitioners and facilitators is first to confront the *Actual*—the initial conditions on the ground at the present time. We then work hard, using the adjacent possible praxis to move dialogue and negotiations past the present dilemma into future scenarios, stories of deep transformation that lead to emergent structures for resilient living on a future planet restored to balance.

I am writing this chapter in the midst of a global pandemic that no one was prepared to handle. The COVID-19 pandemic is a rehearsal for potential breakdowns of global systems. We must be better prepared for the crises ahead, and so I conclude with a suggestion that in order to meet the next crises head-on what we need is a newly designed Sacred Diplomacy that facilitates face-to-face dialogue in numinous, spirit-welcoming spaces. Let us visit the imaginary space where negotiated futures become actualized, based on the adjacent possibles ready to help people and planet flourish in the peaceful future.

REFERENCES

Aasheim, Sissel Småland. 2015. *Post-Normal Science in Practice.* Bergen, Norway: University of Bergen, Centre for the Study of Science and the Humanities.

Abel, G. J., M. Brottrager, J. Crespo Cuaresma, and R. Muttarak. 2019a. "Climate, Conflict and Forced Migration." *Global Environmental Change.* doi:10.1016/j. gloenvcha.2018.12.003.

———. 2019b. *New Study Establishes Causal Link Between Climate, Conflict, and Mitigation.* Luxembourg, Austria: International Institute for Applied Systems Analysis. pure.iiasa.ac.at/15684.

Agence France-Presse. 2018. "On World Food Day, UN Says Hunger, Climate Change and Man-Made Conflicts Creates 'Perfect Storm'." *AFP.com*, October 16, 2018, 23:26:44 IST.

Anthropocene Working Group. 2019. *Results of Binding Vote on AWG.* http://qua ternary.stratigraphy.org/working-groups/anthropocene/.

Barrie, Chris. 2018. "Submission to the Senate Inquiry into Implications of Climate Change for Australia's Nation Security." *AC RAN*, Submission 38, 2018.

Bateson, G. 2000. *Steps to an Ecology of Mind.* Chicago, IL: The University of Chicago Press (Originally published by the Estate of Gregory Bateson, 1972).

Berry, Thomas. 1991. *The Ecozoic Era: Eleventh Annual E.F. Schumacher Lectures.* Great Barrington, MA: Schumacher Center for a New Economics.

Bohm, David. 1996. *On Dialogue.* New York, NY: Routledge.

Cajete, G. 2000. *Native Science: Natural Laws of Interdependence.* Santa Fe, NM: Clear Light Publishers.

Christian, Shirley. 1990. "Ecologists Act to Save Ancient Forest in Chile from Industry." *New York Times*, April 3.

Coates, Ken. 2015. *#IDLENOMORE and the Remaking of Canada.* Regina: University of Regina Press.

Davies, Jeremy. 2016. *The Birth of the Anthropocene.* Oakland, CA: University of California Press.

Eaton, Heather, ed. 2014, *The Intellectual Journey of Thomas Berry: Imagining the Earth Community.* Lanham, MD: Lexington.

Elbein, Saul. January, 2017. "These are the Defiant 'Water Protectors' of Standing Rock." *National Geographic Dispatches.*

Elton-Pym, James. 2018. "Exclusive: Climate Change Warning for Australia's Military." *SBS News*. https://www.sbs.com.au/news/exclusive-climate-change-wa rning-for-australia-s-military.

Enzinna, Wes. 2017. "How a Movement was Born at Standing Rock." *Mother Jones*, January/February.

Extinction Rebellion. 2019. *This Is Not A Drill: An Extinction Rebellion Handbook*. Penguin.

Funtowicz, S., and J. Ravetz. September, 1993. "Science for the Post-Normal Age." *Futures*, 25(7), 739–824.

Guterres, Antonio. September 23, 2019. *United Nations Secretary General, "Remarks at 2019 Climate Action Summit"*. https://www.un.org/sg/en/content/sg/speeches/ 2019-09-23/remarks-2019-climate-action-summit.

Jones, Peter. 2015. *Track Two Diplomacy in Theory and Practice*. Stanford, CA: Stanford University Press.

Kauffman, Stuart. 2020. "The Re-Enchantment of Humanity: The Implications of 'No Entailing Laws'." In *Awakening: Exploring Spirituality, Emergent Creativity and Reconciliation*. Edited by Vern Neufeld Redekop and Gloria Neufeld Redekop. Lanham, MD: Lexington.

———. 2019. "The Shape of History with Stuart Kauffman." *New England Complex Systems Institute*, video.

———. 2008. *Reinventing the Sacred: A New View of Science, Reason, and Religion*. New York, NY: Basic Books.

Lamb, Bob. January 8, 2018. "Collective Strategy: A Framework for Solving Large-Scale Social Problems." *Foundation for Inclusion, Research Brief*, Issue No. 1.Levitin, Michael. 2015. "The Triumph of Occupy Wall Street." *Atlantic Magazine*, June 10.

Lawlor, Maryann. 2005. "Data Farming Cultivates New Insights." *Signal*. https:// www.afcea.org/content/?q=node/975.

Mainau Declaration. 2015. *The Mainau Declaration*. http://www.mainaudeclaration.org/.

McNeill, J. R., and Peter Engelke. 2014. *The Great Acceleration: An Environmental History of the Anthropocene since 1945*. Cambridge, MA: The Belknap Press of Harvard University Press.

McWilliams, Monica. 2015. "Women at the Peace Table: The Gender Dynamics of Peace Negotiations." In *Gender and Peacebuilding*. Edited by Maureen Flaherty. Washington, DC: Lexington Press.

MERIAM. 2018. "Modeling Early Risk indicators to Anticipate Malnutrition." www .actionagainsthunger.org/meriam.

Moore, Jason W. ed. 2015. *Capitalism in the Web of Life: Ecology and the Accumulation of Capital*. New York, NY and London: Verso.

Odum, Eugene. 1953. *The Fundamentals of Ecology*. Philadelphia, PA: W. B. Saunders.

Page, Scott E. 2017. *The Diversity Bonus: How Great Teams Pay Off in the Knowledge Economy*. Princeton, NJ: Princeton University Press and the Andrew W. Mellon Foundation.

———. 2007. *The Difference: How the Power of Diversity Creates Better Groups, Firms, Schools, and Society*. Princeton, NJ: Princeton University Press.

Peat, David. 2008. *Gentle Action: Bringing Creative Change to a Turbulent World.* Italy: Pari Publishing Sas.

Redekop, Vern Neufeld. 2020. "The Emergence of Both Torah and Jesus: Sources of Hope in the Face of Desperation." In *Awakening: Exploring Spirituality, Emergent Creativity and Reconciliation.* Edited by Vern Neufeld Redekop and Gloria Neufeld Redekop. Lanham, MD: Lexington.

———. 2019. "The Emergence of Integrative Peacebuilding: A Complexity-Based Approach to Professional Leadership Development." *The Journal of Peacebuilding and Development,* 14(3). doi:10.1177/1542316619862252.

Ryan, Devon. June 12, 2019. "Stanford-Led Study Investigates How Much Climate Change Affects the Risk of Armed Conflict." *Stanford News.* https://pulitzercenter .org/reporting/scenes-new-cold-war-unfolding-top-world.

Shea, Neil. 2019. "The Thawing Arctic is Heating up a New Cold War." *National Geographic Magazine,* September.

Stanley, Kenneth O., and Joel Lehman. 2015. *Why Greatness Cannot be Planned: The Myth of the Objective.* Switzerland: Springer International Publishing.

Stoakes, Emmanuel. 2019. "Leak Suggest UN Agency Self-Censors on Climate Crisis after US Pressure." *The Guardian,* September 11.

Stocker, T. F., D. Qin, G.-K. Plattner, M. Tignor, S. K. Allen, J. Boschung, and A. Nauels. 2013. "Summary for Policymakers." In *Climate Change 2013: The Physical Science Basis. Contribution of Working Group I to the Fifth Assessment Report of the Intergovernmental Panel on Climate Change.* IPCC.

Stuart, David E. 2014. *Anasazi America.* Albuquerque, NM: University of New Mexico Press.

Thompson, William I. n.d. *The Lindisfarne Fellows 1975–2012.* https://williamirwin thompsonblog.wordpress.com/the-lindisfarne-fellows-1975-2012/.

Thunberg, Greta. 2019. "Transcript: Greta Thunberg's Speech at the U.N. Climate Action Summit." *NPR,* September 23.

UN News. 2017. "Ozone on Track to Heal Completely in Our Lifetime." September 16. https://news.un.org/en/story/2019/09/1046452.

Wallace-Wells, David. 2019. *The Uninhabitable Earth: Life after Warming.* New York, NY: Tim Duggan Books.

Zalasiewicz, Jan, and Colin Waters. n.d. *The Anthropocene.* http://nora.nerc.ac.uk/id /eprint/513436/1/The%20Anthropocene_for%20NORA.pdf.

Conclusion

Oscar Gasana

What a privilege to read *Transforming*! These are nineteen interrelated, well-synchronized, and research-based chapters on various aspects of transforming, showing the virtues of a collective effort to explore a concept in all its dimensions, combining both research and life experiences.

As a concept, transforming is presented as a continuing action that is goal-oriented, process-driven, uneven, and nonlinear at times, but leading to new framings, new actions and possibilities, and reshaping human relations at the individual, group, community, and national levels.

These successive openings of possibilities and surprises has a cumulative influence on people's social, political, economic, religious, and environmental fabric, principally due to their inherent emergent creativity, and the capacity to reflect on the meaning and implications of each action. One important event may pave the way for another, prompting a chain of events converging toward a common and transforming outcome. Finally, transforming is determined by time ripeness—that moment when all the conditions are met for new things to happen, change to take place, awareness and creativity to emerge.

My intention here is not to summarize the book or draw a conclusion—all the joy is yours as you read it through. Rather, I wish to share with you my own transforming journey, and more generally, how events, circumstances, and encounters unexpectedly combine to give transforming a boost, sometimes changing the course of history, with far-reaching implications.

I left Rwanda, my native country, at the age of nine and went into exile in the Democratic Republic of Congo (DRC) under the protection of my older brother, leaving my mother and sisters behind, as only males were being targeted for periodic mass killing. It took me ten years to see my mother again, and for three years I could visit her during vacation time. But this opportunity

441

did not last. Another anti-Tutsi violent episode erupted and the border was closed to me anew. However, in Congo I received a quality education I would not have received had I remained in Rwanda, due to discriminatory policies practices there at the time; these amounted to a similar situation to what was then going on in Apartheid South Africa.

I ended up getting a scholarship to further my education abroad. As I broadened my horizons, I worked in international development, started a family, and had children. But I missed so much that was dear to me: my family of origin and my country. I lacked recognition, being able to travel to all the countries of the world except my own. The situation lasted three decades, and the second generation of Tutsi refugees, mostly born in exile, was coming of age and raising questions about their future.

The Rwandese Patriotic Front (RPF) was formed in late 1980s and in 1990 entered Rwanda through the Northern border with Uganda. We know the rest: a four-year war and a genocide against the Tutsi minority. An unprecedented butchery saw over a million people killed in eighty-four days, the world watching.

The impact on me personally was devastating. I was paralyzed for months, unable to sleep as I gradually learned about the scope of the extermination. Six months after the genocide, I was already on my way to Canada, and my family followed some months later. Depressive anger and obsessive desire for revenge dominated my thoughts at the time. Never would I have imagined then that transforming would be possible to the extent of praying for those who caused me the most horrific loss.

The first step of my transforming journey was my enrolment in the Dominican Pastoral Institute in Montreal. Although a Christian, I had lost trust in God but, at the same time, was tormented by the spiritual emptiness I constantly felt. I expected that the course would answer some of my existential questions about life on earth, God in our lives, legitimacy of vengeance, and the like. Unfortunately, during the three years I studied pastoral theology, nobody was able to provide satisfactory answers to my questions.

My transforming came from unanticipated sources: conversations with individual professors and fellow students, the eyes of children I met during my pastoral work in schools, and occasional encounters with well-wishing people who happened to know that I came from Rwanda. I started seeing humanity in people, something I had totally lost.

At this juncture, we moved from Montreal to the National Capital Region and was introduced to Ottawa's Saint Paul University, where I met Professor Vern Neufeld Redekop. He had been director of the Canadian Institute for Conflict Resolution (CICR) and was now developing a master's program in conflict studies on behalf of Saint Paul University.

This initial conversation with Vern was already transforming. I was gathering information on possible training opportunities, but Vern, knowing where

I came from and the kind of experience I was carrying, devoted his time and energy to actively listening to my story, and generating ideas and possibilities for my recovery and healing. It was a revelation to me, the true beginning of my transforming, one that would take me to the master's program in conflict studies, a Third Party Neutral certificate from CICR, a conflict resolution career in the federal public service, and completion of a PhD in applied social sciences.

Of special significance was my master's research project, directed by Professor Redekop, aimed at bringing together the few willing individuals among Hutu and Tutsi Rwandans in Canada to learn to meet and discuss issues of common interest, including the Tutsi genocide and its implications, and how the two communities could support each other in the healing process.

For someone whose obsession centered around the desire for revenge, who once envisaged spending all his savings to buy nuclear waste to poison all the rivers and lakes of Rwanda, my transforming was real, fragile at times, but steady.

It took me fifteen years before I revisited Rwanda. For I had vowed to never return there. I found a good pretext to go back, namely doing doctoral research. In fact, my transforming was ongoing. The project wasn't easy in the context where I was a researcher and a victim at the same time. It was particularly trying when I went to launch my book, derived from my thesis, and attended a burial ceremony of 1,500 people, including many children, who were killed in a soccer stadium in the Western region of Kibuye. In 1994, they were starved for weeks, before being exterminated using machine guns and hand grenades. A number of my immediate family members were among them. Listening to the few surviving eyewitnesses telling the story was unbearable, and for months I experienced relapses and a resurgence of hateful thoughts. Obviously, transforming as a continuous process may meet obstacles on its way, requiring courage and resilience to allow the transforming process to regain its rightful place.

Ceremonies like the one I attended are common in post-genocide Rwanda, and definitely lead to the outpouring of emotional outbursts. Yet, stories of generative dialogue, forgiveness, and reconciliation between victims and offenders throughout the hills are beyond belief. My hope is that transforming will continue so that the new generation of Rwandese may live in peace and harmony. It is also a personal commitment to devote my retirement time to teaching conflict studies and community-based conflict resolution in Rwanda.

In my capacity as a conflict management practitioner in the Canadian Public Service, I experience transforming in action as I assist employees at all levels and in all roles in dealing with intrapersonal as well as interpersonal challenges, using tools such as facilitated conversation, mediation, and conflict coaching. We have lately put an emphasis on emotional intelligence coaching for managers, to sharpen their ability to understand their emotions and feelings, and those of their employees. The ensuing self-awareness enables them to control their actions, and to experience a transforming impact on employee–manager relationships.

One approach to furthering transforming is to remain sensitive to the suffering of the victims of atrocities, and to imagine constructive ways to deal with them, for atrocities make us hate other human beings and create a spiritual vacuum, triggering depressive behavior. This approach is only possible if we are able to value and uphold the humanity in everyone, and to initiate a dialogue with those who offended us or who are different from us (see Brodeur's chapter on "Interworldview Dialogue").

As Katherine Peil Kauffman's chapter shows, attention to our emotions helps us make sense of our experiences, leading to the integration of our thoughts and our feelings, with a higher capacity to deal with fundamental issues the world is confronted with today, including gender relations, race relations, the integration of Aboriginals and other minorities, and environmental issues.

Transformation manuscripts were handed over to the publisher before another defining event took place: the killing of George Floyd in Minneapolis, Minnesota. On May 25, 2020, the forty-six-year-old African American was killed by the Minneapolis police during an arrest. Derek Chauvin, a white police officer, knelt on Floyd's neck for nine minutes while Floyd insisted he couldn't breathe. Chauvin's fellow officers present either restrained Floyd or prevented bystanders from intervening. Chauvin ignored the pleas from bystanders to remove his knee. And so Floyd died from asphyxia while the world watched, thanks to social media. His death triggered massive U.S. and global protests, denouncing police racist brutality in America and beyond. The words "I can't breathe" rung in the ears of many as that last straw that broke the camel's back. As the demonstrations drew thousands across America and abroad, the mourners called on President Trump to remove his knee from black people's necks by ending systemic injustice in the country.

Obviously, what happened in Minneapolis was part of a systemic problem in America. Floyd was not the first African American man whose death at the hands of the police had led to protests in many U.S. cities. Rallies had been held when Tamir Rice, Michael Brown, and Eric Garner were killed by police, and many others before them.

But this time seemed to be different. Demonstrations were more defiant, were held in all the fifty states, and crossed racial boundaries. The world responded swiftly, with massive rallies in all major European cities and beyond. For the first time, Minneapolis announced a possible dismantling of the police department. Why this time? There isn't one single factor. Several factors combined to enhance transforming.

This was a more obvious and particularly atrocious crime, clearly captured on video as it happened, leaving no ambiguity as to the brutal nature of the act. Nobody could therefore refute the veracity of the crime. The image of the policeman's knee on Floyd's neck was compelling, especially for the younger generation who watched online. The emotional outburst was real and unstoppable. An independent autopsy determined that Floyd's death was a homicide caused by asphyxia, due to neck and back compression, leading to lack of blood flow to the brain.

As transforming and the factors that make it possible are often unanticipated, Floyd's death happened during a pandemic of unprecedented proportions (COVID-19), requiring confinement, causing high unemployment worldwide, and fundamentally changing the way we live, work, and attend to each other's needs. During Floyd's arrest and killing, there were more people than ever sitting home and watching television, and available to take to the streets if need be.

No less important a factor was the fact that Floyd's case followed another series of incidents that raised public outcry. Ahmaud Arbery, and Breonna Taylor, both blacks, were shot and killed in February and March 2020.

On February 23, 2020, Ahmaud Arbery, a twenty-five-year-old African American man, unarmed, was shot and killed in Glynn County, Georgia. As he was jogging, he was being pursued by two armed white residents, Travis McMichael and his father Gregory, driving a pickup truck. The event was recorded on video by a third resident in another car. The killing of Arbery sparked heated debates on racial inequality and injustices against African Americans in the United States.

On March 13, 2020, the twenty-six-year-old Breonna Taylor, a first responder, was shot eight times by Louisville police in Kentucky, inside her apartment, during the execution of a narcotic-related search warrant that turned out to target a wrong home. Once again, the incident became another indication of black people seeing police invade their homes and killing innocent residents.

All the above brought the transforming impulses to a higher level. President Trump was compelled to present a reform bill to tackle police brutality but was short in admitting systemic racism and how to deal with it. Democrats in Congress introduced policing reform bill that went further—the Justice Policing Act—aimed at demilitarizing police and addressing police brutality.

In Canada, rallies were spontaneous in many cities, also asking for a more just society, free from systemic racism. Politicians, Prime Minister Trudeau leading the way, were compelled to take a stand and commit to ending racial profiling and systemic discrimination, particularly in employment. The Floyd phenomenon crossed the Atlantic and was highly visible in European major cities, all chanting the same slogan: end racism. Human rights organizations raised their voices, and Black Lives Matter instantly became multiracial. Sport Leagues in America and globally expressed anger and frustration, and made a renewed commitment to end racism in their ranks. A new history of human relations was in the making, transforming how we look at each other as a human race.

As I read the various chapters at this particular time the themes came alive—compassionate listening, nonviolence, restorative justice, concern for the Other, complex adaptive systems, feedback loops, dialogue, normative violence, broad-based efforts at reconciliation, individual-collective/inner-outer connectivity, and a spirituality of growth, change, and transcendence.

Index

63, 253, 259; Justice Policing Act,
445; restorative, 33, 35, 57, 253;
retributive, 27–28, 57; structural,
371; transitional, 248, 250, 252–54,
257, 261–63, 264n2

Kandahar Provincial Reconstruction
Team (PRT), 174
Kanehsata:ke, 328
Kant, Immanuel/Kantian, 54, 140, 254–
57, 261, 265–66, 383–84
Karpman, Stephen, 122, 133
Kauffman, Katherine Peil, 6, 41, 444
Kauffman, Stuart, 2, 5, 6, 16–18, 29–30,
35n3, 221n1, 407–8, 427–28, 431,
433, 435–36
Kay, Jonathan, 329, 332, 343n2
Keating, Prime Minister Paul, 357
kenosis, 6–7, 69, 73, 78–79, 87n10
kindness, 62, 211, 253, 312, 314, 387
King, Martin Luther, 84, 308
Kitchi-Manitu, 276–77
Klassen, Pamela, 93
Korten, D. C., 44, 60
Kotaletten Soppe (Hamburger Soup), 95
Kraybill, Ron, 164, 178–79, 183
Kronreif, Franz, 80
Krugman, Paul, 402
Kuhn, Thomas, 141
Ku Klux Klan, 4, 308

La Cienega, 425
Lady Gaga, 311
La Loche, Saskatchewan, 333, 335,
343n3
Lamb, Bob, 432–33
Latvia, 86n6, 106
law(s), 41, 60, 75, 246, 264n3, 313, 352,
356, 386, 415, 421; common, 17,
357; electoral, 182; enforcement, 59,
220, 386; entailing, 17; divine, 213;
international, 207; natural, 54, 255,
421, 421; of nature, 64; physical, 52;
of physics, 17
Laws, John, 356

Law(s), Nature's, 386–87; of Courage,
314; of Honesty, 314; of Humility,
314; of Love, 314; of Respect, 313;
Seven Sacred, 313–16; of Truth, 314;
of Wisdom, 314
leadership, 8, 51, 126, 128, 164,
173–75, 177, 180, 183, 188, 193–95,
199–200, 202, 207, 217, 306–7, 333,
383, 399–400, 410, 428–29
Lederach, John Paul, 111, 115, 132,
175, 363–64, 366–69
Lenin, 92–93
Lesotho, 164, 178–82
limbic system, 48
Lindau Nobel Laureate Meetings, 431
Lindisfarne Fellowship, 427–28
linear logical model, 405, 409, 411–12,
416
Lismore, 369
literacy, arts, 9, 225–42
Lithuania, 98
Longo, Guissepe, 17
Los Alamos, 42; National Laboratory,
426
love, 28, 31–33, 42, 44, 47, 50, 63,
72–84, 86nn3,4, 8, 12, 100, 113,
115, 119–20, 122, 124, 127, 131,
132n3, 155, 277, 306, 312, 314;
blessing-based, 33; desire for the
well-being, 32–33, 35; for enemies,
23; as mimetic desire, 32; of truth
and goodness, 289
Lubich, Chiara, 6, 69, 73, 77–81, 84–85,
87n12
Lundy, Patricia, 253

Mabo, Eddie, 357
Machno, Nestor/Machnovites, 93, 96,
101
Macintyre, Lee, 297
Macintyre, Stuart, 354, 357
Maguire, Mairead Corrigan, 427
Maldonado-Torres, Nelson, 258
malnutrition, 352
Manitoba, 191, 273–74, 283, 290n4

About the Editors

Gloria Neufeld Redekop, PhD, is a researcher and author in spirituality and religious social history. Her publications include *Bad Girls and Boys Go to Hell* (or not): *Engaging Fundamentalist Evangelicalism* and *The Work of Their Hands: Mennonite Women's Societies in Canada*.

Vern Neufeld Redekop, PhD, is Professor Emeritus of Conflict Studies, Saint Paul University, Ottawa, Canada. He has published on deep-rooted conflict, reconciliation, teachings of blessing, integrative peacebuilding, protesters and police, conflict studies, René Girard, and mimetic theory.

About the Contributors

Patrice C. Brodeur, PhD, is associate professor, Institut of Religious Studies, Université de Montréal. Past Canada Research Chair on *Islam, Pluralism and Globalization* (2005–2015), he now focuses on contemporary Islamic thought and interreligious dialogue.

Cecil Chabot, PhD, is a postdoctoral research fellow at Concordia University. His interdisciplinary scholarship explores Indigenous, Western, and Christian civilizations and interactions, seeking to engage them in dialogue on fundamental human questions.

Joseph Cleyn, MA (Conflict Studies), was drawn to the field after studying philosophy and traveling in Rwanda. He currently works as a policy analyst with the Federal Government of Canada.

Brigitte Gagnon, PhD, is a consultant doing research, planning, and clinical work in crisis and trauma; as well, she is a Compassionate Listening Facilitator.

Oscar Gasana, PhD, is senor practitioner in informal conflict resolution in Canada's Federal Public Service. He holds a master's degree in conflict studies and a PhD in applied social sciences.

Karen Hamilton, The Rev. Dr., former general secretary, the Canadian Council of Churches; cochair, 2018 Parliament of the Worlds Religions; author, *The Acceptable Year of the Lord*; awarded 2009 North American Catholic Book Award.

Sue-Anne Hess, MA (Conflict Studies), has a strong interest in nonviolent and creative responses to structural injustice. Previously contributed to *René Girard and Creative Reconciliation*, é Redekop and Ryba, 2014.

Iman Ibrahim is a Leadership and Conflict coach and trainer, and former executive director of the Canadian Institute for Conflict Resolution, working with communities, not-for-profits, peace projects, and dialogues. www.ima nibrahimconsulting.com.

Katherine Peil Kauffman is founding director of nonprofit Emotional Feedback System International, whose mission is fostering global emotional wisdom. Introductions to this work can be found at http://emotionalsentience .com/.

Merle Lefkoff, PhD, is FOUNDING director of the Center for Emergent Diplomacy. She is presently developing with her team a "Planetary Balance Playbook" for training facilitators working to prepare local communities around the world to survive and thrive in the next future.

Lauren Michelle Levesque, PhD, is an assistant professor in the Providence School of Transformative Leadership and Spirituality at Saint Paul University, Ottawa, Canada.

Robert Logie, MA (Conflict Studies). As a Foreign Service Officer, he chaired APEC's Economic Committee from 2018 to 2019 and currently works as a Senior Policy Analyst on trade with China.

S. K. Moore, PhD, CAF Padre (retired), after encounters with religious leaders in operational environments, developed the chaplain operational capability of Religious Leader Engagement, now Policy and Doctrine for the Canadian Armed Forces.

Naresh Singh, PhD, International Development Advisor, is an independent practitioner scholar and senior vice president at Global Development Solutions Canada. Among his publications is the book *Legal Rights of the Poor: Foundations of Sustainable and Inclusive Prosperity*.

Petra Steinmair-Pösel, PhD, professor of Catholic Social Ethics, KPH Edith Stein, Feldkirch/Austria, recently published *Im Gravitationsfeld von Mystik und Politik. Christliche Sozialethik im Gespräch mit Maria Skobtsova, Dorothee Sölle und Chiara Lubich*.

Neil D. Theise, MD, is a physician-scientist at New York University—Grossman School of Medicine. With collaborator Menas Kafatos, he is developing an integrative model of "fundamental awareness."

Catherine Twinn has been an Alberta lawyer since 1980. In 2011–2013, Catherine conceived and led the "Braid Strategy," a large-scale collective impact and systems' engagement process to reduce overrepresented Indigenous children in Alberta's child welfare system.

Lissane Yohannes is a seasoned diplomat with decades of experience in negotiation and mediation, serving as the Special Envoy of Ethiopia to Somalia and of the Intergovernmental Authority on Development to Sudan and South Sudan.